Yellowstone & Grand Teton NATIONAL PARKS

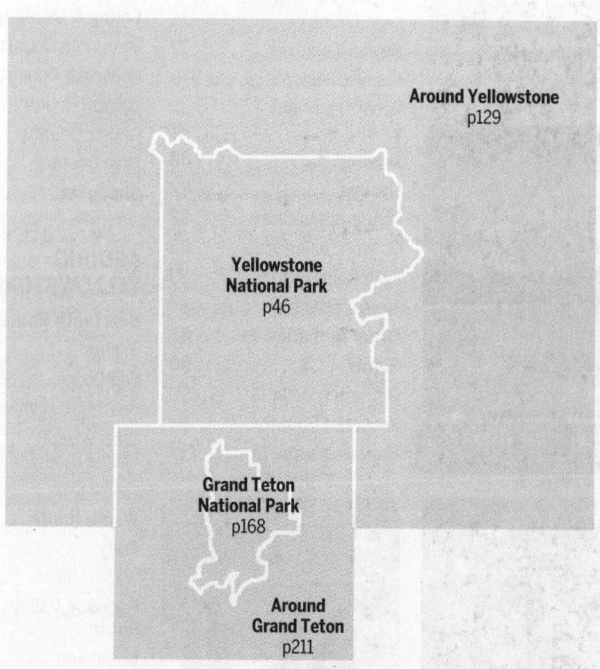

Benedict Walker, Bradley Mayhew, Carolyn McCarthy,
Christopher Pitts

PLAN YOUR TRIP

YELLOWSTONE RIVER P57

Y LIU/EYEEM/GETTY IMAGE ©

OWL, GRAND TETON NATIONAL PARK P168

CHASE DEKKER/SHUTTERSTOCK ©

ON THE ROAD

JACKSON HOLE P221

KEVIN CASS/SHUTTERSTOCK ©

Contents

UNDERSTAND

SURVIVAL GUIDE

COVID-19

We have re-checked every business in this book before publication to ensure that it is still open after 2020's COVID-19 outbreak. However, the economic and social impacts of COVID-19 will continue to be felt long after the outbreak has been contained, and many businesses, services and events referenced in this guide may experience ongoing restrictions. Some businesses may be temporarily closed, have changed their opening hours and services, or require bookings; some unfortunately could have closed permanently. We suggest you check with venues before visiting for the latest information.

SPECIAL FEATURES

Welcome to Yellowstone & Grand Teton National Parks

With its raging geysers and howling wolf packs, Yellowstone stands as one last pocket of a wild, primeval America.

Yellowstone

Yellowstone National Park is the wild, free-flowing, beating heart of the Greater Yellowstone Ecosystem. Its real showstoppers are the geysers and hot springs, but at every turn this land of fire and brimstone breathes, belches and bubbles like a giant kettle on the boil. The park's highways traverse these geysers, through meadows and forests, past roadside herds of bison and campsites aromatic with pine needles and family campfires. In between lies the country's largest collection of elk, the continent's oldest, largest wild bison herds and a pristine wilderness roamed by wolves, grizzlies, moose and antelope. Yep, it's awesome.

Grand Teton & Beyond

South of Yellowstone is Grand Teton National Park, home to probably the most iconic mountain range in the USA. These showy peaks are the picture-postcard image of alpine splendor. Since the first summiting of the Grand in 1898, they have sent a shiver of excitement down the spine of even the least vertically inclined. Get in on the thrill by climbing a Teton peak or backpacking the Teton Crest, then recover under the spell of sophisticated Jackson Hole. Rarely are the delights of the front- and backcountry so close together.

Beyond the Parks

The natural wonders don't stop at the parks' boundaries. The two parks and their surrounding protected areas form a large, interconnected area six times the size of Yellowstone and with a fraction of the crowds. Here you'll find blue-ribbon trout streams, fabulous hiking trails and a scattering of charming Wild West towns with their gaze set firmly on the great outdoors. Budget some time to get a taste of the West in Cody, try Montana's biggest skiing in Big Sky and drive America's most scenic highway across the Beartooth Plateau.

The Essential Outdoor Vacation

Mountain bikers, skiiers, hard-core backpackers, boaters, kayakers and winter enthusiasts will all find a million adventures in Greater Yellowstone. Inside the parks, you'll have to share space with three million visitors a year, but even in summer it's possible to shake the crowds. Some experiences are destined to become indelible memories – the taste of s'mores over a campfire, wrinkled noses at the smell of sulfurous steam and the electrifying thrill of hearing wolves howl. Beyond a great vacation, it's a modern pilgrimage to two of the country's most admirable and enduring national landmarks.

Why I Love Yellowstone & Grand Teton

By Carolyn McCarthy, Writer

ve seen a wolf pack claim a bounding pronghorn, watched a grizzly shake off after his alpine
wim, and logged long backcountry miles to see peaks lapping to the horizon. At a time when
e natural world is facing serious pressure, the Greater Yellowstone region remains one of
e last intact ecosystems of the northern hemisphere. This is the great American wilder-
ess. See for yourself – it's nothing short of sublime. Yellowstone and the Tetons are nature
s it is meant to be: both powerful and restorative.

r more about our writers, see p288.

Above: West Thumb Geyser Basin (p104)

Yellowstone & Grand Teton National Parks

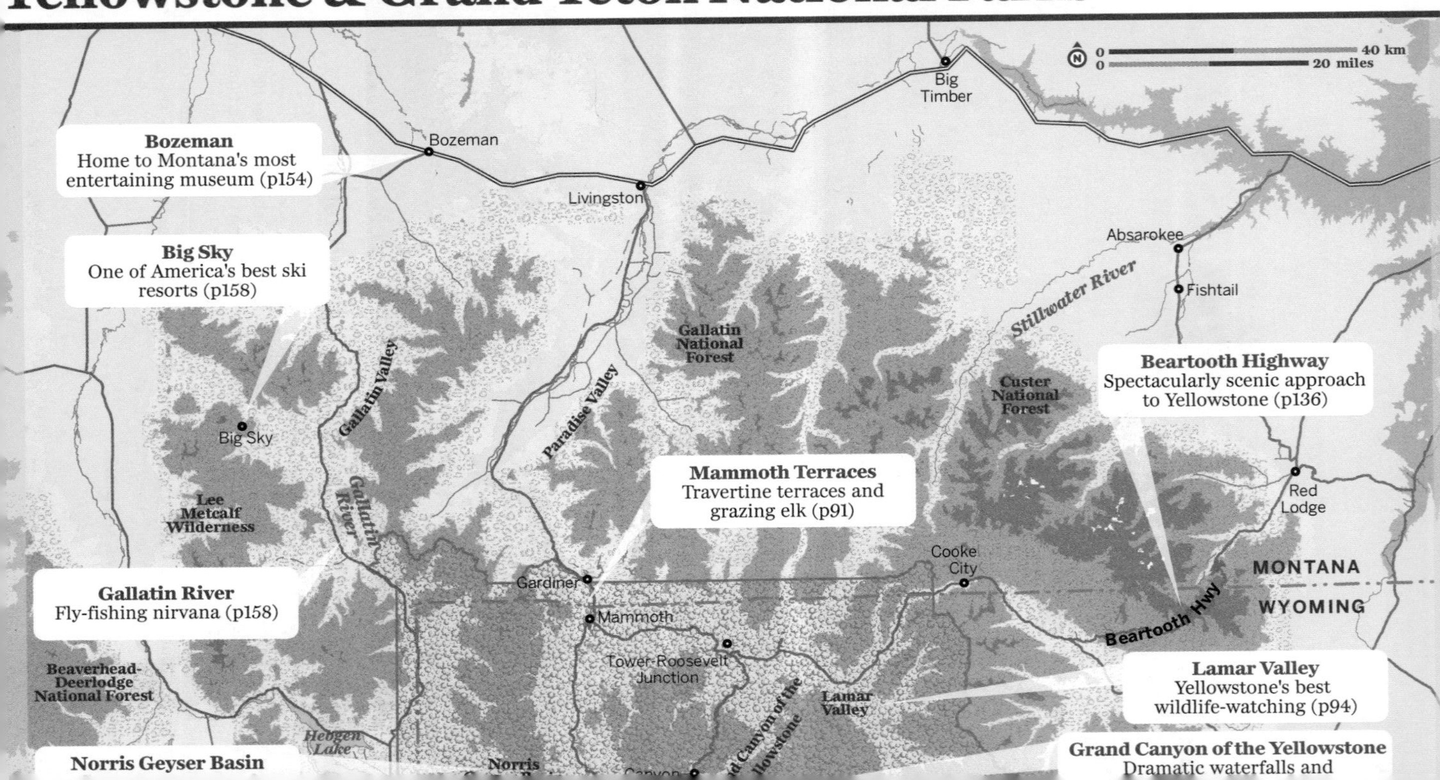

Bozeman
Home to Montana's most entertaining museum (p154)
Big Sky
One of America's best ski resorts (p158)
Gallatin River
Fly-fishing nirvana (p158)
Norris Geyser Basin
Mammoth Terraces
Travertine terraces and grazing elk (p91)
Beartooth Highway
Spectacularly scenic approach to Yellowstone (p136)
Lamar Valley
Yellowstone's best wildlife-watching (p94)
Grand Canyon of the Yellowstone
Dramatic waterfalls and
0
40 km
0
20 miles
Big Timber
Bozeman
Livingston
Absarokee
Fishtail
Stillwater River
Gallatin National Forest
Custer National Forest
Gallatin Valley
Paradise Valley
Big Sky
Lee Metcalf Wilderness
Gallatin River
Red Lodge
Cooke City
MONTANA
WYOMING
Beartooth Hwy
Gardiner
Mammoth
Tower-Roosevelt Junction
Lamar Valley
Beaverhead-Deerlodge National Forest
Hebgen Lake
Norris

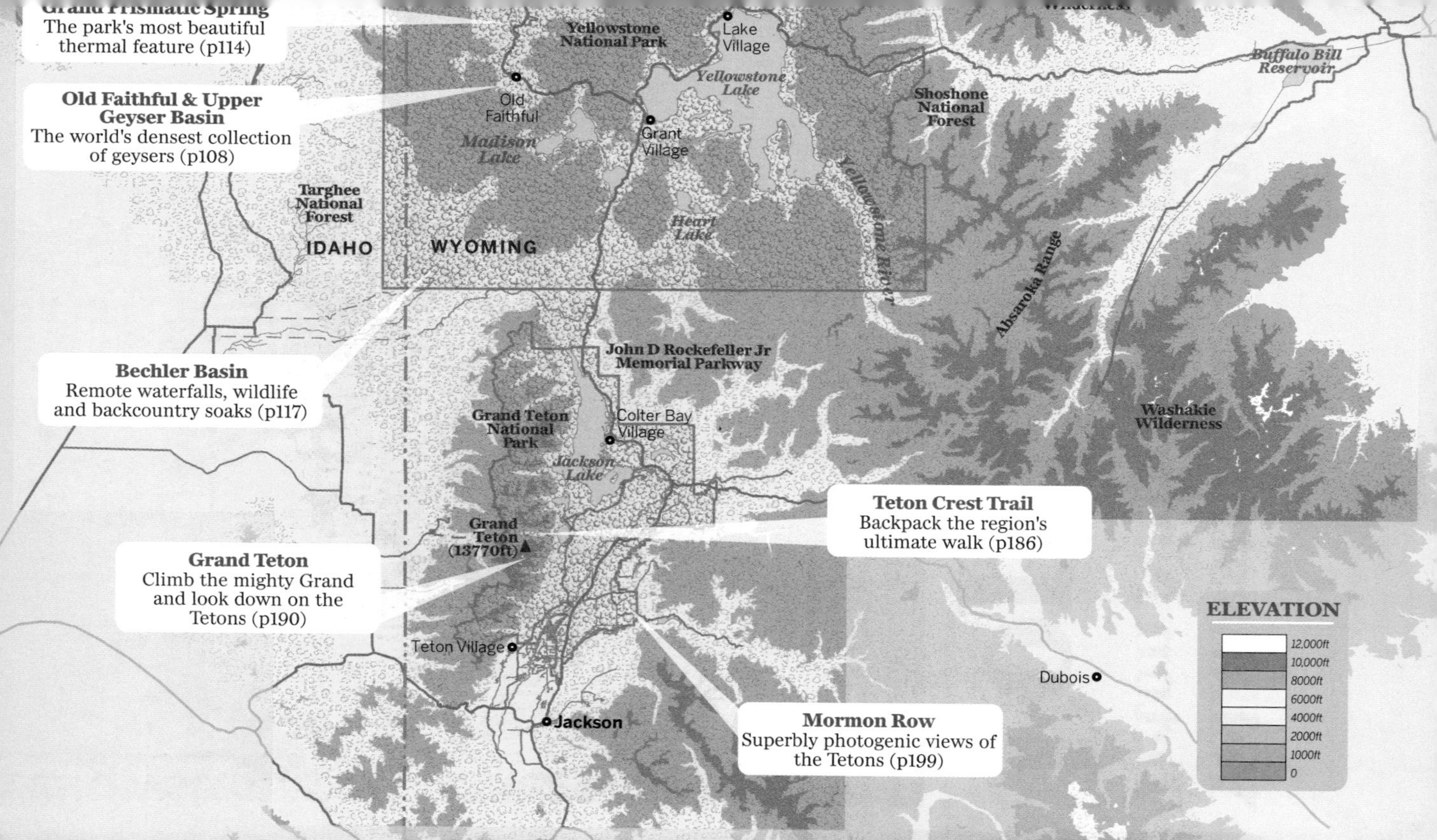
The park's most beautiful thermal feature (p114)
Old Faithful & Upper Geyser Basin
The world's densest collection of geysers (p108)
Bechler Basin
Remote waterfalls, wildlife and backcountry soaks (p117)
Grand Teton
Climb the mighty Grand and look down on the Tetons (p190)
Teton Crest Trail
Backpack the region's ultimate walk (p186)
Mormon Row
Superbly photogenic views of the Tetons (p199)
Yellowstone National Park
Lake Village
Yellowstone Lake
Old Faithful
Grant Village
Madison Lake
Heart Lake
Yellowstone River
Shoshone National Forest
Buffalo Bill Reservoir
Targhee National Forest
IDAHO
WYOMING
Absaroka Range
John D Rockefeller Jr Memorial Parkway
Grand Teton National Park
Colter Bay Village
Jackson Lake
Washakie Wilderness
Grand Teton (13770ft)
Teton Village
Jackson
Dubois
ELEVATION
12,000ft
10,000ft
8000ft
6000ft
4000ft
2000ft
1000ft
0

Yellowstone & Grand Teton National Parks' Top 20

1

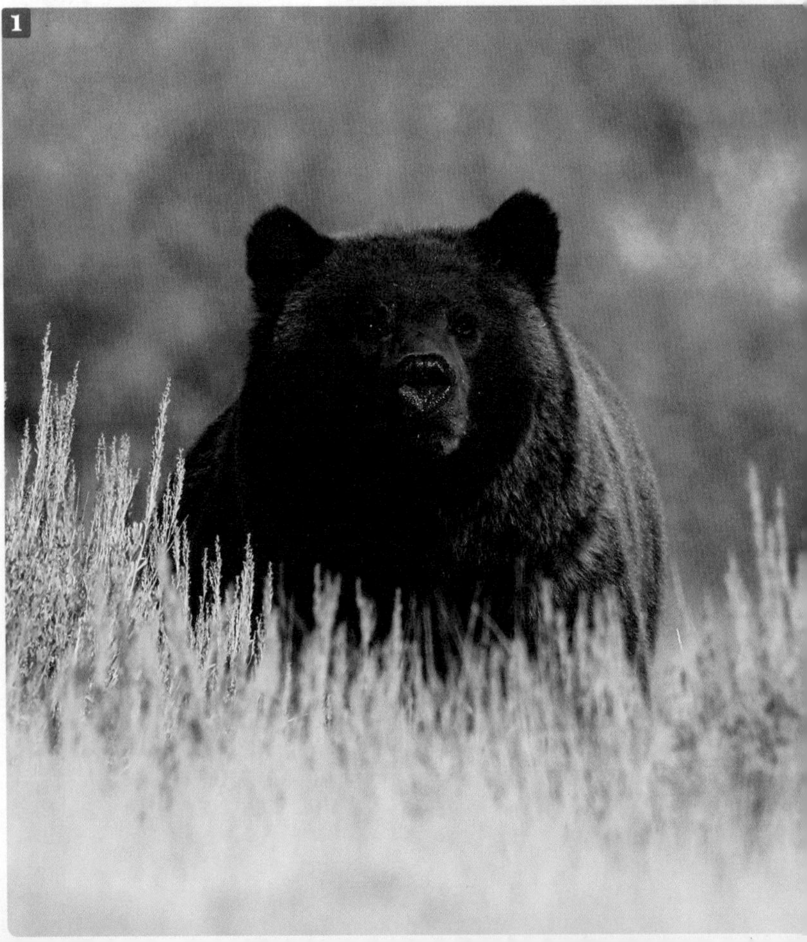

Wildlife-Spotting in the Lamar Valley

1 Known as the 'Serengeti of North America,' the lush Lamar Valley (p94) is home to the densest collection of big animals in Yellowstone. A dozen pullouts offer superb views over grazing herds of bison and elk, but search the tree lines closely with a spotting scope and you'll likely also see a lone grizzly on the prowl or a pack of wolves on the hunt. Come at dawn or dusk or in the company of a biologist guide, and be prepared to stand transfixed as nature plays itself out before your eyes. Below left: grizzly bear, Lamar Valley (p94)

Old Faithful & Upper Geyser Basin

2 The world's most famous geyser (p109) erupts every 90 minutes or so, so you have plenty of time to view it from several angles – from the main boardwalk, from the balcony of the Old Faithful Inn and from Observation Hill. The surrounding geyser basin offers dozens of other spectacular spouters; some that erupt dramatically just once a day, others that thrash continually in a violent rage. Check the visitor center for predicted eruption times and be patient if you want to catch Steamboat, Beehive or Grand, as it may take a while. Below: Old Faithful geyser (p109)

3

JEFF DIENER/GETTY IMAGES ©

4

Paddling the Teton's Alpine Lakes

3 Whether soloing in a kayak or bundling the family into a canoe, paddling (p192) is a great way to glide into nature at your own pace. When your arms tire, shore up on empty beaches for a picnic or a swim. With a permit you can also backcountry camp. Jackson Lake is the Teton's biggest lake; families might prefer the smaller scale of Leigh and String Lakes. For an adventurous multiday alternative in Yellowstone, try gorgeous Shoshone Lake, the region's largest backcountry lake. Above left: Jackson Lake (p192)

Grand Canyon of the Yellowstone

4 The sublime canyon colors and the dramatic 308ft drop of the Lower Falls are the big draws of Yellowstone's very own grand canyon (p97). Views here are spellbinding from all angles. There are several different ways to view the canyon: get close to the drop-off at the Brink of the Lower Falls, take in the big picture at Artist Point or descend steps to feel the spray on your face at Uncle Tom's. Best of all, take the rim's hiking trails to appreciate the views away from the car and the crowds. Above right: Lower Falls (p97)

Backpacking the Tetons

5 Don't expect any breaks; from the trailhead it's all uphill. Bu the payback for overnigh ing (p182) in the Tetons? Rolling glades alight with wildflowers, snow-lipped ridges and clear alpine lakes. Some of the most luscious, life-affirming scenery in the Tetons lies a day's hike in. And once there, who wants to hurry home? Backpackers can spend a week on the pop lar Teton Crest Trail, ram bling over the lofty spine of the Tetons. The shorte but still challenging, Alas Basin has fistfuls of summer blooms and Dall she to keep you company.

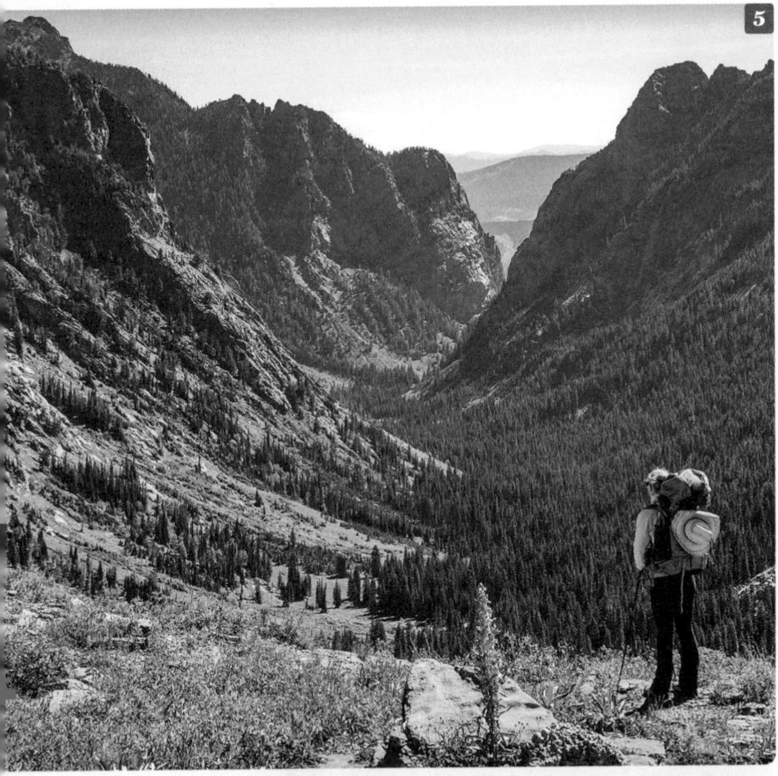

5

Iuseum f the Rockies

6 Greater Yellowstone's most entertaining useum (p155) is the erfect combination of n and learning. Its jaw-opping dinosaur collec-on is what really catches e imagination, from the hibits of sea monsters d fossilized dinosaur ests to the reconstructed *ontanoceratops* and the orld's largest T. rex skull. ere's a fine planetarium d the Yellowstone for ds interactive displays e the perfect place to art or end a park vaca-on. Allow at least half a y to explore the space.

HUGH K TELLERIA/SHUTTERSTOCK ©

6

7

8

Climbing the Grand Teton

7 Buck the trend of roadside viewing and look down on the Tetons on a guided ascent. The birthplace of American mountaineering, the chiseled and weathered Grand (p190) continues to rate among America's premier climbing destinations. The two-day affair starts with a steep 7-mile approach past wildflower fields and waterfalls. Rest up, because a 3am wake-up call heralds summit day, with views of the sprawling wilderness of three states. Climbers need some prior instruction, but it can be gained locally before the climb.

Grand Prismatic Spring

8 Yellowstone's most beautiful thermal feature is this swimming-pool-size hot spring (p114), 10 miles north of Old Faithful. The shimmering turquoise blue waters are impressive enough but it's the surrounding multicolored rings of algae that push it out of this world. As the water temperature changes, so do the colors of the thermophiles, creating a rainbow of oranges, yellows and greens. From above the spring looks like a giant eye weeping exquisite multicolored tears. For the best views, enjoy the new overlook.

ꞁoose-Watching

Majestic, massive and as gawky as overgrown teenagers, moose (p248) ꞁ a sight to behold. Bulls can weigh twice ꞁ much as a Harley-Davidson motorꞁcle, with massive, cupped antlers, each ꞁighing up to 50lb, which are shed after ꞁ fall rut. You'll find moose wherever ꞁlows grow, since it's their food of choice. ꞁey can also be spotted around lakes ꞁd marshes. In the Tetons they're comꞁon around Willow Flats and Cottonwood ꞁeek; in Yellowstone look for them in ꞁ Bechler region and the Gallatin River ꞁainages.

Skiing Jackson Hole or Big Sky

10 Winter is the perfect time to combine a park visit with some serious mountain fun. The region's downhill action centers on Jackson Hole (p221) in Wyoming and Big Sky (p158) in Montana. Jackson Hole offers great runs near Jackson town and airport, whereas Big Sky boasts over 5500 acres of runs and one of the country's best cross-country resorts. Don't limit yourself to skiing – there are dinner sleigh rides and dogsledding in Big Sky and backcountry yurts and heli-skiing options in Jackson Hole.

Above: Jackson Hole (p221)

Bechler Basin Waterfalls

11 Hidden in the remote southwest corner of Yellowstone, close to nowhere and accessed by a single bone-crunching dirt road, Bechler (p117) hides the park's most spectacular collection of waterfalls. Union, Colonnade and Cave Falls are the better-known destinations but there are dozens of other thundering falls, feathery cascades and hidden hot springs that entice hardy backpackers and day hikers to brave the fearsome mosquitoes and boggy trails. Come in August and September for the best conditions. Below: Cave Falls (p117)

Mammoth Terraces

12 Northern Yellowstone's major thermal feature is a graceful coll tion of travertine terraces and cascadin hot pools (p91). Some terraces are bone dry, while others sparkle with hundreds of minuscule pools, coral-like formation and a fabulous palette of colors that cou come from an impressionist painting. Th miniature mountain of thermal action is constant flux. Get bonus views of severa terraces by taking the little-trod Howard Eaton Trail, or ski it in winter, when you'l likely share the terraces with elk.

11

12

GHOST BEAR/SHUTTERSTOCK ©

MARGARETW/SHUTTERSTOCK ©

ormon Row

3 A favorite of photographers, this avel strip of old home-eads (p199) and wind-ashed barns backed by e Teton's jagged pano-ma lies just east of Hwy 1. Sure, you could drive but the ultra-scenic and ncake-flat loop makes one nice bike ride. In e 1890s, early settlers re drawn to this land-ape of lush sagebrush homesteading. The ts are also popular with on and pronghorn; e latter have used this rridor for seasonal grations to the Yukon for er 6000 years.

Wildflowers

14 Break out the hiking boots in June and you'll discover that the hillsides across the region have quietly exploded with a mosaic of attention-grabbing wildflowers (p252). Golden yellow balsamroot, violet lupines and pink monkey flowers are just a few of the spectacular blooms competing for your attention in meadows from the Gallatins to the Tetons. Know your blooms and you might spot more wildlife – grizzlies love beargrass, while hummingbirds are drawn to fire-red Indian paintbrush. Head to higher elevations in July for even more blooms.

Family Hiking

15 Nature trails, hikes to beaches, lookout points, lakes and geysers... adventure just comes naturally to kids, who will be thrilled by their first sighting of a backcountry bison or belching mud pots. These parks do family adventure (p39) right. Junior Rangers can earn badges and nature know-how, while Yellowstone's Young Scientist Program ups the ante by helping kids explore the park with a specialized tool kit in hand. Before heading out, know the endurance level of your kids and choose your trail wisely. Above: Hiking near Grand Prismatic Spring (p114)

BGSMITH/SHUTTERSTOCK ©

Backpacking Yellowstone

16 Perhaps the best way to appreciate the park is to pack up your tent and join the mere 1% of visitors who experience the scale and silence of Yellowstone's backcountry (p70). Only when you wander on foot through wolf and grizzly country do you truly sense the primeval wildness of Yellowstone's remoter reaches. Traverse the Gallatin range in the park's northwest, backpack out to Heart Lake or take an adventurous expedition-style trek as far from a road as you can get in the lower 48.

Yellowstone in Winter

17 Winter is perhaps Yellowstone's most magical season (p88), but come prepared for serious cold. Geysers turn nearby trees into frozen ice sculptures and the wildlife is easier to spot in the whiteness, including the frosty-bearded bison warming themselves by steaming hot springs. Take a snowcoach trip to Canyon, ski past exploding geysers or snowshoe out through the muffled silence to a frozen waterfall, then finish the day sipping hot chocolate in front of a roaring fire at the Old Faithful Snow Lodge.

Beartooth Highway

18 Depending on who's talking, the Beartooth Hwy (p136) is either the best way to ge[t] to Yellowstone, the most exciting motorbike ride in the West or the most scenic highway in the US. We'd say it is all three. Th[e] head-spinning tarmac snakes up the mountainside to deposit you in a different world, high abo[ve] the tree line, onto a rolling plateau of mountain tundra, alpine lakes and Rocky Mountain goats. The views are superb, th[e] fishing awesome and the hiking literally breathtaking. Above: Beartooth Hw[y] near Red Lodge (p134)

orris Geyser Basin

9 Yellowstone's hottest and most active geyser basin and Steam-
at, its tallest geyser (in fact the world's est, at 400ft) are not at Old Faithful : further north in Norris Geyser Basin 05). Boardwalks lead around the 1e-white plain, past hissing fumaroles, blue pools, colorful runoffs and rare dic geysers. The Yellowstone hot spot o close to the surface here that the d actually pulsates. Stay at the nearby npground so you can stroll over from ır campsite at sunset while looking out elk along the Gibbon River.

Fly-Fishing the Gallatin River

20 Montana is sacred ground for fly-fishing enthusiasts, and the region's blue-ribbon streams don't get much better than the Gallatin River (p159), immortalized by Robert Redford in his film *A River Runs Through It*. The region's dozen or so fly-fishing shops are well stocked with lovingly crafted caddis flies and woolly buggers and can fill you in on current best fishing spots, including the nearby Madison, Yellowstone or Firehole Rivers. Most places offer guided trips and some offer casting clinics.

Need to Know

For more information, see Survival Guide (p255)

Entrance Fees

$35/30 per vehicle/motorcycle per park for seven days; $20 per person on foot or bicycle per park. Annual pass $70 per park.

Money

Yellowstone has 24-hour ATMs at almost all hotels and general stores. In Grand Teton look for 24-hour ATMs at Dornan's (p209) and Jackson Lake Lodge (p206), Colter Bay Village (p205) and Signal Mountain (p206).

Cell Phones

Patchy reception in Yellowstone outside of the main junctions. Cell coverage is good in Grand Teton, except the canyons.

Driving

Speed limit is generally 45mph: observe the signs. Parking at popular trailheads fills up by 11am in peak periods.

When to Go

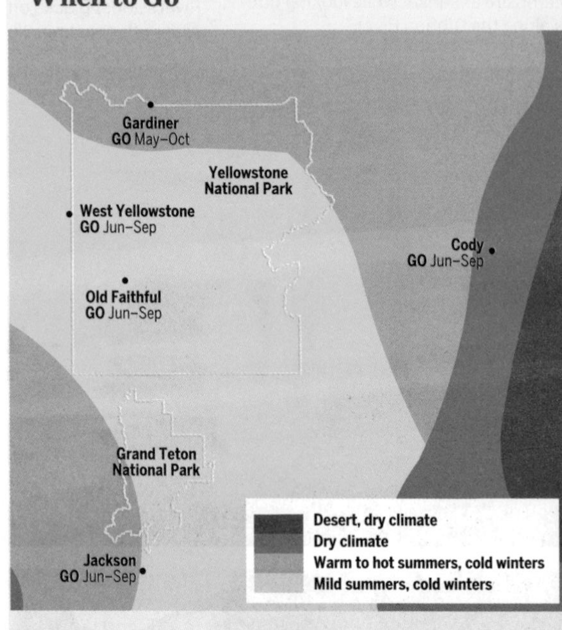

High Season
(Jun–Aug)

➡ Cool nights and hot days (very hot on the plains).

➡ Over half the parks' visitors arrive. Hotel rates peak at gateway towns, park campgrounds fill by lunchtime and reservations are essential.

Shoulder
(Apr-May, Sep–mid-Dec)

➡ Cooler months bring fewer crowds (and more discounts) but unpredictable weather. September is generally excellent.

➡ Some activities and campgrounds close.

➡ Some roads don't open until the end of May.

Low Season
(late Dec–Mar)

➡ Only 5% of visitors see Yellowstone in winter.

➡ Campgrounds are closed and transport is limited to snowcoaches or guided snowmobiles inside Yellowstone, except for the northern Mammoth–Cooke City road.

Useful Websites

Yellowstone National Park (www.nps.gov/yell) Official website.

Grand Teton National Park (www.nps.gov/grte) Official website.

Yellowstone National Park Lodges (www.yellowstonenationalparklodges.com) Yellowstone lodges, campgrounds and activities.

Grand Teton Lodge Company (www.gtlc.com) Lodges, campsites, dining and activities.

Lonely Planet (www.lonelyplanet.com) Destination information, hotel bookings, traveler forums and more.

Important Numbers

Yellowstone National Park	307-344-7381
Old Faithful Visitor Center	307-344-2751
Grand Teton National Park	307-739-3300
Yellowstone National Park Lodges reservations	307-344-7311
Grand Teton Lodge Company	307-543-3100

Exchange Rates

Australia	A$1	US$0.74
Canada	C$1	US$0.76
Eurozone	€1	US$1.17
Japan	¥100	US$0.90
New Zealand	NZ$1	US$0.67
UK	£1	US$1.32

For current exchange rates, see www.xe.com.

Daily Costs

Budget: Less than $150

- Campgrounds: $15–30 per carload, RVs $48–70
- Budget hotel outside the park: $120
- Backcountry permit: $3 per person per night in Yellowstone

Midrange: $150–250

- Rooms in Yellowstone: $177–400, cabins from $96
- Restaurant meal: $20–30
- Rafting/Wild West cookout for a family of four: $220

Top end: More than $250

- Splurge in Jackson and Jenny Lake Lodges
- Guided fly-fishing trip per day in a group of two: $250
- Winter tour in Yellowstone: per person per day from $300

Opening Dates

Yellowstone National Park The north entrance at Gardiner is open year-round, as is the northern Gardiner to Cooke City road via Mammoth and Roosevelt. Park roads open in May on a staggered schedule, closing again in early November. Most campgrounds, park services and visitor centers close October to May.

Grand Teton National Park Open year-round, though most of Teton Park Rd is closed to vehicles in winter. Most campgrounds and visitor centers close October to May.

Park Policies & Regulations

Permits Required for backcountry trips, boating and fishing.

Swimming Prohibited in waters of purely thermal origin.

Wildlife Stay 100yd from bears and wolves, 25yd from other animals.

Food Must be securely stored.

Pets Must be leashed at all times. Restricted access areas apply.

Drones Prohibited in both parks.

Getting There & Around

Jackson, well positioned between Yellowstone and Grand Teton, is fast becoming the region's busiest gateway, closely followed by Bozeman, Billings and, to a lesser extent, Cody.

Jackson Hole Airport is located inside Grand Teton National Park.

Bozeman Yellowstone International Airport is 90 miles from Yellowstone via the Gallatin Valley or 80 miles via Livingston and the Paradise Valley.

Billings Logan Airport is 130 slow, winding miles to Yellowstone via the spectacular Beartooth Hwy.

- It's almost impossible to visit Yellowstone without your own vehicle. All airports in the vicinity of the parks are well represented by car-rental companies.
- It can sometimes be cheaper to fly into a larger hub, like Salt Lake City (390 miles) or Denver (563 miles), and rent wheels from there.
- Park roads can be narrow and many smaller roads are off limits to RVs and buses.
- There's no public transportation of any kind inside the park.

For much more on **getting around**, see p272

If You Like...

Thermal Features

For many, Yellowstone's biggest draw is its other-worldly collection of spouters, gushers, bubblers and burpers, which together constitute over three-quarters of the world's weirdest thermal features.

Old Faithful Try to view this iconic and dependable old geyser from various angles, including Observation Hill. (p109)

Grand Prismatic Spring The park's most beautiful thermal feature is a swimming-pool-sized spring ringed by electric rainbow colors. (p114)

Lone Star Geyser There's something really special about watching a geyser erupt in the solitude of the backcountry. (p68)

Mammoth Hot Springs These graceful tiered terraces and colorful coral-like formations have a subtle but sublime beauty. (p91)

Steamboat Geyser Check to see what's happening at the world's tallest active geyser, in Norris Geyser Basin. (p106)

Chico Hot Springs These open-air mineral hot springs, some 30 miles north of Yellowstone, erase all post-hike aches. (p149)

Ferris Fork Slip into this very private backcountry hot spring while backpacking in the remote Bechler region. (p80)

Wildlife

To spot a grizzly, wolf or bighorn sheep you need to know the terrain, the season and the workings of an animal's brain. Then again, you'll probably see bison, elk or even a bear without having to undo your seat belt.

Lamar and Hayden Valleys Big bison herds, wolf packs and the occasional grizzly make these Yellowstone's prime wildlife-watching hangouts. (p94 and p100)

Grizzly & Wolf Discovery Center If grizzlies and wolves eluded you in the park, see them up close at this nonprofit center. (p163)

Guided tour Learn about Yellowstone's complex ecosystem through a course at the Yellowstone Forever Institute or on a professional naturalist tour. (p34)

Mustang tour For something different, day-trip to spot wild mustangs cavorting on the high Wyoming desert. (p142)

Hermitage Point Hike out to see ospreys diving for their dinner, dozens of water birds, swans and cranes. (p197)

Lake Solitude Hiking Cascade Canyon offers a side of bull moose enjoying the riverbanks in summer. (p202)

Scenic Drives

There's hardly a mile in Yellowstone country that isn't pull-off-the-road, drop-dead gorgeous. These are the ones that make us happy to pay park prices for our gas.

Beartooth Hwy The most scenic road in America is this astounding drive above the tree line. (p136)

Gallatin Valley Scenes from Robert Redford's *A River Runs Through It* paired with mountain ranges and ranchlands. (p158)

Paradise Valley Rolling ranchlands and snowy peaks flank Yellowstone's north entrance. (p149)

Signal Mountain Summit Rd Dramatic panoramas over the Snake River to the Tetons, 800ft above Jackson Hole's valley floor. (p197)

Hwy 191 & Teton Park Rd Fantastic Teton views from the Jackson Hole Valley flats, with roaming pronghorn, deer and moose. (p91)

Geyser Trail Hit the 25-mile route from Old Faithful to West Yellowstone for thermal features galore. (p82)

Backcountry Trips

Yellowstone's wildest corners are as far from a road as you can get in the

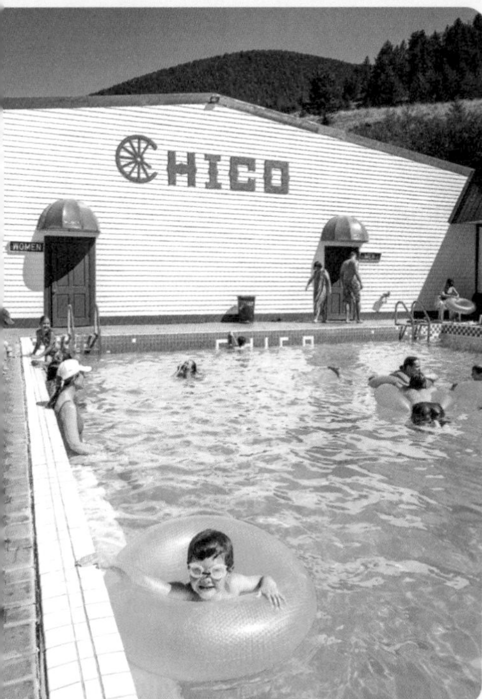

Top: Chico Hot Springs (p149)
Bottom: Gray wolf (p245)

lower 48. A certain know-how is essential here: you need to know what you are doing if you want to bed down with the grizzlies.

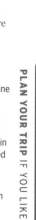

Teton Crest Trail Superlative mountain scenery spurs this four-day trek along the high spine of the Tetons. (p186)

Gallatin Skyline Yellowstone's northwest corner offers superb backpacking trips over mountain passes to lakes and snowcapped peaks. (p81)

Beartooth Plateau Over 1000 lakes dot this alpine tundra with fantastic backpacking routes. (p31)

Shoshone Lake Yellowstone's largest backcountry lake offers golden lakeshore campsites for a great multiday trek or paddle. (p77)

Paintbrush Divide This popular two-day loop takes you up to alpine lakes and craggy peaks. (p182)

Heart Lake Thermal features, a peak ascent and lakeshore campsites, just a day's walk from the road. (p75)

Alaska Basin Approach the Tetons from the lesser-known Idaho side: it's wildflower paradise.

Winter

Only a fraction of Yellowstone's visitors see the park during its most alluring season. Many repeat visitors rank it their favorite season, despite some logistical complications (snowcoaches and skinny skis are the main ways of getting around).

Old Faithful Ski past ghost trees to frozen waterfalls and erupting geysers or drink cocoa at the Snow Lodge. (p109)

Jackson Hole Mountain Resort The region's premier downhill runs also offer excellent Nordic trails and dinner sleigh rides. (p222)

West Yellowstone The region's Nordic skiing and snowmobiling capital is also the kick-off point for Yellowstone snowcoach tours. (p163)

Canyon yurt camp Ride a snowcoach to a private yurt to ski around the wildlife-rich backcountry. (p88)

Mammoth Ski past thermal features or drive the park's only open road for winter wolf-watching. (p89)

Snowshoe with a Naturalist The Tetons offer this excellent park program at Taggart Lake; snowshoe rentals available. (p193)

Jenny Lake XC-ski route Skate or Nordic ski an 8-mile loop along Cottonwood Creek with snowbound Teton views. (p195)

The Good Life

Just because you're in the Wild West doesn't mean you have to rough it all the time. Take a break with the following indulgences.

Piste Mountain Bistro Ride the Bridger Gondola up to the summit for a dinner with an unrivaled view. (p223)

Spring Creek Ranch Resort Snuggle by the fireplace, sink into spa treatments or order sunset cocktails with screaming Teton views. (p217)

Rainbow Ranch Lodge Share one of this luxury lodge's 5000 bottles of wine in the outdoor Jacuzzi. (p161)

Chico Hot Springs Enjoy horseback riding, massages and poolside microbrews at this historic Paradise Valley resort. (p149)

Bin 22 Pair your favorite bottle from the adjoining Jackson wine shop with exquisite Spanish tapas. (p219)

Jenny Lake Lodge Dining Room Indulge in a five-course gourmet meal and Spanish guitar music in this bewitching log cabin. (p209)

Learning

The more you learn about the Yellowstone ecosystem, the more interesting it becomes. With courses from wolf-watching to the inner workings of a supervolcano, you'll never look at the land in the same way again.

Yellowstone Forever Institute Offers a fantastic range of year-round courses, from photography to backpacking 101, led by experts. (p267)

Teton Science School Quality instruction for kids and adults with wildlife tours and immersive programs. (p42)

Junior rangers Kids will love earning their ranger badge through parkwide projects and activities. (p40)

Fly-fishing course The gorgeous waters of the Yellowstone, Gallatin and Madison are ideal for perfecting your cast. (p159)

Kayaking course Gardiner and Jackson outfitters run fun kayaking courses on the Yellowstone and Snake Rivers. (p213)

Ranger talks Both Yellowstone and Grand Teton offer excellent free talks at visitor centers and ranger hikes. (p40)

An Adrenaline Rush

Aside from an unexpected brush with a grizzly, there are plenty of ways to get the pulse racing in the Yellowstone region. Bring a spare pair of underpants.

Climbing Grand Teton This guided climb offers the best views in the West and a real sense of achievement. (p193)

Snow King Resort Walk the tightrope of your limits on this amazing summer adventure course, crafted by experts. (p215)

White-water rafting From wild rides on the Gallatin and Snake Rivers to family floats on the Yellowstone. (p216)

Paragliding Jackson Hole Get unrivaled Teton views on a tandem flight from Jackson Hole Mountain Resort. (p222)

Big Sky Resort Ziplines, trampoline bungees and chairlift-assisted mountain-bike runs ensure summer fun rivals winter at this resort. (p158)

Grand Targhee Resort Check out the mountain-biking opportunities that surround this low-key Idaho resort. (p226)

The Wild West

Montana and Wyoming still carry the ghosts of the American West. It's the proud home to cowboys, ranches, rodeos and Native American powwows.

Cody Trail Butch and Sundance at Old Trail Town and drink up at Buffalo Bill's Irma Hotel. (p141)

Dude Ranches Take in the memorable Western experiences in the Wapiti and Gallatin Valleys and Jackson Hole. (p261)

Roosevelt Country Ride a stagecoach rumble seat before tucking into steak-n-beans at the park's favorite cowboy cookout. (p94)

Jackson Rhinestone cowboys, staged shoot-outs and gourmet chow make Jackson the poster child for Wyoming's New West. (p213)

Mormon Row This historic Tetons district features original log cabins and barns, made famous by Ansel Adams. (p189)

Month by Month

TOP EVENTS

Cody Stampede July

Smoking Waters Mountain Man Rendezvous August

Grand Teton Music Festival July

Plains Indian Powwow June

Custer's Last Stand Reenactment June

March

Mid-March marks the end of the park's winter season, and the snowplows start to clear Yellowstone's roads. Yellowstone's wildlife has the park pretty much to itself.

Spring Cycling

From the second Monday in March to the third Thursday in April, most of Yellowstone's roads are closed to motor traffic, but West Yellowstone to Mammoth road is open to cyclists. There are no facilities and snow is a possibility, but it's a wonderful opportunity to cycle traffic-free.

April

As Yellowstone starts to shake off winter, the park's roads begin to open, starting with the West Entrance and western sections of the Grand Loop Rd.

Backcountry Reservations

On April 1 reservations are taken for Yellowstone's backcountry campsites, so if you have a specific time planned for a popular route, make sure your reservations are in by this day.

May

Rain and snowmelt create high rivers and full waterfalls, with snow at higher elevations. Wildlife viewing is good, with baby elk and bison finding their feet, but many hiking trails are boggy. Focus on the northern half of Yellowstone to avoid spring road closures.

Elkfest Antler Auction

Head to Jackson to kit out your cabin in Rocky Mountain style at Elkfest. In a weekend of activities a week before Memorial Day, boy scouts collect and sell shed antlers to raise money to buy winter feed for the National Elk Refuge. (p216)

Memorial Day

The last Sunday in May heralds high season. Park entrances, roads and access routes are now mostly open and services expand. The last to open is the road between Tower and Canyon over Dunraven Pass (8859ft) and the Beartooth Hwy, if there's heavy snowpack.

June

Summer arrives at last, as average highs hit 70°F (21°C) and wildflowers start to bloom at lower elevations. The last of the park accommodations open by mid-June. Mosquitoes can be bothersome until mid-August.

Plains Indian Powwow

The region's Native American culture is celebrated in mid-June at Cody's Buffalo Bill Historical Center: dancers, drummers and artisans gather at the Plains Indian Powwow in a colorful celebration of Shoshone and other traditions. (p144)

Rodeo!

Rodeo is the major cultural event of the Yellowstone year. The Cody Nite Rodeo kicks off June 1, as does the biweekly Jackson Hole Rodeo, with more rodeos pulling into Gardiner and West Yellowstone mid-month. (p146) (p216)

Custer's Last Stand Reenactment

Hundreds of historical reenactors head to the Battle of Little Bighorn from June 24 to 26 for the anniversary of Custer's Last Stand. Admission to the battlefield is free on the 25th. (p132)

July

Temperatures reach 80°F (27°C) in lower elevations, with Cody and Billings around 10°F (or more) hotter. Afternoon thunderstorms are common but the high country is snow-free, allowing high-altitude wildflowers to bloom. Over one million people visit Yellowstone Park in July.

Cody Stampede

The July 4 weekend brings crowds to the park and rodeo to the park's gateways. The Cody Stampede (www.codystampederodeo.com) is the region's biggest bash but there are also rodeos in Livingston and Red Lodge.

Music Festivals

July is the month for live music. The Grand Teton Music Festival adds some classical class to Teton Village, the Yellowstone Jazz Festival (https://yellowstonejazz.com) funks up Cody, while Targhee Fest (www.grandtarghee.com/event/targhee-fest) brings alt-country to Idaho's Teton Valley mid-month. (p222)

August

As visitor numbers peak, moose and elk retreat into the backcountry. August is a prime hiking month, when wildflowers bloom at higher altitudes and huckleberries and chokecherries ripen.

Smoking Waters Mountain Man Rendezvous

West Yellowstone's mountain man rendezvous is a 10-day reenactment of an 1859 gathering and includes tomahawk-throwing competitions, cowboy poetry and black-powder sharpshooting. Red Lodge has a smaller rendezvous at the end of July, as does Jackson in May.

Crow Fair

More than 1000 tepees of the Apsaalooke Nation are erected in the Crow Agency, west of Billings, on the third weekend in August, for the annual Crow Fair (www.crow-nsn.gov). Highlights include dramatic Native American dances, rodeo and plenty of fried tacos.

September

Fall colors, the sounds of bugling elk, lack of mosquitoes and off-season discounts make September a great month to visit, despite chilly nights. Ranger programs peter out after Labor Day, as park accommodations start to close.

Running of the Sheep

Tiny Reed Point, Montana, hosts the annual 'Running of the Sheep,' an admirably dorky, far less exciting version of Pamplona's Running of the Bulls. A parade and evening street dance ramp up the Labor Day weekend action.

November

All Yellowstone park roads close on the first Monday in November, except for the Gardiner–Cooke City road. In Grand Teton US 26/89/191 remains open all winter to Flagg Ranch but parts of Teton Park Rd and the Moose–Wilson road close, as does Grassy Lake Rd.

Yellowstone Ski Festival

Thanksgiving week heralds the Yellowstone Ski Festival (www.yellowstoneskifestival.com) at West Yellowstone, a great time for ski buffs and newcomers to the sport. Highlights include ski clinics (for kids, too) and gear demos. Nordic skiing kicks off around this time.

December

In the parks, winter conditions have fully set in. Starting in mid-December through mid-March, the XC ski trails for Nordic and skate skiing are groomed in Grand Teton National Park.

Itineraries

Mammoth
Bunsen Peak
Norris Geyser Basin
Yellowstone National Park
Madison River
Fairy Falls
Old Faithful Inn
Yellowstone Lake
Lone Star Geyser
Grand Teton National Park
Jackson Lake
String Lake/ Leigh Lake
Oxbow Bend
Cascade Canyon
Jenny Lake Drive
Mormon Row

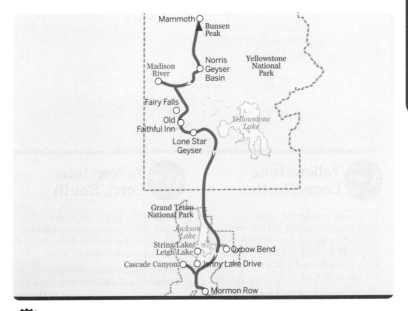

Yellowstone & Grand Teton Overview

Start in **Mammoth**, taking the morning to climb Bunsen Peak for the fantastic views, before paying a brief visit to Mammoth Hot Springs and driving to **Norris Geyser Basin**. Continue to your reserved campsite at Madison for some early evening elk- and bison-spotting or fly-fishing on the **Madison River**.

Spend the next two days in Geyser Country, hiking to either **Fairy Falls** or Sentinel Meadows for backcountry geysers and bison. Stay the night at historic **Old Faithful Inn** to experience the Upper Geyser Basin and the next day cycle out to **Lone Star Geyser** to catch a backcountry eruption.

Drive south into Grand Teton and search for trumpeter swans at **Oxbow Bend**. **Jenny Lake Dr** is worth a linger for its awesome views of the Central Tetons. Enjoy a family trip to forested **String** and **Leigh Lakes** or join the crowds for Grand Teton's most popular day hike up **Cascade Canyon** to Lake Solitude. Finally, cycle around **Mormon Row** for iconic views of barns and bison before heading south to Jackson for some R&R.

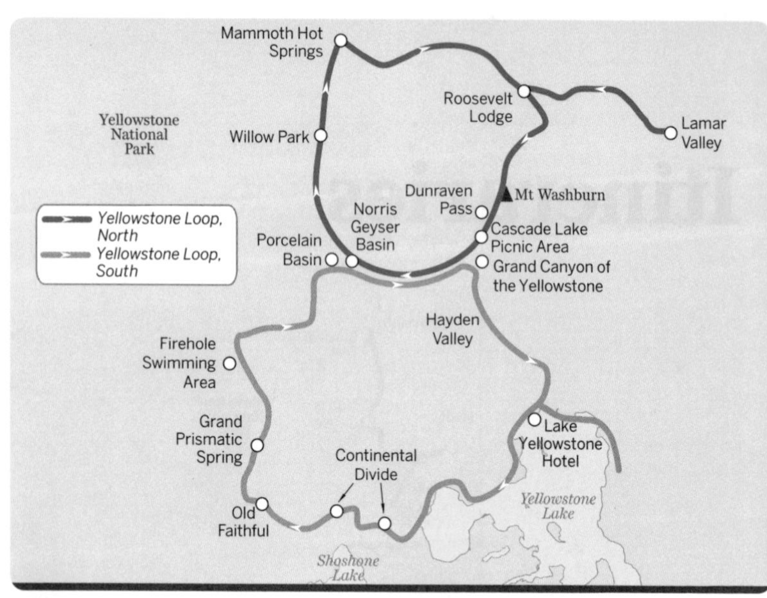

1 DAY Yellowstone Loop, North

This route through the north of the park takes in some premier wildlife-watching, views of the Grand Canyon of the Yellowstone and a sampler of geysers and hot springs. You'll need to start early and stay out late to fit it all in.

Head straight to the **Lamar Valley** around dawn to look for wolves, bears and bison. Grab a 'hiker's breakfast' at **Roosevelt Lodge**, then drive up to **Dunraven Pass** to make the three- to four-hour return hike up Mt Washburn for the park's best views. Picnic amid the pines at shady **Cascade Lake picnic area** or grab lunch on the go at Canyon.

Gawp at the thundering falls and rusted colors of the **Grand Canyon of the Yellowstone** from Uncle Tom's Trail and Artist Point on the southern rim, before driving to the geysers and hot springs of **Norris Geyser Basin**. Then swing north toward Mammoth, stopping en route to watch for moose at **Willow Park**. Stroll the boardwalks at dusk to admire surreal Palette Springs and Canary Springs at **Mammoth Hot Springs**, before collapsing in the bar back at Roosevelt Lodge for a well-deserved Old Faithful Ale.

1 DAY Yellowstone Loop, South

The southern loop takes in epic Yellowstone Lake, the park's greatest geysers and a dip in the Firehole River. Starting in West Yellowstone adds 28 miles.

Start the day with a scenic drive around **Yellowstone Lake** and then branch west from West Thumb over the **Continental Divide** into Geyser Country. Check predicted eruption times at the visitor center to catch **Old Faithful** and others of the Upper Geyser Basin spouters. Head north to Midway Geyser Basin and admire **Grand Prismatic Spring**, then blow off steam with the kids in the thermally heated **Firehole Swimming Area** further north.

Continue north to the **Porcelain Basin** hot springs at Norris, grabbing a quick lunch at peaceful Norris Meadows picnic area, before turning east for views of the **Grand Canyon of the Yellowstone** from Uncle Tom's Trail and Artist Point. Swing south through **Hayden Valley** for some prime sunset wildlife-watching before enjoying the park's best food at **Lake Yellowstone Hotel Dining Room**.

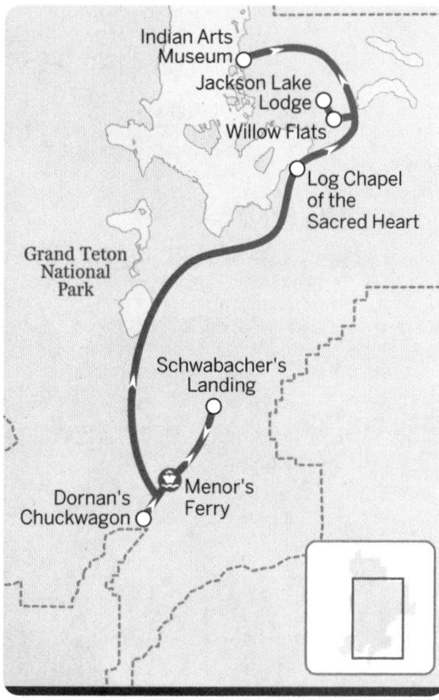

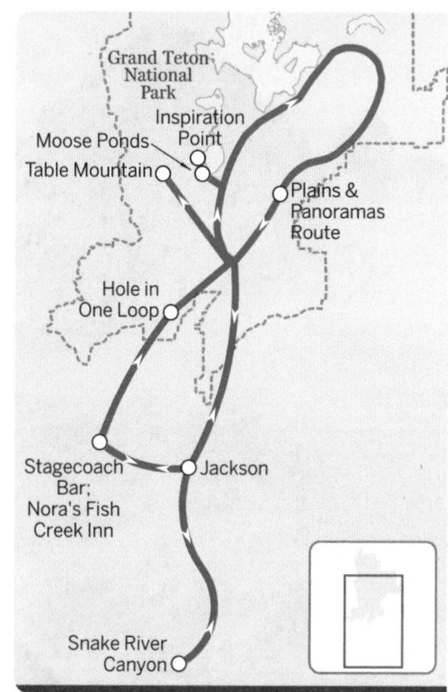

1 DAY Teton in a Day

Start with a hearty breakfast in Moose at **Dornan's Chuckwagon**, a pioneer-style camp serving flapjacks alfresco with great Teton views. Then glimpse the area's fascinating homesteading history at **Menor's Ferry**; audio tours are available for cell phones. For excellent photographs, **Schwabacher's Landing** offers the best panoramas of the Teton's toothy Cathedral group.

Get off the road and into the wilderness with a short hike to the glacial moraines cupping Taggart and Bradley Lakes. Bring swimsuits and take a dip from Taggart's eastern edge if it's warm enough. Afterwards, take the short drive to the **Log Chapel of the Sacred Heart** and spread your blanket for a picnic at the edge of the pines.

Nearby, there's incredible Native American beadwork at the **Indian Arts Museum**. End your outing watching wildlife at **Willow Flats**; there's usually a moose munching in the dusky light. Finally, cap your day at **Jackson Lake Lodge** and down a huckleberry margarita at the Blue Heron.

4 DAYS Jackson Hole & the Tetons

Fuel up with a classic breakfast of pan-fried trout at Wilson's **Nora's Fish Creek Inn**, then saddle your road bike to ride the **Hole in One loop** – extra points for starting from Wilson. Post-ride, opt for a brew at the award-winning Snake River Brewing Co, in **Jackson**.

On day two, hike out to scenic views at **Inspiration Point** and take the ferry back for an easy return. Detour to **Moose Ponds** to snag a glimpse of its namesake ungulates. For sunset views, rumble your pickup along the dirt roads of the **Plains & Panoramas route**.

On day three, take a white-water rafting trip down the **Snake River Canyon**. Later, treat yourself to a pan-roasted elk chop at Snake River Grill and take in some culture at the modern Center for the Arts, both in Jackson.

On your final day, get an early start to power up **Table Mountain** for a challenging hike with big backside views of the Tetons. Make your last night count at the **Stagecoach Bar**, the liveliest roadhouse around.

Above: Cascade Canyon (p202)

Left: Black Pool (p104), West Thumb Geyser Basin

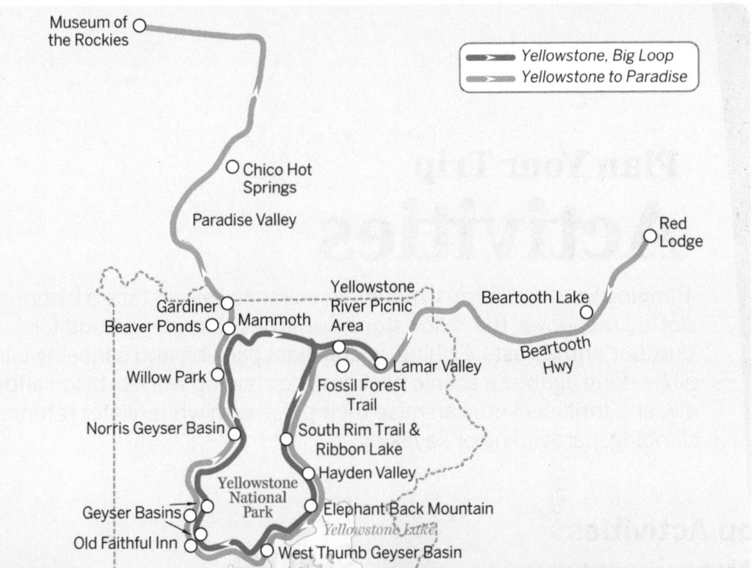

Yellowstone, Big Loop

From Mammoth head to some early morning wildlife viewing in the **Lamar Valley** before enjoying the crowd-free views of the Narrows on the **Yellowstone River Picnic Area** hike. Continue south to Canyon to take the **South Rim Trail & Ribbon Lake** hike before overnighting in Canyon Village.

The next day try some more early morning wildlife-watching in **Hayden Valley** before continuing south to hike **Elephant Back Mountain** for great views of Yellowstone Lake. After a lakeshore picnic on the sand bars around Gull Point, continue south to the hot springs of **West Thumb Geyser Basin** before heading west across the Continental Divide to overnight at **Old Faithful Inn**.

Spend day three visiting the geyser basins, and the next day drive to Mammoth via **Norris Geyser Basin**, arriving at lunchtime to stroll the travertine terraces at **Mammoth**. Either take a guided walk through historical Fort Yellowstone or a dusk hike to spot wildlife on the **Beaver Ponds trail**.

1 WEEK

Yellowstone to Paradise

Add this three-day scenic drive onto the **Yellowstone, Big Loop itinerary** and you'll get a fantastic week of scenic drives, park highlights and even a trip through Paradise.

From Red Lodge, allow half a day to drive the US's most scenic 70 miles, the Beartooth Hwy, stopping to stretch your legs at **Beartooth Lake**. Overnight in Cooke City, then enter the park for some early wildlife-watching in **Lamar Valley** and a hunt for petrified trees on the **Fossil Forest Trail**, before joining the **Yellowstone, Big Loop** itinerary at Canyon for two days' excursions to **Mammoth**.

Heading north from Mammoth on day six, squeeze in a morning rafting trip or horseback ride from **Gardiner** before continuing north through the lovely **Paradise Valley** to relax with a hot soak and gourmet dinner at **Chico Hot Springs**. Continue to Bozeman on your last day to spend a few hours at the **Museum of the Rockies** and do some last-minute shopping.

Plan Your Trip
Activities

Ranging from the Tetons' mountain spires to Yellowstone's bison-dotted meadows, the Yellowstone wilderness is a playground for outdoor enthusiasts. Fishing, hiking, backpacking and canoeing can all be done against a scenic backdrop containing wolves, bison and elk, and thrill-seekers can raise their pulse with white-water rafting, climbing, paragliding or kayaking.

Top Activities

Hiking
Grand Teton packs mountain drama, while Yellowstone brings hot springs and wildlife. And don't forget the Beartooth Plateau.

Canoeing
Paddle the backcountry waters of Shoshone or Leigh Lakes.

Fishing
Perfect the art of fly-fishing while wading in one of Yellowstone's famous blue-ribbon streams.

Horseback Riding
Cross Yellowstone's sagebrush country as it's meant to be done: on a backcountry horse trip.

Skiing & Snowboarding
World-class resorts at Big Sky and Jackson Hole.

Cross-Country Skiing
Glide through a winter landscape of frozen bison and ghost trees.

Mountain Biking
Downhill thrills and flowy rides are outside the parks at Big Sky or Jackson Hole.

Nature Walks
Stroll with a ranger or naturalist guide to score the inside scoop on wildlife.

Summer

Every animal that burrows and snoozes the long winter away snaps to life at the prospect of a Yellowstone summer, and we should be no exception. Exploring the parks on foot is a must and it's well worth setting aside a night or two in the backcountry. When your hiking legs get tired, saddle up, stargaze or explore the region's lakes and rivers by kayak, canoe or raft.

Hiking & Backpacking

A pair of hiking boots opens up Yellowstone, allowing you to escape the crowds, join the wildlife and enjoy abundant alpine vistas, cascading waterfalls and hidden thermal features. Yellowstone National Park boasts over 900 miles of maintained trails, and Grand Teton National Park offers another 200 miles of even more dramatic and vertiginous paths. Although less than 1% of visitors sleep out in the backcountry, popular backcountry campsites fill fast, especially in late summer, so reserve in advance or keep your itinerary flexible.

Closures & Seasonal Restrictions

In Yellowstone, fire outbreaks or bear activity can close trails without warning at any time and there are seasonal restrictions on some trails in early summer. Higher trails may be snow-covered until late July.

In general, you'll find the widest range of hiking options after mid-July. August and September are the driest months, and May and June are the wettest. Ticks proliferate on low-elevation trails between mid-March and mid-July, so wear insect repellent and long pants. Mosquitoes are most intense in June and July, petering out by mid-August. September is the golden month for hiking.

In Grand Teton National Park, higher elevations often remain snow-covered until late July, and high passes such as Paintbrush Divide and Hurricane Pass remain under snow as late as mid-August. Become familiar with using mini-crampons (microspikes) and an ice tool if you plan a high-altitude hike in early summer.

Permits

Backcountry permits are not necessary for day hikes anywhere, but are required for overnight trips in Yellowstone (p71) and Grand Teton (p189) National Parks. These can be obtained at ranger stations a day or two before your trip, according to availability, and cost $35 per trip in Grand Teton or $3 per person per night in Yellowstone.

In Yellowstone backcountry campers must watch a bear-safety video. In Grand Teton backpackers must carry a bear-proof canister for food storage.

Permits for specific backcountry sites or zones can be reserved in spring (online for Grand Teton and by fax or mail for prehistoric Yellowstone), though at least 30% of backcountry sites are kept for walk-in applications.

Hike Ratings

There are hikes for every ability in Greater Yellowstone. In Lonely Planet's coverage, the duration that we list for hikes refers to walking time only and doesn't include breaks. Our trail descriptions follow these guidelines:

Easy Manageable for nearly all walkers, an easy hike is under 4 miles, with fairly even, possibly paved terrain, and no significant elevation gain or loss.

Moderate Fine for fit hikers and active, capable children; moderate hikes have a modest elevation gain.

Difficult For fit and experienced hikers only. Trails might be strenuous, long and even indistinct in places. Expect significant elevation gain, and scrambling may be necessary.

Day Hikes

Almost every part of Yellowstone (p50) and Grand Teton (p172) National Parks offers outstanding day hiking, as do the national forests surrounding the parks. Don't overlook the longer trails – you can fashion short day hikes by following the first couple of miles of a longer trail.

Park trails are well marked and well maintained, often with restroom facilities at the trailhead. In some forested areas, these trails may be marked by a series of blazed trees; in Yellowstone trees bear orange metal tags; on rocky moraines look for cairns.

Overnight Hikes

The wonders and solitude of the remote backcountry make it well worth hauling in overnight gear. Both parks offer backpacking trips for all fitness levels, taking you to remote meadows, mountain crests or backcountry fishing spots.

If you're not used to hiking with a pack, start with one of the easier options (p116). Some backcountry campsites, such as those found at Yellowstone's Ribbon Lake or Grand Teton's Leigh and Bearpaw Lakes, are less than a two-hour hike from the trailhead.

Outside the parks, the best backpacking destinations are the Beartooth Plateau (p136) south of Red Lodge, and the Spanish Peaks (p159) area near Bozeman.

Other areas such as the wild Absaroka Range and Yellowstone's remote Thorofare region are untrammeled wilderness adventures, best suited to the experienced and well prepared. These remote regions are favored by horse packers, because the distances are large, the terrain rugged and the trails seldom used.

Backcountry Safety

Hikers and campers must reckon with Yellowstone's unpredictable weather – you may go to bed under a clear sky and wake up under a foot of snow, even in August. Afternoon weather is particularly volatile in the Tetons, so check the weather forecast and get an early start.

Don't rely on your cell phone for emergency contact, because coverage is spotty in the backcountry. However long your trip, it's important to prepare well, pack bear spray and understand safe backcountry food storage.

THE CONTINENTAL DIVIDE TRAIL

Extending from New Mexico to Canada, this 3100-mile through trail (CDT; www.continentaldividetrail.org) bisects beautiful sections of Yellowstone National Park and the Teton Wilderness, passing through Yellowstone's Upper Geyser Basin, Lone Geyser, Shoshone Geyser Basin, Lewis Lake, Heart Lake and the Snake River Canyon, in 70 miles of epic park trails. This section is a great option for hearty hikers who think big, but there are some logistical problems.

Due to snow, this portion of the trail usually opens around July 1. Obtaining backcountry permits for the Yellowstone section can be tricky, as hikers must know their dates and pick up the permit in advance, but rangers are generally understanding. Old Faithful post office will hold resupply boxes for two weeks if they are mailed there with 'CDT' and your estimated arrival date marked on the package. Mail to: General Delivery, Old Faithful, Yellowstone, WY 82190. Gas canisters and bear spray cannot be posted.

If you're thinking of tackling the trail get the *Continental Divide Trail Guidebook Vol 3*, available from the Continental Divide Trail Society (www.cdtsociety.org).

The most cautious safety measures suggest never hiking alone. Regardless, always let someone know where you are going and how long you plan to be gone. Use sign-in boards at trailheads and ranger stations where available.

Hunters frequent many areas outside the parks in late September and early October, so during this time wear bright clothes and expect campgrounds to fill up.

Rock Climbing & Mountaineering

American mountaineering was born in the Tetons, when Paul Petzoldt built the country's first guiding school in 1929. These huge granite faces continue to be among the US's premier climbing destinations. Excellent short routes abound, as well as the classic longer summits such as Grand Teton, Mt Moran and Mt Owen, and famous routes including the Upper Exum Ridge and Owen-Spalding route. The best season for climbing is mid-July through August.

You can get a sense of what it's like climbing the Tetons through the park's online feature, **eClimb** (www.nps.gov/features/grte/grandteton/eClimb.html).

A prime resource for climbers in the Tetons during summer is the American Alpine Club's Climbers' Ranch (p207). In addition to serving as a hostel for climbers and hikers, the organization's extensive library and knowledgeable staff are excellent resources.

The region's best ice climbing is found at Hyalite Canyon, south of Bozeman, and at the South Fork of the Shoshone River, 40 miles southwest of Cody. The season runs from November to April, with the coldest weather offering the best conditions. The **Bozeman Ice Festival** (www.bozemanicefest.com) in December has climbing clinics for novices.

Recommended Guide Services

The following companies offer guided climbs and courses. For a guided ascent of Grand Teton figure on $750 to $1500, depending on the amount of training, the number of days and whether you want a private or group climb.

Beartooth Mountain Guides (☎406-446-1407; www.beartoothguides.com; 412 N Broadway 8, Red Lodge) Courses and climbs focused on ice climbing, ski touring and mountaineering outside of the parks, including ascents of Granite Peak, Montana's highest point.

Exum Mountain Guides (p193) The region's oldest climbing school, with three-day guided Teton climbs.

Jackson Hole Mountain Guides (p222) An ideal center for instruction or guided climbs in the Tetons and beyond, with kids' programs. A branch office in Cody offers climbing and ice-climbing courses.

Montana Alpine Guides (☎406-586-8430; www.mtalpine.com; 13 Enterprise Blvd, Bozeman) Offers rock- and ice-climbing courses, plus guided climbs outside the parks in Wyoming and Montana.

Montana Mountaineering Association (406-522-0659; www.montanamountaineering.org; 631 E Davis St, Bozeman) Courses on ice climbing in Hyalite Canyon, plus backcountry skiing and mountaineering.

Cycling

Road Cycling

Road biking is possible from late April to October, when the parks' roads, topping out at 8860ft, are free of snow. Cyclists will find discounted campsites reserved for hikers and cyclists at almost all campgrounds in Yellowstone National Park. Most park roads are rough and narrow and do not have shoulders; expect careless drivers with one eye on a bison and another on a map. Riding can be more diverse and less stressful outside the park, away from the RV (recreational vehicle) parades.

In spring, Yellowstone National Park opens its roads exclusively to cyclists; it's a great time to pedal the park. However, snowbanks cover many roadsides until June, making cycling more challenging. Bicycle repairs and parts are not available inside the park; it's typically 20 to 30 miles between services.

In Grand Teton National Park, a multi-use pathway totaling 41 miles runs alongside Teton Park Rd from Jackson to south Jenny Lake.

Cycling Tours

Old Faithful Cycle Tour (p164) This annual 60-mile ride in fall, organized by the chamber of commerce in West Yellowstone, offers a van-supported ride to Old Faithful and back.

RESPONSIBLE BACKCOUNTRY USE

Backcountry environments are fragile and cannot support careless activity, especially in the wake of heavy visitation. We recommend following the principles of Leave No Trace (www.lnt.org/learn/7-principles).

Hiking

- To prevent erosion, always hike on the trail and don't create shortcuts. Staying on muddy trails will prevent damage to the surrounding terrain.

Campsites

- Use old campsites instead of clearing new ones.
- Camp at least 200ft away from the nearest lake, river or stream.

Campfires

- If there is already a fire ring, use it. Don't create new fire rings in the national parks.
- Burn only dead and downed wood.
- Build fires at least 9ft from flammable material (including grass and wood).
- Watch fires at all times and extinguish them completely.

Water & Toilets

- Where no toilet exists, bury human waste in a 6in-deep 'cat hole,' at least 300ft from the nearest lake or watercourse.
- Pack out toilet paper in a sealed plastic bag.
- Avoid soaps and detergents – sand or a kitchen scouring pad clean pots remarkably well. In high-altitude lakes even biodegradable soap may not degrade.
- Disperse dishwater far from streams and separate food residue with a small basin or strainer. Put these residuals in the trash – leaving them or dirty dishes might attract bears.

Access

- Do not camp or collect firewood on private land without permission, and leave stock gates as you find them.

Teton Mountain Bike Tours (☎307-733-0712; www.tetonmtbike.com; 545 N Cache St, Jackson; ⌚9am-6pm) Family-friendly guided mountain-bike tours of Grand Teton and Yellowstone. Half-day tours cost around $75 and include transportation, bike hire and helmet. Mountain bike rentals cost $35/45 for a half/full day.

Mountain Biking

The best bike trip inside the parks is the climb to the summit of Mt Washburn (p83) in Yellowstone. Outside the parks, Bozeman and Jackson are the main mountain-bike hubs, and nearby ski resorts offer lift-serviced downhill trails for the experienced. West Yellowstone's Rendezvous Ski Trails (p165) are a great summer ride for all abilities.

There is also good single track in the Gallatin Range, accessible from near Big Sky. Beartooth Publishing's *Bozeman, Big Sky, West Yellowstone* map details 14 mountain-bike routes in the region. Be sure to yield to hikers and horses on shared trails.

Most of the gateway towns around the parks offer mountain-bike rental (p258).

Regulations

In the national parks, cyclists may ride on all public roads and a few designated service roads, but aren't allowed on any trails or in backcountry areas.

Outside the parks, bikes are restricted from entering designated wilderness areas, but may otherwise ride on select national forest trails and all roads. Trail etiquette requires that cyclists yield to other users.

Wildlife Tours

Joining a naturalist-led tour is relatively expensive but can really bring dividends. A good naturalist knows the best locations for the time of year, has information on recent sightings and can help you understand the complex natural interactions that make up Yellowstone. You'll see and learn more with a naturalist than you ever could on your own.

Start with naturalist-guided trips and courses from the Yellowstone Forever Institute (p267) or the Teton Science School's Wildlife Expeditions (p193).

The recently launched **Yellowstone Day Adventures** (☎406-848-2844; www.yellowstone.org/day-adventures; 308 W Park St, Gardiner; adult/child $79/49) are early-morning wildlife-watching tours, departing from Gardiner's Yellowstone Forever shop. They are accompanied by institute naturalists and participants have access to a Zeiss scope. You may curse the 5am departure but it offers the best chance to see wildlife. Sign up at least the evening before.

There are a number of outstanding private outfits based outside the parks.

Grub Steak Expeditions (☎307-527-6316; www.tourtoyellowstone.com; 1107 Sheridan Avenue, Cody) Cody-based company established by a former park ranger.

Safari Yellowstone (☎800-723-2747; www.safariyellowstone.com; Livingston) Private tours, based in Livingston, MT.

Yellowstone Wolf Tracker (☎406-223-6634; www.wolftracker.com; Gardiner) Biologist-led guided wolf-watching, and supported spring and fall treks, run by Nathan and Linda Varlery, based in Gardiner. Also known as the Wild Side.

Yellowstone Safari Company (☎406-586-1155; www.yellowstonesafari.com; Bozeman) Biologist-led trips and llama treks, based in Bozeman.

Horseback Riding

Yellowstone's sagebrush country was built to be crossed on horseback. If you're eager to break in your Wranglers on a saddle, you'll find a wide range of options throughout the region, from two-hour rides to multiday pack adventures. Guest ranches in the Wapiti, Gallatin and Paradise Valleys offer the most authentic rides and most are open to nonguests.

In Yellowstone park, there are corrals (p85) at Roosevelt and Canyon Junction. Grand Teton has rides from Jackson Lake Lodge and Colter Bay.

Check out the **Dude Ranchers' Association** (www.duderanch.org) for helpful information and links.

Rafting

Cold water, adrenaline and stunning scenery make rafting a prime summer draw. Commercial outfitters throughout the region offer options ranging from inexpensive half-day trips to overnight and multiday expeditions. Paddlers can choose from large rafts for 12 or more people, or smaller rafts for six; pick the latter if you prefer paddling, otherwise your full-time job will be 'holding on.' Half-day trips run around

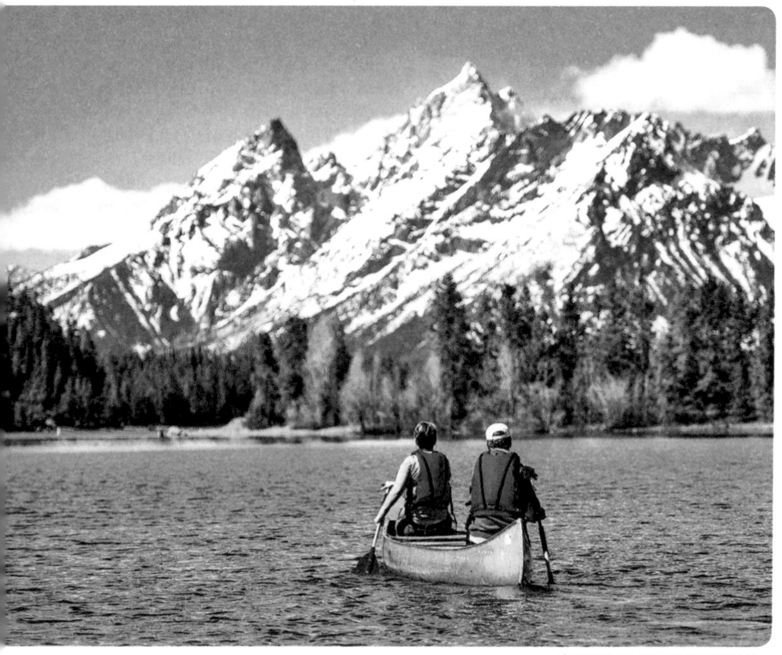

Canoeing on Jackson Lake (p192)

$45 per person and many operations offer activity combos that include horseback riding or ziplining.

White-water trips are not without risk, although serious injuries are rare and the vast majority of trips are without incident. River classifications vary over the course of the year, depending on the water level. Higher water levels, usually associated with spring runoff, make a river trip more challenging until late June.

Best Rafting Destinations

➡ Yellowstone River: the USA's longest free-flowing river courses through Yankee Jim Canyon and the Paradise Valley from Gardiner.

➡ Gallatin River: exciting trips through the 'Mad Mile' start near Big Sky.

➡ Snake River: white-water trips south of Jackson, or slower-paced wildlife-watching trips through Grand Teton National Park.

➡ Shoshone River: west of Cody, it flows through the scenic Absaroka Range.

Canoeing & Kayaking

Both parks offer exciting opportunities for paddlers: families can take a load off little legs and cool off, while romantics can paddle up to hidden camps on remote beaches.

One stunning destination is the pine-rimmed Shoshone Lake, the largest backcountry lake in the lower 48.

Vast Yellowstone Lake offers access to the most remote reaches of the park, but is a serious endeavor; Bridge Bay Marina offers boat shuttles to get you started. For an easier paddle, consider a sea-kayak tour of West Thumb Geyser Basin from Grant Village.

Grand Teton's Jackson Lake offers scenic backcountry paddling. Novice and family paddlers favor String and Leigh Lakes, both of which are perfect for stand up paddle boards (SUPs), while Lewis Lake in Yellowstone is a good family choice. Wildlife-watching is superlative on Grand Teton's Two Ocean Lake.

At Colter Bay in Grand Teton you can rent canoes, but they can't go far because trips are limited to the bay. For a longer trip, it's best to rent from an outdoor shop such as Adventure Sports (p258) at Moose. Kayak rentals and instruction are available in Jackson and Colter Bay in the Tetons, as well as in Gardiner, Cody and Big Sky.

Fishing

Yellowstone offers more than 400 fishable waters with cutthroat, rainbow, brown, brook and lake (Mackinaw) trout, as well as Arctic grayling and mountain whitefish. Fishing season runs from Memorial Day weekend to the first Sunday in November, except on Yellowstone Lake, which opens June 15. Catch and release is standard in many areas.

The Madison, Gibbon and Firehole Rivers in Yellowstone are fly-fishing only, but Yellowstone River and Slough Creek have gained a reputation as angling heaven.

In Grand Teton National Park, Leigh and Jenny Lakes are stocked with lake, brown, brook and Snake River cutthroat trout. One of the best fishing spots is on the Snake River just below the Jackson Lake dam.

Outside the parks, the Gallatin, Yellowstone and Snake Rivers all offer stellar fishing, and all gateway towns have expert fishing shops that offer equipment and guided trips to the region's prime fishing areas.

If you are keen to learn more about fly-fishing, consider a half- or full-day class at Bozeman Angler (p155) in Bozeman, or Yellowstone Fly Fishing School (p148) in Livingston. The latter has a women-only one-day fly-fishing class.

Newbies can also check out the free casting clinics at Jacklin's Fly Shop (p165) in West Yellowstone.

Fishing Licenses

A permit is required to fish in Yellowstone National Park. Anglers aged 16 and over must purchase a three-day permit ($18), a seven-day permit ($20) or a season permit ($40).

To fish in Grand Teton National Park, only a Wyoming fishing license (p193) is required (with a $12.50 conservation stamp for all but one-day licenses).

Winter

While Yellowstone's bears snore away in hibernation and bison huddle in frosted masses, the skiing, snowshoeing and wildlife-watching options are excellent. Though it's an increasingly popular season, winter still only attracts a fraction of summer's visitor numbers, giving you the sense that you are being let in on a park secret. Winter sports are a go from the end of November to April, though February and March generally offer the best snow conditions.

In Yellowstone and Grand Teton National Parks, winter activities include cross-country skiing, backcountry skiing, skate skiing (with short skis on groomed hardpack trails), snowshoeing and snowmobiling.

One useful resource is the **Montana Winter Guide** (www.wintermt.com). Be sure to read up about Yellowstone's limited winter facilities (p88) too.

Downhill Skiing & Snowboarding

Impressive snowfalls and wild and lovely terrain make the northern Rockies a premier downhill destination. Most resorts offer a range of winter activities from snowshoeing to sleigh dinner rides, as well as top-notch ski and snowboard instruction. Cheaper packages are offered in the more precarious early season between November and early December, or the late season from March to April, when the skiing is usually quite good.

The region's premier resorts:

Jackson Hole Mountain Resort (p222) Offers world-class terrain and heart-thumping views.

Big Sky Resort (p158) With vast terrain, Big Sky is Montana's premier resort.

Grand Targhee (p226) Family friendly and famed for deep champagne powder.

Snow King Resort (p215) A mini-resort with tubing and night skiing in downtown Jackson.

Red Lodge Mountain (p135) Thoroughly local, but with expanding terrain, a snowboard park and no lift queues.

Nordic & Backcountry Skiing

Nothing approximates heaven more than gliding through snow-covered wilderness under a sharp, blue sky. Nordic (or cross-country) skiing offers a great workout in stunning settings, and saves bucks on lift tickets. The national park and forest services maintain summer hiking trails as cross-country trails during winter, offering terrific solitude and wildlife-watching opportunities.

In late November, the **West Yellowstone Ski Festival** attracts Nordic skiers

WINTER SAFETY

Backcountry winter trips require extra caution, as streams and geothermal areas can be hidden by snow. Carry a map and compass when you venture off designated trails or roads. Some roads are groomed for snowmobiles and other snow vehicles; exercise caution if you are a skier sharing the road. For weather and avalanche conditions, check the following:

Backcountry Avalanche Hazard & Weather Forecast (recorded information ☎307-733-2664; www.jhavalanche.org) Covers Bridger-Teton National Forest.

Gallatin National Forest Avalanche Center (☎406-587-6981; www.mtavalanche.com)

Mountain Weather (www.mountainweather.com) Jackson Hole reports and links to other resorts with webcams at Grand Targhee.

from around the world and offers demos and clinics. Many resorts offer free trail passes and rentals on **Winter Trails Day** (www.wintertrails.org) in January. Lone Mountain Ranch (p159) at Big Sky offers rentals and lessons for just $5 on that day.

Backcountry skiing takes skiers to more difficult terrain than regular Nordic gear can handle. The equipment – either Telemark (single-camber skis with edges and free-heel bindings) or *randonnée* (an alpine hybrid system allowing for free-heeled ascents), fitted with climbing skins for ascents – allows skiers to travel cross-country and down steep slopes, though Telemark is much better suited to cross-country terrain. Newcomers to the sport should take a lesson (available at most ski resorts) and get in some resort runs before tackling the backcountry. In addition, backcountry skiers must be well versed in avalanche safety.

Experienced backcountry skiers will want to check out Hellroaring Ski Adventures (p165) in West Yellowstone, Teton Backcountry Guides (p196) in the Tetons and Beartooth Powder Guides (p141) in Cooke City.

Dedicated Trails

In Yellowstone, shuttles offer ski drops (p88) in Mammoth and Old Faithful. Stay off the groomed roads meant for motorized travel. Otherwise, skiers will find ungroomed backcountry trails (p89) with orange markers.

Grand Teton National Park grooms 14 scenic miles of track (p195) between Taggart-Bradley Lakes parking area and Signal Mountain. Trails are usually marked with orange flags. Backcountry skiers must take more precautions: avalanches are a major hazard in the canyons and upper areas of the Tetons.

The Best Nordic Trails

- ➡ Rendezvous Ski Trails (p165) in West Yellowstone, the winter training ground for the US Nordic team.
- ➡ A snowcoach (p88) takes you to the Old Faithful Snow Lodge for skiing around the kaleidoscope-hued geyser basins, or around the Grand Canyon of the Yellowstone.
- ➡ Near West Yellowstone, the Fawn and Bighorn Pass Trails connect to form a loop of around 10 miles through elk wintering areas.
- ➡ Lone Mountain Ranch (p159) at Big Sky has almost 50 miles of privately groomed trails.
- ➡ Red Lodge Nordic Center (p135) has 9 miles of trails.
- ➡ Trails around Indian Creek or along the Mammoth–Cooke City Rd in Yellowstone National Park.

Snowshoeing

In Yellowstone and elsewhere you can generally snowshoe anywhere – the problem is getting to the trailhead. Try not to mark groomed cross-country trails with your snowshoes, though; stay a few paces from any groomed areas. You can access trails from the Mammoth–Cooke City Rd all winter, and ski shuttles run to snowbound parts of the park from Mammoth and Old Faithful. Most hotels and gateway towns rent snowshoes.

Rangers lead snowshoe hikes from West Yellowstone's Riverside Trails (p165) – BYO snowshoes – and Grand Teton's Discovery Center (p266), where snowshoes are provided. Lone Mountain Ranch (p159) at Big Sky has exclusive snowshoe trails.

Snowmobiling

The park service enforces a daily cap of snowmobiles in Yellowstone National Park, and the majority must be accompanied by a guide. A small number of non-guided permits (p89) are available through a lottery system (apply at www.recreation.gov). In Grand Teton, snowmobiling is allowed only on the frozen surface of Jackson Lake. A good alternative is found in the surrounding national forests, which offer hundreds of miles of trails.

Snowmobile policies are under constant revision; check with the parks for updates. Yellowstone's snowmobile travel season runs from late December to early March. Book trips well in advance because private companies have a limited daily quota of snowmobile rentals for Yellowstone National Park. All roads except for the North Entrance through to the Northeast Entrance (open only to wheeled vehicles) are groomed for oversnow vehicles. The road from the West Entrance to Madison to Old Faithful is shared with cross-country skiers; ride with caution.

➡ All snowmobiles in both parks must meet best available technology (BAT) standards.

➡ Speed limits are generally 45mph.

➡ Snowmobiles are not allowed in any wilderness areas.

➡ If you are new to snowmobiling, bear in mind that it's much more comfortable to ride solo than to double up.

➡ When renting, check the cost of clothing rental and insurance, and whether the first tank of gas is free.

➡ Backrests and heated handgrips are desirable extras.

Outside the Parks

West Yellowstone is the 'snowmobile capital of the world.' Here you can legally drive snowmobiles in town and attend March's **Snowmobile Expo** (www.snowmobileexpo.com). There are over 1000 miles of snowmobile trails between West Yellowstone and Idaho's Targhee National Forest. One is the popular 34-mile Two Top Mountain Loop, the country's first National Recreational Snowmobile Trail.

Cooke City is another regional hub for snowmobiling activity, either in the backcountry or along the amazing Beartooth Highway.

Snowcoach Tours

Converted vans on snow tracks, snowcoaches (p88) provide transportation in and around Yellowstone National Park in winter, also providing a useful service for skiers. Snow-coach tours depart daily from West Yellowstone and Mammoth; most stop at Old Faithful and all stop for wildlife-watching opportunities. Yellowstone National Park Lodges (p273) and Wildlife Expeditions (p193) operate park-based winter snowcoach tours of Yellowstone. Between Mammoth and Old Faithful, the former's fares are $94/47 per adult/child aged three to 11.

Companies in West Yellowstone offering snowcoach tours of Yellowstone include Buffalo Bus Touring Company (p273), **See Yellowstone** (☎800-221-1151; www.seeyellowstone.com; 217 Yellowstone Ave, West Yellowstone; snow-coach day tour adult/child $145/110) and Yellowstone Alpen Guides (p166). Snow-coach tours from Jackson can be arranged through **Scenic Safaris** (☎888-734-8898; www.scenic-safaris.com; 545 N Cache Dr, Jackson).

Dogsledding

If you have always wanted to travel by paw power, you can try the several companies that offer day and half-day trips in national forest areas.

Absaroka Dogsled Treks (p149) Day trips and a musher's school at Chico Hot Springs.

Continental Divide Dogsled Adventures (p215) Jackson-based operation that runs day trips or overnight trips in yurts (Central Asian–style circular tents).

Spirit of the North (☎406-995-3424; www.huskypower.com) Half-day adventures around Big Sky, costing around $135 per adult.

Plan Your Trip

Travel with Children

If Yellowstone's wonderland of spurting geysers, gurgling mud pots and baby bison turns adults into kids, then imagine its impact on young ones. Sharing these moments will create priceless family memories and, for your kids, a visit to the parks may just kick-start a lifelong love of nature and the outdoors.

Best Regions

Almost every part of Greater Yellowstone has something to offer families. A visit here is an American rite of passage.

Yellowstone National Park

The main attractions: bison spotting, ranger programs, campfires and ice cream, plus belching mud pots.

Grand Teton National Park

Paddling and beaches at String Lake, bike rides, ranger programs and a chuckwagon at Dornan's.

Jackson

Lots of teenage adrenaline fun, with alpine rides, rafting trips, climbing walls, kayak courses, and a staged shootout for the younger ones.

West Yellowstone

A high ropes course for the rambunctious; guaranteed grizzly-spotting; and family-orientated slapstick at the Playmill Theater.

Yellowstone & Grand Teton for Kids

The national parks are as kid-friendly as a destination gets, but the wilderness must be treated with respect. The National Park Service (NPS) looks after its young visitors well, with fun outings, education programs and kid-focused presentations. Children aged under 12 stay free in park accommodations and most restaurants offer kids' menus. Activities ranging from horseback riding to white-water rafting offer shared thrills for all the family.

On the Trail

Consider the following before heading out on a hike:

- Pick a route that offers an easy out. Just in case.
- A cool destination, such as a lake or falls, offers extra incentive.
- Choosing a shorter route gives kids a chance to slow down and explore. Let kids set the pace.
- A scavenger-hunt list, made from features described in hike descriptions, can help keep their attention.
- Outfitting kids with a mini-backpack, a small hiking stick or camera helps them feel part of the expedition.

National Parks Programs

Take advantage of Yellowstone's ranger-led activities, many of which are aimed at families. Most campgrounds run family-oriented campfire programs with lectures in the early evenings and there are hikes to family-friendly destinations, including Storm Point and Mystic Falls. See the park newspapers for details. Grand Teton's campfire program is based in Colter Bay, with campfire talks also at Gros Ventre Campground (p207).

Kids can earn a very cool badge through the **Junior Ranger Program** (www.nps.gov; booklet $3; ⊙Jun-Labor Day; 👪), a renowned and worthwhile program in Yellowstone. Tasks include completing an activity book with questions and games, attending a ranger talk and doing a hike. The program can be completed in two days and is aimed at five- to 12-year-olds (although adults can enjoy it too). For more info, search for 'yellowstone junior ranger program' on the NPS website. Madison's Junior Ranger Station (p128) offers kid-related activities all day.

Grand Teton's Grand Adventure Program (www.nps.gov/grte/forkids/index.htm; donation $1) also trains Junior Rangers; inquire about it at any visitor center.

Junior Rangers and their families can participate in **Yellowstone Wildlife Olympics**, a field day with physical challenges that pit your abilities against those of notable wildlife (no pronghorn are injured in the making of this game). This three-hour activity is held at different visitor centers three times a week at noon; see the park newspaper for details.

Yellowstone's family-friendly Old Faithful Visitor Education Center (p267) also operates the **Young Scientist Program** (www.nps.gov; booklet $5), which lets kids investigate the mysteries of the park with a special tool kit in hand, completing tasks for a coveted patch or key chain. It's for ages five and up.

On **Expedition: Yellowstone!** (www.nps.gov/yell/planyourvisit/expeditionyell.htm; lodging/instruction per day $35/60), kids learn about preservation, the park's natural and cultural history and current issues affecting the Greater Yellowstone Ecosystem. It includes hikes, field investigations, discussions, creative dramatics and journal writing. This four- to five-day curriculum-based residential program is for students in grades four to eight. Badger your teachers to arrange a visit; parents can come along as chaperones. It's based at Lamar's Buffalo Ranch or Mammoth.

Fourth Graders can get a free **Interagency Annual Pass** that gives free entrance to the parks for everyone in their vehicle. Get a voucher from www.everykidinapark.gov.

Private Programs

Inside the parks, concessionaires and nonprofits run a range of family-friendly activities. Short stagecoach rides (p85) from Yellowstone's Roosevelt Lodge travel the sagebrush flats. Trips go several times per day and run from early June to August.

For more in-depth experiences, the Yellowstone Forever Institute (p267) offers a range of excellent year-round family programs. The most popular is Yellowstone for Families, where a qualified naturalist takes families (with children aged eight to 12) animal tracking, exploring and wildlife watching in the park. Other fun stuff includes painting at Artist Point (p99) and taking wildlife photos.

PLAY, LEARN & PLAN ONLINE

If your kids really won't be pried away from their iPads, then get them in the mood for the parks with these online games and interactive activities.

- Test sleuthing skills and try park puzzles at www.nps.gov/webrangers.
- Teens can travel on award-winning electronic field trips at www.windowsintowonderland.org.
- Scavenge for clues about Yellowstone's explosive past or play with jackalopes at the official Yellowstone site: www.nps.gov/yell/forkids/index.htm.
- Find the mystery animal or take the first steps toward the Junior Ranger badge at the official Grand Teton site: www.nps.gov/grte/forkids/index.htm.
- Identify animal tracks and make electronic field trips at www.nps.gov/grte/learn/kidsyouth/parkfun.htm.
- Explore more Junior Ranger fun at www.discovergrandteton.org/junior-rangers.

KEEPING IT SAFE

- Use a checklist for hiking supplies, including water, sunscreen and first aid.
- Kids should carry a flashlight and whistle, and know what to do if they get lost.
- Keep children within sight on the trail.
- Be especially careful roadside when everyone's eyes are on the bison, not the traffic.
- Scenic overlooks with sheer drops require extra attention, especially at the Grand Canyon of the Yellowstone.
- Caution kids about thermal areas before visiting them.
- A pre-trip practice outing helps kids know what to bring and expect.
- Let kids know the proper way to handle an animal encounter.
- Introduce them to Leave No Trace ethics.

Children's Highlights

Adventure

Fishing Cast for cutthroat trout in a pristine mountain lake or river, or take a class. Children under 15 don't need a fishing permit for Yellowstone or Grand Teton.

Grazing elk, Mammoth Families of elk chew nonchalantly on park lawns every day.

Rafting (p34) White water or scenic floats on the Snake, Yellowstone and Gallatin Rivers.

Horseback riding (p34) Mosey through the open range at a dude ranch (kids eight years old and up).

Paddling, String Lake (p35) Rent a canoe or kayak in Grand Teton National Park.

Snow King Resort (p215) Ziplines, alpine slides and a coaster ride in summer or tubing and boarding in winter, just outside Jackson.

Multiuse path, Jackson Hole (p272) Cycle a paved pathway through Grand Teton National Park.

Wilderness Adventures (☎307-733-2122; www.wildernessadventures.com; 4030 West Lake Creek Dr, Wilson; 👪) Operates multisport trips for teens.

Entertainment

Museum of the Rockies (p155) Huge dinosaur skeletons and an interactive Yellowstone for Kids exhibit in Bozeman.

National Museum of Wildlife Art (p213) Make your own art at this studio in Jackson.

Grizzly & Wolf Discovery Center (p163) Try out zookeeper duties and help feed the grizzlies in West Yellowstone.

Geothermal Bathing (p149) Splash about in a spring-fed pool at Chico Hot Springs, or go alfresco at Yellowstone park's Boiling and Firehole Rivers.

Town Square Shootout (p216) Schticky street theater in Jackson is always fun, and there's a version in Cody.

Dining

Chuckwagon dinners Oversize grills and steaming cast-iron cauldrons.

Camping Toasting marshmallows under a canopy of stars.

Picnics Yellowstone has great picnic areas, many of them riverside or lakeshore.

Red Box Car (p135) Burgers and shakes from a defunct train car in Red Lodge.

Running Bear Pancake House (p167) Short stack pancakes in West Yellowstone.

Pioneer Grill (p208) Hot fudge sundaes at a classic diner in Grand Teton National Park.

Montana Candy Emporium (7 S Broadway; ⌚9am-7pm) Sweet-tooth heaven in Red Lodge.

Rainy-Day Refuges

Climbing walls Indoor fun in Jackson, Bozeman and Cody.

Buffalo Bill Center of the West (p142) Kids' workshops and interactive exhibits in Cody.

Yellowstone Giant Screen Theater (p167) Imax-size screen in West Yellowstone.

Old Faithful Visitor Education Center (p267) Aimed at kids; in Yellowstone park.

Coolest Camps

Most ski resorts offer daycare or camp outings.

Teton Science School (☎307-733-4765, 307-733-1313; www.tetonscience.org; Ditch Creek Rd, Kelly) Runs GPS scavenger hunts and ecology expeditions. Also offers outstanding summer camp programs.

Kids Rock (www.jhmg.com/school/kids/index.php) This Jackson Hole Mountain Guides program gives kids aged five to 12 a chance to get vertical (with parents in tow), on a safe and fun day outing.

Playmill Theater (p167) Offers a four-day summer theater camp for children aged 14 to 18. In West Yellowstone.

Jackson Hole Playhouse (www.jacksonplayhouse.com/summercamp) Runs a weeklong theater camp.

Hiking & Cycling

Most kids will enjoy the following Yellowstone hikes (and rides) for little legs; all are within 2 miles of a road. Rangers lead hikes on several of these routes.

Wraith Falls A 79ft cascade on the Mammoth to Tower–Roosevelt road.

Trout Lake Easy fishing destination in the park's northeast corner.

Pelican Creek Bridge A fantastic nature trail to a beach on Yellowstone Lake.

Natural Bridge Trail Pedal an old stagecoach road to a 50ft rock bridge.

Mystic Falls Geysers and hot springs to explore in Biscuit Basin.

Planning

What to Pack

Kids should have comfortable outdoor clothing, a bathing suit, sun hat, shell jacket and warm clothing for chilly days and nights. If you are picky about your bug spray (DEET should be limited to 30%), it's best to bring it from home. Before your trip, make sure everyone has adequate hiking shoes – this could be anything from sneakers to waterproof boots, depending on the range of terrain you'll cover – and ensure they are broken in. Sandals or Crocs can also be useful for around camp. A cheap digital camera or pair of binoculars can provide lots of entertainment since there's so much wildlife to watch. Bring your own marshmallows and toasting sticks.

Most car-rental agencies can add a child's car seat for a nominal fee. Strollers may be harder to come by, so it is best to take yours with you. Baby backpacks are especially handy for getting beyond the boardwalk and onto the trails.

Most bike rental places, including Bear Den Rentals (p258) at Old Faithful, offer children's bikes and even trailers or tandem bikes.

Before You Go

Keep the kids in mind as you plan your itinerary, or include them in the trip planning from the get-go. If they have a stake in the plan, they will be more interested when they arrive, or so the theory goes. Lonely Planet's *Travel with Children* provides good information, advice and anecdotes. If you decide to book a Yellowstone Association program or a popular park activity such as a Yellowstone stagecoach ride, be sure to do so many months in advance. A few ranger programs only admit limited numbers, so it's always a good idea to show up early.

Catering to Teens

The Tetons and Yellowstone offer tons of things for teens to do. If your teens do not have much outdoor experience, it may be wise to enroll them in a course. Bike rentals are available in all gateway towns and Old Faithful Snow Lodge (p266). Climbing gyms usually have short beginner courses appropriate for teens, ski resorts often have mountain biking or alpine slide options and a few places have day-long kayaking courses. Readers suggest whitewater rafting and swimming as perfect activities – there are plenty of alpine lakes that become divine retreats when the temperatures soar. Teens of every skill level can have a blast exploring ski and snowboard runs at area resorts. Most hikes are appropriate for fit teens.

At Yellowstone National Park, the **Youth Conservation Corps** (YCC; www.nps.gov/yell/parkmgmt/yccjobs.htm) offers teens month-long summer jobs in the park, with training in conservation and trail rehabilitation. Weekend activities include hiking, rafting, fishing and assisting scientists or field rangers. The program offers a couple of month-long sessions in a residential setting for young people between the ages of 15 and 18. Only 60 spots are available, chosen from a random draw. Enrollment is six months prior to summer.

Plan Your Trip

Travel with Pets

While vacation-time loyalty to a furry friend is admirable, national parks are challenging places for pets. Strict restrictions limit pets to paved parking lots and picnic areas, which rules out trails or boardwalks. With good reason, too, as these are some of the country's wildest places, where large, charismatic wildlife could be easily threatened by domestic animals (or vice versa). One option for a hassle-free trip is to take advantage of national forest trails, where dogs are allowed on a leash. There are many near Yellowstone and the Tetons, and your dog will thank you for the introduction to a world of new sights and smells.

Rules & Regulations

In the national parks, pets must be leashed at all times. They are not allowed on any boardwalks or backcountry trails, or more than 100ft from roads or paved paths. Needless to say, you will have to clean up after your beloved dog.

Also, you are not allowed to tie your pet (aka bear bait) to objects or leave him/her unattended. If temperatures are cool, a pet may stay inside a ventilated vehicle, but that's rarely the case in summer.

Service animals such as seeing-eye dogs are welcome in park facilities.

Health & Safety

All pets should have their vaccinations before travel. Like people, animals need conditioning for the outdoors. Break your pet in slowly with easier treks where allowed.

Adequate food, shelter and water should always be handy (but never left where it can attract wild animals). Bring a stash of plastic bags to clean up waste and have a water dish. Never let your pet go near

Best Spots for Dogs

Wilderness areas and state parks generally have looser restrictions.

Trails Near Bozeman & Red Lodge

Mountain passes, glacier lakes and basins all on national forest land within a few miles of town.

Jackson Peak

A bare summit with stunning views of the Teton Range, this day hike passes fragrant forests of Douglas fir, and Goodwin Lake in Bridger-Teton National Forest.

Jedediah Smith Wilderness

A remote area strewn with gorgeous alpine lakes and streams north of Grand Teton National Park; access via Grassy Lake Rd.

Jackson, WY

A Fido-crazed town with a pet resort and hip dog park.

thermal features – dogs have died jumping into the seemingly cool pools, and owners have also died trying to save their furry friends.

Trails & Parks

A glance at an atlas reveals city parks or rivers and lakes that can offer pets a refreshing dip. Once there, check signs for restrictions and local leash laws.

Shoshone National Forest, Bridger-Teton National Forest, Custer Gallatin National Forest and Caribou-Targhee National Forest all allow dogs on leashes. In Jedediah Smith Wilderness, dogs must be under voice control at all times. Always have one eye out for wildlife before your retriever exercises its instincts.

Accommodations

Finding accommodations can be a challenge. Pets are allowed in Yellowstone's cabins for a $25 fee, but not in any of the hotels. Most campgrounds allow dogs but do not permit them to go loose.

Our lodging reviews indicate when pets are allowed, usually for a fee ($10 to $35). Reserve these accommodations well in advance, given their shortage.

Run by a local pet-advocacy group, www.pawsofjh.org is a useful resource for finding veterinarians and pet-friendly hotels in the Jackson area.

Kennels

Kennels can be found in most gateway towns. If you don't see one, ask for the local veterinary clinic, where staff can indicate the best local kennels or private dog-sitting services.

Look for kennels that are ABKA (American Boarding Kennel Association) certified. When choosing a kennel, ask for a walk through. Consider the following factors: the size of the sleeping space, the presence of outdoor yards or play spaces, the number of daily walks or play sessions, the number and attentiveness of staff and the kennel's certifications. Some even have webcams, so brooding pet parents won't miss a whimper. Facilities that always keep dogs separate might keep your poodle out of a tussle or prevent it from catching an illness from another dog. Some dogs prefer some canine company to pass the time; in this case, ensure it is well supervised. Kennels may also provide lodgings for cats, birds and fish.

Visitor centers can usually provide information on local veterinary clinics.

Cody Country Bed & Biscuit (☎307-587-3379; www.woofyproducts.com; 134 E Cooper Lane, Cody)

Doggie Daycare & Motel (☎406-763-5585; www.doggiedaycareandmotel.com; 421 Garnet Mt Way, Gallatin Gateway, Bozeman)

Dogjax (☎307-733-3647; www.dogjax.com; 3590 Southpark Dr, Jackson)

Happy Tails Pet Resort (☎307-733-1606; www.springcreekanimalhospital.com; 1035 W Broadway, Jackson)

Kennels at the Smith Family Ranch (☎406-848-7477; www.paradisevalleyvacation.com; 1828 Old Yellowstone Trail South, Paradise Valley)

Querencia Kennels (☎406-333-4500; www.querencia.com; 55 Querencia Dr, Emigrant, Paradise Valley)

Trail Creek Pet Center (☎208-354-2571; trailcreekpetcenter@yahoo.com; 1778 S 1500 E, Driggs; ⏰8am-6pm)

Park Your Paws at Wagging Tails Retreat (☎406-823-9978; 5288 US Hwy 89 S, Livingston)

On the Road

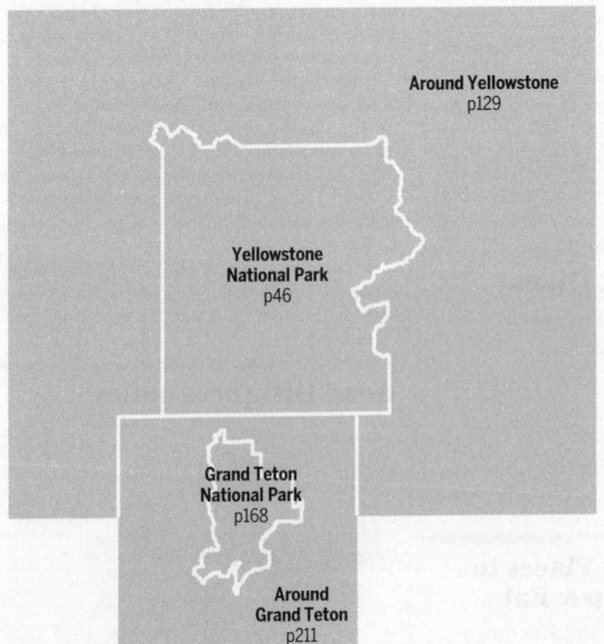
Around Yellowstone
p129
Yellowstone
National Park
p46
Grand Teton
National Park
p168
Around
Grand Teton
p211

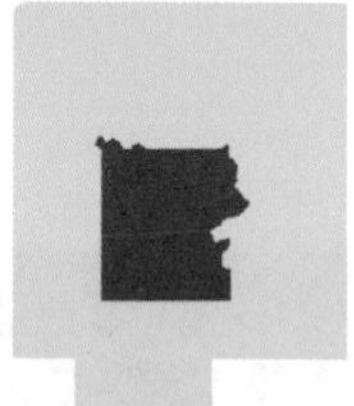

Yellowstone National Park

Includes ➡

Best Hikes

- ➡ Mt Washburn (p61)
- ➡ Bunsen Peak (p52)
- ➡ Yellowstone River Picnic Area Trail (p57)
- ➡ South Rim Trail & Ribbon Lake (p60)
- ➡ Sepulcher Mountain (p56)

Best Places to Sleep & Eat

- ➡ Old Faithful Inn (p123)
- ➡ Lake Yellowstone Hotel (p122)
- ➡ Mammoth Hot Springs Dining Room (p124)
- ➡ Lake Yellowstone Hotel Dining Room (p127)

Why Go?

The sights of Yellowstone are so fantastic that when the first white person to visit described what was there, he was roundly criticized as delirious or possibly a liar. It wasn't until the world saw the paintings of Thomas Moran from the Hayden Expedition some 70 years later that people began to believe such a wondrous place could exist.

Yellowstone is home to over 60% of the world's geysers – natural hot springs with unique plumbing that causes them to periodically erupt in towering explosions of boiling water and steam. And while these astounding phenomena and their neighboring Technicolor hot springs and bubbling mud pots draw in the crowds (over 4 million people each year), the surrounding canyons, mountains and forests are no less impressive.

Teeming with moose, elk, bison, grizzly bears and wolves, America's first national park also contains some of the country's wildest lands, just begging to be explored.

Road Distances (miles)

	Mammoth	Old Faithful	Grant Village	Canyon Village
Old Faithful	50			
Grant Village	70	20		
Canyon Village	30	40	35	
Lake Village	50	35	20	20

Note: Distances are approximate

Entrances

Park entrances are open to vehicles 24 hours a day during open months. The North Entrance station is at Gardiner, MT, and the Northeast Entrance is near Cooke City; both are open year-round. The East Entrance is on US 14/16/20, from Cody, WY, and the South Entrance is on US 89/191/287, north of Grand Teton National Park; both are open early May to early November. The West Entrance is on US 20/191/287 near West Yellowstone, MT, and is open mid- to late April to early November.

DON'T MISS

One of the best free services offered by the park service is its series of ranger-led activities. From boardwalk strolls explaining the interior plumbing of a geyser to short guided hikes, the commentary given by the park's affable rangers will really add to your understanding of the park. Budget constrictions have curtailed some activities in recent years, so check the park newspaper to try to catch a couple of these presentations. At the least, catch the nightly campfire talks given at most park campgrounds, some of which are specifically aimed at young families.

Guided ranger hikes include to Mystic Falls, Storm Point, the southern rim of the Grand Canyon of the Yellowstone and several boardwalk walks around the Upper Geyser Basin. Walks take less than two hours and are free.

When You Arrive

- The park is open year-round, but most roads close in winter. Park entrance permits ($35/30/20 per vehicle/motorcycle/cyclist) are valid for seven days. An annual pass to Yellowstone costs $70.
- Upon entering the park you'll be given a basic map and the park newspaper, *Yellowstone Today*, detailing the excellent ranger-led talks and walks.
- Noticeboards at park entrances indicate which campgrounds are full or closed.

SAFETY

- Stay 30yd (two school buses) from bison and elk; and 100yd (a football field) from bears and wolves.
- Keep on boardwalks at thermal areas.
- Carry bear spray in the backcountry.

Fast Facts

- Area: 3472 miles
- Highest elevation: 11,358ft (Eagle Peak)
- Lowest elevation: 5282ft (Reese Creek)

Reservations

Reserve up to a year and no less than six months in advance for in-park accommodations and Western cookouts, and a couple of months in advance for concessionaire-run campgrounds, especially for high season (June to August). Reservations open May 1 for the following year.

Reservations are not accepted for park-service campgrounds.

Resources

National Park Service (www.nps.gov/yell)

Yellowstone National Park Lodges (www.yellowstonenationalparklodges.com)

Yellowstone Net (www.yellowstone.net)

Yellowstone National Park.com (www.yellowstonenationalpark.com)

My Yellowstone Park (www.yellowstonepark.com)

Yellowstone National Park

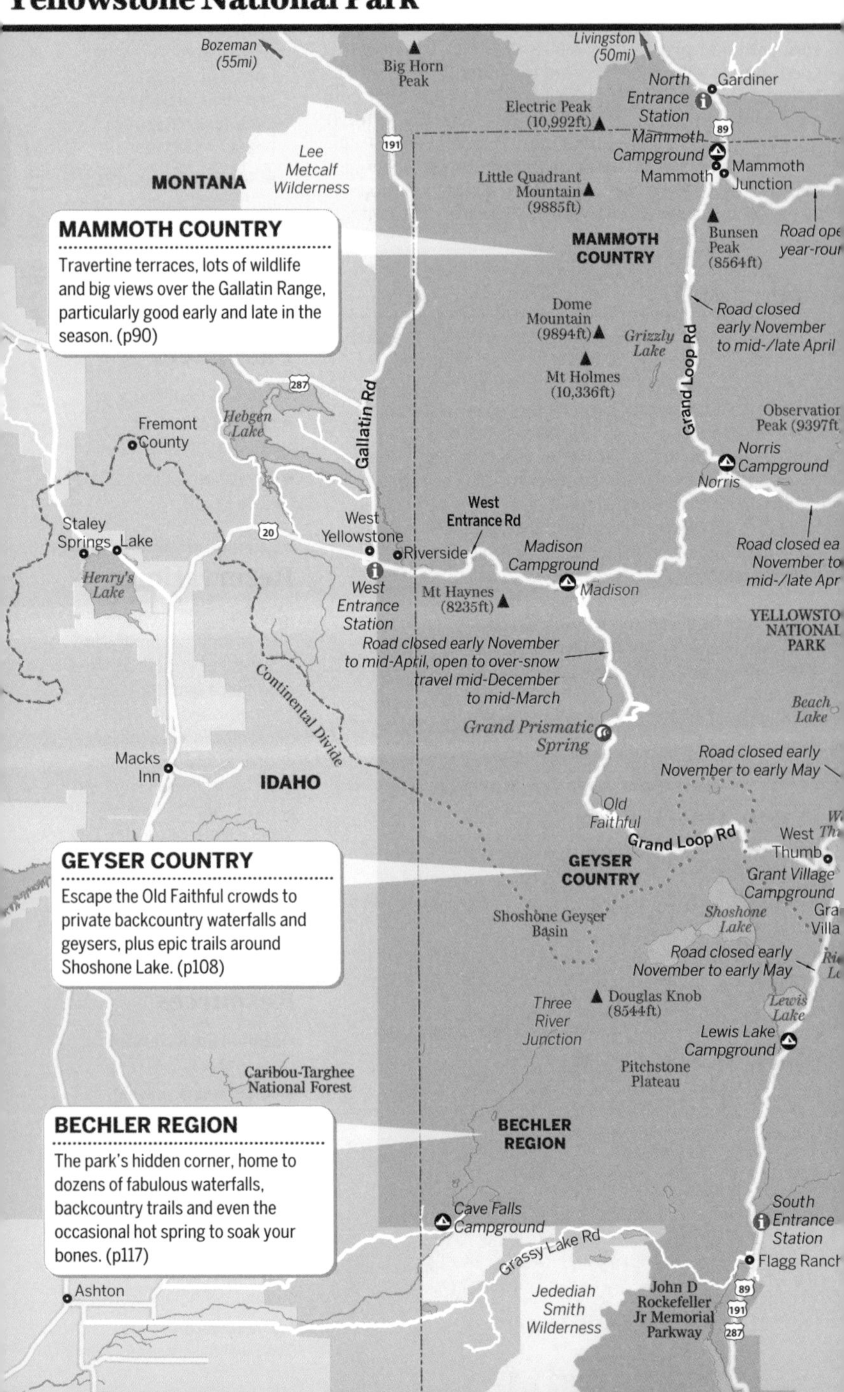
Bozeman (55mi)
Big Horn Peak
Livingston (50mi)
North Entrance Station
Gardiner
Electric Peak (10,992ft)
89
191
Mammoth Campground
Mammoth
Mammoth Junction
Lee Metcalf Wilderness
MONTANA
Little Quadrant Mountain (9885ft)
MAMMOTH COUNTRY
Travertine terraces, lots of wildlife and big views over the Gallatin Range, particularly good early and late in the season. (p90)
MAMMOTH COUNTRY
Bunsen Peak (8564ft)
Road closed early November to mid-/late April
Dome Mountain (9894ft)
Grizzly Lake
Mt Holmes (10,336ft)
Grand Loop Rd
287
Hebgen Lake
Gallatin Rd
Fremont County
Norris Campground
Norris
Staley Springs
Lake
20
West Yellowstone
West Entrance Rd
Riverside
Madison Campground
Madison
Henry's Lake
West Entrance Station
Mt Haynes (8235ft)
Road closed early November to mid-April, open to over-snow travel mid-December to mid-March
Continental Divide
Grand Prismatic Spring
Road closed early November to early May
Macks Inn
IDAHO
Old Faithful
Grand Loop Rd
West Thumb
GEYSER COUNTRY
Escape the Old Faithful crowds to private backcountry waterfalls and geysers, plus epic trails around Shoshone Lake. (p108)
GEYSER COUNTRY
Grant Village Campground
Shoshone Geyser Basin
Shoshone Lake
Road closed early November to early May
Douglas Knob (8544ft)
Three River Junction
Lewis Lake
Lewis Lake Campground
Pitchstone Plateau
Caribou-Targhee National Forest
BECHLER REGION
The park's hidden corner, home to dozens of fabulous waterfalls, backcountry trails and even the occasional hot spring to soak your bones. (p117)
BECHLER REGION
Cave Falls Campground
South Entrance Station
Grassy Lake Rd
Flagg Ranch
Ashton
Jedediah Smith Wilderness
John D Rockefeller Jr Memorial Parkway
191
287

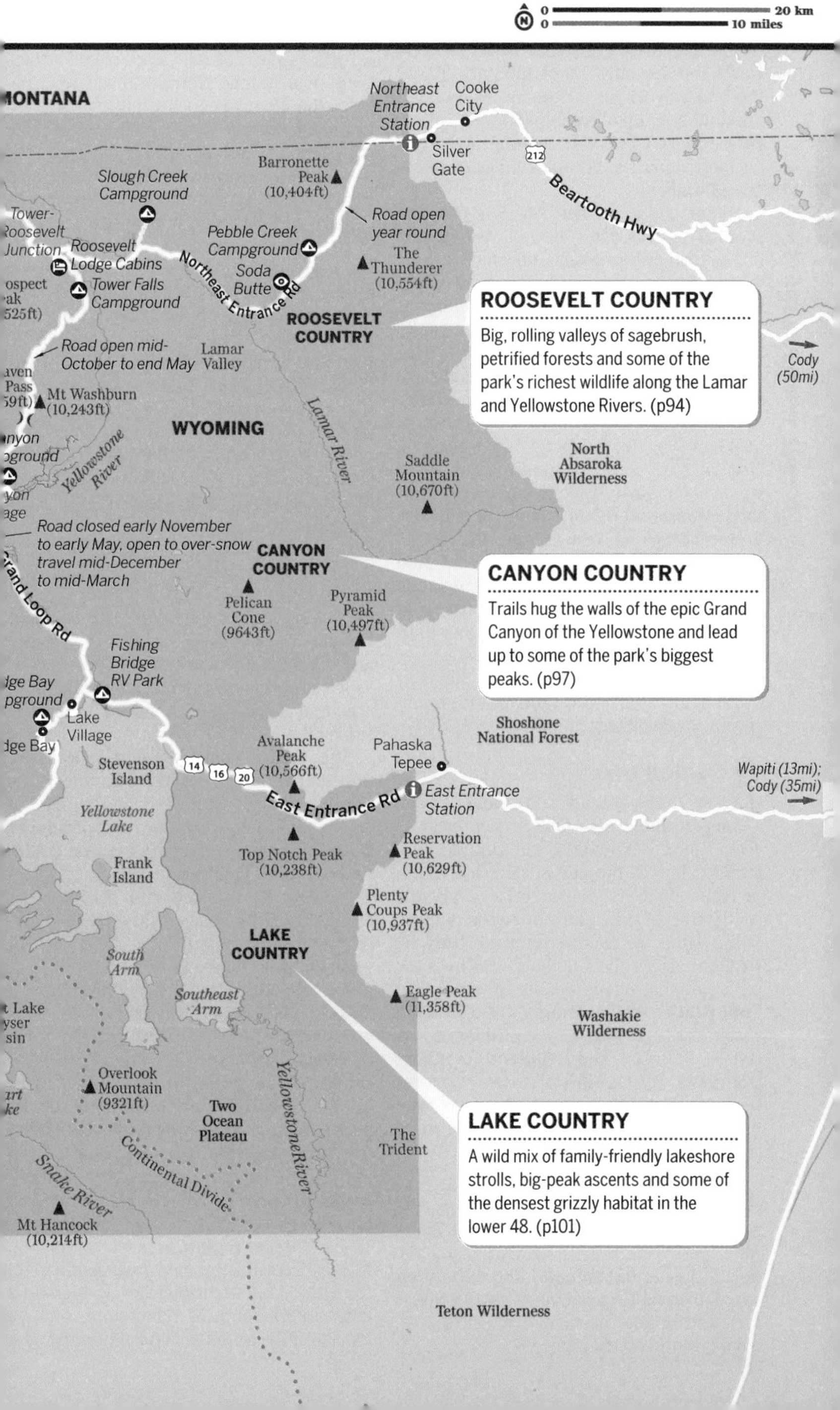

ROOSEVELT COUNTRY

Big, rolling valleys of sagebrush, petrified forests and some of the park's richest wildlife along the Lamar and Yellowstone Rivers. (p94)

CANYON COUNTRY

Trails hug the walls of the epic Grand Canyon of the Yellowstone and lead up to some of the park's biggest peaks. (p97)

LAKE COUNTRY

A wild mix of family-friendly lakeshore strolls, big-peak ascents and some of the densest grizzly habitat in the lower 48. (p101)

0 — 20 km
0 — 10 miles

MONTANA
WYOMING
Northeast Entrance Station
Cooke City
Silver Gate
212
Beartooth Hwy
Barronette Peak (10,404ft)
Slough Creek Campground
Tower-Roosevelt Junction
Roosevelt Lodge Cabins
Tower Falls Campground
Prospect Peak (…525ft)
Pebble Creek Campground
Soda Butte
Northeast Entrance Rd
Road open year round
The Thunderer (10,554ft)
ROOSEVELT COUNTRY
Road open mid-October to end May
Lamar Valley
Dunraven Pass (…59ft)
Mt Washburn (10,243ft)
Canyon Campground
Canyon Village
Yellowstone River
Lamar River
Saddle Mountain (10,670ft)
North Absaroka Wilderness
Cody (50mi)
Road closed early November to early May, open to over-snow travel mid-December to mid-March
Grand Loop Rd
CANYON COUNTRY
Pelican Cone (9643ft)
Pyramid Peak (10,497ft)
Fishing Bridge RV Park
Bridge Bay Campground
Lake Village
Bridge Bay
Stevenson Island
14
16
20
Avalanche Peak (10,566ft)
Pahaska Tepee
East Entrance Station
East Entrance Rd
Shoshone National Forest
Wapiti (13mi); Cody (35mi)
Yellowstone Lake
Top Notch Peak (10,238ft)
Reservation Peak (10,629ft)
Frank Island
Plenty Coups Peak (10,937ft)
LAKE COUNTRY
South Arm
Southeast Arm
Eagle Peak (11,358ft)
Washakie Wilderness
Heart Lake Geyser Basin
Heart Lake
Overlook Mountain (9321ft)
Two Ocean Plateau
Yellowstone River
The Trident
Continental Divide
Snake River
Mt Hancock (10,214ft)
Teton Wilderness

DAY HIKES

Even if you drive every road in Yellowstone you'll still see only 2% of the park. Easily the best way to get a close-up taste of Yellowstone's unique combination of rolling landscape, wildlife and thermal activity is on foot, along the 900-plus miles of maintained trails.

Hiking is also the best way to escape the summer crowds. Only 10% of visitors step off the road or boardwalks, only half of those venture further than a mile and just 1% overnight in the backcountry. It's one thing to photograph a bison from your car; it's quite another to hike gingerly past a snorting herd out on their turf. So pick up a map, pack some granola bars and work at least a couple of great hikes into your Yellowstone itinerary.

Where you hike depends on when you visit the park. Early in summer (May, June) you'll likely have to focus on the north of the park around the Mammoth and Tower-Roosevelt regions. Snowfall and bear restrictions close many higher-altitude hikes and regions around Yellowstone Lake until the middle of July. Many hikes in the centre and south of the park are muddy or snowy until July, so bring appropriate footwear.

Note that the park uses a three-character code (eg 2K7) to identify both trailheads and specific backcountry campsites.

Guided Hikes

If you're a novice hiker consider joining a **ranger hike**. These change from year to year, subject to budget and staffing constraints, but at present rangers lead summertime hikes to Mystic Falls, along the south rim of the Canyon region and to Storm Point, as well as several boardwalk strolls at places like Mud Volcano. Check the park newspaper for details. Alternatively, **Trail Guides Yellowstone** (☎406-595-1823; www.trailguidesyellowstone.com; 2149 Durston Rd, Unit 35, Bozeman) and **Wildland Trekking Company** (☎800-715-4453; www.wildlandtrekking.com; 2304 N 7th Ave, Unit K, Bozeman), both based in Bozeman, offer guided day hikes (from $270) and longer treks.

Orientation

Seven distinct regions make up the 3472-sq-mile park; starting clockwise from the north, they are Mammoth, Roosevelt, Canyon, Lake and Geyser Countries, the Norris area and remote Bechler region in the extreme southwestern corner.

Conceived by Lt Daniel C Kingman in 1886, the 142-mile, figure-eight Grand Loop Rd passes most of the park's major attractions. The 12-mile Norris–Canyon road divides the Grand Loop Rd into two shorter loops: the 96-mile Lower (South) Loop and the 70-mile Upper (North) Loop.

A clockwise drive from the North Entrance begins at Mammoth Hot Springs in the dry, low-elevation northwestern corner of the park. East of here is the sagebrush country of Tower-Roosevelt Junction, a center for Wild West cookouts and trail rides. Further east is **Roosevelt Country**, the wildest part of the park accessible by road and home to wolves and bison in the Lamar Valley. From Tower-Roosevelt Junction the mountain highway climbs south past Mt Washburn (10,243ft) and over Dunraven Pass (8859ft) to **Canyon Junction**, where the views of the 1200ft-deep canyon and the central location make it a popular logistical base.

Continue south along the Yellowstone River through wildlife-rich Hayden Valley and the hot springs of Mud Volcano to Fishing Bridge Junction. This is **Lake Country**, beloved by springtime grizzlies and dominated by the watery wilderness of Yellowstone Lake. Here you'll find lakeshore accommodations and a marina at nearby Bridge Bay.

The Grand Loop Rd skirts the lake's northwestern shore to West Thumb Junction, then heads west over the Continental Divide to Old Faithful in the heart of **Geyser Country**, home to the park's richest collection of geothermal features.

Turning north from Old Faithful, the Grand Loop Rd follows the Firehole River past several beautiful geyser basins to Madison Junction (6806ft) and the popular fly-fishing stretches of the Madison and Gibbon Rivers. From here a road leads west out of the park to the gateway town of West Yellowstone. The Grand Loop Rd continues northeast up the Gibbon River canyon to **Norris Junction**, home to the park's second-most-impressive collection of geysers. From here the road heads north past views of the snowcapped Gallatin Range to the west back to Mammoth Hot Springs.

The **Bechler region**, in the far southwest, is only accessible by road from Ashton, ID, from the John D Rockefeller Jr Memorial Pkwy to the south of Yellowstone, or by a four-day hike from the Old Faithful region.

Mammoth Country

Hikes in the relatively low-elevation area around the park's North Entrance highlight spring wildlife, scenic canyons, panoramic peaks and numerous lakes, streams and waterfalls, all with the backdrop of the Gallatin Range. This is one of the park's hottest regions in summer and is one of the first areas to be snow-free in spring. Consider hiking early or late in the season, or outside of midday.

 Beaver Ponds Trail

Duration 2½ hours

Distance 5 miles

Difficulty Easy to moderate

Elevation Change 350ft

Start/Finish Sepulcher Mountain/Beaver Ponds trailhead (1K1)

Nearest Town/Junction Mammoth

Summary An enjoyable loop hike, perfect if you're overnighting at Mammoth, that climbs to five ponds and offers a good chance of spotting moose and waterfowl.

This loop, with gentle climbs and lots of early-morning and evening wildlife, begins between Liberty Cap and a park residence next to the bus parking lot at Mammoth. The trail ascends through fir and spruce forests along **Clematis Creek** and in 2.5 miles reaches a series of five ponds amid meadows, where beavers and moose emerge in the mornings and evenings. Black bears are also a distinct possibility. Most families will be able to tackle this walk, but bring mosquito repellent.

Before you get started, it's worth pausing at trailside **Hymen Terrace**, named after the Greek god of marriage and one of the prettiest of Mammoth's many hot-spring terraces. The route is clearly signposted and follows the Sepulcher Mountain Trail for the first 0.7 miles, taking a right at the first junction, crossing a wooden bridge. Follow the main trail as it starts to switchback up the hill, avoiding the side trail to the right, and about 20 minutes into the hike you'll reach the signed junction, marking the end of the main elevation gain. Turn right for the **Beaver Ponds Loop** (left for the Sepulcher Mountain Trail).

As the path flattens, it passes through patches of Douglas fir forest and open meadows of wildflowers before a side trail reveals fine views over Mammoth and Everts Ridge. Look carefully at the ridge and you'll see strata of sediment from an ancient sea topped by a tuff of pyroclastic ash from a volcanic eruption. Ten minutes

Mammoth Country – Day Hikes

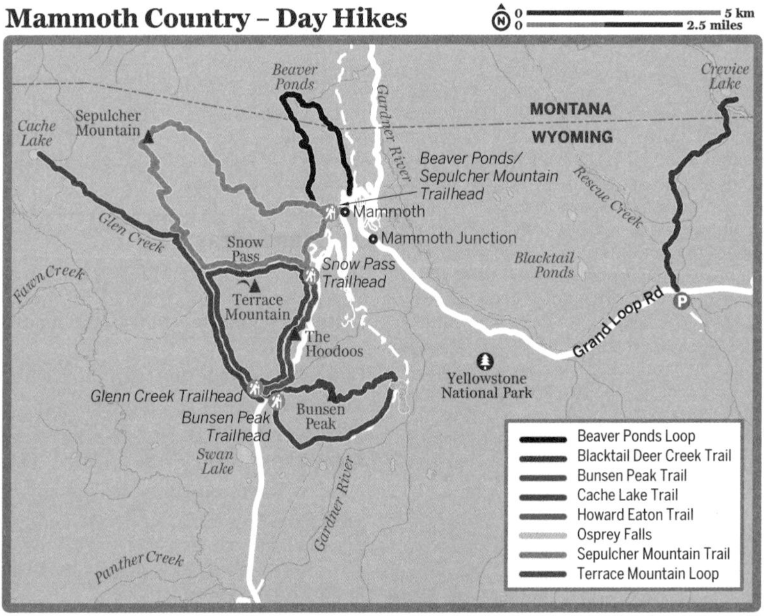

0 – 5 km
0 – 2.5 miles

Beaver Ponds Loop
Blacktail Deer Creek Trail
Bunsen Peak Trail
Cache Lake Trail
Howard Eaton Trail
Osprey Falls
Sepulcher Mountain Trail
Terrace Mountain Loop

YELLOWSTONE NATIONAL PARKS HIKES

NAME	REGION	DESCRIPTION
Bechler Meadows & Falls (p70)	Bechler Region	A solitary walk through lush forest, with big falls & wildlife-watching opportunities
Bechler River Trail (p79)	Bechler Region	A wild backcountry adventure filled with rivers, cascades, hot springs & prolific wildlife
South Rim Trail & Ribbon Lake (p60)	Canyon Country	Fine family hike or a first overnighter to moose habitat & views of the Grand Canyon of the Yellowstone
Mt Washburn (p61)	Canyon Country	The park's most popular trail, offering epic views of Yellowstone caldera, & a mountain-bike route option
Cascade Lake & Observation Peak (p62)	Canyon Country	Wet hike through meadows & past grazing bison, then up the side of a mountain for expansive views
Mt Washburn & Sevenmile Hole (p74)	Canyon Country	Shuttle hike from mountain peak to canyon floor through the heart of grizzly country
Lone Star Geyser (p68)	Geyser Country	Bike or stroll along an old service road to a fine backcountry geyser that erupts every three hours
Sentinel Meadows & Queen's Laundry Geyser (p67)	Geyser Country	Loop hike past bison and hot springs to a historic backcountry geyser, with some off-trail sections
Fairy Falls & Twin Buttes (p68)	Geyser Country	Flat stroll through lodgepole forest to a 197ft waterfall & a little-visited geyser
Mystic Falls & Biscuit Basin (p66)	Geyser Country	Loop hike from a colorful geyser basin to a pretty waterfall, with a more challenging return option
North Shoshone Lake & Shoshone Geyser Basin (p77)	Geyser Country	Part of the Continental Divide Trail to a remote geyser basin & stunningly silent backcountry lake

Wildlife-Watching  *View* 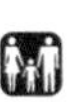 *Great for Families*  *Waterfalls*  *Thermal Features*

later the trail crosses a 4WD service track leading up to a hilltop radio transmitter, before passing a patch of quaking aspens and descending through forest to the first of several beaver-dammed ponds (1¼ hours from the trailhead). The fifth and final pond offers fine views of Sepulcher Mountain in the background and is a good place to spot moose, elk and pronghorn. Look for beaver dams at the lake outflow. Cross the outlet at the far end of the lake and ascend to a small ridge above another long, skinny lake.

From here, the trail continues across an open sagebrush plateau, offering views down on Gardiner town and both the modern and former stagecoach roads to the park, until you reach a ridge with fine views over the orderly buildings and manicured green lawns and white thermal terraces of Mammoth. Continue right for 50yd along the ridge for more views, then descend to the employee parking lot and the 4WD road to Gardiner that leads off behind the Mammoth Hot Springs Hotel. Grab a well-deserved ice cream at the general store before returning to your vehicle.

Bunsen Peak

Duration 2½ hours (six to seven hours with side trip)

Distance 4.2-mile round-trip (10.2 miles with side trip)

Difficulty Moderate (difficult with side trip)

Elevation Change 1300ft (2100ft with side trip)

Start/Finish Bunsen Peak trailhead (1K4)

Nearest Town/Junction Mammoth

Summary A short but steep hike up the side of an ancient lava plug for superb views, with the option of descending to an impressive canyon waterfall.

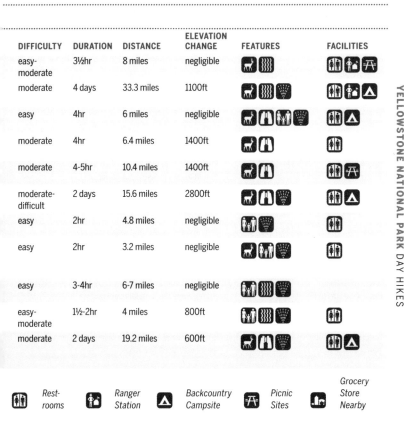

DIFFICULTY	DURATION	DISTANCE	ELEVATION CHANGE	FEATURES	FACILITIES
easy-moderate	3½hr	8 miles	negligible		
moderate	4 days	33.3 miles	1100ft		
easy	4hr	6 miles	negligible		
moderate	4hr	6.4 miles	1400ft		
moderate	4-5hr	10.4 miles	1400ft		
moderate-difficult	2 days	15.6 miles	2800ft		
easy	2hr	4.8 miles	negligible		
easy	2hr	3.2 miles	negligible		
easy	3-4hr	6-7 miles	negligible		
easy-moderate	1½-2hr	4 miles	800ft		
moderate	2 days	19.2 miles	600ft		

Restrooms · *Ranger Station* · *Backcountry Campsite* · *Picnic Sites* · *Grocery Store Nearby*

Bunsen Peak (8564ft) is a popular half-day hike, and you can extend it to a more demanding day hike by continuing down the mountain's gentler eastern slope to the Bunsen Peak Rd and then *waaay* down (800ft) to the base of seldom-visited Osprey Falls. It's also possible to bike 'n' hike (p83) out to Osprey Falls and not visit Bunsen Peak.

The initial Bunsen Peak Trail climbs east out of Gardner's Hole to the exposed summit of Bunsen Peak, offering outstanding panoramas of Mammoth, the Gallatin Range, Swan Lake Flat and the Blacktail Deer Plateau. Even if you just make it halfway up the hill you'll be rewarded with superb views.

Bunsen Peak's trails (especially along the south slope) are free of snow much earlier than those on most other peaks in the park and thus can be negotiated as early as May with some mild glissading. Be prepared for frequent afternoon thunderstorms, which bring fierce winds and lightning year-round.

Bunsen Peak was named by the 1872 Hayden Survey for German scientist Robert Wilhelm Eberhard von Bunsen (after whom the Bunsen burner was also named), whose pioneering theories about the inner workings of Icelandic geysers influenced early Yellowstone hydrothermal research. The mountain is actually an ancient lava plug, the surrounding volcanic walls of which have partly eroded away. So, yes, you are effectively climbing the inside of a former volcano!

From the Mammoth Visitor Center, drive 4.5 miles south on Grand Loop Rd, cross the light-colored rock defile of the **Golden Gate** and turn left into the unpaved parking area on the eastern side of the road, just beyond the Rustic Falls turnout. The parking lot is small and fills up quickly, so get here early, or try the Glen Creek trailhead across the road or continue a little further to Swan Lake Flats.

From 7250ft, the well-trodden single-track dirt trail branches left just beyond a

YELLOWSTONE NATIONAL PARKS HIKES (CONTINUED)

NAME	REGION	DESCRIPTION
Elephant Back Mountain (p63)	Lake Country	Easy ascent following a well-trodden path to fine lake views
Avalanche Peak (p65)	Lake Country	Relentlessly steep ascent above the tree line, offering unparalleled views of the Absarokas & Yellowstone Lake
Pelican Valley (p63)	Lake Country	Bird-watchers favor this rolling stroll through meadows & sagebrush in the heart of bear country
Heart Lake & Mt Sheridan (p75)	Lake Country	Solitude at a backcountry lake near thermal features; challenge-seekers can climb Mt Sheridan
Beaver Ponds Trail (p51)	Mammoth Country	Rolling hike from Mammoth Junction through sagebrush & wildflowers to five secluded ponds
Bunsen Peak (& Osprey Falls; p52)	Mammoth Country	Short uphill climb to mountaintop views, with optional canyon descent to up-close views of a little-visited waterfall
Sepulcher Mountain (p56)	Mammoth Country	Varied & scenic loop with superb views & a peek at Mammoth's hidden thermal features
Monument Geyser Basin (p65)	Norris	Steep but rewarding climb to a little-visited thermal feature, with fine views
Yellowstone River Picnic Area Trail (p57)	Roosevelt Country	Crowd-free views of the lower Grand Canyon of the Yellowstone; a must for amateur geologists
Lost Lake (p58)	Roosevelt Country	Peaceful hike to a secluded lake & a petrified tree – perfect for anyone staying at Roosevelt Lodge Cabins
Fossil Forest Trail (p59)	Roosevelt Country	Steep, unmaintained trail to several 50-million-year-old petrified trees & fine views

Wildlife-Watching  *View*  *Great for Families*  *Waterfalls*  *Thermal Features*

barricade on the left (north) side of unpaved **Bunsen Peak Road**. The trail climbs immediately through sagebrush interspersed with wildflowers, then enters a young Douglas fir and lodgepole pine mosaic. You'll get early views of the Golden Gate Pass below and to the left, and the ash-colored jumble of the limestone Hoodoos to the north. About half an hour from the trailhead a series of meadows offers fabulous views southwest to Swan Lake Flat, Antler Peak (10,023ft), Mt Holmes (10,336ft), Terraced Mountain and Electric Peak (10,992ft).

Five minutes later, at one of the many switchbacks, you'll gain a great view of the eroded sandstone cliffs and spires of **Cathedral Rock**, with vistas down to the red roofs and bleached travertine mounds of Mammoth. The layered sandstone-and-shale mountain of Mt Everts (7841ft), to the north, offers proof that the area was underwater 70 to 140 million years ago.

Beyond the Cathedral Rock outcrop, the switchbacks get steeper on the north side of the mountain and the exposed dome-shaped peak comes into view. Keep your eyes peeled for bighorn sheep.

The trail passes under electricity wires before a small cabin and communications equipment marks the first of three small summits, 2.1 miles from the trailhead. Record your visit in the logbook. Continue east along the loose talus ridge, past the cairns of the middle summit, to the exposed easternmost summit for the best southern panoramas. Electric Peak, one of the highest in the Gallatin Range, looms largest to the northwest, marking the park's northern boundary, with the Absaroka Range to the northeast.

Either retrace your steps down the western slope or wind around the peak to descend the unsigned eastern slope to the Osprey Falls Trail. If you descend the eastern

DIFFICULTY	DURATION	DISTANCE	ELEVATION CHANGE	FEATURES	FACILITIES
moderate	2-2½hr	3.5 miles	800ft		
moderate-difficult	3½hr	4 miles	2100ft		
moderate-difficult	6-8hr	16 miles	negligible		
moderate-difficult	2-3 days	16 miles	345ft (3145ft with side trip)		
easy-moderate	2½hr	5 miles	350ft		
moderate (difficult with extension)	2½hr (6-7hr)	4.2 miles (10.2 miles)	1300ft (2100ft)		
difficult	7hr	11.5 miles	3400ft		
moderate	2hr	2 miles	800ft		
easy	1½-2hr	4 miles	350ft		
easy	2hr	3.3 miles	600ft		
moderate-difficult	2½-3½hr	3.5 miles	800ft		

Rest-rooms *Ranger Station* *Backcountry Campsite* *Picnic Sites* *Grocery Store Nearby*

slope but don't visit Osprey Falls, it's a total 7.2-mile hike of around four hours.

SIDE TRIP: OSPREY FALLS

3–4 HOURS / 6 MILES / 800FT ASCENT

From the south side of the third summit, the trail descends east through the burnt forest and volcanic talus of Bunsen Peak's eastern flank. It's 1.9 miles (one hour) downhill to Bunsen Peak Rd, really just a dirt track. From here head left on Bunsen Peak Rd, snaking down a switchback for 100yd to the junction with the **Osprey Falls Trail**. (If you are coming in the opposite direction it's easy to miss the unsigned trail up to Bunsen Peak; look for the 'Steep Grade' sign as a marker.)

From the marked trailhead, the 1.4-mile Osprey Falls Trail wanders along the cliffs for 10 minutes before dropping like a stone into **Sheepeater Canyon**, losing 800ft in a bit less than a mile on a series of narrow, rocky switchbacks. Finally the trail levels out by the Gardner River to reach the base of the impressive, little-seen, 150ft **Osprey Falls**, set below an impressive basalt cliff and spire. You're more likely to see marmots or water ouzels in the canyon than the namesake bighorn sheep or osprey, which now prefer to nest along the Yellowstone River. The falls are a refreshing spot to linger over a packed lunch and contemplate the relentless chaos and synergy of the park's natural forces.

Retrace your steps out of the canyon and haul yourself for 45 minutes back up to Bunsen Peak Rd, from where it's a 3.2-mile (1¼-hour) trudge along the abandoned dirt road back to the Bunsen Peak trailhead. The road is a popular cross-country ski trail in winter. Look for views of the upper Gardner River en route. In the early morning and evening, hikers often spot wildlife (elk, bison, waterfowl and otters) in the meadows and ponds of **Gardner's Hole**, near the parking area. Look for muskrats in the roadside pond.

Sepulcher Mountain

Duration Seven hours

Distance 11.5 miles

Difficulty Difficult

Elevation Change 3400ft

Start/Finish Beaver Ponds/Sepulcher Mountain trailhead (1K1)

Nearest Town/Junction Mammoth

Summary A long but varied and incredibly scenic loop hike that offers superb views over half the park and allows a peek at hidden thermal features of the Mammoth terraces.

The first half of this day hike is a cardio workout, gaining almost 3500ft before descending through meadows and forest in a long but leisurely stroll back. It's a relentless climb, but it's well graded, offering plenty of interest en route. The hike starts at the same trailhead as the Beaver Ponds hike (p51), near the public toilets, so you can park anywhere in the Mammoth area. Trails Illustrated's 1:63,360 map No 303 *Mammoth Hot Springs* covers the route.

After 20 minutes the Sepulcher Mountain trail branches left away from the Beaver Ponds Trail, then 25 minutes later continues straight at a junction with the Clagett Butte/Snow Pass Trail. Continue up through burnt meadows and dead trees, past a pond on your right, before switchbacking steeply atop a ridge where you'll get your first views of Sepulcher Mountain and the impressive Gallatin Range to the west. The trail swings right and winds below the ridgeline through patches of forest and sagebrush to a viewpoint overlooking Gardiner and the lower Paradise Valley, north of the park boundary. As you continue the ascent, look for a **cairn** marking the path along the ridgeline to the tomb-like rocky outcrops that give Sepulcher Mountain its name. Look for mountain goats here. At a second cairn junction take the right branch for one minute to awesome views of the Paradise Valley and a well-deserved lunch spot. The main trail and actual **summit** (9646ft) are to the left of the cairn junction, past fine views of Electric Peak (10,992ft) and Cache Lake below.

The trail then descends to open meadows and an equally awesome panorama over Gardner's Hole, stretching from Bunsen Peak to Fawn Pass, with views stretching across half the park as far as the Tetons. Descend the grassy hillside on wide, ribbonlike switchbacks before re-entering a patch of forest and the junction with the Cache Lake/Glen Creek/Sportsman Lake Trail; take a left here.

After 15 minutes along Glen Creek you enter an open valley and branch left (east) on a shortcut trail to cross tiny Snow Pass (follow the electricity poles) on a winter cross-country ski trail. Descend past a trail junction, ignoring the left branch signed for the Sepulcher Mountain Trail. As you descend here look for white chunks of travertine beside the forested trail – proof that you're skirting the Mammoth-like destroyed former hot springs of **Pinyon Terrace**.

At the trail junction by the signboard, take the far left branch on the **Howard Eaton Trail**; straight on leads you to the Snow Pass trailhead. The final 1.3 miles take you around the back of the **Mammoth Upper Terraces** – take care if you decide to explore the side trails that lead to extinct cones, sinkholes and caves (emitting deadly carbon dioxide). Past Orange Mound Spring are views of some beautiful hidden white terraces (not visible from Mammoth's Upper Terraces), including New Highland Terrace and Narrow Gauge Terrace. Last, you descend past views over Mammoth to where you started, seven or eight long, but highly enjoyable, hours ago.

Other Mammoth Country Hikes

One enjoyable loop hike is the three-hour **Terrace Mountain Loop**. Starting at the unmarked pullout of Snow Pass trailhead, just south of Mammoth's Upper Terraces, the trail meanders through the interesting limestone Hoodoos, climbing high above the road to views of Rustic Falls, Mt Holmes and Swan Lake Flat, before swinging right through the open sagebrush of Glen Creek and then taking a right turn, following the electricity lines over Snow Pass and downhill past Pinyon Terrace (the last section of the Sepulcher Mountain hike). An alternative is to start at Glen Creek trailhead.

If you can arrange a vehicle shuttle, one excellent, easy and little-seen route (all downhill!) is to follow the 90-minute **Howard Eaton Trail** from Glen Creek trailhead past views of Rustic Falls and the ash-colored Hoodoos, past the junction to Snow Pass and down along the back side of Mammoth terraces to Beaver Ponds trailhead (3.8 miles). This hike follows the first third of the Terrace Mountain Loop.

Cache Lake is a satisfying 11.2-mile, three-quarter-day hike that is long enough to give you a workout but not hard enough to wipe you out. From Bunsen Peak/Glen Creek trailhead (1K3), 4.5 miles south of Mammoth, the trail crosses open sagebrush country, passing turnoffs to Fawn Pass and the Sepulcher Mountain Trail, along the Sportsman Lake Trail. Keep an eye out for moose grazing in the lush, meandering valley of Glen Creek.

Turn right at the final junction with the Sportsman Lake Trail and climb to the lovely lake, ringed by golden meadows and thick forest, with impressive 10,992ft Electric Peak looming to the right. It's about 2½ hours to the lake from the trailhead. Budget some time to savor the lake before retracing your steps. For an ambitious overnighter, continue on to backcountry sites 1G3 or 1G4 and then scramble (not technical) to the summit of Electric Peak the next morning. The peak is not clear of snow until July.

An appealing shorter hike is the 8-mile-return **Blacktail Deer Creek Trail**, 7 miles east of Mammoth. It descends 1100ft from the trailhead north into the Black Canyon of the Yellowstone to join the river near Crevice Lake. The return is all uphill.

Roosevelt Country

Hikes in this region are among the first in the park to be clear of snow and are accessible by road year-round. A fine mix of geology and wildlife is the main draw here.

Yellowstone River Picnic Area Trail

Duration 1½ to two hours

Distance 4-mile round-trip or loop

Difficulty Easy

Elevation Change 350ft

Start/Finish Yellowstone River picnic area (2K7)

Nearest Town/Junction Tower-Roosevelt

Summary A lovely stroll that offers crowd-free vistas over the Narrows, with much historical and geological interest.

Popular with picnickers, this scenic stroll offers fantastic views into the eroded towers and basalt formations of the Narrows and Calcite Springs sections of the Yellowstone valley, and possible glimpses of osprey and bighorn sheep: bring your binoculars. It's a good family hike, but you'll need to watch the little ones because there are lots of sheer drop-offs and no guardrails.

To get to the trailhead, take the Northeast Entrance Rd across the bridge from Tower-Roosevelt to the picnic-area parking lot, 1.5 miles east of the junction. Park in the lot just west of the picnic area, not in the busy picnic area itself.

Several unofficial dirt trails climb the slopes behind the picnic area, but the official (signed) trail leads off from the picnic site left of the vault toilets to ascend a couple of hundred feet and leave you puffing on the rim of the **Grand Canyon of the Yellowstone**. En route the trail passes several large erratic boulders, deposited in the valley over 10,000 years ago from the Beartooth Mountains by slow-moving glaciers. Notice how many of the Douglas firs have prospered in the moist, protective shade of these huge boulders.

The hike traces the canyon's north rim for a couple of miles, providing unobscured views down past the crooked canyon walls to the **Yellowstone River** and north and east beyond rolling ridges to the peaks of the Absaroka Range.

The trail stays in open country on the ridgeline, 800ft above the canyon floor, for the whole route. About 20 minutes from the trailhead you may smell sulfur, a sign that you are about to pass 180-degree views of the **Calcite Springs** thermal area across the canyon. Ten minutes further come fine views of the breccia spires of the Narrows. Look out for bighorn sheep below the basalt columns at **Overhanging Cliff**.

The trail ends abruptly at a bald **hilltop lookout** that offers views down on the site of the Bannock Indian ford, used by the Bannock to cross the Yellowstone River during their annual hunting trips across the park. You can also see the Tower Fall region (but not the falls themselves) to the right and the fire tower atop Mt Washburn in the distance.

From here you can retrace your steps to investigate the views of the canyon for a second time or, alternatively, take the trail left (northeast) for a few minutes to the three-way junction with the **Specimen Ridge Trail**. Take a left at this junction to return downhill back to the road and picnic area. (If you have some excess energy, you could ascend partway up Specimen Ridge along the Specimen Ridge Trail for fabulous views over the plateau.)

Roosevelt Country – Day Hikes

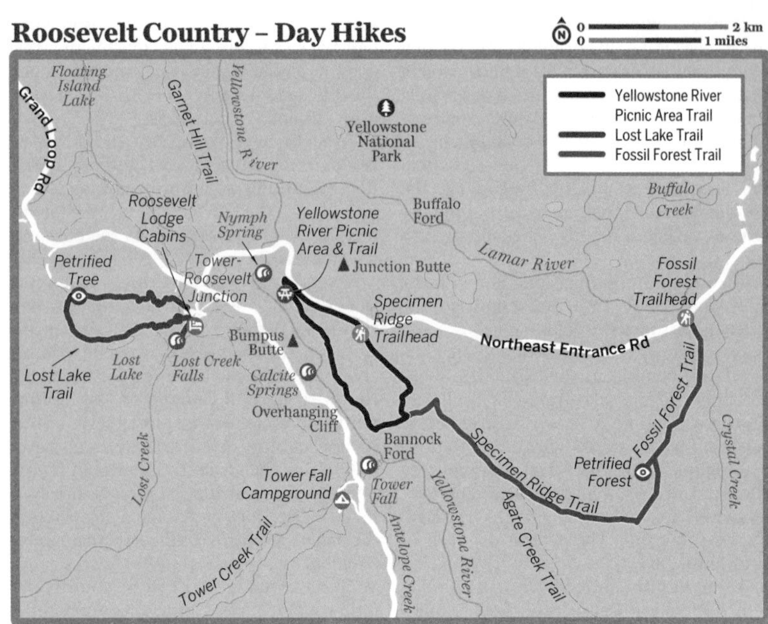

Just before reaching the road, branch left at the trail register and cut cross-country back to the trailhead, paralleling the road to a large erratic boulder. Otherwise, you'll have to hike along the road, an unpleasant end to an otherwise lovely hike.

Lost Lake

Duration Two hours

Distance 3.3-mile loop

Difficulty Easy

Elevation Change 600ft

Start/Finish Roosevelt Lodge

Nearest Town/Junction Tower-Roosevelt

Summary A peaceful early-morning hike to a secluded lake and a petrified tree – perfect for families and anyone staying or dining at Roosevelt Lodge.

The Lost Lake loop trail begins directly behind Roosevelt Lodge (take the right fork), climbing about 300ft past Lost Lake to a petrified tree, from where the trail climbs onto a plateau and then descends to Tower Ranger Station. Before you start the hike, warm up with a quick 10-minute detour left at the trailhead to the small but pretty **Lost Creek Falls**.

From the trailhead the trail crosses a bridge and branches left to switchback surprisingly steeply for the first 10 minutes onto the ridge. Look out for mule deer here in the early morning. Take a right at the junction (left leads to Tower Fall Campground, 2.9 miles away) and you'll come to the meadows surrounding **Lost Lake**, about 30 minutes from the trailhead. The trail traverses the length of the lake, past lily pads and dragonflies, to a good potential picnic spot at the end of the lake. If you're lucky, you might spot moose here.

From here the trail descends through meadows thick with spring wildflowers to reach the parking lot for the **petrified tree**. Take a couple of minutes to appreciate the 50-million-year-old stone redwood (there used to be three such trees here, but early tourists chipped away the other two...). If you started the hike early, you'll have the place to yourself; later in the day the parking lot will be jammed with reversing SUVs.

The trail back to Roosevelt Lodge follows orange markers up the hill from the edge of the parking lot and ascends to an open sagebrush plateau, offering fine views ahead to Junction Butte, Specimen Ridge and the Absaroka Range to the east. The trail then descends to **Tower Ranger Station**. You'll likely see mule deer grazing in the meadows here; at the very least you'll see a John Deere parked by the ranger station. Follow the orange trail markers to detour around the ranger station and in two minutes you'll be back at the cabins of Roosevelt Lodge, where breakfast will be waiting.

Fossil Forest Trail

Duration 2½ to 3½ hours

Distance 3.5 miles

Difficulty Moderate to difficult

Elevation Change 800ft

Start/Finish Unmarked trailhead

Nearest Town/Junction Tower-Roosevelt

Summary A must for amateur geologists, this unmaintained trail climbs steeply to several petrified trees and offers fine views. Listen for howling wolves in the early morning.

This hike leads to a couple of isolated patches of petrified forest scattered along Specimen Ridge, thought to hold the word's largest collection of petrified trees. The forests were buried suddenly in ash around 50 million years ago, or turned to stone by a vengeful Crow medicine man, depending on your beliefs. Paleodendrochronologists (scientists who date fossilized trees) have identified dozens of species of tree here, including tropical avocado and breadfruit, with several ancient petrified forests stacked atop even older petrified forests. Some of the trees were buried where they grew, but others were probably deposited by a mudflow caused by volcanic eruptions about 50 million years ago.

Please don't pocket any of the petrified wood here or elsewhere in the park. If you are desperate for a petrified-wood souvenir, head to Tom Miner Basin in the Paradise Valley, outside the park.

This trailhead isn't easy to find, so be sure not to confuse it with the Specimen Ridge Trail a couple of miles further west. The parking area is marked 'Trailhead' and is just a few hundred yards west of the Lamar Canyon bridge, 5 miles east of Tower-Roosevelt Junction and about 1 mile southwest of the turnoff to Slough Creek Campground. Look for the information board on wolves.

The trail is not formally maintained by the park service, so it isn't as easy to follow as most other trails in the park, though visitor centers do have a handout on the hike if you ask nicely. There is no water along the trail. Keep an eye out for the weather; the exposed ridge is not the place to be during a storm.

From the **unmarked trailhead** the fairly clear path starts off following a dirt double track (a former service road to the nearby Crystal Valley) and then veers right after 100yd to head up the hillside for 45 minutes, through meadows of July wildflowers and past buffalo trails to a small patch of forest. Branch right along the steeper path and, after 10 minutes' uphill climb, you'll reach your first **petrified tree stump** by a bend in the trail. To the right of here on a side trail is a second stump, with a third piece a bit further along the same side trail, branching left and then right. Most of the side trails lead to stumps. Back on the main trail it's more uphill, past a volcanic outcrop enclosing another fossilized tree and into ridgeline meadows.

The main trail continues up the ridge and, after a couple of minutes, branches right on a subtrail, skirting and then traversing a small patch of forest to the stump of a **petrified giant redwood**. This fabulous tree would once have topped out at 200ft! Below the huge stump are two thinner but taller upright trees and views back up toward the redwood's petrified roots. The views over the Lamar and Yellowstone Valleys are superb.

The subtrail continues up the hillside to join the main trail just before a small cairn. Continue for 20 minutes uphill along the ridge to the summit of **Specimen Ridge**, marked by a cairn. There are wonderful views from here of bison herds in the valley below, birds of prey riding the thermals, and Mt Washburn in the distance. Return the way you came for about an hour – the views west are stunning.

One alternative end to the hike is to drop down the back (south) side of Specimen Ridge, veering to the right to hit the Specimen Ridge Trail near a trail marker recognizable by its elk antlers. From here the trail follows the plateau west, past the Agate Creek turnoff, to descend off the ridge and join the Yellowstone River Picnic Area Trail (p57). Figure on 2½ hours from the ridge to the Yellowstone River Picnic Area trailhead. You'd need to arrange a vehicle shuttle to end the hike this way.

Other Roosevelt Country Hikes

From the stagecoach road just north of Tower-Roosevelt Junction, the 7.5-mile **Garnet Hill Trail** is an easy three-hour loop north of the Grand Loop Rd. The trail heads northwest along the stagecoach road and

Elk Creek and then loops around Garnet Hill to return to Roosevelt Lodge. It's a good early- or late-season option. For an extension, take a left at the Garnet Hill junction, then a right to cross the suspension bridge over the Yellowstone River, and drop down to Hellroaring Creek, where there are several backcountry campsites (add 2.5 miles). You can also reach the trail from Hellroaring trailhead, 3.5 miles west of Tower-Roosevelt Junction.

For a good day hike with fine fishing, try the first part of the **Slough Creek Trail**. Head uphill past the patrol cabin to where the trail rejoins the river at the first meadow (a 4-mile round-trip), or continue to the second meadow or nearby McBride Lake (cross Slough Creek) for a 6-mile round-trip hike. Be sure to take the right branch at the junction with the trail that continues up to the Buffalo Plateau. There's also nice hiking along the fishing trails that head up Slough Creek from the campground.

Pebble Creek Trail to Warm Creek trailhead (3K4) is a scenic 12-mile hike that requires a vehicle shuttle. The trail heads up Pebble Creek for 10 miles through burns and lovely wildflowers, crosses a pass (open end of June), then drops down to the Warm Creek trailhead and a nearby picnic area on the Northeast Entrance Rd. The hike includes several river crossings that can prove tricky in early summer.

Specimen Ridge Trail is a popular but long 19-mile hike up and along the ridge, past Amethyst Mountain, then down into the Lamar Valley. Check with rangers beforehand that the Lamar River ford is passable, which is unlikely before July. You'll need to arrange a shuttle.

Canyon Country

Though the surrounding backcountry draws far less attention than the Grand Canyon of the Yellowstone, it is every bit as interesting. Abundant wildlife, good camping, mesmerizing cascades and great vistas await. You can also consider the Sevenmile Hole Trail as an 11-mile day hike.

South Rim Trail & Ribbon Lake

Duration Four hours

Distance 6 miles

Difficulty Easy

Elevation Change Negligible

Start/Finish Uncle Tom's parking lot

Nearest Town/Junction Canyon Village

Summary An incredibly varied hike that combines awesome views of the colorful Grand Canyon of the Yellowstone with a couple of lakes and even a backcountry thermal area.

Southeast of the Grand Canyon of the Yellowstone's South Rim, a network of trails meanders through meadows and forests and past several small lakes. This loop links several of these and makes a nice antidote to seeing canyon views framed by the windshield of your car. Come early in the morning and the canyon is all yours.

Park at Uncle Tom's parking area on the Canyon's South Rim Dr and, after checking out the views of the Upper Falls and the Lower Falls from Uncle Tom's Trail, take the **South Rim Trail** east from Uncle Tom's Trail, along the rim of the canyon to **Artist Point** for some of the finest canyon views available. This section of trail was renovated in 2018.

From busy Artist Point take the trail east toward Point Sublime, taking in the superb views halfway along the trail (tip: the views from Point Sublime itself are actually not as good), then retrace your steps to the junction, where you branch south past **Lily Pad Lake** for 0.3 miles to another junction. Branch left here and descend for 1.2 miles to **Ribbon Lake**, actually two conjoined ponds, with a good chance of spotting moose. For a close-up view of the mouth of **Silver Cord Cascade**, continue on the path to the canyon rim, then head left along the canyon wall to the small falls. (To actually see the falls you'll have to drive to the north side of the canyon and hike a mile from the Glacial Boulder trailhead.) A faint path connects to the main trail at a small footbridge. This is the furthest point of the hike, 3.4 miles from the start.

Two secluded backcountry sites by the lake make for an easy overnighter less than 2 miles from the trailhead (lovely 4R1 is right on the lake; 4R2 is further and on the main trail). Mosquitoes can be a problem here before mid-August, so pack spray.

From Ribbon Lake head back to the junction with Lily Pad Lake and instead of returning the way you came, continue straight, past several minor fumaroles and hot springs to the acidic, spring-fed waters of **Clear Lake**, 1.5 miles from Ribbon Lake. Continue along the Clear Lake Trail and, at the next unsigned junction, take the right branch for the final 0.7 miles back to Uncle Tom's parking area.

Canyon Country – Day Hikes

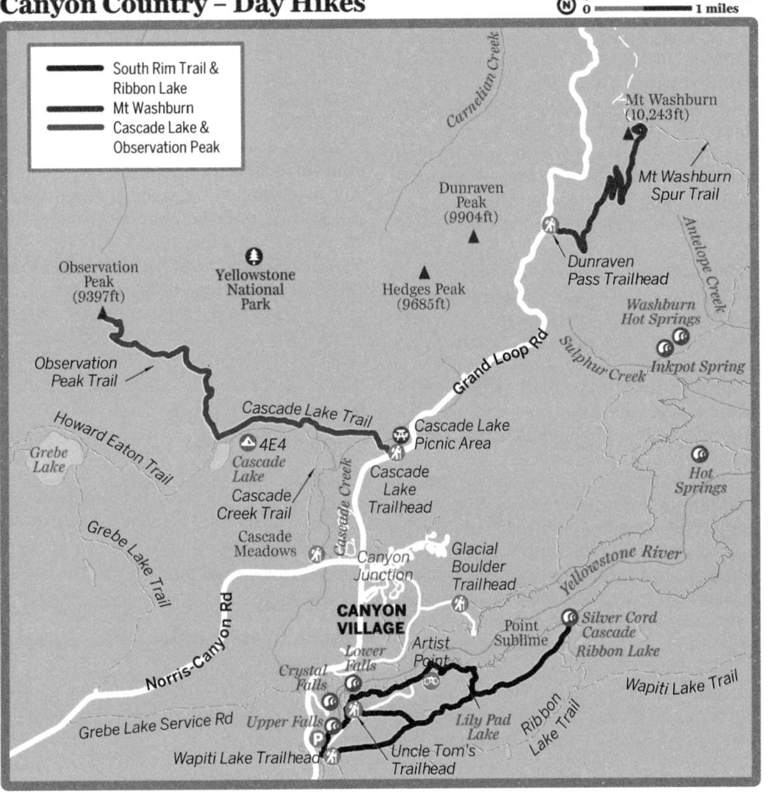

Alternatively, the left branch continues across open grassland (good wildlife-spotting) for just over a mile to the **Wapiti Lake trailhead**, where you can link up with the South Rim Trail by Chittenden Bridge and return through forest to Uncle Tom's, passing fine views of the Upper Falls en route. This longer loop adds 1 mile to the hike, but is a worthwhile option if you have the time.

Mt Washburn

Duration Four hours

Distance 6.4 miles return

Difficulty Moderate

Elevation Change 1400ft

Start/Finish Dunraven Pass trailhead (4K9)

Nearest Town/Junction Canyon Village

Summary Yellowstone's most popular day hike offers unsurpassed 360-degree mountaintop views, with the chance of spotting bighorn sheep and black bears.

This popular return hike climbs gradually to the fire lookout tower on the summit of 10,243ft **Mt Washburn** for some of the park's best views. Over 10,000 hikers tackle this trail annually, so leave early to get trailhead parking. Older teenagers should be able to do the hike.

Mt Washburn is all that remains of a volcano that erupted around 640,000 years ago, forming the vast Yellowstone caldera. Displays in the lookout tower point out the caldera extents, making this a good place to get a sense of the awesome scale of the Yellowstone super-volcano. The peak is named after Montana surveyor-general Henry Washburn, who rode up the peak to see the view during the Washburn, Langford and Doane expedition of 1870.

The route described here starts from Dunraven Pass (8859ft) on the Grand Loop Rd, 4.8 miles north of Canyon and 14.2 miles south of Tower. An alternative route begins from the larger Chittenden parking area (5 miles north of the pass) for a marginally shorter but less interesting hike (but good bike trail) to the summit. Use Trails Illustrated's 1:63,360 map No 304 *Tower/Canyon*.

Snow often obstructs the Dunraven Pass approach through the end of June. Wildflower displays in July and August are legendary. Frequent afternoon thunderstorms bring fierce winds and lightning, so pack a windbreaker even if the weather looks clear and be ready to make a quick descent if a storm rolls in.

Keep in mind that grizzlies flock to Mt Washburn's eastern slopes in large numbers during August and September in search of ripening whitebark pine nuts.

The wide trail follows a rough, disused road (dating from 1905) and so makes for a comfortable, steady ascent, following a series of long, ribbon-like loops through a forest of subalpine firs. After 20 minutes the views start to open up. The fire tower appears dauntingly distant, but the climb really isn't as painful as it looks. Continue northeast up broad switchbacks to a viewpoint, then follow a narrow ridge past a few stunted whitebark pines (look out for bears) to the gravel **Chittenden Road** at the Mt Washburn Trail junction. At the junction the road curves up to the three-story **fire-lookout tower**, about two hours from the trailhead. The side trail right at the junction leads down the Washburn Spur Trail to Canyon Junction.

The viewing platform and ground-level public observation room has restrooms (but no water), a public 20x Zeiss telescope, displays on the Yellowstone caldera and graphics to help you identify the surrounding peaks and valleys. The fire tower was built in the 1930s and is one of three in the park still staffed from June to October. The majestic panoramas (when the weather is clear) stretch over three-quarters of the park, across the Yellowstone caldera south to Yellowstone Lake, Canyon, the Hayden Valley and even the Tetons, and north to the Beartooth and Absaroka Ranges. Below you are the smoking Washburn Hot Springs. Keep your eyes peeled for bighorn sheep basking near the summit. If the crowds get too much, you can always head five minutes down the Washburn Spur Trail for some peace and quiet. From the summit, return the way you came.

ALTERNATIVE ROUTE: MT WASHBURN SPUR TRAIL TO CANYON

6 HOURS / 11.2 MILES / 2340FT DESCENT

If you can arrange a shuttle, or hitch a lift to Dunraven Pass, consider hiking from Mt Washburn down the 5.4-mile Mt Washburn Spur Trail (p74) to the junction with the Sevenmile Hole Trail and on to the **Glacial Boulder trailhead** in Canyon, a total 11.2-mile hike through the heart of grizzly country. You'll ditch all the Washburn crowds and even pass several thermal features en route, notably Inkpot Springs. The lower meadows are often waterlogged until mid-June.

This hike can be done in reverse, finishing at Dunraven Pass, but this adds 850ft of ascent.

Cascade Lake & Observation Peak

Duration Four to five hours

Distance 10.4 miles

Difficulty Moderate

Elevation Change 1400ft

Start/Finish Cascade Lake trailhead (4K5)

Nearest Town/Junction Canyon Village

Summary There's plenty of flexibility here for all levels, mixing an easy hike to Cascade Lake with fine views atop Observation Peak.

There's something for everyone on this trail, which starts just a couple of minutes' drive north of Canyon Village. The full hike climbs 1400ft to Observation Peak (9397ft), but the turnaround at Cascade Lake gives an easy, level hike of only 4.4 miles return (2½ hours). You can also add on a 4-mile return side trip to Grebe Lake, should you wish.

Start the hike at the **Cascade Lake trailhead**, 1.5 miles north of Canyon Junction, or the nearby picnic area of the same name. July is a great time for wildflowers along this route (look for glacier lilies), but the trail can be boggy until July.

The path quickly joins the trail from the picnic area and continues past the trailhead board to enter an open valley frequented by bison. The double-wide track crosses several creeks before swinging into forest to follow a meandering creek. One mile into the hike you'll hit the Cascade Creek Trail that leads here from the Canyon–Norris road, offering a different, drier early-season approach if you can arrange a car shuttle. Take the right branch to **Cascade Lake**.

Ten minutes from the junction, the path leads into a wide valley, past backcountry site 4E4 on the left, to the trail junction at the western end of the lake, less than an hour from the trailhead. The right branch leads to backcountry site 4E3 and Observation Peak; straight ahead takes you to the eastern part of the lake and on to Grebe Lake 2 miles away.

The lake itself opens to meadows on the west and backs on to the Solfatara Plateau and its ghost forest of burnt snags. The lake is worth exploring for its wildfowl and occasional moose. Bison often graze the meadows to the east. The lake's waters drain down Cascade Creek, eventually to plunge into the Yellowstone River over Crystal Falls.

The hike up to **Observation Peak**, part of the Washburn Range, takes about 1¼ hours and gains 1400ft in 3 miles. After 30 minutes the trail crests a saddle and curves to the left, opening up views of the peak ahead. It loops further to a ridgeline, giving you time to catch your breath before the final 20-minute climb to **4P1**, one of the park's most unusual backcountry campsites, in a forested hollow just below the main peak. The site makes a fine place to enjoy dusk and dawn views, but there's no water here, so you'll have to haul up everything you need.

The views from the peak are superb: Cascade and Grebe Lakes sit below you, smoking Norris Geyser Basin is to the west and the Hayden Valley yawns to the south. To the north is the Washburn Bear Management Area, classic grizzly country, so keep your eyes peeled. The ranger hut at the summit is normally closed. The descent back to Cascade Lake takes about one hour, from where you return to the trailhead the way you came.

Lake Country

Lake Country is best known for its boating opportunities, but its great hikes are also worth getting to know. Bear activity in the river inlets to Yellowstone Lake delays the hiking season here (the Pelican Valley, Natural Bridge and Heart Lake Trails are closed until early July), making it a limited early-season option. Check with a visitor center if you are coming in early summer and always hike with others.

The region's other hikes are short but sweet, with good family options to lakeshore views at Storm Point and Pelican Creek (don't confuse this with the Pelican Valley).

Elephant Back Mountain

Duration Two to 2½ hours

Distance 3.5-mile loop

Difficulty Moderate

Elevation Change 800ft

Start/Finish Elephant Back trailhead

Nearest Town/Junction Lake Village

Summary This relatively easy ascent follows a well-trodden path and rewards you with fine lake views near the top.

This hike is a great short-but-sweet picnic option, suitable for families with teenagers. The trailhead is 1 mile south of Fishing Bridge Junction and 0.5 miles north of the Lake Village turnoff on the Grand Loop Rd. From Lake Yellowstone Hotel an alternative side trail cuts 0.25 miles through the woods past Section J of the hotel's cabins to access the trail. Use Trails Illustrated's 1:83,333 map No 305 *Yellowstone Lake*.

The start of this lollipop loop trail parallels the Grand Loop Rd for 100yd, then abruptly ducks into the forest. A few minutes from the road it passes the old water pipes of Lake Village, then crosses beneath a power line and begins a steady climb. The forest floor here is thick with wildflowers, wild berries and fungi. Watch for deer and moose. After passing through 1 mile of lodgepole pines, the trail reaches a junction.

Both trails lead to the **panoramic overlook** (8600ft). The trail to the left (0.8 miles) is steeper than the trail to the right (0.9 miles). Hike clockwise up the steep trail and down the easier trail for an easy-on-the-knees loop. You can picnic with a view at the wooden bench at the top. Looking out, Pelican Valley's meadows lie to the left, Stevenson Island sits in the lake ahead, and the Absaroka Range outlines the horizon in the distance.

Pelican Valley

Duration Six to eight hours

Distance 16-mile loop

Difficulty Moderate to difficult

Elevation Change Negligible

Start/Finish Pelican Valley trailhead (5K3)

Nearest Town/Junction Fishing Bridge

Summary Bird- and wildlife-watchers favor this rolling stroll through remote meadows and sagebrush in the heart of bear country. Restrictions apply.

Lake Country – Day Hikes

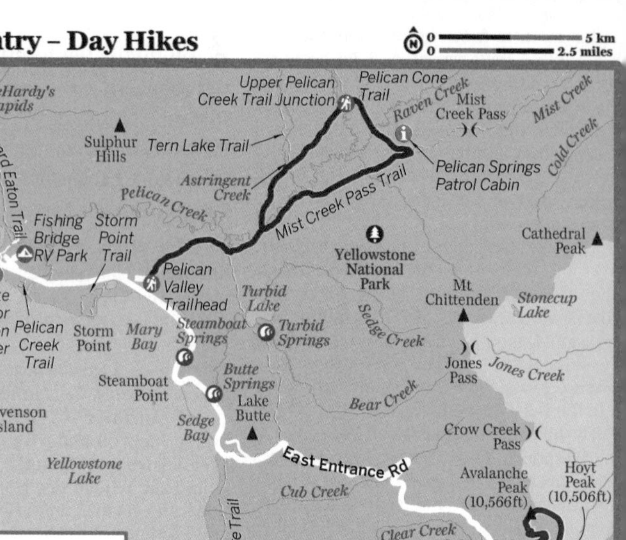

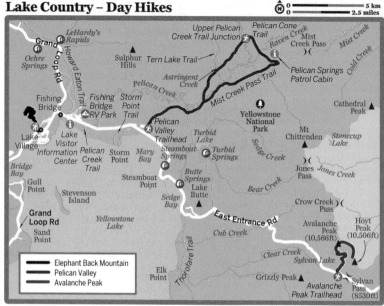

Rangers recommend a minimum party of four hikers for this lollipop loop, through some of the most concentrated grizzly country in the lower 48 states. Backcountry camping is not allowed anywhere in the valley. Bring plenty to drink and a hat, since there's no shade along the trail. Hiking in the morning or late afternoon on overcast, rainy or even snowy days offers the best chance to catch a glimpse of wildlife.

Pelican Valley (including the nearby Turbid Lake Trail) is closed for bear activity from April 1 to July 3 and is open for day use only (9am to 7pm) from July 4 to November 10. The July 4 opening is typically the busiest day in the valley. Off-trail travel is prohibited on the first 2.5 miles of the trail.

The trailhead sits at a gravel parking lot at the eastern end of an old service road. It is off the northern side of the East Entrance Rd, 3.5 miles east of Fishing Bridge and 23.5 miles west of the East Entrance. The lot is across the road from the trailhead for Storm Point and Indian Pond. Use Trails Illustrated's 1:63,360 map No 305 *Lake Yellowstone*.

The **Pelican Valley Trail** follows the abandoned Turbid Lake service road due east for a few minutes, then veers north along the forest edge to an overlook, which provides the first sight of the Pelican Creek drainage, a couple of miles away. Look for pelicans at the mouth of the creek. The trail descends through open meadow to the valley floor, passing through boggy sections. Near the poorly marked Turbid Lake Trail junction, scan the forest edge (and trail) for signs of coyotes, bison, elk and grizzlies.

A mile further on the trail passes the rickety remains of the **Pelican Creek Bridge**. Make the easy ford and climb a terrace for 1.5 miles to the bridge over **Astringent Creek**, just before another junction. The marshy area around a group of thermal springs just south of the trail offers good wildlife-watching. Continue east along the forest edge, scanning the clover patches for bear scat.

Follow the old service road northeast for 1.5 miles to another easy ford of Pelican Creek and the Upper Pelican Creek Trail junction. Stay in the meadows to the right for 0.3 miles to the Pelican Cone Trail junction, where a small stream provides the valley's best drinking water. The ill-defined trail cuts south away from the valley edge, crossing meadows to ford **Raven Creek**. There are plenty of waist-deep swimming holes here.

Beyond Raven Creek the poorly defined trail heads southeast through sagebrush-interspersed meadows. The trail passes through a dormant thermal area fragrant with sulfur. After a patch of unburned forest, follow through rolling sagebrush hills to the

Pelican Springs Patrol Cabin and the Mist Creek Pass Trail junction. From here, it's a well-defined, undulating 5 miles back to the Pelican Bridge junction along the forested southern edge of the valley.

Avalanche Peak

Duration 3½ hours

Distance 4-mile loop

Difficulty Moderate to difficult

Elevation Change 2100ft

Start/Finish Avalanche Peak trailhead (5N2)

Nearest Town/Junction Fishing Bridge

Summary Relentlessly steep, this challenging peak ascent offers unparalleled views of the Absaroka Range and Yellowstone Lake.

This thigh-burner starts off steeply, gets steeper and then continues uphill (steeply) for the entire duration. You can't say you weren't warned... Check for closures; in early fall the trail is frequented by grizzlies foraging for whitebark pine nuts.

During the late-spring snowmelt, subalpine wildflowers peak, leading in midsummer to a profusion of high-alpine butterflies. From midsummer on get an early start, since afternoon lightning storms are common. Regardless of the season, pack your hiking poles and a shell jacket for protection against gusty winds and afternoon thundershowers. Snowfields persist through mid-July, even on the trail's south-facing slopes. July to September are the most reliable months for this hike.

The trailhead sits off the East Entrance Rd, 0.5 miles west of Sylvan Pass, 19 miles east of Fishing Bridge Junction and 8 miles west of the park's East Entrance. Park in the small paved lot on the southern side of the road by Eleanor Lake's west-side picnic area (no toilet). Use Trails Illustrated's 1:63,360 map No 305 *Yellowstone Lake*.

From the signed trailhead (8466ft) across the road, the trail climbs steeply through lush forests of spruce and fir along a small, unnamed stream. Thirty minutes from the road the trail traverses west across an old avalanche chute, then east again into mature whitebark-pine forest.

A little over a mile from the road the trail levels out and emerges at the base of a huge amphitheater-like bowl. At a prominent cairn the main trail veers steeply to the left, climbing along open talus slopes to arrive at the mountain's south ridge. Two trails climb the final section, meeting at a rock shelter, so you can take one route up and the other down.

Above the glacial cirques and well above the tree line, panoramic views extend north to the Beartooths and south to the Tetons. Thousands of acres just west of the peak were burned in summer 2003 after a lightning strike. The true summit (10,566ft) sits to the northeast, along the narrow ridge, by a series of talus wind shelters. After a summit picnic, retrace your steps.

An alternative for the sure-footed is to follow the steep, unstable talus trail down the eastern arm of the peak toward the saddle shared with jagged Hoyt Peak (10,506ft), at the Shoshone National Forest boundary. A side trail climbs to a minor peak, from where you can see the hidden lakes below Hoyt Peak. If you're not comfortable scree surfing down the steep slope, head back the way you came to take the lower path that circles round the back of the peak, offering an easier descent. Descend through a series of sparsely forested rolling hills to rejoin the main trail at the foot of the bowl.

Other Lake Country Hikes

South of Grant Village the 5-mile round-trip Riddle Lake Trail traverses the Continental Divide and drops down to the lake and its marshy meadows, a favorite of moose. The trailhead is off the South Entrance Rd, 3 miles south of Grant Village. Bear activity closes the trail from April 30 to July 15.

Shoshone/Dogshead trailhead offers two ways of getting to lovely Shoshone Lake, the largest backcountry lake in the lower 48. Popular with anglers, the 6.5-mile Shoshone Lake (Lewis River Channel) Trail follows the north shore of Lewis Lake, along the Lewis River Channel, to Shoshone Lake. Return the same way or via the shorter (4.7 miles), forested Dogshead Trail. You can make it an overnighter by booking lakeshore backcountry campsite 8S0.

Norris

In addition to the Monument Geyser Basin hike there are 2 miles of trails leading around Norris Geyser Basin.

Monument Geyser Basin

Duration Two hours

Distance 2 miles

Difficulty Moderate

Norris – Day Hike

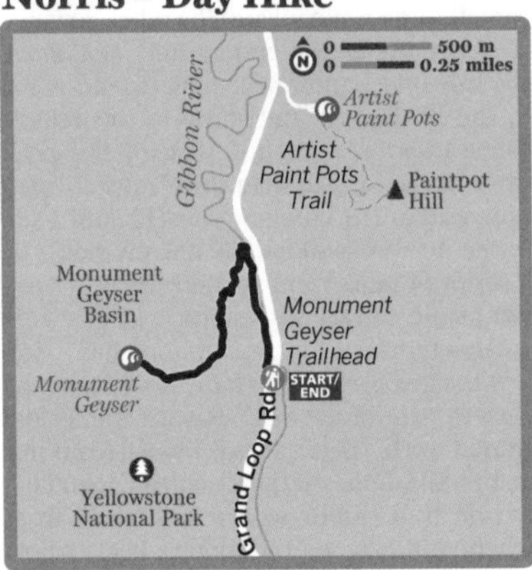

Elevation Change 800ft

Start/Finish Monument Geyser trailhead

Nearest Town/Junction Norris

Summary A steep but rewarding climb to a little-visited thermal feature, with fine views over Gibbon Meadows.

The semi-dormant chimney-like cones of Monument Geyser Basin are among the park's tallest. There's limited thermal action here these days (no geysers or spouters), but you'll likely have the place to yourself.

The short but steep hike follows the **Gibbon River** for 0.5 miles, then heads steeply uphill for another 0.5 miles, offering fine views of Gibbon Meadows and Mt Holmes en route. The most prominent feature in the bleached basin is **Monument Geyser** (also known as Thermos Bottle Geyser), which still lets off steam, unlike the other cones, which have sealed themselves up over the centuries.

To get back to your car, return the same way. Budget around 45 minutes up, half an hour down and 30 minutes to explore the minor springs and fumaroles.

Geyser Country

Even the short hikes described here will get you away from the crowds at Old Faithful to some spectacular backcountry waterfalls and geysers.

Mystic Falls & Biscuit Basin

Duration 1½ to two hours

Distance 4-mile loop

Difficulty Easy to moderate

Elevation Change 800ft

Start/Finish Biscuit Basin (OK4)

Nearest Town/Junction Old Faithful

Summary A short, family-friendly stroll from an interesting thermal basin to a 70ft waterfall, with the option for a longer moderate loop hike that offers views over the Firehole Basin.

The shorter, out-and-back option to the base of the falls is relatively flat and thus popular with families. Due to a lack of shade, the longer loop hike to the overlook is best done in the morning or late afternoon. The trail is closed from the end of the winter season until the last Saturday of May due to the presence of bears.

The Biscuit Basin turnoff is 2 miles north of the Old Faithful overpass and 14 miles south of Madison Junction, on the western side of Grand Loop Rd. Use Trails Illustrated's 1:63,360 map No 302 *Old Faithful*.

From the parking area, head west across the Firehole River bridge. Follow the **Biscuit Basin boardwalk** loop 0.3 miles around to the left, past several notable geysers and hot springs. Just west of Avoca Spring, the wide, sandy **Mystic Falls Trail** (blazed but unsigned) ducks into burned lodgepole forest dotted with wildflowers.

A quieter approach avoiding the boardwalk crowds is to park in the pullout of the main road a couple of hundred yards south of the Biscuit Basin car park. A foot trail leads from here for 10 minutes over a stock bridge to the main Mystic Falls Trail.

The undulating trail parallels, but does not cross, the **Little Firehole River**. Soon you'll reach the signed Summit Lake/Little Firehole Meadows junction. From here it's 0.7 miles to the left on the most direct route to the falls, saving the longer overlook loop – visible on a cliff to the right – for the return trip. After another couple of minutes a second junction leads left to Summit Lake on the Continental Divide Trail, but continue right to the falls. After 10 to 15 minutes the trail arrives at the bottom of the 70ft **Mystic Falls**, 1.2 miles from Biscuit Basin, where several hillside hot springs seep into the river. A series of switchbacks leads to the top of the falls.

Retrace your steps to complete the 2.4-mile family-friendly version. If you're fit, or traveling without children, you can choose instead to complete the loop (which adds a sweaty 500ft elevation gain) by continuing 0.5 miles through more burned lodgepoles to the Fairy Creek/Little Firehole Meadows Trail junction. Turn right and descend to the **Biscuit Basin Overlook** for an expansive bird's-eye view of the steaming Upper Geyser Basin. Follow the switchbacks downhill to rejoin the Mystic Falls Trail, then retrace your steps to Biscuit Basin.

Sentinel Meadows & Queen's Laundry Geyser

Duration Two hours

Distance 3.2 miles return

Difficulty Easy

Elevation Change Negligible

Start/Finish Freight Rd trailhead (OK6), Fountain Flat Dr

Nearest Town/Junction Madison Junction

Summary Some off-trail exploring to a little-visited geyser basin, with a good chance of spotting bison.

This trail is a good choice if you fancy a bit of simple off-route trail finding. It's flat and easy but requires some basic navigation skills. Bring waterpoof boots before July, as trails can be boggy. Park at the end of **Fountain Flat Drive**, just off the main Grand Loop Rd, 6 miles south of Madison Junction and 13 miles north of Old Faithful.

From the parking lot it's 0.3 miles along the dirt road to the **Ojo Caliente spring** (Map p110) and the bridge over the Firehole River, which is where the Sentinel Meadows Trail branches west off the gravel road. You can cycle this first short section and chain your bike to the bridge for your return.

Turning onto the Sentinel Meadows Trail, the route swings away from the Firehole River, passing beneath telephone lines. The soil quickly turns to white, hinting at the thermal features lying ahead. Twenty-five minutes into the hike you pass backcountry campsite **OG1**. The trail climbs a small hill to offer views of the valley, its four smoking thermal features and a probable scattering of bison. **Mound Spring** is the closest and most expansive of the springs, **Steep Cone** is the tallest, and **Flat Cone** is the furthest, across the creek. The trail ascends a second small hill before skirting around a patch of new-growth forest 1.7 miles from the trailhead.

This is where things get tricky. As the main trail bends to the left to hook around the forested hill, look to the right to see the steam of **Queen's Laundry Geyser** – this is your destination. Two faint trails lead here: one directly from the main trail, the other further south (a post in the ground makes a rough marker), which swings northwest, skirting

Geyser Country – Day Hikes

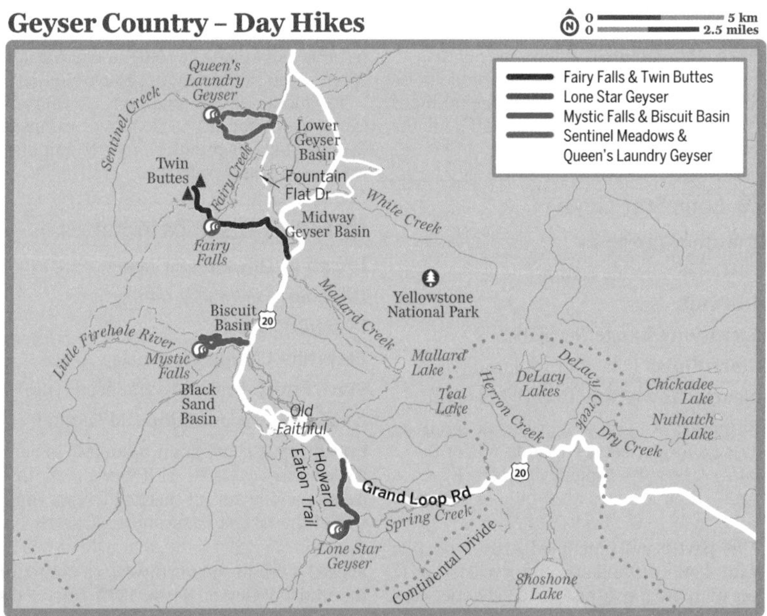

the forest. Both are wet and boggy early in the season, so you'll just have to scout out the driest path. In general, trace an arc counter-clockwise to the right of the bog, staying on dry ground to get to the far northern side of the geyser, by a ruined wooden cabin.

The historic **cabin** is a former bathhouse, built in 1881 by park superintendent Norris as the first national-park building designed solely for public use. The geyser gets its name from the bathing costumes that used to hang to dry on strings beside the bath-house. The deep-blue geyser (really more of a pool) drains past the bathhouse into a wide cascade. Don't get too close to the geyser – act as if the normal boardwalks and warning signs were in place.

Back at the junction you can return the way you came. Alternatively, continue on the main trail as it curves east, past a seasonal pond, across a bridge, over a small rise and then along the edge of Imperial Meadows, beside an open plain favored by bison. After 20 minutes you'll see an orange arrow pointing across the boggy plain. This trail takes a longer route to get to Fountain Freight Rd, so for a shortcut ignore it and continue straight (east) along the forest edge on a social trail until you see a cliff-like butte straight ahead. As the trail peters out, continue straight (east) across the plain toward the right side of the hill. Take a minute to investigate **Boulder Spring**, a perpetual spouter that looks as if it's coming straight out of the hill. Several pools in the river creek offer potential soaking sites here.

Head straight under the telephone poles to rejoin Fountain Freight Rd. The trailhead is a five-minute walk to the left and the parking lot is 10 minutes further.

Lone Star Geyser

Duration Two hours

Distance 4.8-mile return

Difficulty Easy

Elevation Change Negligible

Start/Finish Lone Star trailhead (OK1)

Nearest Town/Junction Old Faithful

Summary An easy, level riverside stroll along a former service road to one of the park's largest backcountry geysers. Even better, do it as an easy 20-minute bike ride.

This paved and pine-lined hike is popular with both day hikers and cyclists (p84), yet it's quite a contrast to the chaotic scene around Old Faithful. Isolated Lone Star erupts every three hours for between 15 and 30 minutes and reaches 30ft to 45ft in height, followed by a steam phase of similar length. The Old Faithful Visitor Center no longer offers predicted eruption times, so you'll just have to bring a book or a packed lunch for the wait. If the parking lot at Lone Star trailhead is full, park at the neighboring Kepler Cascades turnout.

From Lone Star trailhead, above **Kepler Cascades** (where the Firehole River speeds through a spectacular gorge), take the old paved road (closed to cars) past a tiny weir that diverts water to Old Faithful village.

The road crosses the Firehole River bridge and follows the upper Firehole River, heading upstream past the Spring Creek Trail junction (1.6 miles) after 30 minutes to end at the steep-sided, 9ft-tall **Lone Star Geyser** after an easy 2.4 miles. Check the National Park Service (NPS) logbook (in the wooden information box in front of the geyser) to gauge exactly when the next eruption might occur – if you catch an eruption, fill in the log for future visitors. If you have time to kill, consider following the **Shoshone Lake Trail** for 20 minutes to check out the two minor thermal areas along the Firehole River.

To completely avoid the crowds, consider taking the quieter but hillier **Howard Eaton Trail** (OK2) from 1 mile south of the Old Faithful overpass as an alternative 5.8-mile return route. The trail joins the Shoshone Lake Trail 0.3 miles beyond Lone Star Geyser. You could take one route in and the other out if you can arrange a vehicle shuttle.

To guarantee an eruption to yourself, camp overnight at backcountry campsite OA1 or OA2, 10 minutes' and 20 minutes' walk away, respectively.

Fairy Falls & Twin Buttes

Duration Three to four hours

Distance 6 to 7 miles return

Difficulty Easy

Elevation Change Negligible

Start/Finish Fairy Falls trailhead (OK5)

Nearest Town/Junction Old Faithful

Summary A short jaunt to an accessible backcountry cascade, with views over the park's most beautiful thermal feature and one of the largest backcountry geysers.

Tucked away in the northwestern corner of the Midway Geyser Basin, 197ft Fairy Falls is a very popular hike, largely because it's only a short trip from Old Faithful. Beyond Fairy Falls the trail continues to a hidden thermal area at the base of the Twin Buttes, two conspicuous bald hills that offer fine views. The geysers are undeveloped and you're likely to have them to yourself – in stark contrast to the throngs around Grand Prismatic Spring.

The Fairy Falls (Steel Bridge) trailhead is just west of the Grand Loop Rd, 1 mile south of the Midway Geyser Basin turnoff and 4.5 miles north of the Old Faithful overpass. The parking lot fills up early in the day, despite being recently expanded, so get here early. Use Trails Illustrated's 1:63,360 map No 302 *Old Faithful*. The trail is closed until Memorial Day weekend due to the presence of bears.

Cross the **Firehole River** on the silver trestle bridge, then head northwest along Fountain Flat Dr, which is a wide gravel cycling and hiking path. After three-quarters of a mile you'll notice multicolored steam rising from **Grand Prismatic Spring** on the right. You can't reach the boardwalk from this trail, but you can head along the new side trail to your left for 400yd up a gentle ascent for one of the park's greatest views: an astonishing bird's-eye vista of Grand Prismatic Spring.

Back on the main trail, continue 0.3 miles to a junction and turn left onto the narrower **Fairy Creek Trail**. If you are cycling this first section (an excellent idea), lock your bike at the rack here. The trail winds for 1.6 miles past backcountry campsite **OD1** through lodgepole forest burned in the 1988 fires. The campsite is an easy overnight option, just 45 minutes from the trailhead, and offers the chance to get a jump on the crowds the next morning.

At 197ft, **Fairy Falls** is the park's seventh-highest waterfall, but the wispy volume of water is hardly on a par with the falls on the Yellowstone River. Still, patterned streaks of white water blanket the dark lower rocks, and clumps of raspberries and fireweed flourish around a pretty pool, which makes for a fine swimming hole on a hot and sticky summer day.

After crossing a footbridge, the trail continues 0.7 miles northwest toward the prominent **Twin Buttes** and several conspicuous plumes of rising steam. Cross several marshy patches with the aid of log bridges, take a left at the first trail junction and five minutes later take the right branch at a second junction to see the plume emanating from **Spray Geyser**, erupting frequently to a height of 6ft to 8ft.

Continue west, following the outlet from **Imperial Geyser**, which is lined with orange algae. Imperial plays almost perpetually, projecting blasts of water up to 20ft into its large rainbow pool. If you care to climb onto the buttes, head up the hillside trail behind Imperial Geyser. After discovering the collection of five or so lily-choked ponds hidden in a hollow between the two summits, you can continue to either summit, though the right-hand hill is the more appealing. Views to the east encompass the Lower and Midway Geyser Basins, while to the west the trail-free Madison Plateau stretches off toward the park boundary. Retrace your steps to the Fairy Falls trailhead.

Other Hikes in Geyser Country

The best way to get to the shores of lovely Shoshone Lake on a day hike is the three-hour (6-mile) return hike along the **DeLacy Creek Trail**. The meadows en route are good habitat for moose, elk, mule deer, coyotes and sandhill cranes, but bring bug repellent before August. Shoshone Lake was known at one time as DeLacy Lake, after the army engineer who 'discovered' it. The trailhead is east of Craig Pass, near the DeLacy Creek picnic area, halfway between Old Faithful and West Thumb Junction. It's a largely flat walk. Bring a picnic to eat on the lovely volcanic lakeshore beach. Backcountry site 8S3 (no wood fires) is less than 30 minutes from here if you want to make an easy overnight of it.

Bechler Region

Bechler boasts the highest concentration of waterfalls in Yellowstone and some of the best backcountry hot-spring soaks anywhere. Its forests also escaped the worst of the 1988 fires. That said, the region is a long way from anywhere and easiest visited from Idaho or northern Grand Teton Naitonal Park than from other parts of Yellowstone.

The area's remoteness means it's best suited to experienced hikers taking long backcountry trips, but some rewarding shorter hikes are possible. In early summer trails are knee-deep in water, so aim to hike here from August onward. Inquire about conditions at another ranger station before driving all the way out here.

Bechler Region – Day Hikes

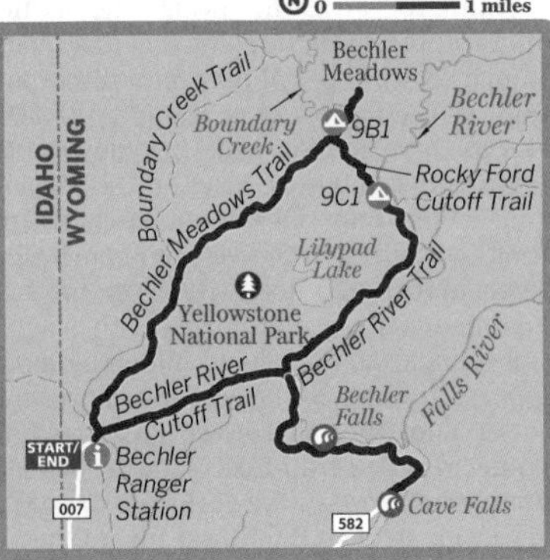

Bechler Meadows & Falls

Duration 3½ hours

Distance 8-mile loop

Difficulty Easy to moderate

Elevation Change Negligible

Start/Finish Bechler Ranger Station (9K1)

Nearest Town/Junction Driggs, ID

Summary A solitary walk through lush forest, with big falls and wildlife watching.

Bechler Meadows' extensive wetlands are a wildlife magnet. Grizzlies and black bears, as well as rare waterfowl such as gray owls and great blue herons, are often spotted. Add substantial cascades to an already spectacular mix by starting from the Cave Falls trailhead, or by taking the Bechler Falls side trip.

This route avoids all fords, but the trails can be wet through July, so bring waterproof shoes. Use Trails Illustrated's 1:63,360 map No 302 *Old Faithful*.

From Bechler Ranger Station, follow the Bechler Meadows Trail 3 miles northeast past the Boundary Creek Trail junction through lodgepole-pine forest to the **Bechler River/Rocky Ford Cutoff Trail** junction. If it's not too buggy, hike an extra 0.5 miles north to **Bechler Meadows**. You will cross a wooden suspension bridge over Boundary Creek past campsite 9B1. It's an ideal spot to look for sandhill cranes and moose, or angle the waters for rainbow trout.

Retrace your steps 0.5 miles back to the junction and then continue southeast 0.7 miles past campsite 9C1 to the wide **Rocky Ford** at the Bechler River Trail junction. Instead of fording the river, trace the river's west bank south for 2 miles to the next junction, where a cutoff leads west 1.7 miles through forest back to the ranger station. The east branch leads to Bechler Falls.

SIDE TRIP: BECHLER FALLS & CAVE FALLS

1½–2 HOURS / 4 MILES / NEGLIGIBLE

Finish your hike with a 3-mile side trip to Bechler Falls and Cave Falls. The worthwhile detour heads 0.5 miles downstream from the Bechler River/Ranger Station cutoff junction to Bechler Falls, one of Bechler's widest and most voluminous waterfalls. Continue east on the riverbank trail 1.5 miles to the broad-spanning Cave Falls (20ft) and its refreshing swimming hole.

From here you can get picked up, hike back the way you came to Bechler Ranger Station, or even cycle 5 miles on the road to the ranger station (leave a bike here en route to the ranger station).

Other Bechler Region Hikes

At the western end of Grassy Reservoir, by the dam, trailhead 9K5 is the start of the 15.5-mile round-trip hike to **Union Falls**, one of the most spectacular in the national park. After a mile the trail branches right, fords Cascade Creek and then branches left (right leads to the Pitchstone Plateau Trail). After another 4 miles the trail fords Proposition Creek and then a mile later branches right onto the Union Falls Trail for another 2 miles. At 250ft feathery Union Falls are the second-highest falls in Yellowstone National Park.

If that seems too ambitious, a shorter 3.6-mile return hike leads from the same trailhead to a lovely series of cascades known as **Terraced Falls**. At the eastern end of Grassy Reservoir a pullout marks the trailhead for the 6-mile round-trip hike northeast to **Beula Lake**, with its two lakeside backcountry campsites. The trail crosses the South Boundary Trail en route.

All hikes are accessed from Grassy Lake Rd, south of the park, and most easily accessed from Flagg Ranch in the John D Rockefeller Jr Memorial Pkwy.

OVERNIGHT HIKES

There's no better way to experience the raw wildness of Yellowstone than on an overnight backpacking trip. Some experience of backcountry camping is important before heading out into the wild, particularly in bear awareness, hanging food and leave-no-trace practices (p33). That said, there's a huge range of challenges available, from easy strolls, to easy backcountry overnights (p116) an hour from the road, to multiday expedition-style traverses of the Thorofare corner or Gallatin Range through some of the remotest terrain south of Alaska. Choose the right trip at the right time of year and arrive prepared, and there's no better way to experience the park.

If you don't fancy organizing a multiday trek yourself, consider a company like Trail Guides Yellowstone (p50) or Wildland Trekking Company (p50), both based in Bozeman, MT, whose backpacking trips cost $255 to $270 per person per day, including meals, guide and transportation from Bozeman. Wildland Trekking Company even offers llama treks.

Backcountry Permits

A backcountry-use permit, available at visitor centers and ranger stations, is required for all overnight backcountry trips (day hikes don't require permits). There is a $3 per person per night charge for backcountry use between Memorial Day and Labor Day weekends. If you are camping for more than eight nights you can opt for a $25 season pass.

About half the backcountry sites can be reserved by mail; a $25 reservation fee applies regardless of the number of nights. Booking starts on April 1, when all existing reservations are dealt with at random, and continues up to 48 hours before your start date. Reservations can be made in person at a backcountry office, by fax to 307-344-2166 or through the mail to Backcountry Office, PO Box 168, Yellowstone National Park, WY 82190. Applications must be on a Trip Planner Worksheet, available at the park website, and you must give two itinerary alternatives.

The downloadable Backcountry Trip Planner (www.nps.gov/yell/planyourvisit/upload/bctrip-planner_2018.pdf) is an essential guide to the park's backcountry sites. To see which sites are available, contact the central backcountry office (p128). Outside of summer call ☎307-344-7381.

Once you've ascertained by phone that the sites and dates you want are available, send the nonrefundable cash, check or money order with your booking. You will receive a confirmation notice, which must be taken to a backcountry office to exchange for a permit not more than 48 hours before your trip but before 10am on the day of your trip departure.

Around 20% of backcountry-use permits are issued no more than 48 hours (effectively three nights) in advance on a first-come, first-served, walk-in basis (no $25 fee). This means you can leave your planning to the last minute, as long as you are flexible with your itinerary. (You may, for example, have to walk one day further than you had planned if your desired site is already booked.)

The most popular areas are the Hellroaring region of the Black Canyon of the Yellowstone in spring, Slough Creek in early summer, Shoshone Lake in August, Bechler region in August/September and Heart Lake throughout summer. You should include a backup itinerary if applying for a popular region or trail in peak season.

There are **backcountry offices** (open 8am to 4:30pm) at nine locations in the park. Check opening hours, as in 2018 several offices were closed two days a week. Most are not open daily until mid-June.

Bechler Ranger Station (☎406-581-7071; 8am-4:30pm)

Bridge Bay Backcountry Office (Map p102; ☎307-242-2413; Bridge Bay Marina; 8am-4:30pm)

Canyon Visitor Education Center (p97)

Grant Village Backcountry Office (Map p102; ☎307-242-2609; Grant Village; 8am-4:30pm)

Mammoth's Albright Visitor Center (p92)

Old Faithful Ranger Station (Map p112; 8am-4:30pm)

Tower Ranger Station (Map p96; 8am-4:30pm)

West Yellowstone Visitor Information Center (30 Yellowstone Ave, West Yellowstone; 8am-8pm mid-May–Aug, 8am-5pm Mon-Fri Sep–mid-May)

Get to the office at least half an hour before closing because you have to watch an 18-minute video on backcountry safety before you can get your permit. Once you've seen the video you don't need to watch it again for subsequent visits. The backcountry-use permit is site and date specific and states the campsite where you must overnight. Part of your permit goes on the dashboard of your car; the main permit stays with you on your pack.

1. Mountain goat (p248)
Keep an eye out for mountain goats perched on the cliffs of Snake River Canyon.

2. Lone Star Geyser (p68)
Time your hike or cycle to coincide with an eruption from this 9ft-tall, backcountry geyser.

3. Yellowstone River (p57)
The USA's longest free-flowing river is a popular destination for white-water rafting and fishing.

4. Hayden Valley (p100)
Spot grazing bison in the vast grasslands of this valley.

4

Canyon Country

Mt Washburn & Sevenmile Hole

Duration Two days

Distance 15.6 miles

Difficulty Moderate to difficult

Elevation Change 2800ft

Start Dunraven Pass trailhead (4K9)

Finish Glacial Boulder trailhead (4K6)

Nearest Town/Junction Canyon Village

Summary Fabulous views, a backcountry thermal feature and a descent into the Grand Canyon of the Yellowstone that feels like it's '5 miles in and 7 miles out.'

This excellent overnight shuttle hike takes you to the top of one of the park's highest peaks and then down, down, down to Sevenmile Hole, a minor hydrothermal area at the bottom of the Grand Canyon of the Yellowstone. It's not a particularly long hike, but it does involve a lot of elevation change (most of it downhill). When the insect hatch is on, the backcountry sites at Sevenmile Hole are very popular with anglers, so book your spot well in advance.

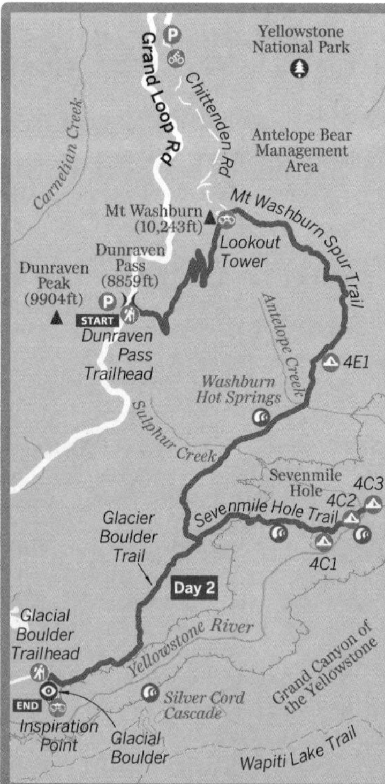

DAY 1: MT WASHBURN & SEVENMILE HOLE

6–7 HOURS / 10.7 MILES / 1400FT ASCENT / 3500FT DESCENT

The popular hike up to Mt Washburn makes up the first couple of hours of this hike.

From the four-way junction just below Mt Washburn, the **Mt Washburn Spur Trail** drops southeast along an undulating ridge past alpine wildflower meadows. After dipping through a saddle to another little gap at the tree line, bear right and descend 2.6 miles from the summit through small clearings to **Washburn Meadow** and campsite 4E1 (campfires allowed).

Keep your wits about you – this is prime grizzly habitat. The **Antelope Bear Management Area**, east of the trail on the mountain's eastern slope, is closed annually from August 1 to November 10 and open May 10 to July 31 only by special permit, so avoid wandering off-trail. The trail descends southwest through boggy grassland grazed by elk and deer to **Washburn Hot Springs**, a small field of inky black mud pots, pools and hissing fumaroles. Proceed past more small thermal areas to the Sevenmile Hole Trail junction, 3 miles from campsite 4E1.

The steep trail switchbacks down 1400ft through Douglas firs, passing a 10ft-high geyser cone before arriving at a more active thermal area. Continue down to the end of the thermal basin and the easily missed turnoff to campsite 4C1 (look for the trail marker lying on the ground), then cross a small thermal stream for the final 15-minute walk to cramped campsite 4C2 beside the **Yellowstone River**.

This entire area is known as **Sevenmile Hole**. Large springs emerge from the reddish chalky cliffs on the river's far bank. To reach campsite 4C3, ford narrow **Sulphur Creek** (can be uncrossable early in the season), then follow the riverbank past a tiny hot pool. Stock animals and wood fires are not allowed at any of the campsites. Unattended food must be out of reach of bears – if you are day-tripping down here, hang (don't dump) your pack at the junction.

DAY 2: SEVENMILE HOLE TO GLACIAL BOULDER TRAILHEAD

4½ HOURS / 4.9 MILES / 1400FT ASCENT

The first section is the hard 1400ft ascent back out of Sevenmile Hole to the junction with the Mt Washburn Spur Trail. Back at the junction, heading southwest, the trail is broader, passing meadow views of Mt Washburn, and leads along the north rim of the 1200ft-deep **Grand Canyon of the Yellowstone** for the final 2.7 miles, passing through lodgepole forest carpeted with fragrant, low-lying grouseberry shrubs.

The views are increasingly spectacular as you pass the unsigned overlook of long, thin Silver Cord Cascade, which drops nearly 1000ft to the canyon floor. The amazing Technicolor swirls of the canyon's eroding sides stretch another mile to the Glacial Boulder trailhead. Canyon Village is 1.5 miles west along paved Inspiration Point Rd.

ALTERNATIVE ROUTE: GLACIAL BOULDER TO SEVENMILE HOLE

5–6 HOURS / 11 MILES / 1400FT ASCENT/DESCENT

An alternative route for day hiking to Sevenmile Hole starts at the Glacial Boulder trailhead (4K6) just before **Inspiration Point**. This out-and-back route is an 11-mile hike and drops 1400ft in 1.5 miles; as always, the hard part is the return trip. It's a decent day hike or a relaxed overnighter – day two of the Mt Washburn and Sevenmile Hole hike in reverse.

Lake Country

Heart Lake & Mt Sheridan

Duration Two to three days

Distance 16-mile round-trip

Difficulty Moderate to difficult

Elevation Change 345ft (3145ft with side trip)

Start/Finish Heart Lake trailhead (8N1)

Nearest Town/Junction Grant Village

Summary A backcountry geyser and thermals, and the opportunity to peak-bag or fish the lake bestow myriad options onto this straightforward hike. July to October are the only feasible months.

While the shores of 2160-acre Heart Lake suffered damage in the 1988 fires, it remains a beautiful, rewarding and popular destination. An extensive thermal field extends from the northwestern shore, showcasing boiling hot pots and a large geyser. Heart Lake provides rich habitat for waterfowl, and there are plentiful stocks of cutthroat and elusive, but record-setting, lake (Mackinaw) trout.

The highest summit in the Red Mountains, Mt Sheridan (10,308ft), rises high above Heart Lake's west shore, providing terrific panoramas. While the extremely fit can knock off Heart Lake in a long day hike, it's worth spending a night (or two) along the lakeshore to relax, watch the bald eagles and osprey, and explore.

The Heart Lake Trail is closed from April 1 to June 30 due to bear activity – reconfirm the opening date with a backcountry office. Elk carcasses from winter hardship tend to pile up here, leading to an early-season grizzly fiesta.

All west-shore campsites have a two-night limit from July 1 to September 1. Snow persists along the trail up to Mt Sheridan until mid-July.

Use Trails Illustrated's 1:63,360 map No 305 *Yellowstone Lake*. Two 1:24,000 USGS maps also cover the route: *Heart Lake* and *Mount Sheridan*. The trailhead is 5.3 miles south of Grant Village and 16.7 miles north of the South Entrance, off South Entrance Rd. There's a toilet at the trailhead.

DAY 1: HEART LAKE TRAILHEAD TO HEART LAKE

3–5 HOURS / 8 MILES / 345FT DESCENT

Follow the sandy, mostly single-track trail southeast through strewn trunks and new-growth **lodgepole forest**. After a few miles, the trail rises slightly over a minor watershed to the first group of smoking fumaroles at the north foot of bald-topped **Factory Hill** (9607ft), 1½ to two hours from the trailhead. Heart Lake, 2 miles downhill, comes into view.

Wind your way down into the intensely active **Heart Lake Geyser Basin**. Numerous spurting springs and boiling pools sit a short way off to the right. The trail crosses warm Witch Creek several times to reach the Heart Lake patrol cabin, just off the lake's north shore (7450ft).

Witch Creek is a prime spot for bathing near thermal spots. You can inquire about this and current fishing conditions at the log-cabin **ranger station** (staffed in summer).

Trail Creek Trail departs left (east) around the lake's northeastern shore; it's a popular jumping-off point for stock users bound for the Thorofare region.

Heart Lake & Mt Sheridan

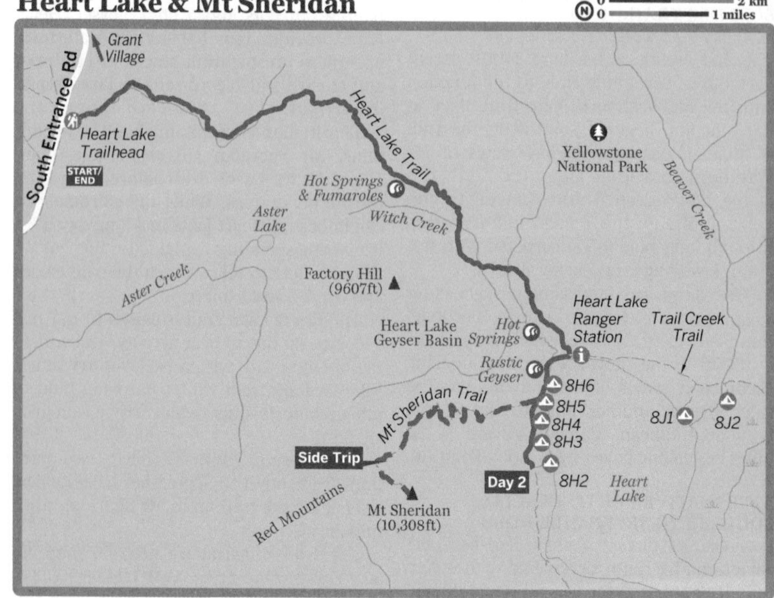

Heart Lake Trail continues right, first following the gray-sand beach to cross the Witch Creek inlet on a log bridge and then tracing the lake's western shore to reach campsite 8H6. This is the first of five sites alongside firs and spruces fringing the shoreline.

Follow the steam along an often-overgrown trail at the tree line behind 8H6 to another fascinating thermal area. Here you will spot the azure **Columbia Pool**. **Rustic Geyser** spouts up to 50ft at irregular intervals, while other springs bubble up into large calcified bathtubs.

The main trail continues past campsite 8H5 to the junction with the Mt Sheridan Trail, then proceeds about another mile south past campsites 8H4 and 8H3 to 8H2 – only 8H2 and 8H3 allow campfires.

There are good views across the 180ft-deep lake east to Overlook Mountain (9321ft) and southeast to flat-topped Mt Hancock (10,214ft). In the evenings, pairs of grebes often dive and court each other with mellow, lilting voices.

There are six additional campsites around Heart Lake: 8J1 (two-night limit) and 8J2 (two-night limit, stock parties only) on its northeastern side, 8J4 and 8J6 on the southeastern shore, 8J3 nearby along Surprise Creek and 8H1 at the lake's southwestern corner. All sites except 8H1 allow campfires. Secluded lakeshore campsite 8J1, which boasts views of Mt Sheridan, is the most coveted.

SIDE TRIP: MT SHERIDAN

4–6 HOURS / 6 MILES / 2800FT ASCENT

The **Mt Sheridan Trail** crosses open meadows briefly before starting its spiraling ascent along a steep spur largely covered in whitebark pines. Bring plenty of water; there's none available on the trail.

You will come to a saddle flanked by wind-battered firs. Continue left (southeast) up the narrowing tundra ridge, over old snowdrifts, to reach the 10,308ft talus-covered summit. The fire lookout (staffed in summer but otherwise locked) scans 360 degrees, taking in Pitchstone Plateau to the west, Shoshone Lake to the northwest, Yellowstone Lake to the northeast and the jagged Tetons to the south. Snowdrifts often persist through mid-July.

DAY 2: HEART LAKE TO HEART LAKE TRAILHEAD

3–5 HOURS / 8 MILES / 345FT DESCENT

Retrace your steps from day one back to the start.

Geyser Country

North Shoshone Lake & Shoshone Geyser Basin

Duration Two days

Distance 19.2 miles

Difficulty Moderate

Elevation Change 600ft

Start Lone Star trailhead (OK1)

Finish DeLacy Creek trailhead (7K2)

Nearest Town/Junction Old Faithful

Summary Follow the Continental Divide Trail on this easy overnighter that combines a backcountry geyser basin with an unforgettable sunset beside silent Shoshone Lake.

Shoshone Lake is one of the park's real hidden gems. Not only is it the largest backcountry lake in Yellowstone, at more than 8000 acres, but it's also the largest lake in the lower 48 states not reachable by road. There are many possible routes around the lake, including loops from three directions (Lone Star, DeLacy Creek and Lewis Lake). Much of the first half of this route follows the Continental Divide Trail, which continues along the southern shore of the lake to the Dogshead trailhead.

The route described here traces the northern shore of the lake and requires a short shuttle or hitch along the Grand Loop Rd. Note that Kepler Cascades turnout is a slightly more secure overnight parking spot than the Lone Star trailhead, since it sees much more traffic. If you are hitching, park at DeLacy Creek trailhead and get the hitching out of the way before you begin the hike; you'll appreciate not having to do it when you're tired at the end of the trek.

Between Lone Star and Shoshone Lake, the trail crosses gentle Grants Pass, which normally isn't clear of snow until late June. The lake is normally frozen until early June and some boater-only lakeshore backcountry campsites are flooded into July. The end of June is the earliest reliable start date for this hike. Mosquitoes can be an irritant until August.

In early summer you'll likely have to ford several streams that can be up to waist height, so bring suitable shoes and trekking poles for stability. Use Trails Illustrated's 1:63,360 map No 302 *Old Faithful*. Two USGS quads also cover the route: *Old Faithful* and *Shoshone Geyser Basin*.

Shoshone Lake is a popular backcountry destination (about one-third of the entire park's backcountry use is concentrated along the shores of the lake), so it's worth reserving sites well in advance. Campsite 8R5 in particular gets booked early because of its proximity to the Shoshone Geyser Basin. Sites open to hikers along the northern shore include 8R5, 8R3, 8R2, 8S3 and 8S2. The latter two sites make a good short overnight trip from DeLacy Creek but are too far to be convenient for your first night on this trip. Sites 8R2 and 8S2 are mixed hiker- and boat-accessible campsites. All of the lakeshore sites are no-wood-fire areas.

DAY 1: LONE STAR TRAILHEAD TO SHOSHONE LAKE

6 HOURS / 11.6 MILES / 400FT ASCENT

Follow the first 2.4 miles along the former road as part of the Lone Star Geyser (p68) hike. Check the logbook at Lone Star Geyser to see if an eruption is imminent.

Proceed past the geyser, following the orange markers, and turn left after 0.3 miles at the junction with the **Howard Eaton Trail** to head southwest. The trail passes the least-desirable campsite, OA1, to cross the Firehole River on a footbridge. From here you follow the **Shoshone Lake Trail** 5.8 miles south to the Shoshone Geyser Basin.

The trail soon passes a small thermal field of scalding-hot pools and hissing steam vents. Past OA1 you'll pass the most attractive off-trail campsite, OA2 (next to a hot spring and with a pit toilet), in 0.4 miles, and finally campsite OA3, in another 0.8 miles. If you got a late start and plan a leisurely three-day hike, break the first day at any of these sites. Campfires are allowed in all three sites.

Climb south over the broad, rolling ridge to cross the unsigned **Grants Pass** (8010ft), which marks the almost imperceptible Continental Divide. The sandy trail heads down through superb stands of tall, old-growth Engelmann spruce and whitebark pine to reach the **Bechler River (Three Rivers) Trail** junction, which is about one hour from OA3 and 2½ hours from the trailhead.

Inviting campsite 8G1 (no campfires) is a short way down the Shoshone Lake Trail, on a rise above the meadows framing Shoshone Creek, 2 miles short of the impressive Shoshone Geyser Basin.

The trail descends through the prime moose and bear habitat of **Shoshone Creek meadows**, crossing the creek twice, either

North Shoshone Lake & Shoshone Geyser Basin

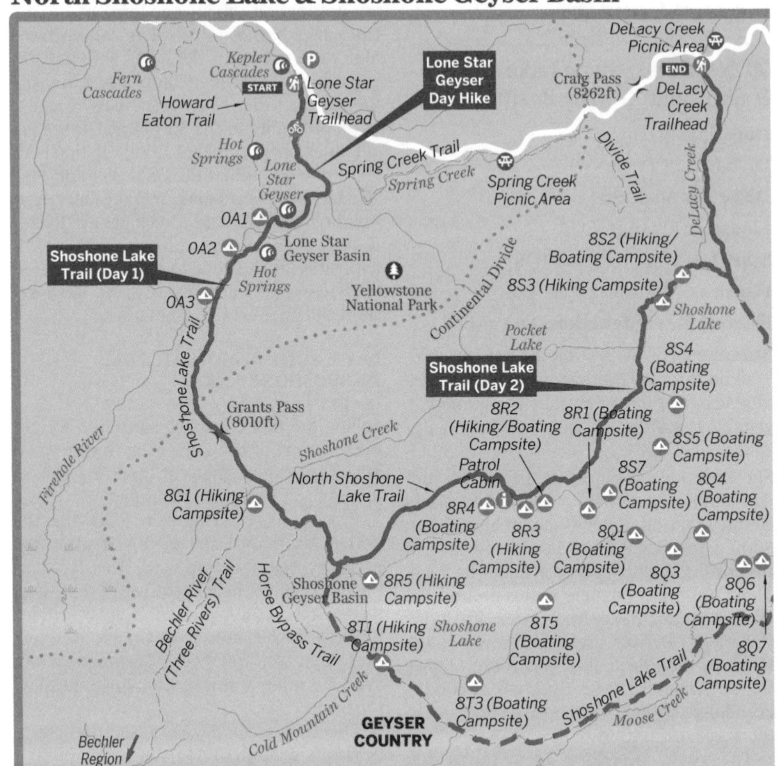

by wading or (later in the summer) on log bridges. One mile from the Bechler junction a stock trail branches right over the creek to avoid the marshy geyser basin.

At the North Shoshone Trail junction (8.5 miles from the trailhead, 8.4 miles to DeLacy Creek) it's worth budgeting an hour to explore the geyser basin. Cross the marshy area on wooden logs and take the left branch to dump your pack in one of the lakeshore bear-proof lockers. Just past here is a small beach, which offers a fine place for a snack overlooking the lake.

Back at the trail junction, continue straight into the geyser basin for around 0.4 miles. The surrounding meadows are fine places to spot moose and other animals at dusk.

Shoshone Geyser Basin is home to over 80 thermal features and was visited in 1839 by trapper Osborne Russell. The main features include **Little Great Geyser**, the **Minute Man group**, **Little Bulger** and the Orion group further south; its **Union Geyser** used to erupt to heights of 100ft. T Scott Bryan's encyclopedic *The Geysers of Yellowstone* details 40 of the basin's geysers, none of which are marked on site. Be careful not to get too close to the brittle crust surrounding the hot springs.

Back at the North Shoshone Trail junction, you'll branch off the Continental Divide Trail after having followed it for 6 miles (just 3094 miles left...). Head northeast along the trail through forest to the backcountry site along the northern shore that you've reserved. Site 8R5 appears after five minutes, 0.5 miles off the main trail, while 8R3 and 8R2 are a further hour away. Just before reaching 8R3 you pass an unmarked trail that leads to a ranger patrol cabin. 8R3 has a cooking area and bear pole by the lake, but camping spots are a bit uphill. Both 8R3 and 8R2 have pit toilets.

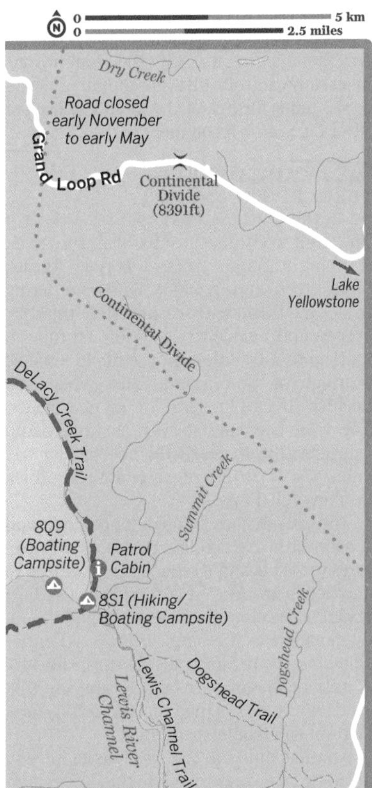

DAY 2: SHOSHONE LAKE TO DELACY TRAILHEAD

4 HOURS / 7.6 MILES / 200FT ASCENT

From sites 8R3 and 8R2 it's another hour's walk through undulating forest to the northern shoreline. The trail parallels the lovely shore for half an hour before dipping back into forest to pass site 8S3. Five minutes further on a lovely little spit offers a superb place to stop and soak up the silence.

Ten minutes later the trail hits site 8S2 and the northern point of the lake as the beach curves to the right in front of large meadows. From here it's 3.6 miles to the trailhead. Follow the beach, looking for the occasional orange metal markers. Early in summer you'll have to ford DeLacy Creek as it enters Shoshone Lake; consider heading inland to cross if the waters are high.

A few minutes later the trail cuts inland to join a trail junction at the northeastern point of the lake. From here it's 3 miles along the lily ponds and meadows of DeLacy Creek to the end of the hike, about 1¼ hours away. The right-hand branch leads 4.2 miles to Dogshead Channel and Lewis Lake.

ALTERNATIVE ROUTES: DELACY CREEK LOOP & DOGSHEAD LOOP

3/4 DAYS / 27 MILES/32 MILES / NEGLIGIBLE

There are plenty of other route options, including the 27-mile, three-day lollipop loop of the lake from DeLacy Creek trailhead, or the 32-mile loop of the lake from Dogshead trailhead near Lewis Lake. Thirteen exclusively boat-in sites along both the northern and southern shores offer paddlers (p87) the option of spending days here.

Bechler Region

Bechler River Trail

Duration Four days

Distance 33.3 miles

Difficulty Moderate

Elevation Change 1100ft

Start/Finish Bechler Ranger Station (9K1)

Nearest Town/Junction Driggs, ID

Summary Traverses wild backcountry filled with rivers, cascades, wildlife and even some hot-spring soaks.

Near the head of Bechler Canyon, your destination here is the Ferris Fork side stream, home to several hidden waterfalls and the park's best hot-springs soak. Sandals and hiking poles are extremely useful for river crossings. Always bring rain gear – Bechler gets three times as much rain as the park's northern range.

Popular with horse-pack trips, backpackers and anglers, Bechler sees fierce competition for backcountry campsites in the prime months of August and September. Campsites may only be reserved for dates after July 15. In-person permits may be granted before this, weather permitting. Ask rangers about river ford and trail conditions – high water and swarms of bugs typically persist along this route through mid- to late July. All of the campsites mentioned here (except 9B9) limit stays to one night.

Waterfall obsessives should pick up *Yellowstone Waterfalls and their Discovery* by Paul Rubinstein, Lee Whittlesey and Mike Stevens, for photos, maps and coordinates of over 250 waterfalls, many in the Bechler region. Use Trails Illustrated's 1:63,360 map

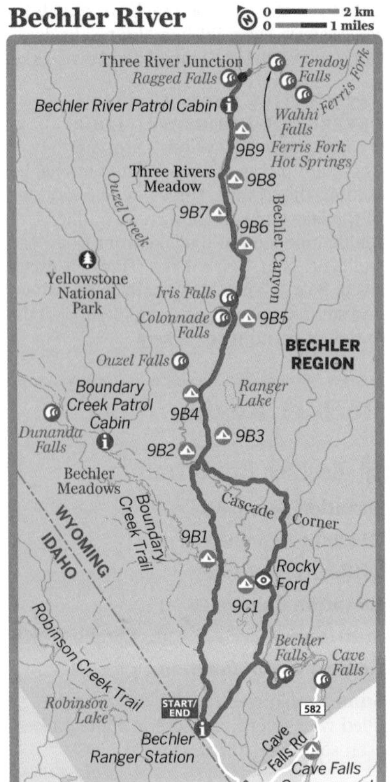

No 302 *Old Faithful*. Three USGS 1:24,000 quads also cover the route: *Trischman Knob, Cave Falls* and *Bechler Falls*.

DAY 1: BECHLER RANGER STATION TO CAMPSITE 9B4

3–4 HOURS / 9.1 MILES / NEGLIGIBLE

Take the Bechler River (Cutoff) Trail from Bechler Ranger Station to Rocky Ford, with the option of a 1.5-mile return side trip to Bechler Falls. The extremely wide crossing of the Bechler River at Rocky Ford is tricky even in low water (from mid-July) and may be completely impassable after heavy rain.

The less interesting, slightly shorter alternative is the **Bechler Meadows Trail**, which requires a shorter, knee- to thigh-high ford near campsite 9B2 (no campfires) and treading some boggy terrain.

Beyond the ford, the Bechler River Trail heads east past the Mountain Ash Creek Trail junction. It then cuts north through forested patches and open grassy plains beside the meandering river to campsite 9B3, at the edge of a broad clearing 8 miles from the trailhead. For the first night's stay, the semi-private, hiker-only campsite 9B4 (no campfires), located 0.5 miles further, at the mouth of Bechler River Canyon, is recommended.

DAY 2: CAMPSITE 9B4 TO THREE RIVER JUNCTION

3½–4½ HOURS / 6.7 MILES / 600FT ASCENT

The trail continues to parallel the river, climbing through fir and spruce forests, birch trees and boulder fields bordering meadows thick with raspberries, thimbleberries and huckleberries. After 1.8 miles a marked side trail descends yards to a scenic overlook of **Colonnade Falls**, where the Bechler River plunges 85ft in two stages. The trail becomes steeper, passing damp campsite 9B5 to reach the spectacular **Iris Falls**, a 40ft curtain of water spraying thick rainbow-filled mist.

The trail ascends through more old fir and spruce forest past gliding cataracts with picturesque islets and riverside campsite 9B6 to another major ford (a 50ft-wide, waist-deep wade). Upstream, the trail sees many muddy moments as it crosses several cold minor side streams before trailside campsite 9B7. A mile upstream, just before campsite 9B8 (and a pit toilet), is the last, less-serious ford, below a patch of burned forest.

Another mile on, the trail passes several algae-rich thermal areas fringing **Three Rivers Meadow**, then passes inviting campsite 9B9 (no campfires and a two-night limit), with a hiker-only site tucked away on the eastern side of the canyon near the base of thundering Albright Falls, which descends from towering **Batchelder Column**. The 9B9 stock campsite and an NPS patrol cabin lie across a bridge on the opposite riverbank.

It's worth the steep extra mile of slog up out of the lovely river flats to the canyon's wild upper valley, where hidden campsite 9D1 (no campfires, sometimes not open until August) awaits beyond a footbridge over the **Bechler's Ferris Fork**. It doesn't get any lovelier than this: camp perched on a peninsula near **Three River Junction**, overlooking the Gregg, Ferris and Phillips Forks' tumbling confluence.

DAY 3: THREE RIVER JUNCTION TO BECHLER RIVER CANYON

3–4 HOURS / 4.8 MILES / 500FT ASCENT

Having made it all this way, you will be giddy if you have booked an extra night in the 9B group of campsites, allowing you a day to explore. Beyond 9D1, the trail switches back uphill half a mile past 45ft **Ragged Falls** to an unsigned (but well-trodden) turnoff on the eastern side of the trail for **Ferris Fork Hot Springs**.

The springs' submerged thermal source emanates from the middle of a 40ft-wide, waist-deep pool, where it mixes with chilly water from the stream's main channel, creating a royal, five-star soak often nicknamed '**Mr Bubbles**.'

After checking out the surrounding thermal features, you might choose to hike another 0.5 to 1.5 miles upstream along the Ferris Fork to explore a quintuplet of seldom-seen waterfalls: 33ft **Tendoy Falls**, 20ft **Gwinna Falls**, 35ft **Sluiceway Falls** and 28ft **Wahhi Falls**.

Retrace your steps down into Bechler Canyon to your chosen 9B series campsite. If you are unable to reserve a campsite for the final night, it's a lengthy but manageable 13.5-mile descent back to the ranger station.

DAY 4: BECHLER RIVER CANYON TO BECHLER RANGER STATION

4–5 HOURS / 12.7 MILES / 800FT DESCENT

Retrace your steps down the canyon to the Bechler Ranger Station, taking a slightly different and more direct route back via the Bechler Meadows Trail.

If you can manage a lengthy vehicle shuttle it's possible to avoid a backtrack by continuing northeast to join the Shoshone Lake Trail just before Grants Pass, near backcountry site 8G1. The next day, hike past Lone Star Geyser to the trailhead of the same name near Kepler Cascades.

Other Overnight Hikes

Mammoth Country

One of the northern Yellowstone's most popular backpacking trips is the 18.5-mile **Black Canyon of the Yellowstone** from the Hellroaring trailhead past the fine fishing waters of the Yellowstone River. This part of the park is said to have one wolf, mountain lion or bear every 2 sq miles. There are 18 backcountry sites along the trail (site 1Y7 is a good halfway spot). You'll need to arrange a vehicle shuttle. The steep final 45-minute section of trail (Yellowstone River Trail No 313) just after you cross Bear Creek was rerouted a couple of years ago to the Eagle Creek forestry service campground.

The 19-mile trail to **Mt Holmes** (10,336ft) begins south of Indian Creek at Willow Flats picnic area and heads west to the summit. Make camp at 1C4 or 1C5 for the first night and tackle the peak the next morning. Radial hikes to Trilobite Lake look tempting, but the trail is unmaintained, with lots of downed trees in the way. This trail has been off-limits for several years due to road construction but should be accessible again by 2020.

Three longer east–west backpacking routes begin west of Mammoth and lead to US 191 in Montana, crossing the Gallatin Range en route: the 19.5-mile **Bighorn Pass Trail** begins from Indian Creek Campground, and the 21-mile **Fawn Pass Trail** and 23-mile **Sportsman Lake Trail** to its north both begin at Glen Creek trailhead, south of Mammoth. Link two of them together for a rewarding loop. Off-trail travel is prohibited in this bear management area.

One exciting high-altitude option is the week-long, 40-mile **Gallatin Skyline** route that crosses the Gallatin Range from west to east, from Dailey Creek in the far northwest to Mammoth, sticking to the high ridges along the Sky Rim Trail via Big Horn Peak, Shelf Lake, High Lake, Sportsman Lake and Electric Peak. You'll need a vehicle shuttle for this life-list trek.

Another great but slightly shorter variant (30 miles) that requires a less lengthy shuttle is to hike the **Sky Rim Trail** from Dailey Creek past Bighorn Peak, Shelf Lake and Crescent Lake as far as High Lake and then swing back to **Specimen Creek trailhead** for a fantastic four-day trip.

Roosevelt Country

The **Bliss Pass** hike, which begins half a mile before Slough Creek Campground, is a pleasant overnight shuttle hike along a popular fishing stream. Head east up Elk Tongue Creek, cross Bliss Pass (8 miles from the trailhead) and descend Pebble Creek to the namesake campground for a total hike of 21 miles. Bliss Pass may be snowbound until mid-July, and fording Pebble Creek can be tricky early in the season. This is a popular horse trail. The first part of the hike follows a historic wagon trail still used by the Silver Tip Ranch – though it lies just outside the northern boundary, the trail is only accessible from the park and enjoys a historic right of access. Backcountry sites along Slough Creek are limited to a maximum stay of three nights between mid-June and mid-September.

DRIVING

There's hardly a single mile on Yellowstone's 142-mile Grand Loop Rd that can't be described as scenic. The views are always fantastic, whether it's mountain panoramas from Dunraven Pass, shore views across Yellowstone Lake or open valley views across meandering rivers and lodgepole forests.

 Geyser Trail

Duration Half-day

Distance 25 miles

Start Madison

Finish Old Faithful

Nearest Town West Yellowstone

Speed Limit 45mph, sometimes dropping to 35mph; 25mph approaching Old Faithful area

Summary The drive south from Madison Campground links several geyser basins and wildlife-watching spots with opportunities to hike, cycle and even swim.

The northern approach to Old Faithful through the heart of Geyser Country offers lots of possible stops, so don't expect to cruise this route in one hit. The drive parallels the Firehole River and there are dozens of potential fly-fishing spots along the route.

Drive south from Madison Junction, past the junior ranger station, and after 2 miles take **Firehole Canyon Drive** to the right. This 2-mile side road takes you past rhyolite cliffs and rapids, Firehole Falls and the popular Firehole swimming area (closed in early summer).

Back on the main road it's another 3 miles south, past fly-fishing turnouts, to **Fountain Flat Drive**, which branches right to give access to the pleasant Nez Percé picnic area, the Sentinel Meadows hike (p67) and the cycleable Fountain Freight Rd (p84).

Back on the main road, 1 mile south, the road crosses Chief Joseph Creek, where an interesting pullout details the flight of the Nez Percé (pronounced 'Nez Purse') tribe, 700 of whom crossed this creek in August 1877 fleeing the US Army.

From here on you'll get your first views of the amazing thermal features ahead. A pullout 1 mile ahead offers a fine view of the smoking geysers and pools of Midway Geyser Basin to the right and Firehole Lake Basin on the left, as well as the meandering Firehole Valley and some of the park's largest bison herds – a classic Yellowstone vista.

Just 1 mile further, take a right into **Fountain Paint Pot** (Map p110; Lower Geyser Basin). Another 1.5 miles south take the left onto **Firehole Lake Drive** (Map p110) and make the leisurely 3-mile drive past Firehole Lake and Great Fountain Geyser to see what's on the boil.

Next up is Midway Geyser Basin, which is worth a stop to see Grand Prismatic Spring (p114). As you continue south, you'll see the colorful runoffs from Excelsior Pool flowing into the Firehole River.

Two miles further is busy Fairy Falls trailhead, a popular starting point for hikes to Fairy Falls (p68), views over Grand Prismatic Spring and bike rides along the gravel Fountain Freight Rd. You'll also likely see bison and fly-fishers in this vicinity.

It's a further 2 miles to the minor thermal sites of Biscuit Basin (p112) and Black Sand Basin (p111), from where cyclists can get out and ride to Old Faithful (p109), 1.5 miles away.

CYCLING

Cyclists can ride on public roads and a few designated service roads in Yellowstone, but not on the backcountry trails. In general, bikes are more useful for short rides on family-friendly paved roads rather than adventurous downhill trips.

Every campground (except Slough Creek) has discounted hiker/biker campsites that rarely fill up.

From mid-March to the third Thursday in April the Mammoth–West Yellowstone park road is open only to nonmotorized travel, creating a vehicle-free playground for cyclists and in-line skaters.

Mammoth Country

The **Old Gardiner Road** between Mammoth and Gardiner offers a traffic-free ride along the late-19th-century stagecoach route into the park. After an initial uphill, the dirt road then descends 1000ft in 5 miles. It's not a stunning ride, but it does offer a rare opportunity to cycle in peace inside the park. Arrange a car shuttle or you'll face a long uphill back. From May to October the road is open to motorized traffic (no RVs or trailers) one way to Gardiner; bikes can travel in either direction. From Gardiner you can continue along dirt roads to Corwin Springs, Yankee Jim Canyon and further into Paradise Valley.

Unpaved **Blacktail Plateau Drive** offers a potential ride, though there can be a fair amount of vehicle traffic.

Bunsen Peak Road & Osprey Falls

Duration One hour (plus a 1½-hour strenuous hike to Osprey Falls)

Distance 6.8 miles return

Difficulty Easy

Elevation Change Negligible (800ft descent on hike to Osprey Falls)

Start/Finish Bunsen Peak trailhead (1K4)

Nearest Town/Junction Mammoth

Summary An easy ride on a former service road, best combined with the strenuous hike down to Osprey Falls.

Now closed to motor vehicles, 6-mile Bunsen Peak Rd is a largely flat twin-track dirt road popular among family cyclists. For active adults the best option is to combine the bike ride with a hike to Osprey Falls. To do this, lock your bike at a rack by the Osprey Falls trailhead, 3.4 miles into the ride. Return the way you came.

From the Osprey Falls junction a shuttle option is to continue downhill to a service road and vehicle-maintenance depot just above Mammoth, from where you can descend along the main road and then a walking trail beside the horse corral to Mammoth Junction. You'd have to arrange a car shuttle for this. Cycling back up the Grand Loop Rd isn't recommended due to the gradient, traffic and the lack of a bicycle lane.

Canyon Country

As well as the easy bike rides around Canyon's north and south rim roads, the Canyon region offers the park's main uphill mountain-bike challenge.

Mt Washburn

Duration Two hours

Distance 5.6 miles return

Difficulty Difficult

Elevation Change 1400ft

Start/Finish Chittenden Rd trailhead (2K6)

Nearest Town/Junction Canyon Village

Summary The park's toughest mountain-bike trip, offering fabulous views from the peak and a thrilling descent.

Mt Washburn is accessed by two former service roads: the southern route from Dunraven Pass is open only to hikers, but the northerly Chittenden Rd is open to hikers, cyclists and the occasional park vehicle delivering supplies to the fire tower atop Mt Washburn. This isn't an easy jaunt you can attempt on a $50 bike from Wal-Mart but, rather, a serious high-elevation climb for well-conditioned cyclists who have the luxury of plenty of low gears to choose from. Even then it's a tough haul. The fire tower offers restrooms (no water), a public telescope and displays on the Yellowstone caldera.

The large trailhead is just over 1 mile off the main Grand Loop Rd and has a vault toilet. The road to the trailhead is sometimes closed at the main road early in the season. In this case you face an extra couple of miles and 500ft of elevation gain.

Access the old service road by the side of the metal gate that blocks the road to cars. This road was originally open to motor vehicles, though the early Model T Fords that attempted the route had to reverse all the way up the mountain because the engines didn't yet come with fuel pumps! The only traffic you'll see today is tourists and the occasional grizzly bear.

The wonderful 1400ft descent is back along the same road. Watch out for hikers and other cyclists on the tarmac-and-gravel downhill run, as there are several blind corners. This is also prime grizzly summer habitat, so keep your eyes open for bears.

Lake Country

Natural Bridge

Duration 45 minutes

Distance 2.4 miles

Difficulty Easy

Elevation Change 110ft

Start/Finish Bridge Bay

Nearest Town/Junction Bridge Bay

Summary A family-friendly ride to an interesting natural feature.

An excellent cycling trail follows an old stagecoach road that once linked West Thumb to Lake Village. The paved road starts opposite the northbound turnoff to Gull Point Dr, just south of the Bridge Bay turnoff. There is parking just to the south. It is 1.2 miles to Natural Bridge, joining en route the hiking trail from Bridge Bay Marina. The flat route leads to rhyolite cliffs forming a natural bridge 51ft above Bridge Creek. You can hike the short uphill trail to the top, but don't walk on the fragile bridge. The trail is closed from late spring to early summer due to bear activity.

Geyser Country

In the Upper Geyser Basin bikes are allowed on the road (not the boardwalk) between Old Faithful and Morning Glory Pool (1.4 miles), and between Daisy Geyser and Biscuit Basin (1.3 miles).

You can hire bikes at Bear Den (p108). Bike trains (a kid's bike that hooks onto the back of an adult's bike) and trailers are also available. Rentals come with helmet and lock.

In addition to the Fountain Freight Rd route, the former service road to Lone Star Geyser (p68) makes for a fine (and flat) 5-mile, round-trip ride, though you'll have to find a tree to chain your bike to as there's currently no rack. Take a packed lunch for the geyser wait. Park in the Lone Star Geyser lot next to Kepler Cascades.

Fountain Freight Road

Duration One hour cycling (up to four hours with excursions)

Distance 7 miles return

Difficulty Easy

Elevation Change Negligible

Start/Finish Fountain Flat Dr trailhead

Nearest Town/Junction Old Faithful

Summary An easy, flat bike ride on a gravel road that allows lots of stops and detours on foot – perfect for families.

The 4-mile Fountain Freight Rd between Fountain Flat Dr and Fairy Falls trailhead offers an opportunity to combine some pedaling with a hike to Fairy Falls and a couple of little-seen backcountry thermal areas.

Just a few hundred yards from the Fountain Flat Dr trailhead, park your bike at the bridge over the Firehole River and check out the Ojo Caliente hot spring on the north bank. Continue south, past the Imperial/Sentinel Meadows trailhead to Goose Lake, the northern shore of which makes for a good picnic spot, either now or on the way back. Pedal south for 1.2 miles to the turnoff to Fairy Falls (p68). You can't cycle this side trail, but you can park your bike at the rack and make the 3.2-mile return hike to the waterfalls.

From the Fairy Falls turnoff continue 0.5 miles and you'll see the blue blur of Grand

BEST WILDLIFE-SPOTTING

The following places offer an excellent chance to get a glimpse of some seriously charismatic megafauna. Maximize your chances by arriving at dawn or dusk and renting a spotting scope from Silver Gate or Gardiner.

Roosevelt Country The Lamar Valley is known as the 'American Serengeti' for its dense population of wolves, bison, grizzlies, pronghorn, elk and trumpeter swans. Try also Antelope Creek for grizzlies and wolves, especially in spring.

Mammoth Country Elk trimming the lawns at Mammoth Junction, bighorn sheep on Everets Ridge between Mammoth and the North Entrance, wildfowl at Blacktail Ponds, moose at Willow Park, and bears and wolves in the backcountry Gallatin Range.

Lake Country Birdlife at Sedge Bay; bison, moose, marmots and waterfowl at Storm Point; springtime grizzlies and moose at Pelican Creek; moose around Lewis Lake; grizzlies around Fishing Bridge in spring.

Norris Elk Park for, well, elk, as well as bison.

Canyon Country Spotters crowd the pullouts of the Hayden Valley at dusk searching for bison, coyotes, wolves and grizzlies (the latter two especially in spring). Ospreys in the canyon; south of Mud Volcano for bison. Mt Washburn for bighorn sheep, black bears and grizzlies.

Geyser Country The Firehole River and Madison Valley for bison, especially in winter.

Prismatic Spring to the left. Park the bike here and make the 400yd hike up to a new park lookout for fantastic aerial views over the colorful spring. From here, turn around and cycle the 3.5 miles back to your car.

With the help of a shuttle driver you could continue 0.5 miles to the Fairy Falls trailhead parking lot, throw your bike in the car to Biscuit Basin, 3 miles away, then pick up the 1.3-mile cycleable trail to Daisy Geyser and continue 1 mile further to Old Faithful.

OTHER ACTIVITIES

Horseback Riding

With its sagebrush scenery and Wild West vibe, the Tower-Roosevelt region of the park is the focus for organised horse rides. Many outfitters based outside the park offer horseback rides of a day or longer inside the park, but these trips don't come cheap. All the following trips are organised by the park concessionaire Yellowstone National Park Lodges (p117). **Stagecoach rides** (Map p96; adult/child under 11yr $15/8; Jun-Aug;) depart from the Roosevelt Lodge corral three or four times daily from June to August and last around 45 minutes. For a treat, ask for the tallyho seat.

Old West cookouts (p124) are a fun family trip, either on horseback (one-hour trips adult/child under 12 $87/72, two-hour trips $94/86) or by horse-drawn wagon (adult/child $63/50). Trips depart daily in the afternoon and travel to the former site of Uncle John Yancey's Pleasant Valley Hotel (1884–87), one of the park's earliest accommodations, for a gut-busting, all-you-can-eat chow-down of steak and beans accompanied by campfire music. The excursion lasts about three hours. Reservations are required months – preferably a year – in advance.

Corrals next to Roosevelt Lodge offer **trail rides** (one/two hours $50/73) three or four times a day through sagebrush country. There are similar rides at Canyon (eight times a day) from the corral south of Canyon Junction. Both operate from June to August. Two-hour rides run just once a day, so reserve these well in advance. Children must be over eight years of age. Rides can be canceled during afternoon storms or after rain.

Private horse-packing parties must obtain a backcountry-use permit ($5 per night per person) for overnight trips. A horse-use permit is also required for day trips. Both are available at most ranger stations. The *Horse Packing in Yellowstone* pamphlet lists regulations. Pack animals include horses, burros, mules, ponies and llamas.

Some backcountry trails are closed to stock, and those that are open may be temporarily closed in spring and early summer due to wet conditions. Overnight pack trips are not allowed until July 1. Stock can only be kept at designated campsites. Hay is not permitted at the trailhead or in the backcountry.

Also try **Yellowstone Wilderness Outfitters** (406-223-3300; www.yellowstone.ws), which is licensed to run half- and full-day rides ($125/225 per person) and multiday pack trips in the park.

> **KAYAKING WEST THUMB**
>
> For a different angle on the West Thumb Geyser Basin, **OARS** (www.oars.com/Wyoming), **Jackson Hole Kayak** (www.jacksonholekayak.com) and **Yellowstone Geyser Kayak Tours** (www.geyserkayak.com) in Jackson offer half-/full-day sea-kayaking tours on Yellowstone Lake ($75/125), as well as sunset paddles ($125) and overnight trips. Tours meet at Grant Village and paddle out 2½ miles to West Thumb and Potts Geyser Basins.
>
> In June 2017 a kayak guide died of hypothermia trying to rescue a client here; it was the first fatality in Yellowstone Lake for 20 years.

Boating

Yellowstone has some epic options for experienced boaters, though the lakes of the Tetons are perhaps better suited to scenic shorter paddles. There are guided kayak trips near West Thumb, and some local boat rentals at Bridge Bay. Companies such as Rendezvous Sports (p213) in Jackson, WY, offer guided multiday kayaking tours on Yellowstone and Shoshone Lakes.

Park Regulations

A boating permit is required for all vessels, including float tubes. Permits for motorized vessels cost $10/20 per week/year, and are available from Bridge Bay Ranger Station, Grant Village Backcountry Office (p71) and the South Entrance.

Permits for nonmotorized vessels cost $5/10 per week/year, and are available from the same offices, as well as the West Entrance, Northeast Entrance, West

JIM BRIDGER'S TALL, TRUE TALES

Jim Bridger is famed as a mountain man and trapper who explored the Yellowstone region in the 1830s, but he was also the West's consummate teller of tall tales. Level-headed low-landers may have dismissed his outrageous stories with a patronizing slap on the back, but, as with most enduring stories, much of the fiction was actually based in fact.

Bridger's most famous tales told of Yellowstone's petrified trees (fact, though he couldn't resist upping the ante to 'peetrified birds singing peetrified songs'); a 'mountain of glass' that acted as a giant telescope (fiction, but based on the volcanic glass of Obsidian Cliff); a river that flowed so fast that friction made it hot on the bottom (actually thermal runoff on the Firehole River); and a spot on Yellowstone Lake where you could throw out a line and reel in a cooked fish (fact, a technique proved by early tourists at Fishing Cone, with the help of an underwater geyser).

He also told of a place where fish could cross the Rocky Mountains (actually Two Ocean Plateau, just south of the park), with a stream atop the Continental Divide branching into two, one leading to the Atlantic, the other to the Pacific. Lake Isa does the same thing between Old Faithful and Yellowstone Lake, but it has no fish.

Yellowstone Chamber of Commerce, Bechler Ranger Station and backcountry offices at Old Faithful (p71), Canyon and Mammoth.

Backcountry permits are required for all overnight boating trips in the park. Get these at Bridge Bay or Grant Village backcountry offices. Other regulations:

- Boating is permitted May 1 to November 1, although some areas may close during the season.
- Motorized vessels are allowed only on Lewis Lake and parts of Yellowstone Lake.
- Sylvan, Eleanor and Twin Lakes, plus Beach Springs Lagoon, are closed to all boating, as are all park streams and the Yellowstone River, except on the Lewis River between Lewis and Shoshone Lakes, where hand-propelled vessels are allowed.
- Launching is permitted only at Bridge Bay, Grant Village (open mid-June) and Lewis Lake. Hand-carried vessels may launch at Sedge Bay on Yellowstone Lake.
- The speed limit on Yellowstone Lake is 45mph. The limit on the south arms is 5mph, while the southernmost inlets are closed to motorboats.
- Landing is not allowed on the thermally affected shore of Yellowstone Lake between Little Thumb Creek and the southern end of the West Thumb thermal area.
- Unlike Grand Teton, waterskiing and jet skis are prohibited in Yellowstone.
- Personal flotation devices (PFDs) are required for all craft.

Efforts are being made in Congress by local paddlers and packrafting advocacy groups to open the park's rivers to non-motorized craft, but at the time of writing the Yellowstone and Grand Teton Paddling Act was in bureaucratic limbo. In the meantime, Yellowstone's rivers remain off-limits to paddlers.

Boating-regulations pamphlets are available at all visitor centers. General boating information is at www.nps.gov/yell/planyourvisit/boating.htm.

Yellowstone Lake

Vast Yellowstone Lake just begs for extended kayak, boat and sailboat exploration, but it is important to plan your outing carefully. Drowning is the leading cause of death in Yellowstone. Water temperatures are very cold, averaging 45°F (7°C) in summer. Sudden winds can quickly churn up 3ft to 5ft waves, capsizing small vessels, so paddle in the early morning or late afternoon and avoid open-water crossings. Prevailing winds come from the southwest, so if you're headed south, you'll need to set off around dawn.

One pleasant, easy trip from Grant Village is the 5-mile return paddle to West Thumb Geyser Basin and Potts Geyser Basin. There's nowhere in the park to rent a kayak, so you'll have to bring your own or rent (p258) from Cody, Gardiner or Jackson. Several companies in Jackson offer guided trips (p85).

From Grant Village, the closest campsites are at Breeze Bay (8 to 10 miles away), some of which are for first- and last-night use only. The canoe and kayak put-in at Sedge Bay (trailhead 5K4) is the closest point from which to access the lake's southeast arm (21 miles), from where you can hike to the park's remote reaches. The nearest backcountry sites start 4 miles away.

If you want to spend a few days paddling around the remote southern arms of the lake, **Bridge Bay Marina** (☎307-242-3876, boat shuttle 307-242-3893; ⊙8am-8pm mid-Jun–early Sep) operates a boat shuttle ($102 per hour, two-hour minimum) for up to six people and their kayaks to docks at Eagle Bay (7L6), Wolf Bay (7L5), Plover Point (7M4), Promontory Tip (5L8) or Columbine Creek (5E6) on the eastern shore of the mouth of the southeast arm. Arrange it in advance and it'll pick you up again after a few idyllic days of remote paddling. There's only one shuttle boat, so book well in advance. The marina has five kayaks to rent ($52 per day) but only if you book its shuttle service.

Certain shorelines are off-limits due to wildlife protection:

- Frank Island and the south end of Stevenson Island are closed from May 15 to August 15 to protect nesting ospreys and bald eagles.
- A 0.5-mile closure around Molly Island protects around 2000 breeding pelicans that summer here between April and September.
- The southern and eastern shorelines are off-limits from May 15 to July 14 to prevent bear disturbance.

The lake also has several anchor-only sites, including two at Frank Island. Boats need to be fully out of the water at some sites; others have docks.

Shoshone Lake

The largest backcountry lake in the lower 48, Shoshone Lake spells paradise for canoeists and kayakers. The serene lake is closed to motorized vessels and is lined with a dozen secluded boater-only campsites. On its far western edge, Shoshone Geyser Basin's pools, thermals and mud pots make up the largest backcountry thermal area in the park. One-third of all of Yellowstone's backcountry use takes place along its shores, which are accessible only to hikers and hand-propelled boats.

Boaters must access the lake up the channel from Lewis Lake. From mid-July to August the channel requires portage of a few hundred yards in cold water (bring appropriate footwear), though in spring you can often paddle through.

Of 20 lakeshore campsites, 13 are reserved for boaters, four for hikers and three are shared. All have pit toilets. Rangers claim the nicest campsites are 8Q4, 8R4 and 8R1. Wood fires are not allowed along the lakeshore.

Most boaters make their first camp on the southern shore (campsites nearest to the channel are reserved for first- and last-night use only). If you need to cross the lake, do so early in the morning and at the half-mile-wide Narrows in the center of the lake. Prevailing winds are from the southwest and pick up after noon. The lake is icebound until mid-June, when flooding is possible at shoreline campsites. Backcountry boating campsites at Shoshone Lake cannot be reserved before July 1 or 15, depending on the site.

Fishing

Yellowstone is justly famous for its fly-fishing, and the park's gateway towns have dozens of excellent fly-fishing shops that can offer expert local advice on current flows, flies and hatches, or arrange fully guided

BE A HERO: GO FISHING

Yellowstone's waters have an astounding 310 million fish that shouldn't be there. The worst offender is the lake trout, also known as the Mackinaw trout, which was introduced to Yellowstone Lake illegally sometime in the 1980s (although the park itself had stocked Lewis and Shoshone Lakes with them earlier). Since they have no natural predators, their Pac-Man-like presence has wreaked havoc on native cutthroat trout. In a year, one lake trout can eat 41 cutthroats – sushi dinners normally destined for grizzlies and bald eagles. If the trend continues, the native trout population may fall to 10% of historic highs, tipping the ecological balance.

With a fishing rod and free time you could help redress the situation. Regulations encourage anglers to catch lake trout and you must kill any you catch. When you get a park fishing permit you'll receive a Volunteer Angler Report card, which provides the park with important biological data on the state of the park's fish resources.

If you do catch lake trout, take your catch (filleted and on ice) to the Lake Yellowstone Hotel Dining Room (p127) and they'll prepare it for you with sides (lunch/dinner $10.95/14.95). The service is also available at Lake Lodge Cafeteria ($9.75 for lunch or dinner; p127). Take your trout to staff before 10am for lunch and 3:30pm for dinner (or one hour before eating for Lake Lodge).

trips. Where else can you cast your line in sight of a grazing bison, or the steam of an exploding geyser?

Cutthroat trout, grayling and mountain whitefish, among 11 species that are native to the park, are catch-and-release only. Some areas (such as the Gibbon River below Gibbon Falls) are open to fly-fishing only. Lead weights are prohibited; only nontoxic alternatives are sanctioned.

Fishing season usually runs from the Saturday of Memorial Day to the first Sunday in November, except for streams that flow into Yellowstone Lake and some tributaries of the Yellowstone River, which open July 15. Other rivers are permanently closed to fishing, including a 6-mile stretch of the Yellowstone River in the Hayden Valley; some may close during the season due to bear activity. The useful *Fishing Regulations* pamphlet details the park's complex rules and regulations. One recent regulation change prohibits felt-soled footwear in an attempt to stop the spread of invasive aquatic species.

A Yellowstone fishing permit is required for anglers aged 16 and older (state licenses are not required). Permits cost $18/25 for three/seven days, or $40 for the season; free permits are required for unsupervised anglers aged 15 and under. Permits are available from ranger stations, visitor centers and Yellowstone general stores.

Detailed fishing information can be found at www.nps.gov/yell/planyourvisit/fishing.htm.

YELLOWSTONE'S WINTER WONDERLAND

Winter is a magical time to visit Yellowstone. The falls turn to frozen curtains of ice, the geysers spurt taller and steamier than in other seasons, and surrounding 'ghost trees' turn into surreal frozen steam sculptures. The warm thermal areas around Old Faithful, Norris and Mammoth become winter refuges for elk and bison, and the thermally heated (and thus still flowing) rivers attract plenty of waterfowl.

The winter season runs from late December to mid-March, and activity centers on Mammoth Hot Springs Hotel and Old Faithful Snow Lodge, the only two accommodations open in the park. Independent travel is more difficult in winter and most people sign up for a lodging and activity package, which often works out cheaper than arranging things yourself. The Yellowstone Forever Institute (p96) runs some particularly good winter programs.

Accessing the park is an adventure in itself. The only road open year-round is the northern Mammoth–Cooke City road via Tower-Roosevelt Junction, plus an extension to Mammoth's Upper Terraces. During the season, Yellowstone National Park Lodges (p273) operates one-way snow-coach tours once daily between Old Faithful and Mammoth (adult/child $123/61.50). It also operates a road shuttle between Bozeman Airport and Mammoth ($75). Private snow-coach companies offer only return day trips from West Yellowstone.

Trips inside the park include day snow-coach tours to Canyon ($166.50) from Old Faithful and Mammoth, half-day tours to Norris from Mammoth ($83) and half-day tours from Old Faithful to West Thumb ($72), the Madison Valley ($83) or Firehole Basin ($62.50).

Mammoth Hot Springs Hotel (p120) and Old Faithful Snow Lodge (p123) and their restaurants are the only places open, though there is limited (and cold!) winter camping at Mammoth Campground (p119). You can snow camp anywhere in the park, with a backcountry permit, but winter camping conditions are for specialists only.

Both hotels rent snowshoes and cross-country skis. You can ice-skate in Mammoth and Old Faithful (with free skate rental). After a day on skis you'll appreciate Mammoth Hotel's hot-tub cabins or a massage at the Old Faithful Snow Lodge.

There are no public accommodations in Canyon, but **Yellowstone Expeditions** (☎800-728-9333; www.yellowstoneexpeditions.com; 536 Firehole Ave, West Yellowstone) runs a winter yurt camp there for its cross-country ski and snowshoe tours. Four-day tours from West Yellowstone cost around $1100 per person, including transportation, heated accommodations, sauna, food and a guide.

Visitor centers at Old Faithful (p109) and Mammoth (p92) are open during the winter season. There are winter warming huts at Mammoth, Indian Creek, Old Faithful (in yurts), West Thumb, Fishing Bridge, Madison and Canyon; the latter two have fast food. Snowmobile fuel is available at Canyon, Fishing Bridge, Old Faithful and Mammoth. Mammoth Clinic (p127) is open weekdays and Old Faithful Clinic (p127) is open periodically.

SNOWMOBILE REGULATIONS

The park service enforces a daily cap of 'transportation events' (ie winter vehicles) into the park. Snowmobilers have to be accompanied by a commercial guide, in a maximum group size of 10, though new regulations now permit snowmobilers to take an online course and get a private permit to enter the park. These limited permits (one per day, up to five snowmobilers) are awarded through a lottery. See www.recreation.gov for details and to apply (there's a $46 fee). Park entry fees are $25 per snowmobile for each national park.

Snowmobiles are banned from all of the park's side roads, including the Lake Butte Overlook, Firehole Canyon Dr and a section of the Grand Loop Rd from Canyon to Tower. All other roads are groomed for over-snow travel. Snowmobile operators must carry a valid state driver's license. The speed limit between the West Entrance and Old Faithful is 35mph; elsewhere it is 45mph. Roads are only open 7am to 9pm and off-road snowmobiling is prohibited.

Yellowstone Lake

Yellowstone Lake is stocked with cutthroat trout, longnose dace, redside shiners, longnose suckers and lake chub. Popular shore- or float-fishing spots include Gull Point, Sand Point picnic area, Sedge Bay, Mary Bay and Steamboat Point.

Fishing is not allowed on Pelican Creek from its outlet to 2 miles upstream, or on the Yellowstone River from 0.25 miles upstream of Fishing Bridge to its outflow from Yellowstone Lake. Hayden Valley is closed to fishing except for two short catch-and-release stretches. All lake trout caught in Yellowstone Lake should be killed.

Geyser Country

The Madison and Gibbon Rivers offer some of the park's best and most scenic fly-fishing. The Firehole (between Biscuit and Midway Geyser Basins), Madison and Gibbon (downstream from Gibbon Falls) Rivers are open for fly-fishing only; lots of pullouts offer access. During hot summers the Firehole is often closed completely to fishing because of high water temperatures.

The pullout beneath Mt Haynes, on the Madison River between Madison Junction and West Yellowstone, offers a good, wheelchair-accessible, riverside fishing spot.

Roosevelt Country

Slough Creek is the sweetest fishing spot in the northeast (closely followed by Pebble Creek and Soda Butte Creek), which is one reason the park's Slough Creek Campground is regularly the first to fill up. Ensure that you make your backcountry reservations early if you want to overnight in any of the Slough Creek backcountry campsites. Other good places include the Black Canyon of the Yellowstone and the Lamar River.

Cross-Country Skiing

All backcountry trails are denoted with orange markers, so you can theoretically ski or snowshoe most of the backcountry trails in the area.

Once in the park, skier shuttles will transport you to and from set trailheads, where you can take a trail or just ski back. Shuttles operate from Mammoth to Bunsen Peak Rd and Indian Creek ($14 each way, three per day Saturday and Sunday). A daily one-way shuttle also runs from Old Faithful Snow Lodge (p123) to Fairy Falls ($22) or Divide trailheads ($28 one way; you must ski back), the latter for Lone Star, Spring Creek and Divide trailheads.

Combined snow-coach and ski/showshoe tours run from Old Faithful to Canyon ($276) twice a week.

Cross-country ski ($26 per day) and snowshoe ($22) rentals are available at Mammoth Hot Springs Hotel (p120) and the Bear Den (p108) at Old Faithful's Snow Lodge, as is ski instruction ($35 for two hours).

The Canyon to Washburn Hot Springs Overlook section of the Grand Loop Rd is open to Nordic skiers.

Mammoth & Roosevelt Country

The north of the park is logistically easier to visit in winter because the road between Mammoth and Cooke City remains open year-round. Around the Mammoth region it's possible to ski from Indian Creek Campground to Sheepeater Cliffs and then along a backcountry trail to Bunsen Peak Trail

GETTING AWAY FROM IT ALL

Shhh...don't tell anyone about these seldom-visited Yellowstone sights.

Bechler Region (p69) The bone-crushing drive deters most visitors from this lush wilderness area, home to half the park's waterfalls. Late summer is the best time.

Fossil Forest Trail (p59) An unmarked turnoff and path leads up to fine views and several petrified tree stumps.

Imperial Geyser (p68) Lose the crowds just 10 minutes past Fairy Falls.

Upper Geyser Basin (p108) Come for a full-moon stroll and the geyser eruptions will seem even more magical.

Yellowstone Lake Picnic Areas There are a few lovely lakeshore picnic tables between Bridge Bay and West Thumb, some signed, others not. Several are right on the beach.

and left to the Mammoth–Norris road (5 miles) or right downhill along Bunsen Peak Rd to Mammoth Upper Terraces. There are also marked loops around Indian Creek (2.2 miles) and partway along the nearby Bighorn Trail (5.5 miles).

The groomed 1.5-mile Upper Terrace Loop Trail follows the Upper Terrace road and is a good place to test out your Nordic legs. A side trail from here follows an old wagon track steeply uphill to Snow Pass and then along Glen Creek back to the Bunsen Peak trailhead (4.2 miles). It's easier in the opposite direction.

In the park's northeastern corner a popular ski trail (3.5 miles) parallels the Northeast Entrance Rd below Barronette Peak (10,404ft) between the Soda Butte Creek bridges. The nearby 2-mile Bannock Trail runs east out of the park from the Warm Creek picnic area along an old mining road to Silver Gate.

Around Tower-Roosevelt, the 8-mile Blacktail Plateau Trail follows the unplowed road of the same name and is a popular shuttle option. The trail climbs gradually to the Cut and then descends for 2 miles to the main Mammoth–Cooke City road.

Rangers lead free guided snowshoe walks around Mammoth Upper Terraces at 2pm on Sunday from December to the end of February (check the park newspaper).

Geyser Country

The area around Old Faithful has the most trails and facilities in winter. Yellowstone National Park Lodges (p117) runs three-hour guided snowshoe tours ($30, with shoe rental $38) twice daily. Half-day guided ski tours ($55) to Lone Star Geyser leave Old Faithful on Sunday.

Upper and Midway Geyser Basins both make for some fine ski trips. You can ski or snowshoe from Old Faithful to Black Sand Basin via Daisy Geyser (4 miles), or to Biscuit Basin via Morning Glory and Atomizer Geyser (5 miles, with a possible extension to Mystic Falls). The frozen Fairy Falls hike is a popular ski day trip – get dropped off at the southern end of Fountain Freight Rd, visit the falls and ski back to Old Faithful (11 miles).

An 8-mile return trip can take you from Old Faithful Snow Lodge and the Mallard Lake trailhead along the Kepler Cascades Ski Trail, crossing the main road to join the main trail to Lone Star Geyser. The Divide ski shuttle will allow you to take the 8-mile Spring Creek Trail (a former stagecoach road) to Lone Star Geyser.

SIGHTS

Mammoth Country

Mammoth Country is renowned for its graceful geothermal terraces and the towering Gallatin Range to the northwest. As the lowest and driest region of the park, it's also the warmest and a good base for winter and early- or late-season activities.

The region's Northern Range is an important wintering area for wildlife, including the park's largest herds of elk, pronghorn, mule deer and bighorn sheep. Around half the park's population of elk winter here, attracted by the lower temperatures and lack of snow on many south-facing slopes (due to the sun and prevailing wind). The poorly aerated and drained soil supports scant vegetation, creating 'dry desert' conditions.

For visitors (and most elk) the focal point of the Mammoth region is Mammoth Junction (6239ft), 5 miles south of the North Entrance, on a plateau above Mammoth Campground. The former park headquarters contains the region's main services, including a visitor center, backcountry office, post office, gas station, medical center and even a church and courthouse. The Mammoth Hot

Springs Hotel has espresso, while the Yellowstone General Store offers groceries, camping supplies, souvenirs and cold beer.

Just south of the junction is Mammoth Hot Springs, the area's main thermal attraction. From here roads go south to Norris (21 miles) and east to Tower-Roosevelt Junction (18 miles).

Mammoth

★ **Mammoth Hot Springs** HOT SPRINGS

(Map p92) The imposing **Lower** and **Upper Terraces** of Mammoth Hot Springs are the highlight of the Mammoth region. An hour's worth of boardwalks wind their way between ornate and graceful limestone pools, ledges and plateaus. **Palette Springs** (accessed from the lower parking lot) and sulfur-yellow **Canary Springs** (accessed from the upper loop, 1km south) are the most beautiful sites, but thermal activity is constantly in flux, so check the current state of play at the visitor center.

The famously ornate travertine formations that characterize the lower terraces of **Minerva Spring** have dried over the years due to earthquake activity but are still among the area's most picturesque. Nearby **Mound Spring** currently has the most beautiful colors and abstract patterns on the terraces. The landscape is so otherworldly that it provided the pre-CGI backdrop for the planet Vulcan during the filming of the 1979 *Star Trek* movie.

The terraces are the product of dissolved subterranean limestone that is continuously deposited as the spring waters cool on contact with air – over a ton of travertine comes to the surface every year. The yellow, orange and brown runoff from the naturally white terraces is due to the different bacteria and algae that flourish in the warm waters.

At the bottom of the terraces, by the parking area, is the phallic, dormant 36ft-high hot-spring cone called **Liberty Cap**, apparently named after the hat style worn during the French Revolution. The former hot spring must have had particularly high water pressure to create such a tall cone during its estimated 2500-year life span.

Across the road, **Opal Spring** is slowly converging on a century-old residence designed by Robert Reamer (the architect of Old Faithful Inn and Roosevelt Arch). Park strategists have to decide which to preserve – the architecture or the spring. The rutting Rocky Mountain elk that sometimes lounge on Opal Terrace in fall are a popular photo subject.

A 1.5-mile, paved one-way road loops counterclockwise around the **Upper Terraces**, 1km uphill from Mammoth; vehicles longer than 25ft will have to park on the main Grand Loop Rd. The overlook affords impressive views of the Lower Terraces and Fort Yellowstone and offers access to Canary Springs and New Blue Spring. Highlights further around the road loop include the spongelike Orange Spring Mound and the perfectly named White Elephant Back Terrace. The loop rejoins the main road near the large Angel Terrace. Rangers lead a 90-minute walk around the Upper Terraces daily at 9am.

For a private perspective on foot, walk the Howard Eaton Trail (p56) from **Orange Spring Mound** (unsigned) down to the lower Mammoth Terraces. Even better, start from the unsigned Snow Pass trailhead pullout two minutes' drive south from the Upper Terraces.

Fort Yellowstone HISTORIC SITE

Mammoth was known as Fort Yellowstone from 1886 to 1918, when the US Army

BOILING RIVER

One of the few places where you can take a legal soak in Yellowstone is **Boiling River** (Map p92), halfway between Gardiner and Mammoth. From the parking area by the Montana–Wyoming border a trail leads 0.5 miles along the river to a point where an underground hot spring surfaces from below a limestone overhang, mixing with river water to create the perfect temperature in several popular artificial pools.

Bring a towel and flip-flops/river shoes. The only changing area is the vault toilet at the parking lot. There's a picnic area across the road. Swimming is allowed only during daylight hours, and food, pets, alcohol and nudity are prohibited. The pools are closed when river levels are high (most commonly in spring and early summer until July). Be aware of the potential dangers of soaking in hot springs.

The turnouts north of here are good places to spot pronghorn in the summer and bighorn sheep and elk in the winter. Also to the north is a sign that marks the 45th parallel, halfway between the equator and the North Pole.

Mammoth Country Area

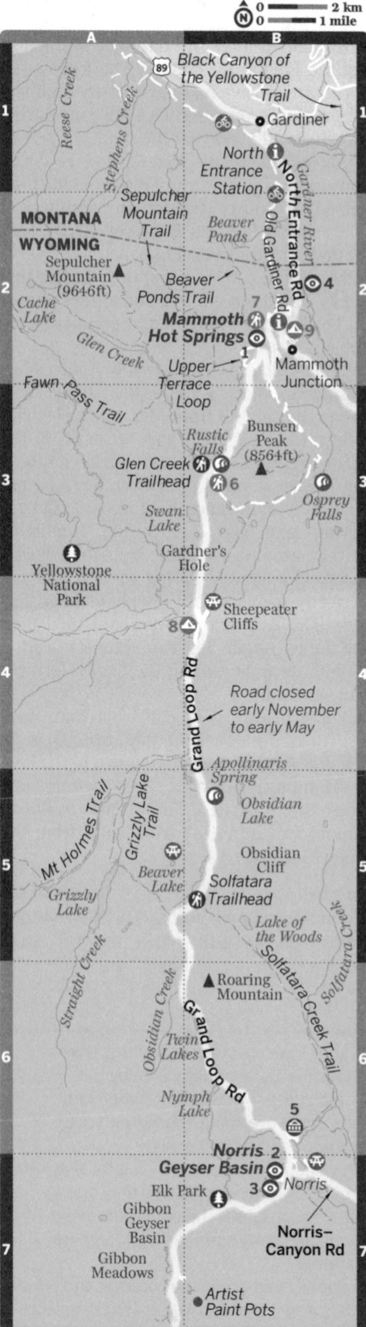

managed the park from this collection of buildings. Elk regularly graze the manicured lawns of the campus-like historic and administrative center, bringing traffic to a standstill, and the high-pitched cries of bugling elk echo around the region in fall.

Mammoth Hot Springs Hotel HISTORIC BUILDING
(Map p92) This hotel is worth a visit even if you're not staying. Piano music echoes around the lobby from 5pm, followed by video or slide presentations in the Map Room at 8:30pm, where you can also check out the huge wall map of the United States assembled using 15 types of wood from around the world. There's also a charming antique water fountain to the right of the gift shop.

Albright Visitor Center VISITOR CENTER
(☎307-344-2263; ⏰8am-6pm mid-Jun–Sep, 9am-5pm Oct–mid-Jun) Mammoth's recently revamped visitor center explores the park's early history and formation – including the role the army played in protecting

Mammoth Country Area

Top Sights
1 Mammoth Hot Springs........................B2
2 Norris Geyser Basin............................B7

Sights
3 Back Basin..B7
4 Boiling River.......................................B2
Mammoth Hot Springs Hotel..(see 1)
5 Museum of the National Park Ranger...B6
Norris Museum ....(see 2)
Porcelain Basin ....(see 2)

Activities, Courses & Tours
6 Bunsen Peak & Osprey Falls...............B3
7 Sepulcher Mountain............................B2

Sleeping
8 Indian Creek Campground..................B4
9 Mammoth Campground......................B2
Mammoth Hot Springs Hotel..(see 1)
Norris Campground ....(see 5)

Eating
Mammoth Hot Springs Dining Room..............................(see 1)
Mammoth Terrace Grill.................(see 1)

Drinking & Nightlife
Map Room Bar & Espresso ....(see 1)

TRUMAN EVERTS

Everts Ridge, northwest of Mammoth, is named after Truman Everts, a member of the 1870 Washburn-Langford-Doane expedition and the subject of a notable early tourist-disaster story.

Separated from his group on the southern shores of Yellowstone Lake in September 1870, the 54-year-old tax inspector soon lost his bearings and promptly broke his glasses. His horse then bolted, taking all Everts' equipment with it, save for a penknife and a pair of opera glasses (not quite as useless as they sound – they helped him make fire). He kept warm at night by cuddling up to hot springs near Heart Lake, but he ended up badly burning himself. At one point he spent the night in a tree as a pacing mountain lion stalked him from below.

After 37 days lost in the wilderness, Everts was finally discovered, shoeless, frostbitten, emaciated, delirious and raving like a madman...but alive.

Yellowstone from poachers and vandals. Don't miss the fine photographs of former superintendent Norris in his trademark buckskins, and mountain man Jim Bridger bearing an uncanny resemblance to country singer Willie Nelson. Rangers give talks several times a day.

Mammoth Chapel CHURCH

(☎307-344-2003; www.gccmt.org/about/mammothchapel) If you're in Mammoth on a Sunday morning, pop into this lovely English-style church (1913), where the stained-glass windows depict Old Faithful and Yellowstone Falls. You can even get married here.

Mammoth to Tower-Roosevelt Junction

The 18-mile road to Tower-Roosevelt Junction heads east from Mammoth over the Gardner River Bridge, where the Gardner River meets the Yellowstone River. By the roadside, just over 2 miles from Mammoth, is pretty, three-tiered **Undine Falls**, aptly named for an alluring water nymph. Get private views of the falls from the north side of the river by hiking less than half a mile along Lava Creek Trail from the nearby Lava Creek picnic area.

The easy 1-mile round-trip walk to **Wraith Falls** is a good family hike through pretty meadows and fire-burn patches. The trail begins at the pullout east of Lava Creek picnic area, 5 miles from Mammoth, and follows Lupine Creek for 15 minutes to the base of a 79ft cascade. Rangers lead walks here twice weekly at 9am.

Just past the **Blacktail Ponds** pullout (good for spotting muskrats and waterfowl) is the Blacktail Creek trailhead, where trails lead down Rescue Creek or into the Black Canyon of the Yellowstone near Crevice Lake.

Two miles past here, the 0.5-mile **Forces of the Northern Range Self-Guiding Trail** is an accessible boardwalk that teaches children about the environmental forces of this part of the park. Kids will get a kick out of placing their hand on a wolf print.

The 6-mile one-way **Blacktail Plateau Drive** detours off the main highway to follow part of the Bannock Trail, a hunting route taken by Bannock Indians in the mid-19th century. The trail originated in Idaho, crossed the Yellowstone Valley at the Bannock Ford and continued through the Lamar Valley to Soda Butte Creek before leaving what is now the park at its northeastern corner and continuing to Bighorn Valley. Along the second half of this drive, near Crescent Hill, is the spot where Truman Everts was finally discovered after wandering lost in the park for 37 days. RVs and trailers are not allowed down the rough, unpaved road, but bikes are an option if you have someone to pick you up at the other end.

Instead of taking Blacktail Plateau Dr, you can continue east on the main Grand Loop Rd. You'll pass **Phantom Lake** (one of three interconnected lakes that are normally dry by July) and an unsigned **scenic overview** of Hellroaring Mountain, Garnet Hill and the Yellowstone River and Hellroaring Creek Valleys. A couple of miles further is the **Hellroaring trailhead**, a short drive down a dirt road and popular with horse packers headed into the Black Canyon of the Yellowstone.

Half a mile past here, **Floating Island Lake** is dense with vegetation, making it a good place to spot birds.

Just before you reach Tower-Roosevelt Junction is the 0.25-mile turnoff (no RVs or trailers) to the heavily visited **Petrified**

Tree, surrounded by a fence like a priceless work of art. The tree is worth a quick look if you've never seen one before, but the parking lot can be cramped and busy. A nicer way to visit the tree is on an early-morning or evening hike from Roosevelt Lodge on the Lost Lake Loop.

Mammoth to Norris

The 20-mile road from Mammoth to Norris has been under repair for the past few years, but construction work should finally be finished by 2020. The initial route passes the Upper Terraces and enters a jumbled landscape of **hoodoos**, formed when the 65,000-year-old travertine deposits of nearby Terrace Mountain slipped down the hillside, breaking into boulder-like fragments. (You can get an up-close look at the hoodoos on the Terrace Mountain Loop hike (p56), or by walking the Howard Eaton Trail from Glen Creek trailhead down to Mammoth.)

The road climbs to the cantilevered road of **Golden Gate**, named after the light-colored welded rock formed from cooled ash flows. The sprouting knob of rock on the outside of the road was actually pulled down and then replaced when the road was widened!

Shortly afterwards a pullout offers views of tiny **Rustic Falls**, a natural funnel that was probably used by the Sheepeater people to trap bighorn sheep. The Sheepeaters, also known as the Tukudika, were a subtribe of the Shoshone famed for their ram's-horn bows and were the park's earliest year-round inhabitants.

The peak rising to the left is **Bunsen Peak** (8564ft), a plug of solidified magma that formed inside a long-since-eroded volcanic cone. Hiking and cycling trails head up and around Bunsen Peak from the busy Bunsen Peak/Glen Creek trailhead. Further along on the right, delightful **Swan Lake**, in the middle of Gardner's Hole, offers good bird-watching (look for trumpeter swans in winter and early spring) and views of the Gallatin Range. A board helps identify the various peaks.

Two miles further south, turn off for the **Sheepeater Cliffs**, an amazing collection of 500,000-year-old hexagonal basalt columns, stacked like building blocks. You'll find a scenic picnic area and strolls along the river to more formations (no buses, trailers or RVs allowed on this road).

The road passes a nice fishing spot and winter warming hut near Indian Creek Campground, then continues to a series of four pullouts at **Willow Park** and **Moose Bogs**, 2 miles further south and a good place to look for some of the park's 200 moose. Soon after comes a pleasant picnic spot at **Apollinaris Spring**, once a popular stagecoach stop for parched travelers headed to Norris.

Obsidian Cliff, to the left of the road, exposes the interior of a 180,000-year-old lava flow. Rapid cooling prevented the formation of crystals and fused the lava into this form of volcanic glass. Obsidian, used for spearheads and arrowheads, was widely traded by Native Americans and was one of the major reasons early people visited the Yellowstone region. The park service was forced to remove the cliffside trails of this National Historic Landmark due to pilfering of the obsidian – leave it alone!

Just 1 mile further, the **Beaver Lake** picnic area offers a fine spot for a picnic and some wildlife-watching. Just past here, isolated fumaroles, hot springs and other thermal features start to appear by the side of the road, heralding the approach of the thermally active Norris region.

Roaring Mountain is a huge bleached hillside pockmarked with hissing fumaroles. During its heyday, around the turn of the last century, visitors could hear the roar of the fumaroles from over 4 miles away. The activity is much reduced today.

From here the road passes pretty North and South **Twin Lakes** and descends to beautiful **Nymph Lake**. The lake's bubbling pools, bleached white shoreline and steaming geysers lend the area a powerfully primeval air – something out of the landscapes of Tolkien or the age of the dinosaurs. Just south of here is the unsigned but superbly named **Devil's Frying Pan** springs. The smell of sulfur stays with you as the road quickly descends into the Norris Geyser Basin.

⊙ Roosevelt Country

President Theodore Roosevelt visited this rugged mountainous area in the park's northeastern corner during a two-week jaunt through the park in 1903, lending his name to the rustic Roosevelt Lodge by Tower-Roosevelt Junction that opened three years later. Fossil forests, the wildlife-rich **Lamar Valley**, its tributary trout streams of

FREE STUFF!

Yellowstone can be a pricey place, especially if you have kids or ravenous teenagers. Fear not, the following can all be had for a song.

- Ranger hikes and winter snowshoe hikes.
- Campfire presentations.
- Films in Old Faithful Visitor Education Center (p109) and museum displays at Canyon and Old Faithful visitor centers.
- Tours of the historic Old Faithful Inn (p109) and Lake Yellowstone Hotel (p103).
- Relaxing in the rocking chairs at Roosevelt Lodge (p120) and Lake Lodge (p122).
- Winter ice skating at Mammoth.
- A tour of the Yellowstone archives at Gardiner.
- Free petrified wood at Tom Miner just outside the park's northern entrance (limits apply).
- Free park entry on certain dates.
- Picnic areas – over 50 in Yellowstone alone, with tables, grills and toilets.
- Hiking is free and overnight backcountry trips cost a paltry $3 per night.

Slough and Pebble Creeks and the dramatic and craggy peaks of the Absaroka Range are the highlights in this remote, scenic and undeveloped region. The rustic cabins, stagecoach rides and Western cookouts at the Roosevelt Lodge add a cowboy flavor to the region's frontier feel. The area is also the birthplace of the park's current bison and wolf populations and one of Yellowstone's great wildlife-viewing areas. Spring is the most popular time to visit, when the valleys are lush and green and pocket-sized baby bison and elk dot the landscape.

The 29-mile Northeast Entrance Rd passes from Cooke City through the Lamar Valley to Tower-Roosevelt Junction (6270ft) and then continues west for 18 miles to Mammoth Junction. This is the only road in the park that remains open year-round. From Tower-Roosevelt Junction the Grand Loop Rd heads south to Canyon Village, over the high Dunraven Pass.

Roosevelt Lodge has accommodations, food, showers, a small grocery store and a nearby ranger station and gas station, as well as a horse corral for trail rides (p85) and hiking trails to nearby Lost Lake (p58).

Northeast Entrance to Tower-Roosevelt

It's 29 miles from the Northeast Entrance to Tower-Roosevelt. A couple of miles inside the Northeast Entrance the road enters Wyoming and follows Soda Butte Creek, offering fine views of the craggy ridgeline of towering **Barronette Peak** (10,404ft) to the west. It was Jack Baronet who rescued Truman Everts for a promised $600 reward. Not only did he not get the reward, but the park misspelled the peak it named after him! This is a good place to look for moose.

Near Pebble Creek Campground at tiny Icebox Canyon, the lovely valley warms up and opens wide. Southeast is a ridgeline known as the Thunderer (10,554ft), after the frequent storms that gather here.

Two miles past Pebble Creek is the trailhead for the short 0.5-mile walk through fir forest and summer wildflowers to scenic **Trout Lake**, named after the abundant cutthroats that spawn here in early summer. The 10-minute uphill hike to the pretty lake is steep enough to leave you puffing, but it's still one of the park's best short family hikes. It's popular also with anglers, who are allowed to keep their catch of rainbow (but not cutthroat) trout. Lose the crowds by following the side trail from the stream inflow for 10 minutes to pretty Buck Lake.

Further along the road, watch (and sniff) for the whitish-yellow travertine cone of **Soda Butte**, the only thermal feature in this part of the park.

The road now joins the mixed sagebrush and grasslands of the Lamar Valley, one of the park's premier wildlife-viewing areas. The roadside turnouts between Pebble Creek and Slough (pronounced 'slew') Creek Campgrounds, particularly the stretch between Lamar River trailhead and the Lamar Canyon, are prime places to spot wolves from the Lamar Canyon pack. Elk and large

Roosevelt Country Area

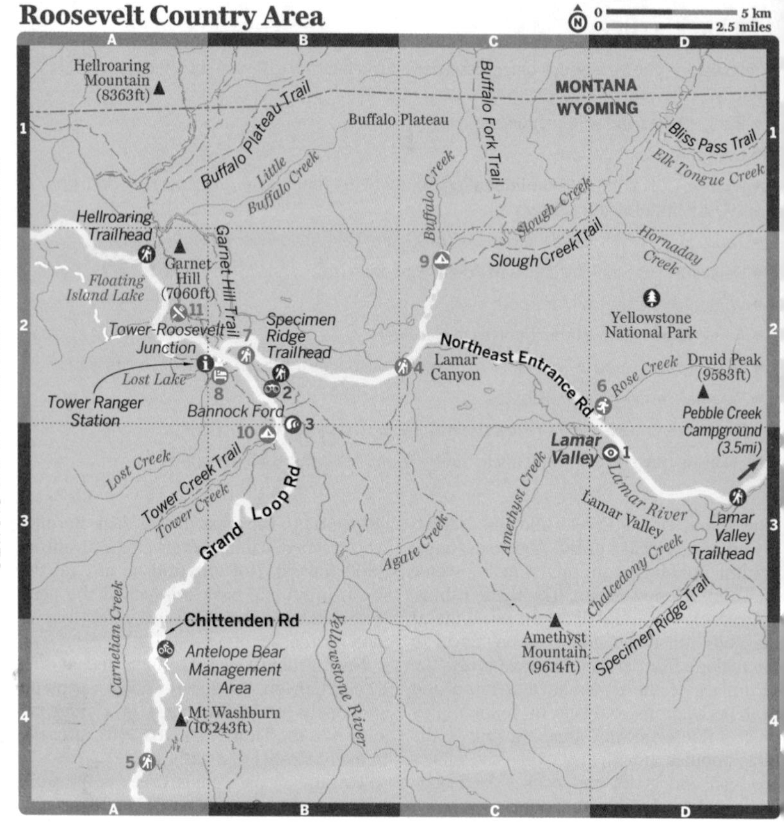

herds of bison also make the broad Lamar Valley their winter range, alongside coyotes, pronghorns and bears.

Also here is the former **Buffalo Ranch**, which almost single-handedly raised Yellowstone's bison herds between 1907 and 1960. The buildings are now home to the excellent **Yellowstone Forever Institute** (Map p96; ☎406-848-2400; www.yellowstone.org; Lamar Valley).

About 6 miles before Tower-Roosevelt Junction, a dirt road turns off north to Slough Creek Campground, offering fishing and hiking access. Further along the main road are several glacially formed 'kettle' ponds, which are periodically closed to protect nesting trumpeter swans.

Just before Tower the road passes the popular **Yellowstone River picnic area** and hiking trail (look for wildlife here) and bridges the Yellowstone River.

Tower-Roosevelt Junction

Calcite Springs Overlook VIEWPOINT

(Map p96) This overlook 1.5 miles south of Tower-Roosevelt Junction offers vertiginous views of a section of the Grand Canyon of the Yellowstone known as the Narrows. A short trail leads to views north of the gorge's sulfuric yellows and smoking sides. All around are vertical basalt columns, part of a 25ft-deep lava flow that covered the area 1.3 million years ago. Below the basalt are glacial deposits; above the basalt are layers of volcanic ash.

Tower Fall WATERFALL

(Map p96) Two-and-a-half miles south of Tower-Roosevelt Junction, Tower Creek plunges over 132ft Tower Fall before joining the Yellowstone River. The fall gets its name from the volcanic breccia towers around it, which brood like a demonic fortress and earn the fall the nickname

Roosevelt Country Area

Top Sights
1 Lamar Valley....D3

Sights
2 Calcite Springs Overlook....B2
3 Tower Fall....B3

Activities, Courses & Tours
4 Fossil Forest Trail....C2
5 Mt Washburn....A4
Stagecoach Rides....(see 8)
6 Yellowstone Forever Institute....D2
7 Yellowstone River Picnic Area Trail....B2

Sleeping
8 Roosevelt Lodge....B2
9 Slough Creek Campground....C2
10 Tower Fall Campground....B3

Eating
11 Old West Cookout....A2
Roosevelt Lodge Dining Room....(see 8)
Roosevelt Yellowstone General Store....(see 8)

'Devil's Den.' A short trail leads to a viewpoint above the fall, but don't bother heading further down as there are no further views of the cascade.

Canyon Country

A series of scenic overlooks linked by hiking trails punctuate the cliffs, precipices and waterfalls of the Grand Canyon of the Yellowstone. Here the river continues to gouge out a fault line through an ancient golden geyser basin, most impressively at **Lower Falls**. **South Rim Drive** leads to the canyon's most spectacular overlook, at Artist Point (p99), while **North Rim Drive** accesses the daring precipices of the Upper and Lower Falls.

The Canyon area is the second-most-heavily-visited part of the park after Old Faithful, due largely to the splendor of the Grand Canyon of the Yellowstone, but also due to the junction's central location and its concentration of visitor services.

Canyon Village

Canyon Village lies just east of Canyon Junction along North Rim Dr. It's the logistical base for the central part of the park and has accommodations, three restaurants, the excellent **Canyon Visitor Education Center** (Map p95; 307-344-2550; Canyon; 8am-8pm Jun-Aug, hours vary Sep-May), well worth a visit for its innovative and interactive displays on Yellowstone's geology; a backcountry office, a general store, an outdoor-gear store and an ATM.

The campground area has showers, laundry facilities and an ice machine.

Grand Canyon of the Yellowstone

After its placid meanderings north from Yellowstone Lake through the Hayden Valley, the Yellowstone River musters its energy and plummets over **Upper Falls** (109ft) and then the much larger **Lower Falls** (308ft), before raging through the 1000ft-deep **Grand Canyon of the Yellowstone** (Map p95). More than 4000ft wide at the top, the canyon snakes for 20 miles as far as the Narrows near Tower-Roosevelt Junction.

Much of the canyon's beauty comes from its subtle range of colors, from egg white to flamboyant salmon pink, a by-product of iron oxidization in the rock – in effect, the canyon is rusting. Whiffs of steam rise from vents in the canyon wall, hinting at the thermal activity that played a major role in the canyon's creation (by weakening the rhyolite rock). Relatively new in geological terms, the canyon was carved out not by glacial erosion but by water supplied by ice dams that melted and flooded the region during the most recent ice age.

The Lower Falls are twice the height of Niagara Falls and are most impressive in spring, when the water volume can be up to 12 times that of fall. An eye-catching green notch indicates a patch of deeper and less turbulent water. At the base of the falls the reds and creams of the canyon walls turn mossy green, fed by the thundering spray of the river. Bring binoculars to spot ospreys that nest in the canyon from late April till early September. In winter, the spray freezes into a giant cone in front of the falls.

Rangers lead hikes daily at 9am from the parking lot above Uncle Tom's trailhead and give short talks several times a day (10am for kids) at Artist Point.

NORTH RIM

★ **Inspiration Point** VIEWPOINT

(Map p95) A side road branches off North Rim Dr to reach busy Inspiration Point, which offers an overview of the length of the Grand Canyon of the Yellowstone and a small section of the Lower Falls. There are a few steps to descend – and there used to

Canyon Country Area

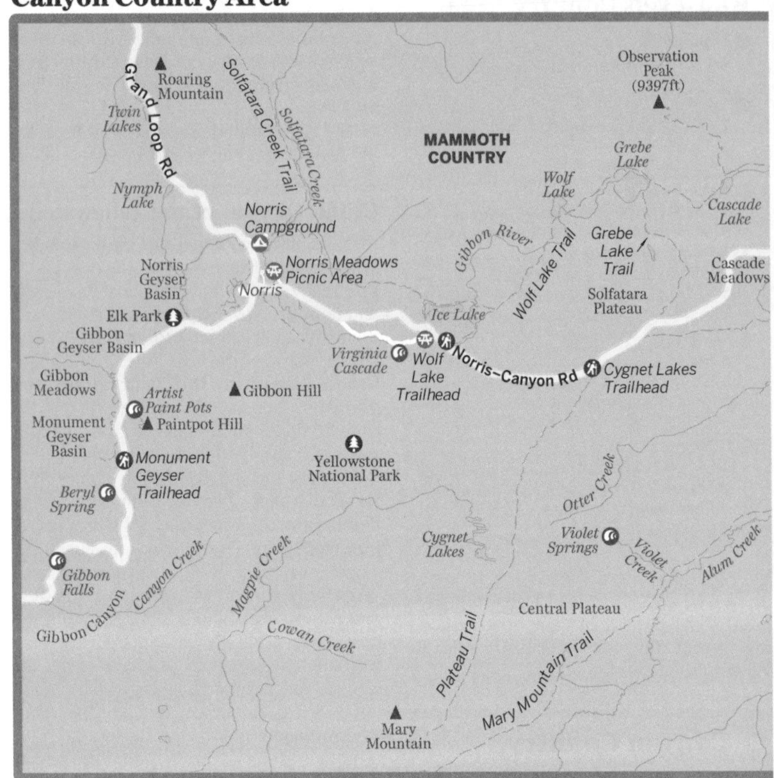

be more, before the old lookout point fell (literally) victim to the canyon's relentless erosion. The site was renovated in 2018.

★ Lookout Point VIEWPOINT

(Map p95) Popular Lookout Point, near Canyon Village, offers the best views of the Lower Falls. An adjacent 0.5-mile trail drops 500ft to Red Rock for even closer views – the average age of the crowd plummets with the elevation (it's hard on the knees). The trails can be very slippery, so watch your step. It was around here that iconic early painter Thomas Moran made the sketches for his famous painting of the canyon, allegedly weeping over the lack of colors in his palette.

Brink of the Lower Falls WATERFALL

(Map p95) The first of the North Rim viewpoints leads down a steep 0.75-mile trail, descending 600ft for exciting close-up views of the tumbling white water as the Yellowstone River rushes over the lip of the Lower Falls. Heading back up isn't half as much fun as going down.

Grandview Point VIEWPOINT

(Map p95) The one-way North Rim Dr leads to Grandview Point, which offers views north over the Grand Canyon of the Yellowstone's colorful smoking walls, though not of the Lower Falls.

UPPER FALLS VIEWPOINT

The Upper Falls Viewpoint is accessible by road: the turnoff is south of Canyon Junction and Cascade Creek on the main Grand Loop Rd to Fishing Bridge. A short walk to the right (south) leads to the **Brink of the Upper Falls**, though the best views of the falls are actually from the Uncle Tom's parking area across the gorge. The brink will close in summer 2019 for trail reconstruction.

A five-minute walk north along the North Rim Trail (a former stagecoach road)

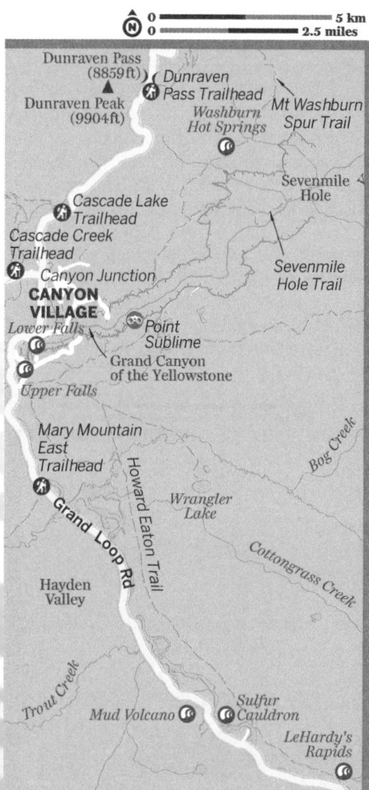

leads to an overview of the much smaller but graceful **Crystal Falls**, the 'Hidden' or 'Third' waterfall of the Canyon region.

SOUTH RIM

South Rim Dr passes the Chittenden Bridge and Wapiti Lake trailhead en route to the canyon's most spectacular overlook at Artist Point. The 3.25-mile **South Rim Trail** follows the canyon rim from Chittenden Bridge to Point Sublime via Artist Point.

★Artist Point VIEWPOINT

(Map p95; South Rim Dr, Canyon) Artist Point is probably the most famous of the canyon's viewpoints, offering a long overview of the Lower Falls and canyon. It was not, as many people assume, named for the spot where Thomas Moran sketched his famous landscape of the falls, a copy of which is on display in the Canyon Visitor Education Center. It was actually named by the park photographer FJ Haynes for its superlative scenic views.

Point Sublime VIEWPOINT

(Map p98) From Artist Point a trail leads 1 mile (45 minutes) to this viewpoint for more fabulous views of the Grand Canyon of the Yellowstone's colorful walls, though the best views are five minutes before you arrive at the point. The 4-mile (two-hour) round-trip hike to Ribbon Lake branches off from here.

Uncle Tom's Trail VIEWPOINT

(Map p95) Near Canyon Village, Uncle Tom's Trail offers the best views of the Upper and Lower Falls. The trail itself is a steep route that descends 500ft down 328 metal steps to the base of the Lower Falls. The trail was constructed in 1898 by early park entrepreneur Uncle Tom Richardson, who led tourists down a series of trails and rope ladders for views of the falls and a picnic lunch. Sadly, the rope ladders are now a thing of the past.

The park service once turned down an application to build an elevator here that would whisk tourists down to the canyon floor, though you may wish it had changed its mind as you make the tough return climb. This is one of the region's largest parking areas. Rangers lead a walk from here along the South Rim Trail at 9am in summer; check the park newspaper for details. The parking lot and trail were renovated in 2018.

CANYON WITHOUT THE CROWDS

Four popular scenic overlooks line the one-way 2.5-mile North Rim Dr. Most people link them by car, but it's also possible to visit them on a scenic hike or even bike ride.

The **North Rim Trail** parallels the road from Inspiration Point to Upper Falls Overlook (2.5 miles), from where you can continue 0.75 miles to Chittenden Bridge on South Rim Dr, where it links up with the South Rim Trail. The only disadvantage to this route is that it's one way, so you'll have to either retrace your steps or arrange a designated driver to pick you up.

One option if you have a bike is to park at the Brink of the Lower Falls, cycle to Inspiration Point (there's a cycle lane) and then walk back along the North Rim Trail. The trail is mostly through forest, but every now and then you'll pop out onto the canyon rim for views that you'll have all to yourself. Figure on two hours with detours and cycling.

Canyon to Lake Village

South of Canyon Junction, Grand Loop Rd winds 16 miles down to Lake Yellowstone via the excellent wildlife-watching opportunities of the Hayden Valley and the interesting Mud Volcano. This section of road makes for a good two-hour bike ride, though, as always, you'll have to watch out for the traffic.

HAYDEN VALLEY

The Yellowstone River is broad and shallow as it meanders gently through the vast grasslands of Hayden Valley, named after the expedition leader whose 1871 survey led to the establishment of the park the following year. This former lake bed was formed in the last ice age when a glacial outburst flooded the valley, turning the region into an arm of Yellowstone Lake. The fine silt-and-clay soil prevents water from percolating into the ground, making the area marshy and impenetrable to most trees. This supports the rich shrubs and grasses favored by bison.

The Hayden is the largest valley in the park and one of its premier **wildlife-viewing** areas. With patience you're likely to see coyotes, springtime grizzlies, elk and lots of bison, plus one of the largest fall ruts. Bird-watching is equally good, with

Canyon Village

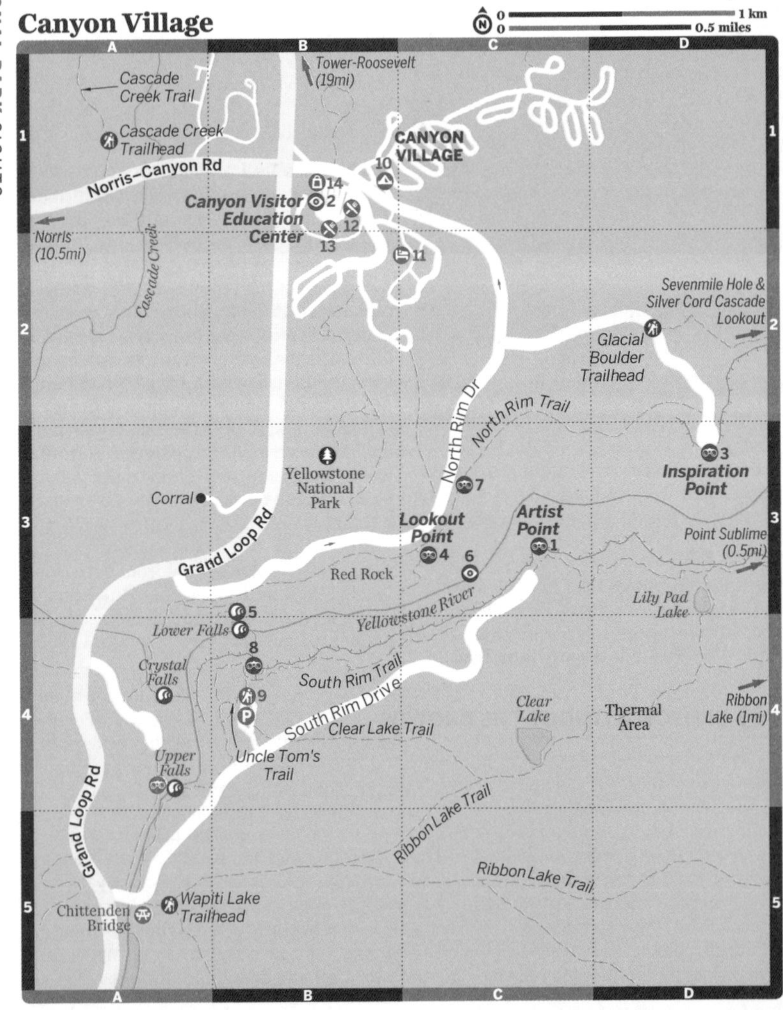

the area home to white pelicans and trumpeter swans, sandhill cranes (also at Alum Creek), ospreys, bald eagles and Canada geese. There are popular viewing areas 1 mile north of Sulfur Cauldron and 1.5 miles north of Trout Creek. Set up your spotting scope early, as the pullouts fill with cars an hour or two before dusk.

MUD VOLCANO

One of the park's most geologically volatile regions, this thermal area 10 miles south of Canyon Junction and 6 miles north of Fishing Bridge Junction contains an assortment of mud pots and other gurgling sulfurous pits. The nearby Sour Creek resurgent dome is the fuel that superheats the mud volcanoes, while the high acidity created by thermophiles breaks down rock into mud pots rather than creating the pressurized geyser plumbing more characteristic of alkaline thermal features. During a series of earthquakes in 1979 the mud pots developed enough heat and gases to literally cook lodgepole pines and grasses on neighboring hillsides. One mud pot recently emerged from underneath the parking lot.

Mud Volcano itself has not erupted since the 1871 Langford-Washington-Doane expedition first encountered it. A crater is all that remains of the original cone. **Dragon's Mouth Spring** gets its name from the deep thumping and crashing that emanates from a hidden lair that looks like it guards the gateway to the underworld. In 1999 the pool cooled and its color changed from green to white and gray and now partially back to green again.

The easiest way to see the other sights is to follow the 0.6-mile loop boardwalk (there are some steps) clockwise, past Mud Geyser and up Cooking Hillside. Halfway up, **Churning Cauldron** is a favorite; waves of water produced by bubbling gas (not boiling water) have created tiny beaches here. The dark colors of this and other pots are due to the presence of iron sulfides.

Black Dragon's Cauldron appeared in 1948 in a crack in the earth and has since moved south 200ft along the crack to produce an elliptical pool. The rolling motion of the water is actually due to rising gases rather than boiling water. Nearby **Sour Lake** looks like a nice place for a swim, but its waters are as acidic as battery acid. Further downhill, **Grizzly Fumarole** changes throughout the year from a fumarole to a mud pot and even a muddy spring, according to the amount of moisture in the ground.

Sulfur Cauldron, just a few hundred yards north, by a pullout in the road, is one of the most acidic springs in the park, at pH 1.3. Other thermal areas, visible across the Yellowstone River, can only be reached by hiking the Howard Eaton Trail from Fishing Bridge.

Rangers lead 90-minute walks around the site at 10am, but sadly no longer go to the **Gumper**, a huge, seething mud pot behind Sour Lake and off limits to visitors.

Canyon Village

Top Sights

1 Artist Point C3
2 Canyon Visitor Education Center B1
3 Inspiration Point D3
4 Lookout Point C3

Sights

5 Brink of the Lower Falls B3
6 Grand Canyon of the Yellowstone C3
7 Grandview Point C3
8 Uncle Tom's Trail B4

Activities, Courses & Tours

9 South Rim Trail & Ribbon Lake B4

Sleeping

10 Canyon Campground B1
11 Canyon Lodges C2

Eating

12 Canyon Lodge Eatery B1
13 Canyon Yellowstone General Store B1
M66 Grill .... (see 12)

Shopping

14 Bear Aware B1

Lake Country

Yellowstone Lake (7733ft) is Lake Country's shimmering centerpiece – one of the world's largest alpine lakes, with the biggest inland population of cutthroat trout in the US. Yellowstone River emerges from the north end of the lake and flows through Hayden Valley into the Grand Canyon of the Yellowstone. The lake's southern and eastern borders flank the steep Absaroka Range and the pristine Thorofare region, some of the wildest and remotest lands in the lower 48. This watery wilderness lined with volcanic beaches is best explored by boat or sea kayak.

A 22-mile section of the Grand Loop Rd hugs Yellowstone Lake's shoreline between Fishing Bridge Junction to the north and West Thumb Junction to the west. Visitor centers and convenience stores are at Fishing Bridge and Grant Village. Grant and Lake Villages offer the most visitor services, including dining. Early-summer bear activity, cold water and lingering snowfields mean that Lake Country is best explored later in the summer, from July onwards.

Bridge Bay Marina (p87) rents outboard motorboats, offers scenic lake cruises and has a fishing/grocery store, dump station, ranger station and picnic area. The busy Fishing Bridge area offers showers and laundry, as well as a gas station, groceries and camping supplies at the Yellowstone General Store.

Lake Village centers on colonial Lake Yellowstone Hotel but also has a post office, medical center and general store.

Yellowstone Lake

The largest high-altitude lake in North America, the deep-cobalt Yellowstone Lake (136 sq miles) has been a human draw for millennia; artifacts found along the lakeshore date back 12,000 years. Traditionally this was only a summering spot for native groups. The lake remains frozen almost half the year, from January to early June, though its average depth is 140ft (maximum 390ft)

Lake Country Area

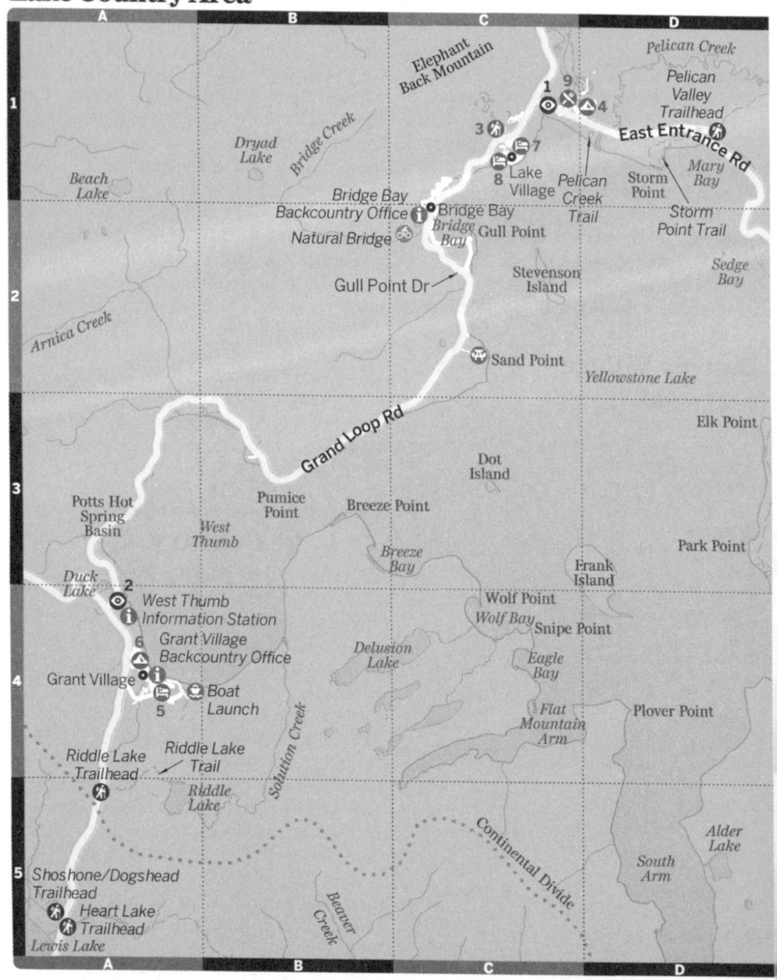

and parts of the lake floor boil with underwater hot springs.

In addition to excellent fishing and boating, the lake also offers prime birding and wildlife-watching. Early summer visitors shouldn't miss an amazing display of spawning cutthroat trout at Fishing Bridge and **LeHardy's Rapids**, 3 miles north of the bridge. As crucial food sources for grizzlies and waterfowl, some spawning areas around the lakeshore are closed during spring and early summer.

Thermal activity rings the lake, and in cold weather steaming thermals blur into the water.

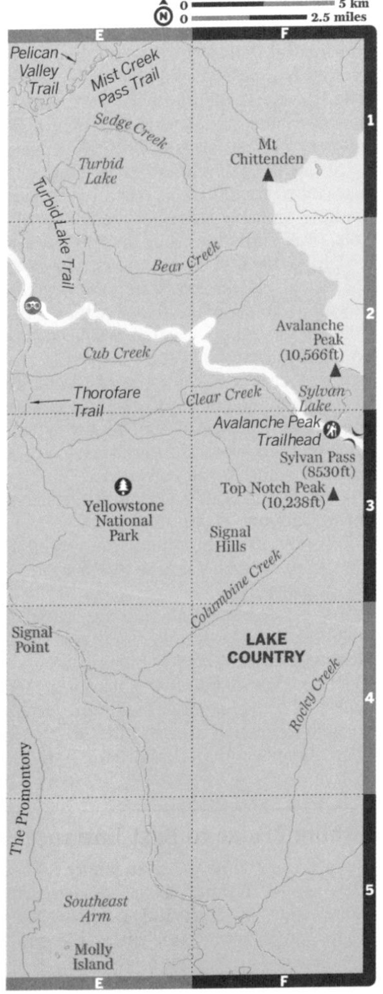

Lake Yellowstone Hotel HISTORIC BUILDING

(Map p102; Lake Village) The buttercup-yellow colonial Lake Yellowstone Hotel, dating from 1891, is the park's oldest building and certainly its most elegant. Robert Reamer (who also designed the Old Faithful Inn) rebuilt the hotel in 1903, adding Ionic columns, a fireplace and false balconies. Swank and expansive, this Southern-style mansion is the perfect setting for pre-dinner drinks.

Fishing Bridge BRIDGE

(Map p102) There has been a bridge at Fishing Bridge since 1902, but it closed to fishing in 1973 to protect spawning cutthroat trout – to the benefit of resident grizzlies. The bridge and surrounding roads are slated for reconstruction in 2019, so expect delays between here and Storm Point until 2020.

Lake Village to West Thumb

You'll find several delightful spots to picnic and/or fish between Lake Village and West Thumb. Near Bridge Bay Marina, 2-mile **Gull Point Drive** (no RVs) is a scenic picnic spot and popular fishing area that also offers a short bike ride for families staying at Bridge Bay. Opposite the turnoff is the road for the 3-mile biking trip to Natural Bridge (p83). An alternative hiking trail leads to the bridge from Bridge Bay Marina.

Bridge Bay Marina itself is a major center for fishing charters and boat rental. If you

Lake Country Area

Sights

1 Fishing Bridge C1
Lake Yellowstone Hotel .... (see 8)
2 West Thumb Geyser Basin A4

Activities, Courses & Tours

3 Elephant Back Mountain Trail C1

Sleeping

4 Fishing Bridge RV Park D1
5 Grant Village A4
6 Grant Village Campground A4
7 Lake Lodge Cabins C1
8 Lake Yellowstone Hotel C1

Eating

9 Fishing Bridge Yellowstone General Store C1
Lake Lodge Cafeteria .... (see 7)
Lake Yellowstone General Store .... (see 8)
Lake Yellowstone Hotel Deli .... (see 8)
Lake Yellowstone Hotel Dining Room .... (see 8)

fancy getting on the water, try the one-hour **sightseeing cruises** (adult/child $18/10.50) from Bridge Bay Marina that travel to Stevenson Island and the wreck of the steamship SS *Waters* (1905). They operate six or seven times daily from mid-June to mid-September and rangers accompany the first three trips of the day. Reserve in advance.

Other nice lakeshore spots include **Sand Point** picnic area, from where trails lead 400yd down to a lagoon and black volcanic-glass beach, and **Pumice Point**, a crumbling promontory and spit of dark-black sand. There are more sandbars and lagoons to explore 2 miles, 4.5 miles and 6.5 miles further toward West Thumb.

West Thumb

Named for its location in the hand-shaped Yellowstone Lake, West Thumb is a small volcanic caldera spawned 150,000 years ago inside the much larger Yellowstone caldera. Yellowstone Lake filled the crater, creating West Thumb Bay, a circular inlet at the lake's western end. The geyser basin pours more than 3000 gallons of hot water into the lake daily.

Back in the early days of the park, visitors would take a steamboat from West Thumb to the Lake Hotel, stopping at Dot Island en route to gawk at the captive elk and bison that were in pens there.

West Thumb Geyser Basin AREA

(Map p102; Yellowstone Lake) Although West Thumb is not one of Yellowstone's prime thermal sites, its 0.5-mile shoreline boardwalk loop (with a shorter inner loop to finish with) passes more than a dozen hot springs. At famous **Fishing Cone**, anglers once used the infamous 'hook 'n' cook' method to prepare their catch, casting fish into the boiling water – a practice now prohibited.

Fluctuating lake levels in spring and early summer sometimes submerge Fishing Cone and Lakeshore Geyser, but you can still see Big Cone. You can spot the underwater features by looking for slick spots or a slight bulge in the water.

Abyss Pool is one of the park's deepest springs. Rangers give a short talk here four times a day. Nearby **Black Pool** is one of the prettiest, with stunning amber-colored runoff, though it's now sapphire blue after years of lower temperatures supported mats of black thermophiles. **Thumb Paint Pots** are struggling to regain the energy that once catapulted boiling mud 25ft into the air.

Smaller thermal areas surrounding West Thumb include the roadside **Pumice Point** and **Potts Hot Spring Basin**.

Grant Village

Grant Village is a sterile scar of blockhouses and tourist facilities named after Ulysses S Grant, the president who established Yellowstone National Park in 1872. Facilities include a gas station, public showers, laundry, post office, marina, visitor center, Yellowstone General Store and backcountry office. The marina is the put-in for kayak tours (p85) of West Thumb.

Grant Village to South Entrance

From Grant Village the road climbs to the **Continental Divide** (7988ft) and drops into a burn area, past several trailheads. **Lewis Lake**, the third largest in the park, comes into view here, and several lake-view pullouts offer nice picnic spots. Boaters use Lewis Lake as the gateway to remote Shoshone Lake. When you hit traffic south of the lake, you have probably arrived at the 30ft **Lewis Falls**. Walk a little way along the north side of the falls for the best views, or along the south side for the closest access. In good weather, look for a glimpse of the Tetons to the south.

To the west, the Pitchstone trailhead cuts over the remote pitchstone (ash tuft) plateau to Grassy Lake Rd, one of the park's least-visited corners. Its roadside meadows are excellent places to spot moose. Pitchstone was formed by the park's most recent lava flow, some 70,000 years ago.

A major burn area signals the start of **Lewis Canyon**. There are lots of pullouts along the roadside, but the southernmost offers the best views. Volcanic rock comprises the canyon walls.

Just before the South Entrance, a small pullout beside a bridge offers access to small **Moose Falls** and Crawfish Creek.

The entrance station is adjacent to the Snake River picnic area. From here it's 18 miles to Colter Bay and 43 miles to Moose Visitor Center, both in Grand Teton National Park.

Fishing Bridge to East Entrance

There are a couple of great family hiking trails west of Fishing Bridge, though road construction in 2019 and possibly 2020 might affect access, so check the park newspaper.

At **Pelican Creek Bridge**, 1 mile east of Fishing Bridge Visitor Center, an easy 1.3-mile loop nature trail winds through lodgepole forest to a pleasant beach and lake views. Keep an eye out for moose and springtime grizzlies in the wetlands. The lakeside ponds south of the bridge offer great bird-watching.

Formed by a giant steam (not lava) explosion, Storm Point, 1.5 miles further east, juts into the north end of the lake. The 2.3-mile (one hour) **Storm Point Trail** loop begins near Indian Pond, winding through diverse wildlife habitats, including meadows, shoreline and old forest. Wildlife, such as bison, moose, marmots and waterfowl, is particularly active around dusk and dawn. Rangers lead a hike here at 4pm. The trail closes in late spring and early summer due to bear activity and can be buggy early in summer.

Just east of Storm Point, a dirt road branches north to the Pelican Valley (p63) trailhead. The lush, meandering meadows here rank among the park's prime grizzly habitats.

Like West Thumb, crater-shaped **Mary Bay** is the result of a thermal explosion. Both Mary Bay and neighboring **Sedge Bay** are peppered with underwater thermal areas, of which roiling Steamboat Point is the most obvious. Sedge Bay beach is a launching point for canoe or kayak trips south along the lake's eastern shoreline and is a fine place for a picnic. Bird-watchers flock to the bay's southeastern corner.

As the East Entrance Rd turns away from the lake, a mile-long paved road (no buses, RVs or trailers) branches north to the **Lake Butte Overlook**, which offers grand sunset views of Yellowstone Lake and the remote Thorofare corner of the park. Further east is the less impressive Yellowstone Lake Overlook.

The main road gradually climbs up the western slope of the remote Absaroka Range past lovely **Sylvan Lake** (with a picnic area and catch-and-release fishing), Eleanor Lake and the Avalanche Peak (p65) trailhead. The road peaks at the avalanche area of **Sylvan Pass** (8530ft), dominated by 10,238ft Top Notch Peak to the south. Look for the Howitzer gun mounted on the southern side of the pass, employed to set off controlled avalanches during the dangerous winter months.

East of the pass the landscape becomes more rugged and impressive. The high, barren walls of Mt Langford (10,774ft) and Plenty Coups Peak (10,937ft) rise to the south. Middle Creek, with several good fishing spots, parallels the south side of the road.

The East Entrance marks the boundary between Yellowstone National Park and Shoshone National Forest. From here the Buffalo Bill Scenic Byway leads to Cody via the Wapiti Valley.

⊙ Norris

The Norris area was a former US Army outpost. Norris is named after Philetus W Norris, the park's second superintendent (1877–82), who is notable for constructing some of the park's first roads and for the shameless frequency with which he named park features after himself.

Norris sits at the junction of roads from Madison (14 miles), Canyon (12 miles) and Mammoth (20 miles). North of the junction is Norris Campground; west is Norris Geyser Basin, with busy bathrooms, an information station and a bookstore. A pleasant 1-mile trail (no bikes) connects the basin and the campground.

Museum of the National Park Ranger MUSEUM

(Map p92; ☎307-344-7353; ⊙9am-5pm Jun-Sep) The historic log Norris Soldier Station (1908), one of only three stations left from the era of the park's army control, now houses this small museum, often staffed by chatty retired NPS employees.

The exhibits detail the evolution of the ranger profession from its military origins, including a fun mock-up of an old ranger cabin and bunk room. See if you can guess which future US president served as a park ranger in Canyon in 1936, before entering the oval office 38 years later.

The Gibbon River flows through meadows in front of the building, making it a pleasant place to look for wildlife. Norris Campground (p122) is right next door.

Norris Geyser Basin

North and west of Norris Junction, the Norris Geyser Basin is North America's most volatile and oldest continuously active geothermal area (in existence for around 115,000 years). It's also the site of Yellowstone's hottest recorded temperatures, where three intersecting faults underlaid by magma rise to within 2 miles of the surface (magma is normally some 40 miles below the surface). Barely 1000ft below the surface, scientific instruments have recorded temperatures as high as 459°F (237°C). Norris is also home to the majority of the world's acidic geysers, fed by the basin's abundant supplies of sulfur, as well as the recently resurgent Steamboat Geyser, considered the world's tallest active geyser. In Norris the ground sighs, boils and rages like nowhere else on Earth.

Norris' geothermal features change seasonally, most commonly in August or September: clear pools transform into spouting geysers or mud pots and vice versa. Thermal activity is also affected by earthquake swarms and other mysterious disturbances, which generally last only a few days before things revert to 'normal.'

The area's only bathrooms are in the parking lot, next to the cold-drinks machines. The parking area and toilets can get crowded, so try to schedule a visit early or late in the day.

Porcelain Basin GEYSER

(Map p92) One mile of boardwalks loop through Porcelain Basin, the park's hottest exposed basin. (The name comes from the area's milky deposits of sinter, also known as geyserite.) The bleached basin boils and bubbles like some giant laboratory experiment and the ash-white ground actually pulsates in places. Check out the overviews from **Porcelain Terrace Overlook**, near the **Norris Museum** (Map p92; ☎307-344-2812; ⏲9am-6pm late May-Sep) – views that, in the words of Rudyard Kipling, made it look 'as though the tide of desolation had gone out.'

As you descend from the museum, veer left before the continually blowing fumarole of **Black Growler Steam Vent**, said to be the park's hottest. As with most fumaroles, this vent is higher than the basin floor and is thus without a reliable supply of water. Below here is the large but currently inactive Ledge Geyser.

Going clockwise, the boardwalk heads left past **Crackling Lake**, which bubbles like a deep-fat fryer, and the **Whale's Mouth**, a gaping, blue hot spring.

The swirling waters of **Whirligig Geyser** and nearby Pinwheel Geyser became dramatically acidic in 2000, helping to support the green cyanidium algae and yellow cyanobacteria that create many of the stunning colors in its drainage channels. The color of these bacterial mats indicates the relative temperatures of the water, from very hot blues and whites (up to 199°F, or 92°C) to cooler yellows and greens (144°F, or 62°C) and even cooler beiges and dark browns (130°F to 80°F, or 54°C to 26°C). Nearby **Constant Geyser** used to erupt every 20 minutes or so but has erupted much less frequently in recent years.

A side path leads past Hurricane Vent to **Congress Pool**, which appeared in 1891 – the year scientists convened in Yellowstone for a geologic congress. The corner of Porcelain Basin at the end of the boardwalk is the fastest-changing and most active part of the basin and offers fine views toward Mt Holmes (10,336ft).

A footpath to Norris Campground leads off from here beside Nuphar Lake.

Back Basin AREA

(Map p92; Norris) Two miles of boardwalks and gentle trails snake through Norris' forested Back Basin. The main show here is **Steamboat Geyser**, the world's tallest active geyser, which infrequently skyrockets to an awesome 380ft (over twice as high as Old Faithful). The geyser was dormant for half a century until 1961 and quiet again for most of the 1990s, but it burst back into life in 2018, erupting every eight days or so during spring. Rangers give a talk here several times a day.

Norris to Madison Junction

The 14-mile Norris to Madison Junction road quickly enters aptly named **Elk Park**, a fine place to spot elk and bison – you'll likely have to navigate a car jam here.

Just under 5 miles south of Norris Junction an easy 1-mile trail leads through burned forest to the fun mud pots and springs of **Artist Paint Pots**, a family favourite. The best mud pots are in the far-right-hand corner.

The road passes through Gibbon Meadows with its pleasant riverside picnic area and abundant bison herds, then passes the trailhead that leads to little-visited Monument Geyser Basin (p65). Next comes pretty, blue-green **Beryl Spring** (where the rolling action of the water comes from escaping gases rather than boiling water).

As the road and river descend off the Solfatara Plateau, you pass **Gibbon Falls**, one of the park's prettiest cascades. For the best views of the 84ft falls you'll have to park and walk downhill along the road. Like so many of Yellowstone's cascades, the falls flow over hard rhyolite that marks the edge of the Yellowstone caldera.

Several picnic areas follow, of which Gibbon Falls is the nicest, offering views down to the river. Tuft Hill picnic area sits at the foot of a wall of rock welded together in a cloud of volcanic ash.

Five miles further west a parking area on the right gives access to **Terrace Spring**, a large pool with a rolling geyser in the corner. Two lovely hot springs above form the namesake terrace. You could safely miss both Terrace and Beryl Springs if you're short on time.

From here the road drops down to **Madison Junction**, with its campground and junior ranger station (p128). The station is a good place to stop if you have kids. There are plenty of kid-friendly activities, bear skins to stroke and talks every half-hour. Spotting scopes offer a close-up look at the elk that frequent the Madison Valley.

Norris to Canyon Village

The 12-mile Norris–Canyon road connects the two parts of the Grand Loop Rd across the burnt forest and cooled lava flows of the Solfatara Plateau. Just past the junction the pleasant **Norris Meadows picnic area** offers some fine bird-watching over the plain of the meandering Gibbon River.

About 2 miles into the drive a one-way side road branches off past **Virginia Cascade**, which, like Gibbon Falls, lies on the caldera boundary. One story goes that the superintendent wanted to name the falls after his wife, Virginia, but the NPS was against naming park features after living people, so they compromised by naming the fall after the state of (ahem...) Virginia. The narrow 2.5-mile road follows the old stagecoach road along the Norris Cutoff and is closed to buses, trailers and RVs.

Back on the main road a small boardwalk trail marks the spot where a freak tornado ripped through the plateau in 1984. This was also the spot of the fiercest of 1988's wildfires.

Ice Lake Trail leads 0.5 miles to the peaceful namesake lake, with a charming wheelchair-accessible backcountry site (4D3) on its southern shore. Sites 4D1 and 4D2 are just a mile or so from the road and make a great first backcountry site for young families, though it's best to avoid the heavy mosquito months of June and July. Camping here feels like owning your own private lake. Trails continue northeast along the border of a major burn area to Wolf Lake (3 miles) and Grebe Lake (another 1.5 miles). There are also some longer hike options to Cascade Lake.

Further down the Norris–Canyon road, you'll pass the Cygnet Lakes and then the Grebe Lake and Cascade Creek trailheads, which offer alternative routes through burnt forest to Grebe and Cascade Lakes.

GEYSER-GAZING STRATEGIES

The first thing to do when you arrive at Old Faithful is check the predicted geyser-eruption times at the visitor center and then plan your itinerary around these. Predictions are made for the region's six main geysers – Old Faithful, Grand, Castle, Riverside, Daisy and the Lower Geyser Basin's Great Fountain – and these are also posted at Old Faithful Lodge (p123), Old Faithful Inn (p109) and the Madison Junior Ranger Station (p128).

You can also get this information on the park service's 'Yellowstone Geysers' app, on the @GeyserNPS Twitter feed, or by phone at 307-344-2751. Another good source on which geysers are currently most active is www.geyserwatch.com.

Remember, though, that geysers rarely erupt on schedule, so take some snacks and sunblock for the wait. Riverside runs to within 30 minutes of predictions, but Grand is only reliable within two or three hours. Still, there's always something erupting in Upper Geyser Basin, and if you're really lucky you'll catch a biggie such as Beehive or Daisy.

Budget at least half a day to see the area around Old Faithful, and a whole day to see all the geyser basins, though you could easily spend a day or two more if you catch the geyser-gazing bug. If time is tight, concentrate on Upper and Midway Geyser Basins and skip Biscuit and Black Sand Basins.

The best loop around the Upper Geyser Basin follows the paved road one way and the boardwalk the other for a total of 3 miles. To this you can add a small hike up to Observation Point for views over the basin. There is a smaller loop around Geyser Hill, but you'll miss many of the best geysers if you limit yourself to this.

One interesting way to see the geysers is to cycle out 1.4 miles along the road to Morning Glory (where there's a bike rack), then continue to Biscuit Basin via Daisy Geyser (1.3 miles). From here you can hike to Mystic Falls or cycle along the Grand Loop Rd to Black Sand Basin and get picked up there. Bikes can be rented at Bear Den Rentals in the Old Faithful Snow Lodge.

Geyser Country

Yellowstone's Geyser Country holds the park's most spectacular geothermal features (over half the world's total), within the world's densest concentration of geysers (over 200 spouters in 1.5 sq miles). It is Geyser Country that makes the Yellowstone plateau utterly and globally unique.

Highlights include Old Faithful and the Upper Geyser Basin and Grand Prismatic Spring. The majority of the geysers line the Firehole River, the aquatic backbone of the basin, whose tributaries feed 21 of the park's 110 waterfalls. Both the Firehole and Madison Rivers offer superb fly-fishing, and the meadows along them support large wildlife populations.

The drive from Madison to Old Faithful takes you plumb through Geyser Country.

The most famous geysers always attract a crowd, but sometimes it's the smaller features that are the most interesting. The smaller geysers make up for their lack of size with great names, such as North Goggles, Little Squirt, Gizmo, Spanker, Spasmodic, Slurper and Bulger (aliases the seven dwarfs might adopt to form a criminal gang).

In the introduction to *A Lady's Life in the Rocky Mountains* (1960), historian Daniel Boorstin attributed Yellowstone Park's enormous appeal 'to the fact that its natural phenomena, which erupt on schedule, come closest to the artificiality of "regular" tourist performances.' So grab some popcorn and check show times at the visitor center.

BEST BACKCOUNTRY THERMAL FEATURES

It's great to see a geyser or hot spring from the boardwalk, but it's quite another thing to explore a steaming off-trail thermal basin. With a bit of legwork you'll likely have the following backcountry secrets to yourself.

Shoshone Geyser Basin (p77) Lakeshore basin best visited on a multiday backpacking or canoe trip.

Washburn Hot Springs (p74) En route from Mt Washburn to Canyon's Glacial Boulder trailhead.

Mr Bubbles (p81) The king of backcountry soaks, in Bechler.

Howard Eaton Trail at Mammoth (p56) Explore Mammoth's terraces and vents from the back side.

Upper Geyser Basin

While Old Faithful receives the most attention, there's lots to explore in **Upper Geyser Basin** (Map p112; Old Faithful), which has the densest collection of geysers in Yellowstone. On Geyser Hill you'll find charismatic **Anemone** and fickle **Beehive Geysers**. If you see a group of backpack- and radio-wielding Geyser Gazers huddled near the latter, stick around for an impressive show. Below, fantastic **Castle Geyser** is one of the largest formations of its kind in the world, and the view from **Daisy Geyser** is excellent.

This heavily visited basin holds 180 of the park's 200 to 250 geysers, the most famous of which is geriatric Old Faithful. Boardwalks, footpaths and a cycling path along the Firehole River link the five distinct geyser groups, the furthest of which is only 1.5 miles from Old Faithful.

Entering the Old Faithful parking area comes as a bit of a shock after you've spent time in the park. As well as the visitor center, the complex boasts two gas stations, three hotels and several general stores, including the original 1897 knotty-pine Hamilton's Store (p125), the oldest structure still in use in the park. Yellowstone General Store, next to the Snow Lodge, has a selection of groceries and sells fishing flies, spotting scopes and fishing permits.

The combined ranger station (p71), backcountry office and medical clinic (p127) are set back from the main parking area, across the west parking lot from the visitor center. **Bear Den Rentals** (Map p112; half/full day $30/40, kids' bikes $20/30; ⏲7:30am-10pm; 👪) at Old Faithful Snow Lodge gift shop offers bike rentals in summer and snowshoe and ski rentals in winter.

Rangers give geology talks in front of Old Faithful eight times a day and offer an evening presentation in the theater at 7pm. There's a short talk for kids at 10am. Daily 90-minute geology walks depart at 5:30pm from Castle Geyser and at 8:30am from the visitor center, with a shorter walk around Old Faitfhul at 2:30pm.

Public showers are available in the reception area of the Old Faithful Inn. There are no campgrounds in the Old Faithful region.

Check out the predicted eruption times of select geysers at the Old Faithful Visitor Education Center before planning your hike. You can easily spend a full day here.

Old Faithful GEYSER

(Map p112) Though it's neither the tallest nor even the most predictable geyser in the park, Old Faithful is the poster child for Yellowstone and a consistent crowd-pleaser. Every 90 minutes or so the geyser spouts some 8000 gallons (150 bathtubs) of water up to 180ft in the air. It's worth viewing the eruption from several locations – the geyser-side seats, the upper-floor balcony of the Old Faithful Inn and (highly recommended) from a distance on Observation Hill.

For over 75 years the geyser faithfully erupted every hour or so – one reason for the name the Washburn expedition gave it in 1870. The average time between shows these days is 90 minutes and getting longer, though this has historically varied between 45 and 110 minutes. The average eruption lasts around four minutes. The water temperature is normally 204°F (95°C) and the steam is about 350°F (176°C). The longer the eruption, the longer the recovery time. Rangers correctly predict eruptions to within 10 minutes about 90% of the time. And no, Old Faithful has never erupted on the hour.

A fairly reliable method of calculating exactly when an eruption of Old Faithful is imminent is to count the number of people seated around the geyser – the number of tourists is inversely proportional to the amount of time left until the next eruption.

If you find yourself twiddling your thumbs waiting for the old salt, pause to consider the power of recycling – you are sitting on a boardwalk made from around three million recycled plastic water jugs.

Old Faithful Inn HISTORIC BUILDING

(Map p112) FREE Designed by Seattle architect Robert C Reamer and built in 1904, this is the only building in the park that looks as though it actually belongs here. The log rafters of its seven-story lobby rise nearly 80ft, and the chimney of the central fireplace (actually eight fireplaces combined) contains more than 500 tons of rhyolite rock. It's definitely a worthwhile visit, even for non-guests.

The Crow's Nest, a top-floor balcony where musicians once played for dancers in the lobby below, is wonderful (but unused since 1959). Look also for the huge popcorn popper and fire tools at the back of the fireplace. The 2nd-floor **observation deck** offers the chance to enjoy fine views of Old Faithful geyser over a drink, and the lobby hosts local artists and authors. Free 45-minute Historic Inn tours depart from the fireplace at 9:30am, 11am, 2pm and 3:30pm.

DON'T MISS

MORNING GLORY POOL

A steamy favorite that's well worth the walk, beautiful **Morning Glory Pool** (Map p112) is named after its flower shape. Unfortunately, the pool is slowly changing temperature and, therefore, color, due to the tons of trash thrown into it by past visitors (the main access road to Old Faithful passed by the pool until 1971). The refuse diminishes circulation and accelerates heat loss. As the pool cools, orange bacteria spreads from its sides, replacing the gorgeous blue tones.

In 1950 park staff induced an eruption to empty and clean the spring, pulling out $86.27 in pennies, 76 handkerchiefs, several towels, socks, shirts and underwear.

The inn's biggest secret? If you make a request when you book your room a year in advance, you just might be one of half a dozen people allowed up on the rooftop to watch the flags being lowered at around 6pm. The geyser-basin views are unparalleled.

Old Faithful Visitor Education Center VISITOR CENTER

(Map p112; 307-545-2751; Old Faithful; 8am-8pm Jun-Sep, 9am-5pm Dec-Mar, hours vary spring & fall;) This environmentally friendly center is all about the thermal features at Yellowstone, exploring the differences between geysers, hot springs, fumaroles and mud pots, and explaining why there are no geysers in Mammoth. Kids will enjoy the hands-on Young Scientist displays, which include a working laboratory geyser. Predicted eruption times are posted for a handful of the park's most famous gushers.

Films are shown 30 minutes before and 15 minutes after an eruption of Old Faithful (the latter on Yellowstone's geysers). Rangers give 45-minute talks in the theater at 7pm.

Yellowstone Art and Photography Center HISTORIC BUILDING

(Map p112; www.yellowstone.org/art; 10am-6pm) This building was constructed in 1927 as one of the original Haynes photo shops. The Haynes family operated 13 photo shops in Yellowstone and produced 55 million postcards and the park's earliest guidebooks, some of which are on display. Displays of historic art sit alongside the work-in-progress of current artists-in-residence.

Geyser Country

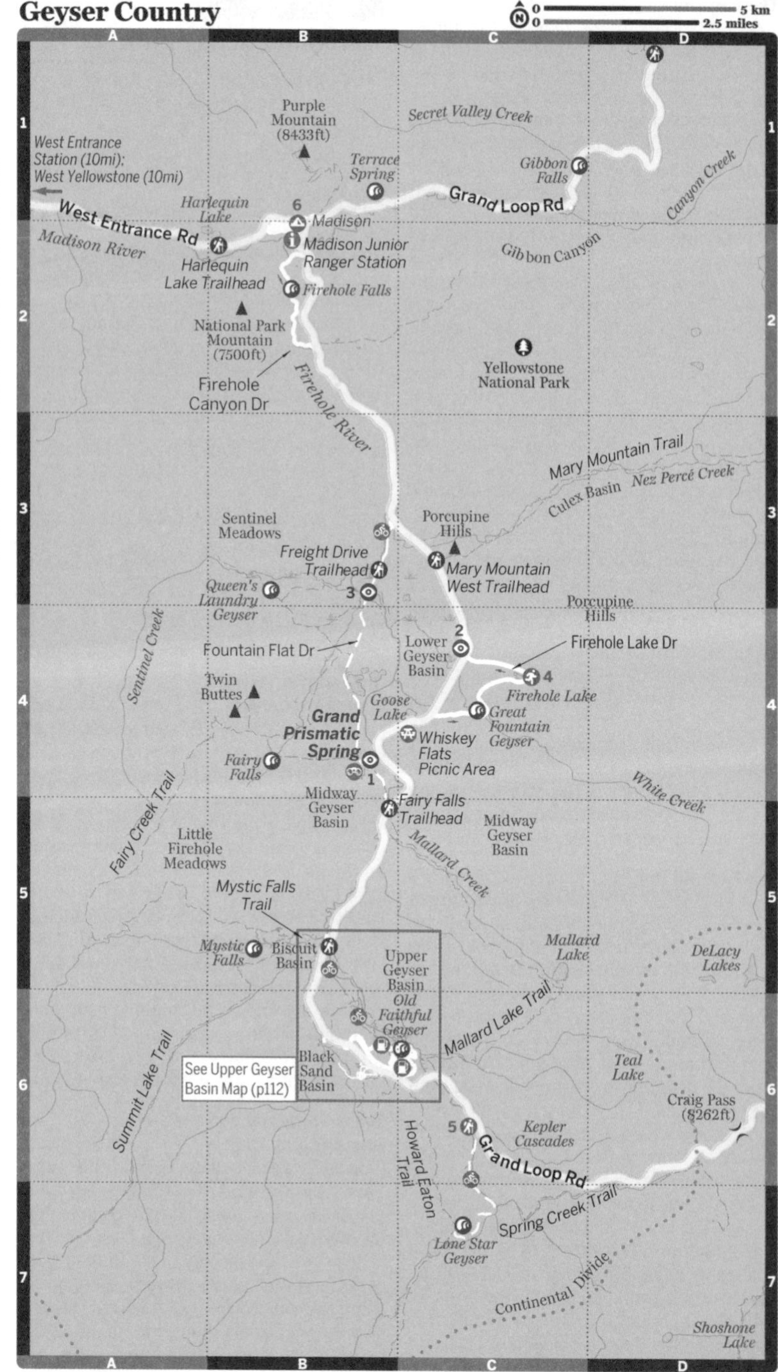
0 5 km
0 2.5 miles
West Entrance Station (10mi); West Yellowstone (10mi)
West Entrance Rd
Madison River
Harlequin Lake
Harlequin Lake Trailhead
Purple Mountain (8433ft)
Terrace Spring
Secret Valley Creek
Gibbon Falls
Grand Loop Rd
Canyon Creek
Madison
Madison Junior Ranger Station
Gibbon Canyon
Firehole Falls
National Park Mountain (7500ft)
Firehole Canyon Dr
Firehole River
Yellowstone National Park
Mary Mountain Trail
Culex Basin
Nez Percé Creek
Sentinel Meadows
Porcupine Hills
Freight Drive Trailhead
Mary Mountain West Trailhead
Queen's Laundry Geyser
Porcupine Hills
Lower Geyser Basin
Fountain Flat Dr
Firehole Lake Dr
Sentinel Creek
Twin Buttes
Firehole Lake
Goose Lake
Grand Prismatic Spring
Great Fountain Geyser
Whiskey Flats Picnic Area
Fairy Falls
Midway Geyser Basin
Fairy Falls Trailhead
White Creek
Fairy Creek Trail
Little Firehole Meadows
Midway Geyser Basin
Mallard Creek
Mystic Falls Trail
Mystic Falls
Biscuit Basin
Upper Geyser Basin
Old Faithful Geyser
Mallard Lake
DeLacy Lakes
Mallard Lake Trail
Black Sand Basin
See Upper Geyser Basin Map (p112)
Summit Lake Trail
Teal Lake
Craig Pass (8262ft)
Howard Eaton Trail
Kepler Cascades
Grand Loop Rd
Spring Creek Trail
Lone Star Geyser
Continental Divide
Shoshone Lake

OBSERVATION HILL

For an alternative view of the Old Faithful eruption, or for a pre- or post-eruption overview of the entire basin, follow a branch trail from the Firehole River up a couple of hundred vertical feet to Observation Point. From here you can descend to Solitary Geyser to rejoin the boardwalk for a 1.1-mile loop.

Solitary Geyser started off as a hot spring until it was diverted into a swimming pool in 1915 (the pool was dismantled in 1950). The lowering of the water level turned the spring into a geyser, triggering eruptions that continue to this day, even though water levels have returned to normal. Small sudden bursts occur every four to eight minutes.

GEYSER HILL

This collection of geysers closest to Old Faithful is most easily visited clockwise on the inner boardwalk loop. If you have limited time, focus on this short loop. If you plan to visit the Main Loop as well, then visit the following at the end of the Main Loop.

Not far from Old Faithful is the unmarked **Chinese Spring**, named after an Asian (actually Japanese) laundry that once operated here. Dirty clothes were put into the spring along with soap, and the owners waited for the clothes to fly out, apparently clean, in an induced eruption. Don't try a repeat performance, unless you want a citation.

From Old Faithful head anti-clockwise and then take the right branch to cross the Firehole River on a bridge. Riverside **Blue Star Spring** was the site of a macabre incident in winter 1996–97, when a young bison fell into the boiling waters and died, causing the pool to smell like beef soup for days.

Seepage from **Giantess Geyser** and **Vault Geyser** has created geyserite terraces that look like scaled relief maps. Giantess springs to life between two and six times a year, though when active the geyser erupts twice hourly for up to 40 hours. The surrounding area shakes from underground steam explosions just before it erupts. Vault Geyser was inactive for a decade until bursting back into life in 1998.

Doublet Pool is known for its deep-blue color, thin scalloped geyserite border and the occasional thumping that emanates from collapsing steam and gas bubbles deep underground. **Aurum Geyser** (*aurum* means gold in Latin) is thought to be connected somehow to water deposits in the meadow behind it. There are some lovely disc-shaped formations here. It erupts to 20ft every 2½ to five hours.

The **Lion Group** is a gathering of four interconnected geysers (two lions and two cubs), whose eruptions are preceded by a roar, hence the name. **Heart Spring** is said to resemble the shape of a human heart.

Beehive Geyser erupts twice a day, rising up to 200ft through its 4ft-high cone-shaped nozzle, and is the second- or third-tallest regularly active geyser in the park. Beehive has an 'indicator' – a smaller vent that, when active, signals the main eruption.

Erupting every 20 minutes, **Plume Geyser** is one of the easiest geysers to catch. It's also one of the basin's youngest geysers, created by a steam explosion in 1922. Interestingly, its eruptions seem to have different phases by night and day. Nearby **Anemone Geyser** erupts every 15 minutes or so.

Rangers lead 1½-hour walks of Geyser Hill daily at 8:30am.

MAIN LOOP

Along the tarmac trail in front of the Old Faithful Inn is **Castle Geyser**, whose huge cone, resembling a bleached sand castle, attests to its status as the oldest geyser in the region, somewhere between 5000 and 15,000 years old (and built atop an even older spring). Castle goes off every 13 hours or so and can be predicted to within two hours – times are posted beside the geyser. The water eruption is followed by a noisy 30-minute steam phase, as the heat and steam energy long outlast the water supply.

Nearby, 42ft-deep **Crested Pool** is almost constantly boiling, at temperatures of around 200°F (93°C). This is one of the best places to get overviews of the basin.

The predictable **Daisy Geyser** lets loose at an angle up to 75ft every three hours or so and can be predicted to within 45 minutes, except when nearby **Splendid Geyser** erupts. Splendid is one of the largest in the

Geyser Country

Top Sights

1 Grand Prismatic Spring B4

Sights

2 Fountain Paint Pot C4
3 Ojo Caliente Hot Spring B3

Activities, Courses & Tours

4 Firehole Lake Drive C4
5 Lone Star Geyser Trail C6

Sleeping

6 Madison Campground B2

Upper Geyser Basin

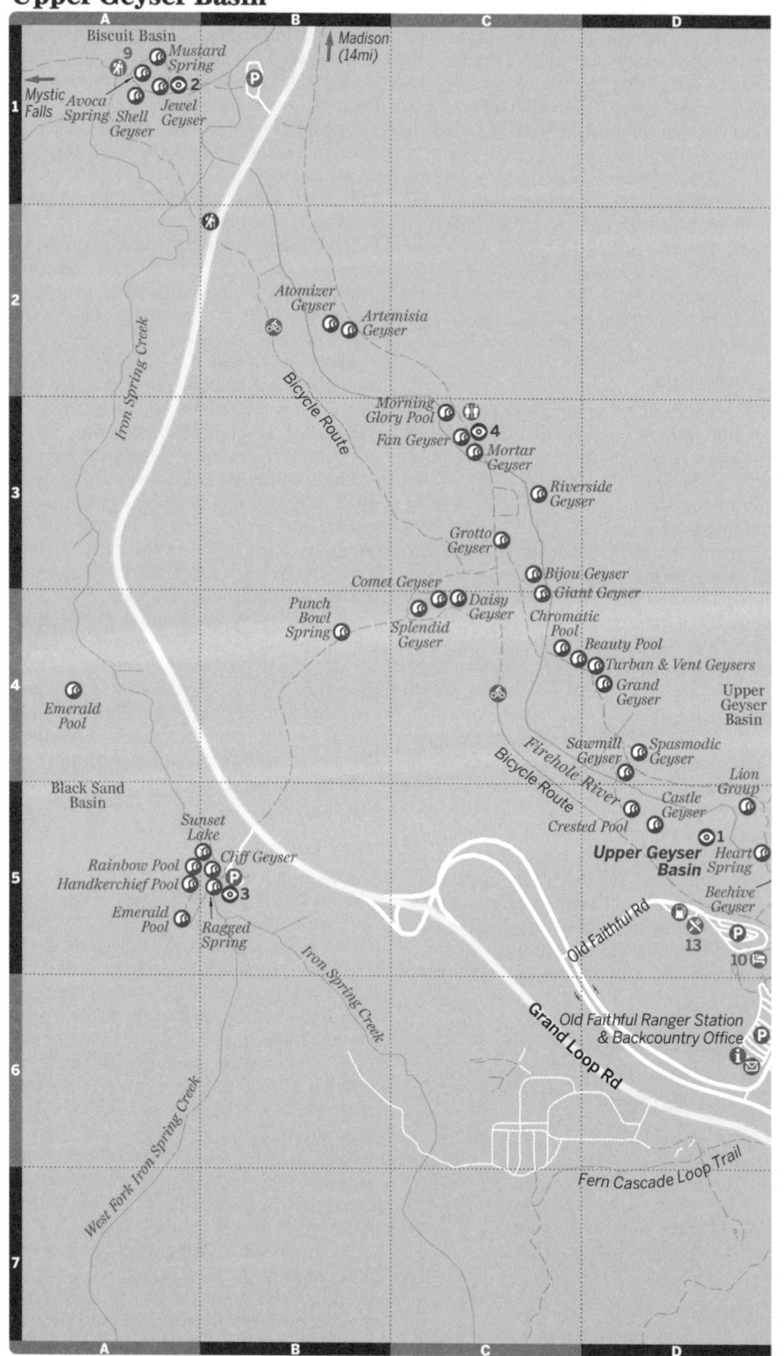

Biscuit Basin
Mustard Spring
Mystic Falls
Avoca Spring
Shell Geyser
Jewel Geyser
Madison (14mi)
Atomizer Geyser
Artemisia Geyser
Iron Spring Creek
Bicycle Route
Morning Glory Pool
Fan Geyser
Mortar Geyser
Riverside Geyser
Grotto Geyser
Bijou Geyser
Giant Geyser
Comet Geyser
Punch Bowl Spring
Daisy Geyser
Splendid Geyser
Chromatic Pool
Beauty Pool
Turban & Vent Geysers
Grand Geyser
Upper Geyser Basin
Emerald Pool
Sawmill Geyser
Spasmodic Geyser
Firehole River
Bicycle Route
Lion Group
Black Sand Basin
Castle Geyser
Crested Pool
Sunset Lake
Upper Geyser Basin
Heart Spring
Cliff Geyser
Rainbow Pool
Handkerchief Pool
Beehive Geyser
Emerald Pool
Ragged Spring
Old Faithful Rd
Iron Spring Creek
Grand Loop Rd
Old Faithful Ranger Station & Backcountry Office
West Fork Iron Spring Creek
Fern Cascade Loop Trail

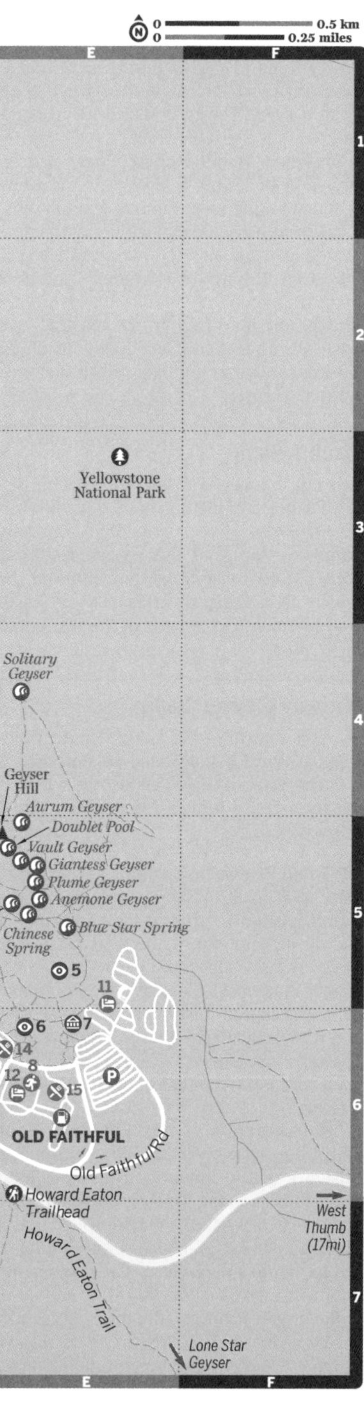

region but erupts irregularly – apparently sometimes triggered by a change in atmospheric pressure, which slightly reduces the pool's boiling point. Don't confuse Daisy with the larger, constantly splashing cone of **Comet Geyser**. All three geysers are linked by underground chambers.

Grotto Geyser erupts every eight hours for anywhere between one and 10 hours. The cone takes its weird shape from trees that have been encased in the geyserite. Increased activity in Grotto generally means less activity in Giant Geyser. The picturesque **Riverside Geyser** puts on an amazing show when a 75ft column of water arcs into the Firehole River, often capped by a rainbow. Twenty-minute outpourings occur about every six hours; water spilling over the cone signals an imminent eruption.

Across the Firehole River, riverside **Fan** and **Mortar Geysers** erupt infrequently but in unison, with Fan bursting water out of 17 individual jets.

Upper Geyser Basin

Top Sights

1 Upper Geyser Basin....D5

Sights

2 Biscuit Basin....A1
3 Black Sand Basin....B5
4 Morning Glory Pool....C3
5 Old Faithful....E5
Old Faithful Inn....(see 10)
6 Old Faithful Visitor Education Center....E6
7 Yellowstone Art and Photography Center....E6

Activities, Courses & Tours

8 Bear Den Rentals....E6
9 Mystic Falls & Biscuit Basin....A1

Sleeping

10 Old Faithful Inn....D5
11 Old Faithful Lodge Cabins....E5
12 Old Faithful Snow Lodge....E6

Eating

Bear Paw Deli....(see 10)
Geyser Grill....(see 12)
Obsidian Dining Room....(see 12)
13 Old Faithful Basin Yellowstone General Store....D5
14 Old Faithful Inn Dining Room....E6
Old Faithful Lodge Cafeteria....(see 11)
15 Old Faithful Yellowstone General Store....E6

Drinking & Nightlife

Firehole Lounge....(see 12)

Next comes beautiful **Morning Glory Pool**, from where hard-core geyser gazers can follow a walking trail to several minor features such as **Artemisia Geyser**, named for its similarity to the color of sagebrush (Artemisia), and **Atomizer Geyser**, named for the large amounts of steam that follow its minor eruptions.

Heading back toward Old Faithful, take the boardwalk that branches off the cycle path to **Giant Geyser**, which produces stupendous eruptions but may be dormant for decades (it erupted several times in 2018). Eruptions can last an hour, reach heights of 180ft to 250ft and expel an astonishing one million gallons of hot water. The cessation of otherwise continuous **Bijou Geyser** nearby signals an imminent eruption of Giant Geyser.

The strikingly colorful **Chromatic Pool** and **Beauty Pool** are linked, so when one drops the other rises.

Next is **Grand Geyser**, ranking as the world's tallest predictable geyser (150ft to 180ft). It spews in bursts every eight hours or so and lasts about 12 minutes. It will often pause after nine minutes and then restart after a minute or so; the subsequent bursts are typically the most spectacular. Grand is a fountain geyser, not a cone like Old Faithful. Nearby **Turban Geyser** acts as a trigger for Grand and, along with **Vent Geyser**, continues to rage for one to two hours after Grand subsides.

Sawmill Geyser is in eruption about 30% of the time, but its extents are highly variable. Water spins violently in its crater like a circular saw. Nearby **Spasmodic Geyser** is also in eruption a third of the time and erupts from more than 20 vents.

Rangers lead 1½-hour walks of the Upper Geyser Basin daily at 5:30pm.

Black Sand Basin

This geyser basin (Map p112), 1 mile northwest of Old Faithful, has a few interesting features. The eponymous black sand is derived from weathered volcanic glass (obsidian). You can access Black Sand Basin by car or, better, by foot from Daisy Geyser. Rangers lead hour-long walks here daily at 1pm.

Cliff Geyser is named for the geyserite wall that separates the geyser from Iron Spring Creek and is a frequent splasher. Nearby **Ragged Spring** frequently joins in the action with 12ft bursts. **Emerald Pool** looks like an exquisite flower with a lovely orange lip and gets its pretty color from yellow bacteria that blend with blue reflected from the sky. **Rainbow Pool** is connected underground to nearby Sunset Lake and is one of the more colorful in the park, though it's hard to see. The ground under the boardwalks here is literally boiling.

Unsigned **Handkerchief Pool**, just to the south of Rainbow Pool, was once one of Yellowstone's most famous features. Visitors would place a handkerchief in the pool and watch it get sucked down and then spat out 'clean' through a side vent. The pool stopped functioning in the 1920s after a dimwit jammed logs into the opening, but it has since restored itself. Today it's illegal to throw anything into any of Yellowstone's thermal features.

Biscuit Basin

Two miles north of Black Sand Basin, Biscuit Basin (Map p112) is named for biscuit-like deposits that surrounded stunning **Sapphire Pool**, but these were destroyed during violent eruptions that followed the nearby 1959 Hebgen earthquake. If you're low on time, this is one basin you could safely miss.

Midway Geyser Basin

Five miles north of Old Faithful and 2 miles south of the Firehole Lake Dr entrance is Midway Geyser Basin. The key sight here is the algae-tinged indigo waters of the Grand Prismatic Spring.

★ **Grand Prismatic Spring** HOT SPRINGS
(Map p110) At 370ft wide and 121ft deep, Grand Prismatic Spring is the park's largest and deepest hot spring. It's also considered by many to be the most beautiful thermal feature in the park. Boardwalks lead around the multicolored mist of the gorgeous pool and its spectacularly colored rainbow rings of algae. From above, the spring looks like a giant blue eye weeping exquisite multicolored tears.

The spring drains into **Excelsior Pool**, a huge former geyser that blew itself out of existence in the 1880s with massive 300ft explosions of water. The last eruptions here were in 1985, when the pool erupted almost continuously for 46 hours before lulling itself back into a deep sleep. The pool continually discharges an amazing 4000 gallons of boiling water a minute into the Firehole River – according to T Scott Bryan's *The Geysers of Yellowstone*, that's enough to fill 300,000 automobile gas tanks every day. More water is expelled here in a single day than Old Faithful releases in two months. You can admire the yellow-and-orange runoff as you approach the basin over the bridge.

The features are linked by a 0.5-mile boardwalk; allow for 30 minutes here, after you find parking.

For the most dramatic photos of Grand Prismatic Spring, drive south to Fairy Falls (p68) trailhead and walk for 1 mile to the new overlook platform on the hillside.

Lower Geyser Basin

Separate roads access the three main sections of this sprawling thermal basin: the main Grand Loop Rd passes Fountain Paint Pot; the one-way Firehole Lake Dr loops off the main road to Great Fountain and other geysers; and Fountain Flat Dr offers access to hiking trails and minor thermal features. The latter two roads both offer the potential for a short bike ride.

FIREHOLE LAKE DRIVE

Firehole Lake Dr is a one-way, 3-mile road starting 2 miles north of Midway Geyser Basin and about 1 mile south of the Fountain Paint Pot parking lot. It passes several pretty pools and large geysers, including lovely Firehole Spring and then huge **Great Fountain Geyser**, which soars up to 200ft in a series of wide staccato bursts every 11 hours or so. Eruption times are predicted by the visitor center at Old Faithful to within a couple of hours, and you'll often find people waiting with a picnic lunch and a good book. The crater begins to overflow 1½ hours before an eruption and violent boiling signals an imminent eruption, which can last one hour.

The nearby 30ft cone of **White Dome Geyser** usually erupts every half-hour or so. Nearby **Pink Cone Geyser** gets its color from manganese-dioxide deposits. A road was built right across the side of this cone in the 1930s.

Firehole Lake is a large hot spring ringed by several small geysers, including the raging waters of Artesia Geyser and the sensuous black-and-tan smoothness of Young Hopeful.

Runoff from Firehole Lake flows into **Hot Lake** (also known as Black Warrior Lake) across the road, which offers more geysers and even a small cascade of boiling water. **Steady Geyser** is in continual eruption through one of two vents.

FOUNTAIN PAINT POT

Roughly midway between Madison Junction and Old Faithful, Fountain Paint Pot Nature Trail takes in four types of thermal features along a 0.5-mile boardwalk loop. The Fountain Hotel, one of the park's earliest lodges, was located here until 1917.

Just past pretty Silex Spring, **Fountain Paint Pot** is a huge bowl of plopping goop that ranks as one of the biggest in the park. The action is sloppiest in spring, with some mud pots drying up by August. The area around the thermal features is slowly being drowned in deposits, while a grassy basin beyond supports the park's largest bison herd.

The mud pots are the top-billed comedians of the show. **Red Spouter** is particularly interesting, since it acts like a muddy hot spring in early summer, only to become a mud pot and then a fumarole later in the year. It only appeared after the huge Hebgen Lake earthquake of 1959. Morning and Fountain Geysers are impressive but infrequent gushers; the latter drains into Spasm Geyser.

Clepsydra Geyser has erupted almost constantly since the 1959 earthquake. The geyser was named Clepsydra (Greek for 'water clock') at the time, when it used to go off every three minutes on the button. **Jelly Geyser** does indeed look like an upside-down bowl of Jell-O.

In 1981 **Celestine Pool** was the site of one of the park's most famous accidents, when a young Californian man dived headfirst into the hot spring to save his dog, which had decided to cool off in the enticing pool. Sadly, both died as a result of their burns.

For a map of Fountain Paint Pot and Firehole Lake Dr, pick up the park-service trail guide ($1). Rangers lead tours here three times a week at 9am.

FOUNTAIN FLAT DRIVE

This former freight road turns off the Grand Loop Rd at the pleasant **Nez Percé picnic area** (with toilets) and continues south for 1.5 miles to a hiking and cycling trailhead. From here the road is accessible to cyclists and hikers all the way to Fairy Falls trailhead, 4 miles away. The trail is wheelchair accessible for 2.2 miles to the Goose Lake (OD5) campsite, one of two wheelchair-accessible backcountry campsites in the park.

FIREHOLE CANYON DRIVE

The one-way Firehole Canyon Dr leaves the Grand Loop Rd just south of Madison Junction. The road passes 40ft-high **Firehole Falls** at the foot of towering dark rhyolite cliffs, but the main attraction here is the lukewarm **Firehole Swimming Area** (no fee), one of the few locations in the park that's open for swimming. The kids will love it. There are two toilets here but limited parking. Note that the swimming area is closed in early summer due to high runoff; a sign at the beginning of the drive indicates whether it's open.

MADISON TO WEST YELLOWSTONE

Madison Junction sits at the confluence of the Firehole, Madison and Gibbon Rivers. Towering above the small junior ranger station is **National Park Mountain** (7500ft), which commemorates the spot where, in 1870, the idea of preserving Yellowstone was allegedly first mentioned.

The Madison Valley is of interest mainly to anglers and wildlife-watchers, though all will appreciate the sublime afternoon light and active herds of deer, elk and bison. Due to the long snow-free season many elk live in the valley year-round, while bison migrate through the valley between their winter habitat near the park's western boundary and summer grazing in the Hayden Valley. The 14-mile road to West Yellowstone is also one of the park's busiest tourist corridors.

Two miles east of Madison, the family-friendly **Harlequin Lake Trail** leads 0.5 miles north to a pond. Rangers lead a hike here on Monday mornings. The trailhead is also a fine place to spot wildlife in the lovely valley to the south. Elk often lie in the meadows, with only their heads poking above the long grass.

From here the road threads between volcanic bluffs, with towering Mt Haynes (8235ft) on the left and Mt Jackson on the right, and past several excellent fly-fishing spots, before the valley opens up to views of the distant Gallatin Range.

Halfway along the road the Seven Mile Bridge are the Madison River picnic area, popular with fly-fishers, and the Gneiss Creek trailhead. The area south of the road is closed to protect a trumpeter-swan habitat. In 1988 this section of the park was engulfed in the North Fork fire, the largest of that summer's giant blazes.

Four miles further, **Riverside Drive** is a 1-mile, two-way road that's useful for fishing access and perhaps some family cycling. Three miles later the Two Ribbons Trail is a 0.75-mile, wheelchair-accessible trail that offers a fairly dull loop or point-to-point stroll through some fire burns.

Shortly after you enter Montana, about 2 miles before West Yellowstone, the dirt Barnes Rd to the north accesses several more fishing spots. And then suddenly, just like that, you are out of the wilderness and in the middle of bustling West Yellowstone.

OLD FAITHFUL TO WEST THUMB

Three miles into the 17-mile drive between Old Faithful and West Thumb is **Kepler Cascades**, where a wooden platform offers fine views of the 125ft falls. Just past the

EASY BACKCOUNTRY OVERNIGHTS

Taking your kids or spouse on their first backpacking trip? The following backcountry sites are all within 2 miles of the trailhead, perfect for easy access and an emergency exit.

Blacktail Creek Site 1A1 is 1.8 miles from Blacktail trailhead; campfires allowed.

Lava Creek 1A3 is 1.4 miles from the Lava Creek picnic area trailhead past Undine Falls. Requires an uphill hike back to the trailhead.

Indian Creek 1B1 is 1 mile from Indian Creek Campground/Bighorn Pass trailhead.

Ice Lake 4D1 and 4D2 are on the lakeshore; 4D3 is an accessible site with a pit toilet five minutes' walk from the road. Buggy before July.

Cascade Lake 4E4 is 1.7 miles from Cascade Lake (p62) trailhead.

Norris Campground 4F1 is 2.3 miles up Solfatara Creek.

Ribbon Lake 4R1 and 4R2 are 2 miles from Artist Point trailhead (p60) in Canyon.

Lone Star Geyser OA1 is within earshot of the geyser (p68) and you can cycle most of the way there.

Fairy Falls OD1 is 2.5 miles from the trailhead (p68) and part of the hike can be done on a bike.

Sentinel Meadows OG1 is 1 mile from Fountain Freight Rd (p67).

cascades turnout is the parking area for the worthwhile hike or bike ride to Lone Star Geyser (p68). The road climbs past Scaup Lake, the Spring Creek picnic area (site of the park's biggest stagecoach robbery in 1908) and the Continental Divide trailhead before reaching **Craig Pass** (8262ft).

Craig Pass is an unassuming spot of deep significance. Lily-choked **Isa Lake** sits astride both the road and the **Continental Divide** and in spring it drains (or rather seeps) into both the Atlantic and the Pacific drainages. The west side of the lake drains year-round into the Firehole River, which flows into the Missouri and Mississippi Rivers before finally reaching the Atlantic to the east; the east side (in spring only) flows into Shoshone Lake and then the Lewis, Snake and Columbia Rivers and thus the Pacific Ocean to the west. The lake was named after Isabelle Jelke, the first park tourist to visit the lake, and it freezes solid in winter under around 15ft of snow.

From the pass, the road descends to the **DeLacy Creek** picnic area and the separate trailhead for hikes to Shoshone Lake (p69) 1¼ hours' walk away. Walter Washington DeLacy was an army engineer and surveyor who helped map Yellowstone's geyser basins. Shortly further on, there's a tantalizing sliver of a view toward remote Shoshone Lake. From here the road ascends back across the Continental Divide (8391ft) before finally descending to excellent views of Yellowstone Lake and the turnoff to West Thumb.

Bechler Region

Visitors must go out of their way to find the Bechler (*Beck*-ler) region. Located in the remote southwestern area of the park, it cannot be reached from the main entrance points or loops. Known for its numerous waterfalls and the park's highest rainfall, the remote region, also known as Bechler Corner or Cascade Corner, is largely the preserve of hardy backpackers, outfitters and horseback riders who brave flooded streams, monster mosquitoes and boggy marshland to access beautiful backcountry with the park's largest waterfalls and outstanding thermal soaking springs. The 19,700-acre meadow is home to diverse wildlife, including sandhill cranes, moose and coyotes. Early-season visits are impractical here – trails are often flooded into July and mosquitoes can be brutal along the river until the beginning of August.

Visitors en route to a hike (p69) in the region, or traveling Grassy Lake Rd, might want to detour by car or foot to the **Cave Falls** cascades and swimming hole.

Bechler is accessed via Bechler Ranger Station or Cave Falls trailhead, both off the mostly unpaved Cave Falls Rd via US 20, 26 miles from Ashton, ID, itself a two-hour drive from West Yellowstone, MT, via ID Hwy 47 and Marysville Rd. Alternative approaches include coming from Driggs, ID, to the south (joining US 20), or the brutal, unpaved Grassy Lake Rd/Reclamation Rd from the turnoff just north of Flagg Ranch, part of John D Rockefeller Memorial Parkway, 2 miles south of Yellowstone's South Entrance – allow at least two hours from Flagg Ranch.

SLEEPING

Although competition for campsites and lodging may be fierce, there's nothing quite like falling asleep to the eerie sounds of bugling elk and howling wolves and waking to the sulfur smell of the earth erupting and bubbling.

You can make reservations for park accommodations and five of the park's 12 campgrounds through the park concessionaire **Yellowstone National Park Lodges** (Xanterra; ☎307-344-7311, 866-439-7375; www.yellowstonenationalparklodges.com). Online bookings are possible and essential for both hotels and campgrounds.

Camping in the Park

Most of Yellowstone's campsites are in natural junctions, areas once frequented by Native Americans as well as early trappers, explorers and the US Army. There are around 2200 formal campsites in the park, plus well over 100 backcountry sites. Noticeboards at park entrances indicate which campgrounds are full or closed.

Aside from backcountry campsites (which require a hike to reach), camping inside the park is allowed in 12 designated campgrounds only; camping is limited to 14 consecutive days in each site from July 1 to Labor Day, and 30 days for the rest of the year. Check-out time is 11am. A maximum of six people are allowed in each site.

The National Park Service has seven campgrounds, available on a first-come, first-served basis only. Call ☎307-344-2114 for recorded NPS campsite information.

Yellowstone National Park Lodges runs five of the park's 12 campgrounds (Canyon, Madison, Fishing Bridge RV Park, Bridge Bay and Grant Village) and these are pricier than the national-park campgrounds. They feature flush toilets, cold running water and vending machines, and a couple have showers (included in the price).

A few sites are reserved for backpackers and cyclists at all campgrounds except Slough Creek and Canyon. Slough Creek fills early, due to popularity with anglers and wolf-watchers. Canyon is popular because of its central location. Boaters favor Grant Village and Bridge Bay; canoeists and anglers often base themselves at Lewis Lake. The Madison Campground is closest to Old Faithful, though Grant Village isn't far off. Fishing Bridge is always full of RVs in midsummer, and reservations are essential.

Lodging in the Park

Today's cabins and campgrounds are direct descendants of classy turn-of-the-century hotels and Wylie tent camps, the latter an affordable early option that opened up the park to budget-minded auto tours. Of the cabin options, rustic Lake Lodge is the most peaceful, and Roosevelt Lodge offers the most authentic Western experience. Lake Yellowstone Hotel and Old Faithful Inn provide the park's most atmospheric and upscale accommodations. For reservations and information, call Yellowstone National Park Lodges.

YELLOWSTONE NATIONAL PARK CAMPGROUNDS

CAMPGROUND	LOCATION	DESCRIPTION	NO OF SITES	ELEVATIO (FT)
Canyon (p121)	Canyon Country	Huge 11-loop site slap-bang in the center of the park	273	7900
Madison (p123)	Geyser Country	Lovely riverside location & the closest campground to Old Faithful	278	6800
Bridge Bay (p121)	Lake Country	Multiple-loop mega-complex appealing to boaters & anglers	432	7800
Fishing Bridge RV Park (p122)	Lake Country	A reservations-essential, RV-only spot, with hookups	340	7800
Grant Village (p121)	Lake Country	Spacious & shady multi-loop complex with conveniences & the lake nearby	430	7800
Lewis Lake (p121)	Lake Country	Shady, quiet campground close to backcountry trails & the lake	85	7800
Indian Creek (p120)	Mammoth Country	Quiet, small, secluded & woodsy	70	7300
Mammoth (p119)	Mammoth Country	Fairly barren spot near the North Entrance, but the warmest site in spring & fall	85	6200
Norris (p122)	Norris	Quiet site with a walking trail to the nearby geyser basin	113	7500
Pebble Creek (p120)	Roosevelt Country	Fairly cramped site, popular with wolf-watchers in the nearby Lamar Valley	27	6900
Slough Creek (p120)	Roosevelt Country	A favorite with anglers, this site fills up the earliest in high season	16	6250
Tower Fall (p120)	Roosevelt Country	Small site that fills up quickly, with several hiking trails	31	6650

* Reservations possible through www.yellowstoneparklodges.com

** Campsite rate includes two hot showers

 *Drinking Water*   *Restrooms*  *Ranger Station*  *Wheelchair Accessible*  *Grocery Store Nearby*

Room prices are for double occupancy, but most lodges have rooms that sleep up to six for an extra $20 per person. All Yellowstone hotel rooms are non-smoking and none have televisions.

Three of Yellowstone's lodges (Canyon Lodge, Lake Yellowstone Hotel, Old Faithful Inn) price their rooms using market rates, so you'll get cheaper rates by booking in low season or well in advance. All other accommodations have fixed prices throughout the year.

Counter-intuitively, the busiest day for accommodations in Yellowstone is Wednesday, not the weekend, as many tour groups and fly-drive travelers arrive in the park midweek.

Mammoth Country

Camping

Mammoth Campground CAMPGROUND **$**
(Map p92; Mammoth; campsites $20; year-round) This barren, sagebrush-covered campground with sparse shade is on a hairpin bend in the road below Mammoth Hot Springs. It gets road noise, but its relatively low elevation makes it the warmest campground and a good choice for early- or late-season visits.

Eating and other facilities are in Mammoth, just to the south, or Gardiner, 5 miles north by the North Entrance. When staffed, the registration office assigns sites, accepts

OPEN	RESERVATION POSSIBLE?	DAILY FEE	FEATURES & FACILITIES
late May-early Sep	yes*	$30**	
early May–mid-Oct	yes*	$25.25	
late May–mid-Sep	yes*	$25.25	
early May-late Sep	yes*	$47.75**	
mid-Jun–mid-Sep	yes*	$30**	
mid-Jun–early Nov	no	$15	
mid-Jun–mid-Sep	no	$15	
year-round	no	$20	
mid-May–late Sep	no	$20	
mid-Jun–late Sep	no	$15	
mid-Jun–early Oct	no	$15	
mid-May–late Sep	no	$15	

Summertime Campfire Program

RV Dump Station

credit cards and offers change. There are several wheelchair-accessible and hiker/cyclist sites, and firewood is for sale between 6pm and 8:30pm. Join one of the ranger talks at the amphitheater at 9pm or 9:30pm, depending on the month.

Sites are first come, first served.

Indian Creek Campground CAMPGROUND $
(Map p92; Mammoth; campsites $15; ⏲early Jun–mid-Sep) Located 8 miles south of Mammoth Junction, this low-key spot is probably the park's most underused campground – most people speed by between Mammoth and Old Faithful – which is one point in its favor. Plus, it's often the last in the park to fill up.

It's set in open forest on a low rise, surrounded by moose territory, and there are several hiking trails nearby – to Indian Creek, along the former stagecoach road, or partway along the Bighorn Pass Trail (look for a handout detailing campground trails). Generators are not allowed, but firewood is sold. Sites are first come, first served.

Lodging

Mammoth Hot Springs Hotel HOTEL $$
(Map p92; cabins $109-183, hotel r $177; ⏲May–mid-Oct, mid-Dec–early Mar) A classy vibe, a good variety of accommodations and a useful location make this one of the park's most popular hotels. The main choice is between the hotel rooms in the main building and cabins out back. The main en-suite rooms echo the historic feel of the hotel, with some rooms boasting antique-style bathroom fittings and claw-foot tubs. Rooms were renovated in winter 2018–19.

The cabins (closed in winter) are mostly duplex units, with a porch to sit on, but if you value your privacy you can request a detached cabin. Families might like the two-bedroom rustic cabins ($213) without bathroom, which can sleep up to six. The cheapest rustic cabins come with a sink but share communal bathrooms in a separate block.

Frontier cabins ($183) come with private bathroom, shower and two double beds. Some have a queen bed and a private outdoor hot tub, enclosed in a privacy fence, for $305. The hotel suites ($587) have a living room and bedroom, the only satellite TV in the park, and can sleep four in two queen beds.

Roosevelt Country

Camping

Pebble Creek Campground CAMPGROUND $
(campsites $15; ⏲mid-Jun–late Sep) The park's remotest campground is set along the banks of a creek in grizzly habitat and surrounded on three sides by the rugged cliffs of the Absaroka Range. It's popular with hikers and wolf-watchers, even though the sites are a bit cramped. It's off Northeast Entrance Rd, 10 miles from the Northeast Entrance, at the lower end of Icebox Canyon.

The nearest showers and supplies are at Tower-Roosevelt Junction. The Pebble Creek hiking trail starts nearby and there's good fishing at Soda Butte Creek. Generators are not allowed. Most sites are pull-through. Sites are first come, first served.

Slough Creek Campground CAMPGROUND $
(Map p96; Tower-Roosevelt; campsites $15; ⏲mid-Jun–early Oct) This remote, peaceful site, 2.2 miles up an unpaved road, is in grizzly habitat along a prime fishing stream. Generators are not allowed. The campground is 10 miles northeast of Tower-Roosevelt Junction. An anglers' paradise that is also popular with wolf-watchers, it fills up by 9am in high season. Sites are first come, first served.

Tower Fall Campground CAMPGROUND $
(Map p96; Tower-Roosevelt; campsites $15; ⏲mid-May–late Sep) This small, secluded single loop of 31 sites is high above Tower Creek in a cool, open pine forest. There are hiking trails up Tower Creek and groceries at nearby Tower Fall general store. Hiker/cyclist sites are available. Sites are first come, first served.

Lodging

Roosevelt Lodge CABIN $$
(Map p96; ☎866-439-7375; www.yellowstonenationalparklodges.com; Tower-Roosevelt; cabins with/without bath $170/102; ⏲Jun-early Sep; 🐾) Founded in 1906 as a tented camp, present-day Roosevelt Lodge was built in 1919 and retains an old-timey cowboy feel, offering 80 rustic cabins, horseback rides and a Wild West cookout in the heart of sagebrush country. Frontier cabins come with private bathroom, while the simpler Roughriders share communal wash blocks offering hot showers and ice.

For groups, families or couples traveling together, the Roughrider cabins are a good deal as some have three beds for the same base rate, meaning you can shoehorn six people in here for around $25 a head! The simple but pleasant wooden cabins come with log-burning stove, though the one-bed cabins are cramped (because it's the same price, book a larger cabin). All beds are doubles rather than queens, so they can be small for couples. There are no en-suite bathrooms and there's no running water in the room.

Frontier cabins are nicely decorated and come with private bathroom, electric heating and two or three double beds, but there are only 12 of these. There are two wheelchair-accessible Frontier cabins with private bathroom.

Cabins should be booked at least six months in advance, though you might find a Roughrider available at shorter notice. There are a few outdoor grills if you want to cook your own food. There's good hiking nearby; the hike to Lost Lake (p58) starts from just behind the lodge.

Canyon Country

Camping

Canyon Campground CAMPGROUND $
(Map p95; campsites $30; late May-early Sep) This huge campground is the most densely forested in the park, but the 11 loops are also some of the most cramped, which makes staying here feel like being churned through a Pink Floyd–style tourism meat grinder. Still, thanks to its central location as a base for day trips to other parts of the park, it's very popular.

There are showers and laundry on site (rates include two showers) and the restaurants and supplies of Canyon Village are nearby. Canyon also offers the most tent-only sites (four out of 11 loops) of any campground. Head to the amphitheater at 9pm or 9:30pm for the nightly campfire programs. Snow can linger here well into June.

Lodging

Canyon Lodges LODGE $$$
(Map p95; cabins $320, lodge r $210-397; Jun-Sep; @) This enormous complex dates from the opening of the park to mass tourism in the 1950s and 1960s, but has seen big changes in recent years. In 2014, 200 of the old cabins were replaced with seven environmentally friendly lodges, which offer modern, comfortable hotel rooms with coffeemakers and small bathrooms.

Here's a tip: premium rooms are marginally older than the pricier superior rooms but are noticeably bigger, so save yourself $50 and opt for the former. Some rooms come with a patio for $10 more.

The remaining cabins are laid out barracks-style, grouped into blocks of four or six, with two queen beds, coffeemaker, porch and tub/shower. A drive around the multiple low-rise, potholed and crumbling loops is like a drive back in time to a classic Middle American suburb.

Check-in is in the Washburn Lodge, which has a morning coffee stand (6:30am to 9:30am), a self-service laundry and a business center with wired internet access for guests.

Lake Country

Camping

Bridge Bay Campground CAMPGROUND $
(campsites $25.25; late May–mid-Sep) This mega-complex adjacent to the marina, 3 miles southwest of Lake Village, appeals to fishing and boating enthusiasts. Some lower sites offer lake views, but the more private ones are in the upper section. Showers and laundry facilities are 4 miles away at Fishing Bridge. There are campfire programs at 9pm or 9:30pm. Tent campers will appreciate the more desirable, forested, tent-only loops (I and J). Loops A, B and C are barren and exposed. Get groceries at the nearby marina general store.

Grant Village Campground CAMPGROUND $
(Map p102; www.yellowstonenationalparklodges.com; campsites $30; early Jun–mid-Sep) On the western shore of Yellowstone Lake, 22 miles north of the South Entrance, this is the park's biggest campground, with a nearby boat launch, an RV dump station and three of the loops dedicated to tent-only sites. Rates include two showers and there's a laundry and groceries. You'll find lovely spots for lakeshore strolls nearby.

The campground only opens when bears have stopped fishing the nearby spawning streams, which can be as late as June.

Lewis Lake Campground CAMPGROUND $
(South Entrance; campsites $15; mid-Jun–Oct) This forested campground is at the southern end of Lewis Lake, about 10 miles north of

DON'T MISS

YELLOWSTONE STARGAZING

The excellent 'Stars Over Yellowstone' interpretive program runs for two weekends in June and July at Madison Campground's amphitheater and is a must for budding astronomers. Astronomers from Museum of the Rockies offer a guided tour of the night sky from 9:30pm and there are all kinds of telescopes on site to play with, courtesy of the Southwestern Montana Astronomical Society. Check the park newspaper for details.

the South Entrance. It's popular with boaters and is near easy access to Lewis Lake and the Lewis River channel. Sites are first come, first served.

Snow often remains here through June because of its high elevation and shaded location, so it may not be the best early-season campground. Bring insect repellent. Generators not allowed.

Fishing Bridge RV Park CAMPGROUND **$$**
(Map p102; www.yellowstonenationalparklodges.com; Fishing Bridge; RV sites $47.75; ⏲ late May-late Sep) This is the only campground with full hookups (water, power, sewer) and due to heavy bear activity only allows hard-sided trailers or RVs. The 340 sites are crammed cheek by jowl and have no privacy. Rates include two showers, and there's a laundry. Reservations are essential.

Most sites are back-ins (some pull-throughs are due to be added in 2019), with a 40ft maximum length. The campground is located near the north shore of Yellowstone Lake, 1 mile east of Fishing Bridge Junction. Planned upgrades will close the park in 2019, but the sites should reopen by 2020.

Lodging

Lake Lodge Cabins CABIN **$$**
(Map p102; Lake Village; cabins $101-246; 📶🐾) The cabins at Lake Lodge are a relatively simple affair. The Western cabins ($246) are spacious, modern and ideal for families, either in forested back loops or (in the A loop) with French windows. The midrange Frontier cabins ($158) are a comfortable cheaper option. Note that Pioneer and Frontier cabins are scheduled to be closed for renovation in 2019, and the cramped Pioneer cabins are to be converted into Frontier cabins.

The best feature is the rustic main lodge, with rockers creaking on the porch, roaring fires inside, a dining hall and a laundromat.

Lake Lodge now also operates the Lake Cottages ($209), formerly run by Lake Yellowstone Hotel and located just behind that hotel.

Grant Village HOTEL **$$**
(Map p102; ☎307-242-3401; www.yellowstonenationalparklodges.com; Grant Village; r $270; ⏲ late May-Sep; 📶) The 300 condo-like boxes with standard hotel interiors at Grant Village are the closest lodging to Grand Teton for those getting an early start, and the rooms were completely updated in 2016. However, some rooms are still smallish and without much natural light.

★Lake Yellowstone Hotel HOTEL **$$$**
(Map p102; ☎866-439-7375; www.yellowstonenationalparklodges.com; Sandpiper r $320, hotel r $515-590; ⏲ mid-May–early Oct; @) Commanding the northern lakeshore, this buttercup-yellow colonial behemoth sets romantics aflutter. It harks back to a bygone era, though the rooms that cost $4 in 1895 have appreciated somewhat. The spacious main-building rooms were upgraded in 2014 and boast the park's only wired internet connections. Lakeside rooms cost extra, sell out first and don't guarantee lake views.

The recently updated Sandpiper annex (a former women's dorm building) lacks the grace of the main building, but rooms are comfortable and more economical. King-bed rooms here are slightly larger. The cottages behind the Sandpiper are now part of Lake Lodge, though they're still maintained by Lake Yellowstone Hotel. The hotel boasts a Green Seal gold rating for sustainability.

Everyone, including non-guests, is welcome to relax in the sprawling and inviting sunroom overlooking the lake. Room service and free valet parking were added in 2018.

🛏 Norris

Norris Campground CAMPGROUND **$**
(Map p92; Norris; campsites $20; ⏲ mid-May–Sep) Nestled in a scenic, open, lodgepole-pine forest on a sunny hill overlooking the Gibbon River and meadows, this is one of the park's nicest campgrounds. Sites are given on a first-come basis and the few loop-A riverside spots get snapped up quickly. Campfire talks are at 7:30pm and firewood is sold between 7pm and 8:30pm. Generators allowed 8am to 8pm.

There are fishing and wildlife-viewing opportunities nearby, Solfatara Creek trailhead is in the campground and the path to Norris Geyser Basin is just 1 mile long. You'll likely face an hour-long queue for sites on summer mornings. Get in the queue by 8am.

Geyser Country

Camping

Madison Campground CAMPGROUND $

(Map p110; 307-344-7311; www.yellowstonenationalparklodges.com; W Entrance Rd, Madison; campsites $25.25; May-Oct) The nearest campground to Old Faithful and the West Entrance occupies a sunny, open forest in a broad meadow above the Madison River. Bison and the park's largest elk herd frequent the meadows to its west, making for great wildlife-watching, and it's a fine base for fly-fishing the Madison. You can (and should) reserve your site in advance.

Tent-only sites are ideally placed nearer to the river. A junior ranger station (p128) and campground amphitheater lie just a short walk away and offer nightly ranger talks. The campground is just west of Madison Junction, 14 miles east of the West Entrance and 16 miles north of Old Faithful. There's an RV dump station, but the nearest food and showers are at Old Faithful.

Lodging

★ **Old Faithful Inn** HOTEL $$

(Map p112; 307-344-7311; www.yellowstonenationalparklodges.com; Old Faithful; Old House d with shared/private bath from $160/260, r $320-390; early May-early Oct) A stay at this historic log masterpiece is a quintessential Yellowstone experience. The lobby alone is worth a visit, just to sit in front of the impossibly large rhyolite fireplace and listen to the pianist upstairs. The cheapest 'Old House' rooms provide the most atmosphere, with log walls and original washbasins, but bathrooms are down the hall.

The lobby is a bit of a zoo during the day, but the day-trippers melt away with the sun. The building (p109) is full of charming hidden corners, with 327 rooms, a lovely balcony, library-style desks and century-old furniture.

The hotel has a vast variety of rooms, including some that are wheelchair accessible, and there are some tips to bear in mind. Old House rooms with two queens are larger than those with one, but they cost the same. Be aware that you can hear every footstep through the creaking wooden ceiling. Easily the best rooms without bathrooms are the two- and three-bed 'dormers' off the 3rd-floor lobby.

The only rooms that have a view of Old Faithful are a couple of 'superior' east-wing rooms ($390); these get snapped up a year in advance. Even if you face Old Faithful, you'll find that the pine trees block most of the view, so get a premium room in the east wing and save yourself dinner money.

The only bum rooms in the hotel are the west-wing lower-level 'garden view' rooms that are below the ground floor. Staff refer to these affectionately as the 'dungeon rooms.' Request a higher floor when booking.

Book well in advance (preferably a year), or you'll find there's no room at the inn.

Old Faithful Snow Lodge HOTEL $$

(Map p112; Old Faithful; cabins $129-219, r $301-323; May–mid-Oct & late Dec-Feb;) This modern lodge was built in 1999 in a 'New Western' style and offers the only winter accommodations available at Old Faithful. The main lodge has a stylish lobby decorated in bear and elk motifs and 134 comfortable, cozy and somewhat bland modern hotel rooms, with two double beds, down comforters, hair dryer, fridge and coffeemaker.

The pine-walled Frontier cabins ($129) are fairly simple but come with shower, sink and coffeemaker. The modern Western cabins ($219) are more spacious, with two queen beds, and are warmer in winter. Winter rates are around 10% higher. The main lodge has a laundromat and there's paid wi-fi in the lobby.

Old Faithful Lodge Cabins CABIN $$

(Map p112; Old Faithful; cabins with/without bath $159/96; mid-May–early Oct;) This 194-cabin lodge was built in 1923 and has its historical roots in Yellowstone's turn-of-the-century tent camps. It's not particularly atmospheric, though the rooms themselves are fine, especially the 66 new Frontier cabins recently converted from employee housing.

The remodeled Frontier cabins ($159) come with new carpet and a private bathroom, but no telephone. Rustic cabins ($96) have sinks with hot water, but the toilets and showers are in outside blocks. Most cabins are in blocks of twos or fours. Cabins 200, 201 and 203 have views of Old Faithful through the windows, while the lower loop backs onto the Firehole River.

Bechler Region

Cave Falls Campground CAMPGROUND $
(208-524-7500; www.fs.usda.gov/caribou; Bechler; campsites $10; Jun-mid-Sep) Situated in the Caribou-Targhee National Forest, just at the southwestern park border, by Bechler's trailheads and Cave Falls, the 23 pleasant woodsy sites line a river cliff offering a slight breeze to ward off mosquitoes. Sites feature picnic tables, fire rings and grills. Vault toilets, bear boxes and water are available.

EATING & DRINKING

Food in the park is split between campfire cuisine, cafeteria food, a couple of fast-food choices and the more pleasant dining rooms of the park's historic inns. The park concessionaire, Yellowstone National Park Lodges, runs most dining options, so don't be surprised if you get a serious dose of déjà vu every time you open a menu. That said, most places are pretty good value considering the prime real estate and there have been significant moves in recent years to add a range of healthy, gluten-free and locally sourced options. You can preview park menus at www.yellowstonenational parklodges.com.

The park's cafeterias are bland but convenient, and reasonably economical for families. All places serve breakfast and most offer an all-you-can-eat buffet that can quickly wipe out even the best-laid hiking plans. Kids' menus are available almost everywhere. Almost all offer sandwiches for lunch and heavier, pricier and more interesting fare for dinner.

There's also fast food at major junctions, plus snack shops and grocery supplies in the Yellowstone General Stores. The Grant Village, Old Faithful Inn and Lake Yellowstone Hotel dining rooms all require dinner reservations.

Mammoth Country

Mammoth Terrace Grill FAST FOOD $
(Map p92; Mammoth; mains $5-8; 8:30am-5:30pm late Apr–mid-Oct;) Line up for MacYellowstone-style burgers, bison brats and ice cream, along with some healthier options and breakfast choices.

★ **Mammoth Hot Springs Dining Room** AMERICAN $$
(Map p92; Mammoth; dinner mains $12-26; 6:30-10am, 11:30am-2:30pm & 5-10pm May–mid-Oct & mid-Dec–early Mar;) There are a few surprises in this elegant place, including a delicious dinner starter of Thai-curry mussels. Dinner is a serious affair, with Montana meatloaf, and pistachio-and-parmesan-crusted trout ($26). For dessert, try the 'Yellowstone caldera': a warm chocolate-truffle torte with a suitably molten center. Reservations only necessary in winter.

The attached **bar** (open until 11pm) has fireside seating in winter and serves restaurant starters if you just fancy a light dinner. Get a flight of four Montana microbrews for $6.25.

Roosevelt Country

Roosevelt Yellowstone General Store SUPERMARKET $
(Map p96; Tower-Roosevelt; 7:30am-9:30pm) Limited groceries and cold beer by the bottle (as well as bear spray) are available at this small store beside Roosevelt Lodge.

Roosevelt Lodge Dining Room AMERICAN $$
(Map p96; Roosevelt Lodge, Tower-Roosevelt; lunch & breakfast $10-12, dinner $14-28; 7-10am & 11:30am-9:30pm early Jun-early Sep) Popular for its applewood-smoked Western-style ribs and Wyoming cheese steak, the meaty menu here stretches to bison burgers and wild-game bolognese but has little for vegetarians. Take a post-lunch or pre-dinner stroll up to Lost Creek Falls, a 10-minute walk behind the lodge. The porch rockers are a fine place for a nightcap.

Old West Cookout BARBECUE $$$
(Map p96; 866-439-7375; Tower-Roosevelt; dinner & wagon ride adult/child $63/50; 3-5pm Jun-early Sep;) The Roosevelt Lodge activities center offers this fun cookout, with steak, beans and the kind of cowboy coffee you have to filter through your teeth. Kids will love it. The price includes a wagon ride out to the site of the former Yancey Hotel in Pleasant Valley. Book at least six months ahead, especially for July or August.

Swap the wagon ride for a one-/two-hour horse ride for an extra $24/31.

Canyon Country

Canyon Lodge Eatery CAFETERIA $
(Map p95; Canyon; meals $10-14; 6:30-10am, 11:30am-3pm & 4:30-9:30pm late May–mid-Sep) Freshened up in recent years, this cafeteria boasts bright orange and teal decor designed to recall the golden era of 1950s Yellowstone. Stations focus on pre-cooked wok dishes and American 'slow food fast' (ribs, country-fried steak), and there are some healthy packaged salads. The nearby Falls Cafe and bar serves pizza-like foot-long flatbreads ($8 to $11), next to an ice-cream stand.

Canyon Yellowstone General Store DINER $
(Map p95; www.visityellowstonepark.com; mains $10-12; 7:30am-8:30pm;) The fun, old-fashioned soda-fountain counter here churns out burgers, chili dogs and root-beer floats, plus there's ice cream and coffee (with refills). Breakfasts include blueberry flapjacks with bacon. The grocery store has fresh fruit and is open an hour later.

M66 Grill AMERICAN $$
(Map p95; 307-344-7311, 307-242-3999; Canyon; dinner mains $17-25; 7-10am, 11:30am-2:30pm & 4:30-10pm Jun-late Sep) This restaurant was recently updated and renamed to commemorate the park's Mission 66 movement, in which Canyon was the main player. Lunch features epic burgers, but the restaurant only truly spreads its chicken wings for dinner, with a famed prime rib *au jus*. Reservations are recommended for dinner.

Geyser Country

Old Faithful Basin

Yellowstone General Store FAST FOOD $
(Hamilton's Store; Map p112; www.yellowstonevacations.com; Old Faithful; mains $10-12; 7:30am-8:30pm May-Sep) The original knotted-pine Hamilton's Store near Old Faithful has a '50s-style diner counter, complete with fountain stools, that serves up burgers, malts and sandwiches. Come at 10am for a brief tour of Charles Hamilton's upper office to see the walls papered in $1.8 million worth of checks. A second, modern **general store** (Map p112; Old Faithful; mains $10-12; 7:30am-8:30pm May-Oct), next to the Old Faithful Snow Lodge, offers flatbreads, breakfast muffins, pre-packaged sandwiches, ice cream and groceries in a cafeteria-style setting.

Old Faithful Lodge Cafeteria CAFETERIA $
(Map p112; www.yellowstonenationalparklodges.com; Old Faithful Lodge, Old Faithful; mains $9-15; 11am-9pm mid-May–early Oct) Providing factory-style functionality rather than fine cuisine, this good-value place churns out solid choices like bison meatloaf and Asian noodle bowls. It's fast, but get here early before the buffet-style food gets too stewed. The best part is the view of Old Faithful from the side windows and porch rockers.

Bear Paw Deli DELI $
(Map p112; Old Faithful Inn; snacks $7-9; 6am-9pm) Just off the lobby of the Old Faithful Inn, the Bear Paw sells unappetizing pre-wrapped sandwiches, continental breakfasts and ice cream. Look for the original etched cartoon murals, which date from 1936, when this room housed the hotel bar.

Geyser Grill FAST FOOD $
(Map p112; sandwiches $5-9; 10:30am-9pm mid-Apr–early Nov & mid-Dec–mid-Mar;) Attached to the Old Faithful Snow Lodge, this fast-food place has breakfasts, burgers, salmon burgers and a bison-bratwurst sandwich. It's the first restaurant near Old Faithful to open in spring. There's nicer outside seating in front of the Snow Lodge.

Old Faithful Inn Dining Room AMERICAN $$$
(Map p112; 307-545-4999; Old Faithful; dinner mains $16-30, breakfast/lunch/dinner buffet $14/16.25/30.25; 6:30-10:30am, 11:30am-2:30pm & 5-10pm early May-Oct;) This buzzing dining room serves good-value steaks, salads and pasta, as well as breakfast, lunch and dinner buffets. The huge fireplace and wagon-wheel chandelier add to the rustic atmosphere, and the classical music on the balcony is an elegant touch. Without dinner reservations you'll end up eating at 5pm or after 9pm; join the waiting list at 5pm.

Obsidian Dining Room AMERICAN $$$
(Map p112; 307-344-7311; Old Faithful; breakfast buffet $14, mains $15-33; 6:30-10:30am & 5-10pm May–mid-Oct & mid-Dec–early Mar, lunch winter only) The quiet dining room at the Old Faithful Snow Lodge serves up a few unexpected dishes, such as the game-sausage sampler and bison ribs braised in Moose Drool Ale (the bison are farmed outside the Yellowstone ecosystem). The cozy fireside seats at the attached **Firehole Lounge** (5-11pm) get snapped up quickly in winter.

YELLOWSTONE NATIONAL PARK OPENING SCHEDULE

Yellowstone's opening schedule is complicated. Pin down specific opening and closing dates from www.nps.gov/yell/index.htm and www.yellowstonenationalparklodges.com.

Year-round The North Entrance at Gardiner and the north road from Gardiner to Cooke City via Mammoth and Tower-Roosevelt Junction. Mammoth Campground is also open year-round.

Mid- to late April The first of the other roads to open are the West Entrance Rd and the western side of the Grand Loop Rd: Mammoth to Norris, Norris to Madison and Madison to Old Faithful. Norris to Canyon opens a week later. Old Faithful Snow Lodge opens.

Early May The South and East Entrances open, followed by the road between West Thumb and Old Faithful over Craig Pass (8262ft). Old Faithful Inn opens. Mid-May Fishing Bridge RV Park, Mammoth Hotel, Old Faithful Lodge and Lake Yellowstone Hotel open.

End May The road between Tower and Canyon Junctions over Dunraven Pass (8859ft) is the last park road to open, usually by Memorial Day. The Beartooth Hwy between Red Lodge and Cooke City normally opens by Memorial Day but can be delayed a week or more by heavy snowfall.

Early June Canyon Village, Lake Lodge and Roosevelt Lodge open. Lewis Lake and Grant Village Campgrounds are the last to open.

September Park accommodations start to close, with Canyon Village and Roosevelt Lodge first to shut.

Mid-October The Beartooth Hwy and Dunraven Pass roads close for the year, as do accommodations at Old Faithful. Slough Creek and Lewis Lake Campgrounds are the last to close, at the end of the month.

November All park roads close on the first Monday in November, except for the Gardiner–Cooke City road.

Mid-December Entrances open to snowmobiles and snow coaches from the third Wednesday in December through to the second Monday in March, when spring plowing starts. Roads are then closed to vehicles but are open to cyclists in April. Old Faithful Snow Lodge and Mammoth Hot Springs Hotel open for the winter until early March.

Lake Country

Lake Yellowstone Hotel Deli DELI $

(Map p102; Lake Village; sandwiches $7-11; ⏲6:30am-9pm mid-May–late Sep) The revamped deli offers superior breakfast bagels and made-to-order sandwiches, Starbucks coffee and carrot-ginger soup, plus beer and half-bottles of wine perfect for a lakeshore picnic.

Lake Yellowstone General Store FAST FOOD $

(Map p102; mains $9-11; ⏲7:30am-8:30pm) Behind Yellowstone Lake Hotel, this branch of the park's general stores dates back 90 years and has a corner soda-fountain feel, down to the period 1938 counter stools. The simple food includes chili and nachos.

Fishing Bridge Yellowstone General Store FAST FOOD $

(Map p102; Fishing Bridge; mains $9-11; ⏲7:30am-9:30pm; 👪) This branch of the parkwide general stores has espresso coffee, waffles and root-beer floats served up at a fun retro soda-fountain counter that dates from 1931. Opening hours may be different when road construction hits in 2019–20.

Grant Village Dining Room AMERICAN $$

(☎307-242-3499; Grant Village; breakfast buffet $14, mains lunch $11-15, dinner $17-30; ⏲6:30-10am, 11:30am-2:30pm & 5-10pm late May-late Sep) The aroma from this high-beamed lodge could draw a band of grizzlies, who would doubtless enjoy the prime-rib sliders. Lunch options include sandwiches, soup and salads. Dinner could be prime rib followed by huckleberry crème brûlée. Dinner reservations advised; grab a perch at the tiny Seven Stool Saloon for a cold brew while you wait.

Lake House CAFETERIA $$

(Grant Village; breakfast buffet $14, dinner mains $10-24; ⏲6:30-10:30am & 5-9:30pm May-Sep) This quiet lakeshore spot offers casual breakfasts and dinners with the best lake views in the park. Dinner includes creative items like huckleberry chicken and wild-game meatloaf. On-site parking is limited; walk down from the main parking area or marina to the lakeshore. Hotel guests can request a shuttle from their lodge.

Lake Lodge Cafeteria CAFETERIA **$$**
(Map p102; Lake Village; dinner mains $12-16; ⏲6:30-10am, 11:30am-2:30pm & 4:30-10pm early Jun-early Oct) Changes are planned in 2019 for this rustic cafeteria at Lake Lodge. Lunch will focus on hand-ground burgers, while dinners will still center on carvery buffet fare such as prime rib, stuffed turkey and trout, plus lighter wraps and salads. Enjoying a drink from the lobby bar while watching the lake from a porch rocker is a pre-dinner highlight.

★Lake Yellowstone Hotel Dining Room AMERICAN **$$$**
(Map p102; ☎307-242-3899; www.yellowstonenationalparklodges.com; Lake Village; dinner mains $16-37; ⏲6:30-10am, 11:30am-2:30pm & 5-10pm mid-May–Sep; ✎) Save your one unwrinkled outfit to feast in style in Lake Yellowstone Hotel's dining room. Lunch options include trout, poached-pear salad and sandwiches. Dinner ups the ante with starters of lobster ravioli and mains of beef tenderloin, elk chops, quail and rack of Montana lamb. Dinner reservations are required.

Breakfast is à la carte, or opt for the blow-out buffet ($16), including smoked salmon and blintzes.

Map Room Bar & Espresso BAR
(Map p92; Mammoth Hot Springs Hotel, Mammoth; ⏲espresso 6:30-10am & 4-9pm) This new bar in the Map Room of the Mammoth Hot Springs Hotel serves espresso in the morning and afternoon, and beer and wine in the evening. For food, you'll have to go to the nearby dining-room bar.

SHOPPING

The nonprofit Yellowstone Forever (www.yellowstoneforever.org) operates bookstores at the park's visitor centers and information stations, and at Norris Geyser Basin. Hiking maps and guidebooks are available, as well as bear spray. Members get a 15% discount.

Yellowstone General Stores (www.yellowstonegift.com) are dotted around the park's major junctions and sell souvenirs, clothes, groceries, fishing licenses, cold beer and liquor. A couple sell fresh fruit and camping supplies such as gas canisters and bug spray.

Bear Aware SPORTS & OUTDOORS
(Map p95; ☎406-224-5367; www.bearaware.com; Canyon Visitor Education Center, Canyon; bear-spray rental 24/48hr $9.50/18.75, 1/2 weeks $28/32; ⏲8am-5:30pm end May-Sep) Rent bear-spray canisters ($50 deposit) from this booth outside Canyon Visitor Education Center and return them at one of the five Sinclair gas stations in the park, at Madison Campground (p123) or Cooke City Visitor Center.

Park Policies & Regulations

- It is illegal to collect plants, flowers, rocks, petrified wood or antlers in Yellowstone National Park.
- Firearms are allowed in the park under valid state or federal laws but are prohibited in park or concessionaire buildings.
- Swimming in waters of entirely thermal origin is prohibited.
- Permits are required for all backcountry trips and activities such as boating and fishing.
- Drones are not allowed in the park.
- Permits are required for overnights in the backcountry, and for boating, fishing and stock use.

Information

MEDICAL SERVICES

Lake Hospital (☎307-242-7241; www.yellowstone.co/clinics.htm; ⏲8:30am-8:30pm mid-May–mid-Sep)

Mammoth Clinic (☎307-344-7965; www.yellowstone.co/clinics.htm; Mammoth; ⏲8:30am-5pm Jun-Sep, 8.30am-5pm Mon-Thu, to 1pm Fri Oct-May)

Old Faithful Clinic (☎307-545-7325; www.yellowstone.co/clinics.htm; Old Faithful; ⏲7am-7pm mid-May–mid-Sep)

MONEY

ATMs at park accommodations and general stores. Cash only for some campgrounds. Tipping expected on horse rides and rafting trips and at dude ranches.

POST OFFICES

Mammoth Post Office (⏲8:30-11:30am & 12:30-5pm Mon-Fri) The only year-round post office.

Old Faithful Post Office (Map p112; ⏲8:30-1:30pm & 2:30-5pm Mon-Fri)

There are also post offices at Canyon, Lake Village and Grant Village.

SHOWERS & LAUNDRY

- Canyon Campground, Fishing Bridge RV Park and Grant Village Campground offer laundry and showers.
- Old Faithful Lodge and Roosevelt Lodge offer showers only, and Lake Lodge and Old Faithful Snow Lodge have laundry.
- Showers cost $4.50, plus $1.50 for a towel, and are open 7am to 1:30pm and 3pm to 9:30pm. Laundry costs $2.75 per load; laundries open 7am to 10pm, with a last load at 9pm.
- Two showers are included in campground fees at Canyon and Grant Village. All facilities close in winter.

TOURIST INFORMATION

Yellowstone visitor centers are usually open 9am to 6pm, with extended hours from 8am to 7pm in summer. Most are closed or open reduced hours Labor Day to Memorial Day. The Albright Visitor Center (p92) at Mammoth is open year-round, and the Old Faithful Visitor Education Center (p109) is open in winter. Check the park newspaper for current visitor hours.

The park produces a series of informative pamphlets ($1) on Yellowstone's main attractions. These are available at visitor centers and in weatherproof boxes at the sites.

Ranger stations (p71) are available at Grant Village , Lake Village, Lewis Lake, Bechler, Canyon Visitor Center, Mammoth, Bridge Bay, Tower Junction, Old Faithful, and the West and South Entrances. These are the best places to get detailed information on trail conditions and to arrange backcountry permits.

Central Backcountry Office (☎307-344-2160; YELL_Backcountry_Office@nps.gov) The central clearinghouse for backcountry permits. Note that permits are not collected here but from a backcountry office or ranger station.

Madison Junior Ranger Station (Map p110; ☎307-344-2821; ⊙9am-5pm Jun-early Oct) The station at Madison is a good place to stop if you have kids. There are plenty of kid-friendly activities, bear skins to stroke and talks every half-hour. Spotting scopes offer a close-up look at the elk that frequent the Madison Valley.

West Thumb Information Station (Map p102; ☎307-344-2876; ⊙9am-5pm late May-late Sep)

Yellowstone National Park Headquarters (Map p92; ☎307-344-7381; www.nps.gov/yell; Mammoth) At Fort Yellowstone in Mammoth. Most of the park's brochures are downloadable from the park website.

Getting Around

Unless you're part of a guided bus tour, the only way to get around is to drive. There is no public transportation within the park, except for a few ski-drop services during winter.

Yellowstone Roadrunner (☎406-640-0631; www.yellowstoneroadrunner.com; West Yellowstone) Taxi and charter service in West Yellowstone that offers one-way drops and shuttles for backpacking trips, though it's not cheap.

DRIVING

The speed limit in most of the park is 45mph, dropping to 25mph at busy turnouts or junctions.

Gas and diesel are available at most junctions. Stations at Old Faithful and Canyon are open whenever the park is open to vehicles. The Roosevelt station closes at the beginning of September, Fishing Bridge in mid-September, Grant Village in late September and Mammoth in early October. Stations are staffed from around 8am to 7pm and offer 24-hour credit-card service at the pump.

Towing, repair services and basic car parts are available at Yellowstone Park Service Stations (www.ypss.com) at the following locations:

Canyon (breakdown service ☎307-242-7644; ⊙May-early Oct)

Fishing Bridge (⊙late May-early Sep)

Grant Village (⊙late May–mid-Sep)

Old Faithful (⊙mid-Apr–early Nov)

Dial ☎307-344-2117 to check road conditions prior to your visit, as road construction, rock- or mudslides and snow can close park entrances and roads at any time.

ORGANIZED TOURS

Yellowstone National Park Lodges (p117) runs a slew of daily tours, all of which offer discounts for children aged 12 to 16 and are free for kids under 12. There are full-day tours of the upper and lower loops, half-day afternoon wildlife trips and dawn photo safaris, as well as trips to the Tetons. Most of these tours are on the wonderful Old Yellow Buses, a refurbished fleet of classic convertible 19-seater touring cars that plied the park's roads between 1936 and 1956. Resuming operation in 2007, they're guaranteed to add a touch of class to your sightseeing. See the 'Things to Do' section of the website for details on all tours.

Rangers also lead free guided hikes and sightseeing walks.

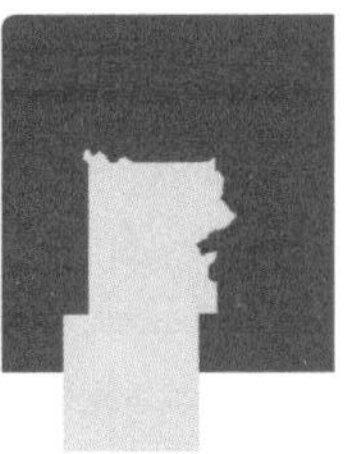

Around Yellowstone

Includes ➡

Why Go?

The 43,750-sq-mile Greater Yellowstone Ecosystem doesn't suddenly end at the park fence. Enveloping the park kernel is a protective cushion of national forests and wilderness areas that offer almost as much scenic splendor as the park itself, but without the crowds and the pesky permits. Try to allocate at least a few days to explore this exceptional area.

Latched onto Yellowstone Park's northern boundaries, the three gateway towns of Gardiner, West Yellowstone and Cooke City serve as functional visitor hubs, good for a bed and a bite to eat, but it's the four corridors that radiate out from the park that offer the real scenic draws. Plan your itinerary to combine the stunning Beartooth and Gallatin routes, or the Beartooth, Wapiti and Chief Joseph Scenic Hwy via the Wild West town of Cody, and you'll have the ultimate add-on to a classic Yellowstone trip.

Best Places to Eat

- ➡ Yellowstone Valley Grill (p151)
- ➡ 2nd St Bistro (p148)
- ➡ Chico Inn Restaurant (p149)
- ➡ Walkers Grill (p133)
- ➡ Red Box Car (p135)

Best Places to Stay

- ➡ Murray Hotel (p148)
- ➡ Chamberlin Inn (p145)
- ➡ Rainbow Ranch Lodge (p161)
- ➡ Chico Hot Springs (p149)
- ➡ 320 Ranch (p160)

Road Distances (miles)

	Billings	Bozeman	West Yellowstone	Cody	Gardiner
Bozeman	145				
West Yellowstone	230	90			
Cody	110	210	135		
Gardiner	170	80	55	130	
Cooke City	130	140	100	75	55

Note: Distances are approximate

Around Yellowstone

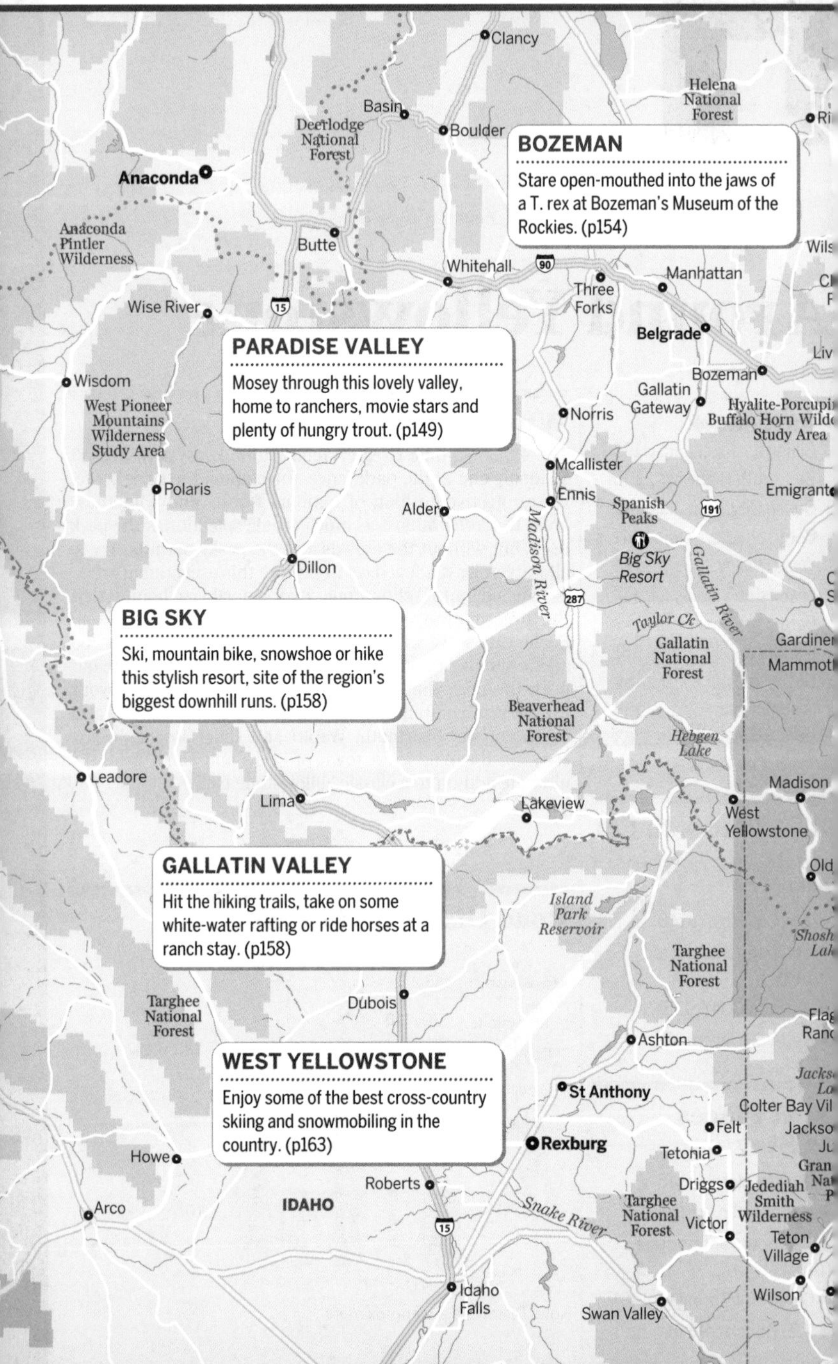

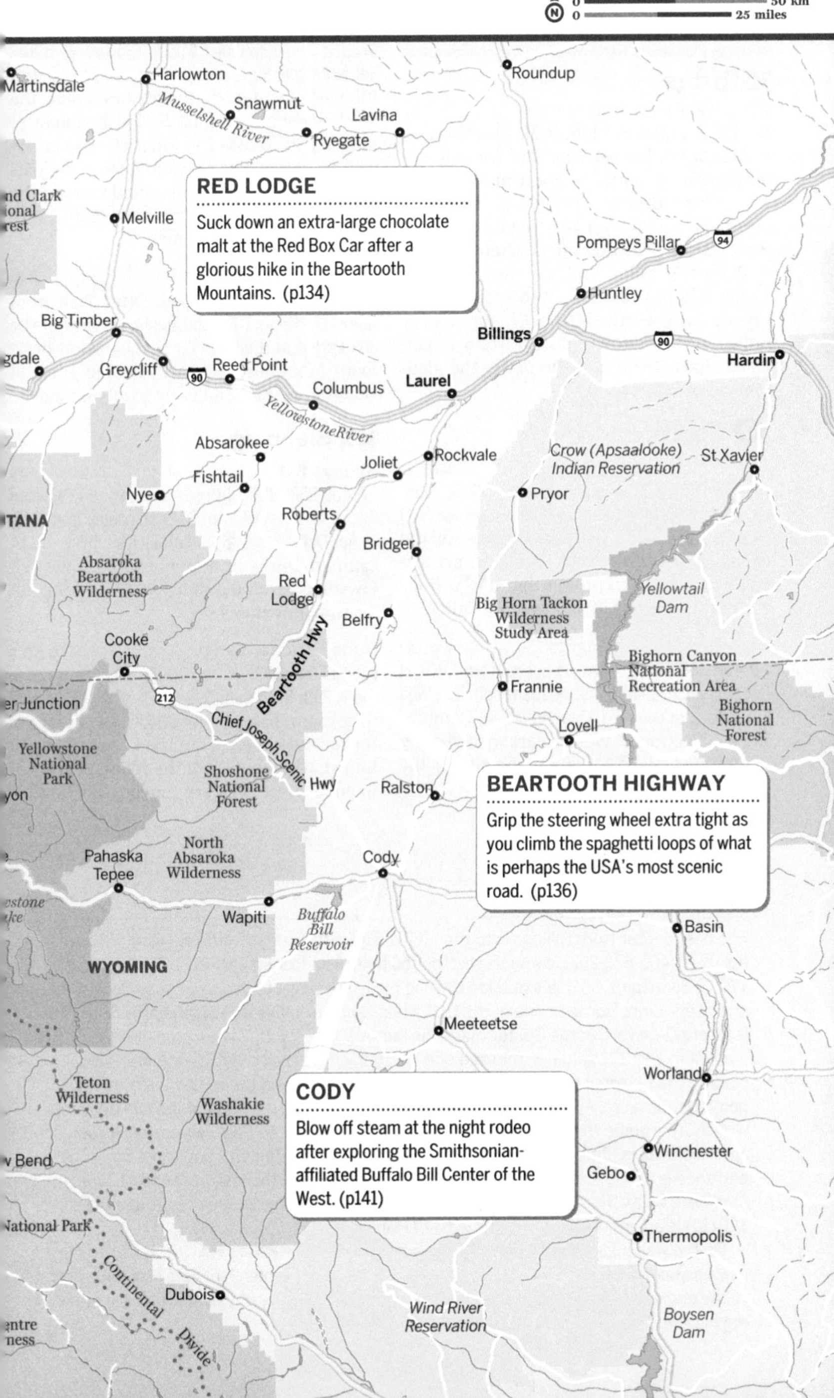

0 50 km
0 25 miles
Martinsdale
Harlowton
Roundup
Musselshell River
Snawmut
Lavina
Ryegate
RED LODGE
Suck down an extra-large chocolate malt at the Red Box Car after a glorious hike in the Beartooth Mountains. (p134)
Melville
Pompeys Pillar
Huntley
Big Timber
Billings
Hardin
Greycliff
Reed Point
Columbus
Laurel
Yellowstone River
Absarokee
Rockvale
Joliet
Crow (Apsaalooke) Indian Reservation
St Xavier
Fishtail
Nye
Pryor
Roberts
Bridger
Absaroka Beartooth Wilderness
Red Lodge
Yellowtail Dam
Big Horn Tackon Wilderness Study Area
Belfry
Beartooth Hwy
Cooke City
Bighorn Canyon National Recreation Area
Frannie
Bighorn National Forest
Chief Joseph Scenic Hwy
Lovell
Yellowstone National Park
Shoshone National Forest
Ralston
BEARTOOTH HIGHWAY
Grip the steering wheel extra tight as you climb the spaghetti loops of what is perhaps the USA's most scenic road. (p136)
North Absaroka Wilderness
Pahaska Tepee
Cody
Wapiti
Buffalo Bill Reservoir
Basin
WYOMING
Meeteetse
Teton Wilderness
Worland
Washakie Wilderness
CODY
Blow off steam at the night rodeo after exploring the Smithsonian-affiliated Buffalo Bill Center of the West. (p141)
Winchester
Gebo
Thermopolis
Continental Divide
Dubois
Wind River Reservation
Boysen Dam

BEARTOOTH ROUTE

Billings

☎406 / POP 110,300 / ELEV 3123FT

It's hard to believe laid-back little Billings is Montana's largest city. The friendly oil-and-ranching center is not a must-see but makes for a decent overnight pit stop, or a point of departure for Yellowstone National Park via the breathtaking Beartooth Hwy.

Pompey's Pillar and the further away Little Bighorn Battlefield National Monuments are worthwhile stops for history buffs, and downtown has a certain unpolished charm for those who prefer the modern West.

Sights

Western Heritage Center MUSEUM

(☎406-256-6809; www.ywhc.org; 2822 Montana Ave; adult/child $5/1; ⏲10am-5pm Tue-Sat) If you have time in Billings, explore the changing exhibits and excellent artifact collection here, representing the various cultural traditions of Yellowstone Valley.

Yellowstone Art Museum GALLERY

(☎406-256-6804; www.artmuseum.org; 401 N 27th St; adult/child $6/3; ⏲10am-5pm Tue, Wed & Sat, to 8pm Thu & Fri, 11am-4pm Sun) Combining a collection of Western art with visiting exhibitions, the YAM is on the site of the 1916 Yellowstone County Jail.

Moss Mansion HISTORIC BUILDING

(☎406-256-5100; www.mossmansion.com; 914 Division St; adult/senior $12/8; ⏲10am-4pm Tue-Sat, noon-3pm Sun Jun-Aug, shorter hours Sep-May) Billings' most interesting historic home, the Moss was built in 1903 by local captain of industry PB Moss. The Moorish-style entryway and atmospheric staff kitchens are particularly interesting. Fans should attend the special behind-the-scenes tour ($30) every second Monday in summer.

The Rims AREA

Cycle or hike Chief Black Otter Trail from near the airport for the best overview of the city (great at dusk) as far as the distant Beartooth Mountains, and to visit the grave of Yellowstone Kelly, an early scout and guide.

Sleeping

Billings KOA CAMPGROUND $

(☎406-252-3104; https://koa.com; 547 Garden Ave; tent/RV sites from $42/51, cabins from $95; ⏲Apr-Oct;) America's first KOA campground is in a scenic spot by the Yellowstone River, 0.5 miles south of I-90, not far from downtown.

Dude Rancher Lodge MOTEL $

(☎406-545-6331; www.duderancherlodge.com; 415 N 29th St; d from $99; @) This historic motor lodge looks a little out of place in the downtown area, but has been well maintained, with about half the rooms renovated to good effect. Western touches like tongue-

WORTH A TRIP

CUSTER'S LAST STAND

The best detour from Billings is to the **Little Bighorn Battlefield National Monument** (☎406-638-2621; www.nps.gov/libi; 756 Battlefield Tour Rd, Hwy 212 off I-90; per car $20; ⏲8am-8pm), 65 miles outside town in the arid plains of the Crow (Apsaalooke) Indian Reservation. Home to one of the USA's best-known Native American battlefields, this is where General George Custer made his famous 'last stand.'

Custer, and 272 soldiers, messed one too many times with Native Americans (including Crazy Horse of the Lakota Sioux), who overwhelmed the force in a frequently painted massacre. A visitor center tells the tale or you can take one of the five daily tours with a Crow guide through **Apsaalooke Tours** (☎406-679-2790; www.crow-nsn.gov/apsaalooke-tours.html; adult/child $10/5; ⏲hourly 8am-4pm Memorial Day-Labor Day). The entrance is a mile east of I-90 on US 212. If you're here for the last weekend of June, the **Custer's Last Stand Re-enactment** (www.littlebighornreenactment.com; adult/child $20/10) is an annual hoot, 6 miles west of Hardin.

On the way back, history buffs can pop into **Pompey's Pillar National Monument** (www.pompeyspillar.org; I-94 exit 23; per vehicle $7; ⏲visitor center 9am-6pm May-Sep), home to the engraved 1806 signature of William Clark and the only physical evidence remaining of Lewis and Clark's famed transcontinental journey.

BILLINGS BREWERY CRAWL

Billings has an impressive collection of craft breweries, all within a few downtown blocks. If you do decide to tackle the following walking tour in one gulp, arrange a taxi and start early – state law means that Montana taprooms can only serve until 8pm. Get a map of a similar walk at www.visitbillings.com.

Start off at the **Yellowstone Valley Brewing Company** (406-245-0918; www.facebook.com/YellowstoneValleyBrewing; 2123 1st Ave N; 4-8pm), referred to locally as the Garage, to sample its range of beers named after fishing flies. You'll often find good live music here.

One block southwest is **Überbrew** (406-534-6960; www.facebook.com/uberbrew; 2305 Montana Ave; 11am-9pm, beer until 8pm), the most polished (and our personal favorite) of the brewpubs and the best place to line your stomach with some pub food. The White Noise Hefeweizen here outsells the other brews three to one.

Continue down Montana Ave to grittier **Carter's Brewing** (406-252-0663; http://cartersbrewingbillings.com; 2526 Montana Ave; 4-8pm), next to the railway tracks, for a De-Railed IPA or a four-taster flight decorated with a rail spike. From here continue down Montana Ave for four more blocks and swing north to **Angry Hanks** (406-252-3370; http://angryhanks.com; 20 N 30th St; 4-8pm Mon-Fri, 3-8pm Sat), where for $3 a pint you can enjoy an Anger Management Belgian Wheat, Street Fight Imperial Red or Head Trauma IPA on the patio. It's worth trying the brown ale just to order a pint of 'Dog Slobber.'

Finally, head up to the restaurant-style **Montana Brewing Company** (406-252-9200; www.montanabrewingcompany.com; 113 N Broadway; 11am-2am) and toast your visit to the Little Bighorn Battlefield with a pint of Custer's Last Stout.

and-groove walls and cattle-brand carpet give it a welcoming rustic feel.

Riversage Billings Inn MOTEL $
(406-252-6800; www.riversageinns.com/billingsinn; 880 N 29th St; r incl breakfast from $108;) Sometimes you don't want an adventure, you just want a clean dependable bed in a spacious box. This budget offering by a local chain delivers exactly that.

Northern Hotel HOTEL $$
(406-867-6767; www.northernhotel.com; 19 N Broadway; r/ste $159/209;) The historic Northern combines its previous elegance with fresh and modern facilities that are a solid step above generic business hotel. Breakfast or lunch is in the attached 1950s diner, and Ten restaurant offers one of the best dinners in town.

Eating & Drinking

Downtown Billings has plenty of solid choices for food, and parking usually isn't a problem, especially in the evenings.

McCormick Cafe BREAKFAST $
(406-255-9555; www.mccormickcafe.com; 2419 Montana Ave; meals $8-12; 7am-3pm Mon-Fri, 8am-3pm Sat, 8am-2pm Sun;) For espresso, granola breakfasts, French-style crepes, good sandwiches and a lively atmosphere, stop by this downtown favorite that started life as an internet cafe.

Caramel Cookie Waffles EUROPEAN $
(406-252-1960; www.caramelcookiewaffles.com; 1707 17th St W; mains $4-8.50; 7am-5pm Tue-Sat;) Better known as the Dutch Brothers, this place bustles at lunch with superb soups, European pastries and the eponymous *stroopwafels*. It's worth arranging your entire Yellowstone itinerary around the weekly seafood bisque.

Harper & Madison CAFE $
(406-281-8550; www.harperandmadison.com; 3115 10th Ave N; mains $7-11; 7am-2pm Tue-Fri, to 1pm Sat) With a hefty dose of Martha Stewart, this sweet cafe does some brisk business. It's no wonder with the excellent coffee, homemade quiches, and gourmet salads and sandwiches. If you're rushing to hit the road, grab some French pastries to go.

★ **Walkers Grill** AMERICAN $$
(406-245-9291; www.walkersgrill.com; 2700 1st Ave N; tapas $7-18, mains $16-32; 4-10pm Mon-Fri, 5-10:30pm Sat & Sun) Upscale Walkers offers good grill items and fine tapas at the bar accompanied by cocktails crafted by expert mixologists. It's an elegant, large-windowed space that would be right at home in Manhattan, though maybe

without the barbed-wire light fixtures – or with. You owe it to yourself to try the duck confit fries.

Doc Harper's BAR
(406-200-7177; http://docharpers.com; 116 N Broadway; 4pm-midnight Mon-Sat) This long, narrow, pretty martini bar was opened by a lawyer who won a (hard-to-get) liquor license in a state lottery and named the place after his dad, a physician who delivered hundreds of babies in the area. Slink up to the mezzanine or sit at the bar and watch the cocktail magic happen.

Shopping

Base Camp SPORTS & OUTDOORS
(406-248-4555; www.thebasecamp.com; 1730 Grand Ave; 9:30am-8pm Mon-Fri, 9:30am-6pm Sat, 11am-5pm Sun) The place for last-minute outdoor gear, topo maps and that lost widget for your stove.

Information

Billings Visitor Center (800-735-2635, 406-252-4016; www.visitbillings.com; 815 S 27th St; 8:30am-5pm Mon-Fri) Can help with hotel reservations and free bike rental in summer. See also www.downtownbillings.com.

Getting There & Away

Downtown Billings is just off I-90 occupying a wide valley of the Yellowstone River. The **airport** (BIL; 406-247-8609; www.flybillings.com; N 27th St) serves major hubs (Salt Lake City, Minneapolis, Denver, Seattle, Portland, Phoenix, Las Vegas and some Montana destinations).

Red Lodge

406 / POP 2240 / ELEV 5568FT

Tiny Red Lodge – hiding in its quiet river valley – is the ideal small Montana mountain town. Once a thriving mining community, the brick buildings lining Main St are now a haven for hikers, climbers and skiers. For travelers, it's a pleasant place to grab a snack and fuel up before tackling the legendary Beartooth Hwy which switchbacks through the imposing mountains southwest of town on its way to Yellowstone National Park.

Sights

Carbon County Museum MUSEUM
(406-446-3667; www.carboncountyhistory.com; 224 N Broadway; adult/student $5/3; 10am-4pm Tue-Sat Jun-Aug, Fri & Sat only Sep-May) Antique guns and mining disasters dominate the exhibits here, but it's the 1912 Model T Ford, Yellowstone stagecoach and horrifying early electroshock machine that really grab the attention.

Yellowstone Wildlife Sanctuary ZOO
(406-446-1133; www.yellowstonewildlifesanctuary.org; 615 2nd St E; adult/child $10/4; 10am-4pm Wed-Mon Mar-Oct;) Families will love this nonprofit refuge for dozens of animals that can't be returned to the wild, including bears, lynx, a mountain lion and a sandhill crane. Check the website to time your visit with animal feeding. It's just northeast of town.

Carbon County Arts Guild Gallery GALLERY
(406-446-1370; www.carboncountydepotgallery.org; 11 W 8th St; 10am-5pm Mon-Thu, to 7pm Fri & Sat, noon-5pm Sun May-Oct, shorter hours Nov-Apr) FREE The old railroad depot on 8th St, one block west of Broadway Ave, is where local artists exhibit paintings, sculptures and mixed media.

Activities

Hiking

A mile south of Red Lodge, just north of the Beartooth Ranger District Office, West Fork Rd turns southwest off US 212 and continues for a bumpy 12 miles up West Fork Creek. Trailheads along the road offer good hikes, including the **Timberline Lake Trail** (9 miles return, elevation gain 2000ft) and **Basin Lakes National Recreation Trail** (trail 61, 7.4 miles return, elevation gain 2000ft). Bear in mind that much of the upper valley was scarred by wildfires in 2008. Nearby **Wild Bill Lake** is a wheelchair-accessible trail to a lake with accessible fishing. The valley has two United States Forest Service (USFS) campgrounds open in summer: Basin ($16) and Cascade ($13).

A rugged option further south is the short but strenuous 3.2-mile return trail to **Glacier Lake**, hidden high up in a glacial valley. Hikers have the option of continuing another mile to Little Glacier and Emerald Lakes. The trailhead is 8 miles southwest of Limber Pine Campground on rough, gravel Rock Creek Rd (Forestry Rd 421). You need fairly high clearance to attempt this road.

The **Lake Fork Trail**, accessed from the end of Lake Fork Rd (turnoff right about 2 miles before Parkside Campground), offers excellent longer day hikes to Lost Lake (5 miles one way) and 1.5 miles further to Keyser Brown Lake. For a rugged overnighter or three-day trek, continue over the 11,037ft

Sundance Pass into the upper West Fork Valley (21 miles). The pass is only open from mid-July and you'll need to arrange a car shuttle between the two valleys.

Winter Sports

Red Lodge Mountain SKIING
(800-444-8977, ski reports 406-425-3334; www.redlodgemountain.com; lifts adult $57, child $24-44; end Nov–mid-Apr) Six miles southwest of downtown, Red Lodge Mountain has a 2400ft vertical drop, serviced by six lifts. With a higher base elevation (7400ft) than any other Montana ski hill, it has some of the state's best spring skiing. Full rentals and excellent-value instruction packages are available.

Red Lodge Nordic Center SNOW SPORTS
(406-425-1070; www.beartoothtrails.org; trail fee adult/child $5/free) Two miles northwest of Red Lodge on Hwy 78, this is Red Lodge's top cross-country resource and a good place for beginners. See the website for other local trails.

Sleeping

South of Red Lodge on US 212 are 10 USFS **campgrounds** (877-444-6777; www.recreation.gov; Hwy 212; tent site $16-17; mid-May–Sep). The nearest are small **Sheridan** and **Rattin**, 6 and 8 miles from Red Lodge, respectively, on the east side of the road. A little further, with shady creekside locations, are the nicer **Parkside**, **Limber Pine** and **Greenough Lake** campgrounds. All can be reserved online. There's also lots of dispersed camping nearby.

Yodeler Motel MOTEL $
(406-446-1435; www.yodelermotel.com; 601 S Broadway Ave; basement r from $106, upper level from $155;) A retro Bavarian theme livens up this friendly '60s-era hotel, down to the in-room wet steam showers and ski waxing room. The spacious upper-level rooms with porches are roomier and brighter than the cheaper basement options. The hosts are enthusiastic hikers who gladly offer advice on local trails.

Pollard HISTORIC HOTEL $$
(406-446-0001; www.thepollard.com; 2 N Broadway Ave; r from $145, ste from $225;) Red Lodge's first brick building, dating from 1893, makes for a fun and elegant place to stay, even if you're paying more for the history than the quality of the room. The cozy lobby and restaurant are hubs of local activity.

Rock Creek Resort RESORT $$
(406-446-1111; www.rockcreekresort.com; Hwy 212; d $144-170, apt $178-230; @) Red Lodge's most upscale accommodation has rooms, condos and a decent restaurant at a quiet creekside location, 4.5 miles south of town, off US 212. The Beartooth Lodge rooms are the freshest and come with balconies.

Eating & Drinking

★**Red Box Car** BURGERS $
(406-446-2152; www.redboxcar.com; 1300 S Broadway; burgers $3.50-12.50; 11am-9pm May-Sep) Without doubt the Yellowstone region's best fast food is served out of a century-old railroad car at the south end of town. The malts and homemade onion rings are unbeatable.

★**Más Taco** MEXICAN $
(406-446-3636; www.eatmastaco.com; 304 N Broadway Ave; tacos $2.95, burritos $7.95; 11am-9pm Tue-Sat, 11am-4pm Sun;) Cranking out fresh tacos from the tiny kitchen including shrimp, *al pastor* (cooked on a gyros-style spit) or the divine *carne asada* – any of

WACKY RACES

Southeast Montana is a proud home to some of the state's more surreal sports. In March, Red Lodge hosts the national **ski-joring finals**, a not-quite-yet-Olympic sport that involves a horse towing a skier around an oval speed track. It's like water skiing. On snow. Except with a horse.

Equally silly is the annual **Running of the Sheep** at nearby Reed Point. Inspired by Pamplona's much more impressive Running of the Bulls, the significantly less dangerous herd of sheep thunders down six blocks of Main St every year during Labor Day weekend.

Finally, summer weekend evenings (Thursday to Sunday) see high-octane pig racing at the **Bear Creek Saloon** (406-446-3481; 2 W Main St, Bearcreek; May-Sep & Dec-Mar), 7 miles east of Red Lodge on Hwy 308. Make a $2 bet, urge your porker over the finish line and round off the evening with a bacon sandwich (only kidding). Proceeds go to charity.

which can be made into a heaping taco bowl. Also has quesadillas or burritos, as well as homemade chips and salsa. It's quick, fresh and tasty, and will get you down the road happy.

Café Regis BREAKFAST $
(☎406-446-1941; www.caferegis.com; cnr 16th St & Word Ave; mains $7-10.50; ⏱7am-2pm Thu-Mon) Locals know this as the best breakfast in town, with good-value blue-plate lunch specials and a very pleasant garden seating.

Red Lodge Ales BREWERY
(☎406-446-0243; www.redlodgeales.com; 1445 N Broadway Ave; ⏱11am-10pm; 📶) From the makers of the regional-favorite Bent Nail IPA come many other well-crafted brews and ciders served in the roomy, family-friendly warehouse of Sam's Taproom on the north side of town. There's patio seating outdoors and grilled sandwiches on the menu. Order the beer sampler to taste the six most popular brews.

Shopping

It's worth setting aside an hour or two for browsing the shops and galleries along Broadway Ave.

Sylvan Peak SPORTS & OUTDOORS
(☎406-446-1770; www.sylvanpeak.com; 9 S Broadway; ⏱9am-7pm) Topo maps, outdoor gear and winter equipment rentals.

Information

Red Lodge Visitor Center (☎888-281-0625; www.redlodge.com; 601 N Broadway; ⏱9am-5pm Mon-Fri, 10am-2pm Sat, 9am-1pm Sun) On the north edge of town, with an RV dump station and road-condition information for the Beartooth Hwy. Check out 'Liver-Eating' Johnston's former cabin just outside.

Getting There & Away

On the west bank of Rock Creek, Red Lodge is 60 miles south of Billings and 65 miles northeast of Cooke City and the north entrance to Yellowstone National Park. It's only accessible by private vehicle.

Beartooth Highway

The breathtaking Beartooth Hwy connects Red Lodge to Cooke City and Yellowstone's Northeast Entrance along a soaring 68-mile road built in 1932. An engineering feat and the 'most beautiful drive in America', according to the late journalist Charles Kuralt, this 'all-American' road is a destination in its own right and easily the most dramatic route into Yellowstone National Park. Motorcyclists in particular love the road, arriving en masse for the Sturgis-like Beartooth Rally in mid-July.

Covering 1474 sq miles, the Absaroka-Beartooth Wilderness stretches along the road, bordering Montana and Wyoming and crossing through Custer Gallatin and Shoshone National Forests, taking in two distinct mountain ranges: the Absarokas and the Beartooth Plateau (the Beartooths). Steep, forested valleys and craggy peaks characterize the Absarokas, while the Beartooths are essentially a high plateau of uplifted three-billion-year-old granite (some of the oldest rock in North America) dotted with more than 1000 lakes and tarns. Together they constitute the most visited wilderness area in the nation.

Most of the wilderness consists of high plateau above 10,000ft. Alpine tundra vegetation is the only thing that grows up here (where snow can last from October to mid-July), lending the landscape a desolate, otherworldly look. In fact, unless you are an outdoorsy type who makes frequent forays above 10,000ft, it probably is another world – you can't usually reach this kind of terrain by car. To really experience the surroundings, you must get out of the car, even if it's just for a few minutes, to suck in the thin, cold air.

The highway has a short driving season and is usually closed between mid-October and late May. For information on weather conditions, hikes and bear sightings, pull into the helpful **Beartooth Ranger District Office** (☎406-446-2103; 6811 Hwy 212; ⏱8am-4:30pm Mon-Fri), just south of Red Lodge on Hwy 212. There's gas at Red Lodge, Cooke City and, less reliably, along the highway at the Top of the World store. For more details see www.beartoothhighway.com.

The political landscape of the highway is as convoluted as the natural landscape. The highway starts and ends in Montana but dips into Wyoming en route. If you are fishing, you'll need to know exactly where you are so that you have the correct state fishing license.

Beartooth Highway Drive

Route Red Lodge to Cooke City

Length 68 miles; three hours

Speed Limit Officially 70 mph, but more like 35mph

Summary From its starting point at Red Lodge, the highway climbs Rock Creek Canyon's glaciated valley before dramatically ascending the valley wall through a series of spaghetti-loop switchbacks, gaining an amazing 5000ft in elevation in just a few miles.

A parking area at **Rock Creek Vista Point Overlook** (9160ft), 20 miles from Red Lodge, has toilets and a short walk (wheelchair accessible) to superb views. The road continues up onto the high plateau, past 'Mae West Curve' and into Wyoming.

In another 7 miles the road passes **Twin Lakes**, where a parking area offers good views of the cirque and the ski lift that comprises the **Beartooth Basin** (www.beartoothbasin.com), an extreme early summer ski area established by Austrians in the 1960s. Another 1.3 miles further, below the road, is **Gardner Lake**. After 0.7 miles, at the start of a series of switchbacks, look northwest across Rock Creek for views of the Hellroaring Plateau and the jagged **Bear's Tooth** (11,612ft; 'Na Piet Say' in the local Crow language), which lends the range its name. A mile later you'll crest the **Beartooth Pass West Summit**, the highest point along the highway at 10,947ft. You'll likely pass deep snowbanks here as late as June.

From this halfway point the road descends past Frozen Lake, Long Lake, Little Bear Lake (the last two with excellent fishing) and then the Chain Lakes (on the left) to the Island Lake and Beartooth Lake Campgrounds. Both offer excellent opportunities for a picnic, day hike or canoe paddle. Between the campgrounds is the **Top of the World Store** (www.topoftheworldresort.com), which offers a reviving coffee (and a fishing license if you need one).

As the road descends, you'll see **Beartooth Butte**, a huge lump of the sedimentary rock that once covered the Beartooths. Two miles beyond Beartooth Lake Campground, 42 miles from Red Lodge, turn right up a 2.5-mile dirt road to the former fire watchtower at **Clay Butte Overlook** (no RVs or trailers). The views from here are fantastic: look for the 'Reef,' a snaking line of sedimentary rock that follows the entire valley, proving that this lofty region was once underwater.

Back on the main road, a mile further on, is an **overlook** offering views of Index Peak (11,313ft) and jagged Pilot Peak (11,708ft). At the height of glaciation, ice sheets would have covered the entire horizon except for the very tip of these peaks. Index was originally given the somewhat unromantic name of Dog Turd Peak. Next up is the **Clarks Fork Overlook** (with toilets) and then a small turnout by Lake Creek Falls.

The turnoff left is for Chief Joseph Scenic Hwy, which leads 62 miles to Cody and accesses Yellowstone's East Entrance via the Wapiti Valley. The Beartooth Hwy descends to several excellent fishing areas on the Clarks Fork and re-enters Montana. Opposite Chief Joseph Campground is **Clarks Fork Trailhead**, a fine place for a picnic, a day hike and a look at the flume of the former mining power station. From here it's 4 miles to Cooke City, via the modest Colter Pass (8066ft).

Activities

Hiking & Backpacking

You can gain about 4000ft of elevation by car and begin your hike right from the Beartooth Hwy, but it's important to allow some time to acclimatize. Also be aware that the barren terrain offers little shade, shelter or wood. In order to protect the fragile alpine vegetation, hikers should not light campfires above the tree line. Grizzly and black bears are not that common in the higher elevations; hikers have a better chance of seeing bighorn sheep, mountain goats or elk.

August is the best month to hike the Beartooths. Snow remains in many places above the tree line at least until the end of July and starts to accumulate again after mid-September. Localized afternoon thunderstorms, with hail, are common in the Beartooths during June (the wettest month) and July. During early summer, you'll also need lots of bug repellent and waterproof shoes to cope with swampy trails. Don't be put off; just be forewarned. With proper preparation, the plateau offers some of Greater Yellowstone's very best hiking.

From Island Lake Campground you can take a wonderful and easy hour-long stroll along the **Beartooth High Lakes Trail** (trail 620) to Island Lake and beyond to Night Lake and Flake Lake. All of these lakes are popular fishing areas. If you can arrange a shuttle, continue downhill to Beauty Lake and then left (south) to Beartooth Lake for a fine half-day hike.

From Beartooth Lake Campground you can make a wonderful half-day 8-mile loop via **Beauty Lake**. Head up Beartooth Creek (trail 619) and then bear right, passing five

Beartooth Hwy

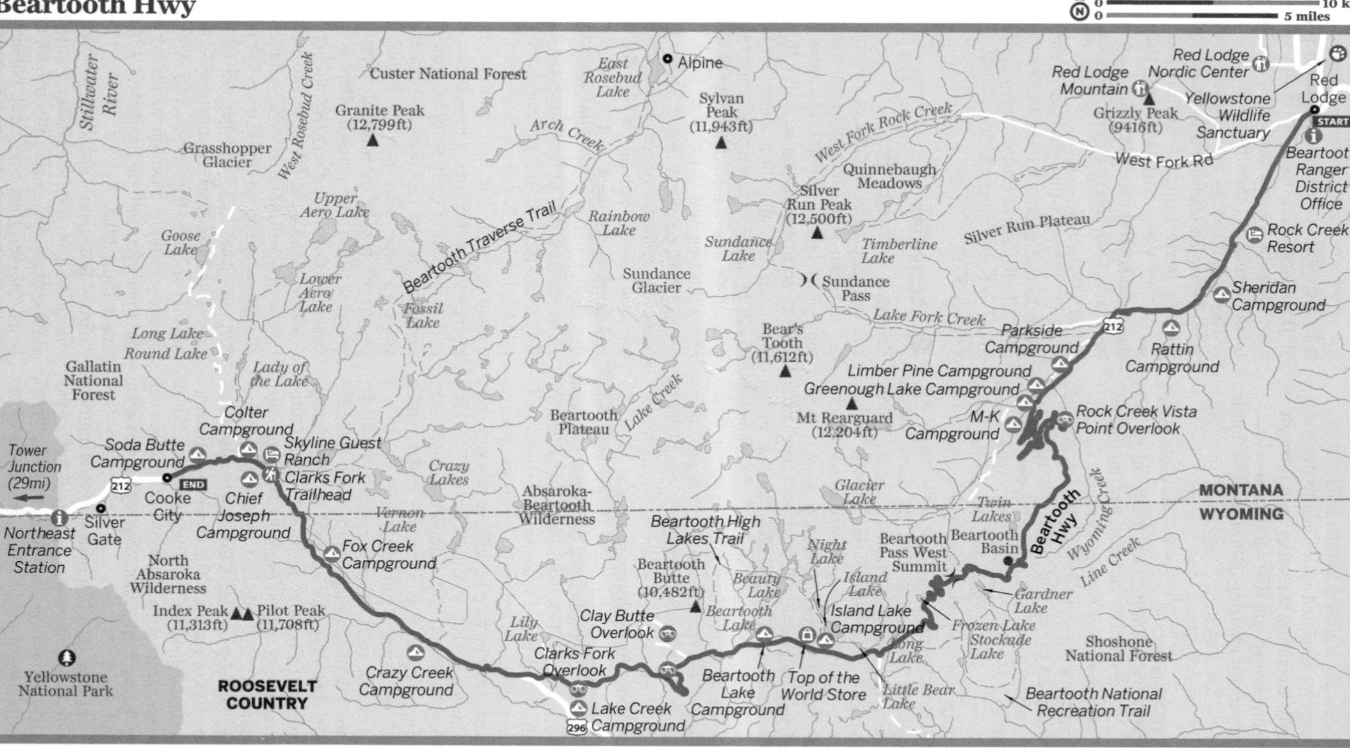

lakes, including Claw Lake (trail 620), to the junction with the Beartooth High Lakes Trail. From here descend right past Beauty Lake (trail 621) back to Beartooth Lake. Parking is limited at the trailhead.

A longer, possibly overnight, option is the 11-mile **Beartooth National Recreation Trail** (trail 613) loop hike, accessed from the highway at Gardner Lake. The trail drops from the lake and loops around Tibbs Butte, initially along Little Rock Creek, past turnoffs to Deep Lake, Camp Sawtooth and Dollar Lake to arrive at Stockade Lake, a fine campsite. From here, continue around the loop past Losecamp Lake back to Gardner Lake, or cut east from Losecamp Lake for 3 miles past Hauser Lake to the Beartooth Hwy by a pullout overlooking Long Lake (this requires a shuttle).

Another easy day hike is the 6-mile return ramble to **Rock Island Lake**, which begins from the Clarks Fork Trailhead. After about 15 minutes, be careful to continue along Russell Creek Trail (trail 567) and *not* turn left along Broadwater Trail. The trail brushes Kersey Lake and branches right up to Rock Island Lake. An alternative hike branches right 1.3 miles from the trailhead up to Vernon Lake (trail 565).

The Clarks Fork Trailhead is also the start of the exciting multiday **Beartooth Traverse** (aka 'The Beaten Path') that runs along Russell Creek Trail to Fossil Lake and then across plateau trail 15 to Rosebud Lake (shuttle required). You need to be fairly experienced for this remote 26-mile wilderness trek.

The contoured 1:100,000 *Absaroka Beartooth Wilderness* map by Beartooth Publishing and the USFS 1:63,360 *Absaroka Beartooth Wilderness* map are both excellent. *Hiking the Absaroka-Beartooth Wilderness* and *Easy Day Hikes in the Beartooths*, both published by Falcon Press and written by Bill Schneider, are also useful resources.

Sleeping

There are 13 basic USFS campgrounds along the Beartooth Hwy between Red Lodge and Cooke City. **Island Lake** (tent sites $15; ⌚ Jul & Aug) and **Beartooth Lake** (tent sites $15; ⌚ Jul & Aug) are up on the high plateau; the latter has a boat launch. Further west are **Crazy Creek** (tent sites $10; ⌚ late May-early Sep) and **Fox Creek** (tent sites without/with electricity $15/20; ⌚ mid-Jun–mid-Sep), the former with a small cascade nearby. These sites come under the Clarks Fork Ranger District (p140) of the Shoshone National Forest.

Closer to Cooke City are Colter and Soda Butte Campgrounds (p141). Only hard-sided vehicles are accepted (no tents) following a fatal grizzly attack at Soda Butte in July 2010. Chief Joseph Campground, 4 miles from Cooke City, is currently closed due to budget issues. Contact the Custer Gallatin National Forest Gardiner District Office (p154) in Gardiner for details.

Skyline Guest Ranch LODGE **$$**
(☎ 406-838-2380; www.flyfishyellowstone.com; 31 Kersey Lake Rd; d incl breakfast $144-179; 📶🐾) The remote Skyline is perfect if you want to get away from it all, experience some Western hospitality and saddle up for some family horseback riding ($40 per hour). Rooms in a three-story lodge are spacious and modern, with nice outside balconies, and the location – 3 miles outside of Cooke City – is officially the middle of nowhere.

Chief Joseph Scenic Byway

The wild and scenic Clarks Fork of the Yellowstone River runs along much of the Chief Joseph Scenic Byway (Hwy 296), linking Cody (via Hwy 120 north) with the Beartooth Hwy and Yellowstone National Park's Northeast Entrance, 62 miles away. It's an astoundingly scenic and largely undiscovered corner of the Yellowstone region that links with the Beartooth Hwy to offer several potential loop itineraries. The highway is named for Chief Joseph of the Nez Percé tribe, who eluded the US Army and escaped through Clarks Fork here in 1877.

The paved highway is open year-round from Cody to just before the Beartooth Hwy, though not as far as Cooke City. The Beartooth Hwy itself is closed mid-October to late May. Fall colors are particularly lovely here.

The 47-mile Chief Joseph Scenic Byway starts 16 miles north of Cody, enters the Shoshone National Forest after 8 miles and climbs to a spectacular viewpoint at **Dead Indian Pass** (8048ft). Native Americans used to ambush game that migrated through the pass between summer mountain pastures and winter ranges down in the plains. The pass is named for a Bannock brave killed here in skirmishes with the army in 1878.

As you descend from the pass, just 0.3 miles before Dead Indian Campground, an unsigned dirt road leads a couple of hundred yards to an unmarked trailhead that offers an excellent short hike to view the 1200ft-deep **Clarks Fork Canyon**. The trail leads north for 2 miles to a scenic overlook – watch for cairns marking the spot shortly after you first see the gorge. The views of the granite gorge and Dead Indian Creek waterfall are breathtaking. The canyon effectively separates the 50-million-year-old volcanic rock of the Absaroka Range from the two-billion-year-old granite of the Beartooth Plateau.

Back on the road, USFS Rd 101 branches southwest into the beautiful **Sunlight Basin**. Its upper branches end at a wall of peaks forming the remote eastern boundary of Yellowstone National Park. Writer Ernest Hemingway spent time grizzly hunting here in the 1930s and wrote an article on the subject for *Vogue* magazine.

Where Hwy 296 crosses Sunlight Creek is the terrific **Sunlight Bridge**, the highest in Wyoming. You can park and walk across the bridge for hair-raising views into the gorge (acrophobes beware!).

Just north of Crandall Creek (named after a pioneer miner who was beheaded by Native Americans), around Swamp Lake and below the Cathedral Cliffs, are six scenic ponds where you might spot sandhill cranes and trumpeter swans.

Hwy 296 continues northwest to the crossbar junction of US 212, where the Beartooth Hwy leads northwest to Cooke City and Yellowstone National Park or northeast to Red Lodge and Billings.

Sleeping

Shoshone National Forest has three simple campgrounds near the Beartooth Hwy: **Lake Creek** (Hwy 296; sites $10; mid-Jun–early Sep), **Hunter Peak** (877-444-6777; www.recreation.gov; Hwy 296; sites $15; late May-Oct) and **Dead Indian** (Hwy 296; sites $10). Contact the **Clarks Fork Ranger District** (307-527-6241) in Cody for details.

K Bar Z Guest Ranch RANCH $
(307-587-4410; www.kbarzguestranch.com; Hwy 296; d cabin $100) Family-run and 28 miles from Yellowstone, this ranch offers horseback rides from $35/175 per hour/day.

Hunter Peak Ranch RANCH $$
(307-587-3711; www.hunterpeakranch.com; Hwy 296; cabin/ste from $152/162;) Just off Hwy 296, 24 miles from Yellowstone, with plenty of summertime horseback riding and fishing.

7D Ranch RANCH $$$
(888-587-9885; www.7dranch.com; 774 County Hwy 7GQ; weekly per person $2240; Jun–mid-Sep) This guest ranch has a fabulous location 8 miles up Sunlight Valley, with only 10 cabins and excellent horseback riding and fishing opportunities. Early September is kid-free and has discounted rates. Rates include all meals and activities.

Cooke City

406 / POP 85 / ELEV 7800FT

Sandwiched spectacularly between two forested ridges of the Beartooth Mountains, just 4 miles from Yellowstone's Northeast Entrance, this one-street Montana town (population 85 in winter, 350 in summer) gets a steady flow of summer visitors en route from the scenic splendors of the Beartooth Hwy and the national park. There's not much here in the way of shops, sights or even trailheads, but the isolated town has a backwoods feel that's more laid-back and less commercialized than the park's other gateway towns, and a population that's as rugged as the surrounding peaks.

Cooke City's isolation is due to geography and the lack of a railroad link. Citizens lobbied to bring the railroad to the original mining town of Shoo-Fly, even going so far as to rename the town in 1880 after the Northern Pacific Railroad's Jay Cooke, but even this blatant flattery failed to overcome hard economics. Oddly, this enclave of Montana can only be accessed from Wyoming.

In winter the road from Yellowstone is only plowed as far as Cooke City, so visitors – mostly experienced backcountry skiers and snowmobilers – tend to check in and stay awhile. Gas prices are the highest in the Yellowstone region. There's no cell coverage in town.

Sights & Activities

In winter the network of mining roads northeast of town are favorites of snowmobilers. Near Colter Campground, the unpaved Lulu Pass–Goose Lake Rd, the Goose Lake Track (trail 3230) and trails to Aero Lakes are all popular, as is snowmobiling the Beartooth Hwy. Several outfits in town rent snowmobiles ($200 to $300 per day).

Cooke City General Store HISTORIC BUILDING
(www.cookecitystore.com; 101 Main St; 8am-7pm May-Sep) This historic 1886 store dates from the town's mining heyday and is a fun

browse. It sells fishing permits, topo maps and almost anything else you can think of.

Yellowstone Trading Post MUSEUM
(209 Main St; ⊙9am-9pm) Kids will like the stuffed animal exhibits in this souvenir store next to the Beartooth Cafe. It's normally free; if not, the small admission fee can be spent in the store.

Hemingway's Yellowstone CULTURAL TOUR
(☎406-838-2109; www.hemingwaysyellowstone.com; tour with meal per person $100-200) Literary travelers will love this day tour focused on locations related to Ernest Hemingway's five summers in the region, offering a unique insight into the great author's work. Locations include Sunlight Creek and the Range Rider in Silver Gate, frequented by Hemingway and his wife in 1938 and 1939. An evening tour and a three-day horse-packing trip are also offered.

Beartooth Powder Guides SKIING
(☎406-838-2097; www.beartoothpowder.com) Come winter these are the people for guided backcountry ski trips, based out of their wilderness yurt or backcountry cabin (accommodations $300 for six to 10 people).

Sleeping

Soda Butte (tent sites $9; ⊙Jul-early Sep) and **Colter** (tent sites $8; ⊙mid-Jul–Sep) campgrounds are just 1.5 miles and 2 miles from town, respectively. Expect hefty discounts from mid-October to mid-December and in April and May.

Alpine Motel MOTEL $$
(☎406-838-2262; www.cookecityalpine.com; 105 E Main St; d $140-155, ste $175-195; 📶🐾) Well-maintained and spacious rooms are the hallmark of this good-value motel with laundry facilities, family suites and discounted spring and fall rates.

Elkhorn Lodge HOTEL $$
(☎406-838-2332; www.elkhornlodgemt.com; 103 Main St; d $160-300, cabins $340-510; ⊙May–mid-Oct, mid-Dec–Mar; 📶) Choose between six rooms in the main building – with pleasant sitting area, coffeemaker and fridge – or the two pricier log cabins with kitchenette. All are fresh and spacious.

Antlers Lodge CABIN $$
(☎406-838-2432; www.cookecityantlerslodge.com; 311 E Main St; cabins $145-245; 📶🐾) This ramshackle collection of 12 old-style pine cabins has quarters in all shapes and sizes (most family-sized and with kitchenettes) and also offers five fresh and spacious motel rooms. The antler-horn chandeliers in the historic main lodge are a bit creepy.

Eating

Bearclaw Bakery BREAKFAST $
(309 E Main St; mains $5-9; ⊙5-11:30am) If you plan to a make an early start into the park, this down-home bakery offers pastries and coffee from 5am and fine scrambles, eggs Benedict and French toast from 6am.

★**Beartooth Café** AMERICAN $$
(☎406-838-2475; www.beartoothcafe.com; 211 Main St; lunch $8-13, dinner $10-27; ⊙11am-9pm late May-late Sep) A bright place for lunch sandwiches (such as a buffalo burger, a 'funk burger,' or lighter portobello sandwich) served on the pleasant front deck, washed down by a fine selection of 130 bottled microbrews. Dinner mains such as ribs, smoked trout and hand-cut steaks are double the lunchtime prices.

Log Cabin Cafe CAFE $$
(☎406-838-2367; www.thelogcabincafe.com; lunch $10-14, dinner $15-40; ⊙5:30am-10pm mid-May–late Sep) In sleepy Silver Gate this unexpectedly cool place serves excellent grilled trout, house-smoked salmon and homemade breakfast pumpkin bread. The cozy cabin dates back to 1937 and there are more cabins ($120 with breakfast) for rent out back.

Information

Bearclaw Mountain Recovery (☎406-838-2040) AAA-endorsed and the people to call if you have a breakdown. Montana fishing licenses are available.

Chamber of Commerce Visitor Center (☎406-838-2495; www.cookecitychamber.org; 206 W Main; ⊙9am-5pm; 📶) A helpful visitor center with public restroom, free wi-fi and an interesting local museum featuring a replica miner's cabin out back. Historical talks take place around the back campfire most Saturdays.

WAPITI ROUTE

Cody

☎307 / POP 9840 / ELEV 4997FT

You have a few choices when it comes to getting into Yellowstone National Park, and approaching from the Cody side of life should be top on your list. Not just for the mesmerizing drive along the North Fork of the Shoshone – which Theodore Roosevelt once called the '50 most beautiful miles in America' – but also for the town.

Cody revels in its frontier image, a legacy that started with its founder, William 'Buffalo Bill' Cody: Chief of Scouts for the army, notorious buffalo hunter, and showman who spent years touring the world with his Wild West extravaganza. The town rallies around nightly rodeos, rowdy saloons and a world-class museum that was started by Buffalo Bill's estate and is a worthy destination all by itself.

Sights

★Buffalo Bill Center of the West MUSEUM
(☎307-587-4771; www.centerofthewest.org; 720 Sheridan Ave; adult/child $19/12; ⊙8am-6pm May–mid-Sep, shorter hours rest of year;) Do not miss Wyoming's most impressive (constructed) attraction. This sprawling complex of five museums showcases everything Western: from the spectacle of Buffalo Bill's world-famous Wild West shows and galleries featuring powerful frontier-oriented artwork, to the visually absorbing **Plains Indian Museum** and a collection of 7000 firearms (under renovation through 2019). Meanwhile, the **Draper Museum of Natural History** explores the Yellowstone region's ecosystem. Look for Teddy Roosevelt's saddle, the busy beaver ball and one of the world's last buffalo tepees.

Entry is valid for two consecutive days – and you'll need 'em. Save a couple of bucks by booking online.

Old Trail Town MUSEUM
(☎307-587-5302; www.museumoftheoldwest.org; 1831 DeMaris Dr; adult/child 6-12yr $9/5; ⊙8am-7pm mid-May–Sep) The hideouts of Butch Cassidy, Kid Curry and the Sundance Kid comprise this unique museum, a collection of late-19th-century wooden buildings relocated here from all over Wyoming. Look for the bullet holes in the door of the Rivers Saloon and the grave of mountain man Jeremiah 'Liver-Eating' Johnson, re-buried here in 1974 with Robert Redford as one of the pallbearers.

Buffalo Bill State Park PARK
(☎307-587-9227; http://wyoparks.state.wy.us; Hwy 14/16/20; day use $6; ⊙year-round) This scenic state park, 6 miles west of Cody, centers on the Buffalo Bill Reservoir and Dam, unveiled in 1910 as the world's highest dam to provide the irrigation for expanding Cody. The reservoir is a hot spot for fishing, windsurfing and boating, and boat launches dot the north and southeast shores. The dam **visitor center** (☎307-527-6076; www.bbdvc.com; 4808 Hwy 14/16/20; ⊙8am-6pm Mon-Fri, 9am-5pm Sat & Sun May-Sep) FREE, just west of the dramatic Shoshone Canyon, offers interpretive exhibits on the dam, Bill and local wildlife.

Activities

No longer just for cowboys, Cody is an excellent base for outdoor pursuits. Apart from the activities mentioned here, Cody also offers some of the best winter **ice climbing** in the US. See www.coldfear.com and www.codyiceclimbingfestival.com, or inquire at Sunlight Sports (p146).

Gradient Mountain Sports KAYAKING
(☎307-587-4659; www.gradientmountainsports.net; 1390 Sheridan Ave; ⊙10am-5pm Wed-Sat & Mon) If kayaking is your thing, head here for rentals, shuttles and information, plus instruction and guided trips. Kayaks, stand up paddleboards (SUP) and canoes cost $40 to $50 per day.

North Fork Anglers FISHING
(☎307-527-7274; www.northforkanglers.com; 1107 Sheridan Ave; ⊙8am-8pm) Anglers should visit Tim Wade's place for local information, flies and guided trips. The website lists current fishing conditions.

Absaroka Bicycles MOUNTAIN BIKING
(☎307-527-5566; 2201 17th St, Kmart Plaza; ⊙10am-6pm Mon-Thu & Sat, to 4pm Fri) Ground central for mountain-bike rentals ($45 per day), repairs, tours (both cycling and hiking) and info on local fat-tire trails, including to the nearby Outlaw and Oregon Basin trail systems.

Red Canyon Wild Mustang Trips WILDLIFE WATCHING
(☎800-293-0148; www.codywyomingadventures.com; 1119 12th St; tour adult/child $40/38; ⊙May–mid-Oct) For something different, take a morning or afternoon van tour out to the desert badlands of the McCullough Peaks Wild Horse Range, a refuge designated for 142 wild mustangs. Photo safaris are also possible. For more information on the horses, visit FOAL (www.friendsofalegacy.org).

Rafting

Just outside of town, the North Fork of the Shoshone River has scenic float trips and excellent class II to class IV white water. Bighorn sheep hang out on the cliffs, and eagles and moose are sometimes spotted. Prices range from $34 for family-oriented lower canyon trips to $75 for a half-day on the North Fork or Clark's Fork.

The rafting season is mid-May to mid-September in the Red Rock and Lower Canyons, and late May to late June for the North Fork.

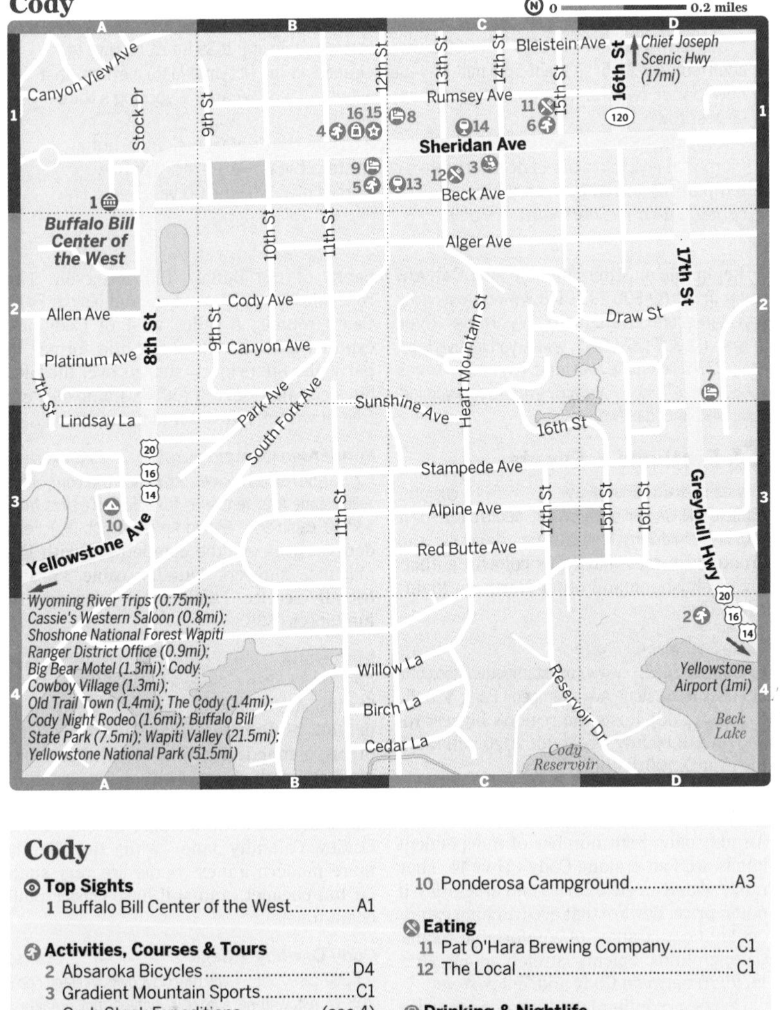

Cody

Top Sights

1 Buffalo Bill Center of the West.............A1

Activities, Courses & Tours

2 Absaroka Bicycles.............D4
3 Gradient Mountain Sports.............C1
Grub Steak Expeditions.............(see 4)
4 North Fork Anglers.............B1
5 Red Canyon River Trips.............B1
Red Canyon Wild Mustang Trips.............(see 5)
6 River Runners.............C1

Sleeping

7 Carter Mountain Motel.............D2
8 Chamberlin Inn.............C1
9 Irma Hotel.............B1
10 Ponderosa Campground.............A3

Eating

11 Pat O'Hara Brewing Company.............C1
12 The Local.............C1

Drinking & Nightlife

13 Juniper.............C1
14 Silver Dollar Bar.............C1

Entertainment

15 Dan Miller's Cowboy Music Revue.............B1

Shopping

16 Sunlight Sports.............B1

WORTH A TRIP

HEARTLAND SECURITY

Following the Japanese bombing of Pearl Harbor, more than 110,000 Japanese-Americans were interned in 10 camps across the US. Taking only what they could carry, around 11,000 Japanese-Americans relocated from West Coast homes to these flimsy tar-paper rooms and made the best of three years of confinement at **Heart Mountain Relocation Center** (307-754-8000; www.heartmountain.org; 1539 Rd 19, off Hwy 14A; adult/student $7/5; 10am-5pm mid-May–Sep, closed Sun-Tue Oct–mid-May), setting up a newspaper, two theaters and a high school in what quickly became Wyoming's third-largest town.

Only the former hospital and chimney remain from the original buildings, but a memorial and barracks-style interpretive center tells the powerful story of how – temporarily seized by xenophobia – the US failed its own citizens 60 years ago. The center is 14 miles northeast of Cody.

Reputable outfitters include **Red Canyon River Trips** (800-293-0148; www.codywyomingadventures.com; 1119 12th St), **Wyoming River Trips** (307-587-6661; www.wyomingrivertrips.com; 233 Yellowstone Ave) and **River Runners** (800-535-7238; www.riverrunnersofwyoming.com; 1491 Sheridan Ave).

Festivals & Events

Plains Indians Powwow CULTURAL
(Buffalo Bill Center of the West; adult/child 7-17yr $10/5; mid-Jun) Drumming, dancing and ornate costumes mark this colorful gathering of Shoshone and other Northern Plains tribes.

Cody Stampede Rodeo SPORTS
(307-587-5155; www.codystampederodeo.com; 519 West Yellowstone Ave, Stampede Park; $20-25; Jul 1-4) Cody hosts the region's biggest rodeo on 4th of July weekend; 2020 will mark the event's 100th anniversary.

Sleeping

An unusually high number of independent hotels are found along Cody's Hwy 14. They range widely in cleanliness and amenities, if not in price. Beware that eye-catching exteriors are no guarantee of comfortable rooms. Campgrounds aplenty stretch along Hwy 14/16/20 between Cody and Yellowstone.

Cody's accommodations are poor value in July and August. You'll find much better deals in spring and fall (summer rates are listed here).

Buffalo Bill State Park Campgrounds CAMPGROUND $
(307-876-2796; http://wyoparks.state.wy.us; tent & RV sites without/with electricity $17/22; year-round) For the nicest camping, skip town for more scenic options along the banks of the Buffalo Bill Reservoir. The roadside **North Shore Bay** and **North Fork** Campgrounds, 6 miles west of Cody, are exposed and shadeless, but the former in particular offers lovely sunsets over the lake. Sites can be reserved online. Campsites are free in winter, but water is not available.

Ponderosa Campground CAMPGROUND $
(307-587-9203; www.codyponderosa.com; 1815 Yellowstone Ave; tent sites from $30, RV sites from $37-50, cabin $65; mid-Apr–mid-Oct;) Ponderosa edges out the competition with immaculate showers, laundry, cable TV and friendly service. Families can overnight in fun tepees ($38).

Irma Hotel HISTORIC HOTEL $$
(307-587-4221; www.irmahotel.com; 1192 Sheridan Ave; r $152-169, ste $225;) Built in 1902 by Buffalo Bill as the cornerstone of his planned city, this creaky hotel has old-fashioned charm with a few modern touches. The original high-ceiling historical suites are named after past guests (Annie Oakley, Calamity Jane), while the slightly more modern annex rooms are very similar but cheaper (and still have classic pull-chain toilets).

Cody Cowboy Village CABIN $$
(307-587-7555; www.thecodycowboyvillage.com; 203 W Yellowstone Ave; r & cabins incl breakfast $179-229; May–mid-Oct;) Popular and well-run, the modern and stylish duplex cabins or stand-alone suites come with small porch, plus there's a large outdoor plunge pool.

Carter Mountain Motel MOTEL $$
(307-587-4295; www.cartermountainmotel.com; 1701 Central Ave; d $135-175;) An unpretentious mom-and-pop-style place, but well

looked after and decent value, with cheery flowerpots, an upper-floor terrace and kitchenette suites.

★ **Chamberlin Inn** INN $$$
(☎307-587-0202; https://chamberlininn.com; 1032 12th St; d/ste from $235/355) An elegant downtown retreat, this historic boutique hotel (built in 1903) has a library and a pretty inner courtyard. The old registry claims Hemingway crashed in room 18 ($295) on a 1932 fishing trip.

The Cody HOTEL $$$
(☎307-587-5915; www.thecody.com; 232 W Yellowstone Ave; d incl breakfast $259-289; ❄📶🏊) Cody's most luxurious hotel combines New Western chic with green credentials, incorporating paneling made with recycled wood from park facilities and offering free bicycles to guests. Pay $10 extra for a balcony room away from the road, or $30 more for a king Jacuzzi suite.

Eating & Drinking

Steak, steak and more steak (and a revolving door of unforgettable Mexican restaurants) sets the tone for dining. A few creative alternatives are trying to buck the trend, and although we appreciate the variety, eating salad almost feels sacrilegious in this Wild West tribute town.

Pat O'Hara Brewing Company PUB FOOD $
(☎307-586-5410; www.patoharabrewing.com; 1019 15th St; mains $10-20; ⏰from 11am Wed-Mon; 📶) Cody's friendliest brewery has 15 local beers on tap and serves up a range of Irish fare, including shepherd's pie and bangers, around a horseshoe bar alive with conversation. Take yourself on a sudsy journey with a flight of six beer samples.

★ **The Local** MODERN AMERICAN $$
(☎307-586-4262; www.thelocalcody.com; 1134 13th St; lunch $10-14, dinner $11-38; ⏰9am-2pm & 5-8pm Tue-Sat; 🖉) 🌿 When Cody's cowboy cuisine starts to weigh on your arteries, find the antidote in the Local's fresh, organic and locally sourced dishes. Think tempeh and avocado wrap for lunch, or grilled scallops and saffron risotto for dinner.

Cassie's Western Saloon STEAK $$
(☎307-527-5500; www.cassies.com; 214 Yellowstone Ave; lunch $9-15, steaks $20-46; ⏰food 11am-10pm, drinks to 2am) This classic roadhouse and former house of ill repute hosts heavy swilling, swingin' country-and-western music and the occasional bar fight. Strap on the feedbag at the attached supper club and tackle tender steaks ranging in size from 8oz to 5.25lb.

Silver Dollar Bar BAR
(☎307-527-7666; 1313 Sheridan Ave; ⏰11am-late) The Silver Dollar Bar is a historic watering hole with lots of TV screens and live music or DJs nightly. The tap list is strong, with lots of great regional craft beers, and the burgers are tasty. In nice weather, an outdoor bar offers excellent views of street life.

Juniper WINE BAR
(☎307-587-4472; www.junipershop.com; 1128 12th St; ⏰4-10pm Wed-Sat) This little oasis is part market and part stylish bar, serving up a sophisticated range of cocktails, wines and whiskeys, alongside house infusions and small plates of tasty charcuterie and cheeses.

DON'T MISS

THE GHOSTS OF BUFFALO BILL

For a thick slice of classic Cody shtick join the crowds at 6pm on the porch of the **Irma Hotel** for the gunslingers' mock **shoot-out**. The shoot-out itself manages to be both hammy and cheesy (sounds delicious), but kids will enjoy watching costumed characters that include Wild Bill Hickok, Buffalo Bill and Wyatt Earp. It runs daily, except Sunday, June to mid-September.

After the shoot-out join the faux-cowboys in their 10-gallon hats for happy hour in the Irma Hotel's **Silver Saddle Saloon**, or better still, head next door to the wonderfully atmospheric **Irma dining room** and grab a stool and a bottle of Bill Cody Beer at the 50ft-long imported French cherrywood bar. Presented to Bill by Queen Victoria, it was transported by stagecoach from Red Lodge and, at $100,000, cost more than the hotel itself.

It's well worth poking around the hallways of the atmospheric **Irma Hotel**. Buffalo Bill built and named the hotel for his youngest daughter, Irma, calling it 'just the swellest hotel that ever was.' He kept two suites and an office for his personal use, and his ghost is said to frequent the creaking corridors.

The delightful back garden terrace has live music Friday and Saturday evenings.

Entertainment

Cody Nite Rodeo SPECTATOR SPORT
(☎307-587-5155; www.codystampederodeo.com; 519 W Yellowstone Ave; adult/child $20/10; ⊙8pm Jun-Aug) Experience a quintessential small-town rodeo at this summer-night Cody tradition. Note that animal welfare groups often criticize rodeo events as being harmful to animals; make your own decision accordingly.

Dan Miller's Cowboy Music Revue LIVE MUSIC
(☎307-578-7909; www.cowboymusicrevue.com; 1171 Sheridan Ave; admission $17; ⊙Mon-Sat Jun-Sep) The historic Cody Theater hosts this Branson-style family show, serving up folk music and cowboy poetry alongside thick slices of Old West nostalgia. Imagine Hannah Montana in cowboy boots, with a fiddle. A combo ticket, including a dinner buffet at the Irma, will save you a couple of bucks.

Shopping

Sunlight Sports SPORTS & OUTDOORS
(☎307-587-9517; www.sunlightsports.com; 1131 Sheridan Ave; ⊙9am-8pm Mon-Sat, 10am-6pm Sun) Cody's most comprehensive gear shop sells standard outdoor equipment including topo maps and bear spray. It offers camping equipment rentals including tents, sleeping bags and backpacks, and staff are excited to share local trail information.

Information

Shoshone National Forest Wapiti Ranger District Office (☎307-527-6921; www.fs.usda.gov/shoshone; 203a Yellowstone Ave; ⊙8am-4:30pm Mon-Fri) Ask for the useful recreation guide.

Getting There & Away

Cody's small **airport** (COD; ☎307-587-5096; www.flyyra.com; 2101 Roger Sedam Dr) connects this otherwise isolated town with Salt Lake City and Denver, and you can thank Buffalo Bill Cody for the scenic byway that bears his name and connects Cody to Yellowstone – a spectacular approach to the park.

Wapiti Valley

Deemed the 'most scenic 52 miles in the United States' by Teddy Roosevelt, **Buffalo Bill Scenic Byway** (US 14/16/20) traces the North Fork of the Shoshone River through the Wapiti Valley from Cody to the East Entrance of Yellowstone National Park. You will find yourself twisting to gape at the volcanic Absaroka Range, a rugged canyon of eroded badlands that gradually gives way to alpine splendor.

The name Wapiti Valley translates as 'pale white rump' from the Algonquin language. Rather than being a jab at homesteaders' backsides, the term distinguishes the lighter-colored elk, or wapiti, from darker-colored moose.

The North Absaroka Wilderness Area sits to the north and the Washakie Wilderness Area (named after a revered Shoshone warrior and peacemaker) to the south. This vast wilderness is home to grizzlies, black bears, deer, elk, moose, bighorn sheep and a few bison. The extensive network of backcountry trails, easy access to Yellowstone National Park's Lake Country and a selection of the region's best dude ranches make the valley an excellent wild route into or out of the park.

Six miles west of Cody, US 14/16/20 emerges from the dramatic **Shoshone Canyon** and tunnel to views of the **Buffalo Bill Reservoir**. Past the tiny settlement of Wapiti, Wyoming's high-desert landscape and open ranchland closes in as the road enters Shoshone National Forest and becomes the Buffalo Bill Cody Scenic Hwy. The roadside information station at the **Wapiti Ranger Station** (☎307-587-3925) has a 3D map of the region, as well as information on grizzly sightings. The national forest here was the USA's first and the nearby 1903 ranger station is its oldest.

From here on, the Wapiti Valley is lined with eerie buttes and dark brown hoodoos. National forest campgrounds, trailheads and guest ranches crop up every few miles as the scenery becomes increasingly rugged.

Two miles before the East Entrance to Yellowstone is the gas station, store, restaurant, bar and corrals of Pahaska Tepee resort, a good place to refuel. Staff lead free tours of the original lodge, built by Buffalo Bill in 1904 as a hunting lodge, and there are local trail rides. Pahaska was Bill's Native American name and means 'Longhair' in the Sioux language, a reference to Cody's long white hair and extravagant goatee.

Activities

Most of the valley's guest ranches offer **horseback riding** (per hour/half-day from $40/100), horse-packing trips and cookouts to guests and non-guests alike. Outstanding **fly-fishing** is easily accessed from the national forest and wilderness areas, and campgrounds.

North Fork Nordic Trails (307-527-7701; www.nordicskiclub.com) offers 12 miles of groomed cross-country trails behind the Pahaska Tepee resort.

Sleeping

Camping

USFS campgrounds line the Wapiti Valley, starting from 29 miles west of Cody. Overflow from Yellowstone fills up the campgrounds on July and August weekends, so try to arrive before late afternoon. All campgrounds border the river, offering easy access to trout fishing. Most are open June to early September but can close any time due to grizzly activity. Call the Shoshone National Forest Wapiti Ranger District Office for details.

Most campgrounds have bear-resistant food storage.

Big Game (www.recreation.gov; sites $10; Jun-early Sep), **Wapiti** (www.recreation.gov; sites without/with electricity $15/20; mid-May–mid-Sep) and **Rex Hale** (www.recreation.gov; sites without/with electricity $15/20; mid-May–early Sep) are all reservable and suitable for tent camping.

Newton Creek (sites $15; mid-May–late Sep), **Eagle Creek** (sites $15; late May-late Sep) and **Threemile** (www.recreation.gov; sites $15; Jul-early Sep) are all suitable for hard-sided camping only. **Elk Fork** (sites $10) is one of the most popular sites and is open year-round.

Lodging

Wapiti Valley's lodges and guest ranches make a great base for exploring Yellowstone or Cody. Most offer fishing, hiking and guided horseback rides. Luxury in proximity to the park doesn't come cheap, but discounted rates are the norm before May and after September.

Lodges East of Yellowstone Valley ACCOMMODATION SERVICES
(307-587-9595; www.yellowstone-lodging.com) Provides information on the Wapiti Valley's numerous family-owned member dude ranches and lodges.

Pahaska Tepee CABIN $$
(307-527-7701; www.pahaska.com; 183 Yellowstone Hwy; cabins $170-230; May–mid-Oct) The historic lodge is close to Yellowstone National Park and a popular place for lunch before entering the park. Despite a great location, the cabins themselves are generally old-fashioned and musty. The cheapest A-frame cabins wouldn't fit a grizzly, but considering the location, that might just be a good thing.

PARADISE VALLEY ROUTE

Livingston

406 / POP 7400 / ELEV 4501FT

In the late 1880s the Northern Pacific Railroad laid tracks across the Yellowstone River and began building Livingston as the main jumping-off point for Yellowstone National Park. Visited by Clark (of Lewis and Clark fame) and at one point a temporary home to one whip-crackin' Martha Canary (otherwise known as Calamity Jane), Livingston is an excellent departure point for rafting and fly-fishing trips on the Yellowstone River.

Bozeman's overflow has brought upscale restaurants, antique shops and art galleries to Livingston's picturesque old buildings, and attracted a community of writers and artists over the years (think Russell Chatham, Jim Harrison, Thomas McGuane and Tim Cahill), but generally it retains its no-fuss, small-town feel.

Livingston is at the north end of Paradise Valley, where I-90 meets US 89. The latter heads south to Gardiner and Yellowstone National Park, 53 miles away.

Sights & Activities

Livingston is home to over a dozen **galleries** ('13 galleries; 3 stop lights'). View them on the afternoon art walk on the fourth Friday of the month in summer. You can get details and a map at any of the art galleries in town.

Livingston Depot Center MUSEUM
(406-222-2300; www.livingstondepot.org; 200 W Park St; adult/child $5/4; 10am-5pm Mon-Sat, 1-5pm Sun May-Sep) The original colonnaded Northern Pacific Railroad depot – built in 1902 by the architects who designed New York's Grand Central Station – is now home to a railroad history-and-arts museum that train enthusiasts will find fascinating.

Yellowstone Gateway Museum MUSEUM
(406-222-4184; www.yellowstonegatewaymuseum.org; 118 W Chinook St; adult/child $5/free; 10am-5pm daily Jun-Sep, Thu-Sun only Oct-May) Livingston's collection of historical

and archaeological treasures is housed in a century-old schoolhouse. Exhibits include a pioneer kitchen and an early Yellowstone stagecoach.

Yellowstone Fly Fishing School FISHING
(406-223-0918; www.yellowstoneflyfishingschool.com; 416 N 8th St) Offers a half-day fly-fishing class for $275/325 for one/two people, as well as land-based casting lessons by the hour and a women's one-day fly-fishing school ($250 per person). There are also youth classes and Yellowstone National Park fishing clinics.

Dan Bailey's Fly Shop FISHING
(800-356-4052; www.dan-bailey.com; 209 W Park St; 8am-6pm) Built on a legacy of Goofus Bugs, Humpy Flies, Green Drakes and Hair Wing Rubber Legs (to name but a few), Dan Bailey's is one of the world's best fly-fishing shops. It offers rentals, guided trips and online fishing reports. It's opposite the Depot Center.

George Anderson's Yellowstone Angler FISHING
(406-222-7130; www.yellowstoneangler.com; Hwy 89; 8am-5pm) Good fly-fishing store with equipment rental and guide service, 1 mile south of town.

Rubber Ducky River Rentals BOATING
(406-222-3746; www.riverservices.com; 15 Mt Baldy Dr; 9am-5pm Mon-Sat, 11am-4pm Sun Jun-Sep) For canoe and kayak rentals and info on local rivers, head to Rubber Ducky, just north of I-90.

Sleeping

The nearest Forestry Service campground is Pine Creek (p150), 15 miles south in the Paradise Valley. Consider also the other excellent options in the Paradise Valley.

Osen's RV Park RV PARK $
(406-222-0591; www.montanarvpark.com; 20 Merrill Lane; RVs $48-53;) Just south of I-90, this place has laundry and showers and is open year-round. RVs only.

★ **Murray Hotel** HISTORIC HOTEL $$
(406-222-1350; www.murrayhotel.com; 201 W Park St; ste $229-239;) Central to Livingston's history since 1904, the Murray is the place to bed down with the ghosts of gunslinger Calamity Jane and director Sam Peckinpah (who lived in a suite for over a year, occasionally shooting holes in the ceiling). The hand-operated lift, original sinks and creaky wood floors set the tone, but the 25 rooms are fresh and modern.

Eating & Drinking

Mark's In and Out FAST FOOD $
(406-222-7744; cnr Park & 8th Sts; burgers $2-5; 11am-8pm Mar-Nov) If your tastes are less merlot and more chocolate milk, Mark's has been churning out quality never-frozen burgers, foot-long chili dogs and malts since 1954, the latter made with Livingston's very own Wilcoxson's ice cream. Roller-skating carhops lay on an extra scoop of nostalgia most summer Friday and Saturday evenings.

Mustang Catering DELI $$
(406-222-8884; www.mustangcatering.com; 112 N Main St; lunch $8.50-10, dinner $18-34; 10:30am-3:30pm & 5-9pm Mon-Sat;) For a top-shelf picnic en route to Yellowstone, combine a fabulous ciabatta sandwich, gourmet salad or hot daily special from this top-notch cafe with a wine-and-cheese grab from the **Gourmet Cellar** (next to Depot Center) and make a beeline for the Paradise Valley.

★ **2nd St Bistro** BISTRO $$
(406-222-9463; www.secondstreetbistro.com; 123 N 2nd St; mains $23-34; from 5pm Wed-Sun) Our personal favorite, located in the historic Murray Hotel, with a superb range of appetizers, cocktails and draft beers, this is a classy but relaxed bistro with an emphasis on quality locally sourced and housemade food. From the pear-and-pumpkin-seed salad to the European-style mussels and fries, you can't go wrong, and there's more vegetarian fare than the average Montanan restaurant.

Chadz COFFEE
(406-222-2247; www.chadzmt.com; 104 N Main St; 7am-2:30pm;) Lose yourself in the comfy sofas for a light lunchtime panini and reviving espresso at this funky coffeehouse.

Katabatic Brewing MICROBREWERY
(406-333-2855; www.katabaticbrewing.com; 117 W Park St; noon-8pm) Suitably named in incessantly windy Livingston, this dog- and family-friendly brewpub has stylishly exposed brick walls and live music on Saturday and Monday. There are normally eight brews on tap, including a crisp pale ale.

Information

Chamber of Commerce (406-222-0850; www.livingston-chamber.com; 303 E Park St; 9am-5pm) Has a very useful website. Try also www.livingstonmontana.com.

CHICO HOT SPRINGS

Thirty miles from Yellowstone National Park, just south of Pray at the mouth of Emigrant Canyon, **Chico Hot Springs** (406-333-4933; www.chicohotsprings.com; 163 Chico Rd, Pray; adult/child $8.50/3.50; 8am-11pm;) was established in 1900 as a luxurious getaway for local cattle barons. The Victorian elegance has been restored, with great attention to rustic detail. It's worth a visit just to poke around and take a plunge in the large outdoor **pool** (adult/child three to six years $7.50/3.50, open 8am to 11pm), fed from hot springs and a toasty 103°F (39°C).

Smallish, creaking rooms in the main lodge, with shared bath, are the cheapest options ($73 to $141), with motel-style fishers' cabins and modern high-ceiling rooms with a porch approximately double those rates. Chalets up the hill have mountain views and mostly sleep four to six. Suites with private Jacuzzi are a great luxury.

The **Chico Inn Restaurant** (406-333-4933; www.chicohotsprings.com; dinner mains $28-38, Sun brunch $21; 7-10:30am Mon-Fri, 7-11am Sat, 8:30-11:30am Sun, 5-9pm daily) is renowned throughout the region, though there's slim pickings for vegetarians. The beef Wellington ($70 for two) gets rave reviews, as does the Sunday brunch, served between 8:30am and 11:30am.

Chico's activity center offers **horseback riding** (half-day rides $130) and **raft trips** ($42) down the Yellowstone. It also offers cross-country ski trips and there's a full spa attached to help you recover. Dogsled tours are operated from Thanksgiving to March through **Absaroka Dogsled Treks** (406-223-6440; www.extrememontana.com; per person $125-450).

Custer Gallatin National Forest Livingston Ranger District (406-222-1892; 5242 Hwy 89 S; 8am-4:30pm Mon-Fri) One mile south of town on I-90, next to Yellowstone Angler.

Paradise Valley

With Livingston as a railroad stop, Paradise Valley became the first travel corridor to Yellowstone National Park. Gardiner, 50 miles south of Livingston and just north of Yellowstone's North Entrance, is still one of the park's most popular entry points. The valley is mostly ranchland and has included at various times such famous residents as Peter Fonda, Jeff Bridges, Dennis Quaid, Tom Brokaw and John Mayer. And yes, a river, the Yellowstone, does run through it.

US 89 follows the Yellowstone River through this broad valley, flanked by the Gallatin Range to the west and the jagged Absaroka Range to the east. If you have time, the scenic East River Rd offers a recommended parallel and quieter alternative to busy US 89. Amazingly, in retrospect, plans were afoot in the 1960s to dam the Yellowstone River and flood much of the lovely valley.

Southern Paradise Valley

South of the Tom Miner turnoff, US 89 winds through Yankee Jim Canyon, a narrow gorge cut through folded bands of extremely old rock (mostly gneiss) that look a bit like marble cake. Yankee Jim George hacked out a toll road through the canyon in the 19th century and made a living from Yellowstone-bound stagecoaches until the railroad put him out of business. This stretch of the Yellowstone River is the valley's hottest white-water spot.

A couple of miles further toward Yellowstone look for the roadside hot springs, which were once channeled into an elegant, turn-of-the-century resort at nearby Corwin Springs. Across the river is the headquarters of the Church Universal and Triumphant (CUT), which built a huge underground nuclear shelter here in the 1980s after its leader, Elizabeth Prophet, predicted the end of the world.

Further south, a pullout offers fine views of the **Devil's Slide**, a superbly named, salmon-pink landslide area consisting of 200-million-year-old rock. Keep an eye out for bighorn sheep here.

Activities

Hiking & Backpacking

Paradise Valley's most popular trail is the 10-mile round-trip hike to **Pine Creek Lake**. The trail starts from the Pine Creek Campground parking area and leads 1.2 miles to Pine Creek Falls, where the crowds thin out for the next 3.8 miles to the lake, gaining around 3000ft en route. Budget at least four hours for the return hike, which is also a good overnighter.

WORTH A TRIP

TOM MINER BASIN

To get off the beaten track, head west of US 89 on Tom Miner Rd, 17 miles north of Gardiner and 35 miles south of Livingston, into one of the prettiest pockets of land in the area. The washboard road ends 12 miles west of the highway at secluded 16-site **Tom Miner Campground** (Tom Miner Rd; sites $7; ⏲ Jun-Oct), which has potable water and toilets.

Trails from the campground lead up through the **Gallatin Petrified Forest**, where remnants of 35- to 55-million-year-old petrified redwood and oak trees lie scattered among the Absaroka's volcanic rocks. A 0.5-mile interpretive trail near the campground winds around volcanic bluffs of fused ash (bear right where a sign says 'Hiker Trail Only') and peters out by a remarkable piece of petrified wood that is lodged in the roof of a small cave.

Visitors are allowed to keep one small piece of petrified wood (maximum 20 cubic inches), with a free permit available at the Gardiner, Bozeman or Livingston ranger offices (and maybe the Tom Miner Campground hosts).

Further south, down Mill Creek Rd, is the trailhead for **Elbow Lake**, 3500ft above the trailhead at the base of 11,206ft Mt Cowen, the highest peak in the Absaroka Range. The strenuous 18-mile round-trip hike (along trails 51 and 48) is best done as an overnighter. From the lake you can continue northeast to a second lake and ascend the ridge on the left for views of Mt Cowen.

Further south, there are more hiking opportunities on the east side of the Gallatin Range. A popular day hike from Tom Miner Campground takes you 3 miles uphill (gaining 1400ft) to meadows at **Buffalo Horn Pass** (clear of snow from July). A viewpoint five minutes' walk south offers excellent views of the Gallatin Valley; Ramshorn Peak (10,289ft) beckons to the north.

Other Activities

The Yellowstone River winds past 19 **fishing** access sites along Paradise Valley, most of which have boat ramps. Experienced anglers can pit themselves against challenging private spring creeks such as Nelson's, Armstrong's and Depuy's. For bookings, fees and conditions contact Livingston's fishing shops.

The Montana Department of Fishing, Wildlife & Parks runs basic **campgrounds** (☎406-994-4042; www.fwp.mt.gov; sites with/without a Montana fishing license $7/12) at the Mallard's Rest, Loch Leven and Dailey Lake fishing access sites. Primitive overnight camping is permitted free of charge at the Bureau of Land Management Carbella and Paradise fishing access areas, by the Tom Miner and Miller Creek turnoffs respectively, but the limited and primitive sites get snapped up quickly. All other access areas are day-use only.

Paradise Valley has some of the best **cycling** in the Yellowstone region. The paved East River Rd from the junction with Hwy 89 to Chico Rd and Chico Hot Springs is a scenic and smooth ride of 24 miles. For something more suited to fat tires, try the 17-mile gravel Gardiner Back Rd between Gardiner and Tom Miner Rd. This route starts from just behind the Yellowstone Heritage and Research Center as a dedicated bike path and follows the old railroad bed and stagecoach road past the Devil's Slide, the narrows of Yankee Jim Canyon and several primitive camping spots. To shorten the ride, turn off at Corwin Springs after 8 miles. Combine these routes, and you'll get a complete traverse of the valley.

Bearpaw Outfitters (☎406-222-6642; www.bearpawoutfittersmt.com; 136 Deep Creek Rd) organizes **horse-pack trips** in the Absaroka-Beartooth Wilderness (half-day $95) and day rides in Yellowstone National Park (from $225).

Sleeping & Eating

There are several useful campgrounds in the Paradise Valley. **Pine Creek** (www.recreation.gov; Luccock Park Rd; sites $15; ⏲ mid-May–Sep) and **Snowbank** (www.recreation.gov; Mill Creek Rd; sites $15; ⏲ mid-May–Sep) campgrounds serve as springboards to local hikes. Snowbank closes first, early in September.

The USFS also operates two simple year-round cabins. **Big Creek Cabin** (www.recreation.gov; FS Rd 132; cabin $50; ⏲ year-round) sleeps 10 and is set a half-mile from Mountain Sky Guest Ranch, up FS Rd 132, on the west side of the valley. **Mill Creek Cabin** (www.recreation.gov; E Mill Creek Rd; cabin $45), which sleeps four, is on the east side of the valley, 12 miles up E Mill Creek Rd, near Snowbank Campground. It has an electric stove and lights, but no mattresses. Call the

Livingston Ranger District (p149) for information. Reserve these up to six months in advance.

KOA CAMPGROUND $
(☎406-222-0992; www.livingstonkoa.com; 163 Pine Creek Rd; tent/RV sites from $30/52, cabins $74-112; ⏱May–mid-Oct; 📶🏊) Nicely situated by Pine Creek between US 89 and the East River Rd, 10 miles south of Livingston, this peaceful spot offers an indoor heated pool, cabins and laundry room. Some spots offer prime river access.

Mountain Sky Guest Ranch RANCH $$$
(☎800-548-3392, 406-333-4911; www.mtnsky.com; Big Creek Rd; weekly rates per person from $4430; 📶🏊) The western flanks of the valley hide this professionally run dude ranch, 4.5 miles up Big Creek Rd and 30 miles from Yellowstone. Rates include food and everything from fly-fishing to fun kids' programs. The dawn horseback rides to catch sunrise over Emigrant Peak are a highlight. There's a one-week minimum stay June to August. Shoulder-season months are adults only.

Yellowstone Valley Lodge LODGE $$$
(☎800-626-3526; www.yellowstonevalleylodge.com; 3840 Hwy 89 S; d $270-320, ste $450-610; 📶) Anglers love this row of modern duplex cabins right on the banks of the Yellowstone River. You can almost cast your line from your private balcony.

★**Yellowstone Valley Grill** MODERN AMERICAN $$$
(☎406-333-4162; www.yellowstonevalleylodge.com; 3840 Hwy 89 S, at Yellowstone Valley Lodge; mains $16-40; ⏱5:30-9pm Tue-Sun) 🌿 The only thing finer than the view of the Absaroka Range rising behind the winding Yellowstone River is the food. Sustainable local ingredients, fresh Napa Valley cuisine and an extensive wine list make this the valley's top restaurant. Make reservations at least two weeks in advance, and try to secure a patio seat.

Gardiner

☎406 / POP 875 / ELEV 5272FT

Gardiner is piled so tightly against Yellowstone National Park's north boundary it looks as if a massive train loaded with souvenir shops, hotels and mediocre restaurants crashed into it. This is a quintessential tourist town that exists solely to house and feed the 785,000 visitors that pour through the park's original entrance every year – a task it does passably well.

The border of the park is marked by the Roosevelt arch, constructed in 1903. Originally, visitors traveled through the arch on the old stagecoach road. Today the highway has to wind awkwardly back on itself to route you through the historic portal.

This is the only entrance to Yellowstone open to automobile traffic year-round. Mammoth Hot Springs is just 5 miles away.

Sights

Roosevelt Arch LANDMARK
Gardiner's most photographed sight is the park's northwestern entry gate, dedicated by Teddy Roosevelt himself on April 25, 1903, and inscribed with Congress' words: 'For the benefit and enjoyment of the people.'

Yellowstone Heritage & Research Center MUSEUM
(☎307-344-2664; www.nps.gov/yell/historyculture/collections.htm; 20 Old Yellowstone Trail; ⏱library 9am-4pm Mon-Fri, 9am-noon Wed) FREE The park's abundant archives (over five million items and growing) moved from Mammoth to this research facility in 2004. Drop-in visitors can peruse the temporary exhibits in the lobby. Alternatively, reserve the hour-long tour that runs at 2pm on Wednesdays (Memorial Day to Labor Day) and takes you into the museum and rare book archives.

Activities

Several outfitters run fishing trips, horseback rides and pack trips into Yellowstone and other nearby mountain areas, though all are primarily hunting operations. Rides start at around $105/170 per half-/full day. Outfitters include **Yellowstone Rough Riders** (☎406-223-3924; www.yellowstoneroughriders.com) and **Hell's A-Roarin' Outfitters** (☎406-848-7578; www.hellsaroarinoutfitters.com; Jardine), which also does cabin rentals, luxury tent accommodations and steak cookouts, courtesy of the Johnson family.

Rafting

Half-a-dozen companies operate family-friendly rafting trips on the Yellowstone River through the class II to III rapids of Yankee Jim Canyon, one of Montana's more famous white-water spots. Half-day rafting trips operate from mid-May to mid-Septxember and start from $43/33 for adults/children aged five to 12, or around $85/65 for a full day. Most companies also offer half-day 'paddle and saddle' combos for around $100/90.

Gardiner

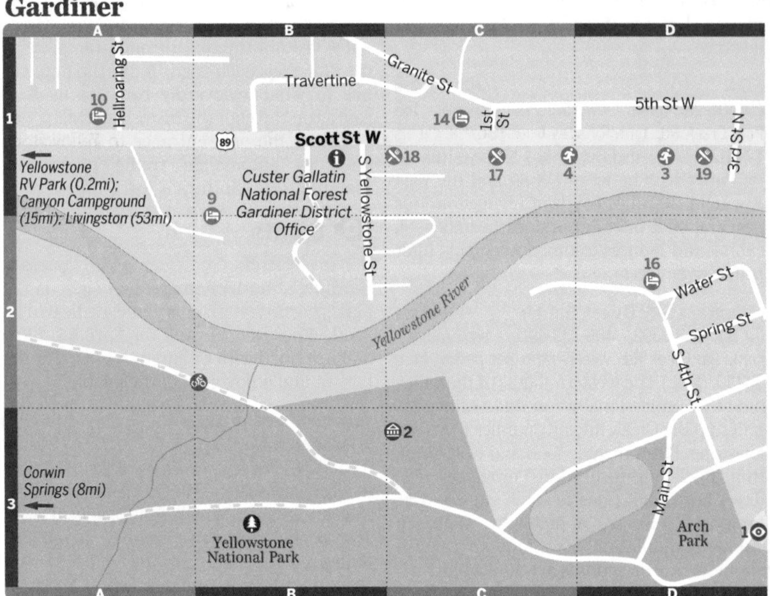

Gardiner

Sights

1	Roosevelt Arch	D3
2	Yellowstone Heritage & Research Center	C3

Activities, Courses & Tours

3	Flying Pig Adventures	D1
4	Montana Whitewater	C1
5	Wild West Whitewater Rafting	E3
6	Yellowstone Day Adventures	E3
7	Yellowstone Raft Company	E3

Sleeping

8	Absaroka Lodge	E1
9	Best Western by Mammoth Hot Springs	B2
10	Comfort Inn	A1
11	Gardiner Guesthouse	E2
12	Hillcrest Cottages	E1
13	Rocky Mountain RV Park	F1
14	Super 8 Motel	C1
15	Yellowstone River Motel	F2
16	Yellowstone Suites	D2

Eating

17	Gardiner Market	C1
18	The Corral	C1
19	Tumbleweed Bookstore & Cafe	D1
20	Yellowstone Grill	E1

Drinking & Nightlife

21	Hi Country Trading	E3
22	Iron Horse Bar & Grill	E2
23	Yellowstone Perk	E3

Yellowstone Raft Company RAFTING
(☎800-858-7781; www.yellowstoneraft.com; 111 2nd St; full day adult/child $86/66; ⊙May-Sep) With over 30 years of local experience, also has half-day kayaking lessons on the river and offers helmet video cams.

Wild West Whitewater Rafting RAFTING
(☎406-848-2252; www.wildwestrafting.com; 220 W Park St; full day adult/child $89/66; ⊙May-Sep) Rafting and gentler scenic floats in the upper Paradise Valley as well as inflatable kayak trips.

Montana Whitewater ADVENTURE
(☎406-848-7398; www.montanawhitewater.com; 603 Scott St W; full day adult/child $82/62; ⊙May-Sep) In addition to rafting and sit-on kayaks, it offers horseback riding and ziplining ($60 to $88), with various combo options. There's a branch in the Gallatin Valley.

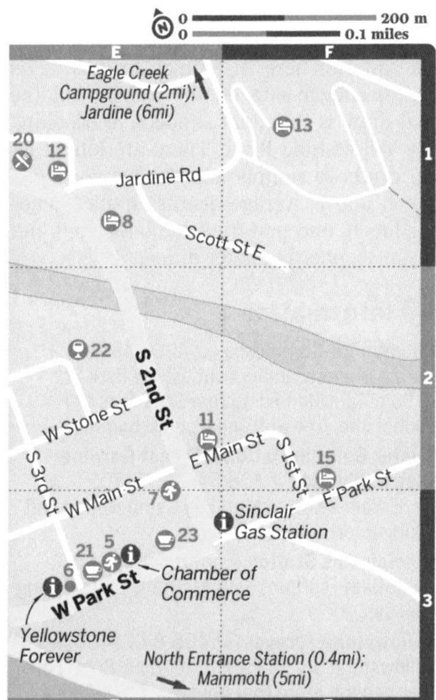

Flying Pig Adventures ADVENTURE
(☎888-792-9193; www.flyingpigrafting.com; 511 Scott St W; full day adult/child $90/69; ⏲May-Sep) Rafting shop that also offers horseback rides, cowboy cookouts, Yellowstone nature safaris and an outdoor-gear shop that stocks bear spray.

Sleeping

Camping

Custer Gallatin National Forest offers three first-come, first-served primitive campgrounds just northeast of Gardiner. Timber Camp and Bear Creek Campgrounds are free but somewhat inconvenient, being 10 and 12 miles respectively from Gardiner and without water.

Rocky Mountain RV Park RV PARK $
(☎406-848-7251; www.rockymountainrvpark.com; 14 Jardine Rd; RV sites $60-67, cabins $75-195; ⏲mid-Apr–mid-Oct;) This friendly place overlooking the river offers showers, laundry, full hookups and fine panoramas of Yellowstone, but little shade. Ask about the one- or two-room cabins that can sleep up to six.

Yellowstone RV Park RV PARK $
(☎406-848-7496; www.rvparkyellowstone.com; 121 Hwy 89; tent/RV sites $35/62; ⏲May-Oct;) At the northwest end of town, this RV park has 46 fairly cramped riverside sites with full hookups, plus showers and a laundry.

Lodging

About half of Gardiner's accommodations close between October and May and those that remain cut their rates by around 50%.

Chain places (all with free breakfast) include **Comfort Inn** (☎406-848-7536; www.choicehotels.com; 107 Hellroaring St; d $255;) and the **Super 8 Motel** (☎406-848-7401; www.yellowstonesuper8.com; 702 Scott St W; d from $190;).

Yellowstone Suites B&B $
(☎406-848-7937; www.yellowstonesuites.com; 506 S 4th St; d without/with bath $135/180;) There's plenty of privacy in this well-appointed, four-room, 100-year-old B&B, which makes a nice antidote to motel overload. There are cozy sitting spaces and views of Electric Peak, but only two rooms have attached bathrooms. Get a deal by renting an entire floor (two rooms).

Hillcrest Cottages MOTEL $
(☎800-970-7353; www.hillcrestcottages.com; 400 Scott St W; d $110, 2-room cottages $150; ⏲May-Sep;) This slightly cramped mini-village features a variety of pleasant if old-fashioned 1950s-era cottages. Most come with kitchenettes and sleep two to seven.

Gardiner Guesthouse B&B $
(☎406-848-9414; www.gardinerguesthousebnb.com; 112 E Main St; d incl breakfast $95-135;) Kid-friendly, pet-friendly and pretty much everyone-friendly, this homey century-old B&B offers two rooms with shared bath and one suite available in the main house, as well as a rustic cabin ($165) in the back. Breakfast is a serious family-style affair.

★ **Absaroka Lodge** HOTEL $$
(☎406-848-7414; www.yellowstonemotel.com; 310 Scott St W; r $190-220;) Modern, but surprisingly unobtrusive hotel with plain rooms that all have great views from their decks above the Yellowstone River. Upstairs rooms are the best and have private balconies.

Yellowstone River Motel MOTEL $$
(☎406-848-7303; www.yellowstonerivermotel.com; 14 E Park St; r $140-167, ste $199; ⏲Apr-Oct;) This is one of the more dependable motels in Gardiner and is clean and friendly with picnic tables and chairs on a tiny 'patio' overlooking the river. The renovated 'new building' rooms are bigger but absolutely generic. They do have a fridge and microwave.

Best Western by Mammoth Hot Springs HOTEL $$$

(406-848-7311; www.bestwestern.com/mammothhotsprings; 905 Scott St W; d $280-300;) It's not 'by Mammoth Hot Springs' (they're 5 miles away), but once you get past that, this is a solid choice, with spacious modern rooms and an in-house tour company.

Eating

For a town practically dedicated to tourism, Gardiner's lack of quality restaurants is something of an enigma. That said, there are a few good options that will get you down the road. Fill up on park supplies at the **Gardiner Market** (406-848-7524; 701 Scott St W; 7am-9pm) across from the Super 8 Motel.

Yellowstone Grill SANDWICHES $

(406-848-9433; www.facebook.com/YellowstoneGrill; 404 Scott St; mains $9-11; 7am-2pm Tue-Sun) This reliable place serves up fine burritos, salads and wraps in a coffeehouse-style industrial-brick interior or on the outdoor terrace. The Yellowstone Scrambler is a heap of yellow goodness that will get you well past lunch. Sit for coffee and cinnamon rolls, or grab and go. Opening hours change frequently, so check the Facebook page in advance.

Tumbleweed Bookstore & Cafe CAFE $

(406-848-2225; http://tumbleweedbooksandcafe.weebly.com; 501 Scott St W; mains $5.50-11; 7am-9pm Jun-Aug, shorter hours rest of year;) More coffeeshop than bookstore, you'll find enough on the menu to fill you up, and just enough on the shelves to entertain you during those lazy days in a hammock at camp, from topical tomes and regional stories to a smattering of easy reading fiction and a (small) wall of children's titles.

The Corral BURGERS $

(406-848-7627; 711 Scott St W; burgers $10-15; noon-9pm Apr-Oct) This old-style malt-and-greasy-burger stand has been proudly clogging arteries since 1960. It's neither gourmet nor all that cheap, but really, where else are you going to dive into a half-pound elk burger followed by a huckleberry shake?

Drinking

Grab your morning espresso at either **Hi Country Trading** (W Park St; 7:30am-9pm), which has some outdoor seating, or **Yellowstone Perk** (208 W Park St; from 7am), which also offers ice cream and a pharmacy.

Iron Horse Bar & Grill BAR

(406-848-7888; 212 Spring St; noon-2am) The interior here isn't much to look at (is that a cougar skin on the wall?!), but the real draw is the great sundeck overlooking the Yellowstone River. There are lots of local drafts to sample and the bar food is a notch above average, featuring elk nachos for lunch, and pan-fried rainbow trout and bison shepherd's pie for dinner.

Information

Chamber of Commerce (406-848-7971; www.gardinerchamber.com; 220 W Park St; 9am-4pm Mon-Fri, to 1pm Sat & Sun;) Tourist info, free wi-fi and a public bathroom.

Custer Gallatin National Forest Gardiner District Office (406-848-7375; 805 Scott St; 8am-4:30pm Mon-Fri) Campground and hiking information.

Sinclair Gas Station (cnr Park & 2nd Sts; 5:30am-9:30pm) Sells Montana state fishing licenses.

Yellowstone Forever (406-848-2400; www.yellowstone.org; W Park St; 8am-8pm) Former general store that houses a bookstore and information desk with a map of recent wildlife sightings in the park. Rent binoculars/spotting scopes here for $15/25 per day. Some courses are also held here.

GALLATIN ROUTE

Bozeman

406 / POP 45,250 / ELEV 4,820FT

Bozeman is what all those formerly hip, now-overrun Colorado mountain towns used to be like. The laid-back, old-school rancher legacy still dominates over the New West pioneers with their mountain bikes, skis and climbing racks. But that's changing rapidly. It is now one of the fastest-growing towns in America and cost of living is on the rise, but it hasn't turned yet.

The brick buildings downtown, overflowing with brewpubs and boutiques, still retain their dusty historic appeal and you can spend days in the surrounding Bridger and Gallatin Mountains without seeing another human.

And, while Big Sky up the forested Gallatin Valley is besieged with condos and townhomes, Bridger Bowl is so underdeveloped you might question whether the place is still open. In short, get here quick so you can tell your kids about the time you were in Bozeman while it was still one of the coolest unknown towns in the Rockies.

Sights

★Museum of the Rockies MUSEUM

(406-994-2251; www.museumoftherockies.org; 600 W Kagy Blvd; adult/child $14.50/9.50; 8am-6pm Jun-Aug, 9am-5pm Sep-May;) The most entertaining museum in Montana should not be missed. It has stellar dinosaur exhibits including an Edmontosaurus jaw with its incredible battery of teeth, the largest T. rex skull in the world, and a full T. rex (with only a slightly smaller skull). Laser planetarium shows are interesting, as is the living-history outdoors section (closed in winter).

American Computer & Robotics Museum MUSEUM

(406-582-1288; www.compustory.com; 2023 Stadium Dr; 10am-4pm Jun-Aug, shorter hours Sep-May) FREE If you have even one bit of computer geek in you (and caught the pun), visit this eclectic collection of artifacts covering landmarks in computer development including binary circuits, vacuum tubes, a chunk of ENIAC, an original Apple I signed by 'the Woz' himself, and a navigation computer from a Minuteman 1 missile – most with painstakingly detailed explanations.

Emerson Cultural Center ARTS CENTER

(406-587-9797; www.theemerson.org; 111 S Grand Ave; most galleries closed Mon) FREE Known around town as the Emerson, the nonprofit art collective occupying an old school is the place to plug into Bozeman's culture scene. Retail galleries, exhibits and studios line the hallway, while an outstanding cafe occupies the southeast corner.

Gallatin History Museum MUSEUM

(406-522-8122; www.gallatinhistorymuseum.org; 317 W Main St; adult/child $7.50/free; 10am-5pm Tue-Sat Memorial Day-Labor Day, 11am-4pm Tue-Sat rest of year) The former town jail does a good job presenting local history and famous residents (including one Gary Cooper).

Activities

Explore Rentals OUTDOORS

(Phasmid; 406-922-0179; www.explore-rentals.com; 32 Dollar Dr; 9am-5pm Mon-Sat, 10am-4pm Sun) Imagine stepping off the plane and there waiting for you is a car complete with luggage box, camping trailer, cook set, sleeping bags, backpacks, tent, bear spray, and full fly-fishing setup – all ready to go for your ultimate outdoor adventure. Or maybe you just forgot your stove. Explore has that and (just about) everything else for rent. Reservations highly recommended.

Spire Climbing Center CLIMBING

(406-586-0706; www.spireclimbingcenter.com; 13 Enterprise Blvd; day pass $18; 6am-10:30pm Mon-Fri, 8am-10pm Sat & Sun) Hone your climbing skills on the indoor walls here before heading off to tackle Grand Teton. Good-value private lessons and weekly classes are offered.

Bozeman Angler FISHING

(406-587-9111; www.bozemanangler.com; half-/full day trip $400/495) Guided fly-fishing trips run to all the nearby rivers, from the Yellowstone to the Missouri, catering to both first-timers and experienced anglers.

Bangtail Bikes CYCLING

(406-587-4905; www.bangtailbikes.com; 137 E Main St; 9am-6pm Mon-Fri, to 5pm Sat) Bozeman's best for buying and repairing bikes (no rentals); it also rents cross-country skis in winter.

MONTANASAURUS REX

It's amazing how much drama you can find in a single 50-million-year-old slab of rock at Bozeman's Museum of the Rockies. From the group of teenage diplodocus who suffocated when their legs became stuck in river mud, to the dinosaur skeleton surrounded by the teeth of the pack of predators that devoured it, these are fossils that come alive before your eyes. We challenge you to stare at the terrifying claws of a deinonychus without feeling a slight shiver run down your spine.

Like all good museums, MOR also shatters preconceptions, reminding you that many dinosaurs were in fact clad in feathers and that sharks once swam the tropical seas covering current-day Montana. Then there's the scale of the beasts – 9ft-long rib bones stand in the corner near huge 20ft-tall reconstructions of horned torosaurus and Montanaceratops (we kid you not). On display here is the world's largest collection of T. rex skeletons.

Even the former curator is larger than life. Paleontologist Jack Horner is widely believed to have been the model for the character Dr Alan Grant in the book *Jurassic Park* and served as technical adviser to all the films. And yes, they *did* extract soft tissue from a Tyrannosaurus thigh bone, right here in Bozeman.

Sleeping

Camping

There are three USFS campsites (all sites $15) 25 minutes' drive southeast of town near the Hyalite Reservoir: **Langohr** (19 sites), **Hood Creek** (26 sites) and **Chisholm** (10 sites). Take Forestry Rd No 62 from south Bozeman. Reserve sites at www.recreation.gov.

Bozeman Hot Springs Campground CAMPGROUND $
(406-587-3030; http://bozemancampground.com; 81123 Gallatin Rd; tent/RV sites from $45/70, cabins $85-100;) Off I-90, 8 miles west of Bozeman in the Gallatin Valley and next to Bozeman Hot Springs (http://bozemanhotsprings.co), this is the only campground in the area open year-round. Admission to the hot springs is free for campers.

Bear Canyon Campground CAMPGROUND $
(800-438-1575; www.bearcanyoncampground.com; I-90 exit 313; tent sites $25, RV sites $34-49; May-Sep;) Bear Canyon Campground is on top of a hill 3 miles east of Bozeman, with great views of the surrounding valley. There's even a pool.

Lodging

Royal 7 Motel MOTEL $
(800-587-3103; www.royal7inn.com; 310 N 7th Ave; d $104-130; @) This little inn really tries. It's dated (squint and it's almost retro cool) but spacious rooms offer large TV, microwave, fridge, continental breakfast, laundry service and a stove for use. Swings are set up in a grassy space for the kiddies.

Lehrkind Mansion Bed & Breakfast B&B $$
(406-585-6932; www.bozemanbedandbreakfast.com; 719 N Wallace Ave; d incl breakfast $170-230;) This sophisticated nine-room Victorian B&B was built by a Swiss-German master brewer and is steeped in period furniture and history (the bricks were actually soaked in beer before construction). The 7ft Regina music box (one of only 25) is a highlight, as are the organic breakfasts and claw-foot bathtubs.

Lewis & Clark Motel MOTEL $$
(800-332-7666; www.lewisandclarkmotelbozeman.com; 824 W Main St; r from $150;) For a drop of Vegas in your Montana, stay at this flashy, locally owned motel. The large rooms have floor-to-ceiling front windows and the piped 1950s music adds to the retro Rat Pack vibe. With hot tub and steam room.

Howlers Inn B&B $$
(406-587-2050; www.howlersinn.com; 3185 Jackson Creek Rd; r $165-180, cabin $225;) Wolf-watchers will love this beautiful sanctuary 15 minutes outside of Bozeman. Rescued captive-born wolves live in enclosed natural areas on 4 acres, supported by the profits of the B&B. There are three spacious Western-style rooms in the main lodge and a two-bedroom carriage house.

The Lark MOTEL $$$
(406-624-3070; www.larkbozeman.com; 122 W Main St; r $240-290;) With a lively yellow palette and modern graphic design, this hip place is a big step up from its former life as a grungy motel. Rooms are fresh and the fine location puts it in walking distance of downtown's bars and restaurants.

Eating

As a college town, Bozeman has no shortage of student-oriented cheap-eats coffee shops. Most are on Main St, but you'll find a few south of campus as well. Several lodges offer dining along the Gallatin River, and there are plenty more options in Big Sky (during summer and winter).

★ **Nova Cafe** CAFE $
(406-587-3973; www.thenovacafe.com; 312 E Main St; mains $10-13.50; 7am-2pm;) A helpful map at the entrance shows you where the food you'll be eating comes from at this retro-contemporary locals' favorite. The hollandaise is a bit on the sweet side for our liking, but still excessively delicious – as is everything else.

Granny's Gourmet Donuts BAKERY $
(406-922-0022; 3 Tai Ln; doughnuts $1; 7am-2pm Tue-Sun) The doughnuts here are utterly addictive, so come in the morning before they sell out and don't be stupid like us and buy only one; you'll only have to return later for more. Look for local Flathead cherry or huckleberry toppings in late summer.

Cateye Café BREAKFAST $
(406-587-8844; www.cateyecafe.com; 23 N Tracy Ave; mains $9.25-12.75; 7am-2pm) The banana-bread French toast and daily specials make the hip and quirky Cateye our favorite Bozeman breakfast. Expect to queue on weekends, but at least you can sip on a coffee while you wait.

Roost Fried Chicken CHICKEN $
(☎406-404-1475; www.roostfriedchicken.com; 1520 W Main St; mains $9.25-12; ⏰11am-9pm; 📶) When two good ole boys from Tennessee first came to Montana to fish, they loved everything but the lack of good Southern fried chicken. And thus, Roost was born. At least that's the story told to us by a grinning grease-smeared local who may have just been drunk on chicken and waffles.

Starky's DELI $
(☎406-556-1111; www.starkysonline.com; 24 N Tracy Ave; mains $12-14; ⏰11am-4pm; 📶) Offering great New York–style deli lunches, including matzo-ball soup and a mean Reuben pastrami on rye, served on a sunny patio. It's perfect for a late lunch.

Dave's Sushi SUSHI $$
(☎406-556-1351; www.davessushi.com; 115 N Bozeman Ave; rolls $7-16; ⏰11am-9:30pm Sun-Thu, to 10pm Fri & Sat) An expanded wooden house, one-and-a-half blocks north of Main St, with a cool counter and patio, offering the best rolls and freshest line-caught fish for miles around.

Plonk BISTRO $$$
(☎406-587-2170; www.plonkwine.com; 29 E Main St; small plates $9-16, mains $22-35; ⏰3pm-midnight) Sometimes you need to kick off the boots, run a comb through your hair and let your inner metro free. Sophisticated Plonk serves a wide-ranging menu from light snacks to full meals, paired with good wine and excellent cocktails.

Drinking & Nightlife

With plenty of breweries and an active live music scene, if you're not having fun in Bozeman, you're doing it wrong. Check the Bozone (www.bozone.com) for a good music calendar.

★**Montana Ale Works** PUB
(☎406-587-7700; www.montanaaleworks.com; 611 E Main St; ⏰4pm-close) Bozeman's former Northern Pacific freight warehouse brings industrial chic to this ever-reliable bar-restaurant, with excellent food (mains $10 to $24), pool tables and people-watching. Staff are happy to let you taste any of the 30 microbrews on tap, including the local Bozones.

Bridger Brewing MICROBREWERY
(☎406-587-2124; www.bridgerbrewing.com; 1609 11th Ave; ⏰11:30am-9pm, beer to 8pm; 📶) This well-run and friendly brewpub with central horseshoe bar draws a loyal combination of beer hounds and local MSU students. The Lee Metcalfe Pale Ale is a firm

ROCKY MOUNTAIN BREWS

The Yellowstone states of Wyoming and Montana are fast developing a reputation among beer hounds for hosting some of the country's best microbreweries.

Snake River Brewing Co (p219) in Jackson is one of the region's most popular brewpubs. Flagship beers include the crisp Snake River Pale Ale, the dark and creamy Snake River Zonker Stout and the Austrian-style Jenny Lake Lager, part of the proceeds of which go to park improvements at Jenny Lake.

Also popular are brews from Teton Valley's Grand Teton Brewing Company (www.grandtetonbrewing.com), which uses local spring water to produce its smooth Old Faithful and Teton Amber ales.

Missoula's **Bayern Brewing** (www.bayernbrewery.com) is the only German microbrewery in the Rockies, serving up amber, pilsner, Killarney and Hefeweizen beers. **Big Sky Brewing** (www.bigskybrew.com), also of Missoula, produces one of Montana's best-selling microbrews, Moose Drool, a creamy brown ale with hints of coffee.

There are dozens of other microbreweries in the Greater Yellowstone Region. Bozeman alone is closing in on 10 microbreweries. Fans of walking and drinking will want to take the Billings Brewery Crawl, a walking tour of six breweries in an eight-block radius. If you are keen on tracking down more Montana craft breweries, try the following:

Lone Peak Brewery (☎406-995-3939; www.lonepeakbrewery.com; Meadow Village, Big Sky; ⏰11am-10pm) A kid-friendly brewpub equipped with a fine shuffleboard and light food menu. The Lone Peak IPA and Nordic Blonde are the most popular.

Bozeman Brewing Company (☎406-585-9142; www.bozemanbrewing.com; 504 N Broadway; ⏰2-8pm Mon-Thu & Sat-Sun, noon-8pm Fri) Drink Bozone brews at the source at this bustling taproom. The four-glass sampler is served on a downhill ski.

favorite and there are lots of food specials, including great pizza ($11 to $21). The not-so-hidden upstairs deck is a top place to hang if you can find a seat. Happy hour is from 2pm to 4pm.

Wild Joe's CAFE
(406-586-1212; www.wildjoescoffee.com; 18 W Main St; 6.30am-7pm Mon-Thu, to 8pm Fri & Sat, 7am-7pm Sun;) Everything a coffeehouse should be: pressed-tin ceilings and comfy sofas in a century-old building, live music on the weekends, pizza by the slice and a fine community spirit. Oh, and great coffee and chai.

Bozeman Taproom & Fill Station BEER GARDEN
(406-577-2337; www.bozemantaproom.com; 101 N Rouse Ave; 11am-close) One of Bozeman's coolest places to grab a pint and fill a growler has an open-air rooftop beer garden. Its 44 draft brews can be combined in as many ways as you like with the 'build your own flight' program. Hot dogs and sandwiches keep your belly full while you sample them all.

Shopping

Northern Lights SPORTS & OUTDOORS
(406-586-6029; www.northernlightstrading.com; 83 Rowland Rd; 10am-6pm Tue-Sat) Everything you need for your next whitewater or fishing adventure.

Chalet Sports SPORTS & OUTDOORS
(406-587-4595; www.chaletsportsmt.com; 108 W Main St; 9am-7pm Mon-Fri, to 6pm Sat, 10am-5pm Sun) A decent selection of outdoor, hiking and camping gear fronts this full-service bicycle shop that rents a range of bikes. It also rents stand up paddleboards.

Information

Custer Gallatin National Forest Bozeman Ranger District (406-522-2520; www.fs.usda.gov/gallatin; 3710 Fallon, Suite C; 8:30am-4:30pm Mon-Fri) Tricky to find in the west of town, with info on campsites and cabins, plus it sells USGS topo maps.

Gallatin Valley

A broad ribbon snaking through big valleys, the Gallatin River leaves its headwaters in the northwest corner of Yellowstone National Park to cascade through the narrow, craggy Gallatin Valley. US 191 traces its path, eventually meeting the Madison, Jefferson and Missouri Rivers at Three Forks. Sandwiched between the scenic Madison and Gallatin Ranges, the route – first forged by Lewis and Clark – is peppered with enough trailheads to make return hikers and skiers arthritic. The commercial heart of the valley is the broad opening connecting Big Sky Resort.

On a clear day, look for a distinct cluster of summits exceeding 10,000ft rising sharply out of the silhouette of the Gallatin Range, west of US 191. These are the Spanish Peaks, the valley's premier hiking and backcountry-ski destination.

Big Sky

Commercial development hits hyperdrive near the turnoff to Big Sky, the Gallatin Valley's main attraction, 18 miles north of Yellowstone National Park and 36 miles south of Bozeman. This world-class winter and summer resort attracts a cosmopolitan crowd more partial to an organic pinot noir than a can of Bud Lite, and multi-million-dollar homes continue to sprout like milkweed.

Big Sky spreads from US 191 to the base of Lone Mountain in four areas: Gallatin Canyon, Town Center/West Fork Meadows, Meadow Village and Mountain Village. Meadow Village and West Fork Meadows offer the bulk of the services, including a dozen restaurants. All are connected by a bike trail and a free shuttle service.

Activities

Big Sky Resort (800-548-4486; www.bigskyresort.com; 50 Big Sky Resort Rd; ski lift $139, bike lift $44) is comprised of Andesite Mountain (8800ft), Lone Peak (11,166ft) and Moonlight Basin (www.moonlightbasin.com), offering an awesome 5500 acres of terrain, with a 4350ft vertical drop, a 15-passenger tram, a gondola and multiple high-speed lifts.

From June to September the Swift Current lift (9am to 4pm) shuttles people and bikes to 10,000ft for $26, from where mountain bikers can choose from a dozen advanced downhill rides. Thrill seekers will love the giant swing ($15) and ziplines ($72 to $92).

For the region's biggest hike, take the Swift Current lift and then walk to the top of Lone Peak. Figure on a couple of hours to the top, which is generally clear from snow by the middle or end of July. Non-hikers can cheat by taking the tram to the summit ($72). Big Sky's other prime hike is the 6.5-mile return to Beehive Basin at the base of the Spanish Peaks range.

Lone Mountain Ranch SNOW SPORTS

(☎406-995-4644; www.lonemountainranch.com; day trail passes adult/child $20/free) Tucked into sagebrush meadows, this is one of the country's top Nordic resorts, with 47 miles of groomed cross-country trails, 20 miles of dedicated snowshoe trails and a full-service, high-end lodge. The 'first-timer' package ($60) is a bargain, including group lesson, trail fee and gear rental. Other standouts include prime-rib-dinner sleigh rides and ski and snowshoe tours of Yellowstone's northwest.

Sleeping & Eating

Inquire about condo, cabin or house rentals in Big Sky through **Big Sky Central Reservations** (☎800-548-4486; www.bigskyresort.com); ski packages are available throughout the winter season.

Hungry Moose Market MARKET $

(☎406-995-3045; www.hungrymoose.com; town center, West Fork Meadows; sandwiches $8-9.25; ⏲6:30am-10pm; 📶☑) If a good cabernet and hot, made-to-order panini would spice up the picnic, check out Big Sky's favorite post-ride or pre-ski stop. There are also hot breakfasts, espresso, smoothies, bulk food and groceries leaning toward the organic and natural.

Information

Big Sky Chamber of Commerce (☎800-943-4111; www.bigskychamber.com; ⏲9am-5pm Mon-Fri) Visitor center by the turnoff to Big Sky on Hwy 191.

Big Sky to West Yellowstone

After passing the Gallatin Canyon, Hwy 191 briefly enters the far northwestern corner of Yellowstone National Park (there is no entry booth here). Several remote park trails offer quiet day hikes and ambitious multiday backpacking trips across the Gallatin Range to the Mammoth region. **Specimen Creek trailhead** leads to Gallatin's petrified forest, created 50 million years ago when lava, ash and mudflows swallowed trees and other vegetation. The **Bighorn Pass** and **Fawn Pass Trails** beckon with more good hiking and hot-springs soaks.

The road leaves the headwaters of the Gallatin River at Divide Lake. The Madison Range and Taylor Peaks of the Lee Metcalf Wilderness lie to the west.

About 12 miles before reaching West Yellowstone you'll see the turnoff to Hebgen Lake (Hwy 287).

Activities

Hiking & Backpacking

Hiking trails – all open to mountain biking – head into the mountains along numerous creek drainages from both sides of US 191. Trails are marked on Beartooth Publishing's *Bozeman & Big Sky's Essential Dayhikes* map, available at local sports stores. It also produces a mountain-bike version.

A favorite dining-and-hiking combo is to hike up to the fire lookout at the top of the **Cinnamon Creek Trail** (6.6 miles return, gaining 2675ft), then have a post-hike beer or dinner at the Cinnamon Lodge, opposite the trailhead across US 191.

The most well-trodden hikes are in the northern half of the valley. The popular 6-mile round-trip hike to **Lava Lake** offers decent trout fishing. The trailhead is at a tight turnoff on a dangerous curve in Hwy 191. The trail climbs about 1600ft, crossing Cascade Creek several times to meadows and then continues up more switchbacks. Good campsites flank Lava Lake's northeast shore, but fires are banned within 0.5 miles of the lake.

A trailhead on Squaw Creek Rd accesses several trails. The 2.5-mile climb to the top of the **Storm Castle Trail** (trail 92) offers great views, but the 1900ft climb is unrelenting, with the last quarter-mile, across loose scree, especially strenuous and tricky.

The equally demanding 8-mile round-trip **Garnet Lookout Trail** (trail 85) leads off in the opposite direction, gaining 2850ft to the top of Garnet Peak, where there is a USFS lookout tower that can be rented as a cabin (bring your own water).

One of the best backpacking destinations is the **Spanish Peaks** area, accessed at the end of USFS Rd 982, about 22 miles south of Bozeman. Camping is allowed at the trailhead and there's a USFS cabin nearby. Most routes are overnighters or multiday loops. A popular loop leads up Falls Creek to the Jerome Rock Lakes (8 miles) and then back down the South Fork. Longer loops take in the Spanish Lakes (8.5 miles from the trailhead) or Mirror Lake (7.5 miles) and return via Indian Ridge and Little Hellroaring Creek.

Fly-Fishing

Ever since Robert Redford and Brad Pitt made it look sexy in the 1992 classic *A River Runs Through It,* Montana has been closely tied to fly-fishing cool. Whether you are just learning or you're a world-class trout wrangler, the wide, fast rivers are always spectacularly beautiful and filled with fish. Although the film – and the book it is based on – is set in Missoula and the nearby Blackfoot River, the movie was actually shot around Livingston and the Yellowstone and Gallatin Rivers.

For DIY trout fishing, the Gallatin River, 8 miles southwest of Bozeman along Hwy 191, has the most accessible, consistent angling spots, closely followed by the beautiful Yellowstone River, 25 miles east of Bozeman in the Paradise Valley. If you'd like a hand, **Gallatin River Guides** (406-995-2290; www.montanaflyfishing.com; Hwy 191; 9am-5pm) offers guided fly-fishing trips, equipment rentals and some women-only trips and tuition.

Other Activities

The Gallatin Valley also offers the best white-water rafting around Yellowstone – most exciting during June's high water. For inspiration, check out the 'mad mile' of white water visible from the main road after the Cascade Creek bridge.

Geyser Whitewater Expeditions RAFTING
(406-995-4989; www.raftmontana.com; US 191) This well-run operation, 1 mile south of the Big Sky turnoff, offers white-water rafting (half-/full day $68/109) and kayaking (half-day $75). Its excellent-value Epic Pass ($159) includes a half-day raft trip, a zipline course and a week of cruiser-bike rentals, paddle boarding and indoor climbing.

Montana Whitewater RAFTING
(406-763-4465; www.montanawhitewater.com; Hwy 191, Mile 64, Gallatin Valley; half-/full day $61/98) Runs white-water trips and scenic floats, as well as a half-day introduction to fly-fishing ($65 per person), ziplining ($60 to $88) and activity combos. See also www.yellowstonezip.com. It has an office in Gardiner.

Jake's Horses HORSEBACK RIDING
(406-995-4630; www.jakeshorses.com; 200 Beaver Creek Rd) Horseback trips, costing about $50 for an hour or $100/160 per half-/full day, plus a steak-dinner ride and horseback trips in Yellowstone National Park. It's 2.5 miles south of Big Sky.

Sleeping

Camping

Numerous USFS campgrounds (open mid-May to mid-September) snuggle up to the base of the Gallatin Range along US 191. All have potable water and vault toilets.

The USFS operates four sweet but simple little cabins in the valley: **Little Bear**, **Spanish Creek**, mountaintop **Garnet Mountain** and **Windy Pass**. The last three are accessible by hiking, skiing or snowmobile only. Great value for self-sufficient groups, most cabins are available year-round for $30 per night, sleep four and are equipped with stoves, firewood, cooking supplies and blankets. Contact the Bozeman District Office (p158) for information. Cabins and campgrounds can be reserved at www.recreation.gov.

Spire Rock Campground CAMPGROUND $
(www.recreation.gov; sites $11; mid-May–mid-Sep) Secluded and away from the road, 26 miles south of Bozeman, then 2 miles east on Squaw Creek Rd No 1321. Has 17 sites, but no water.

Greek Creek Campground CAMPGROUND $
(www.recreation.gov; Hwy 191; sites $15; mid-May–mid-Sep) Doubles as a fishing access site, 31 miles south of Bozeman, with a total of 15 sites on both sides of the highway. Western riverside sites fill early.

Swan Creek Campground CAMPGROUND $
(www.recreation.gov; sites $15; mid-May–mid-Sep) Secluded and popular, with 12 sites backing onto Swan Creek. It's 32 miles south of Bozeman and 1 mile east on paved Rd No 481.

Moose Creek Flat Campground CAMPGROUND $
(www.recreation.gov; Hwy 191; sites $15; mid-May–mid-Sep) Riverside with good fishing and 14 sites, but very close to the road. It's 9 miles north of Big Sky.

Red Cliff Campground CAMPGROUND $
(www.recreation.gov; Hwy 191; sites $15; mid-May–mid-Sep) Ample availability with 63 sites, some with electrical hookups, 48 miles south of Bozeman.

Lodging

Cinnamon Lodge CABIN $
(406-995-4253; www.cinnamonlodgeandadventures.com; Hwy 191; cabins $50-169;) This budget roadside establishment attracts a hodgepodge of RVers, families and fly-fishers. The modest but tidy cabins are perhaps the best value in the valley. It's on the Gallatin River, 11 miles south of the Big Sky turnoff.

★ **320 Ranch** RANCH $$
(406-995-4283; www.320ranch.com; Hwy 191, Mile 36; cabins incl breakfast from $213;) This historic 19th-century ranch occupies a beautiful swath of the Gallatin, 12 miles south of Big Sky by the Buffalo Horn Creek trailhead. Guests stay in spacious duplex log cabins with access to a fishing pond (casting lessons $45), outdoor hot tub and trail rides (activities are

open to non-guests). Couples should splash out on the historic McGill cabin ($270).

★Rainbow Ranch Lodge RESORT **$$$**
(☎406-995-4132; www.rainbowranchbigsky.com; Hwy 191; r $290-400;) Rustic but ultra-chic, it offers a select group of pondside or riverside rooms, most with stone fireplaces, balconies and access to the romantic outdoor hot tub. The Pondside Luxury rooms are easily the most stylish. The lodge is 5 miles south of the Big Sky turnoff and 12 miles north of Yellowstone National Park.

Covered Wagon Ranch RANCH **$$$**
(☎406-995-4237; www.coveredwagonranch.com; 34035 Gallatin Rd; 3-night r & board per person without/with horseback riding from $850/1250) Three miles from Yellowstone National Park, near Taylors Fork, this 1925 ranch feels more rugged than some of the rhinestone-cowboy ranches around. With a strong emphasis on riding, a top offer is the small pack trips into Yellowstone. Stays from three to 14 nights.

Eating

Cinnamon Lodge MEXICAN **$$**
(www.cinnamonlodgeandadventures.com; mains $15-28; ⌚dinner) The Western bar and Mexican steakhouse at the Cinnamon Lodge serves excellent food, including good *chile rellenos* and bacon-wrapped cream-cheese jalapeños, plus there's a nice sundeck for sampling Lone Peak brews from Big Sky.

320 Ranch AMERICAN **$$$**
(☎406-995-4283; www.320ranch.com; Hwy 191, Mile 36; mains $31-47, saloon mains $10-18; ⌚5:30-9:30pm May-Sep;) This ranch-house restaurant and saloon is heavy on game, but the real draws are the fun weekly specials. The popular Wednesday steak chuckwagon dinners start off with a two-hour horseback ride (adult/child $105/95) or 20-minute hay-wagon ride ($55/35). Book the latter in advance.

Rainbow Ranch Lodge AMERICAN **$$$**
(☎406-995-4132; www.rainbowranchbigsky.com; Big Sky; mains $32-60; ⌚5-10pm) The gourmet restaurant attached to its upscale lodge is the best in the valley and the place for a blowout. You won't find Montana morels, fiddlehead ferns or responsibly sourced New Zealand alpine tahr anywhere else.

Hebgen & Quake Lakes

If the Yellowstone park boundary had been drawn differently, this broad lake valley surrounded by snowcapped peaks would be mobbed with tourists. As it is, visitors with a mind to meander will find wild and beautiful backcountry and a slew of recreational opportunities with a fraction of Yellowstone's crowds.

Connected to Quake Lake by a scenic stretch of the Madison River, Hebgen Lake easily merits a few lazy days of hiking, angling and boating. Motorboats are permitted, and are available for rent at the **Madison Arm Resort & Marina** (www.madisonarmresort.com) on the south shore and the **Yellowstone Holiday** (www.yellowstoneholiday.com) and **Kirkwood Resort** (www.kirkwoodresort.com) marinas on the north shore.

Activities

Between the Earthquake Lake Visitor Center and the dam, Beaver Creek Rd turns north off the highway through an area notorious for grizzly sightings, and heads 3 miles to the **Avalanche Lake/Blue Danube Lake trailhead** (trail 222/152). Both Avalanche (11-mile round-trip) and Blue Danube (12.5-mile round-trip) Lakes make excellent day-hike destinations from July onward – the trail splits 4.5 miles from the trailhead. Further along Beaver Creek, the road finishes at Potamogeton Park, the trailhead for an excellent midsummer overnight trip up Sentinel Creek to the dozen-or-so alpine lakes of the **Hilgard Basin** (trail 202/201, 7 miles, 2700ft elevation gain) in the Lee Metcalf Wilderness.

Along the western shore of Hebgen Lake, a couple of miles past Spring Creek Campground, is the trailhead for Watkins Creek and the 10-mile round-trip day or overnight hike (gaining 1700ft) to **Coffin Lakes** (trail 215/209).

The useful 1:63,360 USFS *Lee Metcalf Wilderness & West Yellowstone Vicinity* map marks these and many other trails, as does Beartooth Publishing's *Bozeman & Big Sky's Essential Dayhikes* map.

Sleeping & Eating

On the southwest side of Hebgen Lake, three remote USFS campgrounds serve boaters and anglers. Four miles down a paved road, Lonesomehurst (p166) is the most accessible, with lovely lake views, potable water and a boat ramp. Another 2 and 6 miles, respectively, down a dirt road that turns to rough washboard, are lakeshore **Cherry Creek** and **Spring Creek** (no fee), both primitive sites with pit toilets but no drinking water and reputations as places for teenagers to party. Reach them by turning north off Hwy 20 about halfway between Targhee

WORTH A TRIP

QUAKE LAKE: THE NIGHT THE MOUNTAINS MOVED

Just before midnight on August 17, 1959, an earthquake measuring 7.5 on the Richter scale ripped the landscape of the Upper Madison Valley. As two huge fault blocks tilted and dropped, a massive 80-million-ton landslide pulverized two campgrounds, before rising halfway up the opposite valley wall.

The slip caused Hebgen Lake's north shore to drop 18ft, flooding lakeshore houses and lodges. Gaps opened up in highways, and cars crashed into the gaping holes in classic disaster-movie style.

Hurricane-force winds caused by the slide then rushed down the valley, tearing off campers' clothes from their bodies and creating a huge wave on the lake. Mini-tsunamis called seiches sloshed up and down the lake for the next 12 hours, pouring over the Hebgen Lake Dam, which, amazingly, held firm.

The slide blocked the Madison River, and the waters of newborn Quake Lake soon started to fill, as engineers worked around the clock to cut a spillway and avoid a second catastrophic flood. In a final fanfare, several hundred of Yellowstone's thermal features simultaneously erupted. After the dust settled, it was discovered that 28 people had been killed, mostly in the Rock Creek campsite. Nineteen bodies were never found, presumably entombed under the slide. The quake had been felt in California, and water tables were affected as far away as Hawaii.

Viewing the Site

The best way these days to get to grips with the enormity of the quake, the largest ever to hit the Rockies, is to visit the **Earthquake Lake Visitor Center** (Quake Lake visitor center; 406-682-7620; Hwy 191; 10am-6pm late May–mid-Sep) FREE, atop the landslide area at the end of Quake Lake. Drive or hike up the interpretive trails for a vista of the dramatic slide area and a memorial boulder inscribed with the names of the 28 campers killed in the slide. A dock at the eastern end of Quake Lake allows boaters to glide past the surreal submerged treetops. The following sites, listed west–east, can be seen on the drive back to West Yellowstone:

Refuge Point This is where many of the quake survivors were rescued. In summer rangers often lead a 1.5-mile guided walk from here for an overview of Ghost Village; call the visitor center to check. The ski loop here makes for a great 2.3-mile hike in summer, but the trail is faint so you need to keep a close eye on the blue diamond tree markers.

Ghost Village A half-dozen cabins of the former Halford's Camp lie stranded in the plain here, deposited by the rising waters of the new lake. To get here turn off the highway toward Campfire Lodge and then branch right down a dirt road. The cabins are on the other side of the river.

Cabin Creek Scarp Area Highlights a 21ft-tall scarp that opened up along the Hebgen Lake fault line. One campsite actually straddled the fault, with the picnic table left above the scarp and the fire ring 21ft below.

The Lake That Tilted Ten miles further east along Hwy 287, a road leads off to a parking area and a short trail to Hebgen Lake, where you can see three partly submerged cabins destroyed by the slide.

Pass and West Yellowstone on Denny Creek Rd (USFS Rd 176).

On the southeast shore of the lake is **Rainbow Point Campground** (www.recreation.gov; Rainbow Point Rd; sites $16; mid-May–mid-Sep), 10 miles from West Yellowstone. Rainbow Point and Lonesomehurst are both reservable online. Closer to Quake Lake are two concession-run USFS campgrounds: **Cabin Creek** (www.recreation.gov; Hebgen Lake Rd; sites $15; late May–mid-Sep), 23 miles from West Yellowstone, and the larger, nicer and nearby **Beaver Creek** (www.recreation.gov; Hebgen Lake Rd; sites $15; late May–mid-Sep), near some beaver ponds. Both are reservable. See also www.hebgenbasincampgrounds.com.

Call the Hebgen Lake Ranger District (p167) for information on all of these sites.

Beaver Creek Cabin CABIN $

(www.recreation.gov; Beaver Creek Rd; cabin $30; year-round) A superb base for hiking north of Hebgen Lake, accessible by car in summer, this simple forestry cabin offers bunk beds sleeping four, a stove, utensils, firewood and an ax.

Campfire Lodge Resort CABIN $
(☎406-646-7258; http://campfirelodgewestyellowstone.com; 155 Campfire Lane; tent sites $25-35, RV sites $40-50, cabins $85-330; ⊙Jun-Sep) Just across from Cabin Creek Campground, near Quake Lake, the riverside cabins here sleep up to seven, and there are RV and tent sites, a fly shop and showers. The popular riverside cafe (7am to 2pm) is worth a visit for breakfast or lunch.

Parade Rest Ranch CABIN $$$
(☎800-753-5934; www.paraderestranch.com; 7979 Grayling Creek Rd; room & board per adult/child $296/226; ⊙mid-May–Sep) Ten miles from West Yellowstone, northeast of Hebgen Lake, this historic 1935 ranch offers 15 cabins and plenty of activities. Daily rates include lodging, meals, horseback riding and fly-fishing on Grayling Creek. There's a three-night minimum.

Happy Hour Bar & Restaurant AMERICAN $$
(☎406-646-7281; www.happyhourbar.com; Hwy 287, Mile 4; meals $8-18; ⊙4-10pm Mon-Wed, 11am-10pm Thu-Sun) It's hard to think of a better end to the day than grabbing a basket of shrimp and watching the sun sink over Hebgen Lake from the boat-shaped deck. Drawing locals, fly-fishers, cyclists and campers, it's a colorful slice of rural Montana, down to the collection of eyebrow-raising boob shots on the walls. Wednesday is crab night.

West Yellowstone

☎406 / POP 1340 / ELEV 6667FT

The rambling mountain town of West Yellowstone is smack in the middle of some of the best hiking, fishing, sightseeing and hunting in the Greater Yellowstone ecosystem. It's only 50 miles from Big Sky, 90 miles from Bozeman and 32 miles from Old Faithful, making it almost an ideal base from which to explore the park and countryside; but not quite.

As Yellowstone National Park's busiest entrance – admitting over 1.8 million visitors per year, more than twice as many as the next-most popular south entrance – traffic here can come to a standstill throughout town as everyone funnels through the gates. Expect every hotel to be booked early and restaurants to have a wait. If you do stay here, get up and get out early before the rest of Montana and Idaho arrive.

History

In the early 1900s the Union Pacific Railroad built a rail line to the western edge of the park, then a fledgling community called Riverside. In 1908 Eagle's General Store (still on Yellowstone Ave today) was established, joined by the Madison Hotel in 1912. The frontier-style town, soon rechristened Yellowstone, became a hub of activity fueled by the railroad, until the rise of automobile travel put the line out of business in 1960. The entrepreneurial spirit ruled even during prohibition, when the town exported potent 'Yellowstone Spring Water.'

In 1920 the community changed its name to West Yellowstone after pressure from Yellowstone's other gateway towns.

Sights

From June through August ranger talks are given daily at 2pm at either the Yellowstone Historic Center or the Grizzly & Wolf Discovery Center. There is also a weekly ranger-led slide show at 7pm, and a daily 9:30am wildlife talk at the Chamber of Commerce Visitor Center.

★Grizzly & Wolf Discovery Center ANIMAL SANCTUARY
(☎406-646-7001; www.grizzlydiscoveryctr.org; 201 S Canyon St; adult/child $13/8; ⊙8:30am-8:30pm May-Aug, shorter hours rest of year;) This nonprofit organization offers an alternative for 'pest' grizzlies facing extermination and captive-born wolves that can't survive in the wild. Here they are used for education and product testing (check out the row of shame of non-bear-proof trash containers). The wolves are on continual display in their naturalized enclosures, while the bears are let out individually.

Yellowstone Historic Center MUSEUM
(☎406-646-1100; www.yellowstonehistoriccenter.org; 104 Yellowstone Ave; adult/child $6/2; ⊙9am-9pm mid-May–early Oct) Housed in the 1909 Union Pacific depot, this museum explores early stagecoach and rail travel. Look for the highly unstable-looking early snowmobile with a propeller and three skis parked outside. It closes earlier in May and September.

Oregon Short Line Railway Car HISTORIC SITE
FREE This wonderfully preserved 1903 Pullman car, once used by railroad executives, perfectly sums up the golden age of Western travel. Decked out in velvet, gas lamps and even stained glass, it sits beside the Branch restaurant at the Holiday Inn.

Activities

West Yellowstone hosts a range of cultural and sporting events, from evening **rodeo** (www.yellowstonerodeo.com; adult/child from $12/6; ⏲mid-Jun–Aug) and August's mountain-man rendezvous to the Spam Cup, a series of ski races in which the lucky winner receives a free can of preserved-pork products.

Summer

Both the Rendezvous and Riverside trail systems offer great **mountain biking** and **trail running** from mid-June to mid-October.

West Yellowstone has some of the best fishing shops in the Rockies for information, equipment, rentals and guides.

Free Heel & Wheel ADVENTURE SPORTS
(☎406-646-7744; www.freeheelandwheel.com; 33 Yellowstone Ave; ⏲9am-6pm Mon-Sat, to 5pm Sun) The place for maps, gear and advice on cycling and skiing conditions. In addition to renting mountain bikes ($35 per day), skis and snowshoes ($25), it offers touring and skate-ski lessons and organizes free women's rides.

Parade Rest Ranch HORSEBACK RIDING
(☎406-646-7217; www.paraderestranch.com; 1279 Grayling Rd) Nine miles from West Yellowstone, this dude ranch (p163) offers horseback rides from one to four hours ($60 to $115), including sunset rides and corral rides for kids under seven. There are also fun Western cookouts on a section of the old Bannock Trail overlooking Hebgen Lake on Monday and Friday evenings (adult/child $59/25).

Old Faithful Cycle Tour CYCLING
(www.cycleyellowstone.com; entry $80) The chamber of commerce sponsors this fall cycle tour to Old Faithful, with part of the proceeds going to charity. The fully supported 60-mile trips (with a van and repair assistance) are a lot of fun and are geared toward a range of abilities.

West Yellowstone

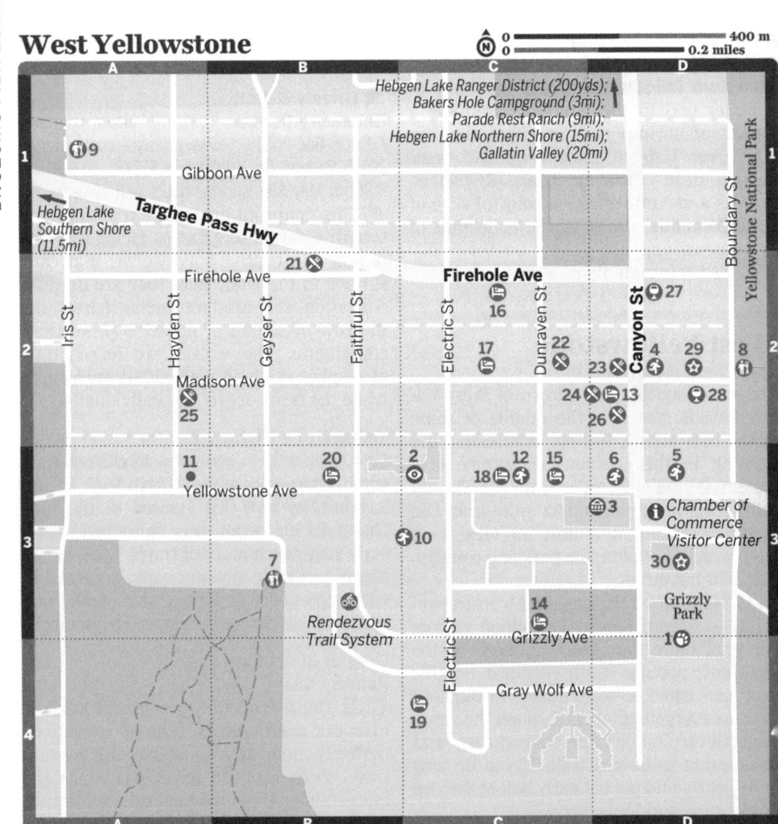

Yellowstone Aerial Adventures ADVENTURE SPORTS
(406-646-5171; www.yellowstoneparkzipline.com; 105 S Faithful St; adult/child $49/45; 9am-8pm Jun-Sep) This high ropes course is a hit with adventurous kids, who inch across rope bridges and throw themselves down ziplines while their parents look on nervously. Kids under 12 can do some of the elements, while even adults will struggle with the upper level.

Big Sky Anglers FISHING
(406-646-7801; http://bigskyanglers.com; 39 Madison Ave) Rents fishing equipment and offers one-day float and walk trips ($550 for two people).

Jacklin's Fly Shop FISHING
(406-646-7336; www.jacklinsflyshop.com; 105 Yellowstone Ave; 8am-9pm) Offers good fishing reports and a free weekly casting clinic on Sundays at 7pm.

Winter

Many of the hotels rent snowmobiles and offer good-value winter lodging and rental packages. Guided snowmobile day tours to the park cost around $225 per person. Several agencies rent snowmobiles for outside the park for $130 to $225 per day, excluding clothing. Rangers lead free snowshoe walks along Riverside Trails from West Yellowstone's Chamber of Commerce Visitor Center at 2pm on weekends.

Rendezvous Ski Trails SKIING
(www.skirunbikemt.com; day/season pass $8/40; Dec-Mar) In November this world-class network of trails becomes the training ground for US Olympic cross-country ski teams, with 30 miles of groomed Nordic skiing and skating trails. Grooming goes through March, when the Rendezvous Marathon Ski Race draws hundreds of skiers. There are also special kids' loops. For more information, visit Free Heel & Wheel.

Riverside Trails SKIING
This small network of trails follows an old stagecoach road for 1.5 miles to emerge on Yellowstone National Park service roads and trails alongside the Madison River. It's also a good short summer mountain-bike ride.

Hellroaring Ski Adventures SKIING
(208-360-0385; www.skihellroaring.com; Dec-Apr) Powder hounds keen to get off the grid should try Hellroaring Hut in the Centennial Mountains, 25 miles west of West Yellowstone. Access is via snowmobile (7 miles), then skiing with skins (3 miles). Hut rental, for a maximum of six experienced skiers, costs $350 per night, and includes snowmobiles, cooking supplies and sleeping bags. Guided trips available by request.

Rendezvous Snowmobile Rentals SNOW SPORTS
(800-426-7669; www.yellowstonevacations.com; 415 Yellowstone Ave) Rents snowmobiles for

West Yellowstone

Sights
1 Grizzly & Wolf Discovery Center D4
2 Oregon Short Line Railway Car C3
3 Yellowstone Historic Center D3

Activities, Courses & Tours
4 Big Sky Anglers D2
Buffalo Bus Touring Company .... (see 20)
5 Free Heel & Wheel D3
6 Jacklin's Fly Shop D3
7 Rendezvous Ski Trails B3
Rendezvous Snowmobile Rentals .... (see 20)
8 Riverside Trails D2
See Yellowstone .... (see 12)
9 Two Top Snowmobile Rentals A1
10 Yellowstone Aerial Adventures C3
11 Yellowstone Alpen Guides A3
12 Yellowstone Tour and Travel C3

Sleeping
13 Alpine Motel D2
14 Explorer Cabins C3
15 Madison Hotel C3
16 Moose Creek Cabins C2
17 Stage Coach Inn C2
18 Three Bear Lodge C3
19 Yellowstone Grizzly RV Park C4
20 Yellowstone Vacations B3

Eating
21 Ernie's B2
22 Food Roundup C2
23 Madison Crossing Lounge D2
24 Old Town Cafe D2
25 Running Bear Pancake House A2
26 Serenity Bistro D2

Drinking & Nightlife
27 Slippery Otter Pub D2
28 Wild West Saloon D2

Entertainment
29 Playmill Theater D2
30 Yellowstone Giant Screen Theater D3

outside the park for $130 to $225 per day, excluding clothing.

Two Top Snowmobile Rentals SNOW SPORTS
(406-646-7802; www.twotopsnowmobile.com; 645 Gibbon Ave) Rents snowmobiles for outside the park for $130 to $160 per day, excluding clothing.

Tours

Yellowstone Alpen Guides TOURS
(800-858-3502; www.yellowstoneguides.com; 555 Yellowstone Ave; adult/child $145/110) Runs 10-person snowcoach tours to Old Faithful, departing daily from mid-December through mid-March. Guided or independent skiing, snowshoeing and kayaking options on Hebgen Lake are also available, as are summer van tours of the park and multiday tours.

Sleeping

As the closest place to Old Faithful outside the park, lodging in West Yellowstone fills up early. Book well in advance.

Camping

Tent camping in town means cramming between rows of powered-up RVs. For more breathing space, don't forget the national forest campsites on Hebgen Lake.

Bakers Hole Campground CAMPGROUND $
(Hwy 191; sites without/with electricity $16/22; mid-May–end Sep) The nearest forestry service campground has 73 pleasant sites on the banks of the meandering Madison River, just 3 miles north of West Yellowstone. There are no reservations and it fills up most summer afternoons.

Yellowstone Grizzly RV Park RV PARK $
(406-646-4466; www.grizzlyrv.com; 210 S Electric St; RV sites $70-83, cabins $110-200; May–mid-Oct;) This RV metropolis is pricey but professional and the friendly service includes help with tours and rentals. Facilities include showers, laundry, cable TV and a recreation room.

Lonesomehurst Campground CAMPGROUND $
(www.recreation.gov; Denny Creek Rd; sites $16; mid-May–mid-Sep) Four miles down a paved road, Lonesomehurst has 26 sites and is the most accessible of several forestry service campgrounds, with lovely lake views, potable water and a boat ramp.

Lodging

Madison Hotel HOSTEL $
(800-838-7745; www.madisonhotelmotel.com; 139 Yellowstone Ave; dm $48, r without bathroom $69-95, with bathroom $150-215; late May–mid-Oct;) It's hard to picture President Hardy or Clark Gable snuggled in one of the basic timber rooms here, but it's this sense of history that might just draw you to this creaky 1912 hostel. Rooms are simple and clean, but with thin walls, and most share a bathroom. Non-guests are free to poke around unoccupied rooms before 6pm.

Alpine Motel HOTEL $
(406-646-7544; www.alpinemotelwestyellowstone.com; 120 Madison Ave; r $109-129, ste $149-189; mid-May–Oct;) The friendly and well-tended Alpine has a rather cramped courtyard, but remains one of the best-value places in town. The suites come with a kitchen and can sleep up to six.

Moose Creek Cabins CABIN $$
(406-646-7952; www.moosecreekinn.com; 220 Firehole Ave; r $200-300, cabins $329-600; Apr-Oct;) This friendly mix of 1950s-era wooden cabins and modern rooms is a good choice. Reception is in the nearby motel with the same name.

Explorer Cabins CABIN $$$
(877-600-4308; www.visityellowstonepark.com; 201 Grizzly Ave; cabins $370-540;) If you fancy a Yellowstone cabin vibe, but can't imagine life without a dishwasher, this group of 50 luxury suburban suites come with a fireplace, porch and even a DIY s'more kit, as well as a kitchen (and, yes, a dishwasher).

Three Bear Lodge LODGE $$$
(800-646-7353; www.threebearlodge.com; 217 Yellowstone Ave; main lodge d $269-299, motel d $209-239;) Rebuilt with reclaimed original wood after a 2008 fire, this friendly lodge offers spacious, stylish hotel rooms, as well as a cheaper motel option. Younger kids will go nuts over the themed 'Goldilocks and the Three Bears' suite ($309).

Stage Coach Inn HOTEL $$$
(800-842-2882; www.yellowstoneinn.com; 209 Madison Ave; r incl breakfast $240-290;) A longtime hub, the Stage Coach has eye-catching stuffed wildlife in the lobby, a sauna and an indoor pool. Deluxe rooms are bigger and fresher than the historic rooms. Winter rates drop as low as $60.

Eating

The selection of diners along West Yellowstone's Canyon St often have lines out the door as frustrated travelers take a break from the line of traffic into the park.

Pick up groceries at the **Food Roundup** (406-646-7501; cnr Madison Ave & Dunraven St; 7am-9pm) supermarket.

Running Bear Pancake House BREAKFAST $
(406-646-7703; www.runningbearph.com; 538 Madison Ave; mains $8-15; 6am-2pm;) Widely regarded as the best breakfast in West Yellowstone, and we see no reason to argue. If the short and tall stacks of buckwheat or buttermilk pancakes, eggs and sausage links don't do it for you, try the banana-walnut bread French toast with the rainbow trout.

Ernie's SANDWICHES $
(406-646-9467; www.erniesbakery.com; 406 Hwy 20; sandwiches $8-16; 7am-2pm;) An unpretentious sandwich maker on the highway between Geyser and Hayden Sts, Ernie's is a popular local stalwart that does good breakfasts, though things get busy at rush hour.

Madison Crossing Lounge MODERN AMERICAN $$
(406-646-7621; www.madisoncrossinglounge.com; 121 Madison Ave; mains $14-34; 5-10pm) West Yellowstone's 1918 school building houses this classy restaurant and bar. Standout dishes include the bison steak salad and blueberry white chocolate pudding, alongside the standard trout and burgers.

Serenity Bistro MODERN AMERICAN $$
(406-646-7660; www.serenitybistro.com; 38 N Canyon St; mains $15-30; 5-10pm) An island of modern upscale cuisine in a sea of chicken-fried steak and gravy, sophisticated Serenity is the place to turn to for a pear-and-walnut salad or orange Thai curry. The dining area is small and intimate so reserve a table, either inside or on the back patio.

Old Town Cafe AMERICAN $$
(406-646-0126; 128 Madison Ave; dinner mains $15-25; 7am-10pm) Grab a counter stool or a booth at this laid-back local diner-bar and feast on authentic down-home beef and trout dinners, or a breakfast of hot cakes, bacon and syrup.

Drinking

A handful of saloons and bars are targeted squarely at the tourist market. Better to enjoy a mellow evening and head into the park early before the crowds.

Slippery Otter Pub PUB
(406-646-7050; 139 N Canyon St; 11:30am-11pm) Beer snobs will want to head here for the region's widest range of craft beers on tap (over 20). Settle in with a selection of five 6oz tasters.

Wild West Saloon BAR
(406-646-7259; www.wildwestpizza.com; 14 Madison Ave; 10am-2am) Live honky-tonk rock packs this divey but fun place on summer weekends, plus you can order in the best pies in town ($14) from the attached pizzeria.

Entertainment

Playmill Theater THEATER
(406-646-7757; www.playmill.com; 29 Madison Ave; tickets $19-27; Mon-Sat Memorial Day-Labor Day;) Churning out light musicals, melodramas and comedies for 40 years, the Playmill is a local institution. Reserve tickets in advance.

Yellowstone Giant Screen Theater CINEMA
(406-646-4100; www.yellowstonegiantscreen.com; 101 S Canyon St; adult/child $9.75/7;) If it's raining head indoors for *Yellowstone*, *Lewis & Clark* and other films on a screen six stories high.

Information

Chamber of Commerce Visitor Center (406-646-7701; www.destinationyellowstone.com; 30 Yellowstone Ave; 8am-8pm;) Friendly traveler assistance, convenient parking and free wi-fi. There's also a ranger-staffed park desk and backcountry office.

Hebgen Lake Ranger District (406-823-6961; www.fs.fed.us/r1/gallatin; Canyon St, West Yellowstone; 8am-noon & 1-4:30pm Mon-Fri) Two blocks north of Firehole Ave, for information on Hebgen Lake campgrounds and trails.

Yellowstone Forever (p154) Houses a bookstore and information desk with a map of recent wildlife sightings in the park.

Getting There & Around

West Yellowstone is south of Bozeman on Hwy 191, and north of Rexburg and Idaho Falls on Hwy 20. There is no public transportation to or around town. Expect traffic jams on holiday weekends and during the height of summer.

Budget (406-646-7882; www.budget-yellowstone.com; 131 Dunraven St) and **Big Sky Car Rentals** (800-426-7669; www.yellowstonevacations.com; 415 Yellowstone Ave) offer car rentals from $60 a day.

Karst Stage (406-556-3540; www.karststage.com) runs buses daily, December to April, from Bozeman airport to Big Sky ($54, up to 90 minutes) and West Yellowstone (around $95, up to three hours). In summer it's charter only.

Grand Teton National Park

Includes ➜

Best Hikes

- Leigh and Bearpaw Lakes (p175)
- Phelps Lake (p181)
- Taggart and Bradley Lakes (p178)
- Cascade Canyon (p175)
- Table Mountain (p178)

Best Places to Stay

- Old Faithful Inn (p123)
- Jenny Lake Lodge (p207)
- Climbers' Ranch (p207)
- Lake Yellowstone Hotel (p266)

Why Go?

Awesome in their grandeur, the Tetons have captivated the imagination from the moment humans laid eyes on them. This wilderness is home to bear, moose and elk in number, and has played a fundamental role in the history of American alpine climbing.

Some 12 imposing glacier-carved summits frame the singular Grand Teton (13,775ft). And while the view is breathtaking from the valley floor, it only gets more impressive on the trail. It's well worth hiking the dramatic canyons of fragrant forest to sublime alpine lakes surrounded by wildflowers in summer.

Designated a National Park in 1929, much of the Snake River Valley was later donated to the park by John D Rockefeller, who acquired it through secret purchases. While their name is often ascribed to French trappers, the range was more likely dubbed for the Thítȟuŋwaŋ band of the Lakota Sioux who inhabited the area long before.

Road Distances (miles)

	Jackson	Moose	Colter Bay (GTNP)	Grand Targhee Resort (ID)
Moose	15			
Colter Bay (GTNP)	40	30		
Grand Targhee Resort (ID)	45	55	85	
Old Faithful (Yellowstone)	100	85	60	130

Note: Distances are approximate

Entrances

The park begins 4.5 miles north of Jackson. There are three entrance stations. The park's south entrance, closest to Jackson, is the Moose Entrance Station (p209), west of Moose Junction. From Teton Village, the Granite Canyon Entrance Station (p209) is a mile or so north via the Moose-Wilson Rd. If driving south from Yellowstone, take the north entrance at the Moran Entrance Station (p209), 3 miles inside the park on US 89/191/287 just north of Moran Junction.

DON'T MISS

Don't miss sunrise from the deck of a canoe. Leigh Lake (p192), our favorite, requires some effort, but it's well worth a short haul in at first light to see Mt Moran hulking in these still, clear waters. More visitors arrive with each hour of the day, but this one is yours.

First, paddle String Lake, entering just off the trailhead (p202). After a short canoe portage, you're on Leigh. Either come early with headlamps or reserve a paddle-in backcountry campsite to make a night of it – though it's only a short trip, the off-trail setting feels marvelously rugged and wild. Bring binoculars to spot wildlife.

Canoes can be rented from Adventure Sports (p193) in Moose, along with life jackets and accessories. Get canoe and backcountry permits (both are required) at Craig Thomas Discovery & Visitor Center (p209).

When You Arrive

- Entrance permits are required to drive on Teton Park Rd (7 days, vehicle/motorcycle/pedestrian $35/30/20). It's free to bring a bicycle.
- Passes grant entry into both Grand Teton and Yellowstone National Parks.
- Keep your receipt to be able to reenter the park if you leave.
- There is no charge to transit the park on Hwy 26/89/191 from Jackson to Moran and out east to the Togwotee Pass including the road to Jackson Hole Airport.
- On arrival you'll receive a copy of the Grand Teton Guide, detailing ranger-led activities, road closures and park news.
- Bear spray is essential and can be purchased from park concessionaires.

GOOD TO KNOW

- The use of drones is prohibited.
- Permits are required for backcountry camping.
- Stay at least 100yd from wolves and bears, and 25yd from all other wildlife.

Fast Facts

- Area: 484 sq miles
- Highest elevation: 13,770ft
- Lowest elevation: 6109ft

Reservations

Grand Teton Lodge Company accepts reservations for the following season starting November 1. The park has three official concessionaires:

Grand Teton Lodge Company (GTLC; ☎307-543-3100; www.gtlc.com)

Spur Ranch Log Cabins (p207)

Signal Mountain Lodge (p206)

Most campgrounds are first-come, first-served but some allow a limited number of reservations.

Resources

Grand Teton National Park (www.nps.gov/grte)

Online Ranger Station (www.tetonclimbing.blogspot.com)

NPS Grand Teton App (www.nps.gov) Search for 'Grand Teton App.'

Park News Releases (www.nps.gov/grte/learn)

Grand Teton National Park

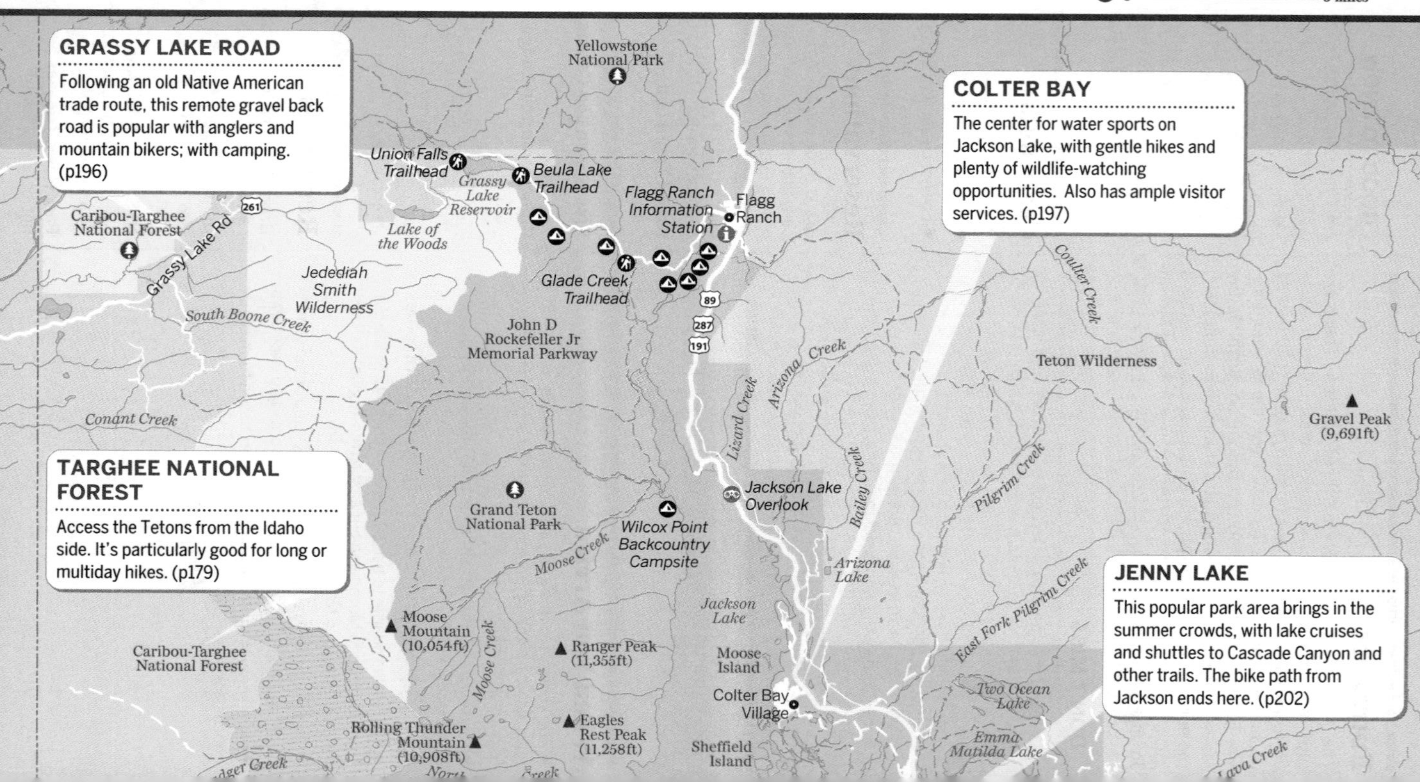

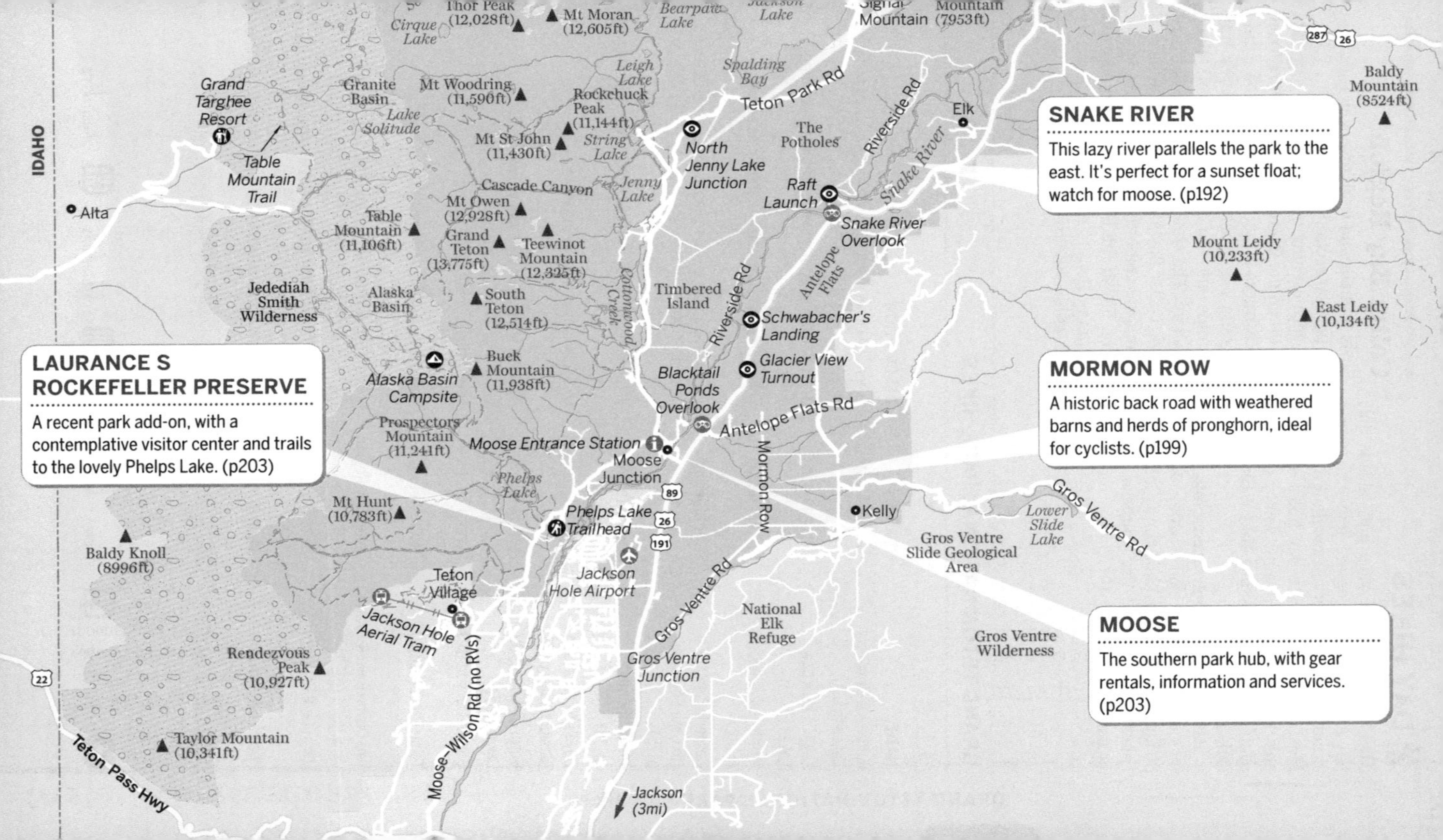

SNAKE RIVER
This lazy river parallels the park to the east. It's perfect for a sunset float; watch for moose. (p192)
MORMON ROW
A historic back road with weathered barns and herds of pronghorn, ideal for cyclists. (p199)
MOOSE
The southern park hub, with gear rentals, information and services. (p203)
LAURANCE S ROCKEFELLER PRESERVE
A recent park add-on, with a contemplative visitor center and trails to the lovely Phelps Lake. (p203)
IDAHO
Alta
Grand Targhee Resort
Table Mountain Trail
Cirque Lake
Mt Moran (12,605ft)
Bearpaw Lake
Mountain (7953ft)
Granite Basin
Mt Woodring (11,590ft)
Leigh Lake
Spalding Bay
Teton Park Rd
Baldy Mountain (8524ft)
Lake Solitude
Rockchuck Peak (11,144ft)
Mt St John (11,430ft)
String Lake
North Jenny Lake Junction
The Potholes
Riverside Rd
Elk
Snake River
Cascade Canyon
Jenny Lake
Raft Launch
Mt Owen (12,928ft)
Table Mountain (11,106ft)
Grand Teton (13,775ft)
Teewinot Mountain (12,325ft)
Snake River Overlook
Mount Leidy (10,233ft)
Antelope Flats
Cottonwood Creek
Timbered Island
Jedediah Smith Wilderness
Alaska Basin
South Teton (12,514ft)
Schwabacher's Landing
East Leidy (10,134ft)
Buck Mountain (11,938ft)
Alaska Basin Campsite
Blacktail Ponds Overlook
Glacier View Turnout
Antelope Flats Rd
Prospectors Mountain (11,241ft)
Moose Entrance Station
Moose Junction
Mormon Row
Phelps Lake
Mt Hunt (10,783ft)
Phelps Lake Trailhead
Kelly
Lower Slide Lake
Gros Ventre Rd
Baldy Knoll (8996ft)
Gros Ventre Slide Geological Area
Teton Village
Jackson Hole Airport
Jackson Hole Aerial Tram
National Elk Refuge
Rendezvous Peak (10,927ft)
Gros Ventre Junction
Gros Ventre Wilderness
Moose–Wilson Rd (no RVs)
Taylor Mountain (10,341ft)
Teton Pass Hwy
Jackson (3mi)

DAY HIKES

The Tetons' extreme verticality means that flat and easy rambles are few. The rating standard of the hikes reflects their difficulty. Most easy-to-moderate day hikes are suitable for families and most walkers. Hikers should adjust the distance they walk to their satisfaction.

Paved **wheelchair-accessible trails** include the Jenny Lake (p202) shoreline, String Lake (p202) shoreline, Colter Bay Lakeshore Trail and the southern edge of Jackson Lake Dam (p197).

Colter Bay Region

Birds, animals and wildflowers all feature in this popular section of the park.

A nice evening or early morning stroll is the 45-minute **Colter Bay Lakeshore Trail**, which traces a figure eight across a causeway onto a small island. Take the forest trail that dips onto the beach or just walk along the shore. The trail starts on a paved road beside Colter Bay Marina, or you can access it from the amphitheater next to the visitor center. Finish the hike at the amphitheater by 7pm or 9pm to catch the evening ranger talk. It's a 2-mile round-trip.

GRAND TETON NATIONAL PARK HIKES

NAME	REGION	DESCRIPTION
Taggart & Bradley Lakes (p178)	Central Tetons	Glacial lakes set in wildflower meadows and pine forest
Leigh & Bearpaw Lakes (p175)	Central Tetons	A fun, flat, family outing to crystal-clear swimming holes
Paintbrush Divide (p182)	Central Tetons	This pretty grind lifts you into the alpine scenery
Cascade Canyon (to Lake Solitude; p175)	Central Tetons	This ultra-popular grind scales to a mountain lake via a gradual climb
Table Mountain (p178)	Central Tetons	Wildflowers and high-alpine scenery without the crowds
Devil's Staircase to Alaska Basin (p179)	Central Tetons	Long day loop with stunning views
Surprise & Amphitheater Lakes (p177)	Central Tetons	A classic leg-burner with valley views
Garnet Canyon (p177)	Central Tetons	The climbers' route to the Grand
Teton Crest (p186)	Central Tetons	The epic hike of Grand Teton National Park
Two Ocean Lake & Grand View Point (p174)	Colter Bay Region	Lush forest, wildflowers and good bird-watching
Hermitage Point (p173)	Colter Bay Region	A wild and windswept point facing the multifanged Mt Moran
Phelps Lake (p181)	Moose-Wilson Rd	A lovely and flat forested amble around a beautiful lake
Death Canyon (p180)	Moose-Wilson Rd	An ethereal river valley flanked by granite climbing walls

 *Wildlife-Watching*   *View*  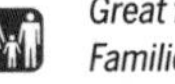 *Great for Families*   *Waterfalls*  *Restrooms*

Hermitage Point

Duration 4½ hours (shorter loop 1¾ hours)

Distance 9.2 miles (shorter loop 3 miles)

Difficulty Easy to moderate

Elevation Change Negligible

Start/Finish Hermitage Point Trailhead

Nearest Town/Junction Colter Bay Village

Summary A wild and windswept promontory with outstanding views of the multi-fanged Mt Moran.

From the Colter Bay Visitor Center, follow the parking lot to the southern end. At first the trail's signage may seem a little unclear, but throughout the hike the junctions are well marked. The trail itself starts by a sign that reads 'Foot Trail Only, No Road.' It follows a former road for less than 10 minutes, turns right, and then turns right again to climb up to the **Jackson Lake Overlook**.

The trail descends and passes along the left (eastern) side of lily-filled **Heron Pond**, where you can look for moose, trumpeter swans and cranes. It branches right, then right again for 2.2 miles to the cairn marking **Hermitage Point** (4.4 miles, 1¾ hours).

DIFFICULTY	DURATION	ROUND-TRIP DISTANCE	ELEVATION CHANGE	FEATURES	FACILITIES
easy-moderate	3hr	5.9 miles	560ft		
easy-moderate	3½hr	7.4 miles	negligible		
moderate	2-3 days	17.8 miles	3775ft		
moderate-difficult	6-7hr	14.4 miles	2240ft		
moderate-difficult	7-8hr	12 miles	3906ft		
moderate-difficult	1-2 days	15.7 miles	2200ft		
difficult	5-6hr	9.6 miles	3000ft		
difficult	9hr	12 miles	4800ft		
moderate-difficult	4-5 days	31-40 miles	6000ft		
easy-moderate	4hr	6.4 miles	400ft		
easy-moderate	4½hr	9.2 miles	negligible		
easy-moderate	3½hr	7 miles	negligible		
moderate	5hr	8-10 miles	1360ft		

 *Ranger Station*   *Backcountry Campsite*   *Boat Shuttle*   *Picnic Sites*  *Drinking Water*

Search the pines for nesting osprey near the point; there can be many here.

This lesser-hiked leg is densely forested and without views. Be sure to announce your presence when approaching blind corners in case of bears. The return leg (4.8 miles, two hours) loops back, taking a right to **Third Creek** and then a left past **Swan Lake**. Keep a watchful eye out for beavers munching on lily pads.

If you don't have the time to tackle the entire Hermitage Point loop, then turn left at the southeast end of Heron Pond to Swan Lake and return on a 3-mile, 1¾-hour loop, which is commonly used by horseback riders and ideal for families with small children.

This is also an easy and enjoyable destination for overnight backpacking. Reserve ahead for backcountry campsite No 9 at Hermitage Point.

Two Ocean Lake & Grand View Point

Duration 4 hours

Distance 6.4 miles

Difficulty Easy to moderate

Elevation Change 400ft

Start/Finish Two Ocean Lake Trailhead

Nearest Town/Junction Jackson Lake Junction

Summary On this unique hike, views take a backseat to the beauty of Two Ocean Lake and the lush surrounding forest.

The park's wildflowers peak in July, when abundant huckleberries and chokeberries make the area prime black bear territory. The tall grass means long trousers are a good idea. Set out by 8am to take advantage of a calm lake and great bird-watching opportunities. Grizzlies frequent this area, so be bear aware.

To reach the trailhead, turn north onto the Pacific Creek Rd around 1 mile west of Moran Junction. After 2 miles turn left onto the rougher Two Ocean Lake Rd and follow the gravel road for 2.5 miles to the parking area.

Follow a clear trail counterclockwise around **Two Ocean Lake** through lovely wildflower meadows with aspens and Teton views. At the west end of the lake (1¼ hours from the trailhead) the trail branches to the right; at the next junction, turn left to continue around the lake. Another option is to take the right branch and then a left branch for 1.3 miles uphill to **Grand View Point** (7586ft).

Colter Bay Region – Day Hikes

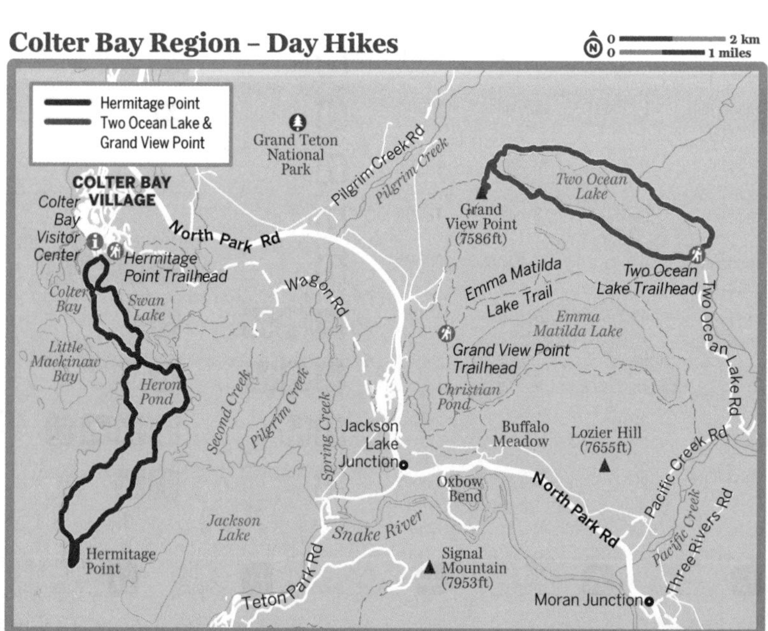

The second hill boasts the best views of Mt Moran, as well as Two Ocean and Emma Matilda Lakes. Return to the main lake trail via the same route.

From the lake junction take a right turn and continue around Two Ocean Lake. Sometimes the trail follows the lakeshore and sometimes it's through conifer forest and open meadow. It's about an hour to the trailhead.

Central Tetons

Though it's the most crowded sector of the park, there's scenery to please everyone here: lakes, waterfalls, glaciers, canyons and viewpoints.

Leigh & Bearpaw Lakes

Duration 3½ hours

Distance 7.4 miles

Difficulty Easy to moderate

Elevation Change Negligible

Start/Finish Leigh Lake Trailhead

Nearest Town/Junction North Jenny Lake Junction

Summary A fun, flat family outing skirting forest-clad, crystal-clear swimming holes.

Leigh Lake Trailhead is at the end of the side road off Jenny Lake Scenic Dr; don't confuse it with String Lake Trailhead. Try to get an early start on this trail, as it's very popular, particularly with young families. Canoeing these lakes (with short portages) is an excellent option on a hot summer's day. Always keep track of your picnic food, since bears are frequently spotted here.

The trail quickly joins the shallow **String Lake**, ideal for swims as it warms up nicely in summer. After around 20 minutes a trail branches left across the outlet to Paintbrush Canyon (and a possible loop of String Lake). Instead, take the right branch and then turn right again to **Leigh Lake**. You may see people carrying their canoes over this portage area.

As you continue north along Leigh Lake, your surroundings open up to fine views of Mt Moran and its Falling Ice and Skillet Glaciers. The dark central stripes in both Mt Moran and Middle Teton (12,804ft) consist of 1.5-billion-year-old lava-injected rock called diabase, which extends 7 miles west into Idaho.

Continue past the lovely lakeside campsites 12A (group site), 12B and 12C, which make easy camping destinations for families with small children. Ten minutes further along the trail you'll pass a picturesque beach, with views of Mystic Island and, from left to right, Rockchuck Peak, Mt Woodring (11,590ft), Mt Moran and Bivouac Peak.

After an hour (about 2 miles) of Leigh Lake views, the trail heads into forest to a meadow junction; take the central path to the west side of **Bearpaw Lake** and campsites 17A and 17C. The trail then veers away from the lake for 0.5 miles to quiet and remote-seeming **Trapper Lake** (an extra 20- to 30-minute round-trip from Bearpaw).

Before you descend too far on the trail back to Bearpaw Lake, watch for a faint path that veers to the left. This drops through forest and over a log bridge to campsite 17B, looping back to join the earlier junction. Return to String Lake the way you came.

Several backcountry campsites are outstanding. On Leigh Lake the most popular sites are 12B and 12C – you'll need to reserve these well in advance. More remote sites 13 and 15 are accessible by foot on an unmaintained trail that leads north from the bridge over Leigh Lake outlet. The nicest site at Bearpaw Lake is 17B, which has fine views of Rockchuck Peak. Site 17A is on the lakeshore below the path; 17C is more private but a bit uphill. Trapper Lake offers the quietest site (18A). These sites are among the few in Teton where campfires are allowed (in fire grates only).

Cascade Canyon (to Lake Solitude)

Duration 6–8 hours

Distance 14.4 miles to Lake Solitude with boat shuttle, 18.4 miles without

Difficulty Moderate to difficult

Elevation Change 2240ft

Start/Finish Jenny Lake Boat Shuttle

Nearest Town/Junction South Jenny Lake Junction

Summary This ultra-popular hike scales to a mountain lake via a gradual climb.

Thanks to wide patronage, this lovely trail (particularly its beginning) lacks the lake's namesake solitude, but still provides a rewarding challenge. Though a long hike with a large elevation gain, it is not especially

Central Tetons – Day Hikes

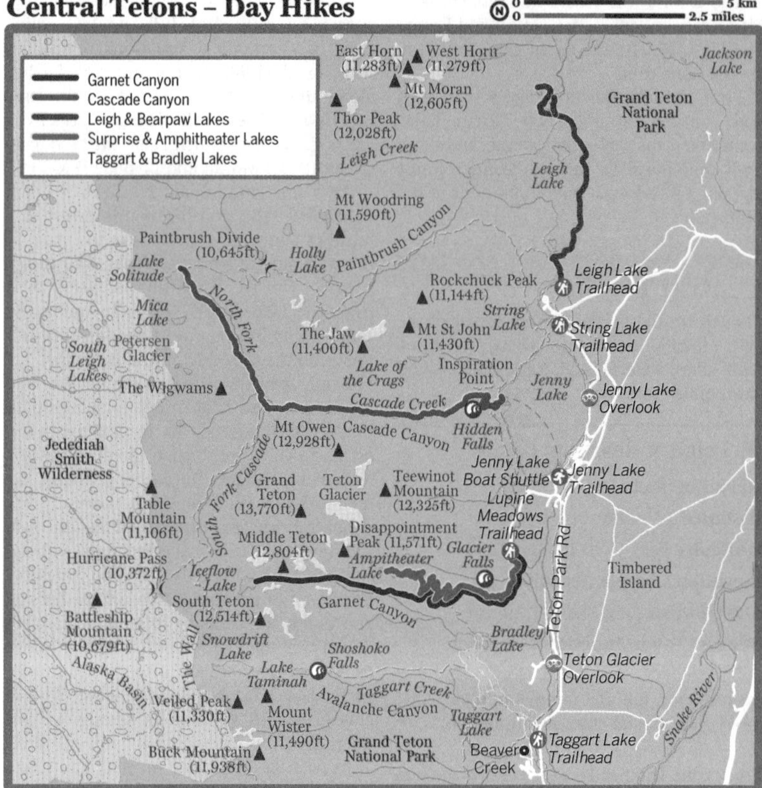

tough since the grade is quite gradual. Gear up for steep sections at the beginning near Inspiration Point and just before Lake Solitude. Moose and bears frequent the area.

The Cascade Canyon (west) dock on Jenny Lake meets a network of trails. If you plan to do the whole hike, taking the Jenny Lake Boat Shuttle (7am-7pm) will cut down on the big mileage.

Head left to pass **Hidden Falls** after 0.2 miles and ascend to **Inspiration Point** in another 0.5 miles. Climbers complete the scenery – Exum Mountain Guides uses this area for training. Soon afterwards, the horse trail from String Lake joins from the right.

The Cascade Canyon Trail continues straight, past a lovely beach and a high cascade, with fine views. About two hours (4.5 miles) from the dock, the valley splits at the **Forks**. The left branch leads to South Fork and Hurricane Pass. Turn right and climb gently for 30 minutes to enter the **Cascade Camping Zone** (12 sites), which stretches for the next 30 minutes. This area can remain quite snowy into early summer; check with rangers on conditions. From the zone's end it's 10 minutes up to the lake, past a small cascade and a hitch-rail marking the end of the line for horses. It's about three hours (7.2 miles) from here back to the dock.

Rimmed by fir and pines and sporting ice until midsummer, **Lake Solitude** (9035ft) is a great spot to loll around (but probably not to swim). To the northeast, the diagonal slash leading up the hillside leads to **Paintbrush Divide** (10,645ft). Camping is prohibited at the lake.

Return to the boat dock the way you came. The terrain, shaded most of the afternoon, is all downhill, affording full views of Mt Owen and Grand Teton.

Surprise & Amphitheater Lakes

Duration 5–6 hours

Distance 9.6 miles (10.2 miles with Glacier Overlook extension)

Difficulty Difficult

Elevation Change 3000ft

Start/Finish Lupine Meadows Trailhead

Nearest Town/Junction South Jenny Lake Junction

Summary One of the park's oldest, this trail is a classic leg-burner. Expect company: great views make it very popular.

Two 1920s businessmen built this trail even before cubicle fever existed. The route should be free of snow by late June. Bring plenty of water since none is available between the trailhead and the two lakes near the top of the climb.

There are three designated campsites at Surprise Lake for those who want to stay overnight, but, due to heavy use, some areas are off limits for regeneration.

The well-worn trail gently winds through pine forest until it mounts a shoulder and the ascent begins in earnest. A junction with the Taggart and Bradley Lakes Trail lies atop the shoulder, 1.7 miles (40 minutes) from the start. Taking in the cheery yellow blooms of arrowleaf balsamroot, keep right and tackle the series of switchbacks up the flank of **Disappointment Peak** (11,571ft). The route offers views over Taggart Lake and Jackson Hole. About 1½ hours (3 miles) from the trailhead there is a signed junction with the Garnet Canyon trail.

The switchbacks ease shortly before the lakes, and after around 2¼ hours of solid climbing, you'll finally reach the inviting, gemstone waters of **Surprise Lake**. Set in a hollow beneath jagged white rocks and cliffs, it is a resplendent payoff for your efforts. The slightly bigger and starker **Amphitheater Lake** lies just 0.2 miles further along the trail. Return the way you came.

SIDE TRIP: TETON GLACIER OVERLOOK

To reach the **Teton Glacier Overlook**, follow the trail around the northeast shore of Amphitheater Lake, staying right at several indistinct forks. Climb between the rocks to the top of a shoulder for breathtaking views of the glacier and into the valley sweeping down from the Grand Teton. A shattered ridgeline between the razor-sharp spires of Teewinot and Mt Owen to the north contrasts with the flatlands visible between sheer valley walls to the south. Vertigo sufferers beware!

Retrace your steps to the trailhead.

Garnet Canyon

Duration 9 hours

Distance 12 miles

Difficulty Difficult

Elevation Change 4800ft

Start/Finish Lupine Meadows Trailhead

Nearest Town/Junction South Jenny Lake Junction

Summary This climbers' route hauls hikers into the world of rock and ice. You must be fit and well acclimatized.

It's possible to hike this trail in a day, but it's best done as an overnighter, camping at either the Meadows or South Fork sites. Set off at first light since afternoon weather is notoriously fickle up here.

For the first 3 miles, follow the Surprise & Amphitheater Lakes trail. At the signed trail junction, branch left instead of right to the lakes. From this junction the trail curves around the hillside to dramatic views of Garnet Canyon and Middle Teton. Just over a mile from the junction, the maintained trail stops and the sometimes indistinct **climbers' path** continues over boulder fields for 20 minutes to the Meadows campsite. If you aren't confident with bouldering and trail finding, this spot makes a good terminus (8.4 miles round-trip, five hours).

The path splits right to Spalding Falls and the base camp for **Grand Teton** and left through indistinct boulder fields to switchback up to a small saddle, where you'll find a couple of campsites. From here, the trail traverses a small snowfield (present until August) and heads up the valley over a series of false saddles.

With several indistinct trails at your disposal, finding the right one involves some guesswork and bouldering. About 2 miles from the meadows you'll finally reach the **saddle** between Middle and South Teton (12,514ft), with fabulous views down to Iceflow Lake and across to the Wall and Hurricane Pass. You will likely meet groups of climbers heading to Middle Teton.

From the saddle it's a 3½- to four-hour return the way you came. Take great care on the rocks and snowfields as you return, as you'll be tired; this is no place to sprain an ankle or worse.

Taggart & Bradley Lakes

Duration 3 hours

Distance 5.9 miles

Difficulty Easy to moderate

Elevation Change 560ft

Start/Finish Taggart Lake Trailhead

Nearest Town/Junction Moose Junction

Summary An easy amble to this pair of glacial lakes that sit at the base of the Tetons, surrounded by grassy areas thick with summer wildflowers and fragrant pine forest.

These lakes were named after surveyors of the 1872 Hayden Geological Survey. The terrain is open from earlier fires, so it's a bit easier to spot wildlife, particularly moose. The trails here offer several easy loop options ranging from around 3 to 5 miles. Plan an early start in summer since much of the trail lacks shade. Don't forget your bathing suit.

The **Taggart Lake Trailhead** is just off Teton Park Rd, 5 miles north of Moose. Follow the trail northwest, past horse corrals, and take the first left at a marked signpost after 0.2 miles. Although this trail is only slightly longer, it receives far less traffic than the other option. After another 1.4 miles, turn right and climb open slopes to a point on the moraine wall overlooking the beautiful, rusty green **Taggart Lake**. Descend the short distance to the lakeshore and use a wooden footbridge to cross the outlet creek. A small, rocky outcropping makes a fine point to swim from. The views of the Tetons are fantastic.

The trail winds around the east shore of Taggart Lake, passing a signposted trail junction for the parking area (a shortcut back if you're tired) to your right. Climb steadily away from Taggart Lake and crest the moraine wall separating Taggart and Bradley Lakes. Descend through the trees to reach the thickly forested shores of **Bradley Lake**. You'll reach a junction just before the trail reaches the shore. Turn right to begin the trip back to the parking area or forge ahead to explore the perimeter of the lake before returning to this junction. The campsite at Bradley Lake is reserved for hikers on multiday loops of the Valley Trail.

You might want to combine your hike with the ranger-led wildflower and naturalist walks that depart every morning from the Taggart Lake Trailhead.

The Tetons via Idaho

The Idaho side of the Tetons offer an access point that's much less crowded, with camping in Caribou-Targhee National Forest and services in nearby Driggs and Victor. While these hikes are technically outside the national park boundaries, they sit within the same range.

Table Mountain

Duration 7–8 hours

Distance 12 miles

Difficulty Moderate to difficult

Elevation Change 3906ft

Start/Finish Teton Canyon Campground

Nearest Town/Junction Driggs

Summary This outstanding hike, starting in Targhee National Forest (part of Caribou-Targhee; p225), offers solitude, wildflowers galore and stunning high-alpine scenery without the crowds found on the eastern side of the range. A long haul, its stream crossings and steep sections make it best for experienced hikers. The trail is optimal after snowpack has melted and crews have cleared winter deadfall (early July through September). The final scramble onto Table Mountain can be slippery – tread carefully.

Heading north through Driggs, take a right at the traffic light (toward Targhee Ski Resort) for 4 miles. Then you will take a right onto a gravel road (6.5 miles) toward Teton Campground; drive through the campground to two parking lots. Park in the first and follow the trail for Table Mountain. Teton Campground (7200ft) provides a good base.

The first section is a thigh-burner. Ascend a steep forested trail to a lovely wildflower meadow dotted with aspens and frequented by moose. The next segment is mellower, with a slow ascent that requires crossing the north fork of **Teton Creek**. Hiking poles and sandals are a great help here. After the stream crossing, the trail winds through a tall pine forest giving way to the open cirque below Table Mountain. Here you ascend steeply – the trail zigzags with breathtaking views of the valley below and the Jedediah Smith Wilderness. Step carefully over patches of snow.

Once you achieve the ridge, the rounded knob of **Table Mountain** (11,106ft) appears so close! But it is still about 1½ hours to its summit. Sighting marmots along the way, follow the trail as it bends left toward Table Mountain. Once there, ascend the steep, crumbly rock with care, using the least steep path.

The flat-top summit of Table Mountain affords great gawping views of the Grand Teton, Alaska Basin and the western slope of the peaks. Spend some time drinking it all in. Photographer William H Jackson took the first photos of the Grand Teton here, during the 1872 Hayden Geological Survey. Head back at a reasonable hour since snowmelt will increase the runoff in the streams and make the crossing more challenging as the day goes on.

Devil's Staircase to Alaska Basin

Duration 1 or 2 days

Distance 15.7 miles

Difficulty Moderate to difficult

Elevation Change 2200ft

Start/Finish Teton Canyon Campground

Nearest Town/Junction Driggs

Summary This long day loop can be done in either direction, but by hitting it counterclockwise you will encounter fewer people in the early leg of the hike and quickly achieve stunning views after ascending the Devil's Staircase. Beware of snowpack in early summer; consult first with Targhee National Forest rangers. You can savor this epic trek by overnighting in Alaska Basin.

This sensitive alpine terrain receives heavy use. Practice leave-no-trace principles, stay on trails and observe fire restrictions. Permits are not required to camp, but campers must be at least 200ft from lakes and 150ft from streams. Bring water tablets or a purifier, sandals for river crossings and ample sunscreen.

To get here from Driggs, head toward Targhee Ski Resort. Take a right onto a gravel road (6.5 miles) when the road forks toward Teton Campground. Just past the campground there are two parking lots; the trailhead is in the second, as are pit toilets.

Tetons via Idaho – Day Hikes

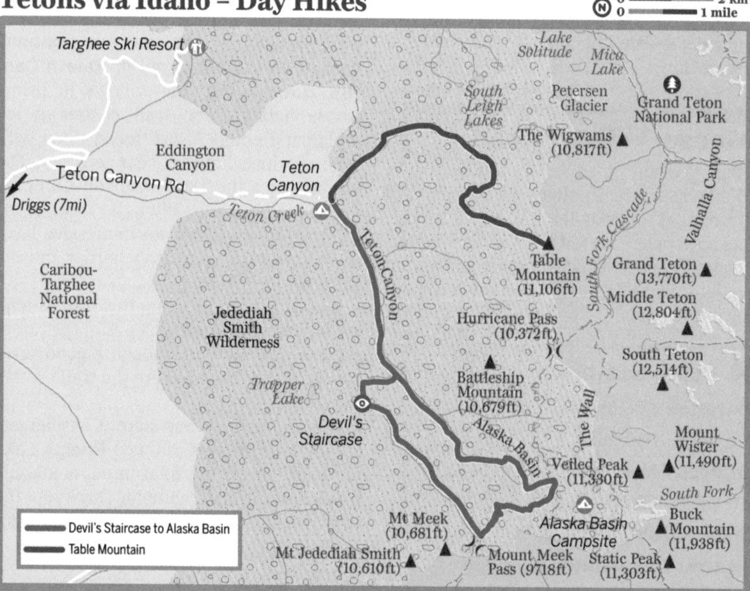

Set aside at least 9 hours. The first 2.7 miles follow an old jeep track at a mellow grade through fir and lodgepole pine. The south fork of Teton Creek parallels the trail. When the trail forks for Alaska Basin and Devil's Staircase, take the right-hand fork, which quickly gets steep. After a few switchbacks, you end up on a gently up-sloping high meadow with views. Heading toward **Mt Meek Pass**, look for Dall sheep on the cliffs that tower to the right. A gurgling brook parallels most of this section, steeped in wildflowers.

The trail splits, with the right fork heading toward Mt Meek Pass and the left dropping down the Sheep Steps into Alaska Basin. Savor the views of Mt Meek (10,681ft), Buck Mountain (11,938ft) and South Teton, before taking the fork to **Alaska Basin** (9200ft). This high-alpine area resembles Alaska's open tundra. There are many good campsites and overnighters have extra time to explore the Basin Lakes.

The rest of the hike follows the valley downhill through switchbacks and stream crossings (either shallow or with stepping stones or a bridge). Polished rock outcrops show evidence of glacial movement. This rocky and sometimes steep forested section can be somewhat tough on the knees.

From Alaska Basin to the signed junction with Devil's Staircase it is 5 miles. Continue toward the parking lot via the entrance trail. If you're hot and sweaty, take advantage of the great swimming holes off short paths to the creek.

Moose–Wilson Road

Moose–Wilson Road is a partially paved 15-mile route (its southernmost 3 miles are gravel) that connects Teton Village to Moose. RVs and trailers are not allowed on this road inside the park, which is quite narrow in sections. Plans are under discussion to pave the entire road.

Death Canyon

Duration 5 hours

Distance 8–10 miles

Difficulty Moderate

Elevation Change 1360ft

Start/Finish Death Canyon Trailhead

Nearest Town/Junction Moose Junction

Summary Lesser-known Death Canyon offers moderate hiking up an ethereal river valley flanked by granite climbing walls.

To reach the Death Canyon Trailhead, take the turnoff 3 miles south of Moose on Moose–Wilson Rd. Go right 1.6 miles down a narrow dirt track in poor condition. If you don't have a high-clearance vehicle, park before the end of the road, where the ruts become larger. The small parking area is often crowded with climbers' and backpackers' vehicles. Nearby, the **White Grass Ranger Station** was once an outfitters' cabin.

The trail climbs 0.9 miles to **Phelps Lake Overlook** (7200ft) and then descends 0.7 miles through lovely aspen forest, passing a springtime waterfall, to a junction; go right here. As you enter the towering gorge, the ascent kicks in – a relentless uphill climb over rocky switchbacks that quickly joins the river, which cascades over large boulders. After a hard slog of about 1.5 miles, the path flattens out. Devoid of the river's roar, the valley seems impressively serene.

The trail hits a junction by an old patrol cabin, 3.7 miles from the trailhead. The right branch climbs steeply to **Static Peak Divide** (10,792ft); if you have the energy, switchback up the trail to the treeline for great views of the peaks and plains (a two-hour detour). Alternatively, continue straight on the main trail up **Death Canyon**, through riverside willows in prime moose habitat. The trail crosses a log bridge and enters a lush forest filled with berries, which indicate bear territory. The campsites of the Death Canyon Camping Area pop up occasionally, as do views of the **Death Canyon Shelf**, an impressive layer of sedimentary rock atop harder granite and gneiss.

You can continue along this trail as long as you wish, perhaps using one of the campsites as a picnic spot, though a good turnaround point comes where the trail crosses the stream.

To exit, retrace your steps. Consider descending to the pine-rimmed **Phelps Lake** for a dip before the final grind, a 1.6-mile hike that includes climbing back up the moraine hill, which somehow seems a lot longer at the day's end.

Phelps Lake Trail

Duration 3½ hours

Distance 7-mile loop

Difficulty Easy to moderate

Elevation Change Negligible

Start/Finish Phelps Lake Trailhead

Nearest Town/Junction Moose

Summary A lovely and flat forested amble around a beautiful lake.

The trail leaves the Laurance S Rockefeller Preserve Center and splits. If you go left over the bridge, you will be on the **Lake Creek Trail**. Go right for the **Woodland Trail**. Before long, the Woodland Trail crosses the main road and continues in a gentle, winding ascent through pine forest and aspens, hitting the junction of the **Boulder Ridge Trail** at 0.7 miles. Continue straight; soon after, views open up and you get a glimpse of Static Peak (11,303ft) and Buck Mountain on its right. It should take 30 to 45 minutes total to reach Phelps Lake. Go the extra 20yd to the lake viewpoint for gorgeous views of the headwall across the lake; there are benches here for resting.

Start the **Phelps Lake Trail** loop counterclockwise. The trail intersects again with the longer Boulder Ridge Trail; continue on the lake loop, going through forested and sometimes bouldery terrain with lake views on the left. About one hour in you'll reach **Jump Rock**, an immense boulder used for launching swimmers into the lake. It's a fine spot to rest or picnic. The rock itself has a 23ft drop and the water is about 30ft deep here, so it's perfect for jumping in.

Ten minutes on, campsites 2 and 1 (respectively) are to the right of the trail. If you want to stay here, obtain a backcountry permit ahead of time. Shortly you will reach

Moose–Wilson Road – Day Hikes

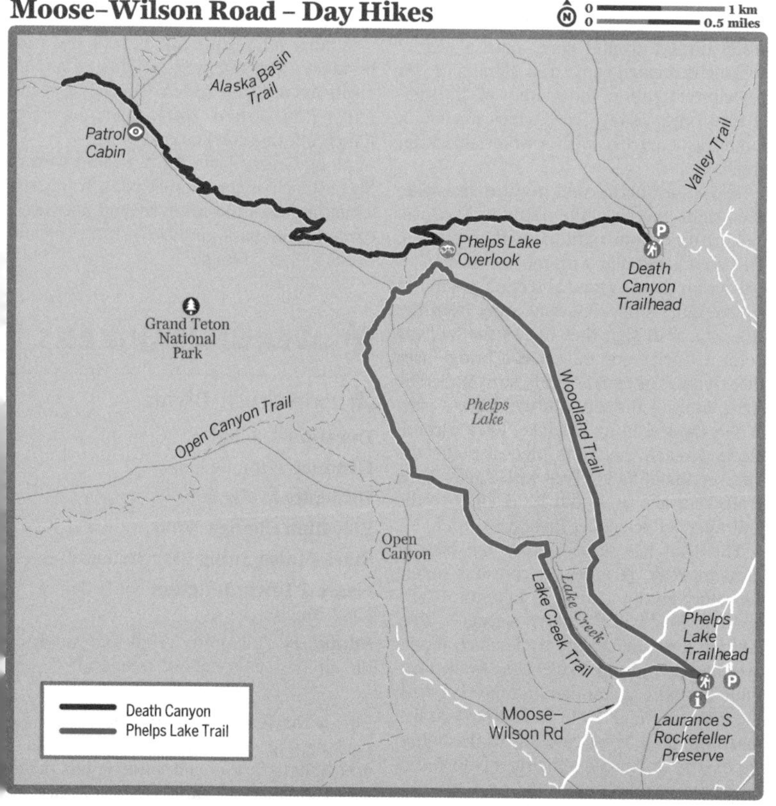

WILDLIFE-WATCHING

Hunker down at dusk or dawn with a spotting scope or binoculars to feast your eyes at the following sites.

Oxbow Bend (p197) A scenic river bend populated with moose, elk, sandhill cranes, ospreys, bald eagles, trumpeter swans, Canada geese, blue herons, white pelicans and…oh, yeah, abundant mosquitoes.

Willow Flats Turnout (p197) Views of a freshwater marsh that's home to birds, moose, elk and beavers.

Blacktail Ponds (Map p200; P) Features ospreys, eagles and moose.

Antelope Flats Bison and pronghorn at home on the range.

Hermitage Point Trail (p197) The spot to see beavers, trumpeter swans and geese at Swan Lake.

the opposite side of the lake. Hikers can get easily turned around here, since a nearby avalanche created some trail detours. If you pay close attention, the route is clear. Briefly turn onto **Valley Trail**, which ascends a humid aspen grove with a waterfall within earshot.

Two short paths veer toward the lake; keep right and continue rounding the lake, looking up to your right to see the waterfall. This area is popular with moose, so keep an eye out for them. A muddy section has round log stepping stones. Ascend away from the lake to a trail sign that marks the halfway point. Go left here and cross a bridge over the stream. The trail ascends, surrounded by ferns, and on the left you will have a view of the creek feeding the lake. Keep ascending and reach the trail's highest point, the intersection of Valley Trail with Phelps Lake Trail. Veer left here, and it's 3 miles to the Laurance S Rockefeller Preserve Center.

The trail has views across the lake to Jackson Peak. A mile on, consider taking the short left-hand trail to lakeside **Huckleberry Point** if it's berry season – they flourish here. Rejoin the trail, which passes over marshlands on a steel boardwalk. Continue straight at another intersection with the Boulder Ridge Trail. Soon after, you will reach the road: cross carefully as it's a blind curve. The trail crosses the river before ending at the Visitor Center.

The parking lot fills up by 9am in summer, so an early (or mid-afternoon) start is helpful.

John D Rockefeller Jr Memorial Parkway

From Flagg Ranch, **Polecat Creek** offers a pleasant stroll. The trail leads across Grassy Lake Rd from the main parking lot, passing two turnoffs to the right and an employee-housing loop before branching right to peaceful Oxbow Meadows. From here you can take a left at the next junction over a small creek to **Huckleberry Hot Springs**. The NPS advises against bathing here due to the high radiation levels in the water (caused by naturally occurring radon), but this hardly deters locals taking post-work alfresco soaks.

You can also get to the springs from a parking lot located one mile west of Flagg Ranch, though you need to ford Polecat Creek on this route, so bring water shoes. This former road used to lead to a hot-springs resort that was torn down in 1983.

A fairly interesting hiking trail also runs beside the volcanic walls of **Flagg Canyon**, northeast of Flagg Ranch. Get the brochure *Flagg Ranch Area Trails* from the Flagg Ranch information station.

Along Grassy Lake Rd, 2.2 miles west of Flagg Ranch, is the **Glade Creek Trailhead**, which accesses the rarely visited northwest corner of the park and its **Berry Creek** and **Moose Creek Trails**.

OVERNIGHT HIKES

Paintbrush Divide

Duration 2–3 days

Distance 17.8-mile loop

Difficulty Moderate

Elevation Change 3775ft

Start/Finish String Lake Trailhead

Nearest Town/Junction North Jenny Lake Junction

Summary This pretty grind lifts you into the alpine scenery above tree level.

This is the Tetons' most popular backpacking trip – perfect if you like a social atmosphere in the backcountry; just make sure you reserve a campsite in advance.

Uber-athletes could zip through it on an epic day hike, though it's worth savoring.

DAY 1: STRING LAKE TRAILHEAD TO HOLLY LAKE

5 HOURS / 6.2 MILES / 2540FT ASCENT

From the String Lake parking lot, take the trail that curves south around String Lake. It climbs gently until the left-hand junction with **Paintbrush Canyon**, 1.6 miles in. This steeper but moderate trail borders a stream flowing over granite boulders, passing through the Lower Paintbrush Camping Zone and some stock campsites. It climbs ever higher to reach an upper basin surrounded by snowy peaks. The first lake is unnamed; continue right of it to reach **Holly Lake** (9424ft). There are two good shady designated campsites at the lake's southeast corner. If these sites are booked, camp in the Upper Paintbrush Canyon Camping Zone.

For a great day hike, you can return via the same route (12.4 miles, 7 hours total), enjoying the lake views framed by the valley above.

DAY 2: HOLLY LAKE TO NORTH FORK CASCADE

3 HOURS / 3.2 MILES / 1235FT ASCENT

Ascend steeply to join the main trail; it's one hour to **Paintbrush Divide** (10,645ft). This is a tricky section with some exposure and a scree field. The pass may be snowy into early July – consult a ranger before going. A mountaineering ice tool could come in handy, even in summer. Enjoy the outstanding views before descending along broad switchbacks to reach **Lake Solitude** after another hour or so. Camp in the nearby North Fork Cascade Camping Zone or continue on.

DAY 3: NORTH FORK CASCADE CAMPING ZONE TO STRING LAKE TRAILHEAD

4–5 HOURS / 8.4 MILES / 2000FT DESCENT

Continue down Cascade Canyon to either the String Lake Trailhead or to Jenny Lake via the shuttle boat below Inspiration Point. If you don't take the shuttle boat across the lake, it's 2 relatively flat miles to the Jenny Lake parking lot. Arrange transportation back to your car in advance, as there's no public services. To return to the String Lake trailhead from Inspiration Point, it's 1.7 relatively flat miles.

From the camping zone, the trail descends through dense forest, which opens up as you head down the canyon. Look for moose, who favor the small ponds and lush banks of Cascade Creek. There's great views of Mt Owen to the south side of the canyon. Berry patches flank the final parts of the trail – be mindful of bears here.

Paintbrush Divide Loop

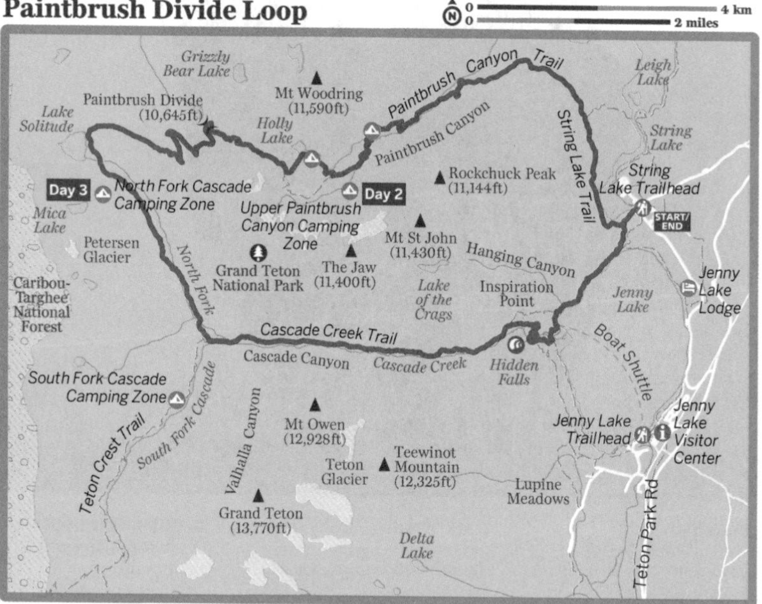

1

1. Bison (p247)
Majestic, free-roaming bison can be spotted against the spectacular Grand Teton backdrop.

2. Elk (p246)
Keep an eye out for this graceful species of large mammal, one of the most abundant in the region.

3. Wildflowers (p252)
June and July are the best times to park's vivid blooms.

2

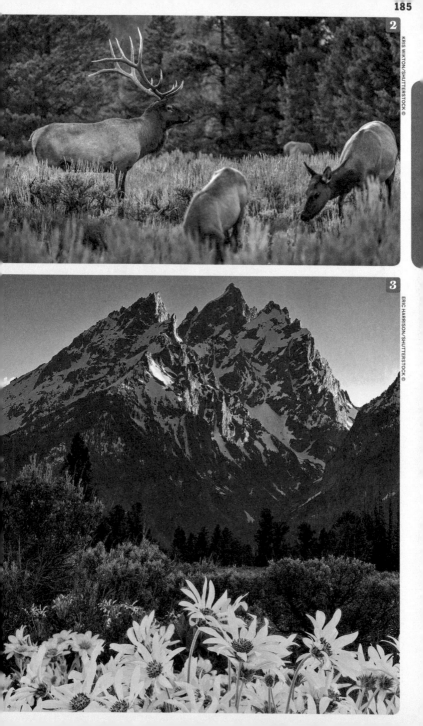

KRIS WIKTON/SHUTTERSTOCK ©

3

ERIC HARRISON/SHUTTERSTOCK ©

Teton Crest Trail

Duration 4 or 5 days

Distance 31.4 or 39.9 miles

Difficulty Moderate to difficult

Elevation Change 6000ft

Start String Lake Trailhead

Finish Granite Canyon Trailhead or Teton Village

Nearest Town/Junction North Jenny Lake Junction

Summary This epic trail takes hikers rambling over the lofty spine of the Tetons for jaw-dropping views and a fair share of high exposure.

This classic route is one to remember. Dipping in and out of the neighboring Jedediah Smith Wilderness, the trail has numerous routes out – namely the canyons and passes that access it on either side. Hikers must arrange for a shuttle or have two cars to leave at the start and end points. Bring plenty of sunscreen – there is almost no shade.

DAYS 1 & 2

Day one is the same as the Paintbrush Divide loop, curving around String Lake and

Teton Crest Trail

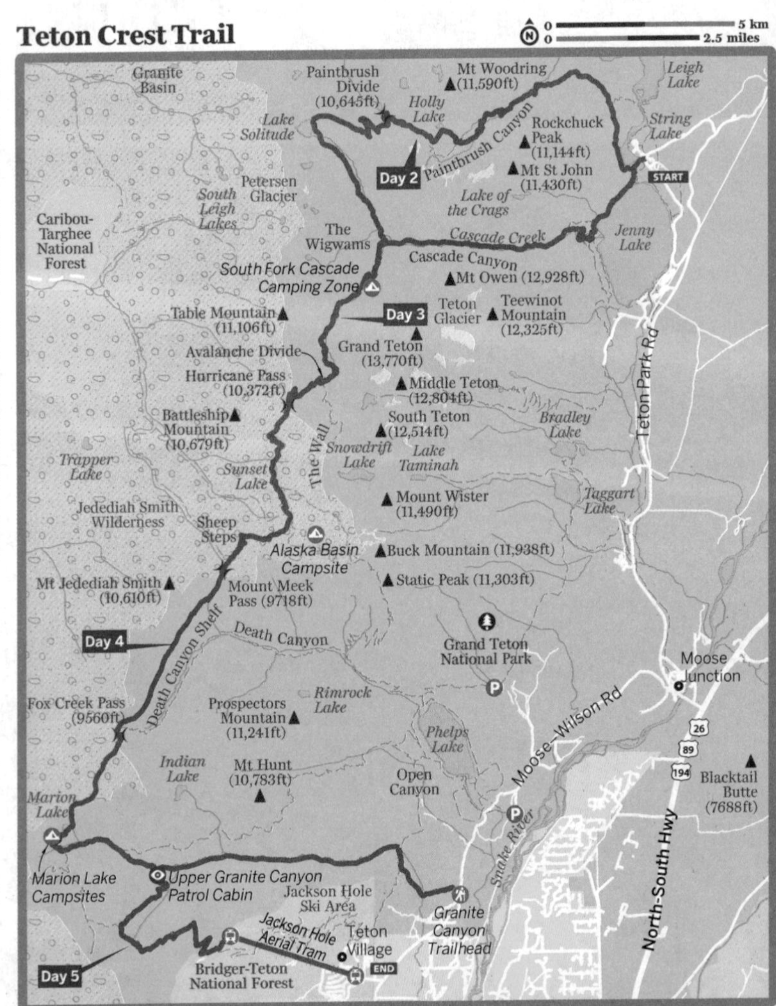

climbing through Paintbrush Canyon to Holly Lake. Day two continues to follow this route, taking you over a scree field to Paintbrush Divide. This section with loose boulders can be sketchy, so take it very slowly. Ice tools may be necessary for the better part of the summer, so check with rangers on conditions before heading out. Follow the divide down switchbacks to Lake Solitude (9035 ft), until the Forks junction between the North and South Forks of Cascade Canyon. Here the trail branches up the South Fork to the South Fork Cascade Camping Zone (19 campsites).

Alternatively, you can start the hike from Jenny Lake, catching a boat shuttle across the lake to Inspiration Point and hiking up Cascade Creek Trail to spend the first night at the South Fork Cascade Camping Zone. With the boat shuttle, this 10.4-mile hike (2050ft elevation gain) shaves off a day. The hike may be longer, depending on your assigned campsite. Allow a minimum of seven hours.

DAY 3: SOUTH FORK CASCADE CAMPING ZONE TO ALASKA BASIN

3–3½ HOURS / 6.1 MILES / 1992FT ASCENT

The trail climbs up to **Avalanche Divide** junction: head right (southwest) to **Hurricane Pass** (10,372ft), which has unsurpassed views of the Grand, South and Middle Tetons. (An excursion from the Avalanche Divide junction leads 1.6 miles to the divide, a scenic overlook above Snowdrift Lake.) From the pass the trail descends into the Jedediah Smith Wilderness, past Sunset Lake and into the **Basin Lakes** of the Alaska Basin, where you'll find several popular campsites. No permits are needed here since you're outside the park, but you must camp at least 200ft from lakes and 150ft from streams.

DAY 4: ALASKA BASIN TO MARION LAKE

4½ HOURS / 8.2 MILES

The trail crosses South Fork Teton Creek on stepping stones and switchbacks up the Sheep Steps to the wide saddle of **Mt Meek Pass** (9718ft) to reenter the park. For the next 3 miles, the trail dips into the stunning plateau of **Death Canyon Shelf** and the camping zone. Past the turnoff to Death Canyon, it climbs to **Fox Creek Pass** (9560ft) and continues southwest over a vague saddle to **Marion Lake** and its designated campsites.

DAY 5: MARION LAKE TO TETON VILLAGE VIA TRAM

5 HOURS / 6.5 MILES TO TRAM TOP / 1400FT ASCENT

The trail descends into the Upper Granite Canyon Camping Zone and continues past the Upper Granite Canyon patrol cabin to the junction with the Valley Trail. From here, head southeast to Teton Village, ascending the backside of the resort to take the Jackson Hole Aerial Tram (p221), or continue east to the Granite Canyon Trailhead (10.3 miles total).

OTHER COMBINATIONS

The Teton Crest Trail can be accessed from the east by several steep canyons. Trailheads (south to north) are: Granite Canyon, Death Canyon, Taggart Lake, Lupine Meadows, Jenny Lake and String Lake/Leigh Lake. Hike canyon-to-canyon to make a combination hike of any length. Options include the following:

Open Canyon to Granite Canyon One-night 19.3-mile loop from the Granite Canyon Trailhead.

Granite Canyon to Death Canyon A two- to three-night 25.7-mile loop via the Teton Crest Trail.

Death Canyon to Open Canyon A 24.7-mile loop from the Death Canyon Trailhead.

Marion Lake & Death Canyon

Duration 2 days

Distance 18 miles (or 23.5-mile loop)

Difficulty Moderate

Elevation Change 3850ft descent (from top of tram to Death Canyon Trailhead)

Start Teton Village

Finish Death Canyon Trailhead

Nearest Town/Junction Teton Village

Summary Downhill but certainly not a downer, this hike's tram shortcut gets you quickly steeped in the backcountry.

DAY 1: JACKSON HOLE AERIAL TRAM TO MARION LAKE

4 HOURS / 6.6 MILES / 1400FT DESCENT

This hike starts with a considerable boost: the Jackson Hole Aerial Tram to the top of Rendezvous Mountain gains 0.8 miles of elevation. From the tram, descend to a junction at the park boundary and turn right to descend into the South Fork of **Granite Canyon**. Take a left at the next

Marion Lake & Death Canyon

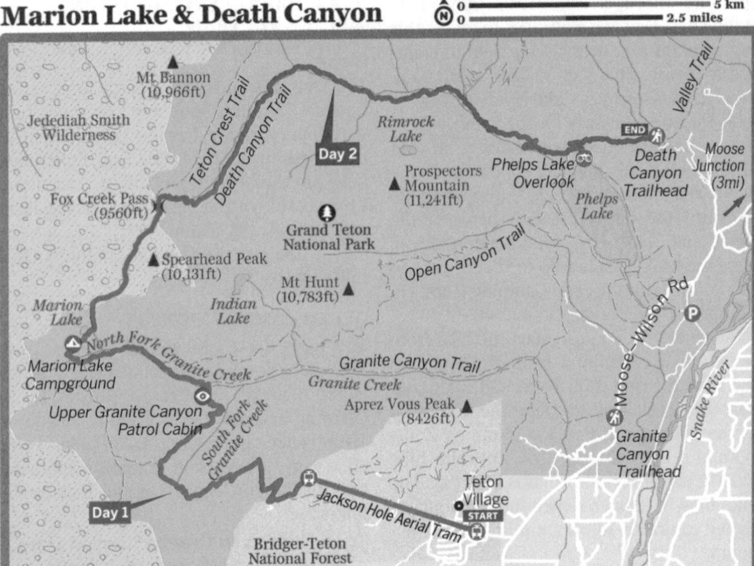

junction and then a right at the next two junctions to descend into the North Fork of Granite Canyon. From here it's a short climb to lovely **Marion Lake**, 6.6 miles from the trailhead, where you'll find three designated campsites.

DAY 2: MARION LAKE TO DEATH CANYON

6 HOURS / 11.3 MILES / 2450FT DESCENT

Today it's 2.3 miles up to **Fox Creek Pass**, then it's all downhill for 9 miles through the forests of Death Canyon to Phelps Lake Overlook and the Death Canyon Trailhead. To avoid a car shuttle, hike south at the junction before Phelps Lake along the Valley Trail to Teton Village (5.5 miles).

By choosing to hike in the opposite direction, you can save a few bucks (the downhill tram ride is free of charge), but you'll gain a lot more elevation.

Other Central Tetons Hikes

Other good options for overnighting include camping at Marion Lake, a 13-mile round-trip from the Jackson Hole Aerial Tram (p221). For an easy overnighter, check out the Hermitage Point (p173) or Leigh and Bearpaw Lakes (p175) hike. Another option is exploring Alaska Basin from the Idaho side (p179).

CYCLING

Cyclists are in less danger from motorists in the Tetons than in Yellowstone National Park because the roads are wider and more open, but it is still best to venture out early to avoid traffic. Grand Teton National Park gets little traffic from September to early October, and the cool temperatures make for pleasant pedaling. In April, Teton Park Rd is open only to cyclists and pedestrian traffic. This is a great time to bike if the snow has cleared.

The best spot for cycling in the park is the **Grand Teton Multiuse Bike Path** (www.nps.gov/grte/planyourvisit/bike.htm; dawn-dusk May-Oct) between Jackson and Jenny Lakes.

Mormon Row

Duration 5 hours

Distance 16-mile loop

Difficulty Easy

Elevation Change 120ft

Start/Finish Gros Ventre Junction

Nearest Town Jackson

Summary A mellow, scenic ride, this 16-mile loop includes terrain beyond Mormon Row.

Start at the Gros Ventre Junction. Go right at the turnoff (if you're coming from Jackson), heading northeast with Blacktail Butte to your north. Take a left at **Mormon Row** (Antelope Flats Rd; P). Bumpy and unpaved, this 3-mile section is probably the only reason not to ride a road bike. Bike north past the intersection with Antelope Flats Rd for a block just to see the historic barns, then return to Antelope Flats and head west toward the Tetons. The road ends at Hwy 191; turn left left (south) here to return to the start.

Shadow Mountain

Duration 2½–3 hours

Distance 6-mile loop

Difficulty Difficult

Elevation Change 1300ft

Start/Finish Antelope Flats Rd

Nearest Junction Moose Junction

Summary Challenge yourself with this strenuous but quick mountain-bike ascent and descent. It may require suspension.

Just east of the park in Teton National Forest (part of Bridger-Teton), the forested **Shadow Mountain** (8299ft) offers a strenuous 6-mile round-trip loop. Set off along a gravel road from the parking lot at the end of paved Antelope Flats Rd. A steady climb, the road is rutted and rocky at points. Open sections offer excellent Teton views. Just over half a mile past the summit there's a single-track path to the left. It splits, and your best option is to stay left, although all trails do lead to the bottom. Be alert for fallen logs, which lie across the path in places.

After this exciting downhill run, join the fire road. Watch for muddy conditions, which make this section a lot trickier. A webbed network of trails here means it is easy to get turned around. For topographical maps, visit Hoback Sports (p216) in Jackson.

Hole in One

Duration 5 hours

Distance 33-mile loop

Difficulty Moderate

Elevation Change 340ft

Start/Finish Jackson, Wyoming

Nearest Town Jackson

Summary Scoot past Jackson Hole highlights on this fun loop with long, flat stretches.

Start in Jackson and head north on Hwy 191 to **Moose Junction**. Go left here and left again to the narrow and winding Moose–Wilson Rd. While it is paved, there are some deep potholes, so stay alert. Horned owls nest along this section. Approaching **Teton Village**, the road becomes smooth and stays

BACKCOUNTRY PERMITS

Backcountry permits are required for all overnight backcountry trips in Grand Teton. Permits for walk-ins are $35, given on a first-come, first-served basis, 24 hours in advance, from the backcountry offices at Craig Thomas (p209) and Colter Bay (p209) Visitor Centers or Jenny Lake Ranger Station (p209). For best results, apply early in the morning the day before your intended departure. A notice board at Craig Thomas Discovery & Visitor Center indicates which backcountry sites are full each day.

About a third of the backcountry sites can be reserved from the first Wednesday in January to May 15 via www.recreation.gov, for a nonrefundable $45 fee.

Park-approved bear-resistant food storage canisters are required. Backpackers can check one out for free when securing their permit.

Backcountry camping is restricted to camping zones. Hikers (with backcountry permits) can choose their own sites inside many of these areas, but in the most heavily used zones all sites are designated (indicated by marker posts). Fires are prohibited, except at some lakeshore sites, so bring a camp stove. Campsites must be at least 200ft from waterways. No bikes or pets are permitted on trails.

No permits are required for backcountry camping in the John D Rockefeller Jr Memorial Parkway (p196), or in the national forest on the Idaho side of the Tetons, though campers must stay a minimum of 1 mile from roads and 100ft from water sources. Fires are generally allowed, but check current regulations at the Flagg Ranch Information Station (p209). Permits for winter camping are free.

WHAT'S IN A NAME?

First impressions are everything... It's thought that French Canadian fur trappers named the three Tetons – South, Middle and Grand – 'les Trois Tetons' (the three breasts) in a lonely moment of Western wandering, though the peaks may in fact be named for the Thítȟuŋwaŋ band of the Lakota Sioux who lived here.

Trapper Osborne Russell claimed their Shoshone moniker was 'Hoary Headed Fathers.' Teewinot means 'Many Pinnacles' in Shoshone – it accurately describes the features of the whole range as well as Teewinot Mountain.

The Snake River also gets its name from the local Shoshone people; the name Snake was mistakenly given to the Shoshone themselves, when the weaving sign for the Shoshone (who called themselves the people of the woven grass huts) was confused with the sign for a snake.

that way. Continue on the flats of Moose-Wilson Rd until you hit a junction with Hwy 22; turn left here. There will be a lot of car traffic on Hwy 22. An early start will help you avoid traffic on the narrows of Moose-Wilson Rd.

SUMMER ACTIVITIES

Rock Climbing & Mountain Climbing

The Tetons are known for excellent short-route rock climbs, as well as classic longer routes to summits such as Grant Teton, Mt Moran and Mt Owen (12,928ft), all best attempted with an experienced guide.

Jenny Lake Ranger Station (p209) is the go-to office for climbing information. It sells climbing guidebooks, provides information and has a board showing campsite availability in Garnet Canyon (p190), the gateway to climbs including the technical ascent of Grand Teton.

An excellent resource and the spot to meet outdoor partners in crime, the member-supported American Alpine Club's Climbers' Ranch (p207) has been a climbing institution since 1970. It also offers lodging.

Grand Teton MOUNTAIN

(Map p200) Crowning glory of the park, the dagger-edged Grand Teton (13,775ft/4199m) has taunted many a would-be mountaineer. The first white men to claim to have summited were James Stevenson and Nathanial Langford, part of the 1872 Hayden Geological Survey. However, when William Owen, Franklin Spalding and two others arrived at the top in 1898, they found no evidence of a prior expedition. So they chiseled their names in a boulder, claimed the first ascent, and ignited a dispute that persists today.

Garnet Canyon HIKING, CLIMBING

(Map p200) Garnet Canyon is the hard-won gateway to scrambles to Middle and South Teton and the technical ascent of Grand Teton – but you need technical climbing skills and an existing familiarity with the routes. However, even non-climbers will find the 4-mile hike to the starting point of the Grand Teton climb a memorable one.

Horseback Riding

Horseback riding is possible at Jackson Lake, Colter Bay and the Flagg Ranch area. Children are charged the same as adults and must be at least eight years old.

Colter Bay Corral HORSEBACK RIDING

(Map p198; 307-543-2811; www.gtlc.com; Colter Bay; 1/2hr trail rides $45/75; 7am-8pm) This corral offers short rides around Swan Lake. Families with small children can check out the breakfast wagon rides (adult/child from $45/35). Make reservations at the activities booth next to the Colter Bay grocery store a few days in advance. Children are charged the same rates.

Jackson Lake Lodge Activities Desk ADVENTURE

(Map p198; 307-543-2811; www.gtlc.com; Jackson Lake Lodge; 6:30am-9pm) Offers guided horseback rides (two hours $75) that loop around the local trails, as well as breakfast and dinner rides by horseback or wagon.

Boating

All private craft must obtain a one-year permit (nonmotorized/motorized craft $12/40). Nonmotorized craft are rafts, canoes, SUPs and kayaks. The Craig Thomas (p209) and Colter Bay (p209) Visitor Centers and Buffalo Fork Ranger Station at Moran Junction issue permits. Display yours on the port side of the vessel at the rear. Permits

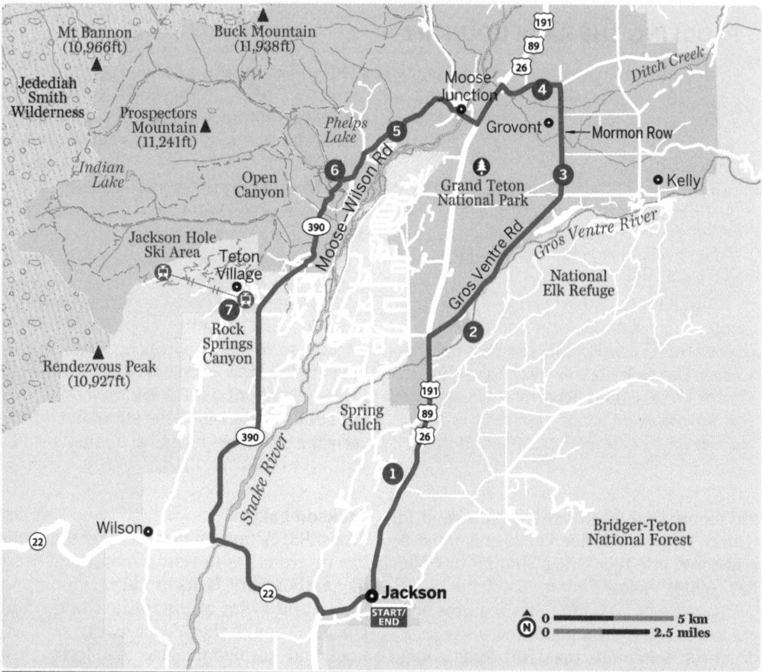

Driving Tour Barns & Bison

DURATION ONE HOUR PLUS STOPS
DISTANCE 40-MILE LOOP
START/FINISH JACKSON
SPEED LIMIT 15–45MPH

A drive through sagebrush flats and forest with picturesque barns and Teton panoramas.

You could say Gros Ventre Butte ruined it for Jackson – there are no Teton views from the park's main hub due to the blockage created by this hump. But this driving tour, not suitable for RVs or other oversized vehicles, is just the remedy. Head out of Jackson on Hwy 191. First stop: the ❶ **National Museum of Wildlife Art**. You may ask, why do this when you have the real thing? Just look. The way these masters envisioned this landscape will change the way you see it yourself.

Continue north on Hwy 191. At the Gros Ventre Junction, take a right and drive along Gros Ventre Rd, skirting the ❷ **Gros Ventre River**, lined with cottonwoods, juniper, spruce and willows. The river ecology contrasts sharply with the dry sagebrush flats to its north, where pronghorn can often be seen, bounding at speeds up to 60mph. At the next junction, take a left to drive north on ❸ **Mormon Row** (p189), a picturesque strip that includes a much-photographed rambling barn. At the end of the row, loop left on ❹ **Antelope Flats Road**, where bison and pronghorn roam the grasslands. It soon meets Hwy 191: go left, then right at Moose Junction.

Before the park entrance gate, take a left onto narrow ❺ **Moose–Wilson Road**. You will need to squeeze onto the shoulder for oncoming traffic: this is why oversized vehicles are explicitly banned. Mind the blind curves, twisting through dense foliage. You will pass turnoffs for Death Canyon Trailhead, Phelps Lake Trailhead and Granite Canyon Trailhead. If you're keen on a swim, these trails will take you to ❻ **Phelps Lake**; it's a 30- to 45-minute walk along the Woodland Trail from Phelps Lake Trailhead. This short section of the road is unpaved but even.

The road spills out near ❼ **Teton Village**, where you can take a gondola (p221) to the top to check out the views or grab lunch. Follow the Moose–Wilson Rd south to Hwy 22. Go left to return to Jackson.

PADDLING THE BACK COUNTRY

Overnight boaters can use backcountry campsites around **Jackson Lake** at Deadman Point, Bearpaw Bay, Grassy Island, Little Mackinaw Bay, South Landing, Elk Island and Warm Springs. Book these sites in advance, especially on summer weekends, when the lake is bursting with powerboats, sailboards, sailboats and canoes. There is a maximum three-night stay.

With dramatic close-ups of the toothy Mt Moran, **Moran Bay** is the most popular destination from Colter and Spalding Bays. While boating you can stop at Grassy Island en route. The following sample distances start from Signal Mountain Marina: Hermitage Point (2 miles), Elk Island (3 miles) and Grassy Island (6 miles); from Colter Bay to Little Mackinaw Bay it's 1.5 miles.

Alternatively, you can paddle from Lizard Creek Campground (p205) to remote backcountry trails on Jackson's northwest shore. Wilcox Point backcountry campsite (1.25 miles from Lizard Creek) provides backcountry access to Webb Canyon along the Moose Basin Divide Trail (20 miles). For a longer intermediate-level trip, paddle the twists and turns of the **Snake River** from Flagg Ranch to Wilcox Point or Lizard Creek.

Predominant winds from the southwest can be strong, especially in the afternoon, when waves can swamp canoes. Morning is usually the best time to paddle.

for Yellowstone National Park are valid for Grand Teton (and vice versa) but must be registered at either Craig Thomas or Colter Bay (p209) Visitor Center.

The state of Wyoming also requires boaters to purchase an aquatic invasive species decal for watercraft over 10ft long to help fund prevention efforts against invasive quagga and zebra mussels. The cost is $10/5 for motorized/nonmotorized watercraft registered in Wyoming, and $30/15 for motorized/nonmotorized watercraft owned by nonresidents. Decals are sold by the **Wyoming Game & Fish Department** (☎307-777-4600; www.wgfd.wyo.gov) online and at automated license agents.

Motorized craft (maximum 7.5HP) are allowed only on Jackson (p192), Phelps and Jenny Lakes. Hand-propelled nonmotorized craft are permitted on Jackson, Two Ocean, Emma Matilda, Bearpaw, Leigh (p192), String, Jenny, Bradley, Taggart and Phelps Lakes, as well as the Snake River 1000ft below Jackson Lake Dam (p197). Sailboats, water skis and sailboards are permitted only on Jackson Lake. Jet skis are not allowed in the park. Floating is prohibited within 1000ft of Jackson Lake Dam. Only hand-powered rafts, canoes and kayaks are allowed on the Snake River. Watercraft are forbidden on other rivers.

On Jackson Lake, fires are forbidden along the east shore from Spalding Bay to Lizard Creek and otherwise permitted only below the high-water mark. See the park's brochures on boating and floating on the Snake River, which can be downloaded from www.nps.gov/grte.

Jackson Lake BOATING

(Map p198) A fun, mellow activity for families or groups is to rent a motorboat for a day and explore Jackson Lake, stopping to picnic and swim at uncrowded inlets and islands. Though they cover less terrain, canoes and kayaks are also wonderful. Ask at Colter Bay Marina or Signal Mountain Marina.

Canoes and kayaks rented at the marinas may not be paddled beyond Colter Bay or Half Moon Bay (from Colter Bay) or Dornan's Island (from Signal Mountain).

String & Leigh Lakes CANOEING

(Map p200) These lakes are perfect for a family canoe trip, stand up paddling or just splashing around. Start on String Lake and make a 120ft portage before Leigh, which offers the most scenic day and overnight paddles. Six beautiful backcountry campsites flank the lakeshore, three of which (16, 14A and 14B) are only accessible by boat.

National Park Float Trips RAFTING

(☎307-733-5500; www.nationalparkfloattrips.com; adult/child US$80/60) The Triangle X Ranch (p207) offers dawn, daytime and sunset floats, plus a four-hour early evening float and cookout. Trips run out of Moose.

Solitude Float Trips RAFTING

(Map p200; ☎307-733-2871; www.solitudefloat-trips.com; Moose; adult/child 5-15yrs US$80/60) This recommended rafting company runs Deadman's Bar-to-Moose trips and sunrise trips, plus shorter 5-mile floats.

Colter Bay Lake Cruises CRUISE
(Map p198; ☎307-543-2811; www.gtlc.com/activities/jackson-lake-boat-cruises; Colter Bay Marina; cruise adult/child 3-11yrs $34/14; ⏲late May-late Sep) Standard 1½-hour cruises three times daily, as well as longer breakfast, lunch and dinner cruises in the shadow of Mt Moran.

Fishing

Fishing is a Tetons draw, with several species of whitefish and cutthroat, lake and brown trout thriving in local rivers and lakes. Get a license at the Moose Village store, Signal Mountain Lodge (p206) or Colter Bay Marina.

Anglers must carry a valid Wyoming fishing license. Fishing licenses are issued at Moose Village store, Signal Mountain Lodge (p206) and Colter Bay Marina. The Snake, Buffalo Fork and Gros Ventre Rivers are closed November 1 to March 31.

In general, anglers are limited to six trout per day, with varying size limitations. Get a copy of the park's fishing brochure for details.

Jackson Lake FISHING
(Map p198) Cutthroat, brown and lake trout cruise the waters of Jackson Lake. On fishing excursions, your catch can be cleaned and most fine-dining restaurants within the park will cook it up for you too. Jackson Lake is closed to fishing in October.

Tour Operators & Equipment

Exum Mountain Guides CLIMBING
(Map p200; ☎307-733-2297; www.exumguides.com; Jenny Lake) Excellent Exum Mountain Guides run the region's oldest climbing school, and can turn you into a safe mountaineer at their lodge by the Jenny Lake shore. They also have base camp at Grand Teton's Lower Saddle (11,640ft).

Grand Teton Lodge Company DRIVING
(Map p198; ☎307-543-2811; www.gtlc.com; adult/child 0-11yrs Grand Teton $75/35, Yellowstone $175/125; ⏲tours 8:30am late May-early Oct) Offers half-day Grand Teton driving tours, full-day tours of Yellowstone or a combination of both parks. Tours depart three times per week, primarily from Jackson Lake Lodge (p206). Private tours are also available.

Wildlife Expeditions WILDLIFE
(☎307-733-1313; www.wildlifeexpeditions.org; 700 Coyote Canyon Rd, Jackson) The Teton Science School runs these half-, full- or multiday naturalist-guided trips and courses.

Adventure Sports OUTDOORS
(Dornan's; Map p200; ☎307-733-3307; www.dornans.com; Moose; ⏲9am-7pm) Rents kayaks, canoes and paddleboards ($55 per 24 hours), mountain and road bikes ($44–65 per day), as well as kids' bikes and racks, with discounted weekly rates. Winter rentals include Nordic skis, snowshoes and sleds.

Colter Bay Marina BOATING
(Map p198; ☎307-543-2811; www.gtlc.com/activities/marina; Colter Bay; ⏲8am-5pm late May–mid-Sep) A busy marina providing fishing gear and licenses, as well as boat rentals. It offers motorboats ($44 per hour), kayak and canoe rentals ($21–25 per hour), as well as guided lake fishing ($92 per hour, two-hour minimum) plus half-day fly-fishing trips (lake/river $110/475 for two people).

Signal Mountain Marina BOATING
(Map p198; ☎307-543-2831; www.signalmountainlodge.com; ⏲7am-7:30pm mid-May–mid-Sep) Rents canoes ($25 per hour), kayaks ($20), motorboats (from $42) and pontoon cruisers ($105); gasoline is extra. Also guides fly-fishing on the lake (half-day for two people $312) and offers scenic Snake River float trips (adult/child US$77/50).

OARS WATER SPORTS
(Outdoor Adventure River Specialists; ☎209-736-4677; www.oars.com; 2-day kayaking trip from $519) Guides kayaking trips around Jackson Lake with instruction for beginners, as well as SUP trips and multiday rafting trips on the Snake River.

Moosely Mountaineering SPORTS & OUTDOORS
(Map p200; ☎307-739-1801; http://skinnyskis.com/moosely-mountaineering; 12170 Dornan Rd, Moose; ⏲9am-7pm mid-May–Oct) This sister store to Jackson's Skinny Skis (p258) sells outdoor clothing and equipment and is useful for rentals of mountaineering equipment, including ice axes, crampons and trekking poles. Also sells topographic maps.

WINTER ACTIVITIES

With the crowds gone, bears tucked away in their dens and powdery snow blanketing the pines, the Tetons make a lovely winter destination. Teton Park Rd is plowed from Jackson Lake Junction to Signal Mountain Lodge and from Moose to the Taggart Lake Trailhead.

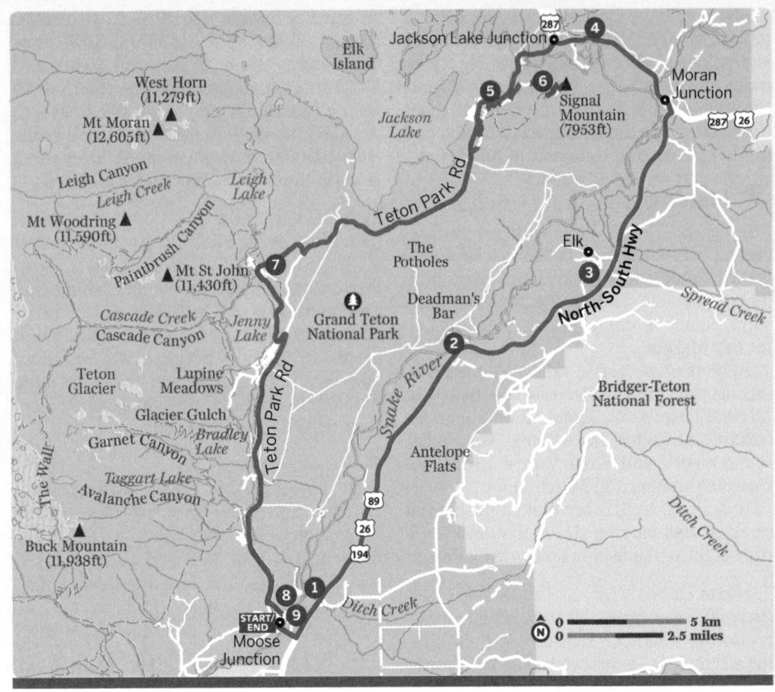

Driving Tour Plains & Panoramas

DURATION 1½ HOURS
DISTANCE 45-MILE LOOP
START/FINISH MOOSE JUNCTION
NEAREST TOWN MOOSE
SPEED LIMIT 30–45MPH

This scenic loop offers fantastic views of the Teton Range from the flats of Jackson Hole Valley. With some luck, you will spot pronghorn, deer or moose. Each year animals are killed on this road, so drive cautiously and watch for animals bounding across the road.

Begin the tour 8 miles north of Jackson at **1 Moose Junction**. Follow Hwy 191 north past Blacktail Ponds Overlook and Glacier View Turnout. Seven miles after Moose Junction, **2 Snake River Overlook** has views of the braided channels of the Snake. Dense cottonwoods, willows and spruce provide an excellent habitat for moose and deer. Spotted sandpipers should be easy to pick out.

Make a stop at **3 Cunningham Cabin**, the site of an 1892 shoot-out when a band of self-deputized locals sought to root out rumored horse thieves. Now the spot is overrun with homesteading ground squirrels.

At Moran Junction bear left, continuing on 191. Mt Moran looms to the west. Stop about 3.5 miles later at **4 Oxbow Bend** to look for fishing eagles, ospreys and trumpeter swans. Long-legged great blue herons stalk the shallows. Head south along Teton Park Rd at Jackson Lake Junction. The rustic 1930s **5 Log Chapel of the Sacred Heart** follows. On your left you will see a sign for **6 Signal Mountain Road**, a 5-mile climb. You can detour here or continue straight ahead.

Turn on the one-way **7 Jenny Lake Scenic Drive**, twisting through a forested area with the spires of the Tetons just across the lake. It will deposit you back on Teton Park Rd. On the left just before Moose Junction, you will see **8 Menor's Ferry Historic District** (p203). The brainchild of Bill Menor, the ferry provided the only transportation across the river. In late summer, when tourists crossed the river to pick berries, Menor charged them 'Huckleberry Rates.' In the same area, the log **9 Chapel of the Transfiguration**, built in 1924, still holds church services. Return to the main road and follow it until it exits the park at Moose Junction.

Grand Teton National Park brochures for Nordic skiing (also appropriate for snowshoeing) and snowmobiling can be downloaded from www.nps.gov/grte/planyourvisit/brochures.htm.

Permits (free) are required for all overnight backcountry trips. Get one at the administration building at **Park Headquarters** (Map p200; ☎307-739-3300; Moose; ⏲9am-4:30pm Mon-Fri) in Moose.

Nordic Skiing

Between mid-December and mid-March, the park grooms 15 miles of track right under the Tetons' highest peaks, between the Taggart and Bradley Lakes parking area and Signal Mountain. Lanes are available for ski touring, skate skiing and snowshoeing. Grooming takes place two or three times per week. The NPS does not always mark every trail: consult at the ranger station to make sure that the trail you plan to use is well tracked and easy to follow.

Remember to yield to passing skiers and those skiing downhill. You can find rental equipment in Jackson.

Jenny Lake XC-Ski Route SKIING
(Map p200; Taggart Lake Parking Area; ⏲Nov-Mar) An easy 8-mile, round-trip, cross-country ski trip. From the Taggart Lake parking area, follow the Jenny Lake trail parallel to Cottonwood Creek and return via Teton Park Rd. There are great views of the Tetons throughout.

Taggart Lake to Beaver Creek SKIING
(Map p200) A moderate-to-difficult trail with some climbing. It's a 3-mile round-trip to Taggart Lake or 4 miles to do the Beaver Creek loop, climbing through a glacial moraine. Use care on the return descent, as the trail may be icy. Leave your vehicle at the Taggart Lake parking area.

Moose–Wilson Road SKIING
(Map p200) To ski Moose–Wilson Rd, it's an easy 5.8-mile round-trip, with some climbing. Park at the entrance to Death Canyon Rd. A 2-mile loop detours to the edge of Phelps Lake. You can also approach via Teton Village, parking at **Granite Canyon trailhead**. Pets are allowed on Moose–Wilson Rd but not on the trails into the park.

Snowshoeing

Snowshoers may use the park's Nordic skiing trails. For an easy outing, try Teton Park Rd (closed to traffic in winter). Remember to use the hardpack trail and never walk on ski trails – skiers will thank you for preserving the track!

From late December through to mid-March, naturalists lead free two-hour, 1.5-mile snowshoe hikes from the Taggart Lake trailhead three times per week. Traditional wooden snowshoes are available for rental (adult/child US$5/2). The tour is open to eight-year-olds and up.

Polecat Creek SKIING
For this easy 2.5-mile loop, park at the Headwaters Lodge at Flagg Ranch. Traveling clockwise, the loop soon arrives at Polecat Creek and Huckleberry Hot Springs. After crossing power lines, in 0.4 miles another trail intersects. Stay right on the loop, continuing south to the lodge.

Snowmobiling

In the park, snowmobiling is only allowed on the frozen surface of Jackson Lake. Snowmobilers will have more options in nearby Yellowstone National Park and West Yellowstone. You must have a valid driver's license and vehicles must have Best Available Technology (BAT) and meet the requirements listed in the NPS snowmobiling brochure.

On the John D Rockefeller Jr Memorial Parkway, Grassy Lake Rd is open to snowmobiles without BAT.

Headwaters Lodge Winter Activities OUTDOORS
(☎307-543-2861; www.gtlc.com/headwaters-lodge.aspx; Flagg Ranch; ⏲Dec-Mar) Offers guided snowmobile tours to Old Faithful (p109) and the Grand Canyon of the Yellowstone (p97), departing at 6:30am. Since the resort is closed to guests during winter, Headwaters Lodge offers hotel pickups in Jackson for its snowmobilers.

Flagg Ranch Information Station (p209) does stay open in winter for those using the trails.

Backcountry Skiing

There is excellent backcountry skiing here, but skiers should have adequate knowledge of avalanche safety and carry a transceiver and shovel, or book a guided tour.

Teton Backcountry Guides SKIING
(☎307-353-2900; http://tetonbackcountryguides.com; 1110 Alta North Road, Alta; 2-person downhill/XC tour $495/380) Guides small groups of one to four on backcountry ski and snowboarding tours for all abilities. Day trips and

TETON WINTER FACILITIES

In Grand Teton National Park, much is closed for winter. Dates for service openings and closures vary greatly from year to year, depending on snow conditions. Get information on weather, road, ski and avalanche conditions from the Jackson Visitor Center (p268). Spur Ranch Log Cabins (p207), which stays open for most of the year, sits close to the center of Moose. There is limited tent and RV camping (December to April 15, US$5) near the Colter Bay Visitor Center (p209), though tent sites may be on snow. On the eastern edge of the national park, Triangle X Ranch (p206) has wood cabins at discount winter rates.

Most of the year, the administrative office of the park is closed to visitors, but Park Headquarters can provide information in winter (November to February) when the Craig Thomas Discovery & Visitor Center (p209) is closed.

multiday tours are available, both within and outside the park. Also operates the only hut system in the Tetons, with backcountry yurts outfitted with wood stoves, and runs safety clinics.

SIGHTS

John D Rockefeller Jr Memorial Parkway

This NPS-managed parkway is a 7.5-mile corridor linking Yellowstone and Grand Teton National Parks. Congress recognized Rockefeller's contribution to the creation of Grand Teton National Park by designating this 24,000-acre parkway in his honor in 1972. Here, the Tetons taper to a gentle slope, and rocks from volcanic flows in Yellowstone line the Snake River. A transitional zone between the two national parks, the area combines characteristics of both, though it's less spectacular than either. Activities focus around historic Flagg Ranch, which was established as a US Cavalry post in 1872.

North–south US 89/191/287 is the main road through the parkway. The turnoff to Flagg Ranch is 2 miles south of Yellowstone's South Entrance Station and 15 miles north of Colter Bay Village. The turnoff to Grassy Lake Rd, which leads west to Ashton, Idaho, is just north of Flagg Ranch.

The Flagg Ranch Information Station (p209) is near the Grassy Lake Rd turnoff. Nearby Headwaters Cabins (p205) offers parkway accommodations, dining, gas and activities. Once a popular winter launch pad into Yellowstone National Park, the resort now closes in winter since stricter snowmobiling regulations have been put in place. Winter trails can still be accessed here.

Grassy Lake Road

The 52-mile, east–west Grassy Lake Rd links US 89/191/287 to US 20 at Ashton, Idaho, offering a remote back way into the national parks. This bumpy gravel road, also a good mountain-biking route, follows an old Native American trade and hunting route. In late fall it closes and snowmobiles take over.

Heading west from US 89, Flagg Ranch is the first landmark on the road. Shortly after crossing the Polecat Creek Bridge, the pavement ends. The graded gravel road parallels the north bank of the Snake River. Camping is restricted to designated sites, and is popular with anglers, hunters and those headed west along the rough Reclamation Rd (USFS Rd 261) to the Cascade Corner in Yellowstone's lush Bechler (p69) region.

Sandwiched between the Winegar Hole and Jedediah Smith Wildernesses, this region is peppered with lakes with great fishing options. The most accessible are the roadside **Indian Lake** and **Loon Lake**, 1 mile down a bumpy track off Reclamation Rd. Further east there's a turnoff for the rough road to stunning **Lake of the Woods**, site of the Boy Scouts' Loll Camp. A mile further east is the 0.5-mile detour south to Tilley Lake. Beyond, the expansive and popular **Grassy Lake Reservoir** has boating, fishing and dispersed campsites. Just after the reservoir, the road enters the Rockefeller Parkway.

There are eight free campsites along Grassy Lake Rd (USFS Rd 261). Depending on spring melt, the road may open later than others in the region. Check with rangers if visiting in May or June, as road conditions may require a 4WD vehicle.

Colter Bay Region

The road south from Yellowstone drops off the Yellowstone plateau at the end of the Rockefeller Parkway, where a startling view of the Tetons soaring above **Jackson Lake** comes into play. Past Lizard Creek Campground (p205), several beaches tucked into nooks offer some of the park's best picnic areas.

Jackson Lake is a natural glacial lake that has been dammed, so water levels fluctuate, dropping considerably toward the end of the summer. **Mt Moran** (12,605ft), named after landscape painter Thomas Moran, dominates the north end of the park. After Moran first traveled this way with the Hayden Geological Survey of 1871, his grand depictions forever became synonymous with the area.

Two Ocean and Emma Matilda Lakes sit east of Jackson Lake, tucked into the hills. Visitor services are concentrated at Colter Bay Village (p206).

Colter Bay

Ask at Colter Bay Visitor Center (p209) about early-morning bird-watching walks. Rangers also lead a daily 8am morning walk from the visitor center to **Swan Lake** (3 miles, three hours) and campfire programs in the evening. The visitor center is also home to the worthwhile **Indian Arts Museum** (Map p198; ☎800-299-0396; Colter Bay; ⏲8am-5pm; P) FREE.

South of the visitor center is the marina and trailhead for hikes to Swan Lake and **Hermitage Point** (Map p198). A popular picnic and swimming area sits just north of the visitor center, though countless other secluded swimming and sunbathing spots are dotted around Jackson Lake.

Around Jackson Lake Lodge

The elegant Jackson Lake Lodge (p206) is worth a stop, if only to gape at the stupendous views through its 60ft-tall windows. In cold weather the cozy fireplaces in the upper lobby are blazing. In summer you can drink in fine Teton views and a cold Snake River Lager while sitting outdoors.

Rangers answer questions on the back deck of Jackson Lake Lodge daily from 6:30pm to 8pm, and there is a free talk on the history of the lodge every Sunday at 8pm.

The willow flats below the hotel balcony are a top spot to catch a glimpse of moose, which flock to willow as a critical food source, particularly in winter. Since the area has become popular with calving elk and bears, it now has a seasonal closure between mid-May and mid-July. During that time you can still enjoy the nearby **Willow Flats turnout** (Map p198), with views of Mt Moran, Bivouac Peak (10,825ft), Rolling Thunder Mountain (10,908ft), Eagles Rest Peak (11,258ft) and Ranger Peak (11,355ft).

A short walk from the lodge, **Christian Pond** is a good place to spot riparian birdlife. The trail to the pond crosses the main road by a bridge just south of the lodge.

About a mile north of Jackson Lake Lodge, a rough dirt road branches east off the main road to a **trailhead** (Map p198), from which it's a 1-mile walk one way (with a steep climb at the end) to **Grand View Point** (7586ft), which offers fine views of both the Tetons and Two Ocean Lake. You can also visit the viewpoint as part of the **Two Ocean Lake hike** (Map p198).

One of Grand Teton's most famous scenic spots for wildlife-watching is **Oxbow Bend**, 2 miles east of Jackson Lake Junction. Early morning and dusk are the best times to spot moose, elk, sandhill cranes, ospreys, bald eagles, trumpeter swans, Canada geese, blue herons and white pelicans. The oxbow was created when the river's faster water eroded the outer bank while the slower inner flow deposited sediment.

Heading south on Teton Park Rd, you'll find interpretive displays along the west shoulder near **Jackson Lake Dam** (Map p198; P). Built in 1916, the dam raises the lake level by 39ft, and was paid for by Idaho farmers who still own the irrigation rights to the top 39ft of water. The dam was reinforced between 1986 and 1989 to withstand earthquakes.

South of here is the rustic Log Chapel of the Sacred Heart, built in the 1930s and renovated in 2002. Open to visitors, it also has a pleasant picnic area.

Signal Mountain Summit

This 5-mile paved road (no RVs) east of Teton Park Rd winds up to the top of **Signal Mountain** (7953ft) for dramatic panoramas from 800ft above Jackson Hole's valley floor. Below, the Snake River, the valley's only drainage, runs a twisted course through cottonwood and spruce. Abandoned dry channels demonstrate the changing landscape.

Views are superb at sunrise, but the best vistas are actually from three-quarters of the way up at **Jackson Point Overlook** (Map p198), a short walk south from a parking area. William Jackson took a famous photograph from this point in 1878, when preparing a

Colter Bay Region

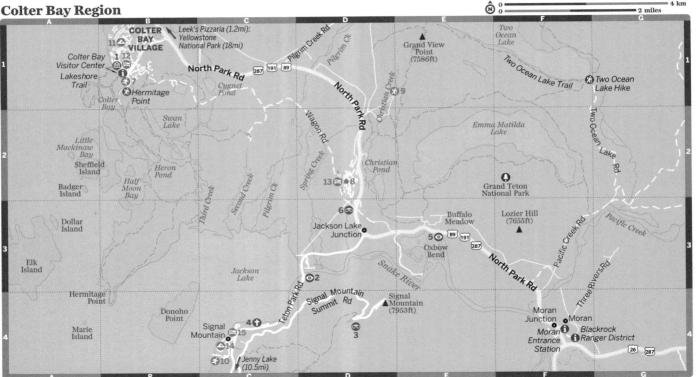

0 – 2 miles
0 – 4 km

COLTER BAY VILLAGE
Leek's Pizzaria (1.2mi); Yellowstone National Park (18mi)
Colter Bay Visitor Center
Lakeshore Trail
Hermitage Point
Colter Bay
Cygnet Pond
North Park Rd
287
191
89
Pilgrim Creek Rd
Pilgrim Ck
Grand View Point (7586ft)
Two Ocean Lake
Two Ocean Lake Trail
Two Ocean Lake Hike
Christian Creek
Wagon Rd
Swan Lake
Little Mackinaw Bay
Sheffield Island
Heron Pond
Half Moon Bay
Badger Island
Third Creek
Second Creek
Pilgrim Ck
Spring Creek
Christian Pond
Emma Matilda Lake
Two Ocean Lake Rd
Grand Teton National Park
Dollar Island
Jackson Lake Junction
Buffalo Meadow
Lozier Hill (7655ft)
Oxbow Bend
Pacific Creek
Pacific Creek Rd
Elk Island
Jackson Lake
Snake River
Three Rivers Rd
Teton Park Rd
Signal Mountain Summit Rd
Signal Mountain (7953ft)
Hermitage Point
Donoho Point
Marie Island
Signal Mountain
Jenny Lake (10.5mi)
Moran Junction
Moran
Moran Entrance Station
Blackrock Ranger District
26
287

single image could take a full hour, using heavy glass plates and a portable studio.

The mountain's name dates from 1891, when politician Robert Ray Hamilton was reported lost on a hunting trip. Search parties lit a fire atop Signal Mountain after he was found dead a week later, floating in Jackson Lake. The summit is also one of the few places in the park with good cell service coverage, which adds modern overtones to its name.

A 6-mile round-trip **hiking trail** leads to the summit from Signal Mountain Campground (p205), through groves of huckleberries. In winter, Signal Mountain Summit Rd offers Nordic skiing (p195) with a fun 5-mile downhill return run. To reach the turnoff, ski 1 mile south from Signal Mountain along a snowmobiling trail.

Eastern Slopes

Highway 26/89/191 traverses the park's eastern flank for about 25 miles from the Moran Junction to the park's southern gate, past sagebrush flats and the occasional ranch – always with the Tetons' sharp spires diverting your gaze westward. The hardscrabble lives of Jackson Hole's early homesteaders are reflected in the valley's characteristic lodgepole buck-and-pole fences.

Moran to Blacktail Butte

Ranchers Pierce and Margaret Cunningham, early major supporters of Grand Teton National Park, cultivated a cattle ranch at Cunningham Cabin in 1890, 6 miles south of Moran Junction. The property is one of the best surviving examples of a homestead cabin; a short trail casts light on local homesteading. Four miles southwest, the Snake River Overlook offers good panoramas of the Tetons and opportunities for wildlife-watching, though forest growth means the photo ops aren't quite as good as when Ansel Adams immortalized the shot.

A better place for photos is **Schwabacher's Landing** (P), a popular rafting put-in 4 miles further south. The jagged Tetons, reflected in the meandering river, rank as some of the park's most sublime scenery. Access the landing via a short dirt road.

East of **Blacktail Butte** (7687ft), an unpaved road great for cycling connects Antelope Flats Rd to the north with Gros Ventre Rd to the south (when not washed out). Its scenic collection of ranches with pioneer barns and cabins is known as **Mormon Row**, where 10 settlers took up residence in the 1890s. A resident bison herd, gorgeous post-dawn light and superb Teton views make this area exceptionally popular with photographers. Two barns sit north of the junction with Antelope Flats Rd and two south, currently under restoration.

Gros Ventre Rd leads east to the **Gros Ventre Slide**, site of a major 1925 landslide.

Colter Bay Region

Sights

1 Indian Arts Museum B1
2 Jackson Lake Dam D3
3 Jackson Point Overlook D4
4 Log Chapel of the Sacred Heart C4
5 Oxbow Bend E3
6 Willow Flats Turnout D3

Activities, Courses & Tours

Colter Bay Corral .... (see 12)
Colter Bay Lake Cruises .... (see 7)
7 Colter Bay Marina B1
8 Grand Teton Lodge Company D2
9 Grand View Point Trail D1
Jackson Lake Lodge Activities Desk .... (see 13)
10 Signal Mountain Marina C4

Sleeping

11 Colter Bay Campground B1
12 Colter Bay Village B1
13 Jackson Lake Lodge D2
14 Signal Mountain Campground C4
15 Signal Mountain Lodge C4

Eating

Blue Heron Lounge .... (see 13)
Café Court Pizzeria .... (see 12)
Mural Room .... (see 13)
Peaks .... (see 15)
Pioneer Grill .... (see 13)
Ranch House .... (see 12)
Trapper Grill .... (see 15)

Central Tetons

South of Signal Mountain, Teton Park Rd passes the **Potholes**, sagebrush flats pockmarked with craterlike depressions known as kettles. The kettles were formed slowly by blocks of orphaned glacial ice, which were left by receding glaciers and stranded under the soil. Just south is the Mt Moran turnout.

Jenny Lake Scenic Drive

Seven miles south of Signal Mountain, the **Jenny Lake Scenic Drive** branches west to begin the park's most picturesque drive.

Central Tetons

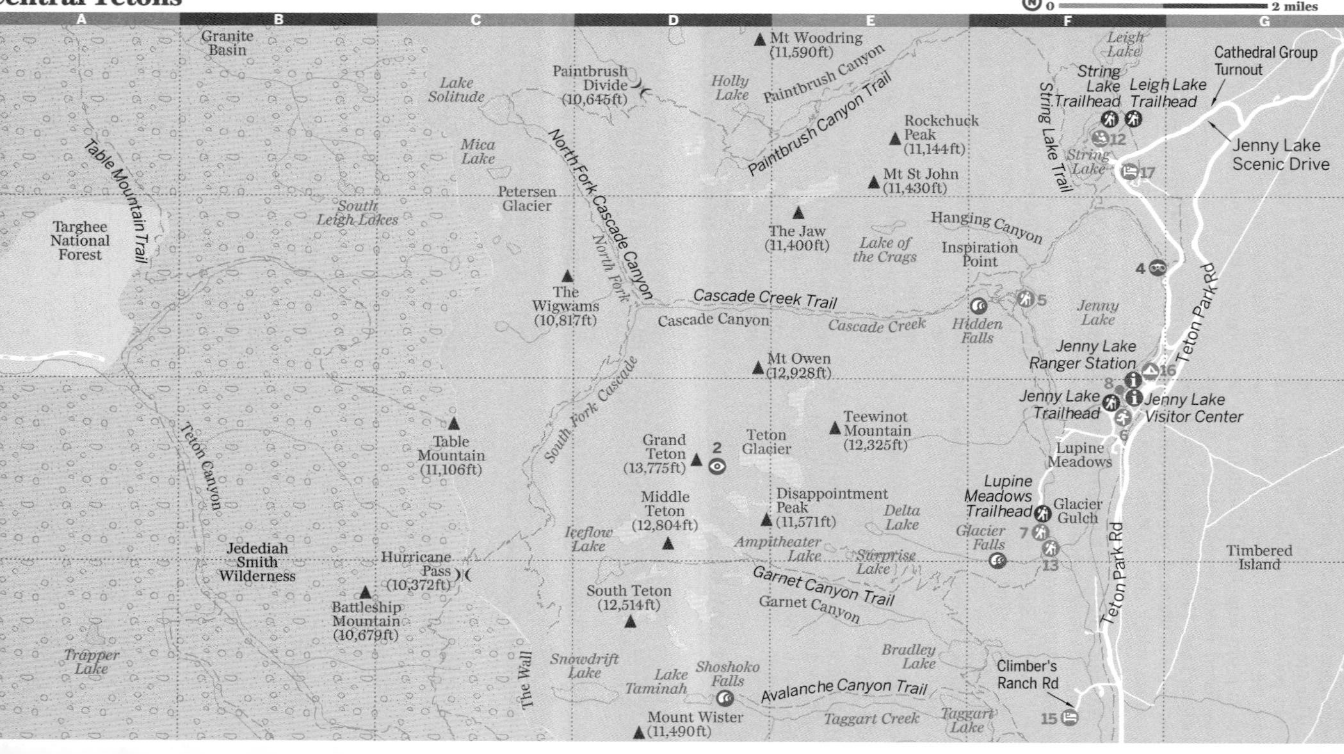

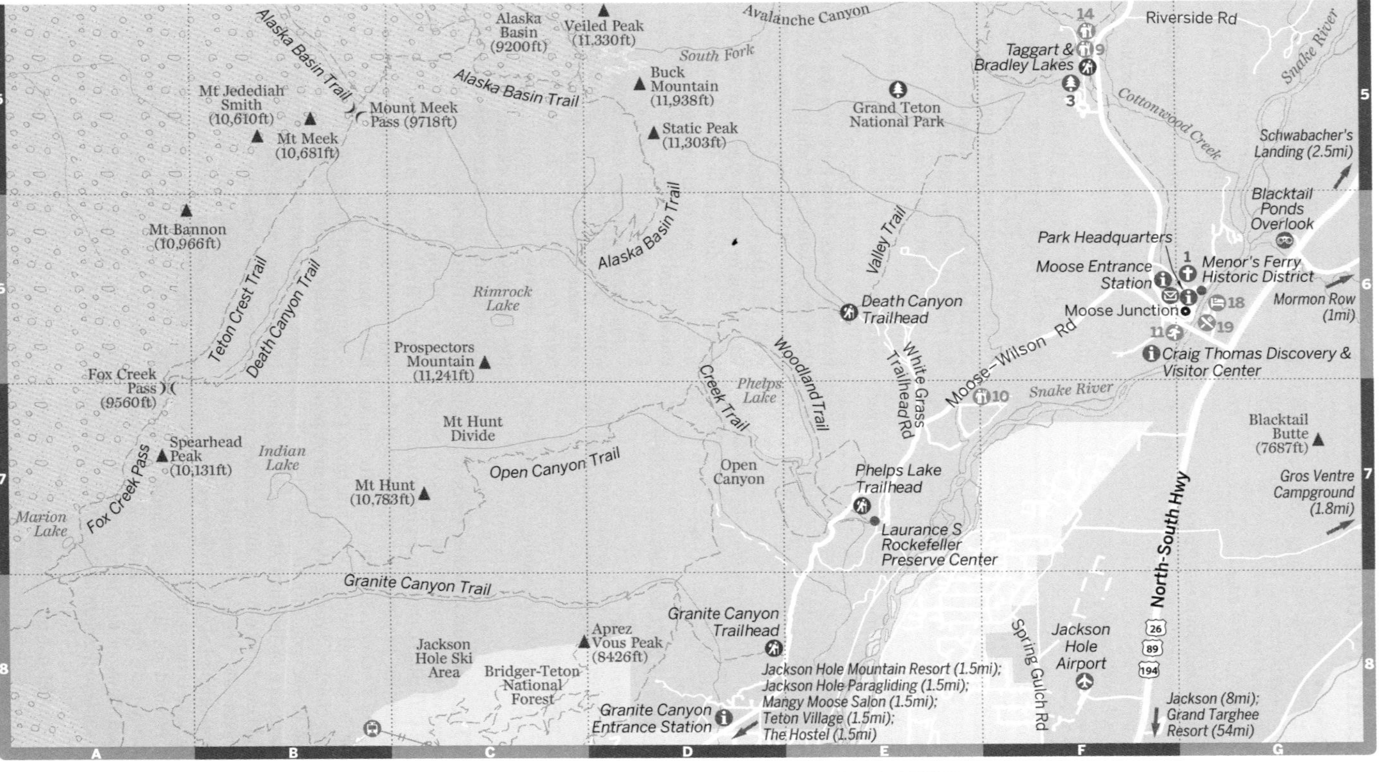
Alaska Basin Trail
Alaska Basin (9200ft)
Veiled Peak (11,330ft)
Avalanche Canyon
South Fork
Alaska Basin Trail
Buck Mountain (11,938ft)
Static Peak (11,303ft)
Mt Jedediah Smith (10,610ft)
Mount Meek Pass (9718ft)
Mt Meek (10,681ft)
Grand Teton National Park
Taggart & Bradley Lakes
Riverside Rd
Snake River
Cottonwood Creek
Schwabacher's Landing (2.5mi)
Blacktail Ponds Overlook
Mt Bannon (10,966ft)
Alaska Basin Trail
Valley Trail
Park Headquarters
Moose Entrance Station
Menor's Ferry Historic District
Mormon Row (1mi)
Moose Junction
Teton Crest Trail
Death Canyon Trail
Rimrock Lake
Death Canyon Trailhead
Prospectors Mountain (11,241ft)
Woodland Trail
White Grass Trailhead Rd
Moose–Wilson Rd
Craig Thomas Discovery & Visitor Center
Fox Creek Pass (9560ft)
Creek Trail
Phelps Lake
Snake River
Mt Hunt Divide
Blacktail Butte (7687ft)
Spearhead Peak (10,131ft)
Indian Lake
Open Canyon Trail
Open Canyon
Phelps Lake Trailhead
Gros Ventre Campground (1.8mi)
Fox Creek Pass
Mt Hunt (10,783ft)
Marion Lake
Laurance S Rockefeller Preserve Center
North-South Hwy
Granite Canyon Trail
Granite Canyon Trailhead
Jackson Hole Ski Area
Aprez Vous Peak (8426ft)
Spring Gulch Rd
Jackson Hole Airport
26
89
191
Bridger-Teton National Forest
Jackson Hole Mountain Resort (1.5mi); Jackson Hole Paragliding (1.5mi); Mangy Moose Salon (1.5mi); Teton Village (1.5mi); The Hostel (1.5mi)
Granite Canyon Entrance Station
Jackson (8mi); Grand Targhee Resort (54mi)

Central Tetons

Sights

1 Chapel of the Transfiguration G6
2 Grand Teton D3
3 Grand Teton National Park F5
4 Jenny Lake Overlook F2

Activities, Courses & Tours

Adventure Sports .... (see 19)
5 Cascade Canyon F2
6 Exum Mountain Guides F3
7 Garnet Canyon F3
8 Jenny Lake Boating F3
9 Jenny Lake XC-Ski Route F5
10 Moose–Wilson Road F7
11 Solitude Float Trips F6
12 String & Leigh Lakes F1
13 Surprise & Amphitheater Lakes F3
14 Taggart Lake to Beaver Creek F5

Sleeping

15 Climbers' Ranch F4
16 Jenny Lake Campground F2
17 Jenny Lake Lodge F1
18 Spur Ranch Log Cabins G6

Eating

19 Dornan's Chuckwagon G6
Dornan's Trading Post .... (see 19)
Jenny Lake Lodge Dining Room .... (see 17)
Pizza & Pasta Company .... (see 19)

Entertainment

Hootenanny .... (see 19)

Shopping

Moosely Mountaineering .... (see 19)

The **Cathedral Group turnout** boasts views of the central Teton spires, known as the Cathedral Group. Interpretive boards illustrate the tectonic slippage visible at the foot of **Rockchuck Peak** (11,144ft), named for its resident yellow-bellied marmots (aka rock chucks). **String Lake** is the most popular picnic spot, with dramatic views of the north face of Teewinot Mountain (12,325ft) and Grand Teton from sandy beaches along its east side. The road becomes one-way beyond String Lake, just before exclusive Jenny Lake Lodge (p207).

Perched on the lake's glacial moraine, **Jenny Lake Overlook** (Map p200; P) offers good views of the Tetons and tall Ribbon Cascade to the right of Cascade Canyon, and **shuttle boats** headed for Inspiration Point. Be careful not to miss the turnout, as you can't back up on this one-way road.

Jenny Lake

The scenic heart of the Grand Tetons and the epicenter of the area's crowds, **Jenny Lake** was named for the Shoshone wife of early guide and mountain man Beaver Dick Leigh. Jenny died of smallpox in 1876 along with her children.

The Jenny Lake Visitor Center (p209) is worth a visit for its geological displays and 3D map of Jackson Hole. The cabin was once in a different location as the Crandall photo studio.

The Jenny Lake area is finishing a massive $19 million restoration to trails and infrastructure. The five-year project unveils in 2019. From the visitor center, a network of trails leads clockwise around the lake for 2.5 miles to **Hidden Falls** and then continues for a short uphill run to fine views at **Inspiration Point**. Once you're here, it's worth continuing up **Cascade Canyon** (Map p200) with a good supply of water for more excellent views. From here, you can return the way you came or continue clockwise 1.5 miles to the **String Lake Trailhead** (Map p200) to make a 3.8-mile circle around the lake. If you're walking the Jenny Lake Trail in the early morning or late afternoon, detour approximately 15 minutes (about 0.5 miles) from the visitor center to **Moose Ponds** for a good chance of spotting moose.

Alternatively, **Jenny Lake Boating** (Map p200; ☎307-734-9227; www.jennylakeboating.com; round-trip shuttle adult/child 2-11yrs $15/8, scenic cruise US$19/11; ⏱7am-7pm Jun-late Sep) runs shuttles across Jenny Lake between the east-shore boat dock near Jenny Lake Visitor Center and the west-shore dock near Hidden Falls, offering quick (12-minute) access to Inspiration Point and the Cascade Canyon Trail. Shuttles run every 15 minutes, but expect long waits for return shuttles between 4pm and 6pm.

Rangers lead **hikes** from Jenny Lake Visitor Center at 8:30am to Inspiration Point (2 miles, 2½ hours) via the Jenny Lake shuttle boat. Numbers are limited to 25, and places are first-come, first-served; arrive at the visitor center by 8am to secure a spot.

Canoes, kayaks and boats with motors less than 8HP are allowed on Jenny Lake. The put-in is by the east-shore boat dock, accessed by a separate road that branches off the Lupine Meadows Trailhead road. Jenny Lake Boating rents kayaks and canoes. It also offers hour-long scenic Jenny Lake cruises throughout the day. Inquire at the dock or call to reserve.

Jenny Lake also offers good fishing and is stocked with lake, brown, brook and Snake River cutthroat trout.

South of Jenny Lake

Just south of Jenny Lake, Teton Park Rd passes the turnoff to the **Lupine Meadows Trailhead** (Map p200), for hikes to **Surprise Lake** (Map p200) and Garnet Canyon (p190). On the east side of Teton Park Rd, watch for **Timbered Island**, an enclave of forested glacial soils stacked atop poorly drained sedimentary soils.

Two miles south of here, **Teton Glacier turnout** offers some of the best views of Teton Glacier, the largest in the park. The **Taggart Lake** (Map p200) turnout is 1.5 miles further on.

Menor's Ferry Historic District (Map p200; Moose; ⌚ early Jul-Aug; P), comprising a short trail and the homestead cabin of William Menor, sits half a mile north of Moose Village, off a paved road. Menor was alone on the west bank of the Snake River for a decade, building a pontoon raft that provided a vital crossing for mule teams and riders who hunted, picked mushrooms and berries, and cut lumber on the Teton side. In 1910 he sold the property to entrepreneur Maude Noble, who started charging a then-brazen $1 to locals and $2 for those with out-of-state plates to cross. Today you can cross in a replica of **Menor's ferry**. Old photographs, restored buggies and the original settlers' wagon offer insight into the lives of early settlers. Stop by the obligatory old-fashioned period store, open 9am to 4:30pm.

The nearby Chapel of the Transfiguration, dating to 1924, has aspen pews and views of the Tetons through the altar window. In summer, Episcopal services are held on Sundays.

Just beyond is Moose Entrance Station (p210) and the Craig Thomas Discovery & Visitor Center (p209), the latter offering interpretive displays, an auditorium hosting excellent speakers and events, and the park's largest selection of books. The park's southern hub, **Moose**, offers accommodations, restaurants and shops, and serves as the jumping-off point for many park activities. It is also the center for wintertime park activity.

⊙ Moose–Wilson Road

Moose–Wilson Road is a partially paved 15-mile route (its southernmost 3 miles are gravel) that connects Teton Village to Moose. RVs and trailers are not allowed on this road inside the park, which is quite narrow in sections. Plans are under discussion to pave the entire road.

Laurance S Rockefeller Preserve Center

For solitude coupled with the most stunning views that don't include the Grand, visitors should check out this newer section of Grand Teton National Park. Once the JY Ranch, an exclusive Rockefeller family retreat, these 3100 acres around Phelps Lake were donated in full by Laurance S Rockefeller in 2001. His grandfather, John D Rockefeller, had been an early park advocate, purchasing the first tracts of land to donate in 1927. Despite strong local opposition, by 1949 he had donated some 33,000 acres of former ranchland to Grand Teton National Park.

With this sector, Laurance Rockefeller's vision was to create a space of refuge and renewal. In contrast to other visitor centers, the beautiful **Laurance S Rockefeller Preserve Center** (Map p200; ☎307-739-3654; www.nps.gov/grte/planyourvisit/lsrpvc.htm; Moose–Wilson Rd; ⌚ 9am-5pm Jun-Sep; P 👪) 🍃 is a meditative experience. Sparely furnished and certified by LEED (Leadership in Energy and

DITCH THE CROWDS

Parking lots at popular trailheads and areas such as Jenny, String, Taggart and Bradley Lakes and Granite Canyon are often packed before 11am. The Death Canyon Trailhead parking stays full since overnight backpackers leave cars for multiple days. Cascade Canyon hums with day-trippers to Solitude Lake in August.

Get an alpine start on your hike (leave before most of your neighbors are even thinking of breakfast) to beat the crowds. It's a good way to see more wildlife too.

Jenny Lake Campground is perennially full, and Signal Mountain Campground fills up early in the day. You can avoid the campground crowds by choosing less-popular grounds such as Lizard Creek (p205) and Gros Ventre (p207).

Two Ocean (p197) and Emma Matilda Lakes, in the northeast section of the park, offer excellent hiking without the crowds.

Environmental Design), the green building features quotes from naturalists and writers etched into walls, giant picture windows to admire the views, and a library with leather armchairs and books on conservation and nature to browse. The center also hosts a full menu of ranger programs.

Little trace is left of the ranch. Homes and cabins have been torn down, roads left to revegetate and an 8-mile network of nature trails has been created. By design, the preserve promotes an intimate experience. To prevent overcrowding, there is no parking allowed nearby on the shoulder of the Moose–Wilson Rd, and the parking lot only accommodates 40 vehicles – come before 10am or after 3pm in summer to ensure a spot. It's located 4 miles south of Moose Junction.

SLEEPING

Accommodation rates are noticeably higher in the Yellowstone region than in the surrounding areas of Wyoming, Idaho and Montana, particularly in the high-season months of July and August. Yellowstone itself remains the biggest headache, with accommodations booked up months in advance. The key is to reserve well ahead.

Campgrounds National Park Service (NPS), concession-run and Forest Service (USFS) all offer the best value and most atmospheric accommodation.

Park cabins Rustic cabins, some without private bathroom, remain the parks' most economical rooms.

Park hotels A mix of grand historic buildings, bland lodges and luxury retreats.

Motels The staple of gateway-town accommodation.

John D Rockefeller Jr Memorial Parkway

Headwaters Campground CAMPGROUND **$**

(Flagg Ranch Campground; 307-543-2861, reservations 800-443-2311; www.gtlc.com/camping/headwaters-campground-at-flagg-ranch; Flagg Ranch; tent/RV sites $38/74, 4-person cabins from $77; May-Sep; P) Among the most expensive campgrounds around, it features pull-through sites, propane for sale, 24-hour showers, laundry and a nightly campfire program.

Sites are generally available the same day, but RV campers should reserve a week or more in advance.

GRAND TETON NATIONAL PARK CAMPGROUNDS

CAMPGROUND	LOCATION	DESCRIPTION	NO OF SITES	ELEVAT (FT)
Gros Ventre (p207)	Central Tetons	Spacious and shady, with plenty of ample spaces; tent sites are on separate loops	318	6783
Jenny Lake (p207)	Central Tetons	The most coveted camp spot amid boulders and trails; tents only	49	6803
Colter Bay (p205)	Colter Bay	Enormous but wooded, with laundry facilities & showers; buzzing with activity	335	6820
Lizard Creek (p205)	Colter Bay	A secluded spot with shade and lake access	60	6768
Signal Mountain (p205)	Colter Bay	Close to shops and restaurants, with lake access and forest shade	86	7593
Headwaters at Flagg Ranch (p204)	Rockefeller Pkwy	Features dining, laundry and showers, but not a haven for tenters	141	6300

  Drinking Water  Restrooms  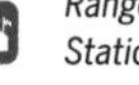 Ranger Station  Wheelchair Accessible  Grocery Store Nearby

Headwaters Cabins CABIN $$$

(Flagg Ranch Resort; ☎307-543-2861; www.gtlc.com/lodges/headwaters-lodge-at-flagg-ranch; Flagg Ranch; d $235-320; ⊙mid-May–mid-Sep; P) This 1910 resort has seen some improvements since its bygone occupation by the US Cavalry: walkways lead to prim log duplexes sporting comfortable Western motifs and featuring rustic log beds, phones, coffeemakers, minifridges and patio rockers. It's pet-friendly ($18 extra) and popular with families and couples stopping between parks. The lodge offers upscale dining, a minimarket and an activities desk.

Colter Bay Region

Camping

Colter Bay Campground CAMPGROUND $

(Map p198; ☎307-543-3100; www.gtlc.com; Hwy 89/191/287; tent/RV sites $31/53; ⊙mid-May–Sep; P) This noisy campground (335 campsites, 103 RV sites with full hookups) on the east shore of Jackson can feel a little oppressive, but often has spots later in the day. Site O333 is the best pick, with direct access to a short lakeshore trail. Sites are available on a first-come, first-served basis.

Lizard Creek Campground CAMPGROUND $

(☎800-672-6012; www.signalmountainlodge.com; off N Park Rd; sites $30; ⊙mid-Jun–early Sep; P) Snug in a forested peninsula along Jackson Lake's north shore, about 8 miles north of Colter Bay Junction, these secluded woodsy sites (60 total) are a great option. Register early since it's popular with boaters. Vehicle length limited to 30ft.

Signal Mountain Campground CAMPGROUND $

(Map p198; ☎307-543-2831; www.signalmtnlodge.com; 501 Signal Mountain Boat Launch Rd; tent/RV sites with hookup $32/54; ⊙mid-May–mid-Oct; P) This popular midsized campground only has one site with a view: #12. Camping can be a little cramped but the place is convenient: a restaurant, bar, grocery store and marina are nearby. Vehicle size is limited to 30ft. There's a dump station for RVs.

Lodging

Colter Bay Village CABIN $$

(Map p198; ☎307-543-3100; www.gtlc.com/lodges/colter-bay-village; Colter Bay; tent cabins $80, cabins with bath $179-265, shared bath $99; ⊙late May-Sep; P) In this busy village, comfortable log cabins, some original, are your best bet,

OPEN	RESERVATION REQUIRED?	DAILY FEE	FEATURES & FACILITIES
early May– mid-Oct	no	tent/RV $29/53	
early May-late Sep	no	$29	
mid-May–late Sep	no	$31	
mid-Jun–early Sep	no	$30	
mid-May–mid-Oct	no	tent/RV $32/54	
late May-late Sep	yes	tent/RV $38/74	

Summertime Campfire Program

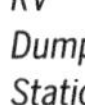
RV Dump Station

CAMPING ON THE CHEAP

Some lesser-known, first-come, first-served sites near the park may have fewer amenities, but they also have openings when NPS campgrounds are bursting, and charge a third to half of the price.

Secluded **Sheffield Campground** (307-739-5500; www.fs.usda.gov; sites $10; late May-early Sep; P) is a five-site USFS (US Forest Service) campground, 2.5 miles south of Yellowstone National Park's South Entrance and just south of Flagg Ranch. Cross the Snake River Bridge, then go a half-mile east on a rough dirt road from a subtly signed turnoff.

Located 7 miles northeast of Kelly on the shores of Slide Lake, **Atherton Creek Campground** (307-739-5500; www.fs.usda.gov; Gros Ventre Rd, Slide Lake; sites $15; P) has 20 sites, drinking water and pit toilets.

Eight free, minimally developed, first-come, first-served campgrounds are strung out along the bumpy and unpaved **Grassy Lake Rd**, which begins just west of the parking lot at Flagg Ranch. The first (and most popular) campground is 1.6 miles along the road and has four riverside campsites. Each of the next three riverside campgrounds, in the 1.5-mile stretch past Soldiers' Meadow, has two sites. The last four campgrounds, spaced out along the next 3.5 miles, are useful for hikes into Yellowstone's southern reaches. All sites have toilets and trash service but no potable water. Camping is only allowed in designated sites.

The tucked-away eight-site **Pacific Creek Campground** (307-739-5500; www.fs.usda.gov; sites $10; late May-early Sep; P) is 12 miles up the graveled Pacific Creek Rd (USFS Rd 30090) from Grand Teton's Moran Entrance Station. It's generally used as a base for backpacking trips into the Teton Wilderness.

Several free dispersed campsites sit on **Shadow Mountain**, on the east edge of the valley. This spot has a dedicated following, so show up early. Don't expect water or toilets, and there's a two-day maximum stay. It's a rough drive anywhere, but you'll be rewarded with stunning dawn views of the Tetons.

available late May through September. Tent cabins (available June to early September) are very basic log-and-canvas structures sporting Siberian gulag charm. Expect bare bunks, a wood-burning stove, a picnic table and an outdoor grill. Bathrooms are separate and sleeping bags can be rented.

★Jackson Lake Lodge LODGE $$$
(Map p198; 307-543-3100; www.gtlc.com/lodges/jackson-lake-lodge; Jackson Lake Lodge Rd; r & cottages $330-449; mid-May–early Oct; P) With soft sheets, meandering trails for long walks and enormous picture windows framing the peaks, the Teton's premier lodge is the perfect place to romance. Nearby, you may find the 348 cinder-block cottages overpriced for their viewless, barracks-like arrangement, though renovations have made them pleasant inside. The secluded Moose Pond View cottages feature amazing porch-side panoramas.

Signal Mountain Lodge LODGE $$$
(Map p198; 307-543-2831; www.signalmtnlodge.com; Teton Park Rd; r $262-368, cabins $218-278, ste $367-408; early May–mid-Oct; P) With a spectacular lakefront location, this complex at the edge of Jackson Lake offers cozy, well-appointed cabins and rather posh rooms. Lakefront suites have stunning mountain views, remodeled bathrooms and patios you'll never want to leave. There's helpful, personalized service, some rooms allowing pets (US$20 extra), and wi-fi in the lobby.

Eastern Slopes

Triangle X Ranch RANCH $$$
(307-733-2183; www.trianglex.com; 2 Triangle X Rd; weekly all-inclusive d from $3800, winter cabins per person $150; P) With a jagged Teton backdrop, this 1926 ranch on the eastern flanks of the park is still run by its founding family, the Turners. There's immaculate wood cabins and activities – including square dancing, trout fishing and Dutch-oven cookouts – to keep you out in the fresh air. Cabins have one to three bedrooms.

Kids get special attention with their own dining hall and a 'Little Wrangler' program, featuring horseback riding, swimming and crafts.

Moose Head Ranch RANCH $$$
(☎307-733-3141; www.mooseheadranch.com; all-inclusive d $880; ⏲Jun-Aug; P) Families rave about this ranch, which has modern log cabins, friendly young staff, a varied and tasty menu and a slew of activities for adults and kids alike. Horseback rides are for all abilities. Visits require a five-night minimum and there are discounted rates for children. It's 18 miles north of Jackson, at 6800ft.

Central Tetons

Camping

Jenny Lake Campground CAMPGROUND $
(Map p200; ☎307-543-2811; www.gtlc.com/camping/jenny-lake-campground; Teton Park Rd; tent sites $29; ⏲May-Sep; P) This tent-only, generator-free campground with 49 sites is the most popular in the park, usually filling before 10am. It sits among the evergreens and glacial boulders, but has no view of the lake itself.

Gros Ventre Campground CAMPGROUND $
(☎307-543-3100; www.gtlc.com/camping/gros-ventre-campground; Gros Ventre Rd; tent/RV sites $29/53; ⏲May–mid-Oct; P) Sprawling but secluded, this campground complex sits near the Gros Ventre River, 11.5 miles southwest of Moose. With the tall cottonwoods for shade and the nearby river, it's fairly attractive. It tends to fill up later in the day, but is usually your best last-minute bet for camping in the park.

Lodging

★**Climbers' Ranch** CABIN $
(Map p200; ☎307-733-7271; www.americanalpineclub.org/grand-teton-climbers-ranch; End Highlands Rd; dm $27; ⏲Jun-Sep; P) Started as a refuge for serious climbers, these rustic log cabins run by the American Alpine Club are now available to hikers, who can take advantage of the spectacular in-park location. There is a bathhouse with showers and a sheltered cook station with locking bins for coolers. Bring your own sleeping bag and pad (bunks are bare, but still a steal).

★**Jenny Lake Lodge** LODGE $$$
(Map p200; ☎307-543-3100; www.gtlc.com/lodges/jenny-lake-lodge; Jenny Lake Scenic Dr; all-inclusive cabins from $736; ⏲Jun-early Oct; P) Worn timbers, down comforters and colorful quilts imbue these elegant cabins with a cozy atmosphere. It doesn't come cheap, but the Signature Stay package includes breakfast, five-course dinner, bicycle use and guided horseback riding. Rainy days are for hunkering down at the fireplace in the main lodge with a game or book from the stacks.

Moose

Spur Ranch Log Cabins CABIN $$$
(Map p200; ☎307-733-2522; www.dornans.com; Moose; cabins $250-350; ⏲closed Nov & Apr; P) Gravel paths running through a broad wildflower meadow link these tranquil duplex cabins on the Snake River. This small family-run resort has 12 cabins with covered porches and grills. Western styling with lodgepole pine furniture and down bedding create a homey feel, but it's views that make it.

EATING & DRINKING

There's fast food, basic markets and even upscale dining in the park. Other options include taking a Jackson Lake dinner or breakfast cruise (p193) or packing a picnic basket. Dornan's Trading Post in Moose offers an impressive selection of wines. Campground diners must store food in bear boxes or cars – never leave it unattended and always dispose of food properly.

John D Rockefeller Jr Memorial Parkway

Sheffield's AMERICAN $$
(☎800-443-2311; Flagg Ranch; mains $10-29; ⏲6:30am-9:30pm, bar to 11pm; 📶) Hungry travelers flock to this friendly but average eatery at Flagg Ranch, the area's sole restaurant, with some vegan options. Breakfast and lunch are casual at this handsome lodge, while dinner goes Western with grilled steaks, elk meatloaf and chicken potpie. The nachos feed two to three people. Whiskey and local brews are served at the saloon.

Colter Bay Region

Colter Bay

Leek's Pizzeria PIZZA $
(☎307-543-2494; Leeks Marina; mains $9-15; ⏲11am-10pm Jun-Sep) Pizza and draft beer on the patio is a fine way to end an active day.

DANGERS & ANNOYANCES

Though people are the greater nuisance, be aware that black bears and a growing population of grizzlies live in the park.

Mid-October to early December is elk-hunting season in areas east of US 26/89/191, west of US 26/89/191 along the Snake River between Moose and Moran Junctions, and the Rockefeller Memorial Parkway. The National Park Service (NPS) *Elk Ecology & Management* pamphlet offers more details and a map.

Issuing limited licenses for grizzly-bear hunting was approved in the state of Wyoming in 2018. Fall hunting may not take place closer than a quarter of a mile from state highways.

North of Colter Bay Village, this casual but cozy eatery also serves soup, salad and sandwiches, and has a basic kids' menu.

Café Court Pizzeria CAFETERIA **$**
(Map p198; ☎307-543-2811; 100 Colter Bay Village Rd, Colter Bay; mains $8-12; ⏰11am-10pm) An airy, plain cafeteria offering salads, burritos, picnic takeout and grill staples. Kids like this place. The service is friendly and the grilled free-range chicken tacos are tasty.

Ranch House AMERICAN **$$**
(Map p198; ☎307-543-3335; www.gtlc.com; 100 Colter Bay Village Rd, Colter Bay; mains breakfast $9-15, lunch $14-17, dinner $18-25; ⏰6:30am-10:30pm May-Sep; 🍷) This Western dining room with a branded bar offers a formal setting, serving wine and beer. Going beyond steak and potatoes, there's miso salmon and shishito peppers in sea salt. Vegetarians are also catered to. The all-you-can-eat breakfast buffet is a pre-hike institution. Dinner often requires a wait.

Jackson Lake Lodge

Blue Heron Lounge BARBECUE **$$**
(Map p198; ☎307-543-2811; www.gtlc.com/dining; Jackson Lake Lodge; mains $11-23; ⏰11am-midnight mid-May–Sep) A must for sunset cocktails, this attractive wraparound bar features knee-to-ceiling windows. Alcohol and tasty small plates consisting of charcuterie and salads are locally sourced. If the weather is good, the outdoor grill offers great barbecue. Occasionally you'll hit on live music.

Pioneer Grill DINER **$$**
(Map p198; ☎307-543-1911; www.gtlc.com/dining/pioneer-grill-jackson-lake-lodge; Jackson Lake Lodge; mains $9-26; ⏰6am-11pm; 👪) A casual and classic diner with a row of leatherette stools, the Pioneer serves up wraps, burgers and salads. For dessert, order a Mt Owen – an oversized profiterole topped with ice cream, hot fudge and whipped cream – to take the burn off that long hike. There's takeout, boxed lunches (order a day ahead) and room-service pizza (5pm to 9pm).

Mural Room AMERICAN **$$$**
(Map p198; ☎307-543-3463; www.gtlc.com/dining/mural-room-jackson-lake-lodge; Jackson Lake Lodge; lunch mains $12-20, dinner mains $22-46; ⏰7am-9pm) In addition to the stirring views of the Tetons and moose ambling in the willow flats, these restaurant walls are adorned with the romantic Rendezvous Murals, depictions of 19th-century life by Carl Roters. Gourmet selections include game dishes and juicy vegetable Wellington. Breakfasts are very good; dinner reservations are recommended.

Signal Mountain

Trapper Grill CAFE **$$**
(Map p198; ☎307-543-2831; www.signalmountainlodge.com; Signal Mountain Lodge; mains $12-20; ⏰7am-2:30pm & 4:30-10pm) Sandwiches, burgers and baby-back ribs, alongside local draft beers, are among the many choices sure to please each picky member of the family. It's the cheaper of the two restaurants at Signal Mountain Lodge (p206), and it has the better view out over the lake. Breakfasts, with sides of ham, bacon or buffalo sausage, are gut busters.

Peaks AMERICAN **$$$**
(Map p198; ☎307-543-2831; www.signalmountainlodge.com; Signal Mountain Lodge; mains $18-41; ⏰5:30-10pm) 🌿 Dine on selections of cheese and fruit, local free-range beef and organic polenta cakes. Small plates, such as wild game sliders, are also available. While the indoor ambiance is rather drab, the patio seating, starring sunsets over Jackson Lake and top-notch huckleberry margaritas, gets snapped up early.

Central Tetons

★ Jenny Lake Lodge Dining Room AMERICAN **$$$**
(Map p200; ☎307-543-3351; www.gtlc.com/dining/the-dining-room-at-jenny-lake-lodge; Jenny Lake

Lodge; 5-course prix-fixe dinner $94; 7:30am-8:45pm) A real splurge, this may be the only five-course wilderness meal of your life, and it's well worth it. For breakfast, crab-cake eggs Benedict is prepared to perfection. Elk tenderloin and daikon watermelon salad satisfy hungry hikers, and you can't beat the warm atmosphere snuggled in the Tetons. Dress up in the evening, when reservations are a must.

Moose

Dornan's Trading Post MARKET $
(Map p200; 307-733-2415; www.dornans.com; Moose; 8am-8pm) The market offering the park's best-quality selection has an excellent deli, with imported cheeses, sandwiches and wildly popular ice cream. The espresso cart parked in front is a godsend. The Wine Shoppe here offers 1700 selections as well as monthly wine tastings.

Pizza & Pasta Company PIZZA $
(Map p200; 307-733-2415; www.dornans.com; Moose; mains $10-13, pizza $9-17; 11:30am-9pm;) If there is a more compelling place for pizza and beers than Dornan's rooftop deck, looking across the Snake River and Menor's Ferry at the towering Tetons, we've yet to find it. Unfortunately service can be slow and the food comes second to the view. One of the only independently owned restaurants in the park, it's open year-round.

Dornan's Chuckwagon BARBECUE $$
(Map p200; 307-733-2415; www.dornans.com; Moose; breakfast & lunch mains $8-16, dinner $9-35; 7-11am, noon-3pm & 5-9pm Jun-Aug) At this outdoor family favorite, breakfast means sourdough pancakes and eggs off the griddle, while lunchtime offers light fare and sandwiches. Come dinner, Dutch ovens are steaming. There's beef, ribs or trout, along with a bottomless salad bar. Picnic tables have unparalleled views of the Grand. Kids get special rates. There's live music from 5:30pm to 8:30pm, Tuesday to Thursday.

Hootenanny LIVE MUSIC
(Map p200; Moose; 6pm Mon mid-Jun–Aug) It's hard to beat the down-home ambience of this free weekly musical gathering out on the lawns at Dornan's Chuckwagon (p209). Popular with locals and kids, there's regional bands mostly playing acoustic and bluegrass music. Bring a blanket or a chair.

Information

Blackrock Ranger District (Map p198; 307-543-2386; Hwy 26/287, Moran; 8am-4:30pm Mon-Fri) A district office of the Bridger-Teton National Forest.

Colter Bay Visitor Center (Map p198; 307-739-3594; Colter Bay; 8am-5pm mid-May–early Oct, to 7pm Jun-Aug) On US 89/191/287.

Craig Thomas Discovery & Visitor Center (Map p200; 307-739-3399, backcountry permits 307-739-3309; Teton Park Rd, Moose; 8am-7pm Jun-Aug, hours vary Mar-May, Sep & Oct;) Provides information and backcountry permits. Ranger programs include map-chats and various guided hikes around Moose.

Flagg Ranch Information Station (307-543-2327; Flagg Ranch; 10am-3pm Jun-Aug, closed for lunch) Provides park information, restrooms and a small bookstore.

Grand Teton Association (www.grandtetonpark.org) This nonprofit organization sells books and maps at all park visitor centers.

Jenny Lake Ranger Station (Map p200; 307-739-3343; off Teton Park Rd, South Jenny Lake Junction; 8am-6pm Jun-Aug) The best place for climbing and mountaineering information. Also offers backcountry permits and backcountry camping information.

Jenny Lake Visitor Center (Map p200; 307-739-3343; Teton Park Rd; 8am-4:30pm Sep-May, to 7pm Jun-Aug) Facilities include a store, geology exhibits and restrooms. With in-depth information on backpacking and trails, it's also the meeting place for guided walks and talks, with activity schedules posted. It's 8 miles north of Moose Junction.

Visitors must pay the entrance fee or show park permits at the following checkpoints:

Moose Entrance Station (South Entrance; Map p200; Teton Park Rd, Moose Village; hrs vary)

Moran Entrance Station (North Entrance; Map p198; Hwy 287; hrs vary)

Granite Canyon Entrance Station (Southwest Entrance; Map p200; Moose-Wilson Rd; hrs vary)

ORIENTATION

Just south of Yellowstone National Park, Grand Teton National Park stretches 40 miles along the compact, 15-mile-wide Teton Range. Its western boundary merges with the Jedediah Smith Wilderness within Targhee National Forest. The Bridger-Teton National Forest sits east. The range's steep eastern flank overlooks Jackson Hole valley, where Jackson Lake catches the Snake River flowing south from its source in

Yellowstone National Park. On the western side of the range, Idaho's Teton Valley features more gradual slopes.

Jackson Lake dominates the northern half of the park, with the Tetons to the west. The popular central Teton peaks, ringed by alpine lakes, are concentrated in the southwest. The most remote and least visited area of the park is the northwest region, accessible only by multiday backpacking. This is the Tetons' prime grizzly habitat, although sightings have extended south and east through other parts of the park.

Before crossing into Idaho, the Snake River winds through flat glacial deposits on the south side of the park. The quieter, less visited east side is bordered by the forested hills of the Bridger-Teton National Forest and the remote trails of the Teton Wilderness.

POST

Post Office (Map p200; ☎800-275-8777; 3 Teton Park Rd, Moose Village; ⏰9am-1pm & 1:30-3:30pm Mon-Fri, 10-11:30am Sat)

RULES & PERMITS

- The use of drones is prohibited.
- Harassing wildlife is not allowed.
- Visitors must maintain a safe distance of at least 100yd from wolves and bears, and 25yd or more from all other wildlife.
- Campers must have a backcountry permit to camp on the trail.
- Motorized and nonmotorized watercraft require a park permit.
- Visitors are not allowed to open-carry firearms in the park. Unloaded weapons may be transported through the park if properly stored.

Getting Around

The speed limit on US 26/89/191 is 55mph; elsewhere it's generally 45mph. Watch for wildlife at dusk, as well as cyclists crossing sections of the multiuse pathway (p188) on Teton Park Rd. Gas stations are open year-round at Moose (24 hours, credit card only 8pm to 8am) and Headwaters Resort, and summers only (June to August) at Colter Bay, Signal Mountain and Jackson Lake Lodge. There is no public transportation.

In winter, the 15-mile section of Teton Park Rd between Taggart Lake Trailhead and Signal Mountain Lodge is closed to vehicles. For seasonal road closures, consult park information offices and entrance stations.

The main north–south route through the park is **US 26/89/191**, contiguous with the east bank of the Snake River between Jackson and Moran Junction. At Moran Junction, US 89/191 joins US 287 heading north along Jackson Lake to the Rockefeller Memorial Parkway; US 26 joins US 287 heading east to Dubois via Togwotee Pass.

Teton Park Rd links Moose Junction to Jackson Lake Junction (and US 89/191/287) via Jenny and Jackson Lakes. The 5-mile **Jenny Lake Scenic Dr** connects North Jenny Lake and South Jenny Lake Junctions; the road is two-way to Jenny Lake Lodge and one-way south of it.

Gros Ventre Rd heads east from US 26/89/191 at the south end of the park to Kelly and out of the park into the Gros Ventre Valley. Antelope Flats Rd is 1 mile north of Moose Junction, east of US 26/89/191.

The narrow **Moose–Wilson Rd** connects Teton Village to Moose; no RVs or trailers are allowed.

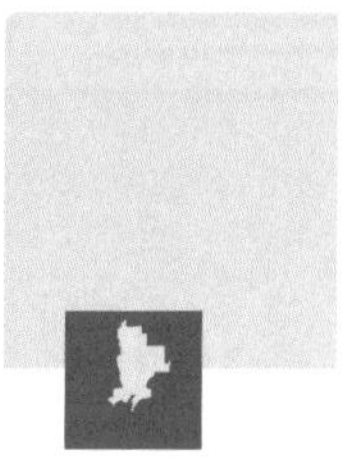

Around Grand Teton

Includes ➡

Best Places to Eat

- ➡ Persephone (p218)
- ➡ Snake River Grill (p219)
- ➡ Teton Thai (p223)
- ➡ Nora's Fish Creek Inn (p221)
- ➡ The Indian (p219)

Best Places to Stay

- ➡ Alpine House (p217)
- ➡ The Hostel (p222)
- ➡ Turpin Meadow Ranch (p224)
- ➡ Wort Hotel (p217)

Why Go?

Outside the park boundaries the landscape doesn't suddenly turn dull. The rampage of beauty continues with cold clear rivers, winding single tracks and steep powder runs. Visit this region in winter and you will find Jackson Hole and Grand Targhee resorts serving up deep, pillowy snow. Lodges light roaring fires and the wilderness becomes a haven for dogsledding, snowshoeing, ski touring and frozen fun.

Posh and popular Jackson serves as the regional hub and base camp, where you can browse for Western baubles, down pints of fresh organic lager or wrap yourself in honey and rose petals. The foodie scene is among the best in the West, with an emphasis on local, farm-raised food. On the Idaho side, rural Teton Valley is another world. If you have come to embrace every scrap of solitude, a trip west across the divide might be in order.

Road Distances (miles)

	Jackson	Teton Village	Moose	Victor, ID
Teton Village	15			
Moose	15	10		
Victor, ID	25	25	35	
Grant Village (Yellowstone)	80	75	65	100

Note: Distances are approximate

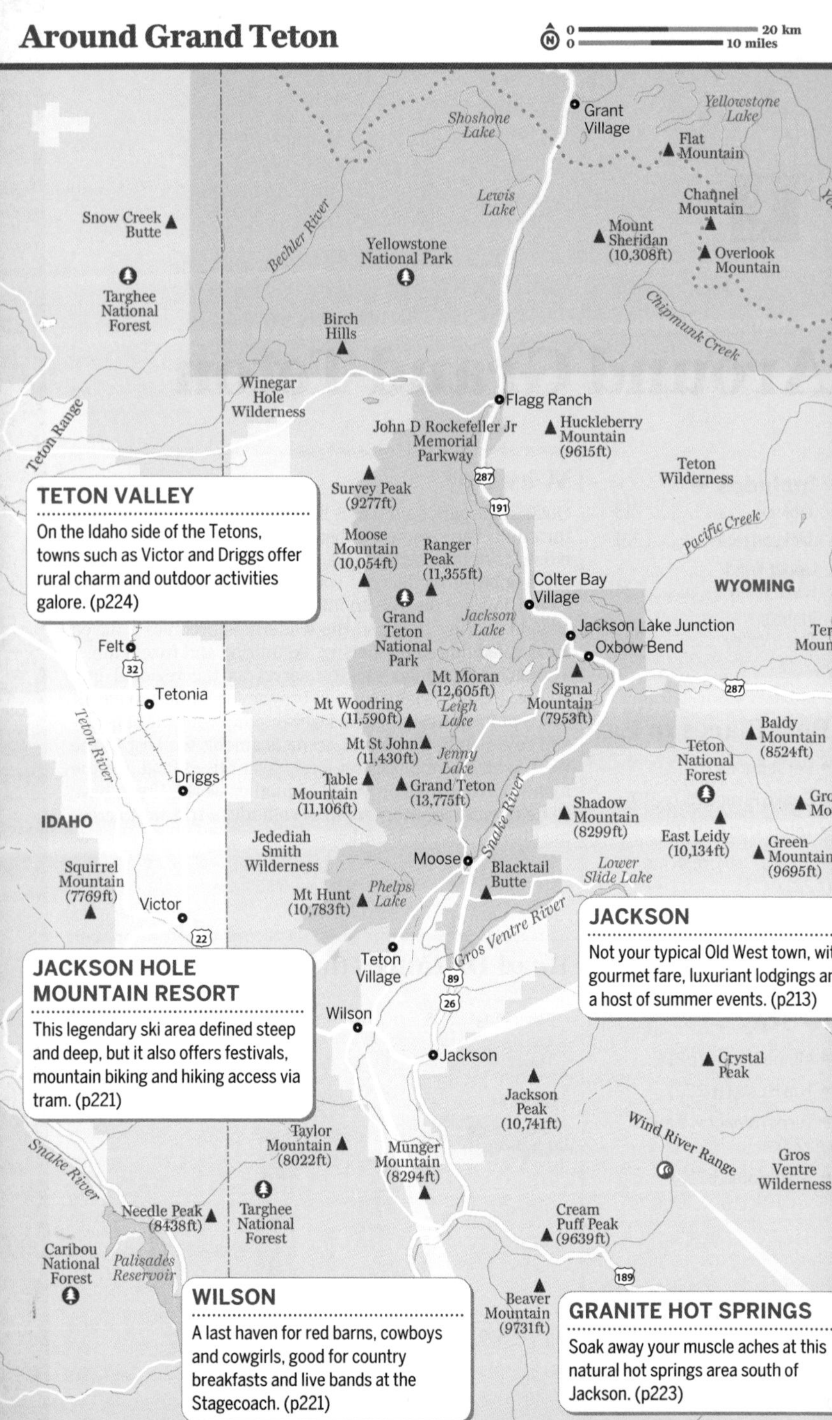
Around Grand Teton
N
0 20 km
0 10 miles
Grant Village
Yellowstone Lake
Shoshone Lake
Flat Mountain
Lewis Lake
Channel Mountain
Snow Creek Butte
Bechler River
Yellowstone National Park
Mount Sheridan (10,308ft)
Overlook Mountain
Targhee National Forest
Chipmunk Creek
Birch Hills
Winegar Hole Wilderness
Flagg Ranch
Teton Range
John D Rockefeller Jr Memorial Parkway
Huckleberry Mountain (9615ft)
287
Teton Wilderness
Survey Peak (9277ft)
191
TETON VALLEY
On the Idaho side of the Tetons, towns such as Victor and Driggs offer rural charm and outdoor activities galore. (p224)
Moose Mountain (10,054ft)
Ranger Peak (11,355ft)
Pacific Creek
Colter Bay Village
WYOMING
Grand Teton National Park
Jackson Lake
Jackson Lake Junction
Oxbow Bend
Felt
32
Mt Moran (12,605ft)
Signal Mountain (7953ft)
287
Tetonia
Mt Woodring (11,590ft)
Leigh Lake
Teton River
Baldy Mountain (8524ft)
Mt St John (11,430ft)
Jenny Lake
Teton National Forest
Driggs
Table Mountain (11,106ft)
Grand Teton (13,775ft)
Snake River
IDAHO
Shadow Mountain (8299ft)
Jedediah Smith Wilderness
East Leidy (10,134ft)
Green Mountain (9695ft)
Squirrel Mountain (7769ft)
Moose
Blacktail Butte
Lower Slide Lake
Mt Hunt (10,783ft)
Phelps Lake
Victor
22
JACKSON
Gros Ventre River
Not your typical Old West town, wit gourmet fare, luxuriant lodgings ar a host of summer events. (p213)
Teton Village
JACKSON HOLE MOUNTAIN RESORT
89
This legendary ski area defined steep and deep, but it also offers festivals, mountain biking and hiking access via tram. (p221)
26
Wilson
Jackson
Crystal Peak
Jackson Peak (10,741ft)
Taylor Mountain (8022ft)
Munger Mountain (8294ft)
Wind River Range
Gros Ventre Wilderness
Snake River
Needle Peak (8438ft)
Targhee National Forest
Cream Puff Peak (9639ft)
Caribou National Forest
Palisades Reservoir
189
WILSON
A last haven for red barns, cowboys and cowgirls, good for country breakfasts and live bands at the Stagecoach. (p221)
Beaver Mountain (9731ft)
GRANITE HOT SPRINGS
Soak away your muscle aches at this natural hot springs area south of Jackson. (p223)

Jackson

☎307 / POP 10,530 / ELEV 6237FT

Welcome to the other side of Wyoming. Hiding in a verdant valley between some of America's most rugged and wild mountains, Jackson looks similar to other towns in the state – false-front roof lines, covered wooden walkways, saloons on every block – but it ain't quite the same.

Here, hard-core climbers, bikers and skiers (recognizable as sunburned baristas) outnumber cowboys by a wide margin, and you're just as likely to see a celebrity as a moose wandering the urban trails.

Although Jackson being posh and popular does have its downsides for the traveler (the median house price is $1.6 million), it does mean you'll find a lively urban buzz, a refreshing variety of foods and no shortage of things to do – both in and out of town.

Sights

Downtown Jackson has a handful of historic buildings.

★National Museum of Wildlife Art MUSEUM

(☎307-733-5771; www.wildlifeart.org; 2820 Rungius Rd; adult/child $14/6; ⏲9am-5pm daily May-Oct, 9am-5pm Tue-Sat, 11am-5pm Sun Nov-Apr; 👪) Major works by Bierstadt, Rungius, Remington and Russell breathe life into their subjects in impressive and inspiring ways – almost better than seeing the animals in the wild. Almost. The outdoor sculptures and building itself (inspired, oddly, by a ruined Scottish castle) are worth stopping by to see even if the museum is closed.

The discovery gallery has a kids' studio for drawing and print rubbing that adults plainly envy. Check the website for gallery openings, book readings, art classes and events.

National Elk Refuge WILDLIFE RESERVE

(☎307-733-9212; www.fws.gov/refuge/national_elk_refuge; Hwy 89; sleigh ride adult/child $23/15; ⏲10am-4pm mid-Dec–mid-Apr) This refuge protects Jackson's herd of several thousand elk, offering them a winter habitat from November to May. During summer, ask at the Jackson visitor center for the best places to see elk. An hour-long horse-drawn sleigh ride is the highlight of a winter visit; buy tickets at the visitor center.

Center for the Arts ARTS CENTER

(☎307-733-4900; www.jhcenterforthearts.org; 240 S Glenwood S) One-stop shopping for culture, attracting big-name concert acts and featuring theater performances, classes, art exhibits and events. Check the calendar of events online. Students get discounts on performances.

Jackson National Fish Hatchery HATCHERY

(☎307-733-2510; 1500 Fish Hatchery Rd; ⏲8am-4pm) FREE Just north of the elk refuge, with daily tours.

Activities

Goodwin Lake & Jackson Peak HIKING

This 9-mile round-trip is one of the closest summits to Jackson with cross-valley Teton views. The bare, pointed summit of Jackson Peak (10,741ft) sits above a lake. Its most secure approach winds left up a gradual saddle. Continue past Goodwin Lake heading southeast, crossing an open field. Take a right at a well-worn but narrow trail marked with cairns. Climb steeply to the ridge, crossing snow patches and rocky outcrops to the peak.

To get here, drive east on East Broadway until it ends, turning left into the National Elk Refuge. The road switchbacks. Bear right at Curtis Canyon for Goodwin Lake (after 9.2 miles) and drive 2.7 miles to the parking lot. The trail climbs steadily through a field of wildflowers, topping out on a level hilltop. Approach the forested shores of Goodwin Lake (880ft), a nice spot for a swim or trout fishing. Return via the same route. Dogs allowed.

Mill Iron Ranch HORSEBACK RIDING

(☎888-808-6390, 307-733-6390; www.millironranch.net; 5 Hwy 89; 2hr ride $80) This fourth-generation operation of a Wyoming ranch family is the real deal. Climbing 2000ft, the two-hour ride in the Bridger-Teton National Forest is rated the number-one trail ride in the US. It also offers dinner rides, sleigh rides and barn dances. To get there, drive south from Jackson on Hwy 89.

Rendezvous Sports KAYAKING

(Jackson Hole Kayak School; ☎307-733-2471; www.jacksonholekayak.com; 945 W Broadway; SUPs & kayaks from $41; ⏲8am-7pm) Offers kayak and SUP rentals and instruction in addition to multiday paddling trips to Yellowstone Lake.

Wyoming Balloon Co BALLOONING

(☎307-739-0900; www.wyomingballoon.com; per person $350; ⏲mid-Jun–mid-Sep) The ultimate float trips are these hour-long flights over the Tetons. Flights are weather-dependent.

Scenic Safaris WILDLIFE WATCHING

(☎307-734-8898; www.scenic-safaris.com; 545 N Cache St; half-day tour adult/child $140/95) Guided wildlife safaris in Grand Teton

Jackson

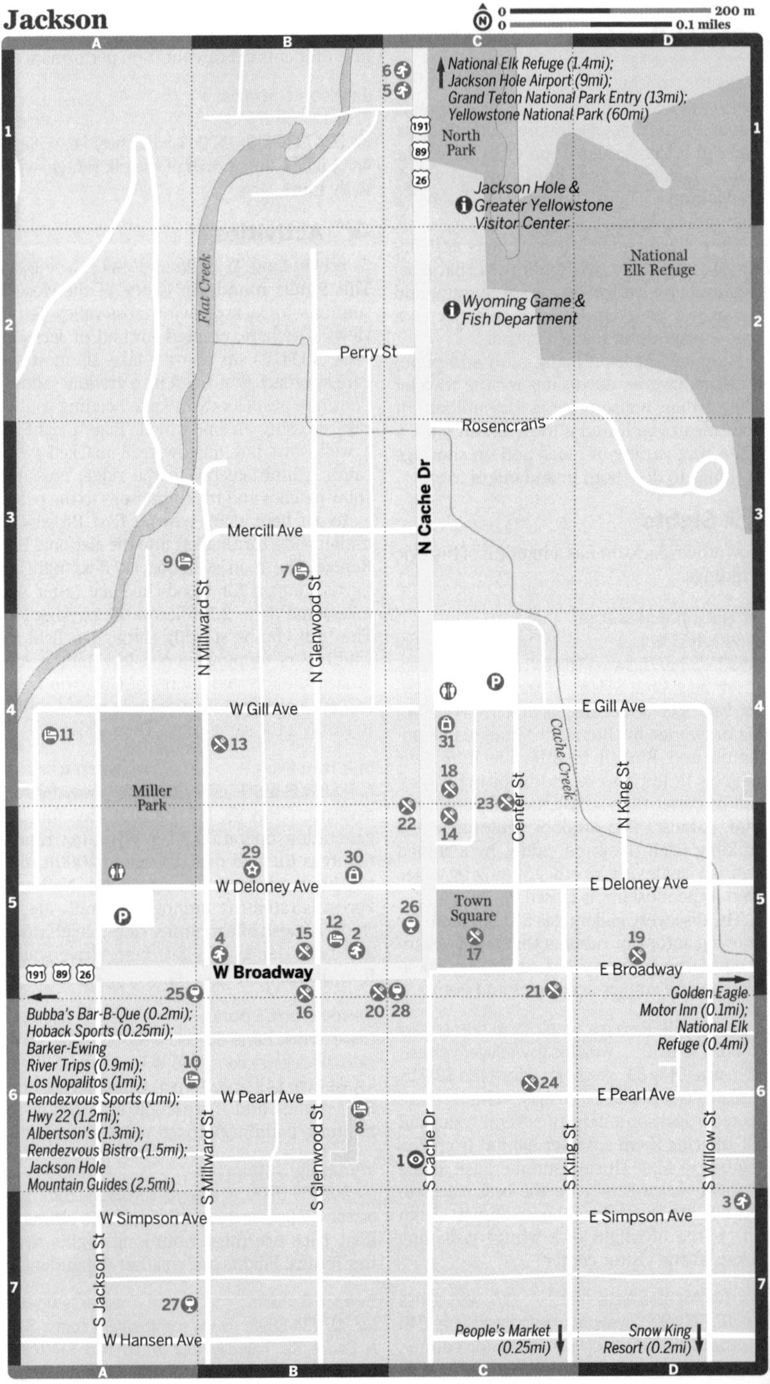

0 200 m
0 0.1 miles

National Elk Refuge (1.4mi); Jackson Hole Airport (9mi); Grand Teton National Park Entry (13mi); Yellowstone National Park (60mi)

North Park

Jackson Hole & Greater Yellowstone Visitor Center

National Elk Refuge

Wyoming Game & Fish Department

Flat Creek

Perry St

Rosencrans

N Cache Dr

Mercill Ave

N Millward St

N Glenwood St

W Gill Ave

E Gill Ave

Cache Creek

Center St

N King St

Miller Park

W Deloney Ave

E Deloney Ave

Town Square

W Broadway

E Broadway

Golden Eagle Motor Inn (0.1mi); National Elk Refuge (0.4mi)

Bubba's Bar-B-Que (0.2mi); Hoback Sports (0.25mi); Barker-Ewing River Trips (0.9mi); Los Nopalitos (1mi); Rendezvous Sports (1mi); Hwy 22 (1.2mi); Albertson's (1.3mi); Rendezvous Bistro (1.5mi); Jackson Hole Mountain Guides (2.5mi)

W Pearl Ave

E Pearl Ave

S Millward St

S Glenwood St

S Cache Dr

S King St

S Willow St

W Simpson Ave

E Simpson Ave

S Jackson St

W Hansen Ave

People's Market (0.25mi)

Snow King Resort (0.2mi)

National Park, with spotting scopes and binoculars provided. Also has Yellowstone options.

Granite Creek Hot Springs HOT SPRINGS
(☎307-690-6323; www.fs.usda.gov/recarea/btnf/recarea/?recid=71639; Granite Creek Rd, Hwy 191; adult/child $8/5; ⏲10am-8pm mid-May–Oct, to 4pm or 5pm Dec-Mar) Head 25 miles southeast of Jackson on Hwy 191 and turn east on gravel Granite Creek Rd. Continue for 10 miles through alpine meadows and forested hills to the the natural hot springs with killer views of the surrounding peaks.

Teton Science Schools Ecology SCIENCE SCHOOL
(☎307-733-1313; www.tetonscience.org) No one beats this nonprofit for fun experiential education, with programs ranging from GPS scavenger hunts to ecology expeditions. Make inquiries through the website.

Winter Activities

Continental Divide Dogsled Adventures TOUR
(☎307-455-3052; www.dogsledadventures.com; half-day $282; ⏲Dec-Apr) Experience Wyoming's wintry backcountry from a dog's point of view with five-time Iditarod veteran Billy Snodgrass. Half-day trips include transportation from your Jackson hotel to Togwotee Pass, where you'll learn dogsled lore and the sport's history while teams of eight to 14 Alaskan huskies whisk you (and a guide) silently through the wilderness. Call for summer tours of the 140-dog kennel.

Snow King Resort SNOW SPORTS
(☎307-201-5464; https://snowkingmountain.com; 400 E Snow King Ave; lift ticket adult/child $55/45) Sling the skis over your shoulder and walk to this tiny 400-acre resort from downtown. Three lifts serve ski and snowboard runs with a vertical drop of 1571ft (15% beginner, 25% intermediate, 60% advanced). This north-facing slope catches less snow than other resorts but is convenient and well suited to families. In summer it offers a host of great activities. Also popular in winter is night skiing (adult/child $25/20; 4pm to 7pm Monday to Saturday) and tubing (adult/child per hour $20/15).

In summer the Treetop Adventure (adult $75, child aged seven to 11 $45), an adventure park designed by pro mountain guides, opens all its attractions (10am to 7pm mid-May to mid-October). It features a fun series of tree-to-tree aerial challenges including wobbly bridges, climbing walls, zip lines, moving skateboards and Tarzan swings that snake through the pine forest with spectacular Teton views. The course has variations for adults and children, and should take between two and four hours.

The Cowboy Coaster carries riders 400 vertical feet up the mountain before speeding downhill at up to 25 miles per hour up to 23ft off the ground, over six bridges and four loops. It runs in both summer and ski

Jackson

Sights
1 Center for the Arts.......C6

Activities, Courses & Tours
2 Barker-Ewing River Trips.......B5
3 Community Foundation of Jackson Hole.......D7
4 Dave Hansen Whitewater.......B5
5 Scenic Safaris.......C1
6 Teton Mountain Bike Tours.......C1

Sleeping
7 Alpine House.......B3
8 Antler Inn.......B6
9 Inn on the Creek.......A3
10 Rawhide Motel.......A6
11 Rusty Parrot Lodge & Spa.......A4
12 Wort Hotel.......B5

Eating
13 Blue Lion.......B4
14 Bunnery Bakery & Restaurant.......C5
15 Coco Love.......B5
16 Dog.......B5
17 Farmer's Market.......C5
18 Lotus.......C4
19 Persephone.......D5
20 Pizzeria Caldera.......B5
21 Snake River Grill.......C5
22 Teton Thai.......C5
23 Teton Tiger.......C4
24 Thai Me Up.......C6

Drinking & Nightlife
25 Bin 22.......A5
26 Million Dollar Cowboy Bar.......C5
27 Snake River Brewing Co.......A7
28 The Rose.......C5

Entertainment
29 Jackson Hole Playhouse.......B5

Shopping
30 Skinny Skis.......B5
31 Teton Mountaineering.......C4

season, with options to drive yourself or go along as a passenger (driver/passenger $21/10).

The scenic 20-minute Snow King Chairlift ride (adult/child $20/15) goes up to 7751ft. Follow the nature trail at the top through wildflower fields and aspen groves. Other diversions include a bungee trampoline and paragliding onsite.

To sample all of the attractions, get a Big King Pass (adult and child $125), which includes access to the 2500ft alpine slide, a bungee trampoline and minigolf.

Cycling

There is excellent mountain biking here. Popular rides in the area include Cache Creek, southeast of Jackson into the Gros Ventre; Game Creek, along USFS Rd 30455 east off US 26/89/191; and Spring Gulch Rd, west of and parallel to US 26/89/191 between Hwy 22 and Gros Ventre Junction. Hard-core riders can try Old Pass Rd, the old route over Teton Pass, south of Hwy 22.

Hoback Sports CYCLING
(☎307-733-5335; http://hobacksports.com; 520 W Broadway Ave; cruiser/mountain bike half-day from $39/69; ⏲9am-7pm) Offers regular and performance road-bike and mountain-bike rentals, tours, repairs and maps of area biking trails.

White-Water Rafting & Floating

You can't swing an oar in Jackson without hitting a rafting company eager to take you down the Snake River. Most offer a mellow 13-mile float through wetlands teeming with wildlife, from the town of Wilson to Hoback Junction, or the more punchy Snake River Canyon with its churning class III rapids.

Only a few outfits offer trips wholly within Grand Teton National Park – if that's important to you – including **Barker-Ewing** (☎307-733-1000, 800-448-4202; www.barker-ewing.com; 45 W Broadway) and **Dave Hansen Whitewater** (☎307-733-6295; www.davehansenwhitewater.com; 225 W Broadway).

Trips typically include transportation and lunch.

Festivals & Events

Jackson Hole Rodeo RODEO
(☎307-733-7927; http://jhrodeo.com; 447 Snow King Ave; adult/child from $20/15; ⏲Jun-Aug) Held at Teton County Fairgrounds, this popular rodeo saddles up at 8pm Wednesdays and Saturdays June through August, with some Friday shows.

ElkFest FAIR
(Antler Auction; http://elkfest.org; ⏲late May) If you need an ungulate rack to provide the finishing touch to your home decor, check out this unique Jackson event which takes place every May around the town square. Boy Scouts collect and sell the shed antlers during the festival to raise money to buy pellet winter feed for the elk – thus the elk financially support themselves during the winter.

Teton County Fair FAIR
(www.tetonwyo.org/fair; 447 Snow King Ave; ⏲late Jul) From pig wrestling to live music and 4H animal shows, it does not get more Wyoming than this. The Teton County Fair takes over the Teton County Fairgrounds in late July.

Jackson Hole Fall Arts Festival ART
(www.jacksonholechamber.com/fall_arts_festival; ⏲Sep) Features live auctions, artist talks and samples of local chefs' culinary wizardry.

Town Square Shootout THEATER
(⏲6pm Mon-Sat Memorial Day-Labor Day) Kids shouldn't dodge this hokey but entertaining street theater. The longest-running shootout in the country happens on Jackson Town Sq, pitting good guys against bad guys – both with impeccably believable timing.

Sleeping

Jackson has plenty of lodging, both in town and at Jackson Hole Mountain Resort (p222), but reservations are still essential in summer and winter high season. Prices, which may double during holidays or weekends, fall precipitously during the spring and fall 'slack' seasons. There are a few camping options scattered in the forest nearby, but most require a long drive, often down poor roads.

Camping

All campgrounds in the Jackson area are first-come, first-serve.

Curtis Canyon Campground CAMPGROUND $
(sites $15; ⏲late May–Aug; 🐾) Conveniently located, this popular 12-site campground, on gravel USFS Rd 30440 (off Elk Refuge Rd), sits 7 miles northeast of Jackson at 6900ft, with splendid views of the Tetons.

East Table Campground CAMPGROUND $
(sites $15; ⏲mid-May–Sep) Toward Idaho on the southeast side of US 26/89 is this roadside, 19-site campground, 24 miles south of Jackson at 5900ft.

SPLURGE: SPRING CREEK RANCH

Embodying every Western fantasy, rustic **Spring Creek Ranch Resort** (800-443-6139; www.springcreekranch.com; Spring Creek Rd; r/ste incl breakfast from $420/480;) gazes smack at the Tetons from the top of a butte ringed in sagebrush. The views are unreal and the vibe is oh-so-relaxed. Guests can rent sprawling mountain villas or little studios with fireplaces. Trails crisscross the property, where you can also ride horses.

Naturalist programs take visitors on dawn or dusk safaris to see bison, wolves and other wildlife. Then grab a juniper massage or mineral-rich seaweed wrap from the lauded Wilderness Adventure Spa.

Hoback Campground CAMPGROUND $
(sites $15; mid-May–mid-Sep) You'll find this shady 13-site campground along the Hoback River, 8 miles east of Hoback Junction and 22 miles southeast of Jackson (6600ft).

Kozy Campground CAMPGROUND $
(sites $15; mid-May–Sep 10) On the east side of US 189/191 is this riverside, eight-site campground, 30 miles southeast of Jackson at 6500ft.

Granite Creek Campground CAMPGROUND $
(sites $15; mid-May–Sep) The signed turnoff for this 51-site campground is 1 mile north of Kozy Campground. The campground itself is 35 miles from Jackson, 9 miles northwest of US 189/191 up (often washboard) gravel USFS Rd 30500, nestled deep in the Gros Ventre Mountains at 6900ft. Has drinking water, flush toilets and shade.

Station Creek Campground CAMPGROUND $
(sites $15; mid-May–mid-Sep) At 5800ft, the 16-site Station Creek is 1 mile west along the Snake River from Granite Creek Campground, 25 miles south of Jackson.

Snake River KOA CAMPGROUND $
(800-562-1878, 307-733-7078; www.srpkoa.com; tent site $32-52, RV site $45-103; mid-Apr–mid-Oct) Grassy Snake River is 12 miles south of Jackson off US 26/89/191 near Hoback Junction. Cheaper, recommended public US Forest Service (USFS) campgrounds are outside town.

Lodging

Pony Express MOTEL $$
(307-733-3835; www.ponyexpresswest.com; 1075 W Broadway; r $187-327;) A proud little motel hidden behind the gas station. Fresh and spacious rooms have pine walls and tucked-away bunks. Outdoors there's a plush lawn with tables and a heated pool. Cyclists can make use of the cleaning buckets and rags.

Rawhide Motel MOTEL $$
(307-733-1216; 75 S Millward St; r $169;) New Berber carpets and pine furniture spruce up these typical motel rooms, which also have flat-screen TVs, hair dryers and coffeemakers. Staff are friendly and one basement room runs $30 cheaper.

Antler Inn HOTEL $$
(307-733-2535; www.townsquareinns.com/antler-inn; 43 W Pearl Ave; r $200-325;) Right in the middle of the Jackson action, this sprawling complex provides clean and comfortable rooms, some with fireplaces and bathtubs. Stepping into the cheaper 'cedar log' rooms feels like you're coming home to a cozy Wyoming cabin, mostly because you are: they were hauled here and attached to the back of the hotel.

★**Alpine House** B&B $$$
(307-739-1570; www.alpinehouse.com; 285 N Glenwood St; r $265-385, cottage $770-1070;) Two former Olympic skiers have infused this downtown home with sunny Scandinavian style and personal touches, like great service and a cozy mountaineering library. Amenities include plush robes, down comforters, a shared Finnish sauna and an outdoor Jacuzzi. Save your appetite for the creative breakfast options, like lemon-ricotta blueberry pancakes or eggs Benedict.

★**Wort Hotel** HISTORIC HOTEL $$$
(307-733-2190; www.worthotel.com; 50 N Glenwood St; r from $444;) A distinctly Wyoming vibe permeates this luxury historic hotel that has only gotten better with age. Knotty pine furniture and handcrafted bedspreads complement full-size baths and Jacuzzis while the best concierge service in Jackson helps you fill out your itinerary with outdoor adventures. Even if staying here is out of your reach, swing by the antique **Silver Dollar Bar** downstairs.

Cowboy Village CABIN $$$

(☎800-483-8667, 307-733-3121; www.townsquareinns.com/cowboy-village; 120 S Flat Creek Dr; cabins $240-310;) Though they're in an urban lot, these cozy log cabins have a spark of yesteryear, snugly furnished with knotted pine, bark beds and animal carvings. It's family friendly, all rooms have kitchenettes and there's a fitness center, outdoor grills and an indoor pool. It's just off W Broadway. Prices drop by $100 or more in winter.

Rusty Parrot Lodge & Spa LODGE $$$

(☎888-739-1749; www.rustyparrot.com; 175 N Jackson St; r from $490;) With a collection of Remington sculptures and amazing Western art, this elegant lodge oozes luxury. Service is top-notch and rooms pamper with well-tended bedroom fireplaces and a plush teddy bear posed on the bed. Those who don't ski will get distracted at the spa, where the arnica sports massages and herbal lavender wraps are pure hedonism.

The gourmet restaurant prepares innovative international cuisine.

Inn on the Creek INN $$$

(☎800-669-9534, 307-739-1565; www.innonthecreek.com; 295 N Millward St; r $309-359; @) Elegant and intimate, this stone inn offers nine handsome rooms. Details include recessed fireplaces, top-quality linens on comfy beds and views of a gurgling creek out back. Some rooms have hot tubs. It's wedged into the edge of town, close to restaurants and shopping.

Snow King Resort HOTEL, CONDO $$$

(☎307-733-5200; www.snowking.com; 400 E Snow King Ave; r from $313;) This expanding resort offers a variety of options ranging from condominiums to luxury suites, with the advantage of being slopeside. Inquire about the attractive seasonal package deals.

Eating

Jackson is home to Wyoming's most sophisticated and diversified food scene. Look for deals dished out for happy hour at many of the bar-restaurant combos.

To see some menus, pick up a free *Jackson Hole Dining Guide,* found in shops and hotel lobbies. Travelers who plan to pack a cooler can shop at grocery stores.

Persephone BAKERY $

(☎307-200-6708; www.persephonebakery.com; 145 E Broadway; mains $8.25-13; ⊙7am-6pm Mon-Sat, to 5pm Sun;) With rustic breads, oversized pastries and breakfast masterpieces, this tiny white-washed French bakery is worth waiting in line for (and you will). In summer the spacious patio provides more room for lingering with your coffee (though at $0.75 a refill, you might not want to linger for that long – go for a pitcher of Bloody Mary instead).

Coco Love DESSERTS $

(☎307-733-3253; 55 N Glenwood St; desserts $8; ⊙10am-8pm) Master dessert chef Oscar Ortega shows off his French training with a pastry case of exquisite objet d'art desserts and handmade chocolates. Do it.

Fiesta MEXICAN $

(☎307-264-1750; 975 Alpine Ln; mains $9-16; ⊙11am-9pm) For anything more authentic you would need a passport stamp. This informal, bare-bones eatery thrives with the local Latin population, especially at lunchtime before the daily specials have run out. Sample the enormous red-mole enchilada or tacos you can dress up at the topping bar. Serves beer and cold watermelon juice.

Pica's Mexican Taqueria MEXICAN $

(☎307-734-4457; www.picastaqueria.com; 1160 Alpine Ln; mains $9-16; ⊙11am-10pm) Cheap and supremely satisfying, with Baja tacos wrapped in homemade corn tortillas or *cochinita pibil* (chili-marinated pork), served with Mexican sodas. Locals love this place; it's the best value around. It's just around the corner from Albertson's.

Dog BREAKFAST $

(☎307-733-4422; 25 S Glenwood St; burritos $8-9.50; ⊙6:30am-4pm) For bomber breakfast burritos, you would be hard pressed to beat this tiny shack whose expert eggman serves them fresh and wrapped in a grilled tortilla: surefire fuel for the slopes.

Bunnery Bakery & Restaurant CAFE $

(☎307-733-5474; www.bunnery.com; 130 N Cache St; mains $10-17; ⊙7am-3pm;) This Jackson mainstay serves breakfast and lunch staples as well as some creative concoctions – all of which should be chased down with a strawberry–cream-cheese croissant or a slice of caramel–apple-crumble pie. Order anything you can O.S.M. style (their flour is made from oats, sunflower seeds and millet) for a hearty rib-sticking start to the day.

Gun Barrel STEAK $$

(☎307-733-3287; http://jackson.gunbarrel.com; 852 W Broadway; mains $19-36; ⊙5:30pm-late) The line stretches out the door for Jackson's best steakhouse, where the buffalo prime rib and elk chop rival the grilled bone-in rib eye for the title of 'king cut.' For a fun game, try to match the meat with the animal watching you eat it: this place was once the wildlife and taxidermy museum, and many original tenants remain.

Thai Me Up THAI $$
(307-733-0005; www.thaijh.com; 75 E Pearl Ave; mains $13-17; from 5pm;) First, the beer. Meet Melvin: the IPA everyone is talking about. He has 19 friends. They're pretty good, too. So is the Thai food. And burgers. And the kung-fu movies work mesmerizingly well with the hip-hop. The reverse-curve bar is a bit cramped, but that's the point. Maybe. Did we mention the tuk-tuk out front? Just check the place out.

Teton Tiger INDIAN $$
(307-733-4111; www.tetontiger.com; 165 N Center St; mains $15-22; 11:30am-2:30pm Mon-Fri, 5-9pm Mon-Sat) Modeled after India's late-18th-century cobra clubs, this chic eatery delivers satisfying curries with texture and smoky undertones. Low-lit, svelte booths set a relaxing mood and service is strong. Start with crispy okra and an icy brew or handcrafted cocktail. At lunchtime, the huge thali meals offer excellent value. There's also worthy pan-Asian options like Mama's midnight ramen.

Pizzeria Caldera PIZZA $$
(307-201-1472; www.pizzeriacaldera.com; 20 W Broadway; pizzas $13.50-17.50, slices $4-5; 11am-9:30pm) Fresh and unpretentious, this upstairs pizzeria serves its pies on the thinner side. Try topping yours with briny kalamata olives or fragrant bison sausage with sage, which begs to be eaten with one of the beers on tap. Salads use locally grown arugula and beets. Slices available until 6pm.

Lotus HEALTH FOOD $$
(307-734-0882; www.theorganiclotus.com; 140 N Cache St; mains $14-26; 8am-9pm;) In a region where steak and potatoes reign supreme, Lotus pushes back with things like plantain torte, vegan burgers and giant grain-and-veg bowls. There's plenty of meat, too – this is Wyoming – but it's all organic.

Finally a place where they won't look at you sideways for asking if your chicken lived a happy life.

Snake River Grill AMERICAN $$$
(307-733-0557; www.snakerivergrill.com; 84 E Broadway; mains $29-66; 5:30-9:30pm) With a roaring stone fireplace, an extensive wine list and snappy white linens, this grill creates notable American haute cuisine. Try the boneless short rib with peanut sauce or the roasted elk chop. Or munch on a cast-iron bucket of truffle fries. Splurge-desserts like Black Forest and cherry compote or homemade ice cream easily satisfy two.

Rendezvous Bistro AMERICAN $$$
(307-739-1100; www.rendezvousbistro.net; 380 S Broadway; mains $18-38; 5:30-10pm Mon-Sat) A sure bet for sophisticated bistro food. The happy-hour menu hits the mark with the well-priced raw bar, including $2 oyster shooters. Mains also show good variety, from comfort foods like fried chicken to blackened catfish with Tabasco butter.

Blue Lion AMERICAN $$$
(307-733-3912; www.bluelionrestaurant.com; 160 N Millward St; mains $23-50; 5:30-9pm) In a cornflower-blue house, the Blue Lion offers outdoor dining under grand old trees on the deck. Its renowned rack of lamb, served in peppercorn rosemary cream sauce, may take a while but wins rave reviews. Or there's tenderloin with artichokes and crab in a blue cheese sauce. Also has early bird specials.

Drinking & Nightlife

From breweries to bars to concerts to theaters, there's no lack of things to fill your evenings in Jackson, especially during the summer and winter high seasons. Consult the *Jackson Hole News & Guide* for the latest happenings, or just head downtown and follow the sound of laughter.

★ **Bin 22** WINE BAR
(307-739-9463; www.bin22jacksonhole.com; 200 W Broadway; 11:30am-10pm Mon-Sat, 3-10pm Sun) Tucked into a wine store stacked deep with wooden crates of the good stuff, this wine bar and tapas restaurant delivers with wonderful wines accompanied by earthy small plates of housemade sausage, organic salads and sumptuous cheeses. Grab a stool at the bar for better service; there's also a pleasant hidden patio.

★ **Snake River Brewing Co** MICROBREWERY
(307-739-2337; www.snakeriverbrewing.com; 265 S Millward St; food 11am-11pm, drinks till late;) With an arsenal of microbrews crafted on the spot (some award-winning), it's no wonder this is a favorite among the younger, outdoor-sports-positive crowd. Food (mains $13 to $19) includes pizzas, bison burgers and pasta served in a modern-industrial warehouse with two floors and plenty of (but not too many) TVs broadcasting the game.

Million Dollar Cowboy Bar BAR

(☎307-733-2207; www.milliondollarcowboybar.com; 25 N Cache Dr; ⊙11am-2am) You know those places that are so outrageously overdone you can't help but have fun? This is Jackson's. Pull on your boots and saddle up at the bar (yes, you read that right) for a shot of Wyoming whiskey and the courage to ask that cute filly or colt to swing-dance to the live music with you. Free dance lessons every Thursday (7:30pm to 9pm) in the summer.

The Rose COCKTAIL BAR

(☎307-733-1500; www.therosejh.com; 50 W Broadway; ⊙5:30pm-2am Thu-Sat, 8pm-2am Sun-Wed) Slide into a red-leather booth at this swank little lounge upstairs at the Pink Garter theater and enjoy the best craft cocktails in Jackson. Encouraged by the success of their libations, they now offer multicourse culinary adventures Tuesday through Saturday from 8pm to 1:30am.

Entertainment

Jackson Hole Playhouse THEATER

(☎307-733-6994; www.jhplayhouse.com; 145 W Deloney Ave) Local theater troupes stage acclaimed Broadway-style musical comedies and provide dinner.

Shopping

Teton Mountaineering SPORTS & OUTDOORS

(☎307-733-3595; www.tetonmtn.com; 170 N Cache St; ⊙9am-8pm) Stocks a good range of books and outdoor gear. Singles seeking climbing partners can check the bulletin board.

Skinny Skis SPORTS & OUTDOORS

(☎307-733-6094; www.skinnyskis.com; 65 W Deloney Ave; ⊙9am-7pm Mon-Sat, 10am-7pm Sun) One of the best backcountry ski shops in the US, with Nordic rentals and many of the other accessories you might need for an outdoor excursion. In the summer they rent backpacks, bags, tents and child carriers, and have intimate knowledge of the best places to use it all, too.

DON'T MISS

FARMERS MARKETS

Get a massage, watch a chef demo and sample some gourmet grub while you're at it.

People's Market (base of Snow King Resort; ⊙4-7pm Wed Jun–mid-Sep) At the base of Snow King, this popular farmers market even sells local beer in reusable glasses. It doesn't get much more Jackson than that.

Farmers Market (www.jacksonholefarmersmarket.com; Jackson Town Sq; ⊙8am-noon Sat Jul–mid-Sep) Local vendors sell produce, cheeses and natural meats, and there are live music performances.

Information

Tune to 90.3 FM (NPR), 93.3 (KJAX) or 96.9 (KMTN) for the local lowdown. Free newspapers include the *Jackson Hole Daily* (liberal) and the *Daily Guide* (conservative).

Jackson Hole & Greater Yellowstone Visitor Center (☎307-733-3316; www.jacksonholechamber.com; 532 N Cache Dr; ⊙8am-7pm Jun-Sep, 9am-5pm Oct-May; 📶) This interagency visitor center is staffed by friendly representatives from the National Park, Forest Service, Fish and Wildlife Service and Chamber of Commerce who collectively know just about everything you could possibly want to know about recreating here. Enjoy a handful of exhibits, pick up hunting or fishing licenses, buy park passes and otherwise plan your visit with expert guidance.

Teton County Library (☎307-733-2164; www.tclib.org; 125 Virginian Ln; ⊙9:30am-8:30pm Mon-Thu, to 6:30pm Fri, to 2:30pm Sat, 12:30-6:30pm Sun; 📶) Great resource for topo maps and local information, with free internet and wi-fi.

Wyoming Game & Fish Department (☎307-733-2321; 420 N Cache St; ⊙8am-5pm Mon-Fri) For fishing licenses and required decals on motorcraft.

Getting There & Away

Jackson Hole Airport (JAC; Map p200; ☎307-733-7682; www.jacksonholeairport.com; 1250 E Airport Rd) is inside Grand Teton National Park 7 miles north of Jackson off Hwy 26/89/189/191. Daily flights direct to Chicago, Dallas, Phoenix, Salt Lake City and Denver, plus many more seasonal flights.

Alltrans (Mountain States Express; ☎307-733-3135; www.jacksonholealltrans.com) runs a shuttle to Salt Lake ($75, 5¼ hours) and Grand Targhee ski area (adult/child $122/94 includes ski-lift pass) in the winter, while **Jackson Hole Shuttle** (☎307-200-1400; www.jhshuttle.com; one-way Jackson/Teton Village $20/30; ⊙24hr) provides regular service from the busy airport to your hotel in the town of Jackson or Teton Village.

Getting Around

The **START Bus** (Southern Teton Area Rapid Transit; ☎307-733-4521; www.startbus.com) system gets you around Jackson (free), to Teton Village ($3) and to Driggs, ID ($8). A bike path

WORTH A TRIP

WILSON

Big barns and open range make this little outpost 13 miles from Jackson feel more like cowboy country, even though the median home price passes a cool million. It's a popular stop before that last push over the pass to Idaho, especially for cyclists and skiers going to Grand Targhee Ski Resort.

A popular mainstay of live music, mingling cowboys with rhinestone cowgirls, hippies and hikers, Wilson's **Stagecoach Bar** (☎307-733-4407; www.stagecoachbar.net; 5755 W Hwy 22; ⊙11am-2am; 📶) is worth the short drive. Daily happy hours start at 4:30pm, Thursday is disco night and every Sunday the house band croons country and western until 10pm.

Local institution **Nora's Fish Creek Inn** (☎307-733-8288; www.norasfishcreekinn.com; 5600 W Hwy 22, Wilson; mains $9-15; ⊙6:30am-2pm Mon-Fri, to 1:30pm Sat & Sun) reels 'em in with heaping country breakfasts. You can skip the wait by taking a seat at the counter. Lunch features fresh trout, an array of sandwiches and homemade cobbler.

runs between Jackson and Jenny Lake in Grand Teton National Park. Major car rental agencies have outlets at the airport.

Jackson Hole

Now that the valley is clad in faux fur, Stetsons and trophy homes, it's hard to remember that the first settlers to Jackson Hole wrangled with harsh winters and a short growing season, not to mention the horse thieves, poachers and elk tuskers that roamed the rural valley.

This is one of the most breathtaking destinations in the country. Moose, elk and bison roam the valley floor against the rugged backdrop of the Tetons. Eagles and ospreys fish the cold, crystalline streams and lakes. Surrounding the valley, the mountainous 3.4-million-acre Bridger-Teton National Forest is the second-largest forest in the lower 48.

Dubbed 'hole' by early European visitors, the broad valley is bounded by the Gros Ventre (grow-vont: 'big belly' in French) and Teton Ranges to the east and west, respectively, and the Yellowstone lava flows and Hoback and Wyoming Ranges to the north and south. The communities of Jackson, Teton Village, Kelly, Moose and Wilson, as well as much of south Grand Teton National Park, lie within the Hole.

Downhill skiing rules winter, but summertime visitors find no shortage of things to do.

Teton Village & Jackson Hole Mountain Resort

Long runs, deep powder and a screeching 4139ft vertical drop may have earned it infamy, but Jackson Hole has quickly become the pet resort of a tony, jet-setting crowd. There are real athletes here too, though, and those with any interest in the outdoors can revel in the fair-weather pursuits of hiking, cycling, white-water rafting, fly-fishing, mountain biking and faux cowboying. This modern year-round resort is at the foot of Rendezvous Mountain, 12 miles northwest of Jackson.

Sights

Jackson Hole's lifts provide a high-altitude piggyback to the high-country trails in Grand Teton National Park. Tickets can be purchased from guest services.

Aerial Tram CABLE CAR
(☎307-733-2292; adult/child $43/28, mountain-biking pass $37, descent free; ⊙9am-5pm mid-May–early Oct) The 60-passenger tram travels 2.5 miles in 12 minutes to the top of Rendezvous Mountain (10,450ft), offering great views of Jackson Hole. Hikers should note that they can hike up (or in via Grand Teton National Park) and take the tram down for free. Paragliding is done from here too. Ordering tickets online will save you a bundle; the same ticket is also valid for the Bridger Gondola and Teewinot chairlift.

Bridger Gondola CABLE CAR
(adult/child $43/28; ⊙9am-5pm early Jun-early Sep) *Via ferrata*, yoga, hiking and paragliding from the headwall (1355ft lower than 10,450ft Rendezvous Mountain). Free evening rides bring diners up to the Deck and Piste Mountain Bistro.

Activities

Hiking and mountain biking are the big summer activities. Resort lifts give a head start into high country. From the Rendezvous summit, hikers can either descend Granite

Canyon Trail or choose from a series of shorter trails: the 0.5-mile Summit Nature Loop, 3-mile Cody Bowl Trail or the 4.25-mile Rock Springs Bowl.

Pick up free bike-trail guides at guest services and rental bikes at the ski shops. Downhill trails can be accessed via the Teewinot chairlift.

★ **Jackson Hole Mountain Resort** SNOW SPORTS

(☎307-733-2292; www.jacksonhole.com; adult/child ski pass $149/91, Grand Adventure pass $73; ⊙Nov-Apr & Jun-Sep) This mountain is larger than life. Whether tackling Jackson Hole with skis, board, boots or mountain bike, you will be humbled. With more than 4000ft of vertical rise and some of the world's most infamous slopes, Jackson Hole's 2500 acres and average 400in of snow sit at the top of every serious shredder's bucket list.

Summer months are active with a bike park, disc-golf course, climbing wall, ropes course and a high alpine *via ferrata* course (starting at $360, half-day) where you tackle mountaineering assisted by cables and ladders. The Grand Adventure Pass gets you access to most activities, including the scenic tram ride (p221). Pro-tip: climb up the 7-mile, 4139ft trail to the top, and ride the tram down for free.

Jackson Hole Bike Park MOUNTAIN BIKING

(www.jacksonhole.com; day pass $37, rental & lift ticket package half-/full-day $129/159; ⊙9am-5pm early Jun-early Sep) The high-speed Teewinot chairlift provides access to downhill mountain-bike trails, jumps and other features for all levels. Don't miss the Friday night bike special: $10 lift tickets from 5pm to 7pm.

Jackson Hole Paragliding PARAGLIDING

(☎307-739-2626; www.jhparagliding.com; tandem flight $345; ⊙May-Oct) The only thing better than being in the Tetons is to be soaring above the Tetons. Tandem rides with experienced pilots take off from Jackson Hole Mountain Resort in the mornings or Snow King (p215) in the afternoons.

No experience is necessary, but age and weight limits apply.

Jackson Hole Nordic Center SKIING

(☎307-739-2729; www.jacksonhole.com/nordic.html) Offers 20 miles of groomed track and wide skating lanes with rentals and instruction.

High Mountain Heli-Skiing SKIING

(☎307-733-3274; www.heliskijackson.com; per person $1350) Delivers advanced skiers and snowboarders to ungroomed backcountry powder. Rates are for one day, including six heli-skiing runs – about 12,000 vertical feet.

Jackson Hole Sports OUTDOORS

(☎307-739-2687; Bridger Center; ⊙8:30am-6pm) Rents and sells downhill gear. In the summer it tunes and rents mountain bikes and can offer the lowdown on area rides.

Jackson Hole Mountain Guides CLIMBING

(☎307-733-4979, 800-239-7642; www.jhmg.com; 1325 Hwy 89, Suite 104) With world-class climbing at your fingertips, Jackson is an ideal center for instruction or guided climbs. This place offers guided Teton rock climbing and programs for kids.

Festivals & Events

Grand Teton Music Festival MUSIC

(GTMF; ☎307-733-1128; www.gtmf.org; Walk Festival Hall, Teton Village; ⊙Jul-Aug) A near-continuous celebration of classical music in a fantastic summer venue. The Festival Orchestra plays every Friday at 8pm and Saturday at 6pm showcasing worldwide musicians and directors. The GTMF Presents program highlights noted talent on most Wednesdays. Free family concerts give you a more informal way to experience the symphony of sound.

Sleeping

Rates vary widely and seasonally; some hotels also levy a resort fee. Rates drop up to 50% in the shoulder seasons (when it is too warm to ski but too muddy to mountain bike). The village has extensive lodging options.

The Hostel HOSTEL $

(☎307-733-3415; www.thehostel.us; 3315 Village Dr, Teton Village; dm $34-45, r $79-139; @ 📶 🐾) This skier's favorite has been here so long it doesn't need a name – everybody knows the Hostel. Budget privates and cramped four-person bunk rooms are smack in the middle of everything. The spacious lounge has a fireplace, pool table and ski waxing station.

Fireside Resort Cabins CABIN $$$

(☎307-733-1177; www.firesidejacksonhole.com; 2780 N Moose-Wilson Rd; cabins $335-665; ⊙May-Oct; 📶) Cabins here are rustic chic, with luxury bedding, TVs, fireplaces and private outdoor fire pits. They're located 2 miles north of Hwy 22 on Hwy 390. There's a three-night minimum stay.

Alpenhof Lodge HOTEL $$$

(☎307-733-3242; www.alpenhoflodge.com; 3255 West Village Dr, Teton Village; r incl breakfast $211-500;

) The classic Tyrolean Alpenhof has snug rooms with thick duvets, hand-painted furniture and wood paneling. The cozy bistro specializes in wild game and schnitzel.

Eating

Teton Thai THAI $$
(307-733-0022; http://tetonthaivillage.com; 7342 Granite Loop Rd; mains $16-18; 11:30am-9pm Mon-Sat) Maybe it's the long hike that kick-started your hunger, but it would be hard to find a more satisfying food stop with craft beer on tap. Chopped larb salad gives just the right bite and the velvet curries burst with flavor. Portions are generous, and vegan options are available.

Calico Italian Restaurant & Bar ITALIAN $$
(307-733-2460; www.calicorestaurant.com; Hwy 390; mains $14-32; from 5pm) Serves original salads, earthy minimalist pizzas, grilled halibut and hearty pastas in a renovated 1905 church. Greens come from the organic vegetable garden out back, and there's also lovely porch seating, a good wine list and $3.50 kids' meals.

Mangy Moose Saloon PUB FOOD $$
(307-733-4913; www.mangymoose.com; 3295 Village Dr, Teton Village; lunch mains $7.50-17, dinner mains $17-33; 7am-9pm, saloon 11am-2am;) For more than half a century Mangy Moose has been the rowdy epicenter for après-ski, big-name bands, slopeside dining and general mountain mischief at Jackson Hole Mountain Resort. The cavernous pub offers a decent salad bar and cranks out bowls of chili, buffalo burgers and steaks from local farms, while the Rocky Mountain Oyster Cafe has your breakfast needs covered.

Bar J Chuckwagon BARBECUE $$$
(307-733-3370; www.barjchuckwagon.com; Hwy 390; adult/child from $25/14; 7pm-late May-Sep) We know it's corny, but all who visit rave about the sing-along chuck-wagon suppers, featuring BBQ beef, biscuits and beans. Pork ribs and steak cost a bit more. Dinner is followed by an hour of stories and songs from the wranglers. Lap-sized kids go free. Reservations are recommended.

Piste Mountain Bistro AMERICAN $$$
(307-732-3177; www.jacksonhole.com; mains $24-46; 5-9pm) Ride the Bridger Gondola up to the summit (free in summer) for a dinner with an unrivaled view. Outdoor tables on the deck may be the perfect place for a drink. During the ski season they do lunch too.

Information

Jackson Hole Guest Services (888-333-7766, 307-739-2753; Tram Bldg; 9am-5pm) Information on activities and tours, located in the tram ticket office in Teton Village. Pick up a free *Jackson Hole Mountain Map & Guide* here.

Jackson Hole Resort Lodging (307-733-3990, 800-443-8613; www.jhrl.com; 3200 W McCollister Dr) Property manager with listings ranging from studio condos to two-bedroom town homes as well as multiple-bedroom houses.

Gros Ventre Slide Area

On June 23, 1925, a vast slide of 50 million cubic yards of rock, one of the world's largest recent movements of earth, plummeted 2000ft down the side of the Gros Ventre Mountains to form a 225ft-high dam, creating a lake atop the Gros Ventre River. Two years later when the dam suddenly gave way, it created a monster wave that killed six and washed away the downstream town of Kelly.

Today the **Gros Ventre Slide Geological Area** offers a 0.5-mile interpretive trail with views over the slide. Amazingly, some trees survived the fall, 'surfing' the slide to reroot on the valley floor. The resulting Upper and Lower Slide Lakes attract anglers and boaters. The turnoff to the slide area is 1 mile north of Kelly. Not far from the junction is the **Kelly Warm Spring**, an undeveloped pool of warm (80°F) water.

The slide sits outside Grand Teton National Park, but is most easily accessed through it by taking Gros Ventre Rd east off Hwy 26/89/191.

Three very attractive and economical **USFS campgrounds** (sites $12-15; mid-May–Sep) are spread out along Gros Ventre Rd beyond the Gros Ventre Slide Geological Area (18 to 23 miles northeast of Jackson). Sites have pit toilets and water but no RV hookups. Twenty-site **Atherton Creek Campground**, 5.5 miles along Gros Ventre Rd at Lower Slide Lake, at the end of the paved road, has a boat dock. If your car can take rough roads, check out the five-site **Red Hills Campground**, 4.5 miles further east, fronting the Gros Ventre River; the six-site **Crystal Creek Campground** is 0.5 miles further east. A 7-mile round-trip day hike heads up to Grizzly Lake from near Red Hills Campground.

Granite Hot Springs

The signed turnoff for the developed Granite Creek Hot Springs (p215) and Granite Creek Campground (p217) is 35 miles southeast of Jackson on Hwy 189/191. Free camping is allowed along the road to the hot springs, but not within 2 miles of the hot springs. In winter, the springs (a delicious 112°F) are accessible by snowmobile or skiing only. In summer the water temperature drops to 93°F. The route south through Hoback Canyon affords views of the stunning south face of the Gros Ventre Mountains.

The campground bumps up against the **Gros Ventre Wilderness** and offers good hiking up Granite Creek. Within walking distance of the campground is the undeveloped **Granite Falls Hot Springs**, accessed from the dirt parking area just below the falls. Reaching the hot springs (on the east bank of the creek) requires an often tricky and always chilly ford, and water levels only allow for soaking from around late May until spring snowmelt submerges the pool. Winter access is by snowmobile or cross-country skis. Please respect the place and enjoy one of Wyoming's best natural soaks.

Upper Wind River Valley

Part of the Wyoming Centennial Scenic Byway, US 26/287 climbs east from Grand Teton National Park's Moran Junction up the slopes of Bridger-Teton National Forest to Togwotee Pass (*Toe*-ga-tee; 9658ft), before dropping into the upper Wind River Valley. To the north is the 914-sq-mile Teton Wilderness; to the south is the more distant Gros Ventre Wilderness. Dubois is the only town in the upper valley, east of which the landscape yields to the semi-arid red sandstone Dubois badlands.

The Bridger-Teton National Forest Blackrock Ranger Station (p209), 8 miles east of Moran Junction, has general information and free maps of the region.

Moran Junction to Togwotee Pass

About 3 miles east of Moran Junction, the paved Buffalo Valley Rd forks off the main highway to offer a 4-mile detour northeast up the Buffalo Fork to the Turpin Meadow Recreation Area, a popular launching pad for local outfitters. There's a USFS campground here and lots of dispersed camping.

For a true wilderness getaway or some of the best Nordic terrain in the region, check out **Turpin Meadow Ranch** (☎307-543-2000; www.turpinmeadowranch.com; 24505 Buffalo Valley Rd, Moran; 2-night d from $770; P), a luxury dude ranch offering acres of cross-country skiing right outside the cabin door, in addition to fat-bike touring and snowmobiling. In summer there's mountain biking, horseback riding, pack trips and wildlife-watching. Cabins feature smart retro decor and fireplaces.

The road loops south as the unpaved USFS Rd 30050 to rejoin US 26/287. Three miles from this junction, just past Togwotee Cowboy Village, a short detour to the left leads to a **scenic overlook** with fine views back to the Tetons. A second viewpoint, the **Togwotee Pass Vista View**, is 5 miles further along; the actual pass is another 12 miles from here. The pass, named for a Shoshone medicine man who led the US Army Corps of Engineers here in 1873, marks the Continental Divide. Just by the pass, the lovely **Wind River Lake** makes a perfect picnic spot.

Six miles downhill, the turnoff to Falls Campground offers access to pretty **Brooks Lake Creek Falls**, with fine views up to the breccia (lava and ash) cliffs of the Pinnacle Buttes.

Across from Falls Campground, unpaved Brooks Lake Rd (USFS Rd 515) winds uphill for 5 miles to gorgeous **Brooks Lake**, a popular base for camping, canoeing, fishing and hiking set at the base of dramatic Pinnacle Buttes. The road passes Pinnacle Campground before it descends to **Brooks Lake Campground** (☎307-455-2466; www.fs.usda.gov; Brooks Lake Rd, Dubois; RV sites $10; P), a boat ramp and a trailhead. From the Brooks Lake turnoff it's 23 miles to Dubois and 31 miles back to Grand Teton.

Idaho's Teton Valley

The west face of the Teton Range soars above this broad valley, which is warmer, sunnier and more tranquil than its well-known Wyoming neighbor. Most of the valley lies in Teton County, Idaho, though a small portion (up to the Teton crest) is in Teton County, Wyoming. In Jackson it's dubbed the 'Tetons' backside,' while in Idaho it's dubbed the 'sunny side.'

Teton Valley (6200ft) was first frequented by Blackfoot, Bannock, Shoshone, Nez Percé and Crow Indian tribes as a summer hunting ground. Lewis and Clark expedition member John Colter stumbled upon it in 1808 while hunting for beaver, finding them in abundance. The valley soon became known as Pierre's Hole, a favored mountain-man rendezvous, until a violent battle with a band of Blackfoot in 1832 caused the fur company's abandonment. Trade ended when beaver hats fell out of fashion (although some await their return with anticipation).

Mountains surround the valley: the Targhee National Forest and the Teton Range to the west, the Snake River Range to the south and the Big Hole Mountains to the southwest. Farming has been the valley's mainstay since Mormon families settled here in the late 19th century, but these once-sleepy ranching towns are now a year-round mecca for outdoor adventure and summer music festivals, with fabulous skiing, hiking, mountaineering and mountain biking. North of Driggs, however, the classic Fords and antique grain silos hark back to days of yore.

Victor & Driggs

A friendly feel, the great outdoors and a growing number of good eats make Victor, Idaho, a growing draw, especially for those who work in Jackson and can't afford to live there. Rapidly growing Driggs (population 1736) is the valley's tourist nerve center and the access point for Grand Targhee Resort.

Sights & Activities

Driggs Geotourism Center MUSEUM
(208-354-2500; www.discovertetonvalley.com; 60 S Main St, Driggs; 9am-5pm Thu-Sat & Mon-Tue, 1-4pm Sun;) FREE This museum and information center packs a lot of knowledge into a small space. Exhibits on the culture, heritage, food, geology and recreational opportunities of the area inspire you to get out and experience them yourself. There are plentiful maps and brochures, and volunteers to answer question. An attached **climbing gym** ($14; 3pm to 9pm weekdays, 1pm to 8pm weekends) offers day passes.

Habitat CYCLING
(208-787-7669; www.ridethetetons.com; 18 N Main St, Driggs; bike rental per day $25-99; 9am-6:30pm Mon-Fri, 10am-5pm Sat & Sun) A hip full-service bike shop that also rents ski and snowboard gear.

Sleeping & Eating

Driggs hosts a few hotels. There are a handful of Forest Service campgrounds at the base of Teton Pass, on Hwy 22 outside of Victor. Currently Driggs has the most shining stars in the restaurant department, but Victor can surprise you.

Teton Valley Cabins CABIN $
(866-687-1522; www.tetonvalleycabins.com; 1 Mountain Vista Dr, Driggs; cabins summer $110-130, winter $79;) This small cluster of cozy pine log cabins are a steal. Each has a private bath and access to the fire pit, volleyball court and horseshoe pits. Great for family reunions or groups of friends looking for a place to base their Teton Valley explorations.

★ **Forage Bistro** CAFE $$
(208-354-2858; www.forageandlounge.com; 285 E Little Ave, Driggs; lunch $15-20, dinner $16-36; 11am-9pm Mon-Fri, from 10am Sat & Sun;) An airy little cafe with a crisp and vibrant atmosphere serving wine, small plates and locally farmed meat and vegetables. Happy hour is 4pm to 7pm and often has great deals on charcuterie boards. Reservations recommended for dinner.

Provisions Local Kitchen CAFE $$
(208-354-2333; www.provisionslocalkitchen.com; 95 S Main St, Driggs; breakfast $7-14, dinner $10-24; 7am-2pm Sun-Tue, to 9pm Wed-Sat;) After developing his palate at many of the fine restaurants in Jackson, head chef Juan Alcantara brought his cooking skills over the mountains for the benefit of the little people. You'll find friendly service and heaping plates of huevos rancheros, steak and eggs, and bison burgers, as well as quinoa and power greens salads for the valley's health conscious.

Drinking & Entertainment

Knotty Pine Supper Club PUB
(208-787-2866; www.knottypinesupperclub.com; 58 S Main St, Victor; 4pm-late) Cranks out an eclectic music lineup that yanks crowds on their feet for frantic fun. It is known for its burgers and microbrews, not its speedy service. Relax, you're in Victor.

Spud Drive-In Theater CINEMA
(208-354-2727; www.spuddrivein.com; 231 S Hwy 33, Victor; adult/child $7/4; Mon-Sat summer) A classic shot of Americana. Grab a malt and fries and get the kids in their jammies for the full experience. Look for the monstrous potato on the back of the vintage flatbed between Victor and Driggs.

Shopping

Victor Outdoor Seconds SPORTS & OUTDOORS
(208-787-2887; 8 N Main, Victor; 11am-5pm Tue-Fri, to 4pm Sat) Quality secondhand outdoor gear and clothing means screaming deals on someone else's short-lived experiment with adventure sports.

Information

Caribou-Targhee National Forest (Teton Basin Ranger District; 208-354-2312; www.fs.usda.gov/ctnf; 495 S Main St, Driggs; 8am-4:30pm Mon-Fri) Provides information on trails and campgrounds, and offers free travel-planner maps.

Grand Targhee Ski & Summer Resort

On the west side of the Teton Range, **Grand Targhee Resort** (307-353-2300; www.grandtarghee.com; Alta, WY, accessed via Driggs, ID; adult/child ski pass $80/36, bike park $39/29) is revered for its incredible powder stashes (more than 500in of snow falls each winter) and its easygoing vibe. Base elevation is 8100ft, and four high-speed lifts to the top of Fred's Mountain (10,200ft) access 1500 acres of runs, with a total vertical drop of 2200ft in 3.2 miles. The runs are suited for families and intermediate-level skiers.

The ski season runs from mid-November to mid-April. Targhee **lift tickets** are a bargain compared with the competition. The ski and snowboard schools offer private and group instruction, as well as telemark and skate clinics. Performance demos and rentals are available. Amenities include a full spa, kids' programs and day care. In summer it is a top-notch mountain-biking destination with extensive trails, a bike park and big-name competitions. Don't be confused by the location: while it is accessed via Driggs, Idaho, it's actually over the Wyoming line.

Activities

Wilderness **snowcat powder skiing** leads intermediate and advanced skiers to Peaked Mountain (10,230ft) for breathless powder runs that average 2000 vertical feet. There are 10 miles of groomed **Nordic trails** (adult/child $10/6) and skating tracks. Other winter activities include snowshoeing, tubing, skating and dogsledding.

When the snow melts muddy trails and wildflower fields replace it and the valley becomes a haven for hiking, climbing and biking. The mountain offers **scenic chairlift rides** (adult/child $15/10; late June to early September) to the summit of Fred's Mountain, with higher rates for lift-served **mountain biking** (day pass $39); a downhill bike is a must.

The resort's **horseback riding** (one hour $40) takes advantage of the stunning scenery at Grand Targhee. Riders amble the dusty trails rimmed by wildflowers in the shadow of the Tetons. Pack trips and lessons on Western and English riding are also available. A one-hour hike affords a spectacular vista of Grand Teton itself; ride the lift down for free.

Frisbee fans take note: there's also free 18-hole disc golf. Kids will enjoy the climbing wall and Eurobungy (a hybrid trampoline-bungy). The activity pass ($32) includes a scenic chairlift ride. Amenities include a full spa, kids' programs and day care.

Festivals & Events

Grand Targhee Bluegrass Music Festival MUSIC
(early Aug) A huge summer music festival with bluegrass, folk and alt-rock.

Sleeping

Rates vary seasonally; contact **Grand Targhee Resort** (800-827-4433; www.grandtarghee.com) about off-season specials and package deals. All lodgings are ski-in, ski-out.

Targhee Lodge HOTEL $
(800-827-4433; www.grandtarghee.com; 3300 Ski Hill Rd; d from $120;) Standard rooms slopeside with two queen-size beds, full bath, TV and phone.

Teewinot Lodge LODGE $$
(800-827-4433; www.grandtarghee.com; 3300 Ski Hill Rd; d from $160;) Snug and luxurious, with deluxe doubles, TV, phone, huge indoor Jacuzzi, outdoor heated pool and ski-in location.

Sioux Lodge CONDO $$
(800-827-4433; www.grandtarghee.com; 3300 Ski Hill Rd; r $175-340;) A steal in summer, these recently remodeled, bright, four-person studios and eight-person two-bedroom units have TV, microwave, minifridge and full bath.

Tower HOTEL $$$
(800-827-4433; www.grandtarghee.com; 3300 Ski Hill Rd; 6-person apt from $460;) The newest lodgings at the resort, these spacious VIP residences are decked in hardwood, with leather armchairs, a fireplace and kitchen.

Getting There & Away

From Driggs head 4 miles east on USFS Rd 025 (toward Alta) to the Idaho–Wyoming state line and continue east 8 miles to Targhee. From the second switchback en route to the resort you get the first glimpse of Grand Teton and an overlook of the Teton Basin.

Alltrans (p220) offers a daily ski bus over the pass to Grand Targhee (adult/child $122/94 including ski-lift pass). Their Mountain States Express (www.mountainstatesexpress.com) line runs daily from Jackson to Salt Lake City airport ($75, 5¼ hours).

Sno'Scape Ski Shuttle (208-529-6597; from Idaho Falls $20) runs a weekly service from Idaho Falls to Grand Targhee Resort; it runs on Wednesdays in winter.

Understand Yellowstone & Grand Teton

The Parks Today

With legendary status, Yellowstone and Grand Teton National Parks attract between four and five million visitors yearly. In a first for the magazine, *National Geographic* dedicated the May 2016 issue to just these parks. It's a far cry from 1872, when the *Yellowstone National Park Act* humbly created a public park or pleasuring-ground for the benefit and enjoyment of the people. Today, this mother of parks straddles an often tense line between preservation and recreation, access and excess.

Best in Print

Walking Down the Wild (Gary Ferguson; 1993) A local writer's 500-mile walk through Greater Yellowstone.

Yellowstone, The Battle for the American West (National Geographic, May 2016) Special magazine edition available at park bookstores.

Come West and See (Maxim Loskutoff; 2018) Fictional stories about passions and divided politics in the rural West.

Best Documentaries

Silence and Solitude (2003) Follows photographer Tom Murphy's winter journey into the Yellowstone backcountry.

The National Parks: America's Best Idea (2009) Ken Burns' engaging visual history.

Yellowstone (1994) IMAX big-screen movie shown daily at West Yellowstone.

Best Maps

Beartooth Publishing (www.beartoothpublishing.com) 1:113,730 – *Yellowstone National Park.*

Trails Illustrated 1:63,360 – hiking maps: *Mammoth Hot Springs, Tower/Canyon, Old Faithful, Yellowstone Lake.*

Trails Illustrated 1:78,000 – *Grand Teton National Park,* with a 1:24,000 inset of Grand Teton climbs.

An American Icon

Over the coming decades, Yellowstone's complex ecological web will be tested like never before. In the forefront, climate change is affecting everything from grizzlies dependent on thinning white-bark pines to bison grazing drying meadows. Introduced species like lake trout have a domino effect on species as distinct as bears, used to fishing for the more surface-dwelling cutthroat trout, to bald eagles, found to be attacking swans now that their favorite fish is off the menu.

In 2016, the National Park Service celebrated 100 years in service. This milestone brought renovations, reflection and renewed energy for the mission of the parks. Yet, Yellowstone's aging roads are still faced with the challenge of carrying traffic that's 30 percent over their maximum capacity. Despite ever-increasing popularity, park funding may be drying up. In 2018, the Department of the Interior faced $16 million in budget cuts and the layoff of 2000 rangers nationwide, with Yellowstone experiencing already noticeable reductions to staffing and services.

Meanwhile, scientific investigation using improved technology is redefining our understanding of the intricate inner workings of the Yellowstone supervolcano. Much is yet to be discovered. For visitors, Yellowstone and Grand Teton continue to deliver wonder and excitement. From the spurting geysers to the jagged Tetons, this intricate wilderness is an essential part of the US national consciousness. Long may it prosper.

Loved to Death

In this rare, wild place, it's hard not to feel that you've come face to face with the eternal. But the truth is, the Greater Yellowstone Ecosystem is a dynamic, changing environment. The visible consequences of climate change have been pronounced here. Human impact is another force that is shaping both the environment and our experience of it.

In the last decade Yellowstone's annual visitation has increased by over 40 percent. With a huge uptick in bus tours, the numbers recall writer Edward Abbey's warnings about 'industrial tourism.' Wildlife regularly creates mob scenes. Wildlife selfies have gotten extreme, with bison butting those who get too close. In 2016, a bison calf had to be exterminated after visitors had ushered it into their vehicle because 'it looked cold.'

Debate rages over how to best manage a well-meaning human influx that isn't wilderness savvy. Higher park fees and timed entrances may be imminent. Encouraging visitation beyond park boundaries is another tactic to combat overcrowding. While public access has been the parks' greatest strength, the absence of a thoughtful approach threatens precisely what we seek out in these magnificent wild places.

Responsible use has become a necessary priority for the parks. In Grand Teton that means seeing to the nitty-gritty, from managing overflowing parking lots to adding volunteer teams to diffuse potential wildlife conflicts in areas of heavy use. With foreign tourists comprising 17 percent of all visitors, the parks now communicate in multiple languages. Mostly, the aim is for visitors to consider their impact in a thoughtful and conscientious way.

Managing Mother Nature (& Other Controversies)

If you want to spark an argument in Yellowstone country, simply start a conversation on grizzly hunting, the park's fire policy, bison hazing, grazing rights or oil drilling. Fractured regional politics means that legal challenges descend on almost every major wildlife policy decision made in Yellowstone. These circumstances can make it hard for Yellowstone to pursue coherent policies.

In 2018, a Wyoming wildlife commission voted unanimously to instate the hunting of grizzly bears. Under the plan, up to 22 bears can be killed in one year. Yellowstone-area grizzlies, a keystone species for a healthy ecosystem, were protected by endangered species status until recently. Montana has voted against hunting while Idaho has approved the hunt of a single male grizzly in fall. Conservation groups, in addition to 200 tribal nations which consider the species sacred, have voiced strong opposition to the plan. The population is by no means secure in its recovery. Grizzlies are known to be among the slowest mammals on earth to reproduce. Despite the plan's approval, pending lawsuits mean the Wyoming decision could still be reversed.

The 1996 reintroduction of wolves to Yellowstone succeeded in restoring ecological balance and integrity to the park. There are now around 105 wolves in the park. Yet, in 2011, wolves also lost their federally protected status. While their presence has been controversial, their appeal has been enormous. *National Geographic* cites that visitors from outside the region spend over $35 million annually in their quest to see wolves.

AREA: **YELLOWSTONE: 3472 SQ MILES; GRAND TETON: 484 SQ MILES**

ELEVATION: **AVERAGE ABOVE 7500FT**

HIGH POINT: **GRAND TETON (13,775FT)**

STATES: **WY, MT, ID**

YEAR FOUNDED: **YELLOWSTONE: 1872; GRAND TETON: 1929**

if 100 people come to Yellowstone

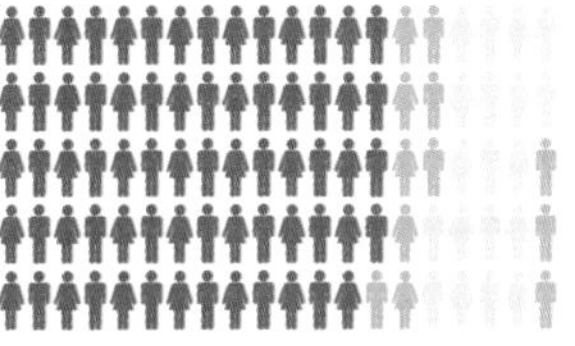

69 visit in Summer
9 visit in Spring
[illegible] visit in Fall
3 visit in Winter

Yellowstone
(% of landscape)

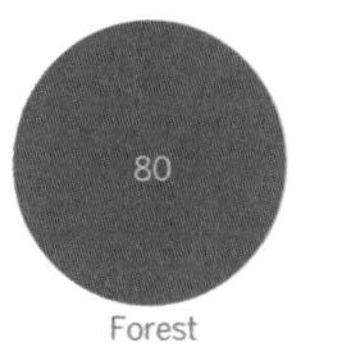

population per sq mile

MONTANA

WYOMING

USA

≈ 1 person

History

As the world's oldest national park, Yellowstone holds a key place in both the historical development of the US National Park Service and the spread of protected wilderness areas across the globe. This is hallowed ground to both environmentalists and tourists, and the tensions between the two form the major theme of the past, present and, doubtless, the future of Yellowstone and Grand Teton.

First Peoples

Recent archaeological evidence unearthed near Pinedale, WY, and excavations from Osprey Beach on Yellowstone Lake suggest that human inhabitation of the Greater Yellowstone region began soon after the Pinedale Glaciation period ended, between 12,000 and 14,000 years ago. Only a few thousand years before that, the Yellowstone region was almost completely covered in glaciers.

To experience Native American culture locally, attend the Crow Fair or the Plains Indians Powwow in Cody; visit Cody's Plains Indian Museum or Colter Bay Indian Arts Museum; or join a Crow interpreter tour of the Battle of Little Bighorn outside Billings.

Archaeologists divide Greater Yellowstone's first inhabitants – ice-age hunter-gatherers who chased spectacular megafauna such as bear-size beavers, enormous camels, gigantic moose, massive mastodons and 20ft-tall bison – into two distinct cultures, Clovis and Folsom, based on the uniquely shaped stone spearheads they fashioned.

The human presence in Greater Yellowstone increased dramatically 1500 to 2000 years ago, coinciding with a more favorable climate, resurgent large mammal populations and development of the bow and arrow, which replaced the *atlatl* (spear-thrower). Sheep traps and *pishkum* (buffalo jumps) were the weapons of choice in the Rockies and Great Plains, respectively. Obsidian from Yellowstone (still visible at Obsidian Mountain on the Mammoth–Norris road) made such durable spear and arrow tips that they were traded for hundreds of miles.

The Tukudika (or Sheepeaters) – a Shoshone-Bannock people who hunted bighorn sheep in the mountains of Yellowstone – were the region's only permanent inhabitants before white settlement, though surrounding tribes such as the Crow/Absaroka (to the northeast), Shoshone (east), Bannock (south and west), Blackfeet/Siksikau (north) and Gros Ventre (south) hunted, traded and traveled seasonally through the region.

TIMELINE

9000 BC–AD 1870

Native American inhabitation of area now known as Greater Yellowstone. Most only entered the high mountains on summer hunting trips to collect food and medicinal plants.

1797

French map makes first reference to the 'R des Roches Jaunes,' or Yellow Stone River, itself a translation of the Minnetaree expression Mi tsi a-da-zi that described the yellow bluffs around Billings, MT.

1805–06

Lewis and Clark expedition passes north of Yellowstone; Clark carves his name on Pompey's Pillar near Billings – today it is the only surviving physical evidence of the expedition.

The Tukudika never acquired horses or iron tools and are often portrayed as a simple and undeveloped people, but they were proficient tanners whose composite sheep-horn bows were powerful enough to send an arrow straight through a bison (it's thought the Tukudika made the horns more pliable by soaking them in Yellowstone's boiling hot springs). The Tukudika, who never numbered more than about 400, spent the summers in camps of *wikiups* (tepee-like frames of leaning lodgepole branches), using dogs to transport their gear. The last of the Tukudika were hustled off the new park territory into the Wind River Reservation in the early 1870s and came under the control of the Shoshone chief Washakie.

One of the region's most extraordinary modern episodes involving Native Americans was the 1877 flight of the Nez Percé, led by Chief Joseph. The Nez Percé fled their ancestral lands in Oregon to escape persecution by the US Army. Today, the National Park Service recognizes formal affiliations with 25 modern Native American peoples.

For a historical chronicle of the park's original inhabitants, try *Indians in Yellowstone National Park*, a slim volume by Joel C Janetski.

Trappers, Traders & Tourists

The first Europeans to come in contact with Native Americans in Greater Yellowstone were French fur trappers from eastern Canada. They encountered the Crow and Sioux in the late 1700s while exploring the upper Missouri River tributaries in search of beaver. It was these lonesome French-speaking trappers who gave the Tetons their name for their highly tenuous resemblance to female breasts. (As one writer wryly noted, that's what happens when you let French fur trappers name mountains!)

The USA's Louisiana Purchase of present-day Montana, most of Wyoming, and eastern Colorado from the French in 1803 led President Thomas Jefferson to commission the famous Lewis and Clark Corps of Discovery in 1804–06. The Shoshone and Nez Percé told the expedition's leaders about a 'thundering volcano to the south' that made the earth tremble, though the expedition only made it as far south as the lower Gallatin Valley (which they named) and the area along the Yellowstone River, east of Livingston, MT.

As knowledge of the American West grew, so did interest in its exploitable resources. Most sought after was the beaver, whose 'plews' (pelts) became known among the trappers as 'hairy dollars.' John Colter, a member of the Lewis and Clark expedition, returned to explore the Yellowstone area during the winter of 1807–08 to try his luck as a trapper. Colter headed south from the Bighorn River into the Absaroka Mountains, into Jackson Hole, over the Tetons (in winter!) and then north past Yellowstone Lake. His epic 500-mile loop hike made him the first white

Colter's most famous exploit was when he was captured by Blackfoot, stripped naked and forced to run for his life. He managed to elude the Blackfoot by hiding in a valley and he walked 300 miles back to civilization, living off berries and roots.

1807–08

John Colter's winter journey into Greater Yellowstone makes him the first 'white man' to travel through the area. Colter's Hell, a series of thermal features along the Shoshone River, are named after him.

1834

Warren Ferris is the first 'tourist' to Yellowstone and the first person to use the word 'geyser' to describe Yellowstone's thermal features.

1835–39

Trapper Osborne Russell travels through Yellowstone three times, eventually penning his story in the classic autobiography *Journal of a Trapper*.

1869

Folsom, Cook and Peterson's month-long expedition into what would later become Yellowstone National Park takes them as far south as Shoshone and Yellowstone Lakes.

person to visit the Yellowstone region, though it's not thought that he saw any of the region's geysers.

After the War of 1812, renewed demand for furs propelled another generation of trappers westward. Legendary 'mountain men' including Jedediah Smith, Jim Bridger, David Jackson (after whom Jackson Hole is named), William Sublette, Kit Carson, Jim Beckwourth (a free African American) and Thomas Fitzpatrick came to know the rugged Rockies' backcountry better than anyone except the Native Americans, with whom many of the men formed beneficial relationships, often learning

THE FLIGHT OF THE NEZ PERCÉ

The discovery of gold in 1877 spurred the US government (under US Army General Oliver Howard) to forcibly relocate the Nez Percé (Nimi'ipuu in their language) from Oregon's Wallowa Valley. After an initial skirmish, the Nez Percé (pronounced 'Nez Purse') set off on what would become an epic 1100-mile flight from the US Army. The route of their journey is now a national historic trail. For more information about this, see www.fs.fed.us/npnht.

By August 23, 1877, 700 of the Nez Percé (of whom only 250 were braves), led by Chief Joseph, crossed the Targhee Pass and entered Yellowstone Park along the Madison River, crossing the Firehole River at modern-day Nez Percé Creek. At that time only 25 tourists were visiting the park, and the Nez Percé somehow managed to bump into all of them, taking six hostage, killing one, and releasing the others near Mud Volcano. Just before reaching Pelican Creek, a band of braves diverted General Howard's men up into the Hayden and Lamar Valleys (at one point camping at Indian Pond) while the bulk of the tribe hurried up Pelican Creek and out of the park's northeast corner. You can visit the spot of two of the group's river crossings at Nez Percé Creek and the Nez Percé Ford.

In September they progressed through Crandall Creek into the Clarks Fork of the Yellowstone, with US forces pressing hard on their heels, and troops led by General Sturgis blocking routes ahead. Sturgis' son had been killed by Native Americans the year before at the Battle of Little Bighorn, and one can only imagine that he was itching for revenge. The Percé once again pulled off a brilliant escape. A group of braves diverted Sturgis' troops while the Nez Percé slipped through the net, passing out of the valley through a gorge thought impassable by the US Army.

Believing they were in Canada, the Nez Percé slowed down just 30 tragic miles before the border, where US troops under General Nelson Miles finally caught up with them at the Battle of Bear Paw. After a 1500-mile, 3½-month chase that included four battles, 87 men, 184 women and 47 children surrendered on October 5, 1877, with Chief Joseph's words: 'From where the sun now stands, I will fight no more forever.' It was the end of a fight they had not sought. Joseph was never allowed to return to his homeland and died in 1904, allegedly of a broken heart.

1870

Washburn-Langford-Doane expedition names Old Faithful, Tower Fall and Mt Washburn, and starts the legend of the founding of Yellowstone National Park.

1871

Hayden leads an expedition to Yellowstone, with photographer William Henry Jackson and artist Thomas Moran, whose images are instrumental in the creation of the park the following year.

1872

President Ulysses S Grant signs the Yellowstone National Park Act on March 1; Nathaniel Langford claims to have climbed Grand Teton.

1877

Philetus W Norris becomes park superintendent and builds the first roads; the Nez Percé, led by Chief Joseph, flee the US Army through Yellowstone National Park.

the languages and taking Native American wives. Annual summer rendezvous – huge trading fairs attended by suppliers, Native Americans and even tourists – began in 1825 at the headwaters of Wyoming's Green River, only to peter out in 1840, as the fur trade hit the skids

For insight into the mountain men, try *The Mountain Men*, by George Laycock, which provides individual portraits of John Colter, Jim Bridger, Jedediah Smith and others, and illuminates the craft of trapping.

Official Explorations

The US defeat of Mexico in the 1846–48 Mexican–American War yielded a bounty of new western territory to explore. The US Corps of Topographical Engineers, guided by ex-trapper Jim Bridger, attempted to explore the Yellowstone Plateau from the south in 1860, but snow-covered mountain passes put the kibosh on their journey.

In the fall of 1869, the private three-member Folsom-Cook-Peterson expedition headed south from Bozeman, MT, for a month to explore the divide between the Gallatin and Yellowstone Rivers. They made it past the Grand Canyon and Yellowstone Lake as far south as Shoshone Lake and returned in fine fettle to write a popular magazine article that refueled interest in exploration among the eastern establishment. Upon witnessing a 150ft eruption of Great Fountain Geyser in the Firehole Lake region, the team wrote: 'We could not contain our enthusiasm; with one accord we all took off our hats and yelled with all our might!'

With considerable foresight, Cook wrote 'We knew that as soon as the wonderful character of the country was generally known outside there would be plenty of people hurrying in to get possession, unless something was done.'

Folsom, Cook and Peterson gained enough notoriety to be invited along for the landmark 1870 Washburn-Langford-Doane expedition, bankrolled primarily by the Northern Pacific Railroad, which was seeking a route across the Montana Territory and publicity to attract investors and tourists. The 19-person party, led by former Montana tax collector Nathaniel Langford and Montana Surveyor-General Henry Washburn, was given a military escort by Lt Gustavus Doane from Fort Ellis (near present-day Bozeman). They successfully traced the route of the 1869 expedition, named many thermal features (including Old Faithful) and returned to the East Coast 40 days later. They received a hero's welcome from the national media, which finally began to take seriously their reports of a landscape 'so grand as to strain conception and stagger belief.' One of Langford's lectures about Yellowstone caught the attention of Dr Ferdinand Hayden, director of the newly formed US Geological Survey (USGS). Hayden soon persuaded Congress, with substantial lobbying muscle from Northern Pacific supporters, to appropriate $40,000 for the first federally funded scientific expedition to the Greater Yellowstone region.

Get a radical retake on the Wild West in *The Empire of Shadows*, by George Black. It's about Yellowstone's creation via forces of exploration, the violent Indian Wars and the 'civilizing' frontier.

1883

Railroad spur line finished to Cinnabar, near north entrance of Yellowstone National Park; Great Plains bison pronounced extinct east of Continental Divide; first bicycle tour of the park.

1890

First tourist guidebook to Yellowstone published; Wyoming becomes the 44th state of the USA, one week after Idaho becomes the 43rd state.

1902

Only 25 bison remain in Yellowstone National Park, despite the passing of the Lacey Act eight years earlier, which prohibited hunting in the park.

1903

President Theodore Roosevelt dedicates Yellowstone National Park North Entrance Arch; Northern Pacific Railroad line reaches Gardiner; construction starts on Old Faithful Inn and Fort Yellowstone.

Historic Hotels

Old Faithful Inn, Yellowstone National Park

Irma Hotel, Cody

Murray Hotel, Livingston

Pollard, Red Lodge

In 1871 the 34-person Hayden expedition set out from Fort Ellis with a full cavalry escort. Hayden's scientific work was fairly pedestrian, but two members of his party, landscape painter Thomas Moran and photographer William Henry Jackson, produced works of art that offered proof of the region's amazing sights and ultimately led to the designation of Yellowstone as a national park in 1872.

The National Park Idea

Portrait artist George Catlin is credited with originally suggesting the idea of a 'national park' during an 1832 trip through the wild Dakota Territory. The US' first nationally protected area was created a few months later at Hot Springs, AR. For decades the park service promoted the romanticized notion that the idea of a Yellowstone national park was born at Madison junction by the members of the Hayden expedition, though the reality was more complex.

In 1872 President Ulysses S Grant signed the landmark *Yellowstone National Park Act,* setting aside 'the tract of land in the Territories of

MILLION-DOLLAR MICROBES

In 1966 microbiologist Dr Thomas Brock isolated a unique enzyme in a thermophilic micro-organism called *Thermus aquaticus*, or 'Taq,' which he extracted from the 158°F+ Mushroom Pool in Yellowstone's Lower Geyser Basin. Brock's discovery ultimately facilitated the replication of DNA for fingerprinting and genetic engineering, sparking an ongoing debate about 'bioprospecting' and the commercialization of public domain resources.

The National Park Service (NPS) continues to issue around 50 free research permits per year to scientists studying microbes. 'Extremeophiles' harvested for free have generated hundreds of millions of dollars of revenue for patent holders, including over $100 million a year for the Taq enzyme alone. Only recently has the NPS begun to gain financially from benefit-sharing agreements.

Not all research efforts are strictly commercial. NASA has studied the biogeochemical signature of cyanobacteria found around hot springs in an attempt to match this signature with a similar one on Mars, which would help to decide where to land on the red planet when attempting to confirm the existence of ancient volcanoes and hot springs.

Other startling discoveries include the DNA sequencing analysis of an organism found in a hot spring in the Hayden Valley. This revealed what is considered to be the living entity most closely related to the primordial origin of life.

Researchers estimate there are at least 18,000 active thermal features in Yellowstone National Park, and that as many as 99% of species present in Yellowstone's extreme environments have yet to be identified. And with more thermophiles estimated to live in one square inch of a hot spring than the number of people living on earth, there's plenty of room for research.

1915

The first car (a Model T Ford) is allowed into Yellowstone National Park; car entry fees cost the modern equivalent of $93 per vehicle.

1916–18

In 1916 the National Park Service (NPS) is created under President Wilson. In 1918 the NPS assumes management of Yellowstone from the US Army, which had governed the park since 1886.

1923

A meeting is held at the cabin of Maude Noble to try to establish Grand Teton National Park; the last gray wolf den in Yellowstone National Park is destroyed by park rangers.

1926

Rockefeller travels through the Yellowstone and Teton region, encouraged by the park superintendent, leading to the purchase of thousands of acres of land later donated to the nation.

Montana and Wyoming, lying near the headwaters of the Yellowstone River,' and 'all timber, mineral deposits, natural curiosities, or wonders... in their natural condition.' The proclamation put a box on the map around what was thought to be the extent of the region's thermal areas but neglected to appropriate any management funds. The park's first superintendent, one Nathaniel Langford (he of the 1870 expedition), was unpaid and only visited the park twice in his five-year tenure. This lack of funding led the park to seek private business partners, such as the railroads, to develop infrastructure and promote tourism; a problem that today's park administrators would recognize well.

The most important legacy of the National Park Service is much greater than simply preserving a unique ecosystem. That the national park and preservation idea has spread worldwide is a testament to the pioneering thinking of early US conservationists.

Jellystone's Yogi Bear, Ranger Smith and Boo-Boo were all inspired by Yellowstone National Park, with a little help from baseball star Yogi Berra.

The US Army & Early Stewardship

A decade of rampant squatting, wildlife poaching, wanton vandalism of thermal features and general lawlessness in Yellowstone National Park preceded an 1882 visit by Civil War hero General Philip Sheridan. Sheridan persuaded Congress to appropriate $9000 to hire 10 protective assistants to aid the park's staff-less superintendent. But park regulations still didn't allow for any substantial punishments beyond expelling trespassers. The jurisdiction of Wyoming territorial law was extended into the park in 1884, but poaching remained rampant.

In the absence of park rangers, the army patrolled the park from 1886 until the handover to the newly created National Park Service and first park superintendent Horace Albright in 1918. At first, troops were stationed in a makeshift fort at Mammoth Hot Springs called Camp Sheridan. Construction of nearby Fort Yellowstone (present-day park headquarters) began in 1891. By the early 1900s, mounted troops were stationed year-round throughout the backcountry. Fighting fires, building roads, protecting desirable wildlife (bison and elk) from poaching and predators, entertaining visitors and preserving the park's natural features were the soldiers' primary duties. Predator control, such as poisoning coyotes, was common, but under the army's rule Yellowstone's environmental status quo was largely maintained. Of the 16 original soldier stations, three remain – at Norris (now a park ranger museum), Tower and Bechler.

Learn more about early park history by taking one of the five daily historic tours of the Old Faithful Inn or a ranger-led historical walk around Fort Yellowstone at Mammoth.

Railroads, Automobiles & Mass Tourism

The Northern Pacific Railroad arrived in Livingston, MT, in 1883, the same year Congress allocated funds to begin construction of the Grand Loop Rd in Yellowstone National Park. Park tourism and the railways

1929 Congress creates Grand Teton National Park; President Hoover extends the east and northwest extents of Yellowstone National Park, adding a further northern chunk three years later.

1943 President Franklin Roosevelt creates the Jackson Hole National Monument, with Forest Service and Rockefeller's land.

1948 Yellowstone National Park receives one million visitors in a single year for the first time, in a post-WWII tourist boom.

1950 Jackson Hole National Monument becomes part of Grand Teton National Park; Mission 66 is launched to radically boost the park's tourist infrastructure.

ROCKEFELLER, ROOSEVELT & THE TETONS

Despite the precedent set by Yellowstone, transformation of the Tetons into a national park was no easy matter, as commercial ranching and hunting interests resisted attempts to transfer private and forestry service lands to the National Park Service. At its creation in 1929, Grand Teton National Park included only the main part of the Teton Range and the lakes immediately below. Distressed at Jackson Hole's commercial development, John D Rockefeller Jr surreptitiously purchased more than 55 sq miles of land to donate to the park (but retained rights to all park concessions), but political bickering prevented the philanthropist's tax write-off until President Franklin D Roosevelt interceded.

Rockefeller's 32,000-acre bequest finally came under NPS jurisdiction when Roosevelt declared Jackson Hole a national monument in 1943. With post-WWII tourism booming in 1950, legislation conferred national park status and expanded the boundaries to include most of Jackson Hole. A final piece of the puzzle slipped into place in 2008 when the Rockefellers' private retreat, the former JY Ranch, was handed over to the park service to become the Laurance S Rockefeller Preserve.

Today, the Rockefeller-founded Grand Teton Lodge Company remains the park's major concessionaire.

were intimate bedfellows and it was the railways that ushered in the era of modern mass tourism in Greater Yellowstone.

Early park visitors rode the rails to West Yellowstone (via the Union Pacific Railroad), Livingston and later Cinnabar (Northern Pacific), Cody (Burlington) or Gallatin Gateway (Chicago, Milwaukee, St Paul & Pacific) and then transferred to stagecoaches for a six-day park tour that still mirrors today's overnight stops. The 'dudes' (tourists) would brave dust clouds and holdups to stay in classy hotels attended by 'savages' (concession employees) and beanery girls, entertained at night by string quartets, while generally behaving badly during the day – throwing handkerchiefs into geysers, bathing in hot springs and (later) feeding the bears.

> To get a sense of the importance of the railways in the development of the park, visit West Yellowstone's Yellowstone Historic Center, the Depot Center in Livingston or Gallatin Gateway Inn – all former railway depots.

The railroad's grand plans to monopolize public access to the park even went as far as a plan to extend rail tracks through the park itself, though Congress put its foot down about this. Ultimately, it was the arrival of the automobile that would scuttle the railroad's bid for domination of concession and transportation interests. Whereas over 80% of Yellowstone's 52,000 visitors in 1915 arrived via railroad, by 1940 nearly all of Yellowstone's half million visitors entered the park in private automobiles.

In 1905 completion of the skeleton of what is known today as the Grand Loop Rd by the US Army Corps of Engineers established the blueprint of the standardized Yellowstone tourist experience. Lobbying by motoring

1959	1963	1968–77	1970
A huge 7.5-scale earthquake hits the Hebgen region, creating Earthquake Lake and causing the eruptions of several Yellowstone geysers.	The Leopold Report is published, and notes that 'a national park should represent a vignette of primitive America.'	Signing into law of the Wild & Scenic Rivers Act (1968), National Trails System Act (1968), National Environmental Policy Act (1969), Endangered Species Act (1973), Clean Water Act (1977) and Clean Air Act (1977).	New bear management plan; last of the bear-feeding garbage dumps closed, emphasizing the shift from recreational use to environmental protection.

clubs persuaded the NPS to admit automobiles in 1915. Constant clashes between cars and stagecoaches over right-of-way on the narrow one-way roads led to the banishment of horse-drawn wagons in 1916.

Establishment of the nation's first forestry reserve, the Yellowstone Timber Reserve (part of today's Shoshone and Bridger-Teton National Forest), in 1891, Jackson's National Elk Refuge in 1912 and Grand Teton National Park in 1929 opened up Greater Yellowstone's south flank to public visitation. East Coast philanthropist John D Rockefeller's 200,000-acre land grant in 1949 added the final pieces of Grand Teton National Park and marked the tipping point in Greater Yellowstone's transition from a resource-based region to a tourist-driven economy.

Modern intensive development of a small area (about 1%) of Yellowstone National Park for tourism, however, has not been without controversy. The park is now home to more than 2000 buildings, thousands of employees and tens of thousands of nightly tourists. Historian Richard White has argued that rather than being a vestige of wild America, Yellowstone is 'a petting zoo with a highway running through it.'

Herein lies possibly the biggest challenge facing Greater Yellowstone today – is it possible for swarms of wilderness- and wildlife-seekers to enjoy solitude and appreciate nature en masse?

You can see examples of Jackson and Moran's iconic artwork at Mammoth's Albright Visitor Center, alongside a copy of the 1872 Act of Congress that created Yellowstone National Park.

Managing Natural Resources

During its formative years, the National Park Service in Yellowstone racked up a – shall we say – checkered history. It poisoned predators, shot wolves, stocked fisheries with nonendemic species, destroyed habitat in the name of development and arranged bear-feeding displays, all of which contributed to the development of an artificial and ultimately unsustainable ecology. Modern managers openly admit that many early park policies were misguided.

Beginning in 1959 with John and Frank Craighead's pioneering studies of Yellowstone's grizzly population, the NPS emphasized scientific study of its natural resources. The landmark Leopold Report, published in 1963, suggested that 'a national park should represent a vignette of primitive America.' The report concluded that a more passive 'natural regulation' regime should replace past policies biased toward hands-on resource manipulation.

The Battle for Yellowstone, by Justin Farrell, tells a gripping story of the park by examining the morality and struggles of its stakeholders.

A major test of that policy was the summer fire season of 1988, when one-third of the park went up in smoke as 25 fires raged through the park for 3½ months. More than 25,000 firefighters were drafted in to battle the flames at a cost of $120 million, and TV anchors proclaimed 'the death of Yellowstone National Park.' The event cast a critical spotlight on the park service's policy of letting natural fires burn. Decades later, a mosaic of meadows and new-growth forest has rejuvenated the

1972

Yellowstone National Park turns 100 and welcomes its 50-millionth visitor – the next 50 million arrive by 1992. John D Rockefeller Jr Memorial Pkwy is established, linking Yellowstone and Grand Teton.

1988

Much-publicized wildfires sweep through the Greater Yellowstone region, burning one-third of the park; the entire park closes on August 20 for the first time in history.

1994

Invasive lake trout in Yellowstone Lake decimate the native cutthroat trout population, affecting bear and osprey food sources. An aggressive eradication campaign spends $2 million annually.

1996

Fourteen Canadian gray wolves are reintroduced to Yellowstone National Park; Yellowstone joins the list of World Heritage Sites in danger.

park. Regardless of an instinctive desire to protect the park, fire is in fact essential to replenish the poor soils of the Yellowstone plateau, and Yellowstone is a healthier place for it.

In Gardiner, the Yellowstone Heritage & Research Center houses precious park archives, with 90,000 photographic prints and negatives, 20,000 books and 35,000 archaeological artifacts. Behind-the-scenes tours take place every Tuesday morning.

Controversy has been no stranger to Yellowstone. One prominent 15-year battle over snowmobile access was resolved in 2013 when new government regulations were announced to allow 51 snowmobile groups per day in the park, with improved technology to curb noise and air pollution.

The management of recovering grizzly, bison and wolf populations continues to provoke controversy, as park regulations are often at odds with those proposed by the three states that surround the park. The diverging interests of tourism, conservation and ranching have pitted neighbors against one another. Even among scientists, it can be difficult to achieve agreement on the best measures to keep this dynamic ecosystem in balance, particularly as climate change plays its own role in shaping the environment.

Given that contradictions are inherent in the park's mandate of both preservation and utilization, high-stakes negotiations will continue to be integral to the future of Yellowstone.

2011

Wolf delisted as an endangered species and control is given over to individual states. Wolf hunts are allowed in Montana, Wyoming and Idaho.

2013

In October, a 16-day government shutdown causes a loss of over $9 million dollars to Yellowstone and its nearby communities.

2014

On March 30, a 4.8-magnitude earthquake hits 5 miles from Norris Basin, the first significant quake since the early 1980s.

2014

A federal judge restores protection for the gray wolf in Wyoming.

Geology

As a supervolcano sitting on one of the foremost hot spots on earth, Yellowstone hosts some of the planet's premier geothermal features. These geysers, hot springs and steam vents offer geologists and visitors a vivid peek into the center of our world. From acidic soils to waterlogged valleys, the environment on this superheated plateau shapes the lives of the plants and animals that call the park home, and has made it one of the leading wildlife destinations in North America.

The Yellowstone Hot Spot

Standing in the park, you are perched atop a thin piece of crust floating over a huge 125-mile-deep plume of molten rock known as a hot spot. This buoyant molten rock, heated by magma deep under the earth's crust, has risen through the upper mantle close to the earth's surface.

Hot spots may be fixed, but as the earth's crust moves over them, it forms a line of progressively newer volcanoes. The North American plate moves southwest one inch per year. Its contact with the Yellowstone hot spot has burned a chain of volcanoes across the West from southeastern Oregon (where it was active 16 million years ago) to northern Wyoming (where it was last active 600,000 years ago). After a few million years, it will slide over to North Dakota.

The Yellowstone region has been sitting atop this hot spot for about two million years, with massive supervolcanic eruptions occurring roughly every 650,000 years. The last three have been centered on Island Park, Henry's Fork and Yellowstone.

What do these eruptions entail? The most recent explosion formed the 1000-sq-mile Yellowstone caldera at the center of the park 600,000 years ago. The explosion spat out magma and clouds of 1800°F liquid ash at supersonic speeds, vaporizing all in its path and suffocating the land in blisteringly hot ash flows. Billowing ash traveled thousands of square miles in minutes, landing as far away as the Gulf of Mexico. The crater roof and floor then imploded and dropped thousands of feet, creating a

Glaciers in the Teton range were formed in the Little Ice Age, a cold period from roughly 1400 to 1850. Numbering around a dozen, they will likely disappear if climate change continues its current path.

PSYCHEDELIC SCIENCE

Given that Yellowstone, with its 10,000 geothermal features, is the world's foremost source of heated water, it comes as no surprise that heat-loving (thermophilic) micro-organisms were first discovered in the park's boiling waters.

A huge variety of microbes and bacteria thrive in these extreme waters, tolerating heat, extremely acidic or alkaline conditions and toxic minerals. One such species has yielded an important enzyme crucial to DNA fingerprinting tests. Other research is revealing important clues about the origins of life on earth and survival of life in outer space.

Much of this activity occurs on a microscopic scale, but visitors can still appreciate the brilliant colors these micro-organisms produce in bodies of water. Each species inhabits a highly specific temperature and chemical zone, so each layer produces the rings and patches of vibrant color that give Yellowstone's waters their psychedelic signature.

smoldering volcanic pit 48 miles by 27 miles wide. Ash circling the globe caused a volcanic winter by reducing the amount of solar heat reaching the earth.

Visitors may be surprised that Yellowstone is not more mountainous; the reason quite simply is that the mountains were either blown away by the explosion or sank into the caldera.

Since the explosion, at least 30 subsequent lava flows, dating from 150,000 to 70,000 years ago, have filled in and obscured the caldera, and forests have reclaimed the area, though you can still make out the caldera in numerous places. Turnouts on the road south of Dunraven Pass provide excellent views of its northern part, and much of the caldera's outline can be seen from the summit of Mt Washburn.

Yellowstone's Thermal Features

Fueled by its underground furnace, Yellowstone is a bubbling cauldron of more than 10,000 geothermal features – more than all other geothermal areas on the planet combined. Maybe it isn't all that surprising. Magma, the earth's molten rock, is just 3 to 5 miles underground, closer to the surface here than anywhere else on earth. The average heat flow from the region is 40 times the global average.

But heat isn't everything. Essential to Yellowstone's thermal features is the addition of water, falling onto the park as rain or, more commonly, snow. This surface water may seep as deep as 2 miles over long periods of time before it drains through the side channels of geysers, hot springs and underground aquifers. The next time you watch a geyser, remember that the water spurting out may have fallen as snow or rain up to 500 years ago.

With Yellowstone's geothermal activity constantly in flux, what seem like permanent features are mere blips on the geologic timescale. Geysers suddenly erupt, or dry up; hot springs gradually appear, or explode so violently that they destroy themselves.

The plumbing beneath the supervolcano has long been mysterious. In 2015, University of Utah seismologists discovered and imaged an enormous lower magma chamber located 12 to 28 miles underground. Over four times the size of an upper chamber, its contents could fill the Grand Canyon more than 11 times. Documented in the journal *Science*, the discovery will help scientists predict potential seismic and volcanic activity.

The Yellowstone Volcano Observatory, created in partnership with the United States Geological Survey (USGS), monitors volcanic and earthquake unrest in the park. See its work at http://volcanoes.usgs.gov/yvo.

GEOLOGIC WONDERS

Grand Prismatic Spring (p114) The park's most beautiful geothermal feature.

Grand Teton (p190) Molten dikes, fault scarps and those peaks!

Hebgen Lake Ponder the awesome result of the 1959 earthquake.

Mammoth Hot Springs (p91) Graceful travertine terraces.

Mud pots Head to Mud Volcano south of Canyon, Artist Paint Pots south of Norris, or Fountain Paint Pot in the Lower Geyser Basin.

Norris Geyser Basin (p105) The region's hottest geothermal area, featuring Echinus Geyser, the park's largest acidic geyser.

Obsidian Cliff (p94) Dark volcanic glass from the interior of a cooled lava flow.

Petrified forests Hike up Specimen Ridge in Yellowstone or take the interpretive walk at Tom Miner Basin in Paradise Valley.

Calcite Springs (p96) Hexagonal basalt columns near Tower Falls.

Upper Geyser Basin (p108) Old Faithful, Morning Glory Pool and other gems.

Scientists are only beginning to fathom these complex underground systems, but it's clear that this is a threatened landscape – unless the broader region is safeguarded thoughtfully. Through conservation, Yellowstone protects about half of the world's geysers, but in areas like Iceland and New Zealand, where geothermal features have been developed as energy sources, geysers and geothermal activity may be altered or cease altogether.

Geysers

Only a handful of Yellowstone's thermal features are active geysers (from the Icelandic *geysir,* meaning 'to gush or rage'), but these still comprise about 50% of the global total, making the park a globally significant resource.

How do geysers form? First, snowmelt trickles into hot rock where it is superheated. The heated water begins to rise, creating convection currents. The earth acts like a giant pressure cooker, keeping the water liquid even though it reaches temperatures of over 400°F. As the water rises, it dissolves silica trapped in the surrounding rhyolite rock base. At the surface this silica is deposited as the mineral sinter (geyserite), creating the familiar ash-colored landscape of Yellowstone's thermal basins.

For a unique angle on thermal activity, check out the aerial photographs of Norris Geyser Basin at http://volcanoes.usgs.gov/volcanoes/yellowstone/yellowstone_gallery_2.html.

What gives geysers their 'oomph' is the sinter seal that junks up the escape valves in geyser chambers. This temporary blockage causes an intense buildup of gas until the seal breaks and releases the accumulated pressure. As the superheated water rushes toward the surface, water pressure drops and the water expands more than 1500 times in a violent chain reaction as it flashes into steam and explodes into the sky. Geysers require walls of hard rock such as rhyolite, which is part of the reason why Yellowstone's geysers are concentrated in the southwest of the park.

Geysers and hot springs are often connected in complex and delicate underground networks and affect each other in ways we don't yet understand. In recent times Steamboat Geyser, the world's tallest erupting geyser located in the Norris Geyser Basin, increased its eruptions. It behaved similarly in the 1960s and early 1980s but it's hard to say what's in store for its future.

Hot Springs

Hot springs occur with a gradual release of hot water. Springs may rage like oil in a deep fryer, churn like giant washing machines or remain completely still. Their crazy colors are a combination of mineral content, which affects the absorption and reflection of light, and water temperature, which supports a range of algae communities. Since algae and thermophiles are very temperature-specific, they may create beautiful concentric bands of colors. Blue pools are the hottest, absorbing all color except blue. Green pools result when the blue is mixed with small amounts of yellow sulfur.

Yellowstone's fascinating geology is laid bare in *Windows into the Earth,* by Robert B Smith and Lee J Siegel.

Mud Pots

Imagine that the sulfuric acid in groundwater is potent enough to dissolve rock, creating a sort of hot spring of viscous bubbling mud. The mud is known as kaolinite, a form of clay. Mud pots form above the water table, where less water is available. Most derive their water directly from rain, snow and condensation, so their consistency depends on precipitation and the seasons. Are they really boiling? No, the bubbling is actually the release of steam and gas. Sulfur and iron content give rise to the nickname 'paint pots.'

Fumaroles

Essentially dry geysers, fumaroles' water boils away before reaching the surface, where they burst with heat. These steam vents also give off carbon dioxide and some hydrogen sulfide (that nice 'rotten egg' smell) with a hiss or roaring sound. Roaring Mountain on the Mammoth–Norris Rd is a huge collection of fumaroles.

Travertine Terraces

The limestone rock of the Mammoth region contrasts with the silica-rich rhyolite found elsewhere in the park. Here, carbon dioxide in the hot water forms carbonic acid, which then dissolves the surrounding limestone (calcium carbonate). As this watery solution breaks the surface, some carbon dioxide escapes from the solution and limestone is deposited as travertine, forming beautiful terraces. They can grow up to an inch per day and are in constant flux.

Oil, gas and groundwater development near the park, and drilling in Island Park, Idaho, and Corwin Springs, Montana, all have the potential to alter the natural function of geothermal systems in the park.

Yellowstone Lake

One of the world's largest alpine lakes, Yellowstone Lake was formed by the collapse of the Yellowstone caldera and shaped by glacial erosion. Hydrothermal explosions have further shaped the shoreline, creating the inlets of West Thumb (a smaller caldera within the larger one), Mary Bay and nearby Indian Pond. Robotic cameras have revealed underwater geysers, 20ft-high cones, rows of thermal spires and more than 200 vents and craters, some the size of football fields, on the lake floor. Mary Bay and the lake floor canyon west of Stevenson Island are the hottest parts of the lake, due to numerous hot springs and vents.

Grand Canyon of the Yellowstone

This canyon is one of the park's premier attractions. It was formed as rising magma lifted the land and the Yellowstone River carved through rhyolite weakened by thermal activity. The fledgling canyon was temporarily blocked up to three times by glaciers (18,000 to 14,000 years ago), and the subsequent glacial flooding created a classic V-shaped, river-eroded canyon. It reached its present form only about 10,000 years ago.

Like many of Yellowstone's waterfalls, the Lower Falls of the Yellowstone tumble over the junction of hard lava bedrock and softer rock, in this case rhyolite and thermal areas. The spectacular colors of the canyon walls are created as hot waters percolate through the rhyolite picking up iron oxides that stain the walls many different colors.

The pink to gray rhyolitic lava that dominates park landscapes owes its hue to silica. The same substance is known to clog up narrow steam vents to create powerful geyser explosions.

The Teton Fault

The Tetons are mere geologic toddlers. Surrounding ranges like the Gallatins and Beartooths were formed 55 to 80 million years ago by volcanic action, as part of the east end of the Basin and Range region that dominates western USA. At this time Jackson Hole was still a high plateau. The Tetons started to rise only 13 million years ago as the earth's crust stretched apart. At that time the current peaks of the Tetons were still some 6 miles underground.

The key to the Tetons' breathtaking profile is the 40-mile-long Teton Fault, which runs along the base of the range. The range was essentially created by a succession of several thousand major earthquakes and slippages. Land east of the fault has fallen, over millions of years, as the west block has hinged and angled upward. The east block has in fact dropped four times further than the peaks have risen. Several of these scarps are visible near Jenny Lake.

As tall as the Tetons appear, their height is actually only a third of the fault's total displacement. Gradual erosion of the peaks, combined with sedimentation in the Jackson Hole valley, has diminished their scale by up to two-thirds.

The very tops of the Tetons consist of limestone, deposited by an ancient sea 360 million years ago. Time has eroded these relatively soft sedimentary rocks, exposing the more resistant granite. To create today's impressive pinnacles, freezing ice wedged and shattered the rock along its weakest joints.

You can note the Tetons' angled faulting by observing the westward tilt of the entire Jackson Hole valley. The west half of Jackson Lake is three times deeper than the east, due to both tilting and glacial scouring. Oddly, the land west of the Teton peaks is drained to the east, unlike the drainage systems in most other mountain ranges.

In 1959 a 7.5-scale earthquake occurred in the Hebgen Lake region just west of the park, causing 300 of Yellowstone's geysers to spontaneously erupt and creating Quake Lake.

Glaciation

As if supervolcanic activity weren't enough, sheets of ice up to 4000ft thick periodically covered Yellowstone and the Tetons, leaving only the tips of the highest mountain peaks visible. The most recent ice sheet, known as the Pinedale Glaciation, covered about 90% of Yellowstone National Park and melted about 13,000 years ago.

Moving glacial ice worked its artistry, sharpening peaks, carving out glacial valleys, scouring walls, and creating ridges of debris (moraines) and lakes. Glaciers shaped the piedmont lakes at the base of the Tetons and the classic U-shaped Cascade Valley, a popular Teton trail. While the Snake River once flowed south out of Jackson Lake, glacial moraines diverted its flow east. South of Jackson Lake, huge blocks of melting glacial ice formed the depressions known as the Potholes.

In Yellowstone's Geyser Basin, ice melted so quickly that large mounds of glacial debris formed low ranges like the Porcupine Hills, while deposits of glacial debris beneath today's thermal features act as water reservoirs for the various geysers and hot springs.

Today's glaciers have largely retreated; their best example are the nearby Wind River Mountains, with the largest glaciers in the lower 48.

Yellowstone's Future

The Yellowstone region has been geologically stable for about 10,000 years now, but the land remains restless. Continued tension in the earth's crust and earthquakes make this one of the most seismically active areas in the USA, with 1000 to 3000 earthquakes occurring each year.

Although a 6.1-scale earthquake rocked the Norris Geyser Basin in 1975, geologists don't expect large earthquakes in Yellowstone National Park because underground heat softens the bedrock and makes it less likely to fracture.

Grasshopper Glacier, outside Cooke City, was named for millions of extinct grasshoppers entombed in its ice. However, most of the grasshoppers have decomposed as the glacier melts due to global warming.

Yellowstone is rising or falling as much as an inch a year, moving 65ft with each slow-motion 'breath,' particularly at Mallard Lake Dome just east of Old Faithful, and Sour Creek Dome, east of the Hayden Valley. These movements in the earth's crust are probably due to the withdrawal of molten rock from twin magma chambers on the rim of the Yellowstone caldera.

No one knows for sure what will happen if (or when) Yellowstone's slumbering giant awakens. The last major Yellowstone eruption dwarfed every other volcanic eruption on the earth's surface for the past several million years, and such an explosion remains beyond human experience. But don't bet on Armageddon just yet. According to the United States Geological Survey (USGS), a supereruption is not imminent. If there is an explosive event, it is likely to be hydrothermal, involving a rock-hurling geyser eruption or lava flow.

For now, we can enjoy the wondrous spectacle of Yellowstone's thermal features. When you gaze up at Old Faithful or down through a hot spring into the bowels of the earth, remember the awesome forces at work below the grandeur.

Wildlife

The 2.5 million acres of Yellowstone and Grand Teton National Parks constitute the biological heart of the earth's largest intact temperate ecosystem. Its significance to wildlife is undisputed. The Greater Yellowstone radiates from its untamed core into 18 million acres of surrounding federal lands and private property to form a vast wilderness among the world's premier wildlife-viewing areas, especially for large mammals.

Animals

Charismatic species living in Yellowstone include the lynx, bald eagle, grizzly bear, whooping crane and the reintroduced gray wolf. Much wildlife also ranges beyond the parks' boundaries into surrounding areas.

Large Mammals

Yellowstone National Park alone harbors 60 resident mammal species, including seven native species of ungulates (hoofed mammals).

Check out the *Yellowstone National Park Journal*, which has information on the park, as well as extensive listings useful for trip planning and travel within the Yellowstone region.

Bears

The black bear roams montane and subalpine forests throughout Greater Yellowstone, hibernating in a den over winter. It's an adaptable, primarily vegetarian forager that sporadically hunts smaller animals. Although they are generally more tolerant of humans and less aggressive than grizzlies, black bears should always be respected.

The grizzly bear once ranged across the western US but in 2009 it returned to the endangered species list. Today its population in the lower 48 has been reduced to fewer than 1200, with 690 grizzlies inhabiting the Greater Yellowstone region. After grizzlies lost endangered species status in 2017, Wyoming approved hunting of the species outside park boundaries. The move sparked controversy, as grizzlies are vital to a thriving ecosystem.

Male grizzlies reach up to 8ft in length (from nose to tail) and 3.5ft in height at the shoulder (when on all fours) and can weigh more than 700lb at maturity. If you find some bear tracks, you might notice that the toe pads of a black bear are widely spaced and form a strong arc, while grizzly bear tracks show closely spaced toes in a fairly straight line, along with impressions from their very long claws. About half of black bears are black in color; the anomalies are brown or cinnamon. Black bears are somewhat smaller than grizzlies and have more tapered muzzles, larger ears and smaller claws.

Omnivorous opportunists and notorious berry eaters, grizzlies have an amazing sense of smell – acute enough to detect food miles away. Their wide range of food sources varies seasonally. After bears emerge from hibernation between early March and late May, they feed mostly on roots and winter-killed carrion, turning to elk calves and then spawning cutthroat trout in late June. A feast of army cutworm moths lures bears to higher elevations in early September. Fall signals the buildup to hibernation, and consumption of whitebark nuts and the raiding of squirrels' pinecone stashes becomes an obsession. Before hibernation, bears can eat up to 100,000 berries in a single day. Scientists are concerned that falling levels of cutthroat trout in Yellowstone Lake and the spread of blister rust fungus, which kills whitebark pines, will have an increasingly detrimental effect on grizzly food supplies in the park.

Male grizzlies generally live alone, require over 800 sq miles of territory, and live for up to 30 years. Females have one to four cubs every three years and are fiercely protective of their young, which stay by their mother's side for two years.

Grizzlies are most active at dawn and dusk in open meadows and grasslands near whitebark and lodgepole pines. They can become extremely agitated and aggressive if approached or surprised, but otherwise they do not normally attack humans. However, they viciously defend carcasses and can outrun a horse when provoked; thus, trails are often closed when a grizzly is feeding nearby on a bison, elk or moose.

Coyotes, Foxes & Wolves

The cagey coyote (locally pronounced 'kye-oat') is actually a small opportunistic wolf species that devours anything from carrion to berries and insects. Its slender, reddish-gray form and nocturnal yelps soon become familiar to hikers. Coyotes form small packs to hunt larger prey such as elk calves or livestock, for which ranchers detest them. While wide-scale coyote eradication programs have had no lasting impact, the reintroduction of wolves (which fill a similar ecological niche) is estimated to have reduced the region's coyote population by 50%.

The small, nimble red fox grows to 3.5ft, weighs up to 15lb and has a brilliant red coat. Foxes have catlike pupils, whereas wolves and coyotes have round pupils. Foxes favor meadows and forest edges and are primarily nocturnal. Although widely distributed, the red fox is not as abundant as the coyote, perhaps because the latter is such a strong competitor.

The gray wolf, aka timber wolf, was once the Rocky Mountains' main predator, but relentless persecution has reduced its territory to a narrow belt stretching from Canada to the northern Rockies. Its successful reintroduction continues to spark much controversy. Wolves roam in close-knit packs of five to eight animals ruled by a dominant male-and-female pair. This alpha pair are the only members of a pack to breed (normally in February), but the entire pack cares for the pups. Between four and six pups are born in April or May, and denning lasts into August.

Wolves eat meat only and, in Greater Yellowstone, tend to focus their predation on elk. Packs communicate via facial expressions, scent markings and long, mournful howls that can be heard from miles away.

Learn more about wolves and advocacy at www.wolfwatcher.org. Kids can track the activities of individual wolves or wolf packs via www.yellowstonewolves.org.

Wolf Politics

Wolves flourished in the West until the late 19th century, when homesteaders' livestock replaced bison herds. Poaching and predator control greatly reduced wolf populations and by the 1920s they had become extinct in Yellowstone. Despite controversy, wolves were reintroduced to restore balance to the ecosystem in the Lamar Valley in 1996 and thrived. Today, the future of wolf populations remains uncertain. Wolves were initially delisted as an endangered species in 2008, and again in 2011 after initial directives were rescinded.

Wolf reintroduction has been contentious. Since 1996 thousands of sheep and cattle have reportedly been killed, and many ranchers compensated for their losses. At the same time 'wolf-watching' now brings in about $35 million a year to the local economy. Wolves have also proven key to keeping coyote populations under control and may have even assisted in the regrowth of key species such as aspen and willow, by limiting elk grazing.

The return of the wolves has been shown to be key to providing balance to native ecosystems, though their restoration to the West remains precarious. In 2015 there were around 104 wolves in Yellowstone and more than 400 in the Greater Yellowstone Ecosystem. Numbers are down from a peak of 275 over a decade earlier – and more than 1600 in the surrounding area. Part of the problem is that states have vastly different approaches to management.

Wolves remain protected in the national parks, but parks are unable to keep these populations from roaming outside their boundaries into unprotected areas, and wolves used to wildlife-watchers are less likely to flee humans. In 2017, Wyoming joined Montana and Idaho in allowing the licensed seasonal hunting of wolves. Yellowstone wolf biologist Douglas Smith published a study in the same year citing that wolf sightings had decreased 45% in the park with trapping and hunting in the region. There is concern that consequences will also be felt in park revenue.

Critics of state plans decry the fact that politicians, rather than wildlife biologists, are deciding on animal management issues. Regions where tourism is the primary focus, such as Teton County, WY, are concerned about the huge impact these policies may have on visitation. For additional info you might consult Douglas Smith and Gary Ferguson's *Decade of the Wolf: Returning the Wild to Yellowstone* or Hank Fischer's *Wolf Wars*.

Elk

Greater Yellowstone's most abundant large mammal, elk (aka wapiti, or red deer in Europe) can weigh 700lb and stand up to 5ft tall at the shoulder. Their summer coats are golden-brown, and the males (bulls) have a darker throat mane. Each year bulls grow impressive multipoint antlers (up to 5ft long, weighing up to 30lb) for the fall rut (mating season), when they round up harems of up to 60 females (hinds) and unleash resonant, bugling calls to warn off other males. Although elk populations were decimated in the 19th century, their numbers have largely recovered – beyond sustainable levels, say some. Elk are cautious and elusive, and prized by trophy hunters who covet the massive rack of antlers that male elk briefly carry each fall.

Elk graze along forest edges; the largest herd in Yellowstone National Park beds down in the meadows west of Madison Campground. September to mid-October is the rutting season, and irresistibly cute calves appear

FINDING WILDLIFE

ANIMAL	HABITAT	WHEN & WHERE	PRECAUTIONS
black bear	forest and meadows	in summer at Tower and Mammoth areas	keep minimum distance of 100yd
grizzly bear	forest and meadows	at dawn and dusk; Hayden and Lamar Valleys; Fishing Bridge to East Entrance	keep distance of 100yd
bison	grasslands	year-round in Hayden and Lamar Valleys; in winter at hydrothermals around Madison River	responsible for more human injuries than bears; a lifted tail signals charge; keep a distance; drive slowly around herds
moose	marshes, lakeshores and rivers	at lower elevations in summer such as Willow Flats (Grand Teton National Park); migrate to subalpine and forests of Douglas fir in winter	don't corner or approach calves, adult may kick
pronghorn	sagebrush and grasslands	in summer at Lamar Valley near North Entrance; in winter between North Entrance and Reese Creek	keep distance of 25yd
wolf	forest and meadows	at dawn and dusk in Lamar and Hayden Valleys	don't feed; keep a respectable distance

in May to late June. An estimated 10,000 to 20,000 elk from seven to eight different herds summer in Yellowstone National Park, and a further 17,000 summer in Jackson Hole. In winter, large herds migrate south to the National Elk Refuge in Jackson. While winter counts of elk have plummeted since wolves were reintroduced, Yellowstone numbers grew in 2015, possibly because of the elimination of a late-season hunt outside the park.

Elk in the Greater Yellowstone are facing a new nonpredatory menace: chronic wasting disease. Found in Western states, it's a fatal neurological disease which accumulates in soil and proves highly contagious among animals. It has created further controversy for winter feeding programs, like those at the National Elk Refuge in Jackson, because they create potential breeding grounds for the disease, which can also infect deer and moose.

Bison

The continent's largest land mammal, the American bison – commonly called 'buffalo' – once roamed the American West in vast numbers (60 million), often migrating to Greater Yellowstone's high plateaus during summer. It is a national symbol long revered by Native Americans, and Yellowstone's bison are some of the USA's last free-roaming herds. Today's herd is wild, descended from ancient bison that roamed the same territory in prehistoric times, unlike other bison in the West which are managed as livestock. Greater Yellowstone is the only region where wild bison have lived since primitive times.

This is a truly majestic animal: full-grown male (bull) bison may stand over 6ft high at the shoulder, have a total length of 12ft and weigh 2000lb. Bison have a thick, shaggy, light-brown coat and a high, rounded back. Both sexes have short black horns that curve upward.

Despite their docile, hulking appearance and 'aloof' manner, bison are surprisingly agile. They become increasingly uneasy when approached. A raised tail indicates one of two subsequent events: a charge or discharge. Statistically speaking, bison are much more dangerous than bears. Every year several visitors are gored and seriously injured by these animals, and sometimes even killed. August is rutting season – keep your distance to avoid becoming an unwilling rodeo clown.

In 1902 there were only 23 wild bison living in the Yellowstone region. Today, herds exist throughout the Greater Yellowstone Ecosystem (an increasing number on private ranches), with three distinct herds ranging in Yellowstone National Park at Lamar Valley, Pelican Valley at the north end of Yellowstone Lake, and along the Mary Mountain corridor between Hayden Valley and Lower Geyser Basin beside the Firehole River. There's another herd in Grand Teton National Park.

Bred back from the brink of extinction, the park's current population of 4300 was culled by over 1100 bison in 2018 as part of a new and controversial program to prevent the spread of brucellosis. The bacterial disease, which causes animals to abort, is one of the ecosystem's hottest issues and was introduced into the region by cattle in the early 1900s. Management plans have called for bison populations to be intensely monitored, with a goal of maintaining Montana's 'brucellosis class-free' status to protect domestic cattle populations. Yet the claim that bison spread brucellosis remains undocumented. Hazing wandering bison back into the park each winter (directing them with noises, helicopters etc) remains controversial.

Park biologists have long argued that maintaining a population of 4000 bison is ideal for the park, while the livestock industry hopes to lower the number to 3000, a plan that has the support of US Interior Secretary Ryan Zinke. However some scientists suggest the focus should shift from bison management to managing contact between livestock and contaminated elk.

Bison & Brucellosis

Some of Yellowstone's 4300 bison are infected with brucellosis, a bacterium that causes domestic cows to abort their calves. Brucellosis spreads from the region's abundant elk population to the bison, who merely carry the bacteria while themselves remaining unaffected.

Bison are protected within the national park but their migration patterns bring them beyond its protective borders and, in 2000, a long-term management plan authorized the extermination of thousands of bison. Bison protectors point out that there are no documented cases of bison transmitting brucellosis to livestock. Advocates with the Buffalo Field Campaign maintain that the herd is headed toward extinction under these policies. Advocates for control counter that the absence of this evidence is due to these stringent actions.

The development of a vaccine has been somewhat impeded by the stringent controls around virus handling due to bioterrorism concerns. After many lawsuits, public dissatisfaction and controversy, ranching advocates have found an ally in former Montana congressman and Secretary of Interior Ryan Zinke. Under his efforts, Yellowstone's bison management plan is moving toward the removal of a thousand more bison from the Yellowstone herd.

Moose

The largest of the world's deer species, moose typically stand 5ft to 7ft at the shoulder, can reach 10ft in length and weigh as much as 1000lb. They have a brownish-black coat and a thick, black horselike muzzle. The male (bull) has massive, cupped antlers, each weighing up to 50lb, which are shed after the fall rut. Moose populations are facing decline, possibly due to a lack of food sources, and fires in the summer ranges of migrating moose.

An estimated 200 moose are found in Yellowstone National Park, favoring marshy meadows like Willow Valley, just south of Mammoth Springs, or on the east side of Lamar Valley. They are also found throughout the Tetons. Moose mainly browse aspen and willows, but also feed on aquatic plants. They are superb swimmers and can dive to depths of 20ft.

Moose may become aggressive if cornered or if defending calves and may strike out with powerful blows from their front hooves.

Pronghorn undertake the longest migration in the lower 48. Since 2007 both Yellowstone and Grand Teton National Parks have been part of a dedicated migratory pathway called Yellowstone to Yukon (www.y2y.net).

Wildlife-Watching Protocol

- Animals have the right of way on roads.
- Never position yourself between an animal and its young.
- Resist feeding animals and never chase one for a photo.
- Stay 100 yards from bears and wolves, and 25 yards from other animals, as per park regulations.
- If you cause an animal to move, you are too close.

Bighorn Sheep & Mountain Goats

Bighorn sheep are arguably the animals that best symbolize the Rocky Mountains. They are robust, muscular beasts, colored grayish brown with a white muzzle tip, underbelly and rump patch. Males (rams) grow up to 6ft long, stand almost 4ft at the shoulder and weigh more than 300lb. Their ideal habitat is alpine meadows or subalpine forests fringed by rocky ridges, which allow them to easily escape predators. Rams have thick, curled horns (weighing up to 40lb), which they use during the fall rut (from mid-September to late October) in fierce head-butting bouts with rivals. Discreet hikers can often closely observe bighorn herds around ridges or alpine valleys; try looking for them on rocky crags between Mammoth and Gardiner.

Introduced to Montana for sports hunting, non-native mountain goats expanded their range into Yellowstone in 1990 and more recently to Cascade Canyon in the Tetons, raising concerns that they might impact the area's fragile mountain meadows and have an adverse effect on the native bighorn sheep population. Surefooted and confident in even the most precipitous terrain, the mountain goat is highly adapted to the harsh environment of the upper subalpine and alpine zones. It has a shaggy, snow-white coat that includes a thin beard and narrow, almost straight, black horns. Mountain goats can reach 5ft, stand 4ft at the shoulder and weigh up to 300lb. Beware where you pee: goats crave salt and will gnaw down vegetation (and anything in their way) in order to satisfy their hankering.

Cats

The solitary, mostly nocturnal, bobcat is a handsome feline (a scaled-up version of the domestic tabby) with a brown-spotted, yellowish-tan coat and a cropped tail. It mainly eats birds and rodents, but when easier prey is scarce it may take small deer or pronghorn. Bobcats are thought to be widespread in the region, and it's not unusual to see one darting across a meadow or into a willow thicket.

Surveys in 2001 confirmed the presence of at least one lynx in Yellowstone. This threatened cat is similar in appearance to the bobcat, but can be recognized by its entirely black tail tip.

North America's largest cat, the mountain lion (aka cougar) prefers remote, forested areas of the park. With a size and shape similar to that of a smallish (African) lioness, the mountain lion may reach 7.5ft from nose to tail and can weigh up to 170lb. Even biologists who study it rarely encounter this solitary and highly elusive creature. It typically preys on mule deer, elk and small mammals, following their summer migrations to higher ground. While curious mountain lions are known to 'stalk' people without harmful intent, they occasionally attack humans.

Curious about that animal or plant that you saw in the park? Download the iNaturalist app to your smartphone. It uses photos and crowd-sourcing to help identify species.

Birds

Boasting 316 recorded winged species (of which 148 stay to nest), Greater Yellowstone offers a delightful bird-watching experience. The American Bird Conservancy recognizes Yellowstone National Park as a 'globally important bird area.' Noteworthy large birds include common ravens, resurgent peregrine falcons, reclusive sandhill cranes, honking Canadian geese and American white pelicans. Smaller birds including pesky black-billed magpies and yellow-headed blackbirds are common sights.

Birds of Prey

This group of birds (aka raptors) includes eagles, falcons, hawks and harriers. Sweeping across lakes, forests or plains in search of fish or small game, they are some of the most interesting and easily watched birds in the area.

The iconic bald eagle is a large raptor, with a wingspan up to 8ft, brown plumage and a distinctive 'bald' white head. Bald eagle pairs mate for life, building their nest close to water. Nests grow with each breeding season to become truly massive structures up to 12ft in diameter. The bald eagle takes fish (or harasses an osprey until it drops its catch), but also preys on other birds or smaller mammals. Nesting eagles are extremely sensitive to human disturbance.

The true 'King of the Rockies,' the gracious golden eagle is sometimes spotted riding thermals high above craggy ridges. Native Americans fashioned headdresses from its golden-brown plumage. Marginally smaller but heavier than the bald eagle, they typically nest on rocky cliff ledges and can easily spot potential prey and predators. They have a varied diet and will swoop on anything from fish and rodents to deer fawns.

The great horned owl is mottled gray-brown with prominent, 'horned' ear tufts, a white throat and a deep, resonant hoot. Its camouflage is so effective that few hikers even notice its presence. Asleep during the day, it preys on nocturnal rodents but also feasts on grouse and other birds.

The fish-eating osprey haunts larger lakes and rivers, nesting in shoreline treetops. Its upper wings and body are dark brown, and its underside is white and speckled on the outer wings. This well-adapted hunter has efficient water-shedding feathers and clamplike feet with two pairs of opposing toes to better grasp slippery, wriggling fish.

Waterfowl

A vast number of waterfowl visit the many lakes, marshes and rivers of Greater Yellowstone; coots, cranes, gulls and some ducks stay to nest.

North America's largest wild fowl, the spectacular trumpeter swan, is hardy enough to winter here in the Henry's Fork and Red Rock Lakes region west of the park. In 1932 only 69 swans remained alive in the lower 48 states, all of them in Greater Yellowstone. Since then numbers have climbed to around 2500, but are declining again. It has proven difficult to wean them from winter feeding to find their own wild foods, and cantankerous Canadian trumpeter populations continue to crowd them out.

Long-legged great blue herons and red-capped sandhill cranes may be seen striding gracefully in wet meadows and along the edges of water, where they use their long bills to capture fish, snakes, frogs and rodents. In the fall and spring, cranes gather into large noisy flocks.

On larger bodies of water the common loon is prevalent, its beautiful mournful wail echoing across tranquil backcountry lakes. Up to 35in long, it has a black-green head with a speckled upper body and white underparts. Its dense body mass enables it to dive to 150ft but also necessitates a long runway for takeoff, which limits it to larger lakes.

Smaller Birds

For a leg up on spotting wildlife carry a field guide such as *Watching Yellowstone & Grand Teton Wildlife*, by Todd Wilkinson.

The boisterous Clark's nutcracker, a member of the crow family, is light gray with black wings and a white tail. It patrols subalpine forests, feeding largely on conifer nuts, which it breaks open with its long, black beak.

The diminutive mountain chickadee is a playful and gregarious year-round resident of subalpine forests. It has a black cap and throat bib, and its onomatopoeic name describes its distinctive call, 'chick-a-dee-dee.'

The red-naped sapsucker is a woodpecker species with a black back, white stripes above and below each eye, and a red chin and forehead. It bores into tree bark (preferably aspen or willow), discharging gooey sap that traps insects, devouring both. Ironically, the bird's activity helps control the even more destructive bark beetle and other noxious insects.

The striking blue Steller's jay has a black crest, head and nape. Its grating 'ack-ack-ack' is unmistakable. Although it consumes pine nuts, berries and insects, it's also an incorrigible scavenger and frequently raids camps for scraps.

Fish

Yellowstone Lake is at the heart of one of North America's most significant aquatic wildernesses, home to 21 gilled species, including nonnatives such as rainbow trout, brown trout, brook trout, lake trout, lake chub and a cutthroat-rainbow trout hybrid. Fish provide critical foraging fodder for bears, waterfowl, otters and raptors throughout the ecosystem.

Yellowstone has more than 220 lakes and at least a thousand streams. Yet when it became a national park, 40% of its waters were fishless. The stocking of some 310 million fish drastically altered the aquatic environment. Current threats to Yellowstone's near-pristine aquatic ecosystem include the illegal introduction of predatory lake trout (the biggest culprits in the decline of endangered native cutthroat) into Yellowstone Lake, and

LAKE TROUT: A YELLOWSTONE NIGHTMARE

First identified in Yellowstone in 1994, when an angler who reeled one in alerted authorities, it wasn't immediately obvious how much trouble the surreptitiously introduced lake trout would cause. By 2012 their numbers had grown to 800,000.

The effects have been devastating, particularly for native cutthroat trout. Aggressive predators, lake trout can grow to up to 35lb. Each lake trout can consume 41 cutthroat trout per year. Since cutthroat trout spawn in rivers, they provide an important food source for grizzlies. Around 40 other species, including bald eagles and river otters, also depend on the cutthroat trout for survival. But lake trout reproduce in the depths of Yellowstone Lake, making them inaccessible to predators.

To preserve the native species and restore the ecosystem, park authorities have had to be aggressive, spending $2 million per year to eradicate the lake trout, mostly through the means of gill netting. Finally, cutthroat numbers may be rebounding. Currently there are around a million in the lake, only a quarter of a healthy population, but one that has recovered from the worst days of the lake trout invasion.

the invasion of New Zealand mud snails, which have been found in densities of half a million snails per square yard and which crowd out native aquatic insects. Invasive mussel species are also a threat.

Today 40 of the park's lakes are fishable, with native sport fish being catch-and-release. It's worth watching cutthroat trout spawn in spring at the outlet of Yellowstone Lake at Fishing Bridge and LeHardy's Rapids.

Plants

Flora from the surrounding mountains, deserts, montane forests, arctic tundra and Great Plains all converge in Greater Yellowstone, where they are grouped into five distinct vegetation zones – riparian, foothills, montane, subalpine and alpine. Yellowstone National Park's herbarium has inventoried 1717 species, 7% of which are considered rare.

Plants of Yellowstone and Grand Teton National Parks, by Richard J Shaw (Wheelwright Press, 2000), is a well-illustrated introduction to the region's rich vegetation.

Trees

Harsh climatic conditions at higher elevations strongly favor hardy conifers. With the exception of aspen, eight conifers dominate these forests and make up 60% of the region's total vegetation.

Douglas firs, quaking aspens, shrubs and berry bushes blanket parts of the landscape from 6000ft to 7000ft. Lodgepole pine forests, which range from 7600ft to 8400ft, cover 60% of the park's broad plateaus. Above 8400ft, Engelmann spruce and subalpine fir predominate, interspersed with lodgepoles. Above the tree line (10,000ft), alpine tundra supports lichen, sedges, grasses and delicate wildflowers.

Aspen has radiant silver-white bark and rounded leaves that 'tremble' in the mountain breezes and turn gold in fall. A regeneration species, aspen tends to reproduce by sending out root runners rather than by seeding. A stand of aspen is mainly cloned from an original parent tree.

Not a true fir, Douglas fir is a tall, adaptable and extremely widespread tree that ranges from the foothills to the subalpine zone and from very dry to quite moist locations. It has flattened, irregularly arranged needles, 4in-long cones, and thick, corky bark that protects it from fire.

True firs resemble spruces, but have flat, blunt needles and cones pointing upward on upper branches. The most widespread is subalpine fir with silvery-gray bark bearing horizontal blister scars.

Many lodgepole pines are dependent on periodic forest fires to melt the resins that seal their cones shut, ensuring seed dispersal after fire has prepared a fertile bed of ash. Lodgepoles sport needles in bunches of two and straight, narrow 'polelike' trunks that make for dense stands in recently regenerated forests.

WILDFLOWER PRIMER

Look for a breathtaking variety of wildflowers peaking throughout June and July.

Trumpet-like gentian A late-bloomer found above 10,000ft in moist arctic bogs, pretty arctic gentian has greenish-white flowers with purple stripes.

Columbine Found at the edges of small, shaded clearings up to 9000ft. Colorado columbine has blue-white flowers with delicate long spurs carrying nectar, attracting butterflies and hummingbirds.

Fireweed A single-stem perennial that grows up to 6ft tall, crowned by clusters of pink, four-petaled flowers about an inch in diameter. It colonizes recent burn areas.

Succulent Indian hellebore (aka corn lily) On subalpine slopes, these 7ft stalks have large leathery leaves crowned by maizelike flower tassels. Native Americans used it as an insecticide.

Delicate, yellow glacier lily (aka dogtooth violet) Blankets entire tundra slopes. Bears eagerly extract their edible bulbs.

Beargrass A fragrant lily relative with white starlike flowers on 4ft stalks in well-drained montane and subalpine clearings. Its waxy, bladelike leaves are favored spring forage among grizzly bears.

Bright red Indian paintbrush Prolific in the Tetons; a food source for hummingbirds.

Found in subalpine zones, the five-needled whitebark pine has smallish, almost round cones that remain purple until maturity. Its seeds provide crucial autumnal forage for grizzly bears. Large individuals stand near Dunraven Pass in Yellowstone and South Cascade Canyon in Grand Teton National Park.

Dominating subalpine forests, Engelmann spruce is a towering, cold-tolerant conifer capable of withstanding winter temperatures of -50°F. Like other spruces, Engelmann has round, slightly pointed needles and pendant cones. Its resonant wood is used to make piano sounding boards.

Shrubs

These small woody plants may grow as heaths, form thickets or stand as single bushes on slopes and in meadows. For herbivores, they are one thing: the bulk food aisle. Know your shrubs and you are one step closer to finding the wildlife.

Shrubby cinquefoil grows in meadows from the foothills to the tundra, sometimes in association with sagebrush. All summer long this multi-branched bush (up to 4ft high) is covered in yellow, buttercuplike flowers with five petals. Deer and bighorn sheep browse the foliage, but only when no other food is available.

Several dozen species of small willows are found in Greater Yellowstone, with fluffy, silky flowers like small bottlebrushes. Shrub willows, including the common gray-leafed willow, form thickets along subalpine and alpine stream basins. Moose eat willow year-round.

The scrumptious blueberry genus includes species locally known as bilberry, cranberry, grouseberry, huckleberry and whortleberry. Almost all produce small, round fruits of bright red to deep purple that sustain bears and other wildlife throughout the Rockies. One of the most common is the fragrant dwarf blueberry, which typically grows among lodgepole pines.

Junipers are aromatic, cedarlike conifers that generally thrive in dry, well-drained areas. Rocky Mountain juniper can approach the size of a small tree, and older shrubs (which may reach 1500 years) are gnarled and knotted. Birds feed on juniper 'berries,' allowing the seed to sprout by removing its fleshy covering.

Strongly aromatic sagebrush thrives on foothills and drier montane meadows. Since grazing mammals shun the bitter foliage, overgrazing results in the spread of sagebrush.

Conservation

For the last century, human presence has branded an indelible mark on the natural habitat of the Greater Yellowstone Ecosystem. How we both preserve and inhabit this region remains of critical importance. From studying the impacts of climate change to preserving native species, managing the region's conservation issues will require a detailed understanding of what they are and a constructive dialogue between diverse stakeholders.

The Bigger Picture

The Greater Yellowstone Ecosystem is among the largest intact temperate ecosystems in the world. We are only beginning to understand the intricate workings of this community, how individual species interact and how best to preserve this amazing environment. For a better understanding, download the free *Yellowstone Issues and Resources* handbook (www.nps.gov/yell/learn/resources-and-issues.htm).

To learn more about sustainable and ecofriendly options in the region, check out National Geographic's 'sustainable visit' map at http://yellowstone.natgeotourism.com.

Protecting Wildlife

Given Yellowstone's mandate to protect wildlife, it's not surprising that some of the fiercest battles are fought over questions of how to manage it. One question is how to protect top-level predators such as gray wolves when they leave the park and run into conflict with local ranchers. Contributing to the confusion is the fact that each state has different laws on these issues. The slaughter of disease-carrying bison that wander out of the park is another vexing topic.

In Greater Yellowstone waterways, invasive species such as whirling disease parasites, zebra mussels and New Zealand mud snails are threatening native species. Currently, the state of Wyoming requires boaters to purchase an invasive-species decal as part of an education campaign. In addition, visiting boats and fishing equipment must be scrubbed of mud and plants that may carry exotics.

Migration Corridors

Protecting migration corridors allows elk and other migratory animals to move from their summer to winter habitats. In 2015 alone, there were 377 wildlife deaths in Jackson Hole as a result of vehicle collisions. As population and road infrastructure increases, corridors become critical to ensure the survival of diverse species. The nonprofit initiative Yellowstone to Yukon (www.y2y.net) supports a dedicated migratory pathway through Grand Teton National Park all the way to Canada. Native pronghorn have been using this corridor for 6000 years to undertake the second-longest animal migration in North America. By modifying livestock fences and creating road crossings, conservationists can help this millennial process continue.

Can Fire Be Positive?

In 1998, 30% of the park blazed in a major inferno that only ceased with the first snows of September. Front-page news, the event was more a public-relations disaster than an environmental catastrophe. In 2016 the Berry Fire became the largest wildfire in Grand Teton National Park history, consuming over 20,000 acres. Today's scientific views on land stewardship are evolving. Fire sparked by lightning strikes is seen as a natural process that has been occurring for thousands of years. In Yellowstone the current policy is to allow natural fires to burn under strict guidelines, as they encourage new growth in plant communities, restore nutrients to the soil and burn off accumulated deadwood.

Climate Change is Local

Climate change may be everywhere, but it appears to be happening at an accelerated pace in the Greater Yellowstone ecosystem. Its consequences are multiple and intricately related. Scientists are predicting major changes by the end of this century.

With average temperatures on the rise, scientists predicted in a 2014 special park report that Yellowstone will be drier than it has been in 10,000 years. The Yellowstone River, a renowned trout-fishing stream, will become a warm-water fishery. Changing water levels affect both life in the park and downstream ranchers, farms and cities. Rising temperatures have also caused whitebark pines to die off at a rate of 85%, which in turn will impact grizzlies as the pine is an important food source. Researchers have also found much longer wildfire seasons, less snowpack and changing habitats.

Get a taste of Yellowstone, see spurting geysers and spy wildlife up close by taking a virtual nature tour at www.nps.gov/yell/learn/photosmultimedia/index.htm.

The specific impacts on wildlife are difficult to predict, but migration patterns are already changing. Grizzlies are denning later, foxes must start adapting to different winter hunting conditions and wolverines may lack enough snow for proper denning.

Sustainability

The Greening of Recreation

In recent years, snowmobile usage in both national parks has been drastically reduced, though proponents decry the regulations' impact on winter tourism. In Yellowstone, snowmobilers are now only allowed on professionally guided tours. In Grand Teton, use has been reduced to the frozen Jackson Lake. Both parks require quieter and more efficient BAT (best available technology) snow machines. In addition the two-stroke engines of rental boats have been replaced with cleaner and more efficient four-stroke versions.

Park Innovation

When the world's first national park approached its 125th anniversary in 1997, Yellowstone began planning for its next 125 years. One result was Yellowstone Environmental Stewardship (YES!), an ambitious project aiming to slash greenhouse gases, electricity consumption, fossil fuel consumption, water consumption and to divert all solid waste from landfills. Solar energy, composting and alternative fuels are a few ways the park has been meeting these goals. As of 2017, the park diverted an average of 45% of the park's solid waste over five years.

The Greater Yellowstone Coalition (www.greateryellowstone.org) works on behalf of every major issue affecting the Yellowstone region, from environmental concerns to species survival.

In Grand Teton National Park, the Zero Landfill Initiative has brought new recycling infrastructure in the park, plans for a composting facility and outreach and education projects. Funded in partnership with private companies, it's an innovative way of addressing budget shortcomings.

Concessions are an area of major improvement, with park concessionaire Yellowstone National Park Lodges employing corn-based biodegradables to help annually divert more than 280,000 plastic bottles from landfills. Gift shops sell greener souvenirs, and dining services pitch in by serving fair-trade coffee, local cheese and naturally raised meats. In both Yellowstone and Grand Teton, park employees use some hybrid vehicles.

LEED-certified park buildings also herald a new era. Efforts for sustainability reach beyond visitor services, as seen in Yellowstone National Park Lodges employee housing. Cleaning practices are getting a makeover too. Yellowstone's Green Housekeeping Program offers visitors discounts on their stay to reduce laundering and save over 300,000 gallons of water per year. To improve environmental health, green cleaning products are also being employed.

Survival Guide

Clothing & Equipment

Deciding what gear is essential for a trip and what will only weigh you down is an art. Smartphone apps, new filtration systems and battery chargers are changing the game. Don't forget essentials, but be ruthless when packing, since every ounce counts on the mountain.

CLOTHING

The Right Layers

Layering is the key to packing for Yellowstone. Locals will tell you there are only three seasons here – July, August and winter – so pack for changeable weather. Even on a cloudless summer day, it's smart to pack a shell jacket and a knit cap.

Synthetic, silk or wool base layers (not cotton) are the most effective. A waterproof but breathable rain jacket and an insulating fleece are musts. A down vest or light jacket is useful in spring and fall, when it can also be useful to have thermal underwear and wind/waterproof shell pants.

Winter and spring travel bring their own specialized equipment demands.

Footwear & Socks

Light to medium hiking boots are recommended for day hikes, while sturdy boots with ankle support are better for demanding hikes or extended trips with a heavy pack. Most importantly, they should be well broken in with a nonslip (such as Vibram) sole.

Snow and boggy meadows in spring and early summer mean you should bring waterproof boots then. In midsummer, running or hiking shoes can work for easier hikes in dry conditions.

Buy boots in warm conditions and walk around while trying them on. Trekking sandals are useful for fording rivers and wearing around camp.

Synthetic and wool-blend hiking socks are the most practical option. They should be free of ridged seams in the toes and heels.

CHECKLIST

The following is a general guideline. Know yourself and what special items you may need on the trail.

- boots
- camp shoes/sandals
- warm hat
- shorts and trousers
- socks and underwear
- sweater or fleece jacket
- thermal underwear
- wicking T-shirt
- bandana or buff

EQUIPMENT

Navigation Equipment

GPS

Originally developed by the US Department of Defense, the Global Positioning System (GPS) is a network of more than 20 earth-orbiting satellites that continually beam encoded signals back to earth. Small, computer-driven devices (GPS receivers) can decode these signals to give users an extremely accurate reading of their location – to within 10m, anywhere on the planet, at any time of day, in almost any weather. The cheapest handheld GPS receivers now cost less than $100 (although these may not have a built-in averaging system that minimizes signal errors). When purchasing, also consider a GPS receiver's weight and battery life.

A GPS receiver is useful only when used with an accurate topographical map. The receiver gives your position, which you must then locate on the local map. GPS receivers only work properly in the open. The signals from a crucial satellite may be blocked (or bounce off rock or water) directly below high cliffs, near large bodies of water or in dense tree cover, giving inaccurate readings. GPS receivers are more vulnerable to breakdowns (including dead batteries) than the humble magnetic compass – a low-tech device that has served navigators faithfully for centuries – so don't rely on them entirely.

Altimeters

An altimeter gives one piece of information: the elevation. Watch altimeters can be easier to use than traditional models with a needle and dial. They help keep track of your progress and pinpoint your location on the map. By noting the elevation of points along the way, it is easier to find these unmarked places again. It is also useful to note progress: if in the first hour you gained 800ft and only 500ft in the second, you can predict your pace for the next 1000ft of a steady slope with better accuracy. And if you summit a peak in the clouds, it's one way to be sure you've truly arrived!

Smartphone Map Apps

Map apps on your smartphone are increasingly popular tools for navigating the backcountry. Keep in mind that you can only find your way as long as your battery lasts. Have all necessary maps downloaded before you get on the trail. Also keep your phone on low power and in airplane mode to conserve the battery. If traveling overnight, a battery charger pack could be a lifesaver.

Backpacks & Daypacks

For day hikes, daypacks (30L to 40L) will usually suffice, but multiday hikes require an internal-frame pack (45L to 90L). Bring a waterproof pack cover if yours doesn't have one built in.

A comfortable fit and padded waistband is essential. A waistband water-bottle holder is a nice extra; otherwise consider a hydration bladder with hose.

Tents & Tarps

A three-season tent will suffice in most conditions. The floor and the fly should have taped or sealed seams and covered zips to stop leaks. Weight ranges from around 2lb for a stripped-down, low-profile tent to 6.5lb for a roomy four-season model.

Dome- and tunnel-shaped tents handle blustery conditions better than flat-sided tents. Bring a tarp and short lengths of rope to make a covered cook shelter in rain.

Sleeping Bags & Mats

Goose-down bags are warm, lightweight and compact, but expensive and of little use if they get wet. Synthetic bags are cheaper and better when wet, but bulkier. Mummy-shaped designs prove best for weight and warmth. The rating (23°F, or -5°C, for instance) is the coldest temperature at which a person should feel comfortable in the bag. A three-season bag should be fine for Yellowstone summer camping. For extra warmth and to keep your bag clean, add a silk liner.

Inflatable sleeping mats, such as those made by Therm-a-Rest, provide more comfort and better insulation from the cold than cheaper foam mats.

Stoves & Fuel

When buying a stove, think lightweight and easy to operate. Most outdoors stores sell and rent stoves. Butane stoves are the easiest to operate, though you are never quite sure how much gas is left and you have to dispose of the canisters properly. Multi-fuel stoves are versatile but need pumping, priming and lots of tender loving care.

In general, liquid fuels are efficient and cheap; look for high-performance, cleaner-burning fuel. Fuel can be found at outdoor gear shops, hardware stores (white gas) and some supermarkets.

Airlines prohibit flammable materials and may well reject empty liquid-fuel bottles or even the stoves themselves – check with airline policies before booking your ticket.

In terms of cookware, titanium or silicone pots are the lightest, toughest and most expensive option. A spork covers all the cutlery bases.

Water Purifiers & Tablets

When buying a filter, note that giardia requires a filter with a rating of 1.0 to 4.0 microns and *E. coli* requires a microfilter rating of 0.2 to 1.0 microns. When filtering, go for clear water in the current of a stream instead of stagnant water. Avoid silty water. A SteriPEN (UV light-based purifier) is a convenient useful alternative.

If you don't plan to be in the backcountry often, chemical tablets are the most convenient and cost-effective solution. Some tablets purify water in 30 minutes, while others take up to four hours,

POPULAR PARK APPS

The following apps will track your park location even when offline, but you have to download the regional map to use them.

Gaia GPS Good maps but downloads are only available with membership.

Yellowstone National Park Official park app.

Grand Teton National Park Official park app with topographical lines.

REI National Parks App Crowd-sourced map information.

Maps.me General maps that also show most trails.

so check when buying. Two-step tablets come with a neutralizing tablet that improves the taste, but you must add this only after the water has been purified.

Buying & Renting Locally

A hotbed for outdoor-gear innovation and consumption, the Rocky Mountain area offers high-quality products, though in-park selection is usually poor. The closer you get to the parks, the higher the rental rates.

All winter resorts have good rental shops with ski, snowboard and Nordic equipment, as well as mountain bikes in summer. Most have a program to 'demo' new equipment models.

Yellowstone & Around

Kayak rentals are available in Cody, Jackson, Livingston and Gardiner. Ski and snowshoe rentals are available at ski centers and popular Nordic locations such as Big Sky and West Yellowstone. Fishing-gear rentals are available in West Yellowstone, Livingston and elsewhere.

Absaroka Bicycles (Map p143; ☎307-527-5566; 2201 17th St, Kmart Plaza; ⏰10am-6pm Mon-Thu & Sat, to 4pm Fri) Mountain-bike rentals, repairs and tours, in Cody.

Bear Den Rentals (Map p112; Old Faithful Snow Lodge; ⏰7:30am-10pm; 👪) This small booth inside the Old Faithful Snow Lodge rents out bikes for kids (half/full day $20/30) and adults ($30/40) during the summer, and snowshoes, skis and other equipment in the winter.

Bridge Bay Marina (☎307-242-3876, boat shuttle 307-242-3893; ⏰8am-8pm mid-Jun–early Sep) Rents outboard motorboats ($57 per hour) for Yellowstone Lake and kayaks to backcountry boat shuttle clients.

Free Heel & Wheel (Map p164; ☎406-646-7744; www.freeheelandwheel.com; 33 Yellowstone Ave; ⏰9am-6pm Mon-Sat, to 5pm Sun) West Yellowstone's center for cycling and skiing advice rents mountain bikes ($35 to $40 per day), kid carriers for bikes, Nordic skis and snowshoes.

Northern Lights (☎406-586-6029; www.northernlightstrading.com; 83 Rowland Rd; ⏰10am-6pm Tue-Sat) Backpacking, kayak and winter rentals, including bear canisters, in Bozeman.

Sunlight Sports (Map p143; ☎307-587-9517; www.sunlightsports.com; 1131 Sheridan Ave; ⏰9am-8pm Mon-Sat, 10am-6pm Sun) Cody's best gear shop offers full backpacking equipment rentals (tents, stoves, backpacks).

Grand Teton & Around

Outside the park, Jackson Hole has a number of outdoor shops selling and renting gear.

Adventure Sports (Dornan's; Map p200; ☎307-733-3307; www.dornans.com; Moose; ⏰9am-7pm) In Moose, rents kayaks, canoes and paddle boards ($55 per 24 hours), mountain and road bikes ($44 to $65 per day), as well as kids' bikes and racks. Winter rentals include Nordic skis, snowshoes and sleds.

Colter Bay Marina (Map p198; ☎307-543-2811; www.gtlc.com/activities/marina; Colter Bay; ⏰8am-5pm late May–mid-Sep) Rents motorboats ($44 per hour), kayaks and canoes ($21 to $25 per hour).

Signal Mountain Marina (Map p198; ☎307-543-2831; www.signalmountainlodge.com; ⏰7am-7:30pm mid-May–mid-Sep) Rents canoes ($25 per hour), kayaks ($20), motorboats (from $42) and pontoon cruisers ($105).

Skinny Skis (☎307-733-6094; www.skinnyskis.com; 65 W Deloney Ave; ⏰9am-7pm Mon-Sat, 10am-7pm Sun) One of the best backcountry ski shops in the US, with summer backpacking rentals and winter Nordic skis.

Teton Mountaineering (☎307-733-3595; www.tetonmtn.com; 170 N Cache St; ⏰9am-8pm) Rents mountaineering and backpacking equipment in summer, plus full ski and snowshoe rentals in winter.

Moosely Mountaineering (Map p200; ☎307-739-1801; http://skinnyskis.com/moosely-mountaineering; 12170 Dornan Rd, Moose; ⏰9am-7pm mid-May–Oct) Rents mountaineering and backpacking gear in Moose.

Charging Electronics

Many people take smartphones and tablets into the backcountry these days, either to view custom maps or guidebooks, or to use the GPS capabilities of their devices to map their route.

To keep devices charged, consider packing a portable or solar charger. When shopping for a solar charger, look for one that sits conveniently on your backpack, works even in partial sunlight and charges multiple devices using a USB outlet. Test your charger before you bring it on the road. A charger that fits into the cigarette lighter or USB port of your car is useful as well.

Pepper (Bear) Spray

Most studies show that pepper spray is the most effective last line of defense against a charging or attacking bear. You should carry bear spray on any hike in Yellowstone. Remember that carrying pepper spray is not a substitute for vigilance or other safety precautions – we suggest keeping a distance of 300ft if you see a bear. Remember to remove the safety tab. When deploying, spray in a slight side-to-side motion.

Airlines do not allow the transportation of bear spray, but outdoor gear shops in the gateway towns and general stores inside Yellowstone National Park sell spray (around $50). UDAP and Counter Assault are good brands. A holster is a worthwhile investment.

You can also rent cans by the day or week from **Bear Aware** (Map p100; ☎406-224-5367; www.bearaware.com; Canyon Visitor Education Center, Canyon; bear-spray rental 24/48hr $9.50/18.75, 1/2 weeks $28/32; ⏲8am-5:30pm end May-Sep) and equipment rental services in Jackson and Grand Teton National Park.

Spray Requirements

- Buy a minimum size of 7.9oz (225g)
- Concentration should be 1.4% to 1.8% capsaicin
- Spray jet should reach 30ft

Proper Use

- Carry within easy and immediate reach, preferably in a hip holster – not in your pack.
- Use when the bear is charging, within 30 to 60 feet.
- Aim at a 45-degree angle toward the ground and remember to disarm the safety cap.
- Make sure you are not downwind.
- And no, it doesn't work like mosquito repellent, so don't spray it all over your tent or body!
- After use, recycle the can at any Yellowstone park visitor center or hotel.

Directory A–Z

Accessible Travel

Yellowstone has many accessible boardwalks and trails, and even several wheelchair-accessible backcountry campsites, including Goose Lake (OD5), south of Fountain Flat Dr (p115) in Geyser Country, and Ice Lake (p107) (4D3) on the Norris–Canyon road, which is 0.5 miles from the trailhead and has a wheelchair-accessible vault toilet. The Madison River, in the west of the park, offers a wheelchair-accessible fishing platform.

The pamphlet *Visitor Guide to Accessible Features in Yellowstone National Park* lists accessible sights and facilities, and is available online at the 'Plan Your Visit' section of the park website. For specific questions call the park's Accessibility Coordinator on ☎307-344-2314. In Yellowstone there are wheelchair-accessible campsites at Bridge Bay, Canyon, Grant Village, Madison and Mammoth.

Deaf visitors can get information at TDD ☎307-344-5395 (Yellowstone) and TDD ☎307-739-3400 (Grand Teton). The parks will provide sign-language interpreters for ranger-led programs if booked three weeks in advance – call ☎307-344-2251.

Wheelchair-accessible trails in Grand Teton include the 6-mile paved trail along String Lake. Accessible accommodations are available at several campsites and all lodging facilities. For more details view the *Accessibility* brochure on the park's website.

Blind and permanently disabled US residents can get a free lifetime access pass, good for all federal parks. Get one at park entrances.

Access Tours (☎208-787-2332; www.accesstours.org) runs tours in Grand Teton and Yellowstone for those with physical disabilities. Based in nearby Driggs, Idaho.

Accommodations

Rates for accommodations are noticeably higher in the Yellowstone region than in the surrounding areas of Wyoming, Idaho and Montana, particularly in the high-season months of July and August. Yellowstone itself remains the biggest headache, with accommodations booked up months in advance. The key is to reserve well ahead.

Campgrounds National Park Service (NPS), concession-run and Forest Service (USFS) all offer the best value and most atmospheric accommodations.

Park cabins Rustic cabins, some without private bathroom, remain the parks' most economical rooms.

Park hotels A mix of grand historic buildings, bland lodges and luxury retreats.

Motels The staple of gateway-town accommodations.

BOOK YOUR STAY ONLINE

For more accommodations reviews by Lonely Planet authors, check out http://lonelyplanet.com/hotels/. You'll find independent reviews, as well as recommendations on the best places to stay. Best of all, you can book online.

Camping

Camping is the cheapest and, in many ways, the most enjoyable approach to a Yellowstone vacation. Toasting marshmallows over an open fire, stargazing in the crisp mountain air and taking in an evening ranger talk are essential parts of the national park family-bonding experience.

Around half the campsites in Yellowstone, and all sites in Grand Teton, are on a first-come, first-served basis. In July and August, campsites get snapped up quicker than you can find them on the map. Establish your campsite in the morning before you head off sightseeing and, once you have a site that you like, hold onto it and use it as a base to visit neighboring sights.

DUDE RANCHES

Dude-ranch history dates back to the late 19th century, when visiting family and friends from eastern cities offered money to the informal accommodations supplied as a sideline by the region's ranches.

These days, you can find anything from a working-ranch experience (5am wake-up calls included) to top-of-the-line resorts frequented by the rich and famous. Ironically, working cattle ranches are increasingly hard to find in the tourist-driven Yellowstone economy.

A few ranches offer nightly accommodations-only rates, but most offer all-inclusive rates and require a minimum stay of three days to a week. Typical weekly rates run $200 to $250 per person per day, which includes accommodations, meals, activities and equipment. Ranches are proud of the connections they form with their clients, many of whose families return to the same ranch generation after generation.

While the highlight of dude-ranch vacations is horseback riding, many ranches have expanded their activity lists to include fly-fishing, hiking, mountain biking and cross-country skiing. Accommodations range from rustic log cabins to cushy suites with Jacuzzis and cable TV. Similarly, meals range from steak and beans to four-course gourmet extravaganzas.

Yellowstone's dude ranches (increasingly called guest ranches) are concentrated in the Wapiti Valley near Cody, Jackson Hole and the Gallatin Valley northwest of Yellowstone. For more information contact the Dude Ranchers' Association (www.duderanch.org), the Wyoming Dude Ranchers' Association (www.wyomingdra.com) or Montana Dude Ranchers' Association (www.montanadra.com).

If you have a tight itinerary and will be moving around a lot, try to plan at least a few overnight stays at Yellowstone's concession campgrounds, run by **Yellowstone National Park Lodges** (Xanterra; ☎307-344-7311, 866-439-7375; www.yellowstonenationalparklodges.com), where you can make site reservations in advance. Gamblers should remember that, even if you manage to score a same-day site at a concessionaire campground, you may have to move out the next day if your spot is booked for that night. Concessionaire campsites are a little pricier than the park-service sites.

If all else fails, you'll find some great USFS campgrounds outside the park, and these generally only fill up on summer or holiday weekends.

Fishing Bridge RV Park (Map p102; www.yellowstonenationalparklodges.com; Fishing Bridge; RV sites $47.75; ⏲late May-late Sep) in Yellowstone, **Colter Bay Campground** (Map p198; ☎307-543-3100; www.gtlc.com; Hwy 89/191/287; tent/RV sites $31/53; ⏲mid-May–Sep; P 📶) in Grand Teton and **Headwaters Campground** (Flagg Ranch Campground; ☎307-543-2861, reservations 800-443-2311; www.gtlc.com/camping/headwaters-campground-at-flagg-ranch; Flagg Ranch; tent/RV sites $38/74, 4-person cabins from $77; ⏲May-Sep; P) in the John D Rockefeller Jr Memorial Parkway are the only places with full hookups, though a couple of grounds have RV dumps. Generators are generally only allowed between 8am and 8pm, and no generators are allowed at any time at Yellowstone's Indian Creek, Lewis Lake, Pebble Creek, Slough Creek and Tower Fall sites.

CAMPGROUND RULES

Some rules to remember from the NPS and USFS:

- Camping in pullouts, trailheads, picnic areas or anywhere except designated campgrounds is illegal.
- Wash dishes, hair, teeth etc away from the spigot. Camp wastewater must be disposed of in waste sinks, restroom sinks (no grease) or the toilet, not chucked into your neighbor's site.
- Campfires must be in established grates. Never leave a fire unattended.
- Cutting trees or shrubs for firewood is prohibited.
- Don't build trenches around campsites.
- A maximum of six people and two cars are allowed at each site (some USFS sites charge extra for a second car).
- No food, ice chests, food containers, utensils or camp stoves may be left outside unattended. If you are tenting, store all food and containers in bear boxes. Don't dispose of food in the camp area; put it in a bag or container and dispose of it in the trash. Don't put trash in the toilets.
- Pets must be physically controlled at all times. Please pick up after your pet.
- Bear restrictions require that only hard-sided campers (no pop-ups) can occupy sites at Fishing Bridge in Yellowstone and certain USFS grounds outside Cooke City and in the upper Wapiti Valley.

PRICE RANGES

The following price ranges are for a double room in high season, without tax.

$ less than $110

$$ $110–$250

$$$ more than $250

YELLOWSTONE CONCESSIONAIRE CAMPGROUNDS

Yellowstone's concessionaire, Yellowstone National Park Lodges (p261), runs five campgrounds, where sites can be reserved in advance. Reservations can be made over the phone, online or from other concessionaire campgrounds or facilities in the park.

Be careful to specify the type of site you want: tent or non-tent, reverse-in or pull-through, and even the length of the site. If your site requirements change, you'll need to change the reservation. Some sites are designated tent-only – you don't *have* to put up a tent in these, but you can't roll up in a giant RV. Site fees are for up to six adults.

➡ When you make an online or phone booking, you must pay by credit card and then receive a booking reference number.

➡ You'll need to show that credit card when you turn up at the campground. Yellowstone National Park Lodges doesn't take checks.

➡ If you cancel your reservation you'll have to pay the first night of each individual reservation.

➡ If the campground office is closed when you arrive, look on the noticeboard for your name on an envelope, which will contain your site allocation.

➡ If you arrive late at night without a reservation, look on the noticeboard to see if any sites are vacant and pay the next morning before 11am.

NPS CAMPGROUNDS

Yellowstone and Grand Teton campgrounds usually have flush toilets (cheaper sites have vault toilets), drinking water, garbage disposal, fire pits (or charcoal grills) and picnic benches. Most hold some kind of nightly campfire talk. Days, times and topics are prominently posted and are listed in the park newspapers.

The process of picking a site varies with the campground, but generally involves picking up an envelope from a box at the entrance, driving around the various loops until you find an available site you like, marking the site with either the tab from the envelope, some camp furniture, or the most agreeable family member, and then filling out the envelope and depositing it with the correct fee back at the entrance. Don't dally trying to find the world's best campsite – by the time you get back, the earlier one you liked may well have been snapped up.

When choosing a site, discerning campers scrutinize its proximity to a bathroom, trash and water supply, whether the ground is level and, most importantly, the neighbors (a scattering of beer cans can be a bad sign). In general, back-in sites offer a little more privacy; parallel sites are little more than car parks by the side of the road. A campground's outer loops are usually the most private.

In larger campgrounds, such as Colter Bay in Teton and **Mammoth** (Map p92; Mammoth; campsites $20; ⏲year-round) in Yellowstone, you register and pay at the entrance and are computer-assigned a spot, so there's no need to mark your site.

➡ Some grounds ask you to keep the receipt tab displayed on your car windshield; others ask you to tag it to the campsite post.

➡ Rangers often come around at night to check receipts against vehicle number plates.

➡ A 'site occupied' sign can be useful to mark your turf, and these are for sale in most campgrounds.

➡ NPS campgrounds generally do not accept checks or credit cards – with the exception of **Signal Mountain** (Map p198; ☎307-543-2831; www.signalmtnlodge.com; 501 Signal Mountain Boat Launch Rd; ⏲mid-May–mid-Oct; Ⓟ) in Grand Teton and Mammoth in Yellowstone – and are self-service, so make sure you bring plenty of $1 and $5 bills.

➡ Interagency Seniors (Golden Age) and Interagency Access (Golden Access) passes give 50% reductions on most camping fees in national parks and national forests.

➡ Most campgrounds sell boxes of firewood ($8) and kindling ($3).

➡ A few campsites are normally reserved for hikers and cyclists at a discounted price.

OUTSIDE THE PARKS

USFS campgrounds are generally less developed than NPS campgrounds – some don't have drinking water and require you to pack out all trash. A few of these sites are free.

Many turn off the water supply about mid-September and then either close or run the site for a while at half-price. At any rate, it's always a good idea to bring a few gallons of water when camping. Checks are accepted at most USFS campgrounds.

Sites can be reserved in certain USFS campgrounds in the Gallatin Valley and in Targhee, Shoshone and Custer (around Red Lodge) National Forests through

Recreation.gov (☎877-444-6777; www.recreation.gov). There is a nonrefundable $9 reservation fee for most sites and a cancellation charge of $10. It's possible to select and reserve specific campsites online, or with the useful app. Sites need to be booked a minimum of three days and maximum of eight months in advance.

Free dispersed camping (meaning you can camp almost anywhere) is permitted in some public backcountry areas. Sometimes you can pull off a dirt road and into a small lay-by where you can camp. In other places, you must be 0.25 miles from a developed campground and often not within 0.5 miles of a major highway. Check with the local district ranger office.

Private campgrounds outside the park are mostly designed with RVs in mind. Tenters can camp, but fees are double the public campgrounds and sites are normally crushed together to maximize profits. Facilities can include hot showers, coin laundry, swimming pool, full RV hookups with phone and satellite TV, games area, playground and a convenience store.

If you don't have kids, you'll find campgrounds to be much quieter outside school summer holidays.

Lodging

If you aren't camping, accommodations in Yellowstone and Grand Teton are limited to concession-run park lodges and cabins. Lodges are often grand reminders of a bygone era, but the rooms have usually been renovated and are generally quite comfortable. Not all rooms are equal, and there's often a vast range of different room permutations available.

Cabins are generally remnants from the 1950s, almost always jammed into a small area and resembling anything from an affluent suburb to military barracks. The cheaper cabins are simple (sometimes without bathrooms), but contain a modicum of rustic charm. The pricier cabins have modern interiors but are pretty charmless.

In general, park accommodations are decent value, considering the premium real estate, but rates are rising year on year. Lodge accommodations start around $160 for a double without bath and $180 for a double with bath. Cabins start at $100 for a double without bath, and $160 with bath. Most rooms are in the $200-300 range.

PARK PASSES

Several types of annual pass grant unlimited access to national parks. The passes admit a private vehicle and its passengers, or the pass holder, spouse and children. You'll need a photo ID to purchase and use the pass.

Annual Park Pass Year-long access to Yellowstone or Grand Teton costs $70 per park. The America the Beautiful Pass is a better deal.

America the Beautiful Pass Excellent-value annual interagency pass ($80) that gives access to any fee-paying site administered by the NPS, USFS, United States Fish & Wildlife Service (USFWS) or Bureau of Land Management (BLM). Space for two signatures means that two people can use the same pass.

Interagency Seniors Pass In 2017, the lifetime senior's pass covering the same areas jumped from $10 to $80. It allows US residents aged 62 and over (and accompanying passengers in a private vehicle) unlimited entry to all sites, with a further 50% discount on many camping and other fees (except Yellowstone's Fishing Bridge RV Park). Existing passes are still honored. Annual passes now cost US$20.

Interagency Access Pass This free pass offers the same benefits to US residents who are blind or permanently disabled (proof is required). If you have an old Golden Age or Golden Access pass, there's no need to replace it with the new passes.

Military Pass Free Interagency Annual Pass for current military personnel and their dependents. You will need to show your Common Access Pass or military ID.

Fourth Graders Pass Fourth Graders can get a free Interagency Annual Pass that covers everyone in their vehicle. Get a voucher from www.everykidinapark.gov.

You can buy the passes at all park entrances. Alternatively, purchase an individual park pass online at www.yourpassnow.com or an America the Beautiful Pass at http://store.usgs.gov/pass. For more information see www.nps.gov/planyourvisit/passes.htm.

➡ There are no TVs or radios in park accommodations; don't panic, bring a book!

➡ Unless otherwise noted, room rates we list are for two people and without tax.

➡ Children under 12 usually stay free.

➡ Check the Yellowstone National Park Lodges website for occasional internet specials, especially discounts of 20% for advance bookings in October and early winter (book before November 1 for mid-December).

➡ In winter you'll save money by signing up for a joint accommodations-and-activities package.

Yellowstone National Park Lodges (Xanterra; ☎307-344-7311, 866-439-7375; www.yellowstonenationalparklodges.com) runs Yellowstone accommodations and some campgrounds.

Grand Teton Lodge Company (GTLC; ☎307-543-3100; www.gtlc.com) runs most of that park's private lodges, cabins and campgrounds.

FREE PARK ADMISSION

Admission to Yellowstone and Grand Teton National Parks is generally free on National Public Lands Day (fourth Saturday in September). There are three or four other free admission days, often including August 25, the anniversary of the founding of the National Park Service, but these change annually – see www.nps.gov/yell/planyourvisit/fees.htm.

OUTSIDE THE PARKS

Accommodations outside the parks offer much greater variety, from hostels to top-of-the-line dude ranches and fly-fishing lodges.

The good news is that you can score great discounts of up to 50% on lodging outside the parks in the shoulder-season months of April, May and October through to mid-December, with winter discounts of at least 30% from January to March, depending on the destination.

USFS cabins are a little-known option and are particularly fun in winter, when you can either snowshoe or snowmobile into a basic cabin equipped with a woodstove, cooking utensils and bunk beds. There are cabins in the vicinity of Hebgen Lake and the Paradise Valley. Book these at **Recreation.gov** (☎877-444-6777; www.recreation.gov).

Houses or condos are available for rent in ski-resort areas and can be good value for large groups or families, as they almost invariably include a kitchen and living room. Most hotels offer multiroom suites with a small kitchen that suit families.

There are several B&Bs scattered around the gateway corridors to the parks, ranging from Victorian houses to wolf sanctuaries. Some offer rooms in the owner's house, while others offer stand-alone accommodations.

Some useful websites:

B&Bs, Inns & Ranches of Wyoming (www.wyomingbnb-ranchrec.com)

Montana Bed & Breakfast Association (www.mtbba.com)

RESERVATIONS

It's essential to reserve park accommodations at least six months in advance, preferably longer if you want a specific type of room. If you find yourself without a reservation, any of the parks' accommodations can tell you exactly what's available park-wide on the spot, and can make bookings for up to two days ahead. If you are desperate, keep heading back to check, as cancellations open up a limited number of accommodations every day.

Outside the parks, the more popular hotels fill up a month or two in advance of high summer (July and

Climate

Mammoth, WY

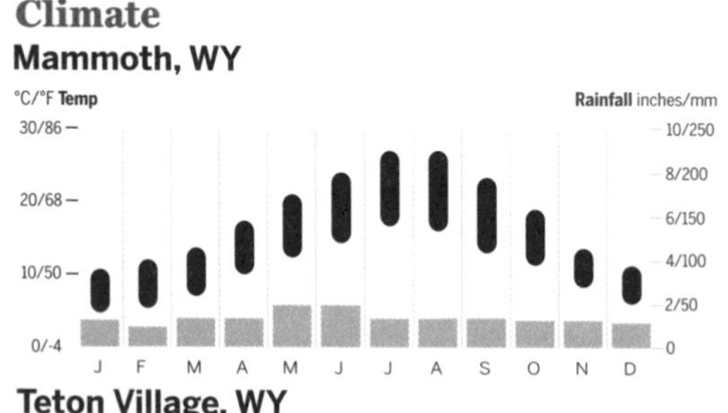

Teton Village, WY

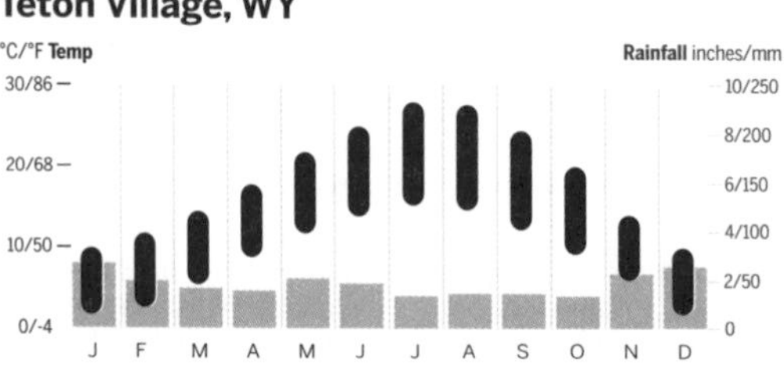

August). You can normally find somewhere to stay if you just roll into town, but it's still a good idea to make a reservation at least a day or two in advance.

Make sure to let the hotel know if you plan on a late arrival – many places will give your room away if you haven't arrived or called by 6pm. Cancellation policies vary; inquire when you book.

Most of the gateway towns surrounding the parks have agencies that will gladly book your entire vacation, from car rental to hotel rooms and excursions.

Jackson Hole Central Reservations (☎888-838-6306; www.jacksonholewy.com; 140 E Broadway)

Yellowstone Tour and Travel (Map p164; ☎800-221-1151; www.yellowstone-travel.com; 211 Yellowstone Ave, West Yellowstone)

Yellowstone Vacations (Map p164; ☎800-426-7669; www.yellowstonevacations.com; 415 Yellowstone Ave, West Yellowstone)

Courses

If Yellowstone's wonderland of spurting geysers, gurgling mud pots and baby bison turns adults into kids, then imagine its impact on young ones. Sharing these moments will create priceless family memories and, for your kids, a visit to the parks may just kick-start a lifelong love of nature and the outdoors.

Discount Cards

Always ask for some kind of discount, whether it be AAA (American Automobile Association), Good Sam, seniors, off-season, shoulder season, multiday or any other even half-credible reason you can imagine. Rates are notoriously flexible in the Yellowstone region. Student cards are of little use.

Electricity

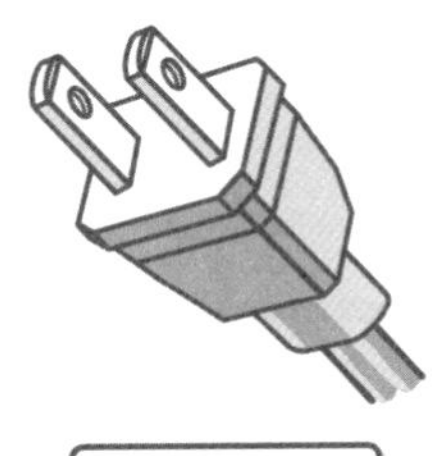

Type A
120V/60Hz

Type B
120V/60Hz

Food

Food in Yellowstone is generally more functional than fun, though you shouldn't have difficulty finding somewhere to eat, whatever your budget. The parks offer a multitude of fast-food outlets and sandwich bars, as well as the occasional need-to-eat-something-different gourmet restaurant.

Outside the tourist-driven eateries in the parks, local cuisine is a stick-to-your-ribs diet of biscuits and gravy, chicken-fried steaks, turkey loaf and mashed potatoes, plus table-shaking half-pound burgers and bloody steaks. One local 'delicacy' that always gets foisted (with a grin) on tourists is Rocky Mountain oysters – deep-fried bison testicles, normally served in pairs.

If you plan on sticking to a strict vegetarian diet while traveling in Greater Yellowstone, you'll have to get used to two things: baked potatoes and grudging looks from local ranchers.

Given the lovely locations and abundant picnic areas, picnicking is a popular option. A cooler is an invaluable piece of equipment during the heat of summer, and ice is available at most park junctions. The majority of campers bring a dual-burner stove to speed along cookouts. At the end of the day, even the blandest can of beans tastes like heaven when cooked over an open fire and under a blanket of stars.

The following price ranges are for a main course at dinner, not including tips or drinks:

$ less than $15

$$ $15–25

$$$ more than $25

Insurance

Foreign visitors to the US should take out adequate travel insurance, purchased before departure. This should include coverage for medical emergencies and treatment (p274), as well as vehicle insurance (p271) including liability coverage if you'll be driving. You should also consider coverage for luggage theft or loss, and trip-cancellation insurance.

Worldwide travel insurance is available at www.lonelyplanet.com/travel-insurance. You can buy, extend and claim online anytime – even if you're already on the road.

Internet Access

Wi-fi and even cell phone data coverage are almost nonexistent in Yellowstone National Park, but slightly better in Grand Teton.

In Yellowstone, the **Albright Visitor Center** (307-344-2263; 8am-6pm mid-Jun–Sep, 9am-5pm Oct–mid-Jun) in Mammoth is the only place offering free wi-fi.

Paid wi-fi is available only in the lobby of the **Old Faithful Snow Lodge** (Map p112; Old Faithful; May–mid-Oct & late Dec-Feb;), **Lake Lodge Cabins** (Map p102; Lake Village;), the lodges at **Grant Village** (Map p102; 307-242-3401; www.yellowstonenationalparklodges.com; late May-Sep;) and **Canyon** (Map p100; Jun-Sep; @), and at the bar at **Mammoth Hot Springs Dining Room** (Map p92; Mammoth; 6:30-10am, 11:30am-2:30pm & 5-10pm May–mid-Oct & mid-Dec–early Mar;), for a fee of $5/12/25 per 1/24/72 hours (consecutive). Call 877-658-5597 for details.

Only **Lake Yellowstone Hotel** (Map p102; 866-439-7375; www.yellowstonenationalparklodges.com; Sandpiper; mid-May–early Oct; @) has wired internet connection in some of the rooms and an internet-connected 24-hour business center free for guests. Connections are slow.

Internet access is due to be improved in Yellowstone over the coming years, though the substantial infrastructure investment required means that progress will be slow.

In Grand Teton the **Craig Thomas Discovery & Visitor Center** (Map p200; 307-739-3399, backcountry permits 307-739-3309; Teton Park Rd, Moose; 8am-7pm Jun-Aug, hours vary Mar-May, Sep & Oct;) offers free wi-fi.

Most hotels, libraries, visitor centers, bookstores and cafes in the neighboring towns offer free wi-fi access.

Legal Matters

Bear in mind the following park regulations during your visit:

- Speed limits are normally 45mph (55mph in some parts of Grand Teton), dropping at major junctions and pullouts. Nighttime speed limits are generally 10mph lower.
- It is illegal to collect plants, flowers, rocks, petrified wood or antlers in the parks.
- Firearms are allowed in the parks under valid state or federal laws, but are prohibited in park or concessionaire buildings.
- Swimming in waters of entirely thermal origin is prohibited in Yellowstone.
- Permits are required for all backcountry trips and activities such as boating and fishing.
- Drones are not allowed in the parks.
- In national parks, federal rather than state law applies, regardless of which state you are in.
- Most park rangers act as law enforcement officers inside the parks and so have the power to arrest you.

LGBT+ Travelers

The conservative red states of Wyoming and Montana are not known for their tolerance of LGBT issues, so discretion would be a good idea when passing through rural gateway communities. That said, gay and lesbian travelers shouldn't face any issues traveling through the national parks.

Companies such as HE Travel (www.hetravel.com) run gay-oriented adventure tours of Yellowstone and Grand Teton.

Opening Hours

Opening hours for all facilities are very seasonal. Outside high season (Memorial Day to Labor Day), you can expect opening hours to be shorter by an hour or two. Park newspapers detail exact opening hours and dates. Occasional federal government shutdowns can close the parks. The following are standard business hours:

Banks, post offices and government offices 9am–5pm weekdays, half-day Saturday

Park visitor centers Generally 8am–7pm in summer (June to August)

General stores 7.30am–9:30pm within the parks

Restaurants 7am–10:30am, 11:30am–2:30pm and 5pm–9:30pm

Shops 9:30am–5:30pm

Post

The only year-round post office in Yellowstone is at Mammoth Hot Springs. Seasonal post offices are at Canyon, Lake and Grant Villages and **Old Faithful** (Map p112; Old Faithful; 8:30-1:30pm & 2:30-5pm Mon-Fri).

In Grand Teton you'll find post offices at Colter Bay (summer only) and Kelly, **Moose** (Map p200; 800-275-8777; 3 Teton Park Rd, Moose Village; 9am-1pm & 1:30-3:30pm Mon-Fri, 10-11:30am Sat) and Moran Junctions.

Public Holidays

On the following national public holidays, banks, schools and post offices are closed, and transportation, museums and other

PARK SUPPORT

Many visitors fall in love with the Yellowstone region, returning with their kids, and again with their grandkids. The following organizations do good work to ensure the parks' future:

Yellowstone Forever (www.yellowstone.org) Supports educational, historical and scientific programs through memberships, book sales and courses at the **Yellowstone Forever Institute** (Map p96; ☎406-848-2400; Lamar Valley). Recently merged with the Yellowstone Park Foundation. Members get 15% off merchandise at park stores, plus off-season discounts at park accommodations.

Grand Teton National Park Foundation (www.gtnpf.org) This organization's mission is to enhance, preserve and protect the park, using member donations to fund park projects.

Grand Teton Association (www.grandtetonpark.org) Book sales and membership dues fund educational, interpretive and scientific programs in Grand Teton.

Greater Yellowstone Coalition (www.greateryellowstone.org) Monitors environmental issues in areas around the park, from snowmobile use to mining concerns.

National Parks Conservation Association (www.npca.org) This national organization strives to protect and enhance America's national parks. Members can subscribe to the magazine or sign up for an association credit card.

services operate on a Sunday schedule. Park visitor centers and facilities are open on the public holidays that fall within their normal opening dates. Holidays falling on a weekend are usually observed the following Monday.

January 1 New Year's Day

Third Monday in January Martin Luther King Jr Day

Third Monday in February Presidents' Day

Last Monday in May Memorial Day

July 4 Independence Day

First Monday in September Labor Day

Second Monday in October Columbus Day

November 11 Veterans' Day

Fourth Thursday in November Thanksgiving

December 25 Christmas Day

Telephone

To call interstate (long distance) dial ☎1 followed by the state code: Montana 406 or Wyoming 307.

To call abroad, dial the international code ☎011.

Toilets

➡ Park junctions, visitor centers, accommodations and most campgrounds have modern flush toilets.

➡ Most trailheads, picnic areas and cheaper park-service campgrounds have vault toilets.

➡ Some backcountry sites have vault toilets; check with the backcountry office when booking your site.

Tourist Information

Visitors to Yellowstone and Grand Teton are well supported with information from various organizations.

Yellowstone & Around

Albright Visitor Center (☎307-344-2263; Mammoth; ⌚8am-6pm mid-Jun–Sep, 9am-5pm Oct–mid-Jun)

Central backcountry office (☎307-344-2160; YELL_Backcountry_Office@nps.gov)

Fire information (☎307-344-2580)

Lost and found (for items lost in Yellowstone lodges or restaurants ☎307-344-5387; elsewhere in the park ☎307-344-2109)

Old Faithful Visitor Education Center (Map p112; ☎307-545-2751; Old Faithful; ⌚8am-8pm Jun-Sep, 9am-5pm Dec-Mar, hours vary spring & fall; 👪)

Park road updates (☎307-344-2117)

Recorded campground and accommodations information (☎307-344-2114)

Yellowstone National Park Lodges (Xanterra; ☎307-344-7311, 866-439-7375; www.yellowstonenationalparklodges.com)

Yellowstone National Park (☎307-344-7381, TDD 307-344-2386; www.nps.gov/yell)

Recreation.gov reservation service (☎877-444-6777; www.recreation.gov)

State road and weather conditions (Idaho ☎208-336-6600, Montana ☎800-226-7623, Wyoming ☎307-772-0824)

West Yellowstone (www.destinationyellowstone.com)

Grand Teton National Park

Grand Teton Lodge Company (GTLC; ☎307-543-3100; www.gtlc.com)

Grand Teton National Park (Map p200; 307-739-3300; www.nps.gov/grte)

Jackson Hole & Greater Yellowstone Visitor Center (307-733-3316; www.jacksonholechamber.com; 532 N Cache Dr; 8am-7pm Jun-Sep, 9am-5pm Oct-May;)

Recorded campground information (307-739-3603)

Recorded weather (317-739-3611)

Visas

Visitors from Western Europe, Australia, New Zealand, Japan and Singapore can enter the US for up to 90 days on a visa waiver program (VWP).

Volunteering

The NPS runs a Volunteer in Parks (VIP) program. See www.nps.gov/volunteer and www.nps.gov/yell/supportyourpark/volunteer.htm for details.

For information about Grand Teton's volunteer program, contact the park's **Volunteer Coordinators** (307-739-3657; www.nps.gov). To find out more, click on 'Get Involved' then 'Volunteer' in the Grand Teton section of the NPS website.

The USFS accepts a wider range of volunteers, from trail maintenance workers to campground hosts, and normally supplies rooms and board with a subsistence wage. Visit www.fs.fed.us/working-with-us/volunteers or www.volunteer.gov.

The **Student Conservation Association** (www.thesca.org) places student volunteers in the parks.

Youth Conservation Corps (YCC; www.nps.gov/yell/parkmgmt/yccjobs.htm) offers month-long programs for teenagers (aged 15 to 18), who work in the park on jobs such as trail construction, often in the backcountry.

Other volunteering options in the region:

Community Foundation of Jackson Hole (303-739-1026; www.volunteerjacksonhole.org; 245 E Simpson Ave, Jackson) Lists opportunities with dozens of local agencies, from therapeutic riding to art and wilderness organizations.

Continental Divide Trail Coalition (303-996-2759; www.continentaldividetrail.org) Volunteers help with trail construction, PR work or fund-raising, with several hands-on maintenance projects in the Yellowstone region each summer.

Yellowstone Forever Institute (Map p96; 406-848-2400; www.yellowstone.org; Lamar Valley) Volunteers at the Buffalo Ranch center assist with courses for summer or winter seasons.

Work

Occasional seasonal jobs (for US citizens only) are available as rangers or laborers with the NPS, though competition for the jobs is fierce. Check for openings at www.nps.gov/personnel and www.usajobs.gov.

Several Facebook groups offer support and advice for

VIRTUAL YELLOWSTONE

You can use a combination of smartphones and your car stereo to liven up the drive to the parks. If nothing else, it solves the festering debate over whose music to listen to!

- You can download the free NPS video podcasts *Yellowstone in Depth, Visiting Yellowstone* and *Inside Yellowstone* from iTunes.
- Yellowstone and Grand Teton National Parks offer several free apps, including the TravelStorysGPS app for Grand Teton.
- Yellowstone (www.youtube.com/YellowstoneNPS) and Grand Teton (www.youtube.com/GrandTetonNP1) have dedicated YouTube channels to get you in the mood.
- Both parks have Facebook pages and Twitter feeds. Yellowstone has the dedicated @GeyserNPS for geyser predictions.
- The GyPSy Guides app (www.gypsyguide.com; $7-10) uses your phone's GPS to give automatic driving commentary through the parks.
- Gaper Guide (www.gaperguide.com) is a stand-alone, GPS-enabled audio guide to Yellowstone. It's not cheap at $45 per day, but you can rent the unit in one gateway town and drop it at another.
- Go old-school with an audio book. Tim Cahill's *Lost in My Own Backyard* is available on audio CD or MP3 and is read by the author.
- The park service operates webcams at Old Faithful and the top of Mt Washburn, among other locations – see www.nps.gov/yell/learn/photosmultimedia/webcams.htm.
- Check out the amazing 360-degree panoramas at www.360panos.com.

INTERNATIONAL VISITORS

Embassies & Consulates

British and Australian consulates are maintained in Denver, but they can't replace lost passports. For all other countries, the nearest options are in Washington, DC or San Francisco.

Entering the Country

If you have a non-US passport, you must complete an arrival/departure record (form I-94) before you reach the immigration desk. It's usually handed out on the plane, along with the customs declaration. On arrival most visitors will have their photo taken and electronic fingerprints made of each index finger; the process takes less than a minute.

No matter what your visa says, US immigration officers have absolute authority to refuse admission to the country or impose conditions on admission. They will ask about your plans and perhaps whether you have sufficient funds. It's a good idea to be able to list an itinerary, produce an onward or round-trip ticket and have at least one major credit card.

If connecting on a domestic flight, you will pick up your bag, go through customs and then place your bag back on a baggage belt before continuing to your domestic gate.

Money

ATMs at hotels and general stores at most park junctions. Some businesses accept US-dollar travelers checks as cash.

Weights & Measures

The US uses the imperial system (miles, yards, pints and quarts). A US gallon is slightly larger than an imperial gallon and the US ton is slightly heavier than a metric tonne. Sadly a US pint is 20% smaller than a British pint.

Time

The Yellowstone region operates on US Mountain Time, which is GMT/UTC minus seven hours. The US subscribes to daylight savings time (DST): on the first Sunday in April clocks are set one hour ahead; on the last Sunday of October, clocks are turned back one hour.

people wishing to work in the parks.

Your first stop should be Coolworks (www.coolworks.com), which is an excellent clearing house for jobs both in and around the parks. Search for 'Yellowstone' or 'Grand Teton.'

The main Yellowstone concessionaire, Yellowstone National Park Lodges (www.yellowstonejobs.com), employs 3000 people in summer and 300 in winter, who do everything from making beds to making soup. Pay hovers around minimum wage and the work is fairly humdrum, though you won't have to go far to find a place to hike on your days off. Employee housing and food cost around $75 per week (a few RV sites are also available). Apply December to March for summer jobs and in August/September for winter positions. Staff are a mix of students, overseas workers (who need to arrange their own work visas) and retirees living in their RVs.

You may also find opportunities with Yellowstone Vacations/Delaware North (www.yellowstonevacations.com/jobs), which runs the Yellowstone General Stores and several hotels in West Yellowstone. It employs around 600 people a year.

The third Yellowstone concessionaire, Yellowstone Parks Service Stations (www.ypss.com), is based in Gardiner and has work for clerical as well as automotive technicians.

For job opportunities in Grand Teton, contact the following:

Dornan's (www.dornans.com)

Grand Teton Lodge Company (www.gtlc.com/the-park/employment)

Signal Mountain Lodge (www.coolworks.com/signal-mountain-lodge/profile)

Transportation

GETTING THERE & AWAY

The main gateways (and airports) nearest to Yellowstone National Park are Jackson (56 miles), Cody (52 miles), Bozeman (65 miles), Billings (129 miles) and Idaho Falls (107 miles). Grand Teton National Park sits right outside Jackson (13 miles).

Depending on your direction of travel, it may be cheaper to land in a larger hub such as Salt Lake City (390 miles) or Denver (563 miles) and rent a car there.

Flights, tours and rail tickets can be booked online at www.lonelyplanet.com/bookings.

Air

Airports

Private planes can land at Jackson Hole Airport and several small airstrips, including Driggs, Idaho and Gardiner, Montana.

Billings Logan International Airport (BIL; ☎406-247-8609; www.flybillings.com; N 27th St) Services to Salt Lake City, Minneapolis, Denver, Dallas, Seattle, Portland, Phoenix, Las Vegas, some seasonal destinations (Chicago and Los Angeles), and other Montana destinations.

Bozeman Yellowstone International Airport (BZN; ☎406-388-8321; www.bozemanairport.com; 850 Gallatin Field Rd) Located at Gallatin Field, 8 miles northwest of downtown Bozeman. Similar connections to Billings.

Idaho Falls Regional Airport (IDA; ☎206-612-8221; www.idahofallsidaho.gov/181/Airport; 2140 N Skyline Dr, Idaho Falls) Services to Las Vegas, Phoenix, Salt Lake City and Denver, plus seasonal flights to Minneapolis and Los Angeles.

Jackson Hole Airport (JAC; Map p200; ☎307-733-7682; www.jacksonholeairport.com; 1250 E Airport Rd) Located 7 miles north of Jackson, off US 26/89/189/191 within Grand Teton National Park. Daily flights to Chicago, Dallas, Phoenix, Salt Lake City and Denver, plus many more seasonal flights.

Yellowstone Airport (WYS; ☎406-646-7631; www.yellowstoneairport.org; ⏲late May-Sep) In West Yellowstone, and the closest airport to Yellowstone National Park. Three daily summer flights (late May through September) to and from Salt Lake City. Closes in winter.

Yellowstone Regional Airport (COD; ☎307-587-5096; www.flyyra.com; 2101 Roger Sedam Dr) Located 1 mile east of Cody; runs daily flights to Salt Lake City, Denver and Chicago (seasonal).

Flights from UK & Ireland

British Airways (www.britishairways.com) and the cheaper budget airline Norwegian Air (www.norwegian.com) have direct flights to Denver, where US carriers connect to Jackson Hole. Also consider American, United, Delta and Virgin Atlantic.

Other useful routes include to Billings or Bozeman on Delta via Minneapolis.

Flights from Australia

Route through Los Angeles or San Francisco before continuing to regional airports. Via the Pacific route, the first leg is 12 to 14 hours. Flying through Asia probably means spending a night or considerable layover time in a connecting city.

Land

Bus

Unfortunately, long-distance bus services are a slow, somewhat infrequent and highly inconvenient way to get to Yellowstone and Grand Teton National Parks. But they will get you to major cities, from where you could then rent a car or bicycle or book a local shuttle.

Companies may charge extra to transport skis or bicycles.

Alltrans Jackson Hole (☎307-733-3135, Mountain States Express 307-733-1719; www.jacksonholealltrans.com) The Mountain States Express shuttles daily between Jackson and Salt Lake City (4½ hours). Reservations are recommended.

In winter, the Targhee Express takes skiers from Jackson and Teton Village to Grand Targhee Resort in Idaho.

Greyhound (☎800-231-2222; www.greyhound.com) Serving Billings, Bozeman and Jackson.

Jefferson Lines (☎800-451-5333; www.jeffersonlines.com) East-west routes to Billings and Bozeman.

Karst Stage (☎406-556-3540; www.karststage.com; to West Yellowstone adult/child 3-12yrs $155/78) Airport shuttle service from Bozeman Yellowstone International Airport to Big Sky and West Yellowstone.

Salt Lake Express (☎800-356-9796; www.saltlakeexpress.com) Daily minibus service to Idaho Falls, Salt Lake City and Boise from West Yellowstone and Jackson.

Car & Motorcycle

A car, RV or motorbike is the way to see the parks. Be aware that soft-shelled vehicles (such as Jeeps) do not provide safe storage for food in bear country, and that parks require vehicles to have proper bear-proof canisters to carry food, although a few sites provide storage boxes.

Car and motorcycle drivers will need the vehicle's registration papers and liability insurance.

DRIVER'S LICENSE

Visitors to the USA must have a valid driver's license from their home country. An International Driving Permit (IDP) may be required, depending on your nationality, and is recommended, especially if your home license doesn't have a photo or is in a foreign language. Your automobile association at home can issue an IDP, valid for one year, for a small fee. You must carry your home license together with the IDP.

To ride a motorcycle you need a US state motorcycle license or an IDP appropriate for motorcycles.

RENTAL

Car rental rates in the towns around Yellowstone vary considerably throughout the year, with summer weekends bringing the highest rates.

Jackson, Billings, Bozeman and Cody have the best selection of rental companies and, thus, slightly lower rates. All the airports have car rentals. The major companies are Hertz (www.hertz.com), Avis (www.avis.com), Thrifty (www.thrifty.com) and National (www.nationalcar.com).

While renting an RV can save money on accommodations and dining out, higher RV campsite fees with hookups and the cost of gas (most RVs average between 5 and 10 miles per gallon) can quickly negate these savings. Camper vans are a convenient smaller alternative.

Campervan North America (☎208-712-8100; www.campervannorthamerica.com) Camper-van rentals with one-way options. Locations in Las Vegas, Denver and Bozeman.

Cruise America (☎800-671-8042; www.cruiseamerica.com) For a range of RVs, Cruise America rents through local dealers in Billings, Bozeman, Denver and Salt Lake City. Renters face a three-day minimum, not including mileage fees. Summer rentals should be reserved well in advance.

INSURANCE

Don't put the key in the ignition if you don't have auto insurance. In most states it's compulsory; moreover, you risk financial ruin if you have an accident without insurance. If you already have auto insurance, make sure it will cover your rental car. Rental companies provide limited insurance, usually charging significantly extra for collision damage. Make sure you also have separate liability insurance, which covers damage to people and other vehicles.

Check to see if your credit card covers collision damage for rental cars; many US cards do and it can save a bundle of money.

If you are booking a rental car from abroad, you might find you get a better deal by choosing a package that includes full insurance. Try online agents such as Kayak (www.kayak.com) and Car Rental 8 (www.carrental8.com).

ROAD RULES

In the parks, practice courteous driving etiquette. If you are driving a slow vehicle, use the numerous pullouts to let faster traffic pass. If you

CLIMATE CHANGE & TRAVEL

Every form of transport that relies on carbon-based fuel generates CO_2, the main cause of human-induced climate change. Modern travel is dependent on airplanes, which might use less fuel per mile per person than most cars but travel much greater distances. The altitude at which aircraft emit gases (including CO_2) and particles also contributes to their climate change impact. Many websites offer 'carbon calculators' that allow people to estimate the carbon emissions generated by their journey and, for those who wish to do so, to offset the impact of the greenhouse gases emitted with contributions to portfolios of climate-friendly initiatives throughout the world. Lonely Planet offsets the carbon footprint of all staff and author travel.

don't want your open driver's side door torn off by a passing bus, pull off the road fully when watching wildlife. Wildlife always has the right of way.

General rules:

- Drive on the right side of the road.
- The speed limit is generally 65mph to 75mph on western highways, 25mph in cities and 15mph in school zones.
- Speed limits in the parks are generally 45mph, dropping to 25mph or less at popular pullouts or junctions. Hwy 191 in Grand Teton National Park has a limit of 55mph.
- Seat belts and child-safety seats are required in every state.
- On motorcycles, helmets are required for anyone aged under 17 in Montana, Idaho and Wyoming.
- Most states don't allow you to transport open containers of alcohol.
- Penalties for driving under the influence of drugs or alcohol (DUI) are severe. Limits vary by state, but a blood alcohol limit of 0.08% or more is considered driving under the influence.
- Littering brings fines of up to $1000.

Train

In its heyday, the *Union Pacific* pulled right into West Yellowstone and Gardiner; now this social event is preserved as a quaint memory by the local historical society. Today the closest passenger trains to Yellowstone are over 300 miles away (Denver and Salt Lake City).

GETTING AROUND

Despite a high volume of traffic trundling through the parks, there appears to be little movement toward developing a mass transit system inside the parks.

Car It's almost impossible to visit Yellowstone without your own vehicle. All the airports have car rentals; Jackson, Billings, Bozeman and Cody have the best selection of rental companies.

Public transport There's no transport of any kind inside the park and only minimal transportation in the gateway corridors.

RVs Offer a classic family vacation, but park roads are quite narrow and some smaller park roads are off limits to RVs and buses.

Bicycle

Touring by bicycle is fairly popular, although cycling through Yellowstone National Park presents its own special challenges. Specifically, many riders report that it can be very unpleasant navigating narrow roads jammed with RVs – whose side mirrors and wide loads present a real danger to the little people. Grand Teton generally has wider roads and even a **bicycle path** (www.nps.gov/grte/planyourvisit/bike.htm; dawn-dusk May-Oct) to Jenny Lake.

Cyclists using national-park campgrounds usually pay the same fee as walk-ins, which can be considerably lower than the fee for a vehicle. Mountain biking in areas around the national parks is outstanding; however, bike travel on national-park trails is severely limited and wilderness areas may also have restrictions.

Bike shops frequently have group rides and can provide information on local trails. Most gateway towns have a bicycle shop. **Better World Club** (866-238-1137; www.betterworldclub.com) offers a bicycle roadside assistance program.

Rental

Long-term bike rentals are easy to find. Rates run from $350 per week and up, and a credit-card authorization for several hundred dollars is usually necessary as a security deposit.

Buying a bike and reselling it before you leave may be a more economical option. Check out local yard sales or message boards in local coffee shops for used bikes, and be sure to tune up your ride before hitting the road.

Bus

Although some long-distance touring companies visit the parks, only Jackson has regular bus service.

Jackson has a free town shuttle that runs every 20 to 30 minutes and the Start Bus (www.startbus.com) runs a service to Teton Village and a commuter service to Driggs, Idaho and Etna.

Alltrans Jackson Hole (307-733-3135, Mountain States Express 307-733-1719; www.jacksonholealltrans.com) operates up to five buses a day in summer between Jackson, Moose, Jenny Lake Lodge, Signal Mountain Lodge, Jackson Lake Lodge and Colter Bay, with one morning service continuing to Flagg Ranch. Rides cost $15 and are unlimited on the daily pass. The service is free for guests of GTLC properties.

Car & Motorcycle

While drivers in this region tend to be lead-footed on the interstate, traffic in the park is exasperatingly slow, typified by lumbering RVs wheezing over the Continental Divide. At the slightest whiff of a bison or moose, traffic slams to a halt. For this reason, it pays to be extra attentive when driving.

Fuel & Spare Parts

Gas prices inside the park are higher than elsewhere in Wyoming and Montana. Prices rise as you get closer to the park, peaking at Red Lodge and Cooke City. Most gateway towns have an auto parts store (Napa or Checker).

Service stations in Yellowstone National Park (p128) can do basic repairs and oil changes, but if your car is struggling, it is best to take it to a shop outside the park.

Road Conditions

Harsh winter conditions create frost heaves and potholes that mar even recently repaved roads. Grand Teton National Park's roads are generally in better condition than Yellowstone's. At Yellowstone, there's usually one section of the Grand Loop under construction, causing delays of up to an hour. Sometimes sections of road are closed between certain hours; make sure you check the parks' newspapers or websites for current road conditions.

Idaho Transportation Department (☎511, 888-432-7623; www.511.idaho.gov) Download the app.

Montana Travel Information (☎800-226-7623; @mdtroadreport)

Wyoming Road Conditions (☎888-996-7623; www.wyoroad.info)

Road Hazards

Every year hundreds of wild animals meet their fate on the grill of a car. Keep an eye out for crossing animals and drive with particular care at dawn and dusk.

Higher-risk areas have signs marked with a deer, though all areas, even those outside the park, may have animals crossing. Bison should be passed very carefully – they are not nearly as passive as cattle.

Hitchhiking

Hitchhiking is potentially dangerous and not recommended. Travelers who hitch should understand that they are taking a small but potentially serious risk. While it is prohibited on highways, you'll see more people hitchhiking (and stopping) on rural roads, especially near hiking trailheads.

If you are hiking a long loop, it's sometimes difficult to encounter a ride for those last few road miles, although more likely at the most popular trailheads.

You can check ride-share boards at ranger stations and in hostels.

ROAD DISTANCES TO YELLOWSTONE

Boston	2450 miles
Chicago	1450 miles
Denver	640 miles
Los Angeles	1010 miles
Miami	2600 miles
New York	2300 miles
Salt Lake City	325 miles
San Francisco	950 miles
Seattle	750 miles
Washington, DC	2200 miles

Tours

Alltrans Jackson Hole (☎307-733-3135, Mountain States Express 307-733-1719; www.jacksonholealltrans.com) Full-day tours of either park from Jackson.

Buffalo Bus Touring Company (Map p164; ☎800-426-7669; www.yellowstonevacations.com; 415 Yellowstone Ave; loop tour adult/child $80/70) Northern or southern loops of Yellowstone from West Yellowstone; free pickup from hotels or campgrounds. Also has winter snowcoach options.

Grand Teton Lodge Company (Map p198; ☎307-543-2811; www.gtlc.com; adult/child up to 11years Grand Teton $75/35, Yellowstone $175/125; ⊙tours 8:30am late May-early Oct) Half-day Grand Teton tours, full-day tours of Yellowstone or a combination of both parks.

Yellowstone National Park Lodges (Xanterra; ☎307-344-7901; www.yellowstonenationalparklodges.com) Park concessionaire runs a wide range of interpretive tours, from one hour to all day. Many are in Yellowstone's classic yellow-colored vintage touring vehicles. The 'Yellowstone in a Day' tour (adult/child aged three to 11 $118/59) starts in Mammoth, Old Faithful Inn or, for slightly more, in Gardiner. Dawn wildlife-viewing tours from Mammoth, Canyon or Roosevelt cost $47.25/94.50, while dusk tours are cheaper. Services should be reserved in advance.

Snowcoach Tours

Converted vans on snow tracks, snowcoaches (p38) provide transportation in and around Yellowstone National Park in winter, also providing a useful service for skiers. Tours depart daily from West Yellowstone and Mammoth.

Health & Safety

Keeping healthy depends on your predeparture preparations, your daily health care while traveling and how you handle any medical problems that develop. While the potential problems can seem daunting, in reality few visitors experience anything worse than a case of sunburn or a skinned knee. Read up in preparation.

BEFORE YOU GO

Medical Checklist

First-aid kits should include:

- acetaminophen (paracetamol) or aspirin
- adhesive or paper tape
- antibacterial ointment for cuts and abrasions
- antibiotics
- anti-diarrhea drugs (eg loperamide)
- anti-inflammatory drugs (eg ibuprofen)
- antihistamines (for hay fever and allergic reactions)
- bandages, gauze swabs, gauze rolls and safety pins
- insect repellent with DEET
- iodine tablets or water filter (for water purification)
- moleskin (to prevent chafing of blisters)
- non-adhesive dressing
- oral rehydration salts
- paper stitches
- pocket knife
- reverse syringe (for snakebites)
- scissors, safety pins, tweezers
- sterile alcohol wipes
- steroid cream or cortizone (for allergic rashes)
- sticking plasters (Band-Aids)
- sunscreen and lip balm
- thermometer

Further Reading

If you're hiking in remote areas, consider the following detailed health guides.

- *NOLS Wilderness Medicine*, by Tod Schimelpfenig and Joan Safford, prepares hikers for outdoor medical emergencies.
- *Medicine for the Outdoors*, by Paul Auerbach, is a general reference with brief explanations of many medical problems and practical treatment options.

Preparation

The best preparation for a hiking vacation is to embark on some regular, dedicated exercise at least three weeks prior to travel. To lessen the chances of getting sore shoulders, blisters and foot fatigue, wear in your boots thoroughly by undertaking long walks with a loaded pack. This also allows you to try different pack adjustments, socks and footwear.

Those coming from sea level should wait several days after arriving before undertaking any strenuous activity at altitude, notably in the Tetons. Prepare your metabolism for acclimation to the higher elevations by drinking more water and laying off the alcohol.

Health Insurance

It's important for travelers to the USA to have comprehensive insurance that covers medical emergencies and treatment, including hospital stays and an emergency flight home if necessary. Medical treatment in the US is of the highest caliber, but the expense could kill you. You will likely have to present your insurance and credit card before you receive any treatment.

RECOMMENDED VACCINATIONS

No vaccinations are currently recommended or required for temporary visitors to the USA. For the most up-to-date information, see the Centers for Disease Control and Prevention website (www.cdc.gov).

IN THE NATIONAL PARKS

Emergencies

Dial ☎911 in any emergency. Emergency messages to friends or family can be posted at park entry stations and at visitor centers.

Availability & Cost of Health Care

Health-care costs will vary widely depending on your insurance. Be sure to travel with your insurance card and know the co-payments and conditions of coverage before traveling. There are three medical clinics in Yellowstone and one in Grand Teton. Bigger facilities are found in Bozeman, Jackson and Cody.

Yellowstone

Lake Hospital (☎307-242-7241; www.yellowstone.co/clinics.htm; ⏲8:30am-8:30pm mid-May–mid-Sep) Summer-only, with 24-hour emergency service through 911.

Mammoth Clinic (☎307-344-7965; www.yellowstone.co/clinics.htm; Mammoth; ⏲8:30am-5pm Jun-Sep, 8.30am-5pm Mon-Thu, to 1pm Fri Oct-May) The only year-round clinic.

Old Faithful Clinic (☎307-545-7325; www.yellowstone.co/clinics.htm; Old Faithful; ⏲7am-7pm mid-May–mid-Sep) Summer-only clinic.

Grand Teton

Grand Teton Medical Clinic (☎307-543-2514; Jackson Lake Lodge Rd; ⏲9am-5pm mid-May–mid-Oct)

Infectious Diseases

Amoebic Dysentery

Fluid replacement is the mainstay of managing serious diarrhea. Weak black tea with a little sugar, soda water, or soft drink allowed to go flat and 50% diluted with water are all good. With severe diarrhea, a rehydrating solution is necessary to replace minerals and salts. Commercially available oral rehydration salts (ORS) are very useful. Stick to a bland diet as you recover.

Lyme Disease

A bacterial infection, Lyme disease is mainly transmitted by the deer (wood) tick. Although the number of cases reported in the US has skyrocketed during the last two decades, Lyme disease remains relatively uncommon over large parts of the Rockies. Early symptoms, which may take months to develop, are similar to influenza – headaches, stiff neck, tiredness and painful swelling of the joints. If left untreated, complications such as meningitis, facial palsy or heart abnormalities may occur, but fatalities are rare. A safe vaccination is not yet available, but Lyme disease responds well to antibiotics.

West Nile Disease

Unknown in the United States until a few years ago, this disease has now been reported in almost all 50 states. It's transmitted by Culex mosquitoes, which are active in late summer and early fall, and generally bite after dusk. Most infections are mild or asymptomatic, but the virus may infect the central nervous system, leading to fever, headache, confusion, lethargy, coma and sometimes death. There is no treatment for the West Nile virus. See affected areas on the US Geological Survey website (http://diseasemaps.usgs.gov/mapviewer).

Environmental Hazards

Altitude

In the thinner atmosphere of the high Rockies, a lack of oxygen may cause headaches, nausea, nosebleeds, shortness of breath, physical weakness and other symptoms. These can lead to serious consequences, especially if combined with heat exhaustion, sunburn or hypothermia. Most people adjust to altitude within a few hours or days. Be careful (especially with children) when driving and overnighting on the Beartooth Plateau, where altitudes reach 10,000ft. In mild cases of altitude sickness, everyday painkillers such as aspirin may relieve discomfort. If symptoms persist, descend to lower elevations.

Bears

Bears live a sedentary life and will typically avoid contact if given sufficient warning of an approaching individual. Yet travelers need to be bear aware. The main causes of human-bear conflict include the animal's instinctual protection of its young, the presence of food and surprise encounters.

Eight people have been killed in Yellowstone by bears since 1872.

- In August 2015, a grizzly sow killed a lone Yellowstone park employee off-trail near Elephant Back peak, near Lake Village.
- In July 2011, a man was killed when he surprised a female with her cubs on the Wapiti Lake Trail.
- In the same summer, a grizzly fatally attacked a lone hiker on the infrequently used Mary Mountain trail for unknown reasons.

In recent years, the population of grizzly bears has increased in Grand Teton National Park, where they were previously rare.

Hikers should follow all suggested precautions. But remember, there's a one-in-three-million chance of being attacked by a grizzly in Yellowstone. You have an almost equal chance of being struck by lightning or killed by a falling tree.

BEARS & HIKING

When hiking in grizzly country, always stay alert and make plenty of noise on the trail. Never hike before dawn or after dusk. While grizzlies have a highly acute sense of smell, they may not catch your scent if you approach from downwind. Some hikers wear 'bear bells' to announce their approach, but bears are better able to hear deeper sounds such as shouting or clapping. The human voice is effective: while some prefer show tunes, many shout, 'Hey, bear!' when approaching a blind corner.

If you encounter a bear at close range:

➡ Do not run – grizzlies can reach 45mph and and will instinctively pursue a fleeing animal.

➡ Do not drop your pack as a decoy – this may teach the bear that threatening humans procures food.

➡ Back away slowly, talking soothingly to the bear while avoiding direct eye contact.

➡ Before charging, a bear may clack its teeth, make a huffing sound, pop its jaw, slap the ground with its paws and lay its ears back. None of these are good signs.

➡ Bears very often 'bluff charge' an intruder, veering away at the last instant.

Using a pepper-based bear spray (p259) is your best bet to deter a charging bear. But if an attack ensues:

➡ Play dead.

➡ Lie down on your belly and shield the back of your neck with your hands. Keep your backpack on and use your legs to avoid being flipped over.

➡ In most cases, the bear will eventually leave the scene once assured that you present no danger.

➡ In extremely rare cases, grizzly bears with clear predatory intent have attacked humans. Such attacks tend to occur around campsites at dusk or during the night, and are the only time when you should fight back against an aggressive grizzly.

BEARS & FOOD

Bears are obsessed with food and rarely 'unlearn' knowledge acquired in finding it. In the past, Yellowstone's bears were regularly fed and given access to garbage dumps while tourists watched in grandstand seating. This tradition has ceased, and today any bear conditioned to associate humans with food is relocated or even destroyed. Don't let your carelessness result in the death of one of these magnificent creatures.

➡ Never leave food unattended, even in a backpack.

➡ Use the bear boxes at developed campgrounds or lock food in your car.

➡ Never store food or eat in your tent.

➡ Prepare and cook food well away from your tent, preferably 100yd away.

➡ Don't sleep in clothes worn while fishing or cooking.

➡ Don't burn food or garbage in your campfire.

➡ Don't camp downwind of your food stash.

➡ There is no evidence linking women's menstruation with bear attacks. Store used tampons and pads in double ziplock bags, hang them as you would food and then pack them out.

In Yellowstone National Park, backcountry campers must hang food and scented items such as garbage, toothpaste, soap and sunscreen at least 10ft above the ground, 4ft from tree trunks and 200ft from their tents. Carry a robust stuff-sack attached to a 35ft length of rope. First weight the sack with a rock and throw it over a high, sturdy limb at least 4ft from the tree trunk. Gently lower the sack to the ground with the rope, stash everything with food smells and perfumes, and raise the sack back up close to the tree limb. Finally, tie off the end of the rope to another trunk or tree limb well out of the way. Backcountry campgrounds all supply a food pole, which simplifies the process.

Grand Teton National Park requires backpackers to use approved bear-resistant canisters instead of hanging food. Backcountry-permitting locations currently loan canisters for free.

Bison, Moose & Mountain Lion

A too-common sight in Yellowstone is that of enthusiastic visitors edging toward a seemingly tame, fuzzy bison for an exclusive photo op. Not a good idea. These 2-ton creatures can sprint at 30mph and have actually harmed more visitors than

WHICH BEAR IS THAT?

TYPE	COLOR	BODY	FACE	TRACKS	AGILITY
Grizzly bears	blonde to black	larger with shoulder hump	dish-shaped face with short, rounded ears	long, straight front claws (2-4in)	can't climb trees well
Black bears	blonde to black	no shoulder hump	straight profile from nose to ears; tall, pointed ears	short, curved front claws (1-2in)	climb trees

bears have. In the summer of 2015 there were four bison attacks in under two months, plus two attacks in July 2018 alone. The message is clear: this is selfie suicide; keep your distance!

Moose usually flee intruding humans, but if a moose feels cornered or otherwise threatened, it may suddenly charge. Moose and elk cows with calves are especially dangerous, as they will aggressively defend their young. Moose can inflict severe injuries by striking out with their powerful front hoofs.

Your chances of encountering an aggressive mountain lion remain extremely small, but as humans encroach on their territory attacks appear to be on the increase. Avoid hiking alone in prime mountain-lion habitats. Keep children within view at all times. If you happen to encounter a mountain lion, raise your arms and back away slowly. Speak firmly or shout. If attacked, fight back fiercely.

There have been no reliable documented cases of fatal wolf attacks on humans for over a century. Attacks on humans by wild wolves are believed to be attributable to either rabies infection or habituation – when a wolf has lost its fear of people.

If you stay aware and keep a respectful distance from all wildlife, most encounters will be avoided.

GEOTHERMALS

You'll see plenty of signs warning you to stay on existing boardwalks and maintain a safe distance from all geothermal features. Thin crusts of earth can break without warning, giving way to unseen boiling water. Even warm springs can be dangerous; temperatures often fluctuate, sometimes dramatically, so what is safe one day may not be safe the next. About 20 people have died in Yellowstone's hot springs since the 1880s; some have backed into hot springs while taking photos, and more than one unknowing pet has jumped into a boiling pool.

The park service warns that hot spring waters can cause a rash and that thermophilic amoebas in the water can transmit amoebic meningitis (though there are no recorded cases). If you do soak in the park, keep your head above the surface and don't take in any water.

Bites & Stings

LEECHES

Sometimes present in lakes, leeches attach themselves to your skin to suck your blood. Salt or a lit cigarette end will make them fall off. Do not pull them off, as the bite is then more likely to become infected. Clean and apply pressure if the point of attachment is bleeding.

MOSQUITOES

Mosquitoes can be a major irritant in early and mid-summer (from mid-June until around mid-August), so remember to carry mosquito repellent. The most effective sprays contain DEET (the higher the percentage of DEET, the more effective the spray). DEET is powerful stuff and should be kept away from plastics and your tent. Citronella is a kinder (to the skin at least) alternative.

SNAKES & SPIDERS

In the history of Yellowstone, there have been only two recorded snakebites. The prairie rattlesnake is the only poisonous snake in the region, found in the dry and warm areas of the Yellowstone River in the northwest corner of the park. There are some spiders with dangerous bites, but antivenins are usually available.

For snakebites, immediately apply a reverse syringe (Sawyer Extractor). Keep the victim calm and still, wrap the bitten limb tightly and immobilize with a splint. Get the victim to a doctor as soon as possible.

TICKS

Ticks may be present from mid-March through August. Always check all over your body if you have been walking through a potentially tick-infested area, as ticks can cause skin infections and other more serious diseases. Ticks are most active in spring and summer, especially where there are plenty of sheep or deer. They usually lurk in overhanging vegetation, so avoid pushing through tall bushes if possible.

To remove, press down around the tick's head with tweezers, grab the head and gently pull upward; avoid pulling the rear of the body. Smearing chemicals is not recommended.

Cold

HYPOTHERMIA

The weather in both Yellowstone and Grand Teton can change quickly and dramatically, even at the height of summer. Hypothermia occurs when the body loses heat faster than it can produce it and the core temperature of the body falls.

It is frighteningly easy to progress from being very cold to dangerously cold due to a combination of wind, wet clothing, fatigue and hunger, even if the air temperature is above freezing. If the weather deteriorates, put on extra layers: always hike with a windproof and/or waterproof jacket, plus a fleece or wool layer and a warm hat. Have something energy-rich to eat and ensure that everyone in your group is fit, feeling well and alert.

Symptoms of hypothermia are exhaustion, numb skin (particularly toes and fingers), shivering, slurred speech, irrational or violent behavior, lethargy, stumbling, dizzy spells, muscle cramps

SAFE WATER

Mountain streams may look crystal clear, but with the prevalence of bacteriological contamination, sipping from the source has the potential to quickly ruin a backcountry trip. Boiling water rapidly for 10 minutes is effective, but uses precious fuel. See p257 for more on filters and purification tablets. Tap water at campgrounds and visitor centers is safe to drink. There are many water-filling stations at all the parks' major junctions so filling up is easy. Most trailheads do not have potable water, so fill up beforehand.

Giardia is a microscopic, waterborne parasite causes intestinal disorders after drinking contaminated water. Symptoms include chronic diarrhea, cramps, bloating and appalling gas. See a doctor if you have symptoms. Treatment requires a course of antibiotics.

and violent bursts of energy. Irrationality may take the form of sufferers claiming they are warm and trying to take off their clothes.

The early recognition and treatment of mild hypothermia is the only way to prevent severe hypothermia, which is a critical condition.

For mild hypothermia, get the person out of the elements, remove clothing if it's wet and replace it with dry, warm clothing. Give hot liquids (not alcohol) and high-energy, easily digestible food. Allow the victim to slowly warm up – don't rub them.

FROSTBITE

If you are visiting the parks in winter, especially if snowmobiling, you need to be aware of frostbite, which refers to the freezing of extremities, including fingers, toes and nose. Signs of frostbite include a whitish or waxy cast to the skin, or even crystals on the surface, plus itching, numbness and pain.

For frostbite, warm affected areas by immersion in warm (not hot) water, or warm with blankets or clothes (only until skin becomes flushed). Frostbitten parts should not be rubbed, and blisters should not be broken. Get medical attention right away.

SNOW BLINDNESS

This is a temporary, painful condition resulting from sunburn of the surface of the eye (cornea). It usually occurs when someone walks on snow or in bright sunshine without sunglasses.

Treatment is to relieve the pain – cold cloths on closed eyelids may help. Antibiotic and anesthetic eye drops are not necessary. The condition usually resolves itself within a few days and there are no long-term consequences.

Heat

DEHYDRATION & HEAT EXHAUSTION

Dehydration is a potentially dangerous and generally preventable condition caused by excessive fluid loss. Sweating combined with inadequate fluid intake is one of the most common causes of dehydration in trekkers, but other important causes are diarrhea, vomiting and high fever.

The first symptoms are weakness, thirst and passing small amounts of very concentrated urine. This may progress to drowsiness, dizziness or fainting on standing up, and, finally, coma.

It's easy to forget how much fluid you are losing via perspiration while you are trekking, particularly if a strong breeze is drying your skin quickly. You should always maintain a good fluid intake – a minimum of 3L a day is recommended.

Dehydration and salt deficiency can cause heat exhaustion. Salt deficiency is characterized by fatigue, lethargy, headaches, giddiness and muscle cramps. Salt tablets are overkill; just adding extra salt to your food is probably sufficient.

SUNBURN

Protection against the sun should always be taken seriously. Sunburn occurs rapidly in the rarified air and deceptive coolness of the mountains. Slap on the sunscreen and a barrier cream for your nose and lips, wear a broad-brimmed hat and protect your eyes with good-quality sunglasses with UV lenses, particularly near water, sand or snow. If you get sunburned, calamine lotion, aloe vera or other commercial sunburn-relief preparations will soothe.

HEATSTROKE

This serious, occasionally fatal condition occurs if the body's heat-regulating mechanism breaks down and the body temperature rises to dangerous levels. Long, continuous periods of exposure to high temperatures and insufficient fluids can leave you vulnerable to heatstroke.

The symptoms include feeling unwell, not sweating very much (or at all) and a high body temperature (102°F to 106°F or 39°C to 41°C). Where sweating has ceased, the skin becomes flushed and red. Severe, throbbing headaches and lack of coordination will also occur, and the sufferer may be confused or aggressive. Eventually the victim will become delirious or convulse.

Hospitalization is essential, but in the meantime get victims out of the sun, remove their clothing, cover them with a wet sheet or towel and then fan continually. Give fluids if they are conscious.

SAFE HIKING

Trail Safety Tips

➡ Allow plenty of time to accomplish a walk before dark, particularly in spring and fall when daylight hours are shorter.

➡ Study the route carefully before setting out, noting possible alternate routes and the point of no return (where it's quicker to continue than to turn back).

➡ It's wise not to walk alone. Always leave details of your intended route, the number of people in your group and the expected return time with someone responsible before you set off; later, announce your return.

➡ Before setting off, make sure you have a relevant map, compass and whistle, and that you know the weather forecast for the area for the next 24 hours.

➡ Time your progress over a known distance to monitor further progress with reasonable accuracy.

➡ Watch the path – look for boot prints, blazes on trees and other signs of previous passage.

Crossing Streams

Drowning is the leading cause of death in Yellowstone's backcountry. In spring and early summer, streams turn into raging rivers and block many trails until July, so always check your route at a backcountry office. Sudden downpours can also quickly turn a gentle stream into a raging torrent. If you're in any doubt about the safety of a crossing, look for a safer passage upstream or wait. If the rain is short-lived, it should subside quickly. Late in the day, crossing may be essential.

➡ Look for a wide, shallower stretch (not a bend).

➡ Keep boots on to prevent injury. Best is to bring river shoes or enclosed-toe sandals.

➡ Store clothes and a towel in a plastic bag near the top of your pack.

➡ Unclip the chest strap and belt buckle of your pack (in case you have to swim).

➡ Use a hiking pole, grasped in both hands, on the upstream side as a third leg.

➡ With a companion, clasp at the wrist and cross side-on to the flow in short steps.

Fire

Fire danger varies from year to year, but is often extreme in July and August. Parts of both parks can become off-limits and you may have to evacuate an area at short notice. Local park and USFS offices can advise hikers about forest fires, and fire warnings are usually posted at wilderness access points. For fire updates contact the park service, stop at a visitor center or check out official websites. Also contact the **National Interagency Fire Center** (☎208-387-5512; www.nifc.gov).

Lightning

Getting struck by lightning during a summer afternoon storm is a real possibility, especially if climbing a summit or ridgeline. Your best bet is to undertake long hikes early. During lightning storms:

➡ Avoid exposed ridges, open areas and lone trees.

➡ Move away from bodies of water or beaches.

➡ If camping, crouch on a sleeping pad with your arms around your knees.

Rockfall

Even a small falling rock could shatter your hand or crack your skull, so always be alert to the danger of rockfall. Don't dally below cliffs or on trails fringed by large fields of raw talus. If you accidentally let a rock loose, loudly warn other hikers below. Mountain goats and bighorn sheep sometimes dislodge rocks, so be vigilant.

Rescue & Evacuation

Search-and-rescue operations are expensive and often require emergency personnel to risk their own welfare. Self-evacuation should be your first consideration.

For serious accidents or illness, seek help, but don't leave the injured party alone. If that's impossible, leave sufficient warm clothing, food and water. Leave a whistle and flashlight too, and mark the position with something conspicuous.

SAFE CYCLING

Yellowstone is not an easy place to bike. Roads are winding, shoulders are slim and many a cyclist has been threatened by an encroaching RV mirror. Additionally, vehicle traffic is heavy most of the time; there are no bicycle paths along main roads; and drivers sometimes pass on hill crests, blind curves or in oncoming traffic. For this reason, it's best to bike early in the morning or after 6:30pm, when traffic thins out. Wearing a helmet and using high-visibility clothing and mirrors is essential. Never use headphones while cycling.

Cyclists should take advantage of shoulder seasons. A good time to bike is between October and mid-November, when there is less traffic and wind. Springtime cyclists can enjoy some roads closed to motorized vehicles: cycling is permitted between the West Entrance and Mammoth Hot Springs from about mid-March (weather allowing) through to the third Thursday in April. Note that high snowbanks from April to June can make travel more dangerous. August is typically the windiest month.

Bison may be a hazard to cyclists. If you come upon some, dismount and walk far around them or wait for a vehicle to drive through (the bison will follow it).

Behind the Scenes

SEND US YOUR FEEDBACK

We love to hear from travelers – your comments keep us on our toes and help make our books better. Our well-traveled team reads every word on what you loved or loathed about this book. Although we cannot reply individually to your submissions, we always guarantee that your feedback goes straight to the appropriate authors, in time for the next edition. Each person who sends us information is thanked in the next edition – the most useful submissions are rewarded with a selection of digital PDF chapters.

Visit **lonelyplanet.com/contact** to submit your updates and suggestions or to ask for help. Our award-winning website also features inspirational travel stories, news and discussions.

Note: We may edit, reproduce and incorporate your comments in Lonely Planet products such as guidebooks, websites and digital products, so let us know if you don't want your comments reproduced or your name acknowledged. For a copy of our privacy policy visit lonelyplanet.com/privacy.

WRITER THANKS

Bradley Mayhew

Thanks to the almost-always professional Carolyn McCarthy for being a dream co-writer, and for joining me on that Shoshone Lake trek. Rick Hoeninghausen and Cameron Walker of Yellowstone National Park Lodges were generous with their time. Cheers to Celeste, Wendy and Sandra for making the Ice Lake author meeting such fun. Goodbye Montana, you have been one of my favorite places and I will miss you.

Carolyn McCarthy

I am very thankful for another opportunity to explore this amazing wilderness and call it my home for a while. Thanks to the Climbers Ranch for providing an excellent base camp. I am also grateful to Andrew White, the Santelices family, Drew Hardesty and the friends who shared my campfire. Lastly, a shout out goes to co-writer Bradley Mayhew for his dedication in the field.

ACKNOWLEDGMENTS

Climate map data adapted from Peel MC, Finlayson BL & McMahon TA (2007) 'Updated World Map of the Köppen-Geiger Climate Classification', *Hydrology and Earth System Sciences*, 11, 1633–44.

Cover photograph: Grand Teton National Park, Dean Fikar/Getty Images ©

THIS BOOK

This 6th edition of Lonely Planet's *Yellowstone & Grand Teton National Parks* guide was curated by Benedict Walker, and researched and written by Bradley Mayhew, Carolyn McCarthy and Christopher Pitts, as was the previous edition. Bradley and Carolyn also wrote the 4th edition. This guidebook was produced by the following:

Destination Editor Ben Buckner

Senior Product Editors Victoria Smith, Kate Mathews

Product Editor Carolyn Boicos

Senior Cartographer Alison Lyall

Book Designer Jessica Rose

Assisting Editors Sarah Bailey, James Bainbridge, Anne Mulvaney, Lauren O'Connell, Maja Vatrić

Cartographers Anita Banh, Corey Hutchison

Cover Researcher Fergal condon

Thanks to Anthony Barreiro, Evan Godt, Nancy Leon, Anne Mason, Clinton Milroy, Theresa Montag, Peter Mutton, Monique Perrin, Alison Ridgway, Ross Taylor

Index

Map Pages **000**
Photo Pages **000**

Map Pages **000**
Photo Pages **000**

H

N

O

P

Q

R

S

T

Map Pages **000**
Photo Pages **000**

Map Legend

Sights

- Beach
- Bird Sanctuary
- Buddhist
- Castle/Palace
- Christian
- Confucian
- Hindu
- Islamic
- Jain
- Jewish
- Monument
- Museum/Gallery/Historic Building
- Ruin
- Shinto
- Sikh
- Taoist
- Winery/Vineyard
- Zoo/Wildlife Sanctuary
- Other Sight

Activities, Courses & Tours

- Bodysurfing
- Diving
- Canoeing/Kayaking
- Course/Tour
- Sento Hot Baths/Onsen
- Skiing
- Snorkeling
- Surfing
- Swimming/Pool
- Walking
- Windsurfing
- Other Activity

Sleeping

- Sleeping
- Camping
- Hut/Shelter

Eating

- Eating

Drinking & Nightlife

- Drinking & Nightlife
- Cafe

Entertainment

- Entertainment

Shopping

- Shopping

Information

- Bank
- Embassy/Consulate
- Hospital/Medical
- Internet
- Police
- Post Office
- Telephone
- Toilet
- Tourist Information
- Other Information

Geographic

- Beach
- Gate
- Hut/Shelter
- Lighthouse
- Lookout
- Mountain/Volcano
- Oasis
- Park
- Pass
- Picnic Area
- Waterfall

Population

- Capital (National)
- Capital (State/Province)
- City/Large Town
- Town/Village

Transport

- Airport
- BART station
- Border crossing
- Boston T station
- Bus
- Cable car/Funicular
- Cycling
- Ferry
- Metro/Muni station
- Monorail
- Parking
- Petrol station
- Subway/SkyTrain station
- Taxi
- Train station/Railway
- Tram
- Underground station
- Other Transport

Routes

- Tollway
- Freeway
- Primary
- Secondary
- Tertiary
- Lane
- Unsealed road
- Road under construction
- Plaza/Mall
- Steps
- Tunnel
- Pedestrian overpass
- Walking Tour
- Walking Tour detour
- Path/Walking Trail

Boundaries

- International
- State/Province
- Disputed
- Regional/Suburb
- Marine Park
- Cliff
- Wall

Hydrography

- River, Creek
- Intermittent River
- Canal
- Water
- Dry/Salt/Intermittent Lake
- Reef

Areas

- Airport/Runway
- Beach/Desert
- Cemetery (Christian)
- Cemetery (Other)
- Glacier
- Mudflat
- Park/Forest
- Sight (Building)
- Sportsground
- Swamp/Mangrove

Note: Not all symbols displayed above appear on the maps in this book

OUR STORY

A beat-up old car, a few dollars in the pocket and a sense of adventure. In 1972 that's all Tony and Maureen Wheeler needed for the trip of a lifetime – across Europe and Asia overland to Australia. It took several months, and at the end – broke but inspired – they sat at their kitchen table writing and stapling together their first travel guide, *Across Asia on the Cheap*. Within a week they'd sold 1500 copies. Lonely Planet was born.

Today, Lonely Planet has offices in Franklin, Dublin, Beijing and Delhi, with more than 600 staff and writers. We share Tony's belief that 'a great guidebook should do three things: inform, educate and amuse'.

OUR WRITERS

Benedict Walker

A beach baby from Newcastle, Australia, Ben turned 40 in 2017 and decided to start a new life in Leipzig, Germany. Writing for Lonely Planet was a childhood dream for Ben: it was a privilege, a huge responsibility and a lot of fun. He's thrilled to have covered big chunks of Australia, Canada, Germany, Japan, Switzerland, Sweden and the USA. Come along for the ride on Instagram @wordsandjourneys.

Bradley Mayhew

Yellowstone National Park Bradley has been writing guidebooks for 20 years now. He started traveling while studying Chinese at Oxford University, and he is the co-author of Lonely Planet's *Tibet*, *Nepal*, *Trekking in the Nepal Himalaya*, *Bhutan*, *Central Asia* and many others. Bradley has also fronted two TV series for Arte and SWR, one retracing the route of Marco Polo via Turkey, Iran, Afghanistan, Central Asia and China, and the other trekking Europe's 10 most scenic long-distance trails. Bradley also wrote the Plan Your Trip and Survival Guide chapters.

Carolyn McCarthy

Grand Teton National Park Carolyn specializes in travel, culture and adventure in the Americas. She has written for *National Geographic*, *Outside*, *BBC Magazine*, *Sierra Magazine*, *Boston Globe* and other publications. A former Fulbright fellow and Banff Mountain Grant recipient, she has documented life in the most remote corners of Latin America. Carolyn has contributed to 40 guidebooks and anthologies for Lonely Planet, including *Colorado*, *USA*, *Argentina*, *Chile*, *Trekking in the Patagonian Andes*, *Panama*, *Peru* and *USA National Parks* guides. Carolyn also wrote the Understand chapters. For more information, visit www.carolynmccarthy.org or follow her Instagram travels @mccarthyoffmap.

Christopher Pitts

Around Yellowstone National Park, Around Grand Teton National Park Born in the year of the Tiger, Chris's first expedition in life ended in failure when he tried to dig from Pennsylvania to China at the age of six. Hardened by reality but still infinitely curious about the other side of the world, he went on to study Chinese in university, living for several years in Kunming, Taiwan and Shanghai. A chance encounter in an elevator led to a Paris relocation, where he lived with his wife and two children for over a decade before the lure of Colorado's sunny skies and outdoor adventure proved too great to resist. Visit him online at www.christopherpitts.net.

Published by Lonely Planet Global Limited

CRN 554153

6th edition – Mar 2021

ISBN 978 1 78868 069 1

10 9 8 7 6 5 4 3 2 1

Printed in Singapore